CYRIL CONNOLLY

By the same author

Playing for Time
Kindred Spirits

The Chatto Book of Office Life

CYRIL CONNOLLY

A Life

JEREMY LEWIS

JONATHAN CAPE
LONDON

First published 1997

1 3 5 7 9 10 8 6 4 2

First published in the United Kingdom in 1997 by Jonathan Cape,
Random House, 20 Vauxhall Bridge Road, London SW1V 2SA

Random House Australia (Pty) Limited
20 Alfred Street, Milsons Point, Sydney
New South Wales 2061, Australia

Random House New Zealand Limited
18 Poland Road, Glenfield,
Auckland 10, New Zealand

Random House South Africa (Pty) Limited
Box 2263, Rosebank 2121, South Africa

Random House UK Limited Reg. No. 954009

A CIP catalogue record for this book is available from the British Library

Papers used by Random House UK Limited are natural,
recyclable products made from wood grown in sustainable forests.
The manufacturing processes conform to the environmental
regulations of the country of origin.

ISBN 0-224-03710-2

Typeset by Pure Tech India Ltd, Pondicherry.

Printed and bound in Great Britain
by Mackays of Chatham PLC

For Petra
who kept us afloat through it all

'What is there to say about someone who did nothing all his life but sit on his bottom and write reviews?' – Cyril Connolly to John Russell, on the subject of Sainte-Beuve

CONTENTS

ILLUSTRATIONS

ILLUSTRATIONS

PREFACE

Boswell excepted, I have never been a great reader or admirer of literary biographies. I far prefer the first- to the second-hand, the immediacy and the intimacy of the autobiography and the memoir, prone as they are to exaggeration, imperfect recollection, blatant prejudice and unashamed untruths; and yet, by some curious irony, writing this particular literary life proved one of the most enjoyable things I have ever done. Much of this, I suspect, has to do with Cyril Connolly himself. Writers, as a rule, should be read and not read about; not because one wants to shield them from prying eyes – though as often as not literary biographies are read, and probably written, as a form of respectable gossip – but because, contrary to popular imaginings, writers' lives are often dull, austere affairs, a matter of long hours put in behind the typewriter, washed down with a good deal of drink and enlivened by the odd flurry of infidelity. Unlike the rest of us, the more diligent among them – W.H. Auden, for instance – know where they want to go, and pursue their calling with the dedication and the single-mindedness reserved for those who achieve great things in life, in whatever sphere of activity.

For all his articulacy and cleverness, Connolly seems a more familiar figure, and this is what makes him so attractive to read and – I hope – to read about. He was haunted by the gulf that separates promise from achievement and by the temptations that await the aspiring writer, though no one who wrote as well as he did can be deemed a failure, however loud his lamentations on that score, unless one measures success in Stakhanovite terms, by the poundage of books produced; whatever his ostensible subject-matter, his abiding topic was himself, and no one has written more vividly, more sympathetically or more honestly about feelings and failings common to us all. I love – and came to love still more – his mixture of romanticism and wit, of bleakness and yearning: my own life could hardly have been more different but, as a writer, I share his autobiographical bias as well as his ambivalence – his belief in 'God the Either, God the Or and God the Holy Both' seems especially congenial – and his delight in gossip and exaggeration; and I felt at times that, far from writing the life of a man I had never met, I had embarked on a superior slice of my own.

I make no apologies for writing about Connolly at almost Boswellian length, and not simply because he shared Dr Johnson's aphoristic wit and his tendency to dominate the company in which he found himself. Clive

Fisher's recent biography covers the facts of his life very adequately, though without quoting at length from Connolly's own writing or examining the small print of the anecdotes and the elaborate jokes that clustered about him like flies, and simply to duplicate his book at a similar length would seem a pointless exercise;* so much of Connolly's writing is out of print, or buried in yellowing piles of newsprint, or has never been published before, and – since the point of a writer is his writing – I have quoted at length from his own works, like a literary archaeologist piecing the shards together; he was obsessed by the hazards and the mechanics of the writer's life, and his dealings with fellow-authors, contributors to *Horizon*, publishers and literary editors provide an extended commentary on the middle section of *Enemies of Promise*; he knew and was loved by an enormous number of people, and since his moods and his jokes and his complicated love affairs were the subject of endless speculation among them, I have quoted extensively from their reactions to him in order to build up a composite picture of a man who combined throughout his life a seer-like wisdom with the emotions of an adolescent. When he was sulking, or being particularly disloyal to one of the women in his life, or making no effort to write a book he'd promised to deliver, or behaving like an over-grown, eloquent baby, I felt at times like giving him a sharp, retrospective kick, but I came to love the man as well as the work. Since I dislike the habit of calling by their Christian names people to whom one has not been introduced, I have referred to him throughout as 'Connolly': inconsistent in this, as in so much else, and swayed perhaps by antique notions of gallantry, I have occasionally broken my own rule where wives and girl friends are concerned.

All this I owe to Cyril Connolly's widow, Deirdre Levi, who asked me to write his authorised biography after Clive Fisher had announced that he was going ahead with his own, unauthorised life. The idea of writing about Connolly had already been suggested to me a year or two earlier by Richard Cohen; and I was eventually recommended to Mrs Levi by Michael Shelden, who had written about Connolly and *Horizon*, and whose help and advice in the early stages were invaluable. He and I had not yet met, though we had spoken on the phone, and, flattered as I was to have my name put forward, I must have represented a fairly long shot on his part. I had spent all my working life on the far side of a publisher's desk, commissioning and editing other people's books; I had no relevant academic or scholarly credentials; the only book I had written was a facetious and supposedly comic slice of autobiography, and when, shortly before our first meeting, Deirdre asked me if I would bring with me to Gloucestershire a copy of

* Though, as Connolly pointed out when reviewing a new life of his hero Sainte-Beuve, 'No two biographies are alike, for in every one enters an element of autobiography which must always be different.'

Playing for Time, I knew that the game was up: quite apart from the contents, the paperback of my book had the worst kind of 'comic' cover, all rolling eye-balls and flecks of foam spraying from the lips; I would be exposed at once as an entirely frivolous figure, quite unworthy of the task that lay ahead. I was working at the time with Alan Ross, the editor of the *London Magazine*, and an old friend of both Connolly and Deirdre; and before I left home I hid my book in a thick pile of *London Magazines*, hoping in vain that Deirdre would forget that she had asked to see it, or that it would acquire some *gravitas* from the company it kept. Two days later, Deirdre rang to say that Cyril would have *loved* my book, that it was all about those parts of Sussex – the Seven Sisters, Firle Beacon, Birling Gap, Mr Rolph's fishmonger's shop in Seaford, and Mary Ranger's second-hand bookshop – that they used to visit together, and that of course I could go ahead. Since then I have received nothing but kindness and co-operation from Deirdre, her son Matthew Connolly (an expert on his father's colourful family tree), and her husband Peter Levi – accompanied, whenever we happen to be near Frampton-on-Severn, by delicious meals and equal measures of drink and laughter, very much in the Connolly tradition of hospitality. I'm very grateful, too, for the enthusiastic support of Cressida Connolly, whose own writing has the wit and elegance of her father's.

No sooner had I signed the contract with Jonathan Cape – here I owe much to its then editorial director, David Godwin, and to my literary agent, Gillon Aitken – than fellow-biographers were urging me to set up interviews with Connolly's contemporaries, some of whom were almost as old as the century. All too often, I'm afraid, these preliminary encounters proved, from their point of view at least, a terrible waste of time. I knew far too little to be able to ask the kind of informed, specific questions that might, with luck, trigger off a flow of reminiscence; and I very soon realised that I was a coward and a humbug, in that I was very happy to play the voyeur in a library, eagerly riffling through the most intimate letters and diaries, but that brought face-to-face with those who had known him I was far too fearful to ask the bold, incisive question, tiptoeing delicately round anything contentious and gasping with relief when the conversation drifted away to cats or children or the weather.

I soon realised, too, how fallible memory is – and that those who had already written about Connolly in their own memoirs or diaries had little extra to add. On one occasion I went to see a distinguished nonagenarian who had been a colleague of Connolly's on the *Sunday Times*. She was very deaf, so I made a funnel of my hands and, leaning forward in my chair, bawled my enquiries into her ear, while below us a Yorkshire terrier fought to untie my shoe-laces. She told me what I knew already from other colleagues on the paper, of how he would come into the office every Wednesday after lunch to read through his proofs and choose a new book to review, after which he might well conduct a kind of informal seminar, reminiscing about writers he had known and the perils of the literary life; and then at some stage I mentioned his having been married. '*Married*?' she said, jolting back in her seat, her bright blue eyes widening with disbelief: 'I never thought of him as a *marrying* sort of man.' Indeed he was, I explained, wondering how she could have forgotten: he had been married three times, with several girl friends in between. 'But whom are we talking about?' she eventually asked; and when I told her she gave a great hoot of laughter and said, 'Oh dear, I thought it was Raymond Mortimer,' who was certainly *not* a marrying sort of man; and with that behind us we agreed to abandon ship, and turn to other things. After that I decided to postpone any more interviews until I'd done my homework in libraries in England and America, read all the books I needed to read, and written a first draft; then, with luck, I might at least know what I was talking about, and be able to ask an intelligent question or two.

Not all my researches were conducted in the calm of a university library. When, in the autumn of 1993, Barbara Skelton decided to move back to London from France, she asked me if I would help her pack up her Paris house and share the driving back to England. One afternoon in early October, very much the worse for wear – the packing had been helped along with generous slugs of whisky, drunk straight from the bottle to save on the washing-up – we loaded her tiny Renault Clio with six pairs of boots, a giant sack of cat litter, two loudly-complaining 'pussers' in a cage, four suitcases, a wicker basket full of bottles, a drawing by Toulouse-Lautrec, innumerable dresses and coats hanging off wire coat-hangers and hurled in the boot and, balanced unsteadily on top of it all, a huge oil painting by Sidney Nolan of a lugubrious-looking wading fowl picking its way through a swamp – and set off unsteadily in the direction of Calais, the car swerving about the road as Barbara removed her hands from the wheel to pull on and then pull off a pair of string-and-leather driving gloves.

Bearing in mind my inadequacies as an interviewer, I would like to thank the following – some of whom, alas, are no longer with us – for talking to me about Cyril Connolly: Lord Annan, the Hon. David Astor, Diana Athill, Anne Baring, Sybille Bedford, Quentin Bell, Michael Berkeley, Peggy Bernier, Caroline Blackwood, Georgiana Blakiston, Melvyn Bragg, the Hon. Dinah Bridge, Michael Briggs, Mrs Horatia Buxton, John Byrne, Susan Campbell, Camilla Cazalet, Sally Chilver, Sir George and Mary Christie, Isabel Colegate, Simon Craven, John Craxton, Rosie d'Avigdor-Goldsmid, Ginette Darwin, the Duke and Duchess of Devonshire, André

Deutsch, Fram Dinshaw, C.J. Driver, Elaine Dundy, Glur Dyson-Taylor, Gavin Ewart, Freya Elwes, Mary Fedden, Magouche Fielding, Desmond Fitzgerald, Ruth Fleminger, Alastair Forbes, James Fox, Viscount Gage, Frank Giles, Lord Gladwyn, Lady Glenconner, Kitty Godley, Wynne Godley, Celia Goodman, Sir Stuart Hampshire, Desmond Hawkins, Lady Dorothy Heber Percy, Sir Nicholas Henderson, Derek Hill, Drue Heinz, Anthony Hobson, Sir Raymond Hoffenberg, Adrian House, Elizabeth Jane Howard, David Hughes, Peter Janson-Smith, the Hon. John Jolliffe, Tim Jones, Mouse Katz, Richard Kershaw, Cynthia Kee, Robert Kee, Veronica Keeling, Catherine Lambert, Joan Leigh Fermor, Patrick Leigh Fermor, James Lees-Milne, R.M. Lockley, the Hon. Fionn Morgan, Anne Dunn Moynihan, John Julius Norwich, Trekkie Parsons, Janetta Parladé, Frances Partridge, Anthony Powell, Dilys Powell, Lady Violet Powell, David Pryce-Jones, Sir Peter Quennell, Michael Ratcliffe, Jocelyn Rickards, Deborah Rogers, Tom Rosenthal, Alan Ross, A.L. Rowse, Sir Steven Runciman, John Russell, Dadie Rylands, Barbara Skelton, Godfrey Smith, Natasha Spender, Sir Stephen Spender, Peggy Strachey, Julian Symons, Chloë Teacher, Pat Trevor-Roper, Ed Victor, Randolph Vigne, Lord Weidenfeld, John Whitley, Michael Wishart, Tony Witherby, Anne Wollheim, Lord Wyatt of Weeford, Francis Wyndham, Victoria Zinovieff.

I am very grateful to the following for their help and advice: Mark Amory, David W. Astor, Judy Astor, Simon Bailey, John Bodley, Neville Braybrooke, Montagu Bream, Julia Brown, David Burnett, Euan Cameron, Sir Raymond Carr, Peter Carson, Artemis Cooper, Ron Cortie, Lord Dacre, Peter Davison, Margaret Drabble, Digby Durrant, Hugh Elwes, Sir Edward Ford, C.J. Fox, Andrew Gailey, Michael Gibson, David Gilson, Geordie Greig, Peter Green, Jasper Griffin, Curtis Harrington, Christopher Hawtree, Lady Selina Hastings, R.M. Healey, Andrew Hewson, Valerie Holman, Miles Huddleston, Richard Ingrams, Virginia Ironside, Howard Jacobson, Kate Jones, Nigel Jones, James Knox, Mr and Mrs Ted Kronfeld, Rebecca Langlands, Hermione Lee, Hattie Lewis, Jemima Lewis, Roger Louis, John Lowe, Andrew Lycett, Candida Lycett Green, Carol MacArthur, Ian Maclean, Sonia MacGuinness, Angus Macintyre, Ian Mackillop, David Machin, Lynda Mamy, James Michie, Pankaj Mishra, Charlotte Mosley, John Murray, Nigel Nicolson, Peter Parker, Roland Phillips, Tom Pomeroy, Gaye Poulton, Isabel Quigly, Rosalin Sadler, Deborah Singmaster, George Sims, Adam Sisman, Tom Staley, Charles Sprawson, Cicely Taylor, Tom Wallace, Michael Wharton, Matthew Wilson, Sara Wheeler, Ian Whitcomb and Martin Whittome, who supplied the photograph of Connolly and Orwell at Eton, taken by his father. Alan Bell read the book in typescript, saving me from solecisms as well as adding invaluable information of his own, as did

John Saumarez-Smith; Dan Franklin and Tony Whittome at Jonathan Cape disproved the current notion that publishers' editors no longer edit; once again I owe a particular debt to James Douglas Henry, who – worried in case my house caught fire – not only locked away photocopies of both drafts in his fireproof safe, but (and this was going far beyond the call of duty, or friendship) read them through, and kept me going with his enthusiasm and his perceptive comments. Sir Isaiah Berlin was also very helpful.

Connolly's library, and then his papers, were sold to the University of Tulsa, where they are immaculately boxed and filed away: I spent seven exhausting but enjoyable weeks in the Special Collections Department of the McFarlin Library, and my every bibliographical whim was gratified by its Curator, Sidney Huttner, and his assistant, Lori Curtis. A mass of other Connolly material is housed at the Harry H. Ransom Humanities Research Center at the University of Texas at Austin, where I was well looked after by Cathy Henderson and Elizabeth Dunn; and, while in America, I visited the Huntington Library in San Marino, home to the papers of Patrick Kinross, where I owe much to Sara Hodson. Back in England, I would like to thank, in particular, Michael Bott of the University of Reading Library, which houses the records of Connolly's first publisher, Routledge & Kegan Paul; Sally Brown at the British Library, with its collection of letters to Evelyn Waugh; Michael Meredith and the Eton College Library; Nick Lee at Bristol University Library, which contains the papers of the long-suffering Hamish Hamilton; and C.S.L. Davies at Wadham College, Oxford, who kindly allowed me to trawl through the contents of Maurice Bowra's tuck-box. I would also like to thank the following institutions for allowing me to consult material held by them, or for providing me with photocopies: the Berg Collection at the New York Public Library, the Beinecke Rare Book and Manuscript Library at Yale University (Connolly's correspondence with Edmund Wilson and Olga Rudge), the Bodleian Library, the BBC Sound Archives at Caversham, the Brotherton Library at the University of Leeds, the Cambridge University Library, Durham University, the University of Edinburgh Library (the Koestler Archive), King's College, Cambridge, King's College, London, the Lilly Library at the University of Indiana (Connolly's letters to Lys Lubbock), Merton College, Oxford, the National Sound Archive, the PEN Club, Penguin Books, the Princeton University Library (Cass Canfield's correspondence with Hamish Hamilton and Weidenfeld & Nicolson), University College, London, Sussex University, and the University of Victoria in British Columbia (Connolly's letters to John Betjeman). Auberon Waugh very kindly lent me material he had collected for his proposed life of Connolly, commissioned by Weidenfeld & Nicolson in 1975 but subsequently abandoned; and I owe a special debt to Anthony Hobson, a friend and a relation by marriage of Connolly's, who not only allowed me to consult his diaries, but the many other Connollyiana he has collected over the years. Last but but not least, I have discovered – like many grateful authors before me – that, as an indexer, Douglas Matthews goes far beyond the conventional call of duty; for which I am very thankful.

Despite the claims of some modern practitioners, biography is the most ephemeral form of literature, with Suetonius, Boswell and Lytton Strachey the exceptions that prove the rule. No one was more aware than Connolly of the ultimate transience of all writing, but if my book revives some interest in this most humane and entertaining of writers I shall feel that that at least was a good deed done.

Jeremy Lewis
December 1996

ONE

Ancestral Voices

In Bath, in the early years of this century, a small boy is being taken to school for the first time, willing each moment to last forever as the horse-drawn cab slowly plods its way uphill towards their destination. He is a striking-looking little boy, memorable rather than conventionally handsome. The upper part of his head is as round as a cannon-ball or a Christmas pudding, seemingly too large for his body; he has straight fair hair, a snub nose, a dome-like brow and overhanging forehead, eyebrows like smudges of theatrical paint, and liquid blue eyes that wear at this stage of his life at least an expression of unusual and unsentimental sweetness, lighting up his entire face and redeeming his somewhat unconventional features. He looks, as he will always look, like a cross between Gibbon, the author of *The Decline and Fall of the Roman Empire*, and a shy, nocturnal mammal from the South American treetops – a lemur, perhaps, like those that would swing from the curtains of his King's Road flat and haunt the pages of *The Unquiet Grave*, or a graceful Capuchin monkey. In later years, as food and good living take their toll, his waistline will steadily expand, giving him a touch of Silenus or Mr Toad waving a large cigar; but for the moment, and for many years to come, he is slim and small and lightly built, his body tapering down over narrow shoulders like that of a tadpole, or a genie summoned from a bottle.

With him in the cab are his father and his aunt. Tall, upright, slightly pop-eyed and sporting a military moustache, one end of which he chews, his father is a professional soldier, subscribing even his most intimate and affectionate letters with the appropriate rank and initials ('M. Connolly, Major'); in the years to come, when he has left the army and devoted himself instead to snails, meat pastes and postage stamps – on all of which he is a world authority – his features will become empurpled with drink, and he will belch and stumble about the house, but now as he sits with his cane between his knees, twiddling its knob between his fingers, he is still a fine and handsome presence. 'Look, there's the Abbey cemetery,' cries Aunt Tots, who is seated beside the boy, as Bath Abbey hoves into view: 'That's where your grandfather is buried and your great-grandfather and your great-grandmother, and all the funny old uncles and aunts.' 'Never left us a penny, damn them!' barks the Major, who will rejoin his ancestors in that same cemetery during the frozen spring of 1947, and whose son will lament far more loudly than he did the fortune that never came his way; and 'Oh, Matt!' sighs Aunt Tots, as the cab turns up a drive and comes to a halt in front of the school, where the headmaster and his wife are waiting and the awful rituals of introduction and abandonment begin ('Well, Sprat, I think you've got everything. Everything that a little gentleman ought to have...').

Even the kindest aunt is a poor substitute for a mother, especially on an occasion such as this; but the boy's mother – once described as 'a charming Irish lady, rather "fey", almost embarrassingly interested in the supernatural' – remains an elusive, shadowy figure, increasingly absent from gatherings that include her husband and their only child; partly because her health is poor – she has weak lungs, and needs to be in hot, dry places as often as she can – and partly because she and the Major find it hard to live together, though she will always remain the love of his life. Over the years Mollie will gradually detach herself more and more from the family circle, eventually moving to South Africa to live with her husband's former commanding officer; and her absence will leave her son with a lifelong dread of being deserted by the women he loves; and an almost fatalistic, countervailing urge to induce them to desert, so that the scabs that cover this self-inflicted wound can be picked at again and again, in his life and in his writings, like the dreams and memories of childhood, of an Eden forever abandoned.

*

Like most of us, perhaps, Cyril Connolly was a man of paradox. He combined an incurable, ever-youthful romanticism – defined in *Enemies of Promise* as 'the refusal to face certain truths about the world and ourselves, and the consequences of that refusal' – with an unwavering, almost masochistic realism about his weaknesses and failings. It is this mixture of restless yearning and terrible honesty that makes him so sympathetic and perceptive a guide to the perils and pleasures of life, evoking again and again feelings and states of mind that are common to us all; his wit was underwritten, as wit so often is, by a corrosive sense of melancholy and loss; he celebrated the pleasures of love and food and literature, yet, like all romantics, he pined for what was lost or out-of-reach; he combined selfishness with generosity, a sense of his own worth with a dread of being snubbed or disliked, an editor's feel for the spirit of the age with an anarchist's urge to react against it. He frittered away his gifts, as he saw it, on ephemeral book reviews, yet – fragmented and fragmentary as it almost always is – his writing when taken as a whole is shot through by recurrent themes and images, and so permeated by his personality and his own experiences that its glittering shards, when pieced together, form an ever-evolving autobiography, that condition towards which all his writing aspired. He spent most of his working life as a literary journalist, a state of affairs he both resented and relied upon; he deplored journalism as a snare for the unwary and the enemy of literature, yet towards the end of his life he was forced to agree – defiantly, since he was contradicting the tenets of a lifetime, but rightly all the same – that 'My journalism is literature'. He dreamed of writing a full-length masterpiece, persuading himself and others that his failure to do so represented a dereliction of duty and a permanent loss to literature; but he remained a sprinter of genius, and *The Unquiet Grave* and *Enemies of Promise* – neither of which bears the marks of a marathon-runner – may well last as long as the novels and poems by contemporaries he so envied and admired. He longed to be a novelist, yet no sooner did he sit down to write a novel than all the sparkle vanished from his prose, and his only completed work, *The Rock Pool*, is a thin, wooden affair, far stronger in its abstract, aphoristic passages than in narrative or characterisation. Pre-empting his critics, he liked to portray himself as a man undone by his own sloth, yet as a reviewer he was diligent and dependable, producing tens of thousands of words every year when not lying in bed or the bath, running through the plots of novels he would never get round to writing, laughing at his own jokes, and feeling suitably guilty about his failure to deliver the books he'd promised himself and his publishers. He mocked academic critics for their narrowness, their ugly prose, their refusal to take risks, yet he dreaded their bad opinion and would cut his own jokes when unnerved rather than risk being written off as a lightweight in the common rooms of Cambridge; no one could be funnier or more charming, yet when he was in a bad mood, and sulking like a baby, he could blight the most genial gathering with his sullen silences. A master of English prose, Connolly once compared himself not unreasonably with Sainte-Beuve, 'who criticises everything and everyone and is a better artist, yet a weaker one, than any of the contemporaries whom he criticises, than Spender-Hugo, or Auden-Lamartine, or MacNeice-Musset', yet he is now best remembered perhaps as the originator of 'the pram in the hall' and a handful of well-turned aphorisms, and as a character – greedy, overweight, lazy, daunting yet wonderfully funny – in the memoirs and diaries and letters of his friends; and that, surely, is the saddest and strangest paradox of all.

Connolly once wrote that 'I hate colonels, but I don't like the people who make fun of them,' and his ambivalence, his sense of pointing in two directions at once, of having his feet in both camps while belonging to neither, has, appropriately enough, an Anglo-Irish flavour to it: and indeed

'My mother, with an English name was Irish, my father with an Irish name was English: the one all insight and imagination, the other an unsuccessful soldier who was also a distinguished scientist; from my father I inherited a clear brain and a good memory, from my mother a romantic heart and a passionate nature.' Although he went through a Celtic phase as a boy, wrestling in vain with the Gaelic and 'reciting "The Dead at Clonmacnois" to myself in a riot of grief', he came to resent being described as an Irishman, something to which American journalists and Evelyn Waugh were prone: but the ambiguity of his origins, like the ambiguity of his class – middle? upper-middle? upper? – exacerbated his writerly sense of being at a slight angle to the world, a passionate observer rather than a mature and responsible participant. Reviewing a book about the Anglo-Irish towards the end of his life, he pondered the matter in public:

> My father's forebears came to England in 1750. Does that make them English? My mother's family, pillars of the Ascendancy, were settled in Ireland in 1660. Does that make them Irish? I was born in Coventry and brought up in Bath, where my grandparents lived and my great grandfather had been rector. I have been called a mick, a paddy, a bogtrotter, a kern and a gallowglass, a wild Irishman, rebel, renegade Catholic etc. I think of myself as a Londoner, or at any rate a Home Counties man, long resident in Sussex where I own about a third of an acre.

As he grew older, and still more so after he had become rather late in life a father for the first time, Connolly became increasingly intrigued by his family origins, sending his old friend Noël Blakiston scurrying into the bowels of the Public Record Office in pursuit of long-forgotten naval men, and not always welcoming the information he unearthed. And although for many years he remained far more obsessed by his elegant, absconding mother, his father, and his father's family, loomed larger in his life and in his genealogical musings than the grander, more remote Vernons of Clontarf.

According to Major Connolly – who took a keen interest in family history, typing up his findings, single-spaced, on the red ribbon of his machine – the Connollys were descended from the ancient kings of Connaught, 'who, in their turn, were descended from a seal'. Be that as it may, by the early nineteenth century, this particular branch of the family was established in Bath: much to Connolly's disappointment, no connection could be made to the celebrated Speaker of the Irish Parliament, who had built, at Castletown in County Kildare, the grandest Georgian house in Ireland and, maddeningly, spelt his name with only one 'n'. According to the Major, the Connollys were 'simple, bluff old sea dogs, with an old-fashioned reverence for primogeniture, heredity and what I may call nomenclature' and restless dispositions, while his son apostrophised them as a 'frugal, blue-eyed, long-lived quiet, tidy, obstinate race of soldiers and sailors'. When Blakiston's researches – undertaken, by a bizarre coincidence, for two members of the Connolly family both enquiring on the same day after the same mutual ancestor, yet neither aware of the other's existence – revealed that Matthew Connolly, fondly believed in the family to have been a captain in the West Indies Regiment, had in fact been a gunner, acquiring his certificate in 1768, Connolly wrote back to say that he was still reeling 'from such a devastating skeleton in the cupboard as a mere gunner for one's great-great-grand-father. How did Lt.Col. V. St G.T. Connolly take it? Smelling salts?'*

In the early summer of 1944, Connolly received a letter from Percy King, an unknown relation who lived in Richmond and described himself as an Anglo-Catholic bachelor who abhorred the modern age. Mr King wrote to say that Connolly had been wrong, in the autobiographical section of *Enemies of Promise*, to claim that his great-grandfather had been the Master of Ceremonies in the Pump Room at Bath. A vigorous correspondence ensued, with Percy King proving a fund of family lore, some of which found its way into the revised edition of 1949, in which the relevant pages were expanded and amended. Connolly's great-grandfather was, in fact, a general, who had commanded the Marines at Woolwich and then retired with his 'vast progeny' to Southsea: he had at least five brothers, all of whom held commissions in the Army, Navy or Marines. Despite his surname, the general was fiercely anti-Irish: his solution to the Irish problem was for the entire island to be 'sunk under ten feet of water – the Anglo-Irish gentry and the Protestant minority having no doubt first been taken off in an ark'. One of his brothers – a 'worldly old man, a blend I imagine of Major Pendennis and Major Bagstock' – was the Master of Ceremonies; another, obsessed by dead bodies, would call in and ask to see the corpse if he passed a house in mourning, after which he would go home and play the Old Hundredth on the violin 'with great devotion'. According to Mr King, the general 'ruled his sons with a rod of iron', while as far as his daughters went, 'that they did not stoop and that they should pull their stockings up straight comprised the

* In an unpublished essay entitled 'Finest Hour', Noël Blakiston described how, in search of his nautical ancestor, Connolly came into the Public Record Office to inspect the relevant muster book. ' "This just links up perfectly," he said. "I am so grateful. Will you come out and have some champagne?" ' Blakiston declined, and went back to work. Not long afterwards a member of his staff popped his head round the door and asked him whether he was prepared to see a Colonel Connolly. Blakiston assumed that this must be his old friend, who had left something behind and promoted himself to colonel as a joke, and asked him to be shown in: but the figure who was ushered in was a complete stranger. His card revealed him to be a Lt. Col. Connolly R.M., and he had come to trace an ancestor – the identical Gunner Connolly. Blakiston beckoned the colonel to the muster book, which still lay open on the desk; it was, he decided, his 'finest hour' at the P.R.O.

whole duty of women'. He was something of a skinflint too: as his funeral cortège passed through Southsea a bystander was overheard to remark that 'There goes a man who never owed a man sixpence or paid a man sixpence' – not the kind of remark that would ever be applied to his great-grandson, who spent much of his adult life fretting over money, borrowing and cadging when need be, yet displaying a disarming generosity whether or not the funds were to hand.

Cyril Connolly's grandfather, Admiral Connolly, was born in 1816 and joined the Navy in 1832. According to his grandson, he had 'a great reputation for good looks of the genial, bearded, crusty, open sort, charm, gallantry, temper and bad language', while his daughter-in-law, Mollie, suggested that 'he was known as the best-looking man in the British Navy – and had the worst or best command of bad language!' He fought in the Syrian Campaign, in New Zealand, where he dispersed some rebel tribes, in the Baltic, and off the Pacific coast of Canada, where he led a party of 450 seamen and marines, equipped with two twelve-pound howitzers, 'for the capture of an Indian in Vancouver's Island': why quite so many men were needed to capture a single Indian remains unclear, but the expedition 'was attended with complete success'. Major Connolly remembered the Admiral as 'a handsome old man of imposing presence and Regency manners', whose progress down the street was retarded by a tendency to stop 'and inform some passing Victorian damsel, in a quarter-deck voice, that she was a "damn pretty girl"'. The author of 'Remarks on Manning the Navy', the Admiral died in 1901 at his home in Marlborough Buildings, Bath, leaving behind him his widow and various journals which 'contained too many scandals to be made public during his life'.

The Admiral's widow, Harriet, was the eldest daughter of Charles Kemble, the Rector of Bath, who had made his mark on the city by restoring the Abbey along regrettably Victorian lines. He could afford to do so, since the Kembles were extremely well-off, though in his great-grandson's opinion the money could have been better spent, or – preferably – not spent at all: 'The fifty thousand pounds he contributed to the restoration of the Abbey was long a bitter warning to his children and formed the basis of a grudge against society which has always haunted me. I never had a break!' A West Country family, the Kembles had made their fortune in the tea trade: Charles Kemble had inherited Cowbridge House, near Malmesbury, from his mother and half a million from his bachelor uncle Edward, which enabled him to build a church in Stockwell before moving on to the Abbey. After leaving Oxford, the Rector joined the Clapham Sect and, although Harriet was High Church, the Kembles as a family tended to the opposite end of the spectrum: Mollie Connolly thought the Rector's children were brow-beaten by their domineering parent, and 'all the aunts except the mater were too humble and meek for their own happiness.' But if they sound a shade low-key after the martial Connollys, one Kemble relation in particular attracted the red-ribboned attention of Major Connolly in his role as family genealogist, since both men – like, in due course, the Major's son – shared an interest in the pleasures of the table. William Kettlewell, who lived in Somerset and was 'something of a crank', brought over from France a team of experts to teach the locals how to make camembert. 'With true English rottenness', the villagers failed to do the job properly: the Major 'introduced these Harptree camemberts into my officers' mess in 1894 when acting as catering officer, and they were well liked at first, but soon became too soft and runny in the middle and too hard outside.'

The Admiral's son, Matthew – better remembered as the Major – was born in Bath in 1872: according to Mollie, 'he was never normal – too old parents, I believe'. Comparing notes after the Major's death in 1947, Connolly and his mother agreed that, given his 'hoarding, collecting passion for dead objects' and his mania for classification, he ought to have become a professional scientist: but the Connollys were expected to join the forces, come what may, and after Haileybury, and some time in France and Germany, Matthew Connolly passed first into Sandhurst in 1890. He passed out with honours, and was commissioned into the King's Own Yorkshire Light Infantry, serving with his regiment in the Channel Islands, Yorkshire and Ireland; and it was while he was in Ireland that he met and became engaged to Muriel Maud 'Mollie' Vernon, the daughter of Colonel Edward Vernon of Clontarf, County Dublin, and his wife Jane, *née* Brinkley.

*

Unkindly described by Connolly's *Times* obituarist as 'a somewhat dismal pedant with a mania for classification' and by Peter Quennell as a 'mildly eccentric and slightly unattractive figure' with bibulous features reminiscent of 'an awful warning in a Victorian temperance advertisement', who spent his spare afternoons in the Windmill Theatre 'appraising and reappraising the same row of nearly naked chorus girls',* the Major, for all his sometimes unattractive ways, comes across as a loyal, sad and touching figure, awkward in his affections and admirable for the diligence with which he pursued his unusual enthusiasms; and although, when he was young, Connolly found him repressive and even repellent, he grew to appreciate him more as the

* Quennell went up in the Major's estimation when he revealed that his second wife had once been a Windmill girl, and had inadvertently toppled over when forming the centre-piece of a theatrical Rolls-Royce.

years went by, and many of his own enthusiasms – for animals, and making lists, and food and drink, and collecting china and silver and first editions – mirrored or resembled those of his seemingly incompatible father. A towering figure in the world of snails, and South African snails in particular, he was to become the author of – among other seminal works – *A Monographic Survey of South African Marine Molluscs*, 660 pages of which were published in 1938, and *The Land Shells of British Somaliland*, as well as of learned papers for the 'Proceedings of the Malacological Society' and the 'Annals of Tropical Medicine and Parasitology' on such matters as *bilharzia* in South-West Africa or the activities of a giant snail in Ceylon which, pestilentially, was given to licking the paint off window-frames. He discovered some thirty new types of snail, including one that lived under railway sleepers; six of these were named after him, and one after his son, Cyril. He became the President of the Conchological Society of Great Britain, and in 1937 he presented his collection of African snails to the Natural History Museum, which offered him in return a room in which to work and the post of 'unofficial scientific adviser'; and when he and Mollie finally drifted apart, he took a room in the Naval & Military Hotel, just over the road from the Museum, and filled it with snails in cardboard boxes lined with cotton-wool.

Snails were not his only interest. While serving in Ireland, he became something of an authority on the pedigrees of thoroughbred horses, and he was a keen philatelist from the age of seven, representing the Irish Free State at the International Philatelic Exhibition in New York in 1936; not long before his son was born, he agreed to give over an afternoon for a 'philatelic chat' with the *Stamp Collector*, an editorial in which hailed him as the 'greatest authority on Railway Parcels stamps'. He was also an acknowledged expert on potted meats and pâtés of every kind. Writing under the anonym of 'A Potter', he was the author of *Pottery: Home-made Potted Foods, Meat and Fish Pastes, Savoury Butters*, which was published by André Simon of the Wine and Food Society in 1946. 'How delicious, to a schoolboy's healthy appetite sixty years ago, was the potted meat at breakfast in my grandmother's old Wiltshire home,' he recalled, before going on to savage those 'faddists' who had 'run amok' in the potting trade with their 'pettifogging restrictions in the name of hygiene'.

Like his son, the Major was well-informed about wine as well as food: but whereas Connolly was always a moderate drinker, his father became increasingly bibulous and befuddled as the years went by and the evenings closed in. Years after the Major's death, Connolly reviewed Beverley Nichols's *Father Figure*, in which Nichols described how he had tried to murder his sadistic and alcoholic father. Connolly saw in this sad story 'an extreme version of my own':

> I was an only child of a father who drank and who made my mother unhappy and whom it was dangerous to approach after nightfall. But he remained a gentleman: I never saw him abuse my mother or saw him pass out.... He was never more than fuddled. But my mother made the same excuse as did Mrs Nichols – that he was 'not himself'; it was not he who said these things; he was poisoned; he would be different in the morning. I soon found my hate of him infiltrated by compassion, that lethal engenderer of irresolution, and when my friends sympathised with me I felt uneasy. Shame rather than hate was my emotion...

Nearly fifty years earlier Connolly – then in his last year at Oxford – found it harder to forgive, and displayed all the thin-skinned intolerance of the young. 'Major Connolly is very vulgar indeed,' he told Noël Blakiston: 'worldliness, meanness, insincerity and vulgarity are his chief vices which is why I hate them so (his next three are cowardice, vanity and greed) – I have rather a streak of vulgarity inherited from him which is what I have tried to suppress.' By then, in the mid-1920s, the Major was drinking a bottle of port a day, 'belching and coughing and lurching to the rears, as well as being fussy and irritable,' his son informed Bobbie Longden: 'He would read my letters if I gave him the chance, and worse than most of his faults are the noises he makes eating and far worse digesting...'

And yet there remains something lovable and touching about a man who can sign off his letters to his son – more often than not including some peppery reproach – with 'Best love, old chap' or 'Best love from Daddy (Major M. Connolly)'. 'I always felt he had had some terrible fright as a child which had warped him,' Connolly wrote to his mother after the Major had been found dead in his frozen room in the Glendower Hotel in South Kensington; and early on in their married life together Mollie was warned that 'Matt will never be happy; he will only play with his toys in the next room.'

*

The Vernons of Clontarf were an old Norman-Irish family, distantly related to William the Conqueror. The castle itself, situated on the outskirts of Dublin, had been granted by Charles II to Edward Vernon, the Duke of Ormonde's quarter-master-general. 'It is noteworthy,' the Major declared for the benefit of his son and heir—with customary thoroughness, he had set himself up as an expert on Mollie's family as well as his own – 'that every one of the Vernon men married a wife who was in no way connected with Irish blood except your grandmother, Jane Brinkley, whose mother, *née*

Harriet Graves, may have been Irish.' Brinkley was to re-surface years later as one of Connolly's *noms de plume*; Robert Graves, with whom Connolly once entered into a convoluted and inconclusive correspondence about mutual ancestors, was his fourth cousin, and Elizabeth Bowen may also have been related. But it was of more immediate interest to the youthful Connolly that his great-aunt Anna Brinkley had married the Earl of Kingston, so becoming the owner of Mitchelstown Castle in County Cork, the 'biggest castle in Ireland'. After the Earl's death, Anna married 'an old Welshman named Willie Webber, who had some very horse-faced lanky daughters, and lost the castle in the Irish rebellion':* but by then the Castle and its Countess had worked their magic on an impressionable and romantically-minded schoolboy, who for a time came to associate Ireland and his grand Irish relations with all that was dashing and stylish and aristocratic, and England and the Major's kin with all that was dowdy and impoverished and irremediably middle-class. In the Major's opinion, 'the Vernons were fine, tall men, usually over six feet in height, and most of the girls very beautiful'. As if that weren't enough, the Castle boasted several suits of armour, and a resident ghost as well. 'It was a friendly ghost and did no harm, usually being most in evidence at times when any of the family were about to leave it,' the Major revealed: his wife-to-be, who was susceptible to such things, once spotted it 'standing by the fire in her room in the middle of the night, but nothing had come of it'.

The seventh child of a seventh child, Mollie herself remains an evasive, almost ghost-like figure, flitting in and out of the lives of her husband and son before vanishing altogether to a new life in South Africa with General Brooke, the Major's former commanding officer. One is left with the impression of sweetness and self-deprecation coating self-interest and a certain ruthlessness: a maddening and disconcerting combination. Peter Quennell remembered her as looking like 'someone one might see at the races', a slight, graceful figure whose elegance embarrassed her son. Throughout his life, Connolly was to be haunted by the spectre of his mother, his early adulation tinged in later years with resentment and even dislike. He loved her with the passion of an only child, but like some tantalising lover who refuses to commit herself, she maddened him and taunted him, and he lived in dread of her leaving, whether for Africa or the Balearics or the final desertion of death: 'It is the loss I dread most,' he told Evelyn Waugh, commiserating over the death of the novelist's mother.

* Mitchelstown Castle was burned down during the Irish Civil War, and subsequently demolished; when Connolly revisited Mitchelstown in 1935, he reported the 'trees felled, lake the local *jardin publique*, nothing but the almshouses and Great-aunt Anna's grave left of the glory of the Lycidas Kings and the Earls of Kingston.'

'Love is the consequence of nursing,' Connolly once suggested: 'All love is for the mother, with fear and admiration for the father a secondary characteristic. All pleasurable experience derives from the mother: food, drink, warmth, sex, art. Death or alienation of the mother is the worst calamity, bringing insecurity and loss of identity.'

No doubt Mollie, for her part, was blighted by the burden of guilt invariably borne by those who abandon their families in order to live their own lives, rather than remain unhappy, dutiful spouses. 'I sometimes think it must seem to you as if I had always deserted you,' she told her son, then in his early fifties, 'but the greatest sorrow in my life was having to go to Banchory because of my lungs and not even being allowed to kiss you because of infection...' As is often the case with unhappily married women who rather despise or resent their husbands, her relationship with her son was almost flirtatious, and in later years she seemed to share his pervasive nostalgia for a paradise lost. Writing to him from South Africa to say that she had belatedly finished reading *The Rock Pool*, published in Paris some five years before, she told him that it reminded her of 'your reading to me out of your diary about the Garden of Eden'. She returned to the subject in 1952, disparaging with motherly tact his adult writings in favour of his youthful outpourings ('To my mind you have never touched the extracts you used to read me out of your diary at the Lock House. The neglected Garden of Eden...'); and four years later she recalled the smell of honeysuckle at Lock House – their last family home, near Farnham – 'and the nightingales when I was saying goodnight. I should have been able to make your childhood there so much happier... I wish you would write the Deserted Garden of Eden again, I would love it...'

'I have had many years of happy friendship with Cris,' Mollie told her son – 'Cris' being General Brooke – 'and perhaps one gives more that way than if one is complacently married'; but guilt and remorse remained, blighting the memories of Eden. The Major was bad with money, frittering away the £10,000 in capital he possessed when they married; Mollie wanted above all to be able to pass on to her son the £4000 she had received as a marriage settlement, but her life, like his in turn, was to be over-shadowed by money worries. 'My charge of you was always frustrated because I had no money'; so much so that she was only able to pay for his school uniform at Eton after her father had died and left her some money of her own.

'She and I do not really trust each other as she is convinced I do not love her, though I do,' Connolly – then in his second year at Balliol – told Noël Blakiston; while to another friend he wrote, after spending some time with Mollie in her flat in St George's Square,

> I found two days of my mother worse really than two weeks with my father because she can be so exacting and unfair and I cannot make the same allowances.... The mother is nearly always disappointed in the husband and tries to drag the child into her own generation as a substitute. They cannot take one as they find one, but go on criticising and fault-finding. They fight with each other and appeal to their child and then criticise him behind his back.

Fathers, he concluded, 'are less exacting but often more tactless or touchy. Still, they do not deliberately cause pain and when alone with one, let one alone.'

For all that, though, he was closest to Mollie. 'I have dreamt about you every night I have had it,' he wrote from his prep school, St Cyprian's, after she had sent him her photograph. When he was younger still, 'Mrs and Master Connolly' had written poems together – including 'The Adventures of Cyril and Hugoline', who were sent to live with an aunt after their mother had left for India, and were supervised by a prim, bespectacled governess.* Connolly's conviction that his mother had deserted him was, according to Peter Quennell, responsible for his 'most "Palinuroid" traits'; and the subsequent sense of loss and longing pervaded his every act and every word he wrote.

*

All this lay in the future. In the meantime, Captain Matthew Connolly and Muriel Maud Vernon, having announced their engagement, were married in Clontarf Church in July 1900. The bride wore a gown of white poplin, brocaded with shamrock; the best man was the Major's cousin, Harold Kemble, who lived at Quenington and would have two daughters, for one of whom Connolly cherished an adolescent crush; the Major's sister, Harriet – Aunt Tots, as she would eventually be known – was a bridesmaid, and a grand reception was held in the Castle. The happy couple looked in love; and in due course a child would follow.

* Hugoline Piggot was – according to Connolly's inscription on the back of a photograph of him and her as children – 'CC's first girlfriend'.

TWO

Intimations of Eden

Cyril Vernon Connolly was born in Whitley Villa, Coventry, on 10 September 1903. His father had been seconded from his regiment to look after the local Volunteers, the Edwardian equivalent of the Territorials, and the family was ensconced in a modest suburban house. According to the first edition of *Enemies of Promise*, his son was named after a cousin, Cyril Cattley, 'who discovered the Cattleya Orchid, immortalised by Proust', but surprisingly, given Connolly's adoration of Proust, whose enormous novel he discovered at Oxford, this was dropped in the revised version. Certainly the Major makes no mention of Proust or orchids in his genealogical researches, noting merely that the Cattleys had made their money from soap, and that Cyril Cattley and his brother Stephen played cricket for Eton, Cambridge and Surrey.

Connolly's father left Coventry two years later to rejoin his regiment in Sheffield. When the King came up to present the King's Own Yorkshire Light Infantry with its colours, Captain Matthew Connolly was in charge of 'G' Company, while Captain C.R.I. ('Cris') Brooke commanded 'C'. In February 1906 he embarked on the first of a series of overseas postings, as a result of which his son was to spend a good deal of time apart from his parents, more often than not with Granny Connolly in Bath. He was put in command of the North Front in Gibraltar until September of that year, when he was joined by his wife and small son, and set sail for South Africa. Although Cyril's first memory – or so he tells us – was of a chemist's shop in Bath, the windows of which were filled with brightly-coloured bottles and a rather sinister-sounding rubber cushion with a hole in the middle, like a surgical doughnut, South Africa, with its dazzling light and its exotic fruit and flowers and animals, was to provide him with an image of Eden, and a passion for hothouse fruit and tropical vegetables and unusual animals and rich, heavily-scented blossoms that remained with him for the rest of his life. Based in Pretoria, Captain Connolly was on reconnaissance duty till the end of 1906, and then served as the Commandant of the School of Signalling until March 1908, when he returned briefly to England. Mollie and Cyril had gone back to England the previous July; but in October 1908 all three returned to South Africa and went to live in Wynberg, where the Major had been appointed the District Signalling Officer for Cape Colony and was soon busying himself discovering new varieties of snail, one of which appeared to have made its way from Bulawayo in the bottom of a flower-pot.

Connolly's two childhood spells in South Africa, brief as they were and young as he was, were to provoke him to lyrical heights it would be rash to emulate: suffice it to say that 'my memories became exotic; arum lilies, loquats, eucalyptus, are the smells which seem to me divine essences, balms of Eden from another life'. He remembered walking to the sea at Cape Point through rushes and white sand, marked with the tracks of lizards; the chameleons in the garden; regimental church parades; the warm smells of tar and pine and eucalyptus. As an only child, he was used to playing by himself and inventing games; and he derived 'something approaching ecstasy from the smell of flowers and fruit and from the sub-tropical scenery'. He shook hands with Captain Scott *en route* for the Pole, saw the fleet at anchor off Simonstown, inspected some giant tortoises, watched a regimental parade on Minden Day; but all these were as nothing to the company of Wups, his dog, and One-Eye, his cat, and a host of imaginary animals as well, or solitary games with tops and fir-cones, or inhaling the scent of wet earth. 'Already my life was a chain of ecstatic moments,' he wrote, in Pateresque vein; and it was of these that they consisted.

The serpent in the garden, insofar as one existed, took the sad but predictable form of the Major. Like many only children, and particularly those whose parents don't get on, young Cyril was spoilt from an early age, above all by old Granny Connolly in Bath, who had a particularly soft spot for her 'darling Spratkins'. 'To me it seemed that the soldier servants obeyed me, my nurse gave in to me, my mother understood and encouraged me, the officers in the regiment tried to amuse me, and only of my father (who represented abstract justice) was I afraid.' The Major's groom taught him to ride on Jess, his mother's mare: but he never liked it, and retained a dreadful memory of 'being stood on a table in the yard, crying, while the two grooms tried to teach me something, either God save the King, or how to semaphore with my arms, I expect. And my father spanked me for walking on a flower-bed. Odious.' But these less congenial memories of life in South Africa were restricted to an early draft of *Enemies of Promise*, in which – significantly – no mention was made of Eden.

In between the two South African excursions, Connolly was taken to Ireland for the first time since he was a baby: to Clontarf, and then, at the high point of the holiday, to Mitchelstown Castle, a huge eighteenth-century Gothic pile, with 30,000 acres of land around it that included a lake and a wishing-well. By now the Earl was no longer alive, but Connolly's grandfather was to be seen wandering in and out with a shot-gun under his arm; when his grandson, enquiring as to his whereabouts, was told that the alarming old gentleman was 'doing his duty', he at once assumed that he must be in the lavatory. Such misunderstandings excepted, this visit 'awoke in me a new passion. I became a snob.' Being an earl's great-nephew was heady enough, even if the earl in question was no longer around, and a further ingredient in the stew was provided by Mollie's favourite sister, Aunt Mab, who had married a rich man: she was beautiful as well as rich, and he came to associate her with exotic smells, and furs, and presents, and moving from one large country house to another, with footmen and romance and (pleasantly, but more prosaically) potato cakes eaten in front of the fire.

In January 1910 Connolly left South Africa for the long journey home, accompanied by his nurse. The immediate cause of his departure was an attack of pneumonia, but towards the end of that year his parents, who stayed on in South Africa, set sail for Hong Kong, where the Major (as he now was) was posted until the following March. 'You must remember that I was away from you in your childhood so much was no fault of mine,' Mollie told her son in after years: 'You had to go home from Wynberg because you got pneumonia and Matt said that if I went home with you he would resign from the Regiment. Looking back now I suppose he was always jealous of you – and Granny was very possessive. She always made me of no account.' And, indeed, Granny Connolly was her son's next port of call, for it had been arranged that on his way back to England he would stop off in Corsica where the old lady and Aunt Tots had taken a villa. Granny Connolly spoiled him, while Aunt Tots would always remain his favourite aunt: an outgoing, cheerful figure, she was some six years younger than the Major, who – citing the colour of her eyes as evidence – liked to believe that she was not the Admiral's daughter, but the work of the family doctor.

By now Connolly had become a fully-fledged if precocious aesthete, obsessed by sunsets and the colours he associated with particular names, words, people and numbers. He went down with a fever and was given orange-leaf tea to bring his temperature down; he went for walks in the *maquis*, sailed boats made from prickly pear leaves in a tank in the garden, and collected transparent Venus's slippers off the beach. One evening he was taken to watch some French destroyers firing their torpedoes and was terrified by the noise. 'From that evening I date a horror of battleships, bands playing, noises, displays of arms and all official functions.'

Equally alarming was taking tea with the daughters of the English consul, and peeing on the floor. 'I have always felt the only child's shame at peeing, and can't do it in public lavatories unless I have a clear field some way each side of me,' he wrote later:

> I can't do it at all with friends near, nor can I ask anyone driving a car to stop because I want to, nor can I leave a room or even a cinema if I feel I should do so ostentatiously. I often think my bladder has burst. Needless to say I did then and do now spend hours in the lavatory, usually late at night, and with a book. My shame at other people being aware of my natural functions increased in proportion to the pride and curiosity I felt in them myself.

More gratifyingly, he fell in love with a Polish boy called Zenon, who was three years older, with a fringe of brown hair and dark eyes. They fought with cardboard swords and shields, and – for this was, indeed, a portentous meeting – 'From that moment I have seldom been heart-free and life without love for me has always seemed like an operation without an anaesthetic. I have been inclined to regard that condition as the justification of existence and one that takes priority over all other ideologies.' Quickly falling into what was to become the pattern of a lifetime, he fell in love again when they moved on to Tangier, this time with a bearded Moorish guide, who gave him a drum. But then it was time to make their way home to Bath; a general election campaign was in progress, and the Connollys wore blue cockades in support of the Conservative candidate.

Exiled from Eden, Connolly amused himself with reading, and collecting stamps and dried flowers, and learning how to play chess. By now he was nearly seven, and – according to *Enemies of Promise* – his 'character began to deteriorate' from that point. No doubt he was a spoilt little brat, adept at exploiting the entire armoury available to a highly-strung, nimble-witted only child, confronted by a doting grandmother – sulking and moping and whining and stamping his foot and, when thwarted, rounding on Granny Connolly 'like a vicious little golden-haired Caligula'; and no doubt he was a rather pampered little boy since, being thought delicate and prone to fevers, he had more than his share of invalid foods, if eggs, butter, tangerines and cutlets are so considered. Whether he was more spoilt or pampered than a good many other little boys of his age is a matter of debate; what mattered was the part it played in the all-important business of creating a *persona*. Throughout his life, Connolly was ingenious and industrious in creating myths about himself, self-exculpatory outriders of his personality which, while always based on shrewd self-knowledge, could be used to justify and explain persistent failures or derelictions, stamp his personality on an occasion, and cajole other people round to his ways of thinking; and, as an avid reader of Freud, like so many of his generation, he was eager to explain and blame the faults of his *persona* on the experiences of childhood. 'To this period I trace my worst faults,' he claimed:

> Indecision, for I found that by hesitating for a long time over two toys in a shop I would be given both and so was tempted to make two alternatives seem equally attractive; Ingratitude, for I grew so used to having what I wanted that I assumed it as a right; Laziness, for sloth is the especial vice of tyrants; the Impatience with boredom which is generated by devotion; the Cruelty which comes from a knowledge of power and the Giving way to moods for I learned that sulking, crying, moping, and malingering were bluffs that paid.

Not before time, perhaps, young Cyril was sent to school – to St Christopher's, in North Road, Bath. According to his literary *alter ego* Jonathan Brinkley* – whose account of being taken to school for the first time has already been quoted – the headmaster had a violent temper and bushy eyebrows, as well as a brace of degrees, while his wife 'seemed always tired and cross'. Connolly, for his part, was, he tells us, a popular boy for the engaging and, in terms of his future development, extremely important reason that 'I had embarked on the career that was to occupy me for the next ten years of "trying to be funny".' In this he almost certainly succeeded: he is best remembered by his friends as an extremely funny man in person as well as in print, constructing ever more elaborate impromptu fantasies about the doings of his friends and his own absurdities and – since he was a brilliant mimic – acting out the parts as well; and from now on his wit, his charm, and his ability to make people laugh were enrolled to offset his unusual looks and slight physique. That said, he was neither particularly good nor particularly bad at games: those who knew him years later as a rather portly magazine editor or food-loving man of letters may well have found it hard to associate him with exercise of any kind, but until he was well into his twenties he would run for miles on end or trek on foot across the Alps or the Pyrenees, and as a child he liked nothing better than to trail through long grass with an 'assegai' in one hand, to waste hours collecting caterpillars and, safely home again, to revel in 'the smell of wet cardboard, drying leaves and insect excrement, the odour of northern childhood'. Susceptible as ever, he became obsessed by saccharine Victorian paintings of the Princes in the Tower, as reproduced in *Little Arthur's History of England*, and would kiss the pages in question with all 'the licence permitted to a small boy in a sailor suit'.

Connolly's 'great love' at St Christopher's was a boy named Hubert Fitzroy Foley, with whom he particularly remembered leaning out of a dormitory window, watching a fireworks display while a band played Gilbert

* A *nom de plume* employed by Connolly under which he wrote unpublished autobiographical sketches, including 'Happy Deathbeds' – on which the opening scene of this book is based – and 'Birds of America'.

and Sullivan. That summer, he 'seemed to be initiated into the secrets of preparatory school life. I came to know the smell of the classrooms, of slates, chalk and escaping gas, and to fear the green baize door which separated the headmaster's part of the house from the boys'. On the one side silence, authority, the smell of savouries; on the other, noise and freedom.' His other friends included two future county cricketers, Reggie Ingles and Ulick Considine, who 'possessed an extraordinary fragrance, which I can only compare to that which Plutarch imparts to the Emperor Alexander', and a boy called Billy Falls, of whom he wrote:

Young Billy would a-wooing go
But Billy only wooed a woe
For every girl that Billy wooed
Said 'William, you're extremely rude.'

At night they made 'tabernacles', stretching their sheets like tents over their beds, or, in the evening light, made animal silhouettes on the wall with their hands; 'and sometimes there were mild sexual experiments, which we called "showing sights".' He enjoyed his work, read voraciously, from Mark Twain and Stephen Leacock to *Comic Cuts*, *Rainbow*, and the *Magnet*, knew – as a keen naturalist and animal-lover – about the ways of aardvarks and Tasmanian Devils, and led the occasional revolt against the masters. He was, in short, 'a typical schoolboy, with a red cap, a belt with a snake (which I slept with under my pillow), a cricket bat, a knowledge of the tracks made by wapiti, skunk, racoon and wolverine, and a happy bitchiness which endeared me, as it was intended to, to my superiors.'

He also wrote 'facetious little Leacockian sketches', in which he was helped by his mother in the holidays. Between them they also displayed a nimble talent for light verse, combining comicality, social observation and a metrical dexterity reminiscent of those nineteenth-century masters of light verse who were to loom so large, much to Connolly's subsequent regret, in the literary pantheon at Eton:

Mrs ABC: 'Oh welcome! Mrs XYZ, I hope you are quite well
Please come into the drawing-room and sing to me a song
(She's dirtying the carpet, I hope she won't stay long)
And how's old Colonel Slapdash, and dear Evangeline
(Will she ever learn to wipe her boots? Or keep her thumb nails clean?)'

Mrs XYZ: 'Oh dear me, Mrs ABC, I've *such* a lot to say
You know our little doggie, I *think* he's run away

I saw him at the garden gate, and now he is not there
(Oh odious Mrs ABC, how *do* you do your hair?)
And then I hear your husband is into debt again?
(I can't see how she likes him, unless she is insane).'

Mrs ABC: 'Alas! Dear Mrs XYZ, your words are but *too* true
(I'd like to kill the odious wretch, I wonder how she knew)
And now, dear Mrs XYZ, I wish to speak to you
(I'll keep this up no longer, the prying scratching screw)'. . . .

Whoever the actual author, Connolly's 'Ode on my own Poetry' was almost certainly too self-effacing:

Scansion unexcellable
Quite unparallelable
Whole thing abominable
A very sad affair
Rhyme is nowhere to be found
Depths of thought are not profound
Sense? It is not there.

What *was* lacking, in the 'Ode' at least, was punctuation: but that would never be his strongest point, consisting as it did of commas and dashes, with all else in short supply. More important than the absence of full stops was his growing love of the written word, though even here he succumbed to the romantic's tendency to enjoy things in retrospect or anticipation rather than at the moment of fruition:

> Ahead of me stretches the evening with my grandmother; the gas lit, the fire burning, the papers unrolled and untied, the peace and security of the literary life though even then I am depressed by the knowledge that nothing I shall find inside them will come up to the sensation of opening them. As with Leopardi's peasants, the eve of the Festival will always bring me more happiness than the Feast itself.

'I don't suppose you remember when you were a small boy being frightened you would have a receding chin and sitting with your underlip stuck out for ages?' Mollie asked her son some forty years later. It seems unlikely he ever forgot, or wanted to be reminded; but chin or no chin, the young Cyril was a sickly youth. A recurrence of malaria added an exotic touch to standard schoolboy items like chicken pox and measles, and so it was decided to take him away from school for a while. 'We shall miss him horribly,' the headmaster informed the Major: 'He is of course a boy *quite* out of the ordinary.'

*

Despite the millionaire rector with his Palladian villa and fourteen gardeners, Granny Connolly was not well off. Both her son and Mollie were often absent – Mollie had returned from Hong Kong with TB, and spent a good deal of time convalescing on the east coast of Scotland and in Switzerland; for a time she was not allowed too close to Cyril for fear of infection – so the doting Granny and her charge were sometimes reduced to living in 'rooms' in Bath, off the Earl's Court Road or, when some sea air seemed in order, on the Isle of Purbeck in Dorset. As he wrote, 'I came to know landladies, and hated them:' he was discovering 'the world of the realist novel, those fuggy rooms with plush sofas and antimacassars, gas mantles, kettles on the hob, and their landladies, overfamiliar women with common voices and ripe bosoms sprayed with jet.'*

He brushed up against the working classes as well, when, with his grandmother, they visited old servants to whom she paid a pension, one of whom was bed-ridden and alcoholic. 'Here,' he felt, 'were horrible things: illness, poverty, old age, and I felt I must make every effort to avoid coming into further contact with them.' In the gardens below the Royal Crescent he used to play with a gang of urchins, hunting for toads on summer evenings. 'Another bitter lesson can be learned from this,' he wrote in an early, unpublished draft of *Enemies of Promise* that displayed an honesty and a self-knowledge that was typical of its author, but must have been rare among the fashionable left-wingers of the late 1930s:

> That when people talk of breaking down class barriers, and making friends, raising up or mingling with the lower classes they always mean with the younger members of it. It is the militant young men, the beddable young women who really appeal to intellectual socialists. The socialism which consists of having personal relationships with the old and sick we leave to the Church . . .

Visiting Ireland with Mollie exacerbated his sense of being a social as well as a national hybrid. He equated 'sordid' England with 'Granny, Lodgings,

* 'Do you know how people like me hate their childhood, the shifts and stratagems of the shabby genteel, the smell of poverty and ugliness on the noses of excruciatingly sensitive only children?' Connolly wrote, years later, in an uncompleted play called *The Founder's Room*.

School, Poverty, Middle Class', and 'desirable' Ireland with 'Aunt Mab, Castles, Holidays, Riches, Upper Class'. With the middle classes he 'felt critical, impatient and sparkling', bridling at the attentions of 'nagging' mothers and the Major's 'hairy' friends, resenting necessary economies and the 'perambulator in the hall' (here acting as an unhappy reminder of social status, rather than a pitfall in the path of an aspiring writer); faced with a phalanx of the upper classes, he felt 'awkward, dowdy, introspective', as well as being uneasily aware, like many another suburbanite or townee, that he might well be looked down upon for hating hunting and shooting, and for feeling out of place in large, noisy families with a weakness for practical jokes. Like many another literary man, or incipient literary man, he viewed upper-class men of action, particularly those who seemed dashing, hard-living, sporting and enviably self-confident, with a kind of petrified fascination, and an improbable longing to be of their number. In due course, this urge to ingratiate himself with those with whom he had little in common would manifest itself in being elected to Pop at Eton and becoming a member of White's; but for the time being, feeling oneself to be born into one class yet condemned to live in another was, in those class-conscious days, 'like an arrow through the heart', or 'having one shoulder too low'.

Mollie, the Major and their son spent the summer and Christmas holidays of 1912 in Ireland. Connolly passed a good deal of his time in the musicians' gallery at Clontarf, playing solitary games of cricket with teams of stuffed animals – which was vastly preferable to Grandfather Vernon's misguided attempts to give him fielding practice on the lawn, or the jocular way in which his grandfather and Great-Uncle Granville pretended to chop off his head with a sword said to have belonged to another remote ancestor, the Irish king Brian Boru. Such joshing made him feel a cissy rather than a soldier, but at the same time aroused an incipient interest in Brian Boru in particular, and Irish mythology and nationalism in general. From St Christopher's he had written home to ask his mother how to spell 'Boru' 'because another boy and I have got up a thing, that he talks Scotch to me and I talk Irish brogue to him; but to make it better we thought we would better have names so he called himself Wallace MacSomething I think it was – MacBane – and I called myself Brian Bru [*sic*] and I thought I ought to know how to spell it . . .'

Eager to cultivate his Irish side, and so distance himself from middle-class England with its dispiriting freight of landladies and antimacassars, he read up about Irish heroes like Wolfe Tone and Lord Edward Fitzgerald, learned to sing nationalist songs, and struggled in vain to cultivate a brogue and even master the Gaelic. None of this guaranteed success with his Irish friends and relations, who refused to appreciate his jokes ('Oh go and eat soap') and teased him about being English – which, it seemed, was synonymous with stupidity, snobbery and a shortage of humour (none of which was a Connollyesque failing). Undaunted, he grilled Great-Uncle Glanville about the real Irish, from whom the Connollys at least – if not the Anglo-Norman Vernons – were surely descended, gratefully tracing his lineage back to Conn, the king of Connaught. He was 'lonely, romantic and affected', shy and very different from his boisterous, outward-going Irish cousins. He longed to be Irish, to be the heir to Castletown, to have a peer for a father: nobody cared, nobody loved him, and 'I would scream and scream with real tears and screams that grew more and more artificial as I had to raise my voice to carry to the dining-room... till at last my mother appeared in evening dress and would sit with me and stroke my head, smelling of chocolates.'

But the world of Clontarf was coming to a close, and with it Connolly's romantic infatuation with Ireland. In the spring of 1913 the Major and Mollie had taken a house in London, and when Colonel Vernon died his widow moved from Ireland and came to live with them there for a time. Brompton Square is made up of handsome early nineteenth-century terraced houses, surrounding a railed-in garden of grass and plane trees reserved for residents' use. The Connollys lived in No. 18, and young Cyril was given a room at the top of the house, looking across to the great Italianate dome of the Brompton Oratory. It contained Admiral Connolly's sea-chest and some animal stories by Ernest Thompson Seton – one of his favourites at the time. A fire was kept burning as late into the night as possible, for 'At night my fear of the dark was still acute. I had to have night-lights and I had a terror of anything "going out" – I could not bear a dying fire or a guttering candle or even a clock to run out – it seemed a kind of death agony.'

Brompton Oratory was Roman Catholic, but behind it stood Holy Trinity, Brompton, an Anglican stronghold, and on Sundays the nearby churches would disgorge their congregations; among them, in the C of E contingent, was young Cyril in his own miniature top hat and Eton jacket, imagining himself as the actor Charles Hawtrey. One day in the winter of 1913 Mollie took her son skating at Prince's, the recently-opened ice-rink on Queensway. Waltzes played as dashing-looking foreigners sped smoothly along, kissing the hands of ladies as they went, and Cyril fell flat on his face and hurt his nose: 'always snub, I now had an explanation for it: "I broke it skating."'

In 1912 the Major – who, much to his regret, had never seen action in his career as a soldier – had been put on half-pay, and in May 1914 he was retired from the Army on grounds of ill health: he was already suffering from rheumatism, and in later years he would hobble between the Naval & Military Hotel and the Natural History Museum with the aid of a rubber-tipped stick. Once again, the Connollys resumed their peripatetic life. When war broke out, they were living in Hythe, in Kent: it was very hot, and Connolly remembered crying at the news in a crypt lined with skulls. Despite his recent retirement, the Major had immediately offered to 'go anywhere in any capacity', and he was ordered to join the 7th Battalion of his old regiment for home duties only. The rest of that year and the early months of 1915 were spent in Woking, Whitley Bay and Harrogate; and then in March 1915 he was appointed an Assistant Officer in the Territorial Record Office in London, in charge of four officers and a hundred clerks, and responsible for paperwork covering the activities of some 100,000 soldiers. After a brief spell back in Brompton Square, the family moved to Gresham Cottage, Brentwood, in Essex. In September a bomb, dropped from a Zeppelin, fell on the Territorial Record Office: the upper part of the building was smashed, but an iron girder prevented any further damage, and since none of the officers or clerks was at work at the time, no one was hurt. In the spring of 1917 the Connollys moved to Empshott Lodge, Farnborough, which they left two years later for the Lock House, Frimley Green, near Farnham in Surrey; and in November 1919 the Major quit the Territorial Record Office, and his days as a soldier were over at last. The Lock House and the Major's unhappy behaviour there were to loom large in Connolly's life and imagination; in the meantime, though, what seemed like a lifetime of schooldays was hovering in the wings, heady with terror and delight.

THREE

St Cyprian's

Unlike the great public schools, the prep schools of England – those private schools, boarding for the most part, to which the sons of the upper and middle classes were sent between the ages of eight and thirteen – have remained relatively unknown and unsung. The single great exception, in literary terms at least, was St Cyprian's in Eastbourne, which flourished between the turn of the century and 1939, when – to the delight, no doubt, of its former inmates – it was burned to the ground. Its alumni included Cyril Connolly, Cecil Beaton, George Orwell and, some ten years later, the writer and naturalist Gavin Maxwell, all of whom produced forceful and at times lurid accounts of the time they had spent there and of its formidable ruling matriarch, and waxed eloquent on the varying degrees to which they had been scarred by the experience.

Until some thirty years ago, the Sussex coast was celebrated for its prep schools. The chalk Downs and the sea air were thought to be alive with health-giving properties, and towns like Eastbourne and Seaford and Bexhill were aswarm with school crocodiles moving purposefully ahead in the teeth of a gale, under the supervision of heavily tweeded masters with baccy pouches in their pockets and golf clubs at the ready. Sheltered from the prevailing south-westerly winds by the great bulk of Beachy Head, Eastbourne was a sleepy, genteel town, much favoured by maiden aunts and retired tea-planters or colonial civil servants who had set aside their modest life savings to buy one of the large, solidly-built Edwardian villas that were springing up behind the sea front and encroaching onto the Downs.

Edwardian prep schools embodied English institutional architecture at its best: rambling, loose-limbed, a riot of gables and mullioned windows and white-painted belfries and weather-vanes and bogus Tudor beams and balconies on which, if the weather was right, mattresses were propped out to dry – Orwell claimed to have been beaten with particular ferocity not long after arriving at St Cyprian's for wetting his bed – with playing-fields all about, decorated with goal posts or cricket nets as the season dictated. By all accounts, St Cyprian's was a typical school of its period, in terms of both the look of the place and the life that was lived within. According to Henry

Longhurst, a contemporary of Connolly's who later became a colleague on the *Sunday Times*, specialising in golf rather than books, it was a 'vast, gabled, red-brick house with a sunken playing-field, complete with a cricket pavilion, known as the Armoury, and a twenty-five-yard rifle-range', while George Orwell – still known to his school-mates as Eric Blair – recalled 'the flat playing field with its cricket pavilion and the little shed by the rifle range, the draughty dormitories, the dusty splintery passages, the square of asphalt in front of the gymnasium, the raw-looking pinewood chapel at the back'.

St Cyprian's had been founded by a recently-married couple, Mr and Mrs Vaughan Wilkes, better known to their charges as 'Sambo' and 'Flip'. Although Orwell later portrayed him as a sadistic monster, lashing out to right and left with a riding-crop or rattan cane, beating with such vigour after the bed-wetting incident that his weapon snapped in his hand (' "Look what you've made me do!" he said furiously, holding up the broken cane'), it has generally been agreed that the headmaster was the junior partner in the enterprise. Orwell remembered him as a 'round-shouldered, curiously oafish-looking man, not large but shambling in gait, with a chubby face which was like that of an overgrown baby', whilst Connolly thought him a 'cold, businesslike and dutiful consort'; a more charitable contemporary, W.H.J. Christie, recalled a 'tall, reserved, shy character', who would probably have been happier as a don or a country gent, with 'ample leisure to play golf and shoot partridges', and whose canings were on the whole something of a 'token performance'. All three agreed, however, that he made effective use of a heavy silver pencil, with which he rapped the inattentive about the head – though Orwell adds, for good measure, twisting the hairs above the ears and some well-aimed kicks below the desk. Gavin Maxwell agreed with his predecessors in pronouncing Mr Wilkes's headmastership 'a courtesy title only', adding that his effective labours were restricted to getting out of bed early enough to supervise cold baths at 7.15 a.m.

Mr Wilkes was in fact a diligent and enthusiastic advocate of his pupils' interests, not least among the smarter public schools, but it was generally agreed that his wife wore the trousers, and that St Cyprian's was 'a strictly matriarchal culture' in which 'the existence of an assertive male at the summit of the hierarchy would have been unthinkable'. As even George Orwell had to concede towards the end of 'Such, Such were the Joys' – the ferocious, posthumously-published essay in which he disinterred and heaped bile upon St Cyprian's and all it stood for, and on the Wilkeses in particular – the monsters of childhood tend to loom larger and more menacing than those of adult life, so that from the safe perspective of middle age Sambo and Flip might well seem no more than 'a couple of silly, shallow, ineffectual people, eagerly clambering up a social ladder which any thinking person could see to be on the point of collapse'; and yet so large did Flip loom in the Lilliputian world of school that one has to assume her to have been a fairly remarkable woman. For Henry Longhurst – a devout admirer, who resented the slurs perpetrated by his more literary contemporaries – she was 'the most formidable, distinguished and unforgettable woman I am likely to meet in my lifetime', as well as being 'the undisputed ruler not only of about ninety boys* but of a dozen masters and mistresses, a matron, under-matron, several maids, a school sergeant, a carpenter, two or three gardeners, Mr Wilkes, and two sons and a daughter.'

The looks and mannerisms of domestic tyrants inevitably engrave themselves on the minds of their subject peoples, and Flip was no exception. Orwell – leading the prosecution once again – conjured up a 'stocky square-built woman with hard red cheeks, a flat top to her head, prominent brows and deep-set suspicious eyes. Although a great deal of the time she was full of false heartiness, jollying one along with mannish slang ("*Buck* up, old chap!" and so forth), and even using one's Christian name, her eyes never lost their anxious accusing look.' Cecil Beaton, who 'regarded Flip with terrified awe', ungallantly recorded her 'rosy cheeks and ape-like grin'; whilst according to Gavin Maxwell, 'the appearance of Flip, her gestures – from her mannish way of lighting and smoking constant cigarettes to her purposeful walk – her voice, sharp with anger or sarcasm or jolly and encouraging', dominated every facet of school life.

Like many absolute rulers, Flip was capricious, volatile and given to favouritism, her charges keenly jostling for position while favours were bestowed or withdrawn on a whim and without a word of warning. Even Henry Longhurst had to agree with Gavin Maxwell's observation that 'to be "in favour" or "out of favour" made the difference between a just tolerable life and a perfect hell,' and W.H.J. Christie suggested that 'no primitive farmers ever scanned the omens of the sky more anxiously than we watched for changes in the climate of Flip's grace and geniality.' Like most courtiers, the favourites of the moment were uneasily aware of the fragility of their own tenure, and even the most awkward and rebellious boys, like Orwell, were far from immune to the blandishments of being in favour: 'Whenever one had the chance to suck up, one did suck up, and at the first smile one's hatred turned into a sort of cringing love,' he wrote, adding that 'I was always tremendously proud when I succeeded in making Flip laugh.' Favourites might be chosen on the basis of charm, or unction, or brain-power, or parental wealth, or important family connections. Cecil Beaton

* Figures differ here, other authorities citing a tally of seventy.

confessed in later life to having been unashamedly servile, pretending to have read books of which she approved – she was something of a literary snob, and copies of *Chum* and the *Rainbow* were hastily concealed at the sound of her tread – as well as offering to mow the lawn and paint her Christmas cards: as a reward he, like other favourites, might be taken shopping in the town and bought slices of coconut cake in Mr Hyde's tea shop, or even allowed to the cinema, returning to school as late as ten o'clock. A particular mark of favour was to be allowed to wait on the Wilkeses and their guests over dinner on Sunday nights, when the maids were off-duty: with the war on, food was in relatively short supply, and the temporary waiters were allowed to polish off the scraps behind the scenes.

Those who had fallen from grace, on the other hand, were exposed to 'the iceberg of Flip's displeasure'. Gavin Maxwell remembered her 'withering her chosen victims with an unerring though often almost sidelong blast', while Connolly recalled how

> When angry Flip would slap our faces in front of the school or pull the hair behind our ears till we cried. She would make satirical remarks at meals that pierced like a rapier and then put us through interviews in which we bellowed with repentance – 'It wasn't very straight of you, was it, Tim? Don't you *want* to do me credit – don't you *want* to have character – or do you simply not care what I think of you as long as you can get a few cheap laughs from your friends and shirk all responsibility?' The example of brothers and cousins now in the trenches was then produced to shame us. On all the boys who went through this Elizabeth and Essex relationship she had a remarkable effect, hotting them up like little Alfa-Romeos for the Brooklands of life.

Connolly went on to say how a parental visit could restore one to favour, as would a word from on high: after being compared before the whole school to the 'tribe of Reuben' – unfavourably, it seems – he was miraculously redeemed following an enquiry after him by Lord Meath, the 'founder of Empire Day' and an acquaintance of the Major's.

And yet, like many tyrants, Flip had her good points as well. Gavin Maxwell had to admit that 'she was basically a kindly person, and certainly an extremely efficient one'; non-sportsmen must have been relieved to learn that sport was taken less seriously than in comparable schools, and that for St Cyprian's to lose a match never provoked those dreaded outbursts of remorse and recrimination, since 'women are notoriously unable to take games really seriously'; and, most importantly of all, she seems to have been an enthusiastic and effective teacher, imparting to her pupils her own love of writing and of literature in particular. With many of the younger masters away at the wars, leaving behind a Mr Chips-like residue, Flip seems to have undertaken a fair amount of teaching herself, including – Mr Christie tells us – French ('impatiently, with hair-pulling and other pains'), scripture, English and history. She encouraged the boys to keep commonplace books, to read widely and well, to learn poetry by heart, and to try their hands at writing themselves; and when, in due course, Connolly and then Orwell published their generally critical accounts of life at St Cyprian's, Christie found in this a pleasing, unintended irony, in that 'I detected, among the excellencies of their writing, some of the qualities – simplicity, honesty, avoidance of verbiage – which we were encouraged by Mrs Wilkes to aim at in the writing of English.'

All this bore fruit in the wider world beyond. With monotonous regularity St Cyprian's carried off the much-sought-after Harrow History Prize, which had been set up by Sylvia Townsend Warner's father, who taught history at Harrow, and was eagerly competed for by prep schools up and down the land; and even if Orwell derided and disapproved of the way in which the brighter 'scholarship' boys were, like so many Strasbourg geese, force-fed and taught by rote whatever they needed to know in order to win scholarships to the leading public schools, so bringing further credit on the school – subjects with no examination value, like geography and science, received short shrift, and even the all-important classics were served up in pre-digested slices – there seems little reason to doubt that, in educational terms at least, St Cyprian's offered value for money.

If Orwell is to be believed, money spoke with a very loud voice at St Cyprian's. Both he and Connolly saw it, in retrospect at least, as a symptom and embodiment of plutocratic, cigar-puffing late-Edwardian England, with its snobbery and its worship of material success and its cheerful acceptance of the mighty gulf that separated the rich from the poor, the few from the many, the son of a peer or a City millionaire from the 'little office boy at forty pounds a year' (the fate with which Sambo threatened Orwell if he failed to win his Eton scholarship). For Orwell, St Cyprian's was quite simply 'an expensive and snobbish school which was in the process of becoming more snobbish and, I imagine, more expensive.' Sambo's two ambitions, he claimed, were attracting titled pupils and winning scholarships to the great public schools; while according to Connolly, Flip would have been quite happy to ship her pupils *en bloc* to Eton, along with her two sons. 'We have an awful lot of nobility i.e. Siamese princes, the grandson of the Earl of Chelmsford, a son of Viscount Malden,' young Cyril reported home in June 1916. Orwell – determined to make his point, perhaps – remembered one of the two titled boys as a 'wretched drivelling little creature, almost an albino, peering upwards out of weak eyes, with a long nose at the end of which a dewdrop always seemed to be trembling', and how, when this unhappy figure had some kind of choking fit at dinner, Sambo laughed the matter off instead of ordering him out of the room, as might have been the case had he been impoverished or a commoner; on the other hand, Henry Longhurst in no way felt himself a second-class citizen in the company of the future Lords Mildmay and Malden, despite his relatively humble origins in Bedfordshire.

Odd lordlings excepted, most of the boys were, according to Orwell – here displaying a different, very English snobbery of his own – 'the children of rich parents, but on the whole they were the unaristocratic rich, the sort of people who live in huge shrubberied houses in Bournemouth or Richmond, and have cars and butlers but not country estates.' Boys of rich parents were, he went on, given preferential treatment in the form of mid-morning milk, riding lessons and exemption from the rattan cane and the riding crop. Bright boys whose parents were less well-off were sometimes taken at reduced fees, an allowance extended to Orwell, and to Connolly as well, as he learned only years later: more thin-skinned than some, Orwell felt that such boys were made only too aware that they were there on sufferance, and that they were expected to sing for their suppers by winning scholarships; but W.H.J. Christie – whose father was also a badly-paid officer in the Indian army, and who was another beneficiary of reduced fees – claimed that no mention was ever made of it at the time, and that, like Connolly, he only learned of it after he had left.

However plutocratic some parents might have been, life at St Cyprian's was an austere enough business for rich and poor alike. Cecil Beaton remembered that it was always cold: as well as getting papillomas on his feet, he suffered terribly from chilblains, brought on in part by having to 'jump into an icy swimming-bath every morning', and exacerbated by clinging on to tepid radiators to try to warm up afterwards. Even the most nostalgic old boys conceded that the food left much to be desired, both in quantity and quality: Christie recalled that 'we were always hungry' despite various 'experimental foods' which were tried out on the boys, while Henry Longhurst's fond memories of his school-days seem all the more surprising given a diet of 'liquefied orange-coloured maize pudding with the coarse husks floating on top' and 'cold pewter pots of porridge with thick slimy lumps, into which I was actually sick one day and made to stand at a side table and eat it up.' Porridge and pewter pots loomed large in the mythology of St Cyprian's school meals: Orwell remembered with a kind of gloating disgust the encrustations of cold porridge caught under the rim of the pewter bowls, and the cargo of hairs and lumps and unidentifiable black objects with which the gruel was freighted. Jam and butter were smeared on bread as thinly as possible and, although on one occasion Connolly made free with the school's supply of honey, Orwell was reduced to stealing downstairs in the middle of the night to raid the larder. Orwell, it goes without saying, was especially eloquent on the 'disgusting' aspects of school life: the hardness of the beds, the slime in the early-morning 'plunge' pool into which they were herded in batches of five at a time, the lockless, dilapidated lavatories, the unwholesome whiff of 'sweaty stockings, dirty towels, faecal smells blowing along corridors, forks with old food between the prongs...' Small wonder that Connolly found himself longing for 'the oasis of bed, the obscurity, the peace, the liberty after stormy seas', and yearning for 'the enforced silence of winter evenings when there was no noise but the turning of pages, the plopping of gas mantles, the wind under the door, and no sensation of cold, of dread of Monday, of finding skin on my bread-and-milk and being made to drink it'; or that he should have retained a lifelong aversion to milk.

But even Orwell had to admit that life at St Cyprian's had its brighter moments – consisting, in his case, of expeditions to Beachy Head or to bathe at Birling Gap, brilliant sunlit mornings reading in bed while the other inmates of the dormitory slumbered on around him, strolling about the grounds on luminous summer evenings, or collecting caterpillars on the Downs above the town. Carpentry was a popular recreation for boys with a practical turn of mind, and the school had an enviable record on the miniature rifle range, carrying off the trophies in inter-school competitions; and if gym proved a trial to those who were not so inclined – Cecil Beaton's arms invariably gave out half-way up the rope, leaving the unhappy child suspended in mid-air – senior boys were allowed to ramble as far as Alfriston, blackberrying as they went. Favourites were allowed to write their letters in Flip's 'big oak-lined cigarette-smelling sitting-room', with its brown leather armchairs and sofa, and brown plush curtains: Flip insisted on inspecting their handwriting, so instituting an informal system of censorship.

In the month before Connolly joined St Cyprian's the First World War broke out, and for the next four years not even the most sheltered schoolboys could fail to be aware of events in the world beyond. On days when the wind was right, the rumble of guns could be heard from across the Channel; able-bodied masters enlisted; old boys on leave from the Front came down to revisit the scenes of their youth, and the names of those who had been killed were printed in the *St Cyprian's Chronicle*, along with sporting fixtures, records of academic prowess, and lists of scholarships won. The Cadet Corps assumed an unprecedented importance, forming a useful part of the 2nd Home Counties Brigade, Royal Field Artillery: a month or two before the real war broke out, Lieutenant Loseby – one of the masters who later joined up – organised a mock battle between members of the Corps and some Zulu impis who had been discovered lurking in the bushes, and were massacred to a man; and after manoeuvres on the Downs, during which they engaged the 'grey-uniformed veterans of the Volunteer Reserve', the boys – equipped with puttees, drill rifles, four buglers and a drummer, and drilled by a retired sergeant-major – would be lined up for inspection by a visiting colonel or general, who submitted an approving report to Mr Wilkes, now doubling up as a captain. The Corps band was under the expert supervision of Sergeant-Major Moody, while Sergeant Barnes taught boxing as well; he had once been the middleweight champion of the army, and liked to take on three boys at once in the ring.

Outside the school gates was a camp for convalescent soldiers, clad in uniforms of blue; the boys would save their pocket-money to buy them sweets and Woodbines, receiving regimental badges and buttons in exchange. As their contribution to the war effort, the boys were encouraged to grow vegetables and to knit, graduating – according to Longhurst – 'through simple long khaki scarves to three-needle socks and plain-and-purl balaclavas'. One especially industrious boy was transmogrified into a 'human knitting-machine', turning out blue and khaki socks by the score. He became unpopular in his dormitory as he insisted on knitting far into the night, wrapped in an eiderdown, and in the morning his fellows were woken to the remorseless click of his needles.

*

Such, then, was the school that Connolly joined in September 1914. Whether, like Henry Longhurst, he was collected at Eastbourne Station in a charabanc powered by 'a gas balloon on the roof' is something we may never know; but no doubt, like Cecil Beaton, he came equipped with twelve pairs of socks, six ditto of pyjamas, a blazer, three pairs of football shorts, a napkin ring and a Bible, plus the everyday uniform of a green jersey with a light blue collar, a cap with a Maltese cross on the front, and corduroy breeches which, Gavin Maxwell noted, 'rubbed with a purring noise as we walked'; while his favourite belongings from home were crammed into a wooden tuck-box with black metal corners and his initials stencilled on the lid. Like Beaton, he was miserably homesick at first, crying a good deal under the sheets at night; and he too suffered dreadfully from the cold, 'haunting the radiators and the lavatories, and waking up every morning with the accumulated misery of the mornings before'.

Despite the tears and the cold, he seems to have made a good start, and was soon enjoying himself and impressing his contemporaries. 'I am *very* pleased with your boy, I consider that he has made a good start,' Sambo informed the Major in Connolly's report of December 1914. School reports are seldom illuminating about their subjects' real feelings, but the following March Connolly felt free to confide to his mother that 'I like St Cyprian's very much': it may be that Flip was wielding the censor's pencil under the guise of approving his handwriting, for he went on to say how much he enjoyed going to chapel – later he remembered the chaplain for 'his grizzled cheek-tufts and his gospel of a Jesus of character who detested immorality and swearing as much as he loved the Allies' – and that he had no complaints about the early-morning plunge. In his report at the end of that term, Mr Wilkes told the Major that he hoped to be able to move his son into the scholarship form as soon as a vacancy occurred: surprisingly, perhaps, in view of his later francophilia, French was proving his weakest subject. That July, Charles Grant Robertson – a Fellow of All Souls and Tutor in Modern History at Magdalen, Oxford – made his annual descent on the school, and his findings were, as ever, given a good deal of space in the *Chronicle*.* 'I came down to St Cyprian's and took all the forms in *viva voce*,' he pronounced: 'The results were quite satisfactory. The answers were given quickly and correctly, and though of course there are always some boys in every form who fail to give the right answers, there was no falling-off in the good results I have observed in previous years.' By now Connolly had made it into the scholarship class, and both he and Eric Blair, Dr Grant Robertson informed the headmaster, 'have done very promising work, and they have a good prospect of obtaining next year distinction for themselves and their school.'

That term Connolly also carried off one of the three prizes awarded for 'boys who read the best list of books during the term'. Eager like everybody else to curry favour with the capricious Flip, he triumphed by putting Carlyle's *French Revolution* at the top of his list: improbable reading for even the most precocious twelve-year-old, it had the desired effect until the prize-winner – displaying precocity of a different kind – was caught reading Blair's copy of Compton Mackenzie's *Sinister Street*, then notorious for its intimations of homosexual goings-on at Oxford. According to Orwell, 'there was a fearful row about bringing "a book of that kind" into the school, and the momentary favourite was plunged into disgrace. Undaunted, he and

* It's hard to imagine a modern Fellow of All Souls taking time off to examine ten- and twelve-year-olds: Robertson's involvement with the school was, perhaps, indicative of the smallness of what would later be known as the 'Establishment', as well as the lengths to which the Wilkeses were prepared to go in order to advance their pupils' careers and the reputation of the school.

Blair continued to share reading-matter. 'Do you remember one or other of us getting hold of H.G. Wells's *Country of the Blind*... and being so enthralled by it that we were constantly pinching it off each other?' Orwell wondered, almost a quarter of a century later: 'It's a very vivid memory of mine, stealing along the corridor at about four o'clock on a midsummer morning into the dormitory where you slept and pinching the book from beside your bed.'

Scholarly success is far from synonymous with social success, but Connolly seems to have made his mark there as well. Orwell's childhood friend, Jacintha Buddicom, remembered Blair quoting Connolly's sayings during the school holidays, and Orwell himself recalled that 'Of course you were in every way much more of a success than I'; and – though allowances must be made for the fact that boys who go on to become famous names tend to be better remembered by writers of memoirs than the great majority who sink swiftly into oblivion – Cecil Beaton considered Connolly to be, of all the boys in the school, 'certainly the strangest, most fascinating character to me. He seemed so grown-up. Even his face was dotted with adult moles; and his long fingers ended with filbert nails.'* 'I got a bit of a shock,' Beaton went on,

> when I discovered how much he knew about life. A few of us vaguely realised that someone's parents were rich or titled, or had a large motor car. But Cyril knew which of the masters had a financial interest in St Cyprian's, and which were only there on sufferance. He said it helped you to know how to behave towards them.

Such worldly wisdom sometimes took a more Bunterish vein, as Beaton nervously recorded:

> What made me tremble was that Cyril's greed seemed stronger than his sense of self-preservation. When it came to food, he did the most dangerous things... Cyril's taste in literature being far above everyone else's, his standing with Flip kept him "in favour". Yet after breakfast, during Flip's alarming scripture lesson to the whole school, Cyril seemed unable to resist continual nibblings at the bread and honey. While we still sat at our places in the dining-room, Flip, from one end of the central table, would instruct various boys to recite the collect for the day. Her beady eyes darted through the hall, quick to discover anyone not paying attention. Cyril, barely two yards from her, surreptitiously extended a filbert-nailed

* A lifetime later, at a dinner in John Julius Norwich's house following the presentation of the Duff Cooper Prize to the poet Roy Fuller, Connolly suddenly referred to a poem in which Fuller had mentioned 'my filbert nails, my moles' – and then 'held out his hand to display his fingernails – which were, indeed, remarkably grained, brown and convex'.

> hand towards the big bowl of rough honey in front of him. Dip went the sop into the stickiness. Then it was brought by slow motion across the table, over his green sweater front, and up to his mouth. By the end of the meal, it seemed as if a hundred snails had been travelling backwards and forwards between Cyril and the honey-bowl.

Of the masters at St Cyprian's, Connolly's particular champion was Mr Ellis, 'a peppery, gruff, boy-loving master with an egg-shaped bald head': Connolly referred to him, waggishly, as 'the barking Wuf-wuf of the forest', 'Thor the Thunderer, Norwegian God' and the 'Author of the Cave Man's Guide to Algebra', but he was more widely, if dully, nicknamed 'the Egg'. He had a sandy moustache, wore baggy plus-fours and highly polished brown shoes, and carried a walking-stick which he would wave wildly about his head and bring crashing down on the desks of inattentive boys, apologising profusely as soon as the storm had blown over. Mr Ellis was convinced that the Germans deserved to win the war on account of their superior efficiency; he thought 'Cyril' an inappropriate name for his pupil, calling him 'Tim' instead and building up his *persona* as a carefree, laughing Irish rebel.

The only other master who counted at all as far as Connolly was concerned – 'the rest were makeshifts thrown up by the war' – was Mr Sillar, who had been with the school from its earliest days and remained with it to the end, and was responsible for its triumphs on the miniature rifle range. A Chips-like figure with white hair and a drooping white moustache, he was – according to W.H.J. Christie – 'one of those invaluable assets to a preparatory school, an elderly Socrates with the heart of a boy, and completely lacking in condescension to the young'; Gavin Maxwell recalled him as 'the one master whose real goodness I recognized,' while Henry Longhurst assumed him to be the one character 'about whom even poor Orwell could scarce have found anything vile to write'. He encouraged the boys to share his love of drawing, and of butterflies and moths. He loved to read aloud to the school, and his rendition of *A Christmas Carol*, accompanied by lantern slides, regularly marked the end of the Michaelmas term.

For all his worldly wisdom and the reading of *Sinister Street* under the sheets, Connolly remained the quintessential nimble-witted prep-school boy: clever, funny and articulate in the way that bright boys are, but still engagingly childish and facetious. Writing as 'Signor Veridotti' in his private version of the *St Cyprian's Chronicle* – 'Visitors are requested to call an ambulance before entering these pages,' he warns those rash enough to read these 'attempts at wit on the part of Tim Connolly' – he provided a boisterous display of schoolboy humour. Under the heading of 'How to be popular by being funny', he suggested as a 'sample joke', to be unleashed on a Saturday night in the presence of Mrs Wilkes and the assembled school, '"Why is St Cyprian's like a rotten apple?" "Because it has a rotten Corps (core)"'. Other 'good jokes' included hiding Mr Ellis's blackboard duster and – rather more controversially – asking Mr Wilkes 'if he missed all his birds when he went shooting *as usual*': the corollary of which was 'I see you haven't retired at sixty-three, as some schoolmasters do...' In a section entitled 'On Habits', Connolly resolved to clean his teeth and brush his hair every day, and never to lie except to avert punishment or 'damage the character of a friend'; useful objects advertised for sale include 'elastic envelopes for secreting inedible school puds', 'potted essays for Mrs Wilkes', available in exchange for two apples, and dusters for use as anti-beating devices; among the headlines of the day – by now, Mr Ellis is Prime Minister, and Connolly himself a member of the Cabinet – are samples from *John Bull* ('THE FACTS ABOUT THE PREMIER – Ellis the boy-whipper! Shocking testimony of pupils maimed for life by the monster's kick! ELLIS MUST GO!') and the *Daily Mail* ('Loss of Temper in Cabinet. Premier calls Sir Vernon Connolly a STINKER!'). In 'How to Write an Essay' Connolly displayed, at an early age, the lethal eye for polysyllabic obfuscation that he would later bring to bear on the works of academic literary critics ('When we consider the reconstruction of the factors which did, or did not, as the case may be, at the time of the war co-operate with the continental party when owing to the prevalence of unnatural conditions they were coordinated without in any way compromising the inaugural function and good will of either party in spite of the determined opposition of each to the other...'); and he continued to exercise the gift for light verse that he would lose at Eton and Oxford, and only fitfully regain towards the very end of his life:

Rain is drizzling on the windows
Mist is sweeping o'er the Downs
All the world is black and dreary
(What on earth of English nouns
Can I find to rhyme with Downs?)

he wrote in 'Ode on St Cyprian's Weather', while in 'The Degeneracy of St Cyprian's' he warned his readers that

The school is going to the dogs
So all the masters say
There's no one left worth talking to
Save Tomlinson and Keay

And when I heard the news I cried
O where are Crawford, Quick and Hyde
  Connell, Crawford, Quick
    And Hyde...

His verses were not immune from that fascination with his own all-too-familiar weaknesses which was to prove one of the hallmarks of his later writings:

You know I try
To be too funny
I know you sigh
And say 'Oh sonny
You always lie,
Not worth my money
Don't be so funny' –
Then I reply
'Goodbye my honey...'

Connolly's histrionic gifts, and his ability to make people laugh, were put to good use in school plays. In December 1916 he appeared as Miss Wardle – Eric Blair took the part of her father – in 'Mr Jingle's Wooing', a dramatised version of some of the Dingley Dell scenes from *Pickwick*: as well as parents and friends, nearly a hundred wounded soldiers attended one of the performances and were treated to supper afterwards. According to the *Chronicle*, the evening 'revealed an artist of most exceptional merit in Connolly as the much desired and quite undesirable mature spinster. His acting was of the highest quality and more than deserved the recognition it obtained; his entire performance was exquisite.' Other items on offer that evening included 'Pinafore Potted', in which Cecil Beaton played the part of 'Little Buttercup'. Beaton remembered Connolly playing a bar-keeper's daughter in 'mob-cap and curls' in an 'end-of-term curtain-raiser' by W.W. Jacobs – perhaps this was the occasion on which W.H.J. Christie noticed 'Tim Connolly's unruly cow's lick of hair, crammed under a Dickensian mob-cap' – and on another occasion he took part in a production of *The Mikado*, with Beaton in the lead. 'The whole school was mad about Gilbert and Sullivan,' he reported home, though he went on to suggest that the dutiful parents may not have shared its enthusiasm:

The parents came to see the play
A very stuffy audience

In fact so dull the people say
They should be called
The bored-ience...

Elsewhere, in his private version of the *Chronicle*, Connolly recorded how a deputation had waited on Beaton, begging him to 'perform his part and songs before the play commenced and to tell the audience, who remained outside, when he had finished. This was a rash proposal. Beaton finished his songs about a week ago and is now giving imitations of famous actors. The audience is still outside...'

Earlier that year, in June 1916, Field Marshal Lord Kitchener was drowned in the North Sea. He had been a national hero – his blazing eyes, waxed moustache and jabbing, accusatory forefinger glared angrily out from innumerable recruiting posters – and, suitably moved, Mrs Wilkes set his untimely end as a subject for the boys, to be commemorated in verse or prose. Connolly sent his poem to Mollie for her approval. 'I got the chap who is considered the best poet to criticise,' he told her: Blair – the poet-turned-critic in question – 'did a very good poem which he sent to a local paper'. Before submitting his own effort to the *Henley and South Oxfordshire Standard* – which was more than happy to publish so patriotic a piece – Blair showed it to Connolly, asking for 'stern criticism, please'. 'My dear Blair!!' Connolly wrote in the first of many items he was to write about his school friend, 'I am both surprised and shocked. *Dashed* good. Slight repetition. Scansion excellent. Meaning a little ambiguous in places. Epithets for the most part well selected. The whole thing is neat, elegant and polished.'

Four months later, the war intruded once again when George V descended on Eastbourne, accompanied by Field Marshals French and Robertson, to inspect the Summerdown Camp for convalescent soldiers. Doubtless to Captain Wilkes's delight, the St Cyprian's Cadet Corps provided a guard of honour for the King. 'The whole thing was rather a failure,' Connolly informed his mother, in a letter which somehow seems to have evaded the censor:

> We got our uniforms on and everything and went out to line the roads, when it began to reign [*sic*] and there was a biting wind. We stood at attention for an hour in the rain. I could hardly move my legs, they were so stiff. Then the King came passed [*sic*] in 3 taxis at about 60 miles an hour. I saw someone's hat in one of them. The wounded soldiers, there were about 1000, all leant on a fence when they saw him, so that it broke and they all fell down a bank into the mud. But the worst part was when that fat ass Sammy suddenly took us all away home because our uniforms

were wet! The other schools shrieked with laughter when we passed, and that morning Flip had lectured us on discipline etc . . .

Not surprisingly, perhaps, no mention was made in the *Chronicle* of the collapsing fence or the merriment displayed by the rival schools: the Cadet Corps, its readers were informed, had been 'summoned by the Municipal Authorities to line the road leading into the Camp and to keep the road clear for the Royal cars', a duty that was 'thoroughly appreciated by the Cadets'. The following day, the writer continued, the Corps was inspected by Colonel H.S. Follett, who gave the boys 'a most inspiriting address'. This was followed by a march-past, drill and 'an attack in extended order', after which the Corps 'then marched round the field in columns of four led by the Band'. Connolly must have been among the marchers: indeed, he may have been in a position to bark out an occasional order, since at some stage in his school military career he was promoted to the rank of corporal.

Although back in the summer Mrs Wilkes had taken her class to see *The Scarlet Pimpernel* in an Eastbourne theatre (it proved 'simply spiffing'), Connolly found that remaining in favour was proving a hazardous affair. Despite Sambo's references to his 'admirable' conduct, and improved performance on the cricket field, the autumn – usually Connolly's favourite season – brought fluctuations in his fortunes. 'I have been turned out of the fifth form again,' he told his mother, this time for ragging in the passage:

Punishment for aforesaid crime – sent to bed (by master on duty)
" " being sent to bed – sent out of the Fifth Form (by Flip)
" " being sent from Fifth Form – general bad favour (by Flip)

To make matters worse, he lost his way while out blackberrying on the Downs, and Sambo suspected him of smoking behind a gorse bush.

Bad behaviour and academic prowess are perfectly compatible, however, and back in the summer the headmaster asked the Major whether he would like to engage a special tutor in the holidays to help prepare his son for the Harrow History Prize. Whether his offer was taken up remains unclear, but in any event Connolly won first prize that year, with Eric Blair in second place and Steven Runciman – a contender from another school – and another St Cyprianite as runners-up. That year the Prize's founder and presiding genius, George Townsend Warner, died. 'He often visited us at Eastbourne,' Sambo wrote in the *Chronicle*: '. . . he used laughingly to say that he was tired of always awarding it to St Cyprian's and that *caeteris paribus* he should give it to a boy from some other school!' Sambo had no intention of letting this happen; as for the prize itself, it consisted, Connolly told his mother, of 'three rather dry books'.

That December C. Grant Robertson, writing from All Souls, once again presented his findings. The war had regrettably prevented him from examining the boys in person, but 'I have inspected the papers sent to me with particular care.' Of the pupils in the Scholarship Class, Connolly and Blair invariably topped the bill. At Greek they both did well, though Blair was far better at grammar; at Latin, they were neck-and-neck at grammar, but Blair pulled ahead at composition; Blair triumphed at French translation, Connolly at grammar; Connolly forged ahead at arithmetic and divinity; at the English essay – the subject of which was 'What is a national hero?' – Connolly provided 'the best and fullest' contender, winning 48 out of 50, with Blair lagging behind on 43. At the prize-giving that followed, Blair was presented with the Form VIA classics prize, and Connolly with the prize for English: parents were deputed to hand over the prizes, among them the Earl of Essex, Major M. Connolly, who presented Lord Pollington with the Form II Prize for French, and a Mrs Hyde, who awarded Cecil Beaton the Drawing Prize.

In February the following year, Sambo wrote to the Major to say that he would be entering his son for the Eton and Charterhouse exams in early June. Mrs Connolly had enquired tentatively after Wellington, but that, the headmaster suggested, was a '*very* poor school'. Only the best would do for a boy of Connolly's calibre, and the best was what he would get.

*

Looking back at St Cyprian's in *Enemies of Promise*, written and published some twenty years after he left, Connolly suggested that St Wulfric's, as he called it,

> was typical of England before the last war; it was worldly and worshipped success, political and social; though Spartan, the death-rate was low, for it was well-run and based on that stoicism which characterised the English governing class and has since been underestimated. 'Character, character, character' was the message which emerged when we rattled the radiators or the fence round the playing fields, and it reverberated from the rifles in the armoury, the bullets on the miniature range, the saw in the carpenter's shop and the hooves of the ponies on their trot to the Downs . . .
>
> Muscle-bound with character the alumni of St Wulfric's would pass on to the best schools, reporting their best friends for homosexuality and seeing them expelled, winning athletic distinctions – for the house rather

> than themselves, for the school rather than the house, and prizes and scholarships and shooting competitions as well – and then find their vocation in India, Burma, Nigeria and the Sudan, administering with Roman justice those natives for whom the final profligate overflow of Wulfrician character was all the time predestined.

None of this – apart from the best public school and the scholarships – seemed a probable prognosis for 'Tim' Connolly, whom Flip liked to introduce as 'our dangerous Irishman' and 'our little rebel'; nor was he alone in standing out against the prevailing cult of Character. Of his two particular friends, Connolly wrote, Blair demonstrated Intelligence, and Beaton Sensibility, as alternative modes of behaving and seeing the world. Whereas he remained, he felt, a 'stage rebel', Blair was – even as a schoolboy – the genuine article: 'Tall, pale, with his flaccid cheeks, large spatulate fingers, and supercilious voice, he was one of those boys who seem born old.' Though Blair himself denied it, Connolly claimed that, despising St Cyprian's and all it stood for, he was immune to the whole degrading business of paying court to Flip and striving to remain in favour. They walked the Downs together discussing literature and, as schoolboy poets, compared their imitations of Stevenson, Longfellow and Connolly's particular favourite, Robert Service, well-known for his camp-fire verses about manly exploits in the Yukon, redolent of billy-cans and grizzly bears. Alone among their contemporaries, Connolly later claimed, Blair was an intellectual: he read Shaw and Samuel Butler, 'and rejected not only St Wulfric's, but the war, the Empire, Kipling, Sussex and Character'. 'Of course, you realise, Connolly,' he told his companion one day, 'that, whoever wins this war, we shall emerge a second-rate nation.'

Cecil Beaton, the epitome of Sensibility, could hardly have been more different. Good at neither games nor work, 'he had a charming, dreamy face, enormous blue eyes with long lashes and wore his hair in a fringe. His voice was slow, creamy and affected.' He escaped persecution 'through good manners and a baffling independence'. Ten years later Beaton confided to his diary, apropos his old school friend, that 'He is extraordinarily intellectual but I think has no sense of beauty. One feels he has no fundamental basis and he always falters when he talks about beauty' – a fair enough judgement, perhaps, when it came to the visual arts, but way off beam as far as writing was concerned – but in the meantime Beaton taught Connolly about art, just as Blair taught him about literature, while the two boys pretended to polish the brass in the chapel, or ate gooseberries in the kitchen garden, or mowed the lawn with the help of an aged pony.

The high-point of Beaton's St Cyprian's career occurred when – 'faced with a sea of blue flannel uniforms and scarlet ties' – he sang 'If You Were the Only Girl in the World' to the convalescent soldiers from Summerdown Camp; and as he did so,

> the eighty-odd Wulfricians felt there could be no other boy in the world for them, the beetling chaplain forgot hell-fire and masturbation, the Irish drill sergeant his bayonet practice, the staff refrained from disapproving, and for a moment the whole structure of character and duty tottered and even the principles of hanging on, muddling through and building empires were called into question.

As well as playing Nanki-Poo in *The Mikado*, Beaton enjoyed illustrating scenes from Gilbert and Sullivan, and gave Connolly a 'ravishing Japanesey water colour of "on a tree by a willow a little tom-tit etc" which became my favourite picture'. But although Beaton's singing and drawing 'kept him far too busy to show the slightest interest in sex', Connolly, on the other hand, already dwelt – as he was to dwell for most of his life thereafter – in a state of heightened romantic susceptibility; and for the last years of his time at St Cyprian's the object of his adoration was a boy called Terry Wilson, referred to as 'Tony Watson' in *Enemies of Promise*. In retrospect, Wilson seemed 'the one reality' of Connolly's time at the school, as well as being 'one of the best friends, and certainly the worst enemy, to make at school'. He was

> small and brown and wiry, with an untidy fringe, a small and wonderful mouth and superb brown eyes. He had a green overcoat and we used to get far ahead of the walk and come back together. He was a beautiful boxer and runner and diver and played football very well and I used to coach him for the Common Entrance and he used to grin at me when I went up and received prizes at the end of term. We used to rag among the pegs at night and sometimes climb out of a window and run out to the lawn, but mostly he would sit drawing which he did beautifully and making me tell him stories – which if I did well would lead to a lovely picture of a fox howling . . .

Wilson was in a lower form, and 'moved in a fast-moving set of hard-smoking and hard-swearing cronies from whom he protected me'. He shared Connolly's love of animals, and accepted homage in the form of a poem:

> Wilson the silent, Wilson the merciless,
> Speaking but little from noon till dawn
> Prince of all ragers, dancers and artists,
> There's pride in your sulking and hate in your scorn.

Wilson the dreamer, lover of animals,
Thirsting for stories from night to morn,
Ragging at noontide, drawing at eve,
Dreaming the night out with thoughts forlorn.

The two boys vowed blood brotherhood, cutting crosses on their left hands and pressing the scratches together: ' "Now we are blood brothers," he said, "and we will see if you love me." He took up a pinch of salt and rubbed it in my cut, watching my face with serious interest.' Sometimes, 'after a night of pillow-fighting, gang reprisals and smoking on the roof' – the hearty had taught the aesthete how to smoke, much as he hated it – Wilson would climb into Connolly's bed:

> We slept together every Sunday for two terms when our rooms were near; biting or growling, Red Fox hurled himself at his enemy and his sharp fangs met in the other's shoulder; for long they struggled in the sharpness of the den. 'Pax,' Tim said and they lay side by side, licking their wounds . . .

Wilson would tickle his companion, 'but a consideration for my innocence prevented him from going any further; it hung round my neck like an albatross, and must have irritated him almost as much as it depressed me.' On one occasion, in a bathroom, Wilson 'tried to kiss me, wearing a towel round my waist, his brown skin shining, his hazel eyes very soft and his little lips parted.' Connolly was overcome by 'spinster modesty' and spurned his companion's approach; rebuffed, Wilson turned away and never repeated the offer, while for weeks after Connolly 'lay awake angry and miserable'.

Though evidently a heady brew, Wilson was 'never a bad influence on me, who was thought to have reformed him, nor were we anything but sentimental and chaste.' They never met again after they had gone their separate ways, Wilson to Repton and Connolly to what his friend referred to as 'Eaton', but they continued to correspond for a while. Connolly much looked forward to Wilson's letters, with their curious misspellings and carefully coloured drawings of animals, and remembered hugging them to him as a new boy at Eton 'through tea of bread and margarine and plopping gas lights and the smell of stale food'; and he stored them carefully away, for 'they were in fact a kind of religion, a religion of loyalty, romanticism, of faith defying time, of friendship triumphing over other distractions. If I failed him, I failed myself and all that I meant by love . . .' In due course, however, 'the awkward letters, with their clinging to a shrinking ice-flow of common experience and their scribbled kisses at the end, ceased, and we probably both breathed more freely. I was brotherless again.'

Wilson, Connolly later told a friend, 'was more faun-like than anyone else I have ever seen;' and in *Enemies of Promise* he uses 'Tony Watson' to introduce his celebrated theory about the 'four types' of people, of either sex, to whom he was susceptible – the Faun, the Redhead, the Extreme Blonde and the Dark Friend. The Faun, he warns us, is a type 'that has recurred through my life and which gets me into trouble;' it has a touch of cruelty and madness, is narcissistic and nimble at adapting its way to those of clever people, and tends to a 'small mouth, slanting eyes and lemon-coloured skin'. It exercises a fatal power, and the damage it does is made worse by its ability to mislead those infatuated by it into believing that their feelings are reciprocated. The other three types were mercifully rather less disruptive, though the calming effect they produced could be undone in an instant by the appearance of yet another Faun. Extreme Blondes are 'quiet, intelligent, humorous, receptive', brick-like, dependable figures who are seemingly unmoved by sudden displays of temperament; the Dark Friends, with their 'brown eyes and oval faces', are the most sympathetic of all, laughing at one's jokes and consoling the afflicted, but seldom provoking romantic adoration; the Redheads, of the 'gay, thin, dashing green-eyed variety', are a trickier proposition, in that they are often as soothing as the Extreme Blondes, but can also, quite suddenly, be as 'deleterious' as the Fauns.

Connolly's typology remains, as it must, an essentially private affair, not entirely accessible to the outside world: but it embodies an aspect of the romantic sensibility that formed so crucial an element in his character, and was to intensify and bedevil his relations with those whom he loved. As an only child, he tells us, he 'romanticised sisterhood', and longed for a sister of the same age while pining too for an imaginary brother. So strong was his desire for a sibling that he 'came to see existence in terms of the couple; in whatever group I found myself I would inevitably end by sharing my life with one other, driven by an inner selection through a course of trial and error till after forming one of a group of four or five, and then of a trio, I achieved my destiny as one half of a pair.' He called this search for the ideal partner the 'Pair System', and later, he went on, he became fascinated by Plato's belief that each one of us was seeking for a romantic counterpart; and this intense romanticism, which included among its contradictory ingredients a tendency to fall in love at first sight, a nostalgic yearning for past or abandoned loves, a restless dissatisfaction with the present, and an apparent ability to be in love with two or more people at once, was to remain with him for the rest of his life, suffusing his work with elegiac melancholy and a pervasive sense of loss.

*

By now the time had come for the scholarship boys to launch themselves at the major public schools, and despite Sambo's caveats both Connolly and Blair went up to Wellington to sit the entrance exam. Connolly thought it a dismal spot, hemmed in by pines and rhododendrons, and was no doubt relieved when he failed; Blair got his scholarship, and spent an unhappy term there before transferring to Eton, again on a scholarship and a year ahead of his friend. In June 1917 Connolly went up to Eton to sit for a Foundation Scholarship. The exam lasted two and a half days, and part of it consisted, unnervingly, of a *viva voce* conducted by a panel of four, drawn from the Provost, the Vice-Provost, the Headmaster, the Master in College, and assorted Fellows. It was customary for candidates to be accompanied by their prep school headmasters, like boxers' trainers hovering anxiously behind the ropes. Sambo took charge of the St Cyprian's contingent, taking his protégés to tea with old boys already installed as boys or masters.* Although he later went on to win a scholarship at Charterhouse, after taking the exam in a cellar, during an air raid, Connolly knew with almost mystical certainty that Eton was the place for him:

> I had a moment on Windsor Bridge; it was summer, and, after the coast, the greenness of the lush Thames Valley was enervating and oppressive; everything seemed splendid and decadent, the huge stale elms, the boys in their many-coloured caps and blazers, the top hats, the strawberries and cream, the smell of wisteria. I looked over the bridge as a boy in an outrigger came gliding past, like a waterboatman. Two Etonians were standing on the bridge and I heard one remark, 'Really that man Wilkinson's not at all a bad oar.' The foppish drawl, the two boys with their hats on the backs of their heads, the graceful sculler underneath, seemed the incarnation of elegance and maturity.

Much to his relief, and the Wilkeses' delight, he did pass, coming twelfth out of thirteen. History and English had been his special subjects, and when early the following year Flip visited Eton, she was told by Mr Marten, the history master, that although Connolly had written a 'phenomenal' history paper, he had in fact been elected on his English. A month later, Sambo suggested in his school report that if Connolly decided to take up his place at Eton the following year, it was essential that he should be able to hold his own with his fellow-Collegers, or scholarship boys. Mr Ellis reported him as being untidy and unmethodical, but interesting to teach and 'good in all branches requiring originality, thought and perception, rather than mere

* The Wilkeses' son, who was a year older than Connolly, had won a scholarship to Eton; in later life he taught at the school and married the daughter of C.A. Alington, the Headmaster in Connolly's day.

adherence to rule'; and over the months that followed, the Wilkeses did all they could to ensure that when he finally arrived at Eton, he did so in prime condition. Writing to the Major in April 1918, Sambo warned that Connolly was 'a little inclined to write for effect' and to 'fly off at a tangent and not finish one book before beginning another': boys at Eton were left to work on their own – a discipline calling for reserves of 'grit' – and he was encouraging him to study Horace and Homer 'just as if he were at Eton', so as to make sure that he wouldn't lag behind the rest of his year, or 'election'.

With his place at Eton assured, Connolly could afford to enjoy the remainder of his time at St Cyprian's. By now he was a 'good mixer', famous for his 'repartee' and waggish turns of phrase, and head of the Sixth Form, which had its own sitting-room; the other occupants were Ned Northcote, the captain of the school and an Extreme Blonde, Frankie Wright, a Dark Friend, and the faunlike Nigel Kirkpatrick, who captained the football team and later disapproved of Messrs Connolly and Orwell's accounts of the school. They formed a 'little clique at the head of the school . . . gay, powerful, introspective and absorbed in each other's impressions': they were 'about as civilised as little boys can be', seldom caning junior boys, writing to each other in the holidays, and treating each other with exemplary politeness. Connolly saw them in retrospect as a 'kind of "Souls" of St Wulfric's', but their behaviour often had more in common with Billy Bunter than with A.J. Balfour or Raymond Asquith.

Feeling he could confide in his mother 'as you will not write to Mrs Wilkes as some mothers would', he reported a night-time adventure in which he lost his way in the dark, fell down a flight of stairs, and found himself in the matron's room *en route* for the school pantry and its supply of buns. Matrons loom large in the mythology of prep schools, and St Cyprian's was no exception. She used to creep about the corridors in rubber-soled shoes, hoping to surprise boys talking in the dorms after lights-out; or, as Connolly put it,

Stalk and sneak, stalk and sneak,
Maid of the rubbered shoes
Sneak, sneak, every week,
Maid of the rubbered shoes
Over the cubicle wing you go
Hearing the red room whisp'ring low
Low as a murmuring sea . . .*

* In the version printed in *Enemies of Promise*, 'maid' had become 'Maud' – a suitably Tennysonian touch.

One terrible evening three of the 'Souls' were caught by Matron talking in Connolly's cubicle, the door of which had been bolted with a toothbrush. Their crime was reported at once, and they were taken downstairs to be caned by Sambo; and the following day further disgrace ensued, with all three losing their sergeants' stripes in the Corps and their places in the Sixth Form.

'My lack of character was now a permanent feature,' Connolly commented:

> I was *unreliable*. For that reason I was head of the sixth but not captain of the school; I occupied already the position I was so often to maintain in after life, that of the intellectual who is never given the job because he is 'brilliant but unsound'. I was also a physical coward, though I learned how to conceal it, a natural captain of second elevens, and a moral coward by compensation, since, in an English community, moral cowardice is an asset.

If Character was the quality that made for conventional success, 'Character plus Prettiness' was an even more effective combination in the tiny world of prep school. Connolly was lamentably short on Character, nor was he pretty like Terry Wilson or Nigel Kirkpatrick: but he knew how to charm and to make people laugh, and he was clever and articulate: qualities that he would exploit to the full in the wider world that opened up after Sambo had, in a final peroration at the end of the Easter term, exhorted those boys who were leaving, and those going on to Eton in particular, not to play with themselves, or go for walks with boys from another house, or make friends with older boys, and to report at once any boys who tried to climb into their beds – all eyes swivelling in Connolly's direction, since it was assumed that literary types were prone to that kind of thing. Tearful farewells were exchanged with the 'Souls' and a suddenly benevolent Flip; and life at St Cyprian's claimed him no more.

*

Flip and Sambo might well have felt that they had done with Connolly, and done him proud, but he was far from done with St Cyprian's. Twenty years after Sambo's exhortatory address, he returned to his prep school in the autobiographical section of *Enemies of Promise*; and hardly had the book been published than Mrs Wilkes wrote from Midhurst, whence the school had decamped following the disastrous fire. 'Dear Tim,' she wrote,

> The makers of St Cyprian's are optimistic (though not easily disheartened) and yet it lay in your power to do one of them at least serious

> phshlogical [*sic*] damage. Other damage too which I find it hard to think you did deliberately to two people who did a very great deal for you, one of whom at least always defended you against all detractors and understood your particular difficulties though you did not (like most small boys) realise this at the time and has always been your friend and supporter in spite of what was said against you later at Eton and Oxford. I suppose that is why your book got me rather badly . . .

Not only had the book 'hurt my husband a lot when he was ill and easily upset', but 'your apparent opinion of me is so far removed from all I have ever tried to be and do and credited me with motives that never even occurred to me . . .' Despite her bruised feelings and curious grammar, her old resilience soon resurfaced in a request that he should write a short piece for the *Chronicle*.

As might be expected, old boys of a Character-free kind reacted rather differently. Cecil Beaton wrote to say how thrilled he was by Connolly's account of the school – 'I am deeply impressed by your having seen through all the futilities and snobbishnesses of Flip and her entourage whom I hope are alive to read of what they unsuspectingly nurtured.' Orwell's reaction was bleaker, less jubilant and vindictive: 'I wonder how you can write about St Cyprian's. It's all like an awful nightmare to me, and sometimes I think I can still taste the porridge (out of those pewter bowls, do you remember?)' That said, Orwell went on to produce a far more damning account of prep schools in general, and St Cyprian's in particular, in his celebrated – or notorious – essay 'Such, Such Were the Joys', which 'I originally undertook as a sort of pendant to Cyril Connolly's *Enemies of Promise*, he having asked me to write a reminiscence of the preparatory school we were at together for *Horizon*.' The essay was never published during his lifetime: although he was keen to see it in print, he felt this should wait until 'the people most concerned' were dead, and he was worried about the risk of libel. Not long after his death, however, it was published in America. Henry Longhurst, who unwisely bought a copy in Honolulu, was 'so shocked that I have never read it again'. In a letter to Connolly, A.S.F. Gow, who had taught at Eton while Connolly and Blair were there before becoming a don at Trinity, Cambridge, and who had urged Orwell's widow not to include the offensive item in the four-volume *Collected Essays, Journalism and Letters*, rose to Flip's defence. She was, he suggested,

> capable and motherly in a way which jarred on you and Orwell. But they were decent people and genuinely anxious to do the best they could for the school and the boys. No other prep school proprietors in my

> experience took so much trouble to see the boys at Eton and to enquire how they were getting on; and if some of their methods at Eastbourne now seem out-of-date I should doubt if they were more different from those of other prep schools at the time.

Connolly had already admitted in print that he had 'never dared to re-read' Flip's reproachful letter, but that re-reading old reports and letters had made him in old age unhappily aware of 'the immense trouble she had taken to help me win my scholarship to Eton'. The Wilkeses were 'true friends and I had caricatured their mannerisms . . . and read mercenary motives into much that was just enthusiasm'. The publication of Orwell's writings prompted a fresh reappraisal: 'History, if it can be bothered, will probably show Mr Wilkes to have been an extremely conscientious, though perhaps unimaginative and unlovable man; and Mrs Wilkes to have used too much physical violence and emotional blackmail, and to have vented some personal bitterness on the boys. Yet she was warm-hearted and an inspired teacher.'

Three years earlier the old lady had written to 'Cyril/Tim' to ask if he could help Charles Rivett Carnac, a school contemporary, to find a publisher for a book he had written about the Mounties. By now she was living in Eastbourne, in a lodge at the end of what had once been the school drive. She died in August 1967, aged ninety-one. Not long before her death, Henry Longhurst paid her a visit. He found her as sprightly as ever, doing the *Times* crossword, and able to remember every detail of the boys who had passed through the school. Connolly attended her funeral, but 'Nobody spoke to me.'

FOUR

'Aut Colleger aut Nihil'

Whereas St Cyprian's had been in existence only for a couple of decades when Connolly left it in the summer of 1918, Eton had been founded by Henry VI in 1440: it was, as it still is, the grandest if not the oldest of the great English public schools, in which middle-class boys like Connolly rubbed shoulders with the sons of earls and foreign potentates. Endowed, as often as not, with a particular blend of stylishness, charm, arrogance and self-confidence, Etonians went on to rule the Empire, to occupy as if by right the highest positions in the land, and to make an impact out of all proportion to their numbers on every aspect of British life, from sport and soldiering to law and literature. Eton was still a small country town, just over the river from Windsor, where the huge royal castle frowned greyly down from its heights. It consisted of a main street, with narrow pavements lined with shops and private houses, all apparently built for dwarves, at the far end of which, where the road suddenly widened, a baffled foreigner or new arrival would in term time find himself suddenly swamped by surging tides of schoolboys between the ages of thirteen and eighteen, incongruously clad for the most part in grubby black tail-coats, black-and-white striped trousers, scuffed black shoes, black waistcoats, white shirts and white tuck-in ties, and, as if to complete the resemblance to youthful undertakers, black top hats. *'Mais qu'est que c'est que çela? C'est une punition?'* an appalled André Gide asked Connolly when, years later, they stopped at Eton on their way back from staying with Lord Berners, and found themselves surrounded by these graceful, crow-like figures.* Among them moved some older, graver-looking figures, usually clad in grey, with academic gowns hanging from their shoulders and mortar-boards on their heads, who were known to the boys as 'beaks' or 'ushers', to the world at large as schoolmasters. During the afternoon the tail-coats and stiff white collars of the swots heading for the School Library would be replaced by the more flamboyant hues of the sportsmen: in summer by the white flannels and dazzling blazers of the

*According to Diana Mosley, on the other hand, Connolly and Gide called in at Eton after Gide had been awarded an honorary degree at Oxford; and Gide's comment – on watching some Collegers about to eat their evening meal – was *'Cela me coupe l'appétit.'*

cricketers, *en route* to Agar's Plough, the great playing fields that lay between the school and the river, bordered by giant, soporific elms, or the shorts and scarves of the 'wetbobs', as schoolboy oarsmen were known; in the Easter half by soccer-players clunking over the cobbles in their cleated boots, and in the autumn by players of the Field Game. All around – for the school straddled the main street – were the buildings of Eton itself: an elegant, red-brick, very English hotch-potch of styles and periods, from mediaeval to Victorian, in which high fifteenth-century chimneys and Georgian doors, white-painted mullion windows and Elizabethan diamond panes jostled one another. At the heart of it all was the School Yard, a huge cobbled quadrangle reminiscent of Hampton Court or a Cambridge college, and guarded, as such places always are, by implacable porters at the gate: in the centre of the Yard stood a railed-off statue of the school's royal founder, and beyond him loomed Lupton's Tower, a fine Tudor gatehouse with four finials at each corner. A separate building in the cloisters housed the College Library and its priceless collections. To the right of the School Yard, approached by a broad swathe of steps, stood the College chapel, a Perpendicular masterpiece similar to, though smaller than, the great chapel at King's, Cambridge, a sister foundation to which many Etonians made their way in due course; to the left were the mediaeval buildings of College, the oldest part of the school, which included Lower School, a still-functioning fifteenth-century classroom with skeletal wooden desks blackened by age; while the side of the Yard that ran along the street was possibly the work of Sir Christopher Wren, with a pillared arcade or loggia and, above it, a long, dusty, narrow room called Upper School, the blackened panelling of which was carved with generations of schoolboy names, where debates were held and plays performed and the school as a whole could be addressed. School Yard and its adjacent buildings formed the historical core of the school; in the streets around stood the gaunt, mostly Victorian Gothic houses in which the great majority of Etonians lived, under the supervision of a housemaster and a resident 'dame', or matron.

The buildings, the river, the playing fields in summer, the lush green vegetation, the boys themselves in their curious uniforms, both clerical and urbane, the sense of history and the long list of Etonians past and present who had made their marks in the world – all these proved a heady mixture for most, sometimes the headiest of their lives; and no one (except perhaps the poet Thomas Gray some two hundred years earlier) was to hymn its delights with a more elegiac sense of loss than Cyril Connolly, for whom 'Eton was our Eden and gave us grace, greenness and security, the security to rebel, the greenness to worship, and the grace to love'; while his contemporary Henry Yorke – the novelist Henry Green – struck a similarly prelapsarian note, recalling how 'Those days belonged to adolescence, when one's heart was the world's... We were fresh and saw opening out before us as a promise what stretches at our feet now forever unredeemed.' Not all Etonians were as rhapsodic: Christopher Hollis, who was a year or two older than Connolly and an important figure in the school, thought it in retrospect 'an absurd but lovable place', in a dull part of the country and far too near Slough for its own good. Etonians tended, however democratic their intentions, to see themselves as almost a caste apart, but Hollis professed – a shade disingenuously – to be unable to see why those who had left tended to go on and on about their time there, since it wasn't really any different from anywhere else; but he did agree with Connolly that 'it encouraged both extravagant conformity and extravagant eccentricity.... Precisely because it was so sure that the vast majority would conform, it was prepared to allow the individual not to conform.'

Towards the end of his life, Connolly remembered how

> Eton publishes a list of all the boys with their home addresses and the names of their parents or guardians, and these we used to study with fascination as the assemblies in School Yard, to be called over, brought out all the boys, athletes in their splendid plumage, scholars in their gowns, new boys in their short jackets.
>
> Although we were supposed not to be snobs, except about those who were good at games, some of those addresses were unforgettable: 'c/o H.M. King of the Belgians'; 'Duke of Hamilton, The Palace, Hamilton'; 'Sirdar Charanjit Singh of Kapurthala, Charanjit Castle, Jullundur City, India'...

Despite such heady company, the novelist Anthony Powell, the son of a professional soldier, who went to Eton in the summer of 1919, claims to 'recall no sense of inferiority on account of many boys' parents being richer and grander than my own', and that it was only when he moved on to Oxford that he was exposed to the withering impact of snobbery and riches. Intellectual ability, on the other hand, did differentiate a small minority – which included Connolly – from their fellow-pupils. Of the 1100 boys in the school, seventy were 'Collegers' or King's Scholars, who wore the initials 'K.S.' after their names and were housed in College, in the ancient heart of the school; whereas the rest, known as 'Oppidans', were scattered between the red Victorian houses in the town. Collegers were known unflatteringly as 'tugs',* often preceded by the epithet 'dirty': although Powell thought that 'the supposed difference between Oppidans and Collegers is often exaggerated,' the stereotypes had it that Collegers were middle-class swots who

* From *toga*, a gown.

spent an unhealthy amount of time poring over their books, and were rightly looked down upon by the Oppidans, a flamboyant or aggressive minority of whom were thought to be richer, better connected, better at games, and a good deal more worldly and dashing. Connolly remembered how, as a very junior Colleger, he was regularly kicked by an Oppidan called Mosley ('brother of the Leader'), and how, since Collegers' fees were a quarter of those paid by the rest, some Oppidans

> grudged the 70 scholars access to the privileges and education for which their parents paid £400 a year, they imagined them to be of inferior social class, to be dirty, and to be as unpleasant as must be expected when a collection of people are chosen for their intelligence. I was a standing argument in support of their prejudices.

Although Connolly, as he grew older, was to develop a familiar, ambivalent attitude towards the Oppidan grandees – half-contemptuous, half-admiring, disdainful yet longing to be accepted – he retained, as did many of his fellows, a very strong sense of Collegers as a people apart, a closely-knit group whose friendships and animosities had an intensity and a rarefied self-absorption unknown in the more humdrum houses beyond. 'You will find all Oppidans worldly . . .' he once advised a fellow-Colleger, adding that 'I detest worldliness more than any other trait;' and a year or two later that same friend, by now an undergraduate, wrote to his old mentor in the elegiac tones with which this particular group, momentarily forgetting the miseries of their early days, came to look back on their days in College. 'College is the only possible preparation for any life whatsoever. College is the only real proof I know of the existence of God – *aut Colleger aut nihil*,' he told Connolly: 'I have not passed a night since I left in which I have not dreamt either about College or some of the happy souls still there.'

Not all Collegers were quite as star-struck, or had quite so hyperbolic a view of College's role in the cosmos, but it must have been hard to resist the physical attractions of College, with its mixture of ancient buildings, cloisters and cobbles, and its great dining-hall with a high table at one end and eminent old boys in oils gazing down from the walls. The writer and editor John Lehmann, who entered College in 1921, the year before Connolly left, remembered the insidious 'romantic charm' of College, 'a charm derived to a large extent from the sense of living in history, in a nest of ancient buildings,' and recalled how

> The light of autumn evenings falls with peculiar beauty on the older buildings of Eton: under the darkening rose- and flame-coloured skies,

with the yellow leaves drifting from the elms, the boys returning from practice at the Wall Game, mud spattered on their striped stockings and shirts, huge woollen scarves wrapped round their necks, might have been the young Greek warriors seen through the eyes of a mediaeval chronicler . . .

Writing to an old College friend from Balliol in 1923, Connolly – racked with nostalgia for the 'perfect beauty' of his last two summers at Eton – used similar language to Lehmann's, conjuring up 'the echoes of ancient tongues that link College to the youth of Athens or the age of Ronsard. The vanity, the affectation, the introspection, the truth of it all . . . '; but in the meantime, as a new arrival in the autumn of 1918, he found himself 'quite lost and friendless' in a far from Arcadian world.

The fifteen junior boys in College lived in a long, barn-like room called Chamber, which was divided into stable-like stalls, separated from one another by wooden partitions, each about ten feet high and carved all over with the names of former inmates. Each stall contained a chair, a desk (known as a 'burry', short for 'bureau'), a bed which pulled down from the wall, and a basin in which the occupant could wash in cold water. A passage ran the length of the room; half-way down was a fireplace and a large round table, which was used for 'siphonings' by the Captain of Chamber, who, though the same age as his fellows, was allowed to administer seven strokes with a rubber tube for particular misdemeanours. Further unpleasantnesses also associated with this otherwise harmless table were 'Chamber singing' – boys were made to stand on it and sing before the assembled company, which presented no problems to melodious extroverts, but was a torment to the timid and the tuneless – and a ritual, common to most public schools, whereby new arrivals were subjected to a ferocious grilling about school lore and hierarchies and similar important matters, and duly punished if they failed to produce the right answers. And it went without saying that boys in Chamber were expected to 'fag' for older boys, who could steal what little spare time they had by sending them on unwelcome chores, and beat them for their mistakes. Who could beat whom, and who could even talk to whom, raised the whole question of authority; for Eton, in those days at least, was an intensely hierarchical institution, with often baffling and countervailing structures of command.

At the top of the adult hierarchy was the Provost, an honorific post, and below him the Vice-Provost and then the Headmaster. Although Connolly claimed in later life to have been on book-borrowing terms with the then Provost, M.R. James – better remembered as a writer of ghost stories – neither he nor the Headmaster, C.A. Alington, a Church of England clergyman who had been appointed in 1916, loomed large in his life at Eton. Far more important, given the self-contained nature of College life, was the Master in College, J.A. Crace. Although Mr Crace displayed, in his school reports at least, a shrewd and sympathetic understanding of Connolly's strengths and weaknesses, he was viewed by his subject with a far more jaundiced eye. 'The Master in College who governed us was not the ordinary schoolmaster type,' Connolly once suggested:

> He was a jesuitical, conscientious and deceitful man, not at peace with himself, and perpetually torn between an idealistic and a cynical attitude to boys. He was religious, unmarried, Celtic, a Browning addict and, like myself, obviously a virgin. He would come round, when I had been beaten, whistling in a quizzical way; it was unnerving to discover that he knew all about it, and perhaps had even suggested it. He loved tickling small boys, and the squeals of the tickled were agonising music for the bullied and the persecuted like myself. I was never really tickle-worthy.

Elsewhere he conjured up the hapless Master on holiday, 'brooding, a sinister figure, among the frowning beeches and bleak moorland of his ancestral home – there in the massive hall walking up and pacing down, at times emitting soft trills and squeaking with compressed lips . . .'

Particularly arrogant or snobbish boys tended to look down on the 'beaks' as unusually well-educated servants, fawning members of the middle classes who could be relied upon to pander to their more aristocratic pupils in the hope that they might thereby ingratiate themselves with the parents and wangle an invitation to the ancestral home, and be patronised accordingly. Doubtless such attitudes were rarer than Connolly liked to suggest – most of the masters had been to the school themselves – but it may well be true that, compared with other schools, the balance of power tilted towards the senior boys rather than the masters, and not simply because the boys were allowed to beat one another, whereas the masters were restricted to issuing lines, detentions and 'tickets' for misbehaviour.

The most powerful body in the school was Pop – more formally known as the Eton Society – a self-selected oligarchy of some twenty-eight boys, mostly sportsmen and swells, who were allowed to wear coloured waistcoats, braid on their tail-coats and, for purposes of identification, blobs of sealing-wax on their top hats; they were further entitled to carry tightly-rolled umbrellas and to walk arm-in-arm about the streets. An *ex officio* member of Pop was the Captain of the School, a Colleger who corresponded to the Captain of the House in an Oppidan house and – in theory – ruled the school in conjunction with the Sixth Form, which itself consisted of ten

Collegers and an equal number of Oppidans, who were entitled to employ fags, cane junior boys and wear stick-up collars on their shirts. Within College itself, power lay with him and the nine other College members of the Sixth Form. Below them was a small group of boys known as 'Liberty'; then those who had escaped the thraldom of fagging and occupied an indeterminate area between powerlessness and power; and at the bottom of the pile were the boys in Chamber, such as the newly-arrived Connolly K.S. Like layers of sediment, Collegers were divided into 'elections', according to the year in which they had won their scholarships; and when they arrived each election was supposed to keep to itself, and fraternisation with one's 'senior' or 'junior' election was frowned upon. Trying to explain all this years later for puzzled laymen, Connolly employed a suitably mediaeval analogy: members of Pop represented the feudal over-lords, with assorted Sixth Formers and captains of games occupying the ranks below; the masters embodied the countervailing power of the Church, the fags stood in for the serfs, and the rest lay uneasily between.

Connolly's first year was spent as a 'complete nonentity'. He was sixty-ninth in College, one from the bottom; his fagmaster failed to observe the convention whereby 'fagmasters were usually chivalrous to their own slaves,' if not to other people's; and far from extending a fraternal hand, Godfrey Meynell – the ex-St Cyprianite whom Sambo had chosen to keep an eye on his protégé – turned out to be an inventive and industrious bully, whose activities were approved by the elections above on the grounds that he was that elusive entity, a 'good influence'. 'A tousled wire-terrier of a boy' who loved reading Homer, Meynell made Connolly dance on the mantelpiece above the fire in Chamber, waving a red-hot poker between his legs and submitting him to the kind of ritual beloved of bullies (' "What is your name?" "Connolly" "No – what is your real name? Go on. Say it." "Ugly." "All right, Ugly, you can come down." ').

Equally unendurable, and equally reminiscent of *Tom Brown's Schooldays*, were the beatings to which junior boys, and not only junior boys, were subjected. Connolly recalled how, at Prayers, the eyes of Sixth Form would swivel round in the direction of the damned, and how, after the eighteen-year-olds had eaten supper in a room of their own, they would send a fag to collect the wanted boy from where he stood – half-undressed, perhaps, and about to step into the bath – and take him away to be beaten over a chair by the Captain of the School or some other member of Sixth Form. Occasionally a mass beating would take place, and all the fags would be beaten for being 'generally uppish' or, on one occasion, because an unexplained sponge had fallen from a window and landed on a master's head. The Captain of the School, Marjoribanks, was a passionate flogger, and when Meynell handed in an anonymous, suggestive note to his fagmaster and no culprit could be found, the entire lower half of College was subjected to the lash.

Not surprisingly, Connolly took shelter as often as he could in the School Library, immersing himself in the Celtic Twilight; and he fell in love with a faun-like little Oppidan, 'who was quick to divine in the little black-gowned, dirty Colleger a potential admirer, even as a beautiful orchid accepts the visits of some repulsive beetle'. The beatings and bullying were affecting his work, and he loathed having to present the dreaded 'tickets' to his tutor, the long-term effect of which was that 'To this day I cannot bear to be sent for or hear of anyone's wanting to see me about something without acute nervous dread'; but he found salvation, once again, in his ability to make people laugh. Meynell began to find him funny, and so too did his sidekick Hopwood; the bullying gradually died away; and by the end of his second term Connolly was indulging in some mild bullying himself, the Goebbels – as he later put it – to Meynell's Hitler and Hopwood's Goering.

In his autobiography, Anthony Powell – himself an Oppidan – suggested that, quite apart from being a 'poor advertisement for self-government by learned persons', the bullying that went on in College was 'preparatory school bullying unlike in kind, rather than degree, what went on in the rest of the school. At the same time these hardships collectively produced an indestructible corporate feeling, of which Connolly himself possessed a strong sense.' But after *Enemies of Promise* was published, Connolly received letters from two well-known Old Etonians, both expressing surprise at the brutalities he had so luridly described. 'I was staggered by your account of College,' Maurice Baring wrote: 'I had always taken it for granted that College was like a larger house which possessed all the urbanities and the grown-up-ness of Oppidan life without the conventionality and Philistinism. I thought College was peopled by spontaneous scholars who loved scholarship for scholarship's sake and worked because they liked it. Now comes your book . . .' And Maynard Keynes was equally amazed: according to him, 'the old College customs you suffered from all came in *after* my time and were unheard of in my day – frequent and mass beatings, College Pop privilege in Reading Room, all the politics of your period. No mass beatings had ever been heard of in or before my time – we should have been profoundly shocked . . . There was no rule of non-intercourse with the elections, except (not very rigidly) in Chamber . . .'

The war was one reason for this new severity: not only had the Officers' Training Corps been made compulsory, but according to Hollis, discipline had become far stricter in every area of school life. With perfect if unconscious timing, Meynell asked Connolly to call him by 'Godfrey' shortly after the Armistice had been signed. The end of hostilities was to have an effect on Eton life, and College life, as well as in the wider world beyond. The Officers' Training Corps collapsed into 'total anarchy'; revolutionary views received an unexpected airing, with fifteen out of the sixteen boys in Eric Blair's English class voting to include Lenin among the ten greatest men alive; some senior boys, with Hollis to the fore, 'decided that the traditional customs of punishment were barbaric and refused to punish the boys under our authority'. Armistice Day was a half-holiday, during the course of which – according to Connolly's most flamboyant contemporary, Brian Howard –

> a riot commenced, all the school rushed up and down the streets yelling and screaming, one person was beating a bath-tub, another a tea tray, and you never *heard* such a noise, then for two or three days cheering and singing and fireworks continued and I nearly burnt the house down, then Mr Booker gave a banquet, with fruit salad and chicken and pheasant and cider . . . and then we carried a maid up and down the house and sang songs till nearly 10 o'clock. Japanese lanterns were hung outside the house, and the place was covered in flags.

According to Orwell, on the other hand,

> Our elders had decided for us that we should celebrate peace in the traditional manner by whooping over the fallen foe. We were to march into the school yard, carrying torches, and sing jingo songs of the type of 'Rule Britannia'. The boys – to their honour, I think – guyed the whole proceedings and sang blasphemous and seditious words to the tunes provided.

A conflict broke out within the school and within College itself between the reactionaries – supported, in Connolly's view, by the masters, the Master in College and 'certain Vile Old Men who wished to wrest from the boys all liberty and independence' – and the liberals, who wanted to relax the austere and authoritarian regime that had come in with the war, abolish the election system, modify the fagging system, place less emphasis on games and colours and the OTC and, within College itself, reduce the privileges of College Pop; and it was fought with all the ideological vigour that divides those who believe in the inherent wickedness of man from those who would rather appeal to reason, goodness and common sense. The dominant figures in Connolly's senior election – the boys in the year ahead of him in College – formed an 'oasis of enlightenment' between the reactionaries in the year above, and the cowed conformists from the year below. These potentially kindred spirits included Denis Dannreuther, who eventually became an enlightened Captain of the School and subsequently a Fellow of All Souls; Roger Mynors, later to become a Professor of Latin at both Cambridge and Oxford; Bobbie Longden, who was to become one of Connolly's closest friends; and, rather aloof and very much a loner, Eric Blair, who spent his days reading Shaw and Samuel Butler, and sneered at 'They' – by whom he meant the established order at Eton. Though thought to be a 'bad influence' by Connolly's parents after their son had been described in a report as 'cynical and irreverent', he had come to his old school mate's rescue after Hopgood had been discovered administering some torture, and knocked his assailant down. Towards the end of his second year, Connolly was taken ill, and shared a sick-room with Roger Mynors. Although he could be beaten for talking to a boy in an election above him, they became friends; Connolly was exposed to the civilising influence of his seniors, and the barriers began to crumble.

Connolly still suffered the occasional onslaught from Meynell and Hopwood combined, but before long they were to lose what little sway they had once possessed. Hopwood – 'a big, neat, handsome boy, good at games, a fast bowler, fond of girls and dirty stories' – was sent down for two terms for laying hands on a confirmation candidate; Meynell got pneumonia and was exiled to the sick-room for a month, and while he was away Connolly formed an alliance with three other 'trampled satellites' – Charles Milligan, Jackie O'Dwyer and Kit Minns – so as to withstand the tyrant on his return; but he came back quieter and harder-working. 'Untidy, lazy yet energetic, sentimental and self-reproachful, a puritan with a saving grace of humour, a border baron half converted to Christianity whose turbulent life fitted exactly into the Eton feudalism for he was an example of character and prettiness in authority', Meynell had dominated the boys in his election: Connolly was to remember how inspiring it had been to play football under his captaincy, tears of rage rolling down his cheeks if their team had been defeated, and how, in their first year, he would beat him for untidiness, 'half miserable at having to flog his best friend, half pleased at fulfilling a Roman duty'; and Meynell's death on the North-West Frontier half a generation later – he was awarded a posthumous V.C. – inspired in his friend a touching tribute to the time they had spent together:

> Such an end seems remote from the literary life, yet it was the end of one of my own age, with whom for four years I had been shaken about like stones in a tin. To a parent passing through College there must have seemed nothing to choose between Godfrey and myself, two small boys in

Eton jackets cooking their fagmaster's sausages, both untidy, noisy and mouse-coloured and yet in each a fate was at work; two characters, reacting differently to the same environment, were shaping their lives. The qualities I admire are intellectual honesty, generosity, courage, and beauty. Godfrey was grave. I was not.

Such was the reward of leadership, the destiny of character – not the position of business responsibility which St Wulfric's had promised us, but a premature and lonely death with the barren glory of a military honour.

*

As a junior boy Connolly was, in his own words, 'dirty, inky, miserable, untidy, a bad fag, a coward at games, lazy at work, unpopular with my masters and superiors, anxious to curry favour and yet to bully whom I dared'. The misery and the fagging would soon be behind him, but the grubbiness and the poor academic record were all too apparent. 'His work like his hair is always unkempt, and, like his hands and face, frequently dirty. Indifference to personal appearance is no doubt a virtue but I cannot think it is good for a boy to be so grubby. It is certainly bad for his mathematics, in which he seems to have no ambition; otherwise a friendly and cheerful individual,' reported Mr Coneybeare; while Mr Crace informed the Major that 'I have had sometimes to send him out of pupil room to wash his hands or change his very dirty collar – and I think he is old enough to have emerged from this grubby stage . . .' He made regular appearances near the bottom of his class, and his marks and percentages were shamingly low; he was the kind of boy who, maddeningly, combined indolence and carelessness with occasional flashes of brilliance. 'The boy certainly has a vein of great originality – he is very quick to see a point, thinks for himself with decided independence, criticises and comments well, and has a really remarkable gift for "occasional" verse . . . But it is all very undisciplined at present,' was the end-of-year verdict of the Master in College: he had obtained poor results 'in all work that calls for precise and accurate knowledge. And if his ability is to grow up to something better than cheap journalism he must tackle the training of it in habits of thoroughness and accuracy of thought.' That his mathematics should have been 'intolerable' was unsurprising: but his knowledge of French grammar was 'infantile', while 'the weakness of his documentary classical grounding' repeatedly let him down, despite all Sambo's cramming, and 'it remains extraordinary that a boy who has such an adept ear for English should be so slow in picking up Latin metres.' Even on the uncontentious subject of confirmation in College chapel, Crace returned, like a harbinger of doom, to the perils of journalism, and not for the last time: 'He has a keen and a sincere mind but not one to which reverence comes very naturally. I do not think devotion comes easy to him . . . And he has not any romantic ideals – intellectually, for instance, his point of view is more that of a journalist than that of a scholar or scientist.' Connolly was and remained a sceptic as far as organised religion was concerned, and the spectre of journalism was to haunt him all his life; but Crace was quite wrong about the absence of romantic ideals, even if these were, for the time being at least, confined to reading Housman, James Elroy Flecker and the earlier poems of Yeats.

Any moment now, romance and romantic ideals were to sweep all before them, transforming Connolly from a grubby little boy into a lovelorn adolescent: but a last, engaging glance of Connolly the child is provided by the Proceedings of the Chamber Debating Society for the 4th of October 1919. Godfrey Meynell was in the Chair, Charles Milligan as Secretary wrote up the minutes in a large, leather-bound volume, and Connolly himself moved the motion, the subject of which was 'Ancient and Modern Torture'. Called upon to open the debate, he 'suggested the torture of the treacle and ants in which the victim was covered with treacle and was pegged onto an ant's nest and gradually eaten.' Not to be outdone, the President suggested covering the victim with wire netting and slicing away the flesh as it bulged through the holes, whilst Hopwood proposed that a rat in a cup be attached to the victim's naked body, and the Secretary, more conventionally, came up with boiling oil. A vote was taken, and Hopwood's solution prevailed. Two years later, as members of the more august College Debating Society – College Pop – Connolly and his friends would be debating weightier matters, such as whether 'All gentlemen in College be allowed to turn down their coat collars' (Proposer: Roger Mynors) and whether the *Illustrated London News* and the *Spectator* should be dropped in favour of the *Bystander*, *Country Life* and *Workers' Dreadnought* (they were): but by then they dwelt in a different world, and were no longer the boys they had been.

Rather surprisingly, perhaps, Connolly was sixteen when he moved the motion in the debate on torture ancient and modern: the same age at which Collegers like himself came to be taught by one of the best-known and most influential of Eton masters, Hugh Macnaghten. Connolly came to believe that Macnaghten was one of five masters who embodied, like the priests of some arcane and ancient mystery, the 'inner culture' of Eton, to which only a few favoured boys were ever admitted. The constituent parts of this 'inner culture' were 'the pure eighteenth-century tradition of classical humanism' – given, in Macnaghten's case, a Pre-Raphaelite and Tennysonian overlay –

and an adulation of Socrates so pervasive that 'Socrates roamed through the classes like a Government inspector and even Virgil and Tennyson withdrew before him.' An enthusiastic, reverential teacher of literature, Macnaghten was – as his own appalling poems make plain – 'an ogre for the purple patch'. He pronounced his 'r's like 'w's, giving a Nineties twist to his incantations of all that was most lavishly doomed and despairing in nineteenth-century Romantic verse; according to Connolly's contemporary, Alan Pryce-Jones, 'his sensibility, we were told, was so acute that, whenever the word "little" was spoken in his presence, he wiped away a tear.' More will be said later about what Connolly came to see as the stultifying and retarding effect of Eton's 'culture of the lilies' – and Macnaghten's influence in particular – on his own literary tastes and development; in the meantime, though, 'there was no doubt that the teaching of the inner cult encouraged homosexuality', or that it was 'the forbidden tree round which our little Eden dizzily revolved'. The draft version of *Enemies of Promise* is blunter on the subject than either of the published editions: boys caught having sexual intercourse with one another (whatever that might involve) were expelled on the spot, and even to be suspected could be fatal; 'the majority of the school floundered through on masturbation, surreptitious experiments and dirty jokes,' much as they did elsewhere, while the 'sentimental friendship', of the kind to which Connolly would become so addicted, was 'permitted in some houses, forbidden in others'. Yet nothing was quite as clear as it seemed: Macnaghten, 'Spartan in body as he was soft in mind', would deliver lectures in which he attacked sentimental friendships like those described in Plato's *Euthyphro*, while at the same time making his class put into Latin verse a sentimental poem addressed to the Captain of the Eleven. 'In the preaching of the careful Pater beckon the practices of Wilde,' wrote Connolly, persuaded from the vantage-point of thirty-five that that particular aspect of an Eton education benefited a potentially homosexual boy. In Anthony Powell's opinion, although 'romantic passions were much discussed' between the boys, 'I should have thought that physical contacts were rare;' be that as it may, Connolly – susceptible, romantic, a boy who had never been kissed but yearned to fall in love, to 'lay my personality at someone's feet as a puppy deposits a slobbery ball' – was about to enter a fickle, flirtatious world in which boys pined away in the absence of those they were 'gone on', and 'the toughest member of army class thought as much about veiled glances and hinted assignations as an aristocratic señorita in a Spanish convent'.

FIVE

The Dream Brother

Like many aspiring writers, the young Cyril Connolly spent a fair amount of time and energy, particularly in his early and mid-twenties, starting novels which then petered out after a page or two. As is so often the case, most of these fragments dealt with young men adrift in London who can't make up their minds what to write about, or whom to fall in love with, but one – written in the back end of a Mediaeval History notebook, elsewhere crammed with the details of Papal schisms – is set in Ancient Greece. It reads like a cross between Petronius Arbiter and Margaret Kennedy – the *Satyricon* was a long-standing favourite, Kennedy's *The Constant Nymph* a shorter-lived and less explicable passion from the 1920s – and within a paragraph or two the hero, Gorgias, spots a beautiful youth in the market-place. He had, we are told,

> brown hair, not very dark, and rather a round face, a delicate nose and a brown skin and an exquisite mouth with the lips parted in a smile and a row of white teeth showing. It was a perfect face and though every feature was delicate and small there was nothing doll-like in its beauty but rather a tousled Dorian charm which the brown untidy hair and the small firm chin and the roguish laugh intensified... The affection in the hazel eyes, the mischief in the tousled hair and the intolerable beauty of the slim brown arm and the bony elbow fused and mingled in his heart...

Above the piece is written 'Noël, Sunset from Alhambra': the 'Noël' in question was Noël Blakiston, the son of a Lincolnshire vicar, and it seems fair to assume that the Greek youth looked very much like him (apart, perhaps, from the 'roguish laugh'), and that Gorgias' reactions to him were very similar to those of Connolly when, in the summer of 1920, he first set eyes on 'the one person who would be David to my Jonathan', or so he hoped. According to *Enemies of Promise*, this first happened 'by the letter slab' in College, but elsewhere we learn that 'I first noticed you looking very cool and brown and charming and chewing a daisy in the May sun.' Either way, Blakiston, with his green eyes and yellow skin and the 'wistfulness of a minor angel in a Botticelli', seemed the Faun incarnate, the dream brother made flesh; and he was to remain his strongest romantic attachment for the next seven years or so. Connolly being Connolly, such matters were – as they always would be – more complicated and more agonised than usual, but it seems fair to say that Blakiston was the first great love of his life, and that his passion for him bore all the hallmarks of his future infatuations, from seventeen to seventy: a perfectly genuine ability to be in love with more than one person at once; a tendency to run down the beloved behind his or her back without in any way diluting his attachment, combined with an equally strong desire to please, to tell the person of the moment what he or she wanted to hear; a love of intrigue, the more complicated the better, and an irresistible urge to play games; a passion for gossip, and a fascination with his own doings, and those of his friends, that, in the last resort, was probably stronger and more absorbing than any other interest in his life.

Blakiston was two years younger than his new admirer. Under the rules of the election system, Connolly could consort with his junior election, but could certainly not be seen with someone from his sub-junior election. Apart from furtive or coincidental meetings at meals or on Chapel steps, one way round this was to get on good terms with his junior election, and meet him through them. Quite apart from providing a raft of new friends – among them William le Fanu and the red-haired Freddie Harmer – this aligned him still further with those liberal elements in College who wanted to do away with the election system altogether. With love providing a spur to his instinctive liberalism, Connolly also cultivated the liberals in his senior election, and even in his super-senior election; and when, in the summer of 1920, members of the Officers' Training Corps were sent to their annual camp at Mytchett, firing blanks at one another, creeping through the bracken and sleeping under canvas, he brought home to dinner at the Lock House not only contemporaries like Godfrey Meynell, but a contingent of more senior boys that included the future historian Steven Runciman (later remembered as a tall, quiet boy, 'so generous with bananas and cream'), Dadie Rylands, and Robert Longden, with whom Connolly would later have a friendship as close as that with Noël Blakiston.

According to *Enemies of Promise*, Connolly was – like a debutante at her coming-out ball – 'launched' in the autumn term of 1920. But although he began to make his mark, 'I never felt well in the summer term,' he wrote:

> The Thames Valley climate was lowering, I was enervated by the profusion of elms and buttercups and sheep turds, the heat and the leisure. The summers at Eton were too pagan, one collapsed halfway through. Those hot afternoons punctuated by the 'toc toc' of bat hitting ball when I sat

> with a book in the shade of Poets' Walk, a green tunnel that has etiolated so many generations of poets, or wandered through the deserted College buildings, where the chalky sunbeam lay aslant the desk, were deleterious.

He came to associate autumn with making a fresh start, though the Easter term – when he played squash and fives, the games he was good at – remained his favourite.

'A charming, feline boy' with 'the kindness and cruelty of a cat and as luscious as a feather bed', 'Dadie' Rylands – who went on to become a long-serving Fellow of King's and a junior member of the Bloomsbury set – was a keen admirer of Rupert Brooke and the Georgian poets, and lent Connolly their work as it appeared in the form of chap-books. Both boys were members of the College Literary Society; Connolly was greatly pleased when a poem he had written which ended with the lines

> And winging down the evening sky,
> The herons come to the heronry

was greatly admired, Rylands comparing it favourably with Rupert Brooke. At this stage in his life, Connolly 'worshipped' the older boy, but the traffic was not all one way: over sixty years later Rylands remembered of his young admirer that 'His wit and range of reading were an education to me – almost persuaded me that I was a philistine.' By the time he left Eton, Connolly 'knew by heart something of the literature of five civilisations' – but in the meantime he and his new friend Terence Beddard, also from super-senior election and a 'foppish, melancholy and ironical dandy', invented a bogus Georgian poet called Percy Beauregard Biles, whose doggerel ranged from the lushly romantic ('I have dwelt in spirit in Grecian vales/ Where Daphne fled from the nightingales') and amorous effusions ('And Noël Blakiston whom I loved so / With lips of strawberry, skin of cream') to schoolboy jokes about spots and nose-picking, replete with rollicking chorus lines.

Beddard shared Connolly's fascination with Noël Blakiston; but – judging by *Enemies of Promise*, and Connolly's correspondence with his friends – Etonian passions were quite as intense and capricious as those encountered in later life, and his feelings for his beloved were suitably volatile. Blakiston was a cricketer and a Christian, embarrassing his admirers with outbursts of tearful sentimentality and religiosity, and when Connolly found the 'heartless, soulful Noël' spoilt or unattainable or passive or simply rather tedious, he might well be 'gone' on little Freddie Harmer instead – particularly in winter, since Harmer had 'one of the few rooms that had a fire instead of a radiator where we often had tea among sheets of graph paper, an unemptied bath, and a moraine of towels and football clothes.'*

Anthony Powell once suggested that, given his strong beliefs and his own 'very definite ideas of how he wanted to pursue his life', Blakiston was 'perhaps the only person who was ever able, relatively speaking, to cope with Connolly'. It's a large claim to make, but an example of what Powell had in mind occurred in the spring of 1921. Although Connolly tended to be dismissive of Blakiston to other people – 'He's one of the few people who go down in my opinion when I meet him and go up again soon afterwards when I go away,' he told Harmer – he was 'gone' on him again, with Harmer consigned to the reserves, and he decided to send him a signed photograph, and a long letter spelling out his philosophy of life. In it

> I said I thought I lived for the best form of happiness: learning to appreciate the first-rate and know the sham, learning to look for beauty in everything, sampling every outlook and every interest (bar stinks and maths), trying to stop people being lukewarm and liking the second-rate, trying to make other people happy, but not doing so at the cost of my own happiness, or concealing it when I am being generous . . .

He concluded by asking its recipient to 'treat me as a nice dog, not worship or despise, but sympathise'.

It was a philosophy to which Connolly would adhere for the rest of his life, but Blakiston was neither amused nor impressed. 'Dear Connolly,' he wrote back – there was no question of 'Cyril', despite its use on the signed photograph –

> I feel very honoured that you consider me worthy of ink. You see I don't think you are [his reply was written in pencil]. I did not ask for the picture, but as you have sent it there remains no other course than to say 'thank you'. By the way, I wish you would leave paragraphs in your so-called letters.

Although he felt a 'pitying affection' for his admirer, he found his frivolity 'utterly despicable and repulsive to my principles'. Connolly was a 'waste-paper basket for wrong ideas': he would not allow him to come before his work or his religion, but felt it his duty to improve his spiritual condition, preferably by means of some 'systematic Bible-reading'.

* By a pleasing coincidence, Harmer's father, who worked at the Natural History Museum, was an expert on slugs. As such he was known to the Major, but 'their paths only crossed when some tactless explorer produced a shell-less snail or a hermit slug, and in their rare meetings they seemed like God and the devil disputing the soul of a late-repenting sinner.'

'A wonderful letter for a boy of fifteen,' Connolly commented to Beddard, before going on to bolster his battered self-esteem by pointing out that, whatever Blakiston might say, he was becoming 'quite a Socrates in lower College'. Blakiston was in danger of becoming an 'awful Puritan': Connolly's riposte to Bible-reading would be to try to interest his young friend in 'poetry, painting etc', and to win him round to his superior ideals, based as they were on the assumption that 'there is no conscious immortality, that happiness is the mean between good and evil, that the greatest happiness is to be found in novelty'. 'Perfection in Happiness' was now his ideal, and 'I must try and be a Stoic in adversity, and Epicurean in prosperity'.

With Blakiston put in his place, Connolly went on to tell Beddard about a 'curious communication' he had received from Eric Blair, whom he reported as drinking tea from an 'insidiously hissing' samovar 'amid a litter of cigarette ash'. 'I am afraid I am gone on Eastwood,' Blair confessed ('*naughty Eric*' was Connolly's comment), and he thought Connolly was too. He was not jealous of his rival ('*noble Eric*'), but he knew that Connolly had strong 'proprietary instincts' as well as influence over Eastwood; and he ended by begging him not to set Eastwood against him ('Please don't do this I implore you. Of course I don't ask you to resign your share in him only don't say spiteful things'). Connolly's reaction to this pathetic, unexpected plea from his usually aloof and austere old friend has the arrogance and the brutality of the lover who has been bruised and rejected himself, but is also increasingly aware of his own power and attractions, and his ability to dominate those around him; it is redolent of a hothouse world in which romantic ideals were combined with bitchiness, Machiavellian amorous manoeuvres with straightforward sulking and stamping of the feet. He had been far too involved with Blakiston and Harmer, Connolly told Beddard, to see Eastwood as anything other than an 'exploitable sideline', who made a useful partner at squash and fives and 'might perhaps gratify some of my peculiarly sensual moods'; but he would have no compunction about stealing Eastwood off Blair, 'who deserves no commiseration, when gone on someone you do not ask for a half share from the person you think owns the mine. It is a business . . .' Or, as Percy Beauregard Biles put it in the same long letter, written while on holiday at the Lock House:

> Oh to be back at school again
> To gossip and laugh and swear
> To love the curve of Milligan's hips
> And Noël Blakiston's proud lips
> And Freddie Harmer's hair
>
> To fight and jeer and run down Crace

To scorn the spiteful Blair
To love Maud's smiling youthful grace
To gain the love of each new case
And stroke forbidden hair

To feel the squeeze of Eastwood's arm
To like a pretty face...

Relations with Blakiston continued tempestuous throughout the summer of 1921. The younger boy seemed interested only in cricket and getting his colour, and Connolly felt himself neglected and unloved. He told Blakiston it must be All or Nothing; Blakiston chose Nothing, adding that Connolly was a 'dirty scug' (an unkind epithet for a boy without a colour for games); Connolly stormed off in hysterics and worked off his fury by smashing a chair. For the remainder of that term, Blakiston continued to ignore his advances; spurned for the first time in his life, Connolly decided to make himself seem the most 'useful and desirable' person in the school, to humiliate Blakiston while at the same time making himself indispensable to him. To achieve this, he began to cultivate a wider circle of friends, including some oarsmen, two of whom were in the school Eight, and the footballing acquaintances of a new friend, Denys King-Farlow. King-Farlow was a fellow history specialist with whom he studied the Renaissance, and together they elaborated a cult of Machiavellianism whereby boys were to be cultivated for the sake of advantage, and their passions and their weaknesses played upon accordingly. He worked harder than hitherto; he consciously exercised his charm, winning people round by asking them about themselves and seeming to be interested in their answers; following the fashion of the time, he lined up on his mantelpiece signed photographs of his friends, 'like an old hostess collecting celebrities' – including one of Blakiston, which he had somehow appropriated. He cultivated an equally fashionable philosophy of scepticism and pessimism, luxuriating in a self-pitying sense of the brevity and futility of life, and already exhibiting – in a leaving poem written for another boy – a kind of anticipatory nostalgia, a sense of loss for a time that has yet to come:

Now years three and 'halves' ten
Have hastened by and flown
And there will soon be other men
But I shall be forgotten then
My very name unknown.
And no more careless evening hours
Of slippered armchair ease

No glimpse of tea-things in the towers,
No cans, no steam, no shouts from showers
No shorts, nor muddied knees.

At Corps Camp that year, Connolly's lyrical melancholia was in full spate. He shared a tent with King-Farlow, who was driven wild with irritation ('Here, Private Connolly, you who appreciate the beauty of our English hedgerows, you who claim that pleasure and pain are the same thing, go and empty this bucket!).* Neither Harmer nor Blakiston was there, and to console himself he borrowed a motor-bike and drove off to drink port with his new-found rowing friends.

'To this day I can tell whether a person is school-minded,' Connolly informed readers of *Enemies of Promise*, nearly twenty years later:

> whether they are cowardly, gregarious, sensitive to pupil-teacher relationships, warm, competitive and adolescent – or whether they are school-proof. The art of getting on at school depends on a mixture of enthusiasm with moral cowardice and social sense. The enthusiasm is for personalities and gossip, for a schoolboy is a novelist too busy to write.

Mussolini, Winston Churchill, Sir Hugh Walpole were all 'school-minded', according to an early draft of the book, whereas Hitler, Stalin, Sir John Reith and Somerset Maugham were 'school-proof'. Of more immediate importance was the fact that whereas boys like Blair, 'with his "*non serviam*"', and Steven Runciman, who divided people between stupids and sillies, lacked the 'ape-like virtues' necessary to enjoy life at a public school, Connolly had decided to go with the stream; and that summer, as a mark of his new-found social advancement, he was elected to College Pop, along with Milligan, O'Dwyer, Eastwood, Meynell and the uncompromising Blair.

The war between the reactionaries and the liberals was now at its height, with the Head of the School and his fellow Bourbons under siege from Dannreuther, Mynors and the other enlightened spirits from the year above Connolly's. An epidemic of beating broke out, during the course of which – according to Connolly's subsequent version of events – eighteen-year-olds

* Earlier in the summer, King-Farlow recalled, he, Blair and other members of their election were lazing on that part of the river that was known, in Eton parlance, as 'Athens'. There they were joined by

> our self-appointed jester, Cyril Connolly, whom we had, disregarding a strict College custom, taken up from our junior election year. Blair, knowing Connolly from preparatory school . . . warned us that we could expect to hear plenty about a 'Connolly's (probably no family connection) marrying in 1758 the second Duke of Richmond's third daughter.' We did.

like Blair and King-Farlow were beaten on trumped-up charges by boys of their own age.* The new, outgoing Connolly, in the meantime, was establishing himself as someone to be reckoned with. In a telegraphic self-portrait, he wrote of his

> intolerable selfishness... brutality... scathing wit... works selfishly and unscrupulously for his own ends, name generally mentioned in scorn – overdoes sentiment and sensual too – is bored – is wrapped up in fresh fields and partners new – is bored by gossip... is too frank to observe ordinary decencies... is purely cynical and selfish, is cold-blooded...- three parts sensuality in his idea of friendship, only feels the need for sensual attachment... manners are atrocious... evil gossip about himself and his dealings with the smaller boys...

while in another notebook he wrote of how 'at school his oscillating between beauty and satire had been sweeping and rudimentary. It rang deafening changes on Byronic cynicism and Celtic and mystical aesthetic – both were sentimental and vulgar.' Few writers have been more delightedly or self-absorbedly aware of their own weaker and less agreeable traits, and no doubt his unflattering self-portraits were heightened by the cult of melancholic pessimism: but, for all his gaiety and charm, Connolly at seventeen – like Connolly at seventy – could be a moody, atmospheric and capricious figure who needed to be handled with care, and bestowed and withdrew his favours on an alarmed and awestruck circle of admirers. 'I don't know what the power is that Cyril has got over other people's emotions,' wrote one school friend to another, after mentioning that Connolly had reduced Freddie Harmer to tears: 'I suppose it's animal magnetism; anyhow it's very disconcerting.' 'His conversation is as butter and honey after bread and dripping,' wrote William le Fanu after a momentary estrangement, while elsewhere he remarked that 'Even people one would never suspect of it seem afraid of Cyril, speaking of him only in hushed whispers.' He was and would remain

* Shortly after publication of *Enemies of Promise*, Connolly received a curious spate of letters from King-Farlow on the subject of these beatings. Connolly's references to them had come as a rude shock after so many years. The beatings he had witnessed at Eton had left him with a loathing for the whole business – which, later, 'came out in the form of a mild delight in the flagellation of young women'. He could only assume that Connolly was taking a belated revenge for an incident that same summer, when the two boys went for an illicit swim after cricket: Connolly had owned up and been beaten, whereas he had kept quiet and avoided the lash. Connolly's reference to the incident was a grave and wounding libel, and Farlow was consulting his solicitor.

Thirty years on – and by now a neighbour of the Connollys' in Sussex – King-Farlow was still smarting over the reference: Connolly had expressed 'contrition' but had done nothing about removing the offending passage, which had made him an object of ridicule, especially in America. By a curious coincidence, King-Farlow, an oil executive, worked for some years in Tulsa, Oklahoma, where Connolly's library and papers – including King-Farlow's reproachful letters – ended their days.

the kind of man whom people – half-gladly, half-resentfully – always set out to please, putting their best feet forward; and if he froze them with his sulking and displeasure, he as quickly wooed them back with his cleverness, charm and wit. Even the noble-minded Denis Dannreuther, whom Connolly worshipped for his cleverness, was far from immune to 'a charm in your outward manner which makes people forget all the selfishness and jiltings that have gone before, and weakly rejoice in a momentary reconciliation.'

*

College politics and College love affairs may have provided life with its savour, but the school's more humdrum purposes could not be altogether ignored – much as he might have liked to, since to be seen to work or 'sap' was to incur the contempt and disapproval of the other boys, and even Collegers were anxious not to be seen as highbrows or intellectuals. 'Intelligence was a deformity which must be concealed; a public school taught one to conceal it as a good tailor hides a paunch or a hump,' Connolly once wrote, seeing in this a variant on 'the English distrust of the intellect and prejudice in favour of the amateur'; while elsewhere he confessed that

> Becoming ashamed of working, which seemed anti-social and vulgar, was to make me unhappy for the next twenty years, for work, love and friendship are the only refuge of the over-sensitive from the world, and of these love and friendship, which I plumped for, destroy work, but work brings with it both love and friendship.

No doubt much to the Major's dismay, Connolly's reports in his third and fourth years were all too similar to those of the opening two. In April 1920 Crace reported that he had come last in his election exams by a long way, and once again he sounded the journalistic warning bell:

> He is in danger of achieving nothing more than a journalistic ability to write rather well about many things, if he is impatient of real study and thoroughness, and if he has not at least the desire for, and respect for, scholarly knowledge of *some* subject. He can criticise, and enjoys finding fault or voicing a grievance, but I sometimes feel that a little more humility of mind would help him onwards.

Three months later, Crace – who had earlier asked the Major not to withhold his son's allowance, since he did at last appear to be trying – admitted that although he often had cause to quarrel with Connolly, 'constantly the saving feature is the boy's independence of thought and his complete sincerity – he is absolutely candid, with a fearlessness that it is impossible not to like.' He hoped Connolly would try for a history scholarship at Oxford; in December he reported with pleasure that their son had indeed decided to become a history specialist, not least because 'in leaving classics as a special subject, he has come to a literary interest in them with a quite new zest.' Sloppy work remained a problem: 'It is odd that a boy with rather developed literary interests in some ways should be so careless and slovenly about the literary side of his own work. He writes essays which are often both original and thoughtful, yet leaves them written with hardly a stop in them and no regard for paragraphs and such-like considerations.' As for the future, 'Cyril is a person who may find it specially difficult, I think, to find his right opening' – though it would be a pity if the Major insisted on his following him into the army.

As a history specialist, Connolly came under the influence of C.H.K. Marten and G.W. 'Tuppy' Headlam, both of whom he included among the five masters in the school whose teaching really mattered – the others being Hugh Macnaghten, with his worship of literary excellence; C.M. Wells, who taught the classical specialists, as well as being a first-class cricketer and salmon-fisher, and an authority on claret; and the Headmaster, a worldly divine and a Fellow of All Souls, with whom Connolly, like other senior boys, would occasionally be invited to dine. Under their influence he began, at last, to do some work, like a huge Russian river unfreezing in the spring, for 'they were teachers whose rebukes of one boy enlisted against him the sympathy of the class, and "to do poorly" up to Headlam, or be "tiresome" with Marten was distressing for at last we were attaining a level where it was not impermissible to work.' Marten was clear and enthusiastic, the 'sanest of schoolmasters', but Headlam exercised the greater influence. A product of Balliol, he seemed, in retrospect at least, to provide welcome evidence of 'a pre-Ruskinian culture of the eighteenth century'. Dark, handsome and rather fat, he was worldly and tolerant, while at the same time abhorring indolence, inefficiency and schoolboy smugness. Connolly found his sense of irony and the faint ridicule in which he appeared to hold the pronouncements of authority entirely congenial; and, above all, 'In the aestheticism which was gathering round me, part backwash of the Nineties, part consequence of my Celtic romanticism being worked upon by the Pre-Raphaelite background of the Eton lilies, Headlam's sober intellectual energy, his Roman values, offered a gleam of mental health.' Just as Eton's upper echelons found room for both Headlam and Macnaghten, so he combined within himself realism and romanticism, clear-headed *realpolitik* with the dreams and the ideals of youth.

*

Near the disused and overgrown Basingstoke Canal, the Lock House was

> not a 'place' but rather a large small house, mostly eighteenth-century but skilfully added on to and with a lovely garden now rather run to seed, abiding in a hollow by still water and encircled by protecting trees. My father does not like it because it is damp and because it is out of the way, but my mother loves it more than me. It is full of nice creatures, birds that my mother knows all about, squirrels and rabbits and even foxes and very kindly trees...

Although Connolly was to spend many unhappy hours there alone with the drunken Major, his beloved Lock House was to provide him with another image of Eden, of greenness and trees and water, a dream of home that was to haunt him throughout a restless and peripatetic life. 'I am very fond indeed of our house, and I love all our furniture and pictures and "know" them all almost physically – china and chairs and tables and pictures of Africa and various portentous wooden ships my ancestors commanded – as well as all the rooms and the garden and all that green and water and the hidden inaccessible house in the trees,' he once wrote; and to another friend he confided 'We are so shut in with trees that they make a noise like rain all the time – the faint hum of mosquitoes, the ticking of a clock and the scratching of a physically introspective Pekingese are all that is to be heard.' He loved the damp red-brick house for its remoteness and its silence, for the way the trees cut it off from 'the military horrors of Aldershot, the suburban advance of Woking', for light shining through lattice windows into a darkened garden at night.

Life at the Lock House was far from luxurious, and still less so as Mollie spent more of her time away from home with 'Cris' Brooke, who had won a DSO in 1915, and had retired from the army in 1920 with the rank of lieutenant-colonel.* The Major became increasingly solitary and bibulous. To more than one correspondent he was to compare the house to Mariana's Moated Grange:

> Damp is in the house, ceilings bulge, halls sweat and paper strips and peals. Mice scamper at night and there are rat holes in the table cloth. Plaster falls and leaves black splodges and white flakes on chintzless chairs. Outside the ragged edges of unclipped yew hedges appear through clouded panes, roses turn to briars, and leaves and fallen branches cover the garden in which nothing stirs but burrowing moles and occasional

* On retirement, he was given the honorary rank of brigadier-general.

> squawking jays. We have no comforts, baths are impossible, light fails, the gramophone is broken, when I see a human being I retreat, scared . . .

For all its damp decrepitude, he loved the house with a passion, and longed to show it to friends from Eton and, later, from Oxford. For him, at least, the garden was criss-crossed with the railway lines of the Beesnest Express, and holidays could be given over to drawing up elaborate route maps, with the stations carefully marked, or providing potential travellers with much-needed information about the new 'Forest' route, stopping at Mousehole, Beesnest, Swing-seat, Pondgate, etc; and until he was well into his twenties he loved nothing better than to set out on long, solitary runs through the pine trees and bog- and heather-covered heath-land of the country round about, clad in his holiday uniform of shorts and a roll-top sweater and carrying in his right hand, lifted above his shoulder, his favourite assegai.

Writing to Terence Beddard, Connolly revealed that a female cousin – presumably one of Harold Kemble's daughters from Quenington – was coming to stay at the Lock House: so far he had been 'foolishly afraid' to kiss her, but he hoped her arrival would provide an opportunity to advance his 'romantic education'. No more was heard of this particular encounter, but that summer matters were marginally advanced when the Major took him to Paris, and then on via Bruges to Knokke on the Belgian coast. Despite his romantic entanglements at school, girls were evidently much on his mind. He told Dannreuther that he was determined to 'flirt and if possible fall in love' while in Paris, capitalising on the fact that Blakiston had provided him with 'a fair knowledge of "*grandes passions*" '. Even so, the whole adventure had in anticipation a touch of the dutiful ordeal about it: 'I hope I enjoy my romantic education though I am not looking forward to it – but long practice with HNB [Blakiston] has taught me the *beau geste* – but I shall take it all much too seriously with all the deadly lack of humour and abundance of sentiment peculiar to calf love.' More important in retrospect was the fact of his going abroad for the first time since he was a small child. 'I am a great believer in unconscious influences on character and my early voyages of which I hardly remember anything made me adore travelling in any sort of country which resembles the veldt,' he told Dannreuther. Neither Paris nor the Belgian coast bore a strong resemblance to the veldt; but his journey with the Major marked the beginning of a lifetime's addiction to travel, and of a passion for those countries – more often than not Mediterranean – which shared the warmth and the flowers and the fruit and the bright light that he remembered from his childhood Eden in South Africa.

Connolly and the Major stayed off the rue de Rivoli, eating their meals together in restaurants separated from the pavements by tubs of 'sooty privet'. Despite his later infatuation with the city, Connolly was not greatly taken with Paris: he was frightened, it was too hot, and the Parisians had smelly feet. He liked Notre Dame, Versailles and the Louvre, but found plodding round art galleries a wearisome business, while the Venus de Milo and other well-known pieces of Greek sculpture 'produced no sudden ecstasy, only the usual bitter-sweet of all beautiful things'. And the whole place seemed 'as full of whores as Camp was of wasps', he told Jackie O'Dwyer, before moving on to the far more gripping topic of College politics, and who was blackballing whom in the elections for College Pop. One hot evening, though, he underwent 'a truly Michael Fane experience which I just escaped all right to the tune of 100 francs' – Michael Fane being the rather *risqué* hero of *Sinister Street*. Ask any Parisian the way, Connolly told William le Fanu, and he will 'be telling you the nearest "*halles de nuit – filles de joie vous comprenez – Oh mais sûr on s'amuse*" – to walk away huffily I think would be rude and priggish.' Walking back to his hotel after dinner, he was accosted by a pimp in a straw hat, who first offered to take him to a music hall, and then – according to *Enemies of Promise* – lured him into a brothel, where the girls paraded before him and the terrified youth, convinced that he would end up in a crate *en route* for Buenos Aires, drained a bottle of champagne. It was then suggested that he might like to go upstairs with the girl of his choice, but that before he could do so he must settle the bill, which came to almost ten pounds. Connolly explained in a trembling voice that he had no money on him, but he told the Madame that he would bring her the money as soon as he could, left her a card on which he had written the address of his hotel, and scuttled gratefully away. The rest of his stay was blighted by the thought of the madame and her straw-hatted pimp turning up at the hotel and demanding payment; luckily his grandmother sent him some money for a present, and as soon as it arrived he hastened round to the brothel and pressed the notes on another madame altogether.

His misadventures as described to Dannreuther took a slightly different turn, in that – having gone out during an interval at the theatre to get some fresh air – he was clutched tight by a lovely girl who chucked him under the chin and tried to lure him back to her apartment, and he only managed to escape when, out of the corner of his eye, he spotted the Major advancing towards them; either way, the canals and churches of Bruges must have come as a relief.

Far more importantly, he soon found himself back at Eton for the beginning of his final year, and life looked good indeed. He was in 'messing' with Charles Milligan, with a fag to make them tea; he had won his 'shorts' for football, which meant that Blakiston was prepared to talk to him again;

the reactionary election that had beaten and tyrannised the term before had gone their separate ways, and although the Captain of the School was a 'clerical reactionary', he was an isolated figure, easily offset by Mynors, Dannreuther, Longden and Connolly's other cronies from the year above his own.

SIX

Pop and the Permanent Adolescent

Writing to his friend and former pupil Rupert Hart-Davis in the early summer of 1961, George Lyttelton – a former Eton master who, as an Old Etonian with private means had escaped the patronising assumption on the part of grander boys that 'most of the staff had never held a gun or worn a tailcoat' – told the publisher that he had been reading *Enemies of Promise*; and that apart from being mistaken in his belief that the book had been banned at Eton, Connolly had been 'much too favourable' in his view of 'Tuppy' Headlam. 'T.H. never had "much the best house" at Eton,' he suggested, 'and if as C. says he "hated idleness" he got over it: for in his last years he was conspicuously idle in school (golf at Swinley *every* Sunday!), partly because he had formed the opinion that history was not a good subject for teaching to the great majority of boys. And he may have been right.' Be that as it may, Headlam and what he seemed to stand for – worldly success combined with academic excellence – loomed large in Connolly's final year at Eton.

Unexpectedly he won the Rosebery History Prize. The material reward for this consisted of twenty pounds' worth of books, which he chose to take instead in the form of Medici Society prints to hang in his room. More importantly, in terms of his own standing in the school, he was as a result co-opted into Division One, the top academic stratum in the school. This was an honour usually reserved for winners of the Newcastle Prize, open only to classicists: but history was becoming a fashionable subject, and Connolly's triumph made him an altogether better-known figure.

As well as teaching history to the senior boys, Headlam was also a housemaster; and an enviable one at that, since eight of the twenty-eight or so boys who belonged to Pop were from his house. After he had won the Rosebery, Connolly began to be noticed by the grandees of Pop, and, for the first time, he began to make friends among the Oppidans. Just as a term or two earlier he had cultivated oarsmen and football-players in his bid to impress and humiliate Noël Blakiston, so he now turned his attention to a wider world beyond the intense, incestuous self-absorption of College. Oppidans in general he found to be 'easy-going extroverts', whose friendships were less demanding than those between Collegers: meeting them was 'like going to smart luncheons where people seem more intimate than they are'. Once again, he exploited his ability to make people laugh; inspired by the example of Petronius Arbiter, who seemingly 'idled into fame', he cultivated the image of the 'brilliant idler', working hard on his books by night, and busily socialising by day. He had, he discovered, an excellent memory, he had no problems in learning things by heart and, like a good reviewer-to-be, he could 'gut a book in an hour and a half of arguments, allusions and quotations, like a Danube fisherman removing caviare from the smoking sturgeon'. He helped less nimble-witted boys with their work, artfully combining friendliness with a certain reserve.

Before long it was time to move on after bigger game. 'As a little boy, on my way through the classroom, down corridors where rows of hats hung on pegs,' he wrote,

> I would often feel a mystical thrill as I noticed a silk hat covered with dark blobs of sealing wax on the rim. It was a Pop privilege to seal hats, for quick identification, and it meant that in that form room a member of the Eton Society was at work, perhaps one of my heroes, Michael Davies or Peter Lindsay: I felt like a naturalist who finds a tuft of giant panda fur. Now I was in a division [Headlam's] where nearly all the hats bore the magic imprint.

Of the members of Pop, four stood out for Connolly's especial admiration: Antony Knebworth, Nico Davies, Teddy Jessel and Lord Dunglass. Knebworth and Davies were 'the most successful types of normal schoolboy: they were all in the Eleven, ran their houses, were able and rather lazy at their work, conventional, intolerant, and sentimental.' They drank and smoked and invited debutantes down for tea, and 'were easily moved to rage or tears, like Homeric heroes'. Though generally good-natured in a patronising way, they were merciless beaters. Knebworth nicknamed Connolly 'Spud'; the name caught on, but although he 'preened when so addressed by a Pop', he wouldn't allow anyone in College to use it. The other two 'feudal princes' were less school-minded; 'they were dandies in the pure sense, with a sober worldly gravity.' Better known in after-life as Sir Alec Douglas-Home, Dunglass captained the cricket eleven and was President and Keeper of the Field; he was, Connolly wrote in a passage that would be widely quoted when Sir Alec succeeded Harold Macmillan in No 10 Downing Street,

> a votary of the esoteric Eton religion, the kind of graceful sleepy boy who is showered with favours and crowned with all the laurels, who is liked by

> the masters and admired by the boys without any apparent exertion on his part, without experiencing the ill effects of success himself or arousing the pangs of envy in others. In the eighteenth century he would have become Prime Minister before he was thirty; as it was he appeared honourably ineligible for the struggle of life.

Antony Knebworth, on the other hand, was to be killed in a flying accident at the age of twenty-nine. His father, the Earl of Lytton, memorialised him in a book entitled *Antony*, and Connolly was sent it to review by the *New Statesman*. He recalled his erstwhile hero in his prime, as someone 'remarkable for his vitality, which was often boisterous, his fits of melancholy, his ability and his charm'; he was 'a beautifully built and slightly stooping athlete, an incarnation of that adventurousness and courage which is so alluring to intellectuals and which usually ends in them breaking their legs'. Knebworth had won the Rosebery History Prize and been a brilliant sportsman, but his life after Eton had proved a sad disappointment. Like Connolly after him, he was disappointed by the 'dismal emptiness and ugliness of Oxford'; after graduating, he moved restlessly from one thing to another, serving as an ADC to his father in India, skiing and playing polo, flying, sitting briefly as a Conservative MP, and – anti-climactically – working in the Army and Navy Stores. All this time he was steadily moving to the right, eventually embracing fascism. Connolly saw in the brief life of his former friend not simply an awful warning about the dangers of being too successful at school – something from which he had 'only recently' recovered – but a sad example of the way in which the ruling classes had 'persistently underestimated the intellect'. Knebworth had inhabited a world in which 'ability, self-interest and shrewdness, heavily coated with good fellowship and charm, are what matter': cut off from 'the life of the mind, from all genuine aesthetic experience', lacking in ideals and frozen in the attitudes and tastes of a schoolboy, he had missed out entirely on 'the two great conceptions of our day: that of artistic integrity, the life of the spirit, and that of social justice, "the palpable and obvious love of man for man".' Such reservations lay in the future, however, and in a very different world: in the meantime, the 'droll, idle, timorous little beetle' of yesteryear had become an altogether more assured and flamboyant creature, eager above all to consort with Lord Knebworth and his kind.

That winter, in the Christmas holidays of 1921, Mollie took her son skiing at Mürren in Switzerland. Connolly loved skiing, and the hotel was full of pretty girls; he fell in love with one of them, but promptly forgot her as soon as he got back to school. Knebworth was staying in the same hotel, and amused himself by muddling up all the shoes that had been put outside bedroom doors for polishing overnight. He and Connolly got on well together, and he was able to report back to his fellow grandees that Connolly appeared not to live in the dirt and squalor in which it was assumed most Collegers passed their days.

Back at Eton, it was decided that Connolly should try for a history scholarship at Oxford or Cambridge. King's, Cambridge, had closed scholarships reserved for Etonians: Dadie Rylands and Denys King-Farlow were already there, and were joined later by Freddie Harmer and William le Fanu. The previous summer, however, Crace had told the Major that he thought Oxford would suit his son better; Headlam agreed, and out of respect for him Connolly decided to try for Balliol, specialising in the obscurities of the Dark and Middle Ages. Eager to sustain his pose of the brilliant idler, and relishing the remoteness and the futility of his subject matter, he worked by candlelight, devouring Gibbon, and Milman's *History of Latin Christianity*, and versing himself in gloomy mediaeval heresies. When the time came to take the Balliol scholarship exams, he stayed in college with Denis Dannreuther, Roger Mynors and Bobbie Longden and sat two papers a day, including an English essay on the subject of Compromise. Balliol struck him as dingy and dispiriting: he was given a room overlooking the Victorian neo-Gothic front quadrangle, which compared unfavourably with the view from his room in College, and was furnished with a 'blokey' armchair and a table with a dark green table-cloth covered in burns. Back in Eton, much to his relief, he and Bobbie Longden played fives for College in the inter-house matches, and were beaten; and then the news came through that he had won the Brackenbury History Scholarship at Balliol, where he would be joined by Mynors and Dannreuther on classical scholarships, with Longden winning a classical scholarship to Trinity, the next-door college to Balliol.

Connolly had started the term with two ambitions: to win a scholarship and, an altogether more improbable proposition, to be elected to Pop. The problem here was that he had no sporting achievements or colours to display, nor was he in Sixth Form. According to Christopher Hollis – who managed to be elected without any sporting distinctions other than playing cricket for College – Pop was 'a bad institution, for it encouraged shameless and degrading toadying by those who wanted to get in to those who were already in', and Connolly, apart from exploiting his talents as a comedian, busied himself cultivating and being seen with the two Pops who were already in College. Of these, the most important to his story was Bobbie Longden, 'one of those angel-faced Athenians whom the school delighted to honour'. His father was an admiral; Kenneth Clark, his contemporary at Trinity, remembered him as 'a handsome red-haired Etonian' who had 'an immense zest for life, and told longer and funnier stories than anyone I have ever known', while James Lees-Milne found him a 'man of angelic disposition', and A.J. Ayer as 'good-looking, enthusiastic, boyish in manner and with an air of success about him'. Although Connolly always found Longden physically extremely attractive – disruptively so, at times – his admiration for his mind and his looks tended to be tempered by a note of derision: in some notes on Eton contemporaries, made towards the end of their time at the school, he wrote of his being 'good-natured and cheerful', with a 'mind like a well-kept allotment'. Longden, he noted disapprovingly, 'stoops to take Pop seriously, is amazingly overjoyed at getting in': but now that he too wanted to join the elect, Longden was someone to be seen with.

Gratifyingly, Connolly's politicking paid off. He was put up for Pop by Longden and the other Colleger; the existing Pop met in conclave, and candidates' names were proposed and seconded and blackballed; and then, quite suddenly, a group of Pops in parti-coloured waistcoats, with flowers in their buttonholes and rolled umbrellas, came thundering up the wooden stairs to Connolly's room to congratulate him, 'and after they had left only the faint smell of Balkan Sobranie and Honey and Flowers mixture remained to prove that it was not a dream'. 'I cannot tell you how divine it is being in Pop and how happy I am,' Knebworth had reported home after his election, and doubtless Connolly felt the same. In chapel next morning he felt that the eyes of the school were upon him, the younger boys staring particularly hard since not to know the names of all the Pops could earn them a beating. Only the austere and high-minded Dannreuther failed to join the congratulations: he had been co-opted into Pop as Captain of the School, but it was not an institution he admired, and he failed to understand why Connolly wanted to join so reactionary a body. Nor were all the Oppidans impressed. Hubert Duggan, one of the richest and grandest of school swells and the stepson of Lord Curzon, unkindly enquired when the news broke of Connolly's election, 'Is that the tug who's been kicked in the face by a mule?'

*

In the spring holiday, Connolly went down to St Cyprian's, where his triumphs had been reported in the *Chronicle* under the name of 'Conolly'. From Eastbourne he travelled along the coast to Newhaven, where he met Charles Milligan, 'an Extreme Blonde with delicate features and an air of neatness and languor'. They crossed to Dieppe on the boat, and from there they took the train to Paris. They visited the Folies Bergères, and during the interval they bought drinks for a couple of prostitutes. Clad in blue suits, camel-hair waistcoats and waisted navy-blue overcoats, and puffing large cigars as they leaned back in their chairs, they felt very much men of the world: but back in their hotel, Connolly's face began to itch, and Milligan began to scratch, and both boys were overcome by that familiar schoolboy dread, more often associated with lavatory seats, that they might have 'caught something' off their drinking companions. But all was forgotten next day when they took the train south, and Connolly saw for the first time a part of the world that he was to revisit again and again, in person and on paper: the country round Avignon, and the south-west corner of France where it runs into Spain. His candle-lit studies of the mediaeval Antipopes, who had based themselves in the city for over a hundred years, had already whetted his appetite for Avignon. It was all that he had dreamed of. 'I know only that they are sacred places,' he was to write in *Enemies of Promise*, 'that the country between the Mont Ventoux and the Canigou, from Avignon and Vaucluse to Figueras and Puigcerda, is the expression of the complete south, the cradle of my civilisation.'

They hired bicycles, and although Milligan was tempted by the casinos of the Riviera, they decided to head towards Spain, since it would be cheaper. They visited Narbonne, and the marshes that run along the coast, and Roussillon and Cerbère; they looked across to Spain, but could go no further without a visa. By now Connolly was pining for Eton, and they began a long, unpleasant journey home. Both boys had run out of money, and they had to travel separately; Connolly spent his last five shillings on a meal in Soho before bedding down for the night in St Martin's-in-the-Fields.

Back at Eton for their final term, Connolly and Milligan were summoned by the Headmaster and given a wigging for visiting the Folies Bergères. Connolly's copy of *La Vie Parisienne* was confiscated by his tutor, together with *Tristram Shandy* and an uncut Rabelais; perhaps this was also the occasion on which he had to surrender his copy of *Crome Yellow* by Aldous Huxley, an Old Etonian who had taught French during Connolly's time at the school: he had been mocked by the boys on account of his great height and extreme short sight as he moved unsteadily along the High Street.

Although Connolly was 'messing' with Milligan, for the first few weeks of the summer term he consorted almost exclusively with Oppidans and his grand new friends in Pop. 'Get into Pop if you can but use it as a means to being intellectual and popular in spite of it. I realised that I could do most good for the Intellectual by being sought after by the Worldly,' he advised a friend; but for the time being at least the Worldly seemed a good deal more alluring than the Intellectual. César Franck and Ravel were abandoned in favour of the fox-trot; fellow-Collegers seemed suddenly 'insipid and dowdy', Milligan and O'Dwyer excepted; he strolled arm-in-arm with his new friends, a privilege extended only to members of Pop, and smoked and drank with them in the garden of a Windsor hotel before they returned to their separate houses to breathe port and tobacco fumes over their house-masters; the Captain of Boats was persuaded to give him a rowing colour so as to bring him in line with his more sporting colleagues; 'for a month I was a model member of that corrupt and glittering eighteenth-century clique and I forgot for the first time in my life that I was a "highbrow", and that highbrows are cut off from the world.'

All this was heady stuff, as Anthony Powell remembered. He was invited to tea one day by Brian Howard, the most outrageous and sophisticated Etonian of his time, who happened to mention, in an offhand manner designed to impress, that Connolly might be looking in as well. Powell was suitably awed, for 'Connolly was in Pop, and – although to walk arm-in-arm with Connolly would not, in snobbish terms, have rated anything like as high as with the Captain of the XI, Keeper of the Field or Captain of Boats – to run across him in this informal manner would nevertheless grade as a manifest social success'. As it turned out, Howard had committed the grave solecism of leaving his postcard of acceptance, with its Pop letterhead, too obviously on display on his mantelpiece; nor did Powell ever meet him at school, though

> I knew him, of course, by sight. It was impossible not to notice Connolly as he passed in the street, or loitered in School Yard. He looked like no one else. Even so, his personality made no very definite impression until one afternoon when I was walking back from the tree-shaded playing-field called Upper Club. The picture remains a clear one in my mind. Connolly himself mentions that, after becoming a member of Pop, he experimented in wearing a dinner jacket (instead of blazer or tweed coat) with flannel trousers, 'a fashion that was not followed.' In this guise I first took him in as a formidable entity. Arm-in-arm with another Colleger (one not in Pop), he was strolling towards the elms of Poets' Walk. Connolly was laughing and talking a lot. I felt conventional misgiving at the dinner jacket as an innovation in school dress.

John Lehmann, whose career as a writer and editor was to parallel and intersect with that of his senior at school, provided a vivid picture of Connolly at about this time:

> He occupied an isolated room on the other side of the corridor from my own room: it was notorious among us, dangerous, shocking and exciting at

the same time. The perfume of Sin that seemed to rise from it was compounded in my imagination from the curling smoke of Turkish cigarettes, powerful liqueurs produced from secret hiding-places, risqué discussion of *avant-garde* books that one could never imagine finding in College Library, and lurid stories of the forbidden world of cabarets, night-clubs, and dancing-girls. Cyril was already fairly high in the school, and under the tolerant College regime of the time did more or less as he liked; one of the things he liked was to invite one or two boys from my Election to come to his study and join the privileged circle of his friends in emancipation. I was appalled by this; I felt responsible for the boys – as Captain of Chamber a certain respect was due to me, but my authority was rather like that of the Paramount Chief of a small African tribe under British colonial rule, and I could in fact do nothing – and I was convinced that they were being corrupted by an evilly cynical worldliness, a tone associated with the faster and more disreputable Oppidans, only worse because much more intellectually sophisticated. No doubt this feeling cloaked a longing to be one of the initiated myself, and Cyril divined it. In any case he was much amused by my studied disapproval: he would stand at the door of his room, slim, self-assured, smartly attired, with a teasing look on his puggish face, and when I passed would say, in a tone which made the simple greeting heavy with malice and mockery, 'Well, Johnny Lehmann, how are *you* this afternoon?' I passed on, head in air, a blush stealing to my cheeks, with as much dignity as I could muster, back to the seat of my miserable authority.

Not even Anglo-Ireland was immune to the grandeur of Pop. There were Anglo-Irish boys at Eton, some of them cousins he had met with his aunt, the Countess of Kingston; but now it was their turn to look up to him, and his ignorance of guns and horses no longer left him feeling inadequate and incurably middle-class. Clontarf Castle suddenly shrunk to 'an ugly and unimportant house in a Dublin suburb', and as for the Anglo-Irish themselves, 'I felt about them from then on as many North Americans must have felt about Southerners, that they were a charming and attractive society, but too envious, vain, ignorant and pig-headed to survive in a not unreasonable world.'

On the Fourth of June – the great day in the Eton social calendar – Connolly, in his new-found role as a 'wet-bob', was one of six Collegers to take part in the ceremony of boats; clad in the traditional garb of black bum-freezer jacket, pink-and-white striped shirt, white flannel trousers and a boater covered in flowers, he and Bobbie Longden formed part of the crew of the *Monarch*, standing awkwardly to attention in the narrow shell of the boat while fireworks burst above the river and crowds of boys and parents milled along the banks. Triumphs of a different kind awaited him in a College production of *She Stoops to Conquer*, run over two days in Upper School in aid of the Eton Mission for Infant Welfare Work. Dannreuther played Mr Hardcastle, and Mynors his daughter; Connolly took the role of Mrs Hardcastle, and on the last night 'the house was crammed and from all accounts it was Cyril who moved the whole thing.' Even more gratifying were the 'signatures on my programme at the extreme moment of dandyism', including as they did a clutch of Pop grandees (Dunglass, Jessel and Knebworth among them), and Brian Howard, who, with Harold Acton, was becoming well known as the school's resident aesthete.

Nemesis lay round the corner, however, ready to pounce on an unhappy combination of indolence and the desire to show off. One of the advantages of being in College Pop was that its members had no need to stamp or post their letters, but could get a fag to do it for them. As keeper of the stamps, it was up to Connolly to ask his fellow-members for money to cover their cost. Flushed by his recent triumphs, he announced that he would pay for them himself; but when the supply ran out, and unposted letters began to accumulate, he suddenly remembered that letters could be posted through Pop, and sent a fag down to the Eton Society with a bundle of post. His ruse was detected when another member of Pop riffled through the outgoing letters and noticed that many were addressed to the parents of Collegers. Unkind remarks were made about Collegers living in villas in Tooting: for a time it was assumed that Dannreuther was the guilty man; Connolly lay low, but in the end he had to confess his crime. Nico Davies and Knebworth drew him aside for a word, and all his feelings of social insecurity came surging back: he had let down his friends in Pop, he had never belonged, he was 'like a Labour Party Prime Minister agonising over whether the cut of his tail coat would be passed at Londonderry House.'

Bruised and unnerved by this encounter with Worldliness made flesh, he took refuge in the familiar, unalarming world of College. The summer before he had been a sceptic, wallowing in pessimism and melancholy broodings on the futility and brevity of life; now he became an aesthete, reading Pater's *Marius the Epicurean* and Huysmans' *A Rebours*, and doing his best to burn with a 'hard, gem-like flame'. He read Baudelaire and Verlaine and Mallarmé, gazed intensely at white roses at the Windsor flower show, and wrote a brief but heart-felt poem about them in French. He also made the acquaintance of Brian Howard.

Brian Christian de Claiborne Howard – the name should be remembered when reading Connolly's best-known parody, 'Where Engels Fears to Tread' – was the son of an American from the Deep South; he was languid, waspish, precocious, fashionable and unashamedly camp. Henry Yorke remembered him as 'the most handsome boy I'd ever seen', a brilliant talker who was also 'a terrible poseur and a wild snob'; according to Harold Acton, his friend and fellow-aesthete, 'His big brown eyes with the long curved lashes were brazen with self-assurance: already his personality seemed chiselled and polished, and his vocabulary was as ornate as his diction . . . He had an intuitive gift for the malice that could stab and fester beneath the skin. Scarcely anybody was spared the shafts of his ridicule.'

Connolly was introduced to Howard by Teddy Jessel, and found himself confronted by a boy with 'a distinguished impertinent face, a sensual mouth and dark eyes with long lashes'. Howard asked him to tea, and Connolly, as we have seen, wrote to accept on a Pop post-card. Finding this propped on Howard's mantelpiece, he felt, once again, that he had done wrong by his fellow-Pops, and, after wolfing down the *foie gras* and the strawberries and cream, he fled the scene 'like a lady who is offered a swig by a madman in a tunnel'.

Unnervingly advanced in his literary tastes, Howard was already reading, writing about, and even meeting modern writers of the kind that Connolly would be championing in ten years' time but had now barely heard of. He was two years younger than Connolly, and in 1920, when he was still only fifteen, had written a piece entitled 'The New New' in which he had referred favourably to such outriders of modernity as Wyndham Lewis, the Vorticists, the Sitwells, Ezra Pound and Aldous Huxley; this had been accepted for publication by the influential editor A.R. Orage, whose magazine *The New Age* was an early champion of the Modern Movement. The following year Howard was discovered by Edith Sitwell, of whom Connolly would later become an enthusiastic devotee.

For all his precocity, Howard never fulfilled his early promise, and he is remembered not for his indifferent poems and occasional book reviews, but in the memoirs of his contemporaries at Eton and Oxford, as Ambrose Silk in Evelyn Waugh's *Put Out More Flags* and Anthony Blanche in *Brideshead Revisited*, and as Christian de Clavering in 'Where Engels Fears to Tread'; but in the Eton of the early 1920s he was an astonishing phenomenon, all the more remarkable when in the summer of 1922 he and Harold Acton produced the single issue of what must be the most extraordinary school magazine ever published. Printed on thick, hand-laid paper with margins as wide as the type panel, bound in thick pink cardboard, and priced at 2*s* 6*d*, *The Eton Candle* not only included poems by Brian Howard and Harold Acton, and a drawing by Anthony Powell, but a sonnet by Edmund Gosse and an Old Etonian supplement that included contributions from Huxley, Sacheverell Sitwell and Shane Leslie. But although the magazine had a

Nineties flavour to it, redolent of the *Yellow Book* and Max Beerbohm, it was also an advocate of Modernism. Howard himself contributed an essay entitled 'The New Poetry' in which he attacked the Georgian poets associated with J.C. Squire and the conservative *London Mercury*, and the notion that rhyme and the 'subtle cramp of metre' were indispensable to true poetry. He ridiculed the English antipathy to *vers libre*, of which he claimed Ezra Pound was the greatest exponent, and heaped praise on the Imagists and the writers associated with *Wheels*, and on Amy Lowell, H.D., F.S. Flint, Richard Aldington, Edith Sitwell and Aldous Huxley. Unlike most school magazines, *The Eton Candle* was reviewed in *The Times Literary Supplement*, and by Edith Sitwell, who came to give a lecture at the school. 'I hear that Gow and Lyttelton – Lord God damn and shrive their smelly souls! – kept nudging and grinning,' Howard informed his fellow-editor: she delivered her views in little better than a whisper, and at the end 'the beastly old Vice-Provost – Macnaghten – got up and advised *Edie to speak louder in future*!'

Harold Acton was a tall, courteous, benign-looking boy with a large, domed forehead and Chinese-looking eyes, and in both his background and tastes he was as exotic and sophisticated as Howard. Both boys shared a passion for the Russian Ballet, and would 'leap into riotous dances' when the gramophone struck up; and both were founder-members of the Eton Society of the Arts, together with Acton's brother William, Anthony Powell, Robert Byron and Henry Yorke. The Society was addressed from time to time by luminaries like William Rothenstein and Roger Fry, 'neither of whom seemed very sparkling' as far as Powell remembered, and among those who attended were Oliver Messel, Alan Clutton-Brock and Connolly, who 'puffed cynically on our fringe'. As well as being the 'most fashionable boy in the school', Howard belonged 'to a set of boys who were literary and artistic but too lazy to gargle quotations and become inoculated with the virus of good taste latent in Eton teaching'; in retrospect at least, they should have provided more congenial company for Connolly than the scholars of College or the bloods of Pop, but 'my moral cowardice and academic outlook debarred me from making friends with them.'

Despite his subversive reading of *Crome Yellow*, Connolly's literary tastes were as yet far more conventional and traditional than his later reputation as a champion of the Modern might suggest, and were to remain so until after he had left Oxford: to a later generation of Etonians he revealed that he didn't remember being asked to contribute to the *Candle*, that he would have been too shy to have put himself forward – and, besides, 'most of us had not yet caught up with Brooke and Flecker'. From St Cyprian's onwards, he had been brought up to believe that 'literature meant the romantic escape, the purple patch'; and Eton teaching, as embodied in Hugh Macnaghten, had encouraged him to linger in the euphonious romantic melancholy of 'the full Tennysonian afterglow'. By the time he left Eton, Milton was – as he would remain for many years – the poet he loved above all others. He knew little Shakespeare apart from *Hamlet* and the Sonnets, adored Webster, relished Donne and Herrick and Marvell, knew little – as yet – of the eighteenth century before Blake. He looked, above all, for 'the authentic romantic thrill and the prestige of obscurity': both were provided in abundance by Tennyson and Matthew Arnold, though he had little time for the Romantics, finding Shelley flatulent, Keats saccharine, Byron vulgar and Wordsworth prosaic. Among the moderns he admired A.E. Housman, who came down to lecture the boys on Erasmus Darwin, Rupert Brooke, the early Yeats, Ralph Hodgson, John Masefield, and Robert Bridges's *The Spirit of Man.* Flecker was to become a particular favourite: John Maud, a fellow-Colleger, urged him to go and see a production of *Hassan* in Windsor under the direction of Basil Dean, and as late as 1925 Connolly was claiming Flecker as 'a classic master', urging Blakiston to read him since 'no modern poet has such an absolute range both of subject and treatment, Flecker was romantic at heart but imposed on himself the classic (Parnassian) discipline.' He still felt the same about Housman, but ten years later he was to savage his old idol in the *New Statesman*, provoking a ferocious counter-blast from the poet's best-known advocate, John Sparrow.

In later years Connolly was to claim, loudly and often, that early deprivation of Ezra Pound, and the 'culture of the lilies', in which Tennysonian romanticism was combined with the cult of decorous light verse as practised by Calverley, Praed and that much-admired Old Etonian, J.K. Stephen, had retarded his appreciation of the changes that were taking place in the wider literary world – 1922 was, after all, the year of *Ulysses* and 'The Waste Land' – and made it impossible for him to realise his potential as a poet; and that his immersion in the classics had left him able to write in any language but his own. Even Homer and Virgil, the two pillars on which the educational edifice was built, were romanticised in the 'cribs' or authorised translations without which most boys found it hard to struggle through to the end. Butcher and Lang rendered the *Odyssey* into a bogus saga prose, so that its 'Mediterranean clarity' was 'blurred by a Wardour Street Nordic fog'; J.B. Mackail infused Virgil with a 'morbid distress', redolent of London in the 1880s or the Grecian paintings of Alma-Tadema rather than the ancient world, while his translations from the *Greek Anthology* – which Connolly continued to read and admire for many years after – were 'even more deleterious'. 'One of the sacred books of the inner culture, the very soil of the Eton lilies,' Mackail's renditions 'exhaled pessimism and despair, an over-ripe perfection in which it was always the late afternoon or the last stormy sunset of the ancient world'. As a result,

> a sensitive Etonian with a knowledge of Homer and Virgil through these translations and a good ear, would be unable to detect in poems like *Tithonus, Ulysses* or *The Lotus Eaters* any note foreign to the works of Homer or Virgil... The two classics had been 'romanticised' for him, impregnated with the cult of strangeness, of the particular rather than the general and of the conception of beauty characteristic of the Aesthetic Movement as something akin to disease and evil.

Connolly's own reading still tended to the pessimistic. He preferred the Old Testament to the New, and particularly enjoyed *Ecclesiastes* and the *Song of Solomon*; he adored the *Odyssey* but not the *Iliad*, and relished the lyric poets and, in particular, the sceptical epigrams about love and doomed youth. Despite a lifetime's Latin, he found it hard to enjoy Horace and Virgil until the Loeb translations were published: his favourite Roman poet was Catullus and his favourite prose-writer Petronius Arbiter – he owned four editions of *The Satyricon*, one of which, bound in 'black crushed leather', he kept in his pew in chapel for reading during the sermon, and held up in place of a prayer book.

*

Like all romantic anarchists, Connolly tended to react against the prevailing order, even if he found its principles sympathetic and had campaigned in its cause while in opposition. The liberals were now in power in College; beatings had stopped, little fagging was actually done, and the election system was in abeyance. As an uneasy member of Pop, he was a school prefect, but since he was not in Sixth Form he was not a house prefect; displaying to the end an admirable shortage of 'character', he slipped into a state of aesthetic irresponsibility, riling the ruling triumvirate of Dannreuther, Mynors and Longden, calling all the boys in College by their Christian names, consorting with the fags – one of whom he hired to sing Gregorian chants outside his room – on the grounds that he wanted them to be happier than he had been at their age, and ridiculing the horrors of the past by staging mock beatings at which the cane had been thoughtfully sawn in half, and snapped at the first stroke. No doubt all this made him something of a hero to the junior boys, but among his contemporaries he was regarded as a formidable and even alarming figure. John Maud – who went on to become an eminent civil servant, chairing endless committees and ending his days as Lord Redcliffe Maud, the Master of University College, Oxford – confessed later that he was 'always conscious' of his 'immense intellectual and aesthetic inferiority' to Connolly, of whom he was 'invariably frightened': Connolly, for his part, regarded Maud as 'frightfully pushing', with an 'air of hypocritical piety', unkindly comparing him to 'a cake of soap that one has left in one's bath'.* Even Dannreuther admitted that whereas Connolly's election to Pop had made him his 'worldly superior', his Balliol scholarship 'made you even more convincingly than before my intellectual superior', and that his last 'half' had been made wretched by his fear of losing Connolly's friendship. Dannreuther's misery was heightened by his not being asked to Connolly's leaving tea, though 'Your idea of friendship is three parts sensuality, while I can respond to any amount of sentiment but am utterly unsensual.' Six pairs of boys attended the tea: they were, Connolly told Dannreuther, 'all musical and all gone on each other . . . how could you have fitted in?'

Freddie Harmer had been Connolly's other half at the leaving tea. Like Blakiston and O'Dwyer and Milligan, he had aroused in Connolly passionate emotions, but whether rhetoric was ever converted into action seems unlikely. Connolly tells us in *Enemies of Promise* that he left Eton without having masturbated, let alone moved on to the next stage; writing to Blakiston in the autumn of 1922, he shared the younger boy's regrets that they couldn't get married, but went on to say that although he was 'very sensual', he didn't 'consider any sins of the flesh'. The year before, at Camp, he had 'lain' with Jacky O'Dwyer, but 'I did not do him or anything – I was not gone on him but in the dark one face is very much like another and it was the perfect understanding that arose out of such close embrace that I valued so much . . .' With O'Dwyer his relationship seems to have been particularly 'sensual': the two boys addressed each other in letters as 'My darling Cyril' and *vice versa*, with a line of crosses subjoined, and no doubt a certain amount of actual as well as epistolary kissing took place: but although Connolly may have snuggled up at night with O'Dwyer and other boys at Camp or even in College ('My God if Crace caught us sleeping together next half!' O'Dwyer once exclaimed), caution almost certainly prevailed. 'You never resisted me (above the belt!),' O'Dwyer told Connolly, who in turn suggested that these schoolboy relationships were essentially emotional affairs, in which humiliation and domination were curiously combined in a self-immolatory yearning for another:

> I always hanker to be second fiddle to one person . . . I like to abdicate all my personality into someone weaker really than myself – that is the theory

* John Sparrow once observed of him that 'With Maud one has to take the smooth with the smooth.'

> of being gone on someone as opposed to hero-worship . . . for instance I always tried for Charles [Milligan] to run me when I was gone on him – ditto HNB – though when not gone on them I did not look up to them . . .

As Connolly later admitted, although he knew all about such matters as infibulation through his reading of the classics, he had no idea how sexual intercourse was performed or how babies were born; and despite the ripeness of his conversation, 'I was supposed to be much more "immoral" than I really was.'

Although he had become increasingly bored with College life and needed to move on, he dreaded having to leave what seemed 'a private civilisation of reason and love at a temperature warmer than the world outside'. He attended chapel for the last time, refusing to bow his head during the Creed and reading Petronius undetected, and a last meeting of Pop, at which their successors were chosen: Charles Milligan was among them, and Connolly put up Noël Blakiston although he was not elected until the following year. ' "It's all very well, Spud," ' he remembered one of the dimmer Pops complaining,

> 'but I just don't see anyone I can damn well put up – I mean who is there? We're nearly all leaving, and there's a hell of a lot of vacancies. Well, I just don't see anyone to fill them . . . I said to Alec Dunglass "After all, why take the trouble to fill the bloody vacancies?" – but you know what Alec is, he didn't seem properly awake while I was talking . . .'

And finally he went for the last time to Camp, where – he told Jacky O'Dwyer – he and another boy

> kissed each other feverishly all night like I did when I thought you were asleep as if you'd vanish any moment and like one does one's pillow sometimes – once in the night he woke up and said in a small voice 'Please could you come a little closer?' – so the midsummer madness got hold of him – I had kissed him in his sleep (from remorse) the time we were on the same paliasse – Christ did I enjoy Camp – what it would have been like if I had had you passeth all understanding.

And then it was over, and

> So it has come and I have gone
> And never more shall I
> With Jacky, Michael, William, John,

All nice and good to look upon,
Beguile the winter sky . . .

*

And yet it was far from over: Eton and his memories of Eton not only inspired some of Connolly's finest autobiographical writing, but exercised a profound influence on his character and the ways in which he behaved and thought about the world. Nor, in the short term, had Connolly finished with Eton, though Eton, it seems, was ungratefully anxious to be finished with him. Unhappy and homesick at Balliol, he pined for his vanished Eden. 'I am terrified of being forgotten by them,' he wrote to William le Fanu, apropos the Collegers he had left behind: 'Find out if my fags miss me and give my love to little Freddy.' 'I have cried since seven o'clock and have had no dinner,' he told the same school friend, after bursting into inelegant if heartfelt verse:

And now are all so far away
And still are drifting with the tide
Which takes them further on their way
And I must stay with hands tied –
For all the paths where friends divide –
For all that fades when it is fair –
For faces wherein youth has died –
Criez 'Jouvence ou la chimère'

For all the stars of our night who shine,
For little Freddy and Peter Pan,
Noël Blakiston, Jackie and John,
Raymond, Randy and Charles who ran
And William who called me a charlatan
For Freddy Harmer with fiery hair,
For every boy that becomes a man –
Criez 'Jouvence ou la chimère'

Such sentiments would have cut little ice with the Master in College and his fellow-beaks, many of whom clearly regarded Connolly as a bad influence who should be kept firmly at arm's length, not least where fags were concerned. Jacky O'Dwyer reported that 'Crace and the Head Usher have been talking to me about your writing to fags, and the HU said he would probably go and see you next time he was in Oxford. They both practically made me promise I would not hand on any letters' – this in reply perhaps to a letter in which Connolly had suggested coming down to Eton to 'corrupt the fags from the security of the Cloisters'. 'Tuppy' Headlam was then drawn into the fray, as was the Balliol don 'Sligger' Urquhart: 'I do not wish to interfere in what is not my business, but I gather that perhaps it would be wiser and kinder on your part not to come here on Sunday, or at any rate if you do come not to go into College: come and see me if you like in the morning with Sligger but let the boys rest...' By now College must have seemed more like a city under siege than a peaceful seat of learning, with emissaries carrying messages between its defenders and the enemy without. 'Tuppy told me not to come to Eton,' Connolly told Mynors: 'Bobbie, Sligger and Chris [Hollis] have all gone to investigate and defend me.' Ever the dutiful friend, Longden reported their findings to the pariah in Balliol: Crace had told him that Connolly had promised not to write to the fags, and would far sooner he kept away. Even so, Connolly visited the school in December, and Harmer wrote to say what a success it had been, 'bringing our friendship down (or up?) to a more practical level'. And the following summer Connolly suggested a meeting with Blakiston, either at the school or at the Eton and Harrow match.

Such frenzied attempts to regain the past and resist the passing of time were not unusual: Antony Knebworth, now up at Magdalen, Oxford, found it impossible to keep away, for 'There is not a thing about it that isn't absolutely perfect. I don't wonder that people live on and on there'; as for Oxford, 'it's not a quarter as good as Eton' – it might be 'a good interesting place for old men of forty, but for boys, why I'd rather be at a girls' school for knitting'. But such nostalgic visits soon petered out as the boys in the year behind left in their turn, and other interests began to exert their claims: and in fact Connolly kept away for many years thereafter, terrified that he would be chased from the premises by angry beaks brandishing copies of *Enemies of Promise*. However the image of Eton as Eden grew ever stronger in his mind, together with the notion – familiar to generations of public-school Englishmen, albeit in cruder, more boisterous form – of life thereafter as intrinsically anticlimactic. While still in his mid-twenties he began asking Eton friends to return his letters to him as the basis for an autobiographical evocation of the lives they had shared in Paradise. 'Reading about Eton in old letters always plunges me back into the golden age,' he wrote in a notebook of 1927:

> Is this because it is so remote or because of its intrinsic value? I think the latter, which explains why I have never really looked forward. Few things are more disturbing than the barren aspect of the present world when the taste of honeydew still lingers in the mouth. Eton and Camp so Greek, so

> rich in the luxury of love's desperation and philosopher's despair. This wild world of tears and hatred, epigrams and kisses, seems really to have died with us.

It hadn't, of course: but the concept of paradise lost reinforced his innate romanticism, his carefully cultivated sense of the sad futility of life and most endeavour. Four years earlier, the twenty-year-old Connolly, already on the look-out for corroborative correspondence, told le Fanu of how

> I labour under the delusion that I have steadily deteriorated since I was seventeen – the Rosebery, my scholarship and Pop being stages in the decline, with their ever-increasing publicity, advertisement and solace of the world, and Bobbie only in the year that follows to keep me from sheer ruin, you may see how eagerly I cling to any documentary evidence of what I was like at the time.

Yet Connolly's romanticism and nostalgia were tempered even then by realism, by a shrewd awareness of what he was up to; of how, for the romantic, life was at its most heightened in anticipation or, more probably, in retrospect. Eton, he told Blakiston, had been 'nothing without one's friends . . . nothing but hostile and dessicating stillness in the dark shades and dancing dust shafts of New Buildings silent and suppressed beneath the fixed eye of the invigilating sun . . .' A 'sense of living in a sequel' had blighted his time at Oxford, yet 'even at Eton one was always bitterly envying the Attic boyhoods of Lysis and Alcibiades and the fields that cool Ilissus laves . . .'

Looking back on his time at Eton in the closing pages of *Enemies of Promise*, Connolly enunciated his famous 'Theory of Permanent Adolescence', according to which

> the experiences undergone by boys at the great public schools, their glories and disappointments, are so intense as to dominate their lives and to arrest their development. From this it results that the greater part of the ruling class remains adolescent, school-minded, self-conscious, cowardly, sentimental, and in the last analysis homosexual.

For many of his school friends, now in their early thirties, life was effectively over, and nothing would quite be the same again; and for this 'Once again romanticism with its death wish is to blame, for it lays an emphasis on childhood, on a fall from grace which is not compensated for by any doctrine of future redemption; we enter the world, trailing clouds of glory, childhood and boyhood follow and we are damned.' Only the artist was exempt from this subversive nostalgia, this refusal to grow up; and the fact that artists, like some foreigners, were prepared to accept maturity was what made them so unpopular.*

'For my own part,' he went on,

> I was long dominated by impressions of school. The plopping of gas mantles in the class-rooms, the refrain of psalm tunes, the smell of plaster on the stairs, the walk through the fields to the bathing places or to chapel across the cobbles of School Yard, evoked a vanished Eden of grace and security.

He had left Eton, he said, with a sense of the transitoriness of all delights; hubris and retribution were forever waiting in the wings. Politically he was a 'liberal individualist': he hated power, loved freedom and justice, but had no time for politics and 'wished for nothing better than to talk to my friends, travel abroad, look at Old Masters and Romanesque churches, read old books and devote myself to lost causes and controversies of the past.' A hater of Competition (which set friends against each other) and Worldliness (despite his flirtation with Pop), he had ended his days there 'an affected lover of sensations which I often faked, a satirist in self-defence, a sceptical believer in the Heraclitan flux, an introspective romantic – sensitive, conceited, affectionate, gregarious, and, at the time of leaving Eton, the outstanding moral coward of my generation.'

By the time he came to write *Enemies of Promise* – that rueful, horribly exact account of the pitfalls that lie in the path of the writer of promise – Connolly had come to see himself as the embodiment of his hapless subject matter. 'Somewhere in the facts I have recorded,' he wrote, looking back on his childhood and schooldays,

> lurk the causes of that sloth by which I have been disabled, somewhere lies the sin whose guilt is at my door, increasing by compound interest faster than promise (for promise is guilt: promise is the capacity for letting people down); and through them run those romantic ideas and fallacies, those errors of judgement against which the validity of my criticism must be judged.

* The maturity of artists seems open to doubt, and Connolly himself was often, and rightly, to lament the immaturity of English poets and novelists of the nineteenth century when set against their French equivalents: Thackeray and Dickens and Tennyson versus Flaubert and Stendhal and Baudelaire, for instance. One sees what he means, but it doesn't quite tie up with the Theory, and neither Dickens nor Tennyson were exposed to the luxuriant rigours of a public school.

Two years after publication of *Enemies of Promise*, Connolly's old school friend George Orwell referred, somewhat scathingly, to the 'Theory of Permanent Adolescence' in his essay about the British intelligentsia, 'Inside the Whale'. Expressing amazement that Connolly could seriously suggest that the lives of grown men could be dominated by their schooldays, Orwell – whose experiences since Eton had included a spell in the Burma police, living rough in London, Paris and the North of England, and fighting in Spain – wrote that

> Cultured middle-class life has reached a depth of softness at which a public-school education – five years in a lukewarm bath of snobbery – can actually be looked back upon as an eventful period. To nearly all the writers who have counted during the thirties, what more has ever happened than Mr Connolly records in *Enemies of Promise*? It is the same pattern all the time: public school, university, a few trips abroad, then London. Hunger, hardship, solitude, exile, war, prison, persecution, manual labour – hardly even words.

And of course he was right, in his brisk, commonsensical way; and yet for many of us – some leading sheltered, conventional lives, others more adventurous or exposed – Connolly's elegiac sense of the sadness of life, of the passing of youth, the slow diminution of hopes and the narrowing of horizons, remains all too touching and true.

SEVEN

Blokey Balliol

Perhaps the most remarkable feature of Connolly's generally undistinguished Oxford career, and almost certainly the one that gave him the most pleasure, was the amount of travelling he managed to fit into his three years at university. This was, of course, a golden age for young, footloose Englishmen, eager to trade in the rain, the fog, the humbuggery and the waterlogged vegetables of post-war England for summer shores, where the wine was cheap, the food an improvement and the natives (or so it was fondly believed) life-loving and spontaneous, with none of the hypocritical reserve that blighted life on the other side of the Channel. The roads were still empty, hotels and meals cost next to nothing and, best of all, the pound was worth its weight in gold, a pillar of strength and sobriety when set against unreliable and ever-depreciating foreign currencies. Over the next few years Connolly was to become a passionate, almost obsessive traveller, moving about the Mediterranean, more often than not alone, in knee-length shorts and an Old Etonian tie, and combining in letters and postcards home the realist's unillusioned eye with the romantic's sense of travel as a form of yearning for what lies beyond the horizon, in which the actuality of the moment never quite matches up to the promise of what lies ahead. Travel, he wrote, is the 'only lasting homesickness', an illusion of action whereby the anonymous voyager asserted his right to run away, a 'flight from oneself and into oneself'; it was also, more prosaically, a matter of dirt and boils and dust and sea-sickness and missed connections and money running out, all of them unpleasant at the time but soon forgotten when the vacation came round again, and with it the urge to move south once more.

Anxious to build up his reserves before facing the rigours of Balliol, Connolly spent some weeks before term began travelling in Germany, Austria and Hungary – initially as part of a family group, and then by himself. 'I hanker after narrow dirty old streets with cobbles sweating in the sun and houses smelling of corruption,' he told Jacky O'Dwyer, but in the meantime he had to put up with his mother's irritating habit of comparing everything they saw with Wynberg or Deep Cut, as well as arguing with both parents over the colour of Roger Mynors's hair, and whether or not a

Captain Cornelli of the Italian Navy was in fact an Austrian. 'My ambition is to find a place which can't be compared to anywhere else,' he confided to his journal; and to escape the interminable chatter, he rowed out alone into the Moselle off Trier and ostentatiously read a poem by Ausonius, one of the Latin poets he had studied at Eton under 'Muggins' Macnaghten. No doubt it was a relief when the family party – which incongruously included 'Cris' Brooke – headed home and left him to his own devices, armed as he was with five shillings a day, a German dictionary, the *Odyssey*, La Rochefoucauld's *Maxims*, Bergk's 'Fragments' of Greek lyric poets and a mandolin, which was plucked in Donaueschingen but remained silent thereafter. He went to the passion play at Oberammergau, but was too 'cold, tired and depressed' to enjoy it; in Munich the Oktoberfest was in full frenzy, much beer was drunk and an amorous waitress encountered; a bounderish-looking Englishman met in a hotel turned out to be the son of the Master of the Quorn and the brother-in-law of a peer, so they sat down to dinner together, working their way through caviare, *pâté de foie gras*, an asparagus omelette, a partridge each, peach melba, champagne, Grand Marnier and a 'terrific cigar', for all of ten shillings each. Old friends, though, were for ever in his mind. 'Christ I do miss you,' he told O'Dwyer: 'I admit I haven't blubbed since Thursday last (after all I *am* going to be a man) but you are hardly out of my thoughts,' so much so that he wondered whether he mightn't come down to Eton on his return and 'nip up Crace's back stairs during Prayers'. O'Dwyer would soon be going on to Woolwich and a career in the Army, and their paths would diverge thereafter, but an earlier and longer-lasting love was not forgotten by the lonely traveller: 'I would like to write a symphony to our friendship,' he told Noël Blakiston, 'beginning like Beethoven's Sixth with very light pastoral for that time when I first noticed you looking very cool and brown and charming and chewing a daisy in the May sun'.

Deep in Beethoven country, he took a train from Salzburg to Vienna, and so on to Budapest. For some curious reason a letter from O'Dwyer aroused the suspicions of the customs officials at the Hungarian frontier, but when he explained that it was in fact a '*lieber briefe*' he was quickly waved through. Adrift on the interminable *puszta*, he slept in hay-stacks, and worried about putting on too much weight after breakfasting with farmers on bread, sausage, coffee, wine and cognac. He borrowed a horse, equipped with a saddle but no stirrups, on which he set off across the flat, green Hortobágy, with its wells and acacias and low white houses and uncorralled herds of oxen, covering fourteen miles, incongruously clad in a 'lounge suit' and getting soaked in rain and mud in the process. Despite his spotting in a Budapest bookshop window 'a tempting book *Reserche aux temps perdus* or some title like that – Vol IV Sodom & Gomorrah,' his new-found sophistication let him down when confronted by the 'head girl' in a café ('Oh for more courage, less consciousness of self'), but after booking into the Astoria Hotel he resumed his amorous education. Feeling 'dauntless *à la* Cyrano', he carried on a 'long conversation about the immortality of the soul' with an English officer in a brothel, interrupted by 'French kisses etc' from the employees, while a band played briskly in the background. Eventually he retired upstairs with a girl who became 'very passionate and took her stockings off – she enjoyed it I think. I love it I must say and said I had never been so happy before – tried several "ways of love" afterwards, "*comme animal* etc".' He staggered back to his hotel at four in the morning, but next day he felt miserable, depressed and 'very limp'.

Reflections on the ultimate ends of life were not restricted to conversation in brothels with random English officers. Like many of us, Connolly combined – and would always combine – vague religious urges with an intellectual inability to accept the tenets of any organised religion. He had been contemplating a conversion to Rome, he told le Fanu as he headed home via Vienna, Nuremberg, Frankfurt, Brussels and Bruges, but

> My trouble is to simulate the necessary piety to get started when I only want the Romance and Peace of the mother church and can't believe any more than before. My gods are Pan and Apollo, Nemesis and Fortune.... I worship the frail plants who bud and bloom and die in the garden of Mortality, and Beauty that wounds and fadeth, and Truth that allures and hideth.

Not long after his return he wrote again to le Fanu, a letter from whom had brightened his 'cheerless arrival in this horrible hole' – the hole in question being Balliol College, Oxford. Balliol was one of the oldest Oxford colleges – as it happened, Connolly was twenty-second in descent from its mediaeval founder, John de Baliol – and it was almost certainly the ugliest, many of its original buildings having been torn down and replaced by mid-Victorian Gothic of the most gleamingly hideous kind; it also enjoyed a unique reputation within the university thanks to the labours of its celebrated former Master, Benjamin Jowett, an eminent Victorian who converted Balliol from a smallish, rather middling college into a formidable forcing-house, the products of which were expected to combine intellectual distinction with worldly success, academic excellence with an almost automatic access to the sources of power and influence. At a time when the great majority of undergraduates were drawn from the public schools, Balliol had a more meritocratic reputation than most other colleges, welcoming (in theory at least) boys from humbler backgrounds, and becoming well-known within the university for its intake of Indians, and even the occasional black man; but like Christ Church and Magdalen, both of which were grander, larger and more elegant, it was also much favoured by Etonians, a gaggle of whom once set on Sir Philip Sassoon (who, though rich, was also Jewish) and drove him from the quad with horse-whips. According to Anthony Powell, who joined the college a year or two later, 'Balliol stood out in bleakness'; Dannreuther warned Connolly that 'Balliol is the home of sensuality, selfish aggrandisement, cynicism and cleverness, and I see little chance of keeping afloat except by sacrificing principle.'* Comparing his beloved College favourably with Balliol, Connolly reckoned that the spirit of College was 'antagonistic to Balliol in its suppression of the political, its lack of emphasis on conversation, its hatred of giants at play, and attention to reading and to reading of dead rather than living authors. It appears more akin to Cambridge in some respects.'

Of his fellow-Etonians at Balliol, Roger Mynors soon proved himself 'indispensable'; as for Dannreuther, 'Denis I would never look at if he was in another college, but he is the only man in this I know well enough to sit up with after midnight.' Collegers of an older generation such as Christopher Hollis tried to make him feel at home: but Hollis, who later converted to Catholicism, and became a well-known writer on Roman Catholic matters as well as a publisher and MP, spent too much time reading Chesterton's paradoxical poems, and Connolly soon tired of his 'Chesterto-Wembley view of life'. Among his fellow-Etonian freshmen he particularly disliked John Heygate and Alfred Duggan. Duggan – who moved in a grand Oppidan circle that included Oliver Messel, Billy Clonmore and the Acton brothers – soon established himself at the centre of Balliol social life: this revolved around 'unlimited drink', and 'one usually has to assist in putting him to bed.' Looking back in old age on the young Connolly, Maurice Bowra, by then the Warden of Wadham, suggested that Balliol was 'a little too hard, too worldly for him, and it had almost nothing to offer as he explored his sensibility'; but part of his squeamishness was probably old-fashioned snobbery, and Evelyn Waugh may have been right in suspecting that Connolly, like Waugh himself, would have been happier in a grander, more beautiful college such as Christ Church. Within Balliol, Etonians clung together like exiles in a foreign land, and it was only gradually that he got to know a few non-Etonians, like Kenneth Clark, the future art

* This formed part of a letter in which Dannreuther charged his friend with just those qualities he attributed to Balliol, and hoped that – even though a mutual friend had warned him that Connolly would find him 'very useful for a bit until he got into a new set' – they could now resume their friendship on more equal terms.

historian, who had been to Winchester and was now at Trinity with Bobbie Longden. As it was, Connolly regarded most of his 'blokey' fellow-undergraduates, with their pipes and tweed jackets with leather patches on the elbows, and grey flannel trousers and college scarves and baccy jars emblazoned with the college coat of arms, with suspicion and disdain. He couldn't face dining in hall, he told Freddie Harmer – who was, presumably, enjoying a more College-like existence at King's – and lived instead off 'biscuits and oranges, of which Roger has a crate': nothing, it seemed, could be more dismal than 'Balliol hall on a smelly evening, the burble of many accents though one tongue, ugliness expressed in every inmate . . . ' 'Every single person is quite bloody bar Roger (and Denis),' he wrote, with sweeping exclusivity: 'if they haven't bloody voices they have bloody faces, and if they haven't those they make up by their conversation.' For the rest of his life he loathed the sound of bells, which reminded him of dank, dismal, tedious Oxford afternoons. 'If it were a monastery it would be all right,' he informed le Fanu: ' – a sleepy place where one could follow the advancement of learning, peopled only by Bobbie, Roger, Miles and Randy, books and fires and nice food and dreamy dons – but it bristles with acquaintances, bridge, tea parties, debts and people who gloat with joy like John Wilkes and Chris Hollis, who ask Bobbie to lunch and dinner and bridge . . . My theory is to have no acquaintance – the sort of frightful people whom you make conversation with – and confine myself to the Middle Ages, about which I am accumulating an immense library.'

Young men who like to think of themselves as being more rarefied and sensitive than most will often disguise commonplace feelings of fear and alarm, induced by new and unfamiliar surroundings, by affecting a refinement of spirit, a hermit-like aloofness, and by cultivating, and often imitating, older men who provide less of a challenge than boisterous, beer-swilling contemporaries and enable the acolyte to distance himself from the vulgar horde, with its footer boots and crossword puzzles and pewter mugs of ale. Even as a rather precious undergraduate, Connolly was too realistic and too self-aware to allow the affectations of the poseur to become a somewhat fraudulent way of life: but throughout his time at Oxford he kept himself apart from the conventional undergraduate pleasures and opportunities, cultivating a small circle of friends, some younger dons among them. He may have been, in Kenneth Clark's words, 'without doubt the most gifted undergraduate of his generation', but in terms of measurable achievements – academic, literary, artistic, social or sporting – he held himself at bay. 'I don't think you had a breakdown at Balliol,' Maurice Bowra told him years later, but 'I think you were going through in a very acute form the transition from the confidence of boyhood to the considered behaviour of manhood ... You left a great deal behind and were too critical and too clever to accept what was offered you in its place. Anyhow at such a time history was an absurd subject to take, and the Balliol people ought to have known better.' Despite his enthusiasm for the Dark Ages and mediaeval heresies – the darker the age and the obscurer the heresy, the happier he was – his academic career soon languished irremediably; and although in later years he would automatically be associated with such Oxford contemporaries as Evelyn Waugh, Graham Greene, Anthony Powell, John Betjeman and Henry Green, he remained, as at Eton, an observer (if that) as far as the university's literary life was concerned. Waugh, Tom Driberg, Robert Byron, Christopher Sykes and John Betjeman all edited *Cherwell* during their university careers, but featured not at all in the life of the future founder of *Horizon*; he continued to write dense, old-fashioned, heavily romantic verse, but none of it found its way into the annual edition of *Oxford Poetry* (its editors then included Harold Acton and Peter Quennell, its contributors Graham Greene, David Cecil, L.P. Hartley, Christopher Hollis, Richard Hughes, A.L. Rowse and C. Day Lewis) or Harold Acton's short-lived *Oxford Broom*, for which Waugh provided the cover illustration as well as a piece within.

Despite his Etonian loyalties, Connolly was not associated with the more flamboyant and extravagant manifestations of post-war gilded youth – one memorable example of which was the twenty-first birthday party of his future friend Harry d'Avigdor-Goldsmid, a Harrovian who went up to Balliol a few years later and, according to Osbert Lancaster, hired a river steamer 'complete with a brass band and loaded to the Plimsoll Line with champagne' – or with the antics of what came to be known with wearisome familiarity as the 'Brideshead Generation': that widely celebrated world of plovers' eggs and high Victorian camp, of Oxford bags and grey bowler hats, of Brian Howard fluttering his eyelashes and calling everyone 'my dear' and Harold Acton – most famously of all – reciting *The Waste Land* through a megaphone from his room in Christ Church's Meadow Buildings to puzzled-looking oarsmen and elderly passers-by. Fifty years after the event, Connolly joined other elderly survivors – Waugh, Harold Acton, Bob Boothby and Roy Harrod among them – on the Brighton Belle to celebrate the anniversary of John Sutro's Oxford Railway Club, but there is no evidence of his having taken part at the time; nor was he a member of the notorious Hypocrites Club, which met above a bicycle shop in St Aldate's and whose founder-members – stolid, pipe-smoking Rugbeians and Wykehamists – had been ousted by hedonistic, Sitwell-loving Etonians, and whose walls were soon redecorated by Robert Byron and Oliver Messel. 'Connolly was no less further removed from such everyday Oxford spheres as indicated by the names of the Union, OUDS or Bullingdon,' Anthony Powell recalled: 'Even by Balliol standards he lived a life apart . . .'

'Anything connected with Oxford turns me queer inside,' Connolly told his new friend Patrick Balfour, later Lord Kinross, and a Wykehamist from Trinity; and, as he had for much of his time at Eton, he turned his back on the world in favour of intense, introspective, passionate personal relationships. According to Bowra, he reacted against his earlier enthusiasm for bloods and the kind of young men he had consorted with in Pop – Teddy Jessel, he told le Fanu disapprovingly, seemed interested only in golf and gambling – 'and to make up for it he applied his acute and sensitive intelligence partly to finding a selected circle of close friends, with whom he could live in intimate ease, partly to extending his knowledge of literature and foreign countries . . . He had lost his old stance and was looking for another, and this meant that at times he was unhappy, unsure of himself and in need of support.' Throughout his life Connolly was an avid maker of lists, not least of his friends and lovers, and the margins and blank pages of his mediaeval history notebooks were spattered with the names of his friends, repeated over and over again or set out in ever-changing orders of preference; and, as in College, much agonising went on over who was edging ahead of whom, or slights received, or favourites jostling for position. Already he combined wit and charm with a disconcerting moodiness, boyishness with a worldliness well beyond his years. Bowra remembered him as being 'slim and slight, with a large head, a fine forehead, eager, questing eyes, a face that registered every change of feeling, and a soft, hypnotising voice: although his own behaviour was far from faultless, he expected high standards from his friends.' And although 'he had a great capacity for enjoyment, he could be exacting about it. If you asked him to luncheon or dinner, you had to be careful that he would like the other guests' – a trait that remained with him for the rest of his life, marking him out as a far better host than guest, and triggering off spasms of nervous anxiety on the part of those who invited him, lest he be overcome by boredom or irritation, and make his feeling plain. He expected much, and was easily disappointed. 'His worries about personal relations occupied much of his time and kept him even further from the mass of his contemporaries', but he liked nothing better than to fantasise and speculate and gossip, building up elaborate myths about the goings-on of his friends: 'he was extremely quick to notice changes of mood or small betrayals of character, and on them he would build bold edifices of speculation.' 'I have never known anyone of his age who was in so many ways mature and yet kept the freshness, both sad and glad, of youth,' Bowra remembered, while to Kenneth Clark he was 'obviously an extraordinary person, with a width of knowledge and a maturity of mind of an entirely different class to the rest of us:'

> He had read the Greek and Latin authors, including those of the Silver Age, with a subtle, questioning mind; he had read the French poets and critics of the nineteenth century; he had even read the Christian Fathers. All this learning was almost entirely invisible below a surface of wit and intellectual curiosity. He was a master of parody, who could improvise anybody's style in the course of conversation.

But although he was widely considered brilliant, 'this label did not suit Cyril, partly, I think, because his voice had a curious matt tonality, partly because he never attempted to shine or exert himself.' Within his small circles, he was both formidable and unpredictable. 'He was a protean character,' wrote Peter Quennell, a lifelong friend from Balliol days towards whom Connolly always felt a certain ambivalence, and

> nobody had a livelier wit or, if annoyed, a sharper tongue. His cynical *bons mots* were apt to stick like burs. Yet his pensive romanticism was just as conspicuous as his cynicism.... Whatever the subject that confronted him, he had his own immediate response; and I frequently admired, not just the spirited quickness of his mind, but the readiness with which he managed to produce some startlingly original opinion.

Fellow-Collegers were not immune from Connolly's disapproval or disdain. 'It's been *extremely* nice of you to go on stolidly being nice to me, with only dullness and politeness in return,' John Maud wrote from New College, where he once invited Connolly to dinner, warning him that the meal might not be up to scratch since 'my scout is of extreme age, suffering from rheum, asthma and delirium tremens': maybe the meal was beyond endurance, for before long the unhappy Maud found himself being cut at a social function, hurriedly writing to assure his erstwhile friend that he had never dreamt of patronising him. Beneath this alarming exterior the soul of a schoolboy still lurked, rather reassuringly, in a watery addiction – not to elegant oarsmanship of the kind conventionally associated with the heartier undergraduates, or even languid punting up the Cherwell, but to the altogether humbler canoe. Anthony Powell was once asked if he liked adventures, and then joined Connolly in an attempt to canoe upstream against some rapids, the bottom of the boat bumping over the rocks; while Peter Quennell – who remembered how Connolly always relished the odder aspects of Oxford, and his gift for 'lending colour and poetic significance to the smallest episode' – shared a canoe on a nocturnal expedition round the dark, unglamorous wastes of the Oxford Canal, where (according to his leader) 'the squat tower of the castle looks more like Provence than anything I have seen in England and where the water eddies beside old houses and flowers of chestnut and may and lilac hang over the dirty water and music comes from ancient inns.'

As well as cultivating his own exclusive circle of friends, Connolly enjoyed the company of certain dons – and of two dons in particular, both of whom were well known within the university for their patronage of clever, well-connected and reasonably good-looking undergraduates. Evelyn Waugh, who was disrespectful to dons and extremely hard-drinking, and felt, in retrospect at least, that the temperate Connolly was 'too fastidious for the company I then kept', believed that Eton had given Connolly 'a taste for the society of dons'; and not long after his arrival Connolly reported that 'I am glad to find I have not lost my capacity for hero-worship and lay it on fairly thickly on the dons here.' Among the recipients of this hero-worship – though he could hardly have been a less heroic figure – was the Dean of Balliol, F.F. Urquhart, commonly known as 'Sligger', whom Connolly pronounced 'wonderfully refreshing after the beaks at Eton', a 'Dean whom you can pinch, put your arms round his neck and call Sligger without any self-consciousness at all.'

Then in his mid-fifties, Urquhart was the quintessential bachelor don. Kenneth Clark remembered him as a 'kindly-looking man with white hair and the pink complexion of a baby', Anthony Powell as 'mild, monkish, white-haired, withdrawn, elusive in manner . . . a devout Roman Catholic, conversationally inhibited'. He had a large room over the West Gate, which Clark recalled as 'an authentic relic of Victorian Oxford, filled with threadbare settees and dowdy-looking books, most of them mediaeval charters and the like'. Earlier in the century, 'Sligger' – a corruption of the 'sleek one', according to Bowra – had appeared to endorse Balliol's high-minded and relatively democratic principles by suggesting that 'we should get the best men (in several ways) from our public schools and let them mix with intelligent men from Birmingham etc'; but rhetoric was less often matched to practice, and whereas the public schoolboys were accorded the warmest of welcomes, an emboldened Birmingham man was likely to receive short shrift: ' "What book have you come to borrow, Thompson?" ' he would be asked, according to Christopher Hollis, before being 'summarily ushered out again'. A.L. Rowse – a genuine working-class lad, albeit enrolled at the grandest college of all – unkindly noted his 'lascivious blue lips and hooded erotic eyes (repressed of course)', but for those who passed the test Sligger proved a benign and kindly presence, a kind of academic mother-hen clucking anxiously round the 'earnest young scholars, minor royalty, priests, budding poets and a few lonely nonentities' who made themselves at home in his rooms, celebrated by Kenneth Clark as a 'reservoir of kindliness and tolerance'. No drink was available there, which 'kept out the more spirited undergraduates', and after Waugh had been offered barley water he mounted his celebrated and hurtful offensive against the Dean, culminating in his standing outside the main gate of the college chanting 'The Dean of Balliol lies with men!' to the tune of 'Nuts in May'. And the fact that Sligger was responsible for the closure of the Hypocrites Club made him still more unpopular with his elfin persecutor.

No doubt the Dean dreamed of sleeping with a good many of the handsome young men with whom he surrounded himself, but it seems unlikely that dreams were ever converted into reality; in Graham Greene's opinion, Sligger gathered round him young men 'who attracted him by their looks and who played, if only superficially, the comedy of homosexual inclinations'; while Maurice Bowra, who ran a rival salon, albeit with a fiercer and more worldly tone, thought him 'cultivated but not highbrow', the kind of maternal don who exerted his influence through 'the tolerance and gentleness which he extended to a number of highly-strung young men much in need of them. He would calm them down, give them unobtrusively good advice, and help them in their troubles. One met all sorts in his rooms, where he gave little dinner parties at which no one ate or drank too much.'

Although Balliol fielded its due quota of active heterosexuals – among them Graham Greene, who tried to persuade himself that he was in love with a waitress at the George, and Peter Quennell, who was eventually sent down for what Anthony Powell described as his 'down-to-earth approach where the opposite sex was concerned', – many undergraduates continued to haunt the same unisexual and sometimes homosexual world familiar to them from their public schools. According to Hollis, the immediate post-war generation, many of them ex-soldiers, showed a flicker of interest in women, but by the time Connolly came up old ways had reasserted themselves. Girl students were in short supply and strictly chaperoned; male students lived in an entirely masculine world in which those set in authority over them were often unmarried and likely to remain that way; most students were, in Quennell's words, 'content to live in a society as confined as it had been before the coming of the railways and to indulge in light flirtations during the holidays and deep friendships during the term'. Not surprisingly, 'sentimental homosexual friendships' flourished. For the most part they represented a 'phase' to be grown out of in due course, and the authorities were prepared to avert their gaze provided the platonic friendships didn't become so intense as to lead to an 'overt physical act', in which case 'horror was unbridled and the punishment of expulsion instant and unrelenting'. Connolly himself fitted almost exactly into the pattern described by Quennell, and while in Oxford was perfectly happy to 'adopt the mores of an Hellenic city-state'; as he wrote to Noël Blakiston towards the end of his time at Balliol,

> As to women I came into the world with no natural inversion [meaning, in the jargon of the time, homosexual leanings] except a romantic conception of friendship but Eton and Oxford and the study of Greece have confirmed it and though women flatter me and make me feel a chap against my better judgement, apart from the vanity of coping with them I find the male form more beautiful, the male mind more true, and in the love of friends more good – a certain austerity of taste has made me always revolt from the curves of the feminine shape and the professionalism and the wiles of the daughters of Eve!

Within Balliol, the historian Kenneth Bell – a tutorial fellow whom Connolly regarded with affection – represented, in Greene's opinion, Sligger's polar opposite. Described by Hollis as a 'strange, roistering character', whose Balliol career was abruptly terminated after he abandoned his wife for another woman, and who ended his days as a vicar in Coventry, 'praying away like mad', Bell gathered round him undergraduates who were 'aggressively heterosexual and inclined, like himself, to drink large quantities of beer'; and whereas Sligger tended to slip away from college feasts, Bell invariably got drunk – so drunk that, on one occasion, he began to hurl coal at passers-by from the windows of his room, and had to be hidden under his bed by Alfred Duggan for fear that he might have his fellowship removed.

Such pranks were far removed from Sligger's dainty, maidenly world; but although in Bowra's opinion the Dean was 'kind and generous' to Connolly, soothing his anxieties, 'he did not give him quite the incitement that he needed, or discuss with sufficient knowledge or insight the subjects that absorbed him.' If a stronger, more invigorating draught was called for, the Dean of Wadham was the man to provide it; and whereas the kindly Sligger faded from Connolly's life within a year or two of his leaving Oxford and aroused, as often as not, a kind of affectionate derision ('From Sligger comes, like flushing rears,/ The noises of advancing years'), the more combative and demanding Bowra was to remain, often uneasily, a lifelong acquaintance.

Five years older than Connolly, Bowra had been born in China, and educated at Cheltenham and New College. In 1917 he had joined the Royal Field Artillery, and his experiences during the third battle of Ypres, at Cambrai and during Ludendorff's March 1918 offensive, marked him for life, helping perhaps to explain the brusque, seemingly self-confident face he presented to the world: 'Whatever you hear about the war, remember it was inconceivably bloody – nobody who wasn't there can ever imagine what it was like,' he once told Connolly, and in his autobiography – a milder, duller and more endearing document than the legend of Bowra might lead one to expect – he admits that 'I was not nearly so sure of myself as I should have liked, and this made me present a brassy face to the world and pretend to be more hard-boiled than I was... I developed a mocking, cynical way of treating events because it prevented them from being too painful.' He was haunted by his inability to write as well as he spoke, and by his homosexuality; but to those undergraduates whom he favoured with his presence and his patronage, he seemed a daring, disruptive force, an irresistible combination of academic brilliance and epigrammatic worldly wisdom. A classicist, he had been made a Fellow of Wadham in 1922, together with Lord David Cecil, and was appointed Dean shortly afterwards; and within a short time he had established himself as a forceful figure on the Oxford scene, well known beyond the walls of his adopted college. 'Noticeably small, this lack of stature emphasised by a massive head and tiny feet, Bowra – especially in later life – looked a little like those toys which cannot be pushed over because heavily weighted at the base,' Anthony Powell recalled; while Noël Annan, a friend from later years, remembered how 'When you were with him the large Johnsonian face was for ever mobile, responding to your remarks, giving expression to his own, alight, amused, domineering. But one feature in his face never smiled: his eyes. They were pig's eyes, fierce, unforgiving, unblinking, vigilant.' Not only was he, Isaiah Berlin wrote, 'passionately opposed to the conventional wisdom and moral code of those who formed pre-war Oxford opinion,' but 'He loved the sun, the sea, warmth, light and hated cold and darkness, physical, intellectual, moral... His passion for the Mediterranean and its cultures was of a piece with this: he loved pleasure, exuberance, the richest fruits of nature and civilisation, the fullest expression of human feeling, uninhibited by a Manichaean sense of guilt.' For the young, he was a 'major liberating force', because he 'dared to say things which others thought or felt, but were prevented from uttering by rules or conventions or personal inhibitions.' Kenneth Clark – who was uneasily aware that Bowra thought him, as an undergraduate, a bit of a dry stick – recalled how his 'priggish fears and inhibitions were blown to smithereens' by Bowra: 'the chief quality of his wit was its audacity. He said all the dreadful things one longed to hear said, and said them as if they were obvious to any decent man.' For Anthony Powell, 'Here was a don – someone by his very calling (in those days) suspect as representative of authority and discipline, an official promoter of didacticism – who, so far from attempting to expound tedious moral values of an old-fashioned kind, openly practised the worship of Pleasure'; while Osbert Lancaster recalled how he could 'stimulate the brilliant response even among those whose reactions were not normally lightning-quick; with the Dean everything seemed speeded-up, funnier and more easily explicable in personal terms ... our most daring flights were never censored for being too outrageous; only if they were quite clearly prompted by a desire to shock were they pointedly ignored.' 'To meet him,' Noël Annan wrote, 'was like downing tumblers of brandy rather than savouring a bottle of wine. One left reeling.'

Quite apart from calling on 'great reserves of lung power to gain a conversational advantage', relations with 'Mr Bowra the boarer' (Connolly's epithet) were not always easy, and were often unnerving. He often took offence, inhabiting an incestuous, catty world, the denizens of which could all too easily find themselves charged with making 'bad blood'. Anthony Powell – who met him for the most part at dinner parties of between six and eight people, at which no other dons were present and a great deal was drunk – recalled that there was 'always a slight sense of danger'; much was made of conversational brilliance – Bowra liked his undergraduates to be clever, but not necessarily academic – and witty epigrams, often unkind, were at a premium, so that, according to Hollis, 'even those who were at heart kindly and genial did not forbear to say wounding things about their fellows.' Those who had given offence or fallen from favour could find themselves nominated for the Bête Noire club, and so open to persecution. 'The Bowra innovation,' Powell suggested,

> was not only to proclaim the paramount claims of eating, drinking, sex (women at that early stage somewhat derided, homosexuality and auto-eroticism approved), but to accept, as absolutely normal, open snobbishness, success worship, personal vendettas, unprovoked malice, disloyalty to friends, reading other people's letters (if not lying about, to be sought in unopened drawers)* – the whole bag of tricks of what most people think, feel and often act upon, yet are ashamed of admitting that they do, feel and think.

Bowra liked to think of himself as fearless and worldly-wise and up-to-date, the kind of don who 'gave tutorials with a bottle of whisky by the armchair and a girl in the bedroom'; and yet there was something sad and vulnerable about him. Like many academics, he was ill-at-ease in the wider world, and although he liked to see himself as doing battle single-handed

* Isaiah Berlin remembers discussing with Connolly the ethics of reading other people's letters: Connolly told him he always kept a kettle at the ready.

against the parochialism and the timidity and the humbuggery of his colleagues, he remained *au fond* a conventional Oxford figure for whom university life was an end in itself, regarding the outside world with that familiar academic mixture of fearfulness and affectations of familiarity: when Anthony Powell, while still an undergraduate, confessed that he was miserable at Oxford, and longed for it all to be over, Bowra was so shocked by such heresy that it took thirty-five years for their friendship to be fully restored. Nor was his homosexuality a source of positive pleasure: although he 'always talked as if homosexuality was the natural condition of an intelligent man', Powell doubted whether he ever enjoyed a full homosexual relationship with the undergraduates he so admired.

Given his wit, his gift for mimicry, his passion for poetry and the classics, his love of gossip and intrigue, and his own gift for the waspish or wounding turn of phrase, Connolly was a natural member of Bowra's circle; they had many friends in common – Kenneth Clark and Bobbie Longden among them – and no doubt Connolly found congenial his mentor's unashamed addiction to pleasure and the sun and the Mediterranean virtues. But it may well be that Bowra's strongest influence was on his literary tastes. Although he was a dull and uninspiring writer, Bowra's polyglot enthusiasm for, and knowledge of, poetry in particular was both genuine and contagious. In his memoirs he tells of how he and Connolly were brought together by their shared admiration for the Greek poets and the moderns, such as Yeats and Eliot; but Connolly himself was more than happy to admit that, as far as the Modern Movement was concerned, Bowra was the master and he the willing pupil. Peter Quennell, who had come up to Balliol as a published poet – a friend of the Sitwells and Edmund Gosse, he had been published by Eddie Marsh in *Georgian Poetry*, and his first book had appeared when he was seventeen – wrote in his autobiography of how he and his contemporaries venerated *The Waste Land*, but two years after its appearance Connolly, evidently a late convert, was tentatively urging a friend to give it a go: 'It has the most marvellous things in it – though the "Message" is quite unintelligible'; the whole thing was 'thoroughly decadent', its 'sterility disguised by expert use of quotation and obscure symbolism'. Bowra urged him to persist with Eliot, introduced him to the harsher, bleaker world of the later Yeats and, in due course, to Proust's interminable masterpiece – he recalled how Connolly relocated and repopulated *A la Recherche*, 'comparing himself with Swann, Sligger with Françoise, a great friend with Albertine, a socially pretentious young man with Odette, the Morrells of Garsington with the Verdurins and David Cecil with the Duchesse de Guermantes' – but, for the most part, Flecker and Housman still prevailed; and for all his sophistication, Connolly remained, in literary terms at least, a rather old-fashioned Oxford undergraduate.

EIGHT

Minehead and After

No sooner were the Christmas celebrations over than, in January 1923, Connolly joined a 'pack of freshers' on a tour of Italy. Chaperoned by Sligger – who fussed and clucked about them, irritating Connolly by his tendency to 'call a masterpiece jolly to avoid the embarrassment and humiliation of contemplating beauty' – a party including Bobbie Longden, Roger Mynors and Denis Dannreuther made their way south via Florence, Rome and Naples. Pompeii, Connolly reported back to William le Fanu, was 'revoltingly tawdry and dull besides a number of bad frescoes and some pictures as unblushing in their cheap obscenity after 1800 years as anything written in a public rears.' He loved the Greek temple at Segesta – he was writing from Sicily, for which he retained an affection denied the rest of Italy – but the Romans were 'bloody' and the Coliseum a 'consecrated charnel house'.

Back in Balliol, he attended a table-turning session with John Sutro, smuggled a gramophone into the Master's garden, argued with Christopher Hollis over G.K. Chesterton, sailed on the river, gave a performance on the mandolin through which Hollis unashamedly slept, and fell briefly in love with a 'nice, odd, child-like boy with nice hands and mouth' called Richard Pares. A good-looking Wykehamist whose 'floppy light hair' had already excited Sligger's interest, Pares was in his second year at Balliol – which, Connolly told Mynors, 'makes me able to behave like his fag without showing it'. A few years later Pares turned away from the companions of his youth to become an austere and dedicated scholar, a Fellow of All Souls and, in Isaiah Berlin's words, 'perhaps the most admired and looked-up-to of the Oxford teachers of his generation'; but for a short time he seems to have wreaked havoc among his more susceptible contemporaries. Evelyn Waugh was, for a time, passionately in love with him, and tried to convince him of the manly delights of heavy drinking – according to Hollis, he even persuaded him to address the Union in the cause of insobriety. He resented Connolly's interest in the person he later described as his 'first homosexual love'; and although Hollis encouraged Connolly's friendship with Pares on the grounds that at least he wasn't an Etonian, he may well have had mixed feelings about Connolly's short-lived infatuation, since he too was 'gone' on the alluring youth. Years later Bowra told Connolly that Pares hadn't been right for him since 'he was at heart a puritan and rather a prig, censorious about things that don't matter and, despite his external brightness, not gay at heart'; in the meantime, however, Connolly found it hard not to thrill with pleasure when Pares took his arm outside the London County and Westminster Bank, and when Hollis told him that Pares 'had become a complete prostitute more from obligingness than anything else' but felt so miserable as a result that he was contemplating suicide, this merely made him more 'dog-like and devoted than ever'. Although, in Connolly's case, far more formidable competition was readying itself in the form of Bobbie Longden – who, Mynors was told, still referred to his school friend as 'Connolly', so provoking 'the old thrill of hoping to be called "Cyril" instead' – the end of term was marked by the two young men taking tea at Rumpelmayer's before moving on to Westminster Cathedral, where they attended compline and Pares, overcome by emotion, wept profusely.

Two days later, on March 20th, Connolly took the ferry to Holland with a fellow-undergraduate called Miles. They visited Middelburg together, and when Miles took the ferry home, Connolly made his way to Paris, and then on to Bordeaux, which was to become one of his favourite French cities and the home of his favourite restaurant, Le Chapon Fin. In Bayonne he encountered a 'Gloucester Road colonel with an Earl's Court wife', who spent their time bickering, and bought himself a staff with a leather-looped handle and a tip made of horn. Staff in one hand and a tam o'shanter on his head, he climbed slowly up the French side of the Pyrenees, through woods of Spanish chestnut and over ridges on which he dozed in the sun, and down the Spanish side to Roncesvalles, where he left some photographs to be developed and posted on to Balliol, before boarding a bus to Pamplona. The following day was Good Friday, and he joined an enormous crowd watching a procession of cowled and black-robed Franciscans and tableaux representing the Stations of the Cross as it inched its way along the narrow streets. On Easter Day there were more processions; he attended Mass in the cathedral and, overcome by a sudden nostalgia for Eton, he dreamed of water-meadows and buttercups while the sermon droned about his ears. Two days later he took a bus out to the monastery of San Domingo de Silos. It was set in a bleak 'African' country of gorges and basalt hills, and as he looked about it Connolly cried out '*O terra pulcherrima*' and '*O beata solitudo, O sola beatudino*,' which – as he noted in his diary – impressed the monks a good deal. After impressing them still further with his prowess on a mule – riding with the stirrups crossed, and jumping a ditch – he was shown to his cell, which had bare boards and stone walls and looked onto the cloister. There were two other guests staying in the monastery, one from Oxford and one from Cambridge, 'one an imbecile and the other a snob'. Before dinner the visitors' hands were washed by the abbot; they ate in silence while a monk read episodes from the history of the Church from a pulpit in the gallery. The food and wine were excellent; afterwards Connolly discussed the Albigensian heresy with the guest-master, and having out-snobbed the snob he felt he could relax. Next morning, after listening to the monks singing a Gregorian chant, he showed off again, climbing boldly about on the rocks, and – since money was, as ever, in short supply – wondered whether he could touch the snob for a pound.

From the monastery he travelled through the snow to Burgos, where the manager of a hotel – taking pity on his finances – gave him a free lunch; later he picked out some carols on the piano, but doing so made him pine for Jacky O'Dwyer, and he had to give up. Feeling 'brown, fit and hardened', he made his way to Hendaye, and back by train to Paris and London.

'Spain of all countries best enforces on the traveller that strict regime of boredom, loneliness and apathy which he must undergo like a cure,' Connolly wrote some years later. It appealed to the romantic in him in a way that Italy never could, or did; perhaps its gloomy, rather hopeless fatalism coincided with that Celtic side of his temperament to which he so often referred. Travelling alone in Spain, he came to relish 'the long dull mornings, the empty cafés, the shuttered shops . . . an ordeal by ennui, an agony of empty heart-searching.' Lying on his bed after a late and indigestible lunch, with nothing left to read, 'I recall my grievances – the real and fancied rebuffs that a young man fond of sex and society sees or thinks he sees in an indifferent world.' Drinking alone in a hotel restaurant, he spots an English couple in evening dress:

> He bows, and props his paper up . . . When I have finished my bottle of red wine with wire round it, eaten a fig from the wicker basket, I rise pink in the face and warm with appreciation for my friends at home. The waiters bow me out. The English stare. Last year's engineering supplements are laid out in the reading-room. It is dark. It is time for bed. I am in Spain.

Undeterred by such lonely, lugubrious delights, he made his way to Spain once more the following July. 'I am Catholique and Irlandais when abroad,' he informed Bobbie Longden from Toulouse, where he was waiting to catch the train south, after rain had forced him to abandon his attempts to cross the Pyrenees by foot once again: but judging by his outfit he must have looked an irremediably English figure. The upper man was clad in 'a new blazer, very cool, a white shirt and OE tie (for towns only)'; his legs were encased in a pair of 'Pop shorts', which again were 'marvellously cool but I wish my knees weren't so hairy'; on his feet he wore a pair of 'delicate lady's stockings (grey khaki)', a pair of Hall's socks – Hall's being the Oxford tailor where, like other undergraduates, Connolly bought his clothes on tick – and rope-soled shoes, which proved 'noiseless and light and perfect for mule tracks'. His head was covered with a Hall's hat or a Portuguese beret; over his shoulder was slung a school Corps haversack containing two clean shirts, his washing things and a bar of soap, a bottle of eau de Cologne, a Baedeker, socks and stockings, a jersey, a silk scarf, his diary, his wallet and a phrase book; in one hand he carried his ash staff, as high as his shoulder.

Once again, he spent his time exploring the monasteries and the countryside of north-east Spain – the landscape that Hemingway was to evoke so vividly in *The Sun Also Rises*, a novel Connolly came to admire in due course. 'I look very sleuth-like at present – lantern-jawed and loose-limbed,' he told Bobbie Longden, whom he planned to meet in Avignon as soon as his solitary Spanish adventures were over; nor was he suffering from loneliness to anything like the same extent as he had in the spring. He carried a wineskin 'in which anything I put turns well over lukewarm in about ten minutes and tastes of leather'. Despite the heat, he walked every morning between eight and one; by the afternoon exhaustion was setting in, but the flies prevented him from sleeping and he would drag himself on 'over aching ridges and agonising valleys', dreaming of iced drinks like a man adrift in the desert. He was badly bitten by fleas, and on one particularly dreadful day he covered twenty-five miles without breakfast or lunch, and was nearly sick over his dinner. 'I never see a soul,' he wrote,

> – only a man on a mule will suddenly appear and stare and ride away or a cart drawn by a row of mules will lumber by and stare, or some gypsies will go by, oval-faced and slant-eyed and almost black with long matted hair and dirty ragged children and scarlet shawls. Then the sun sets very slowly and the glare off the paths is softer and the cicadas are quieter and the butterflies settle and the bells of goats sound from some hidden pasture and a great ox lumbers into the river all alone – and I begin to feel that after all it is something to go alone into a strange country in the hottest time of the year...

The Spain he was discovering was still that of Richard Ford and George Borrow, as he found when

> it gets dark and I come round a bend and know the moon is trying her best to give me a shadow and can't quite and in front is a hill with a brown fort

> on the top and houses underneath and I climb up and look back on the silver green of the moon on the river and the last golden glow of the sun on the far mountains and then forward again and up narrow cobbled streets through an old gate in the walls and all the Catalans are sitting at their doors or on vine-shaded balconies and the first lights are lit and the streets are full of children playing . . .

From Spain he made his way – doubtless by wooden-seated third-class railway carriage – to Avignon, where he extended the patronage of the seasoned traveller to Bobbie Longden, who had 'never known the squalor and sordid desires of real poverty'. Despite the perennial shortage of cash, Connolly seems to have lashed out in Provence in his anxiety to shield his friend from 'all the dimmer side of being abroad – asking the price of a room before you book one, only lunching when one has seen the price on the menu, third-class everywhere' and – worst of all – having to endure the unconcealed contempt of waiters and the like. His finances suffered a further setback as a result of buying a tin of pâté for the Major: Longden was a dutiful family man, taking endless trouble over elderly aunts, and the tin was bought partly from a sense of duty and partly because Connolly knew it would please his friend. But the pâté still had some way to go before it ended its days on the dining-room table, subject to much expert sniffing and sampling from its recipient.

In 1865, David Urquhart had built a wooden chalet at St Gervais les Bains, in the French Alps, under the shadow of Mont Blanc. Sligger inherited the Chalet des Mélèzes while still an undergraduate, and every summer from 1891 until 1931 he took a select party of undergraduates out to the chalet to spend some weeks together walking and reading and working and communing with nature; after his death in 1934 it was bequeathed to Roger Mynors. Chalet life was a fairly austere business: according to Bowra, 'Work was the order of the day, broken by a piece of chocolate in the middle of the morning and occasional walks up and down the mountain.' Kenneth Clark went once, and that was more than enough: he disliked the regime of cold showers and mountain-climbing, and couldn't face spending the rest of the day over a book; the food was so bad that out of desperation he escaped to a local restaurant while the rest of the party scaled Mont Blanc. After a week of 'pulses and stale bread', hunger, boredom and constipation – to which, according to Mynors, he was unhappily prone – he made his excuses and left. Nor was the available reading matter as exciting as some might have wished: earlier that year Sligger had written to Patrick Balfour asking him if he would bring some more tea when he came, and 'as regards books I have here Stubbs's *Introduction to Rolls Series* and McKechnie's *Magna Carta* and Vinogradoff's *Growth of the Manor*.'

Connolly and Bobbie Longden joined the party some time in August; apart from Sligger, they included Gladwyn Jebb, the future diplomat, 'cold and haughty-looking but seems rather nice and intelligent', Richard Pares, Christopher Hussey and 'an unctuous peer' named David Balniel. When, in due course, Bobbie left for home – to minister after an ailing aunt, perhaps – Connolly was overcome by grief and lay on Longden's bed and wept; his own bed was occupied by the sedentary form of Sligger, who urged him to pray for his departed friend. A day or two later the little party crossed over to Courmayeur and the Val d'Aoste in Italy, and indulged in a little light glacier-climbing. Connolly and Balniel separated themselves from their companions and made their way back via Mont Blanc – 'a fitting excursion for the last days of my teens' according to Connolly, who was clad in Gladwyn Jebb's white silk pyjamas and those mysterious Pop shorts. They enjoyed eating their evening meal in a hut at 10,000 feet before starting back over the glacier at 3.30 in the morning, a porter carrying a lantern to light them on their way.

Before he left the chalet in mid-September, Connolly gave Longden's discarded pillow a farewell scratch ('Goodnight, Bobbie'), and, in traditional boy-scout vein, hid in a hollow tree an envelope weighted down with a twenty-centime piece and bearing the inscription 'CVC *in mem* RPL'. Bobbie's departure, and the sad scenes that ensued, were celebrated in the 'Chalet Vale':

And then I start to write to you
And then at last we go to bed
And there the coverlet was spread
With sheets for one but not for two

And Sligger came and found that shirt
Then he sat down and stroked my hair
I wept and thanked him for his care
And said that sorrow did not hurt...

Kind as he was, Sligger was to tax his young friend's patience to the limit in the days that lay ahead, for – unwisely, perhaps – Connolly had agreed to join him on a motoring tour of southern France before returning to Oxford. In this they were joined by a middle-aged friend of Sligger's called Bill Farrer, a hearty, grey-haired solicitor who was pleasant enough, but whose jocular talk of 'turning in' for the night and making a 'good effort' grated on the nerves of their younger travelling companion. Sligger had hired an open-backed car and a chauffeur for a week, and after dropping off Pares at Annecy the foursome set off in a westerly direction, Connolly in front with the chauffeur while the two old-timers sat in the back. In Annecy, Connolly had already endured the horrors of sharing a room with Sligger – he had cleaned his teeth very loudly, with a good deal of spitting, before announcing 'Well, my dear Infant, from what I have seen of you you seem very happy sharing a room, so we'd better always have one,' after which his companion had leapt into bed and never turned from the wall all night – but further irritations lay in store. Quite apart from his 'intolerable canniness in choosing bad hotels', all of them supervised by 'buxom but dowdy whores', the Dean entertained his companion with a remorseless stream of clichés and banalities, from 'The waxing moon, behold, my dear Connolly' to 'Truth is stranger than fiction' and 'Which end does a rainbow end?' 'Sligger's taste is awful – he loves "jolly valleys" – cows and chickens and green fields and farms with wooded hills on either side,' Connolly reported.

Back in London, he lit candles in Westminster Cathedral, and introduced Blakiston to Sligger: the meeting was not a great success, since Blakiston said nothing but merely gazed 'decoratively into space'; afterwards he told his admirer that although he awarded him low marks for prayer, he would pray for him all the same. His depression at being back was deepened by a visit to his father, who was now installed in the Naval & Military Hotel in South Kensington, surrounded by drawers-full of snails laid out on beds of cotton-wool: no mention was made of the pâté, and the Major chided him for his restlessness, for always wanting to move on to something new. Overcome by 'tristesse d'automne, schoolboy scepticism, tedium vitae or acedia and that ghastly loss of vitality that makes action impossible and utterance hard', he spent an unhappy week walking Charles Milligan's dog in the Park before heading back for his second year at Balliol.

That December, he was off on his travels again. He joined his parents in Alassio, on the Italian Riviera. 'An invincible mania for the dance drags me out tired and aching to rob me of one more night of sleep,' he told Longden; his preferred partner was a girl called Philippa Hanbury, but she was keenly guarded by her mother, and Connolly found himself in disgrace for arranging to meet her in the garden of the hotel, where they occupied themselves, innocuously enough, picking oranges and tangerines. Shortage of cash was, once again, a problem, but Bobbie Longden came up trumps: 'I am much poorer than I thought, so it will have to be a pound only,' he told his prodigal friend: 'Can't you and your mother between you induce your father to spend a little less on drink and more on you?' Eschewing the festive spirit, he set off by train on Christmas Eve *en route* for Sardinia and Tunis. Philippa, he confided to his diary, seemed sad to see him go, but his mind was soon elsewhere: as the train trundled along the coast to Genoa he remembered the Major's cautionary words about the perils of Arab girls, while an Italian in the seat opposite described in sign language the bosoms of Italian matrons. After sending Roger Mynors a dirty postcard, he boarded a boat for Sardinia: there were only two other passengers on board, the sea was high, he was violently sick, and the night was punctuated by banging noises and occasional cries of anguish.

Nor was dry land much of an improvement. Barely had the boat touched the quayside at Cagliari than 'Christ! a horrible Sardinian face is leering in at me through the porthole'; and even when the leering face had thoughtfully removed itself, he could see only 'a swarm of filthy children and dirty stiffs spitting into the water about a yard away'. Rousing himself, he rushed down the gangplank shouting 'Malado!'; but the gangplank was, as yet, unattached, and he fell off it into the arms of a Sardinian. Cagliari seemed a hell-hole, dirty, windy and sordid: clouds of dust blew in all directions, everything still swayed in front of his eyes, the locals were 'very dark and very dirty and all look extremely sour and sinister' and reputedly ate cats.

A day later he caught his first sight of Africa since his childhood when, off Bizerta, a pilot was taken on board; in his brown robes he looked like a Franciscan, and Connolly was thrilled by the realisation that he was, in fact, an Arab. Once on dry land, he inspected the souks and the kasbah, where he bought a carpet for his room in Balliol. The locals, he reported, were either 'fat, sordid, elderly Arabs in mud-coloured garments' or 'sleek unctuous younger men', while the women 'all looked deformed lumps wrapped up in sheets'. He inspected a brothel – the inmates were 'incredibly ugly' and fat, and business was understandably slack – consumed chocolate cake at a *thé dansant*, and had his hand read; and then it was time, once again, for the long, reluctant journey home.

Back in Oxford for the spring term of 1924, he found himself 'happier than I have been for some time,' he told William le Fanu: 'all last vac I was brutally anti-intellectual and anti-Oxford, but I like it more than I have before – if only my vitality would not decay under this dead sky.' Living in college, he had 'a gem of a room, painted nominally primrose yellow, in reality burnt orange.' Around the walls he had hung six reproductions in black frames of fifteenth-century paintings, and in one corner stood a bracket, surmounted by a sixteenth-century angel he had bought in Italy. A Florentine candlestick served as a lamp, there was a gramophone in one corner, and tea was served from a Chinese tea set. 'I glory in being exclusive and am rapidly forming a small but exclusive clique' – the members of which were Mynors, Longden, Balfour and Clark.

Mynors comes across as a quiet, scholarly, rather reserved figure, with precise, formal, old-fashioned handwriting. Longden often irritated Connolly with his heartiness and his restlessness and his habit of practising imaginary golf strokes; in his letters he seems a bit of an old woman, forever fussing about his health and the nuts and bolts of life, but despite his rather prosaic qualities he exercised a powerful emotional and physical hold over his former school friend. 'As you know, I only tolerate Oxford because I couldn't be with Bobbie otherwise and every term and every vac alike I have wished I was not there,' Connolly told Patrick Balfour: 'I want nothing except to live with him where nature is at its loveliest . . . I would rather keep a flock of goats on the island of Cos with Bobbie than any other career I have come across.' To what extent romantic yearnings were converted into physical passion is not certain. 'I always want to sleep with you more than anything but it is not very practicable at Oxford,' he told Longden in 1925. 'Please don't sleep with Ronnie, he is too tall for you,' he begged on another occasion, though who the lanky Ronnie was remains unclear, while to Mynors he explained, confusingly, how 'Of course the purely mystical and religious sense that physical relations with him has taken for me is enough to make no image visible but a carnal one, like an ex-communicant deprived of his celebration.' Connolly's relationship with Longden was a more physical affair than that with the other great love of his school and undergraduate years, Noël Blakiston: or, as Anthony Powell suggested many years later, 'I agree about Noël Blakiston having a probably prim relationship, but I don't think that was the case with Bobbie Longden. One was always led to suppose that a great deal of manual labour went on . . . Cyril made Maurice Bowra his confidant in such matters (Maurice himself being by no means without interest in Bobbie Longden) and the matter was widely ventilated at Bowra dinner parties by the host.'

Connolly's relations with Patrick Balfour, on the other hand, were a good deal less ambivalent, less subject to romantic gush and platonic idealising. A worldly young man who later became a gossip columnist and an authority on modern Turkey, Balfour was unashamedly homosexual, and no dainty circumlocutions were called for. First encounters seem to have been somewhat prickly: Balfour was keen to buy a blue overcoat off Connolly, and when the vendor wrote to suggest a price of one guinea, he added in a PS 'The brown curtains that were in my bedroom I would certainly let you have at the price you asked if you had not adopted that tone of social patronage which we, less noble, more honourable Balliol men have grown to expect of you.' But before long Connolly, learning that Balfour was going through a bad patch, was inviting him to join him and Peter Quennell for dinner at the Mitre, and later to share a lobster in his rooms: 'I do not know if it is a cock or a hen and it might embarrass it to enquire. Anyhow it has some mayonnaise so please come and eat it.' Later they became extremely fond of each other, in an uncomplicated way: after Connolly's death Kinross told James Lees-Milne that his old friend had been extremely attractive as a young man, that he was the first person he 'slept with' at Oxford, and that 'the next day Cyril left him a note, merely saying "Alpha and Omega". However he repeated the performance.'

None of these problems applied to the fourth close friend of the time, since Kenneth Clark was keenly heterosexual, even though – according to Bowra – he kept his girl friends apart from his Oxford intimates for fear that they might not go down well in such an exclusively male society: on one occasion he had to hide Jane, his future wife, in a cupboard when Sligger strolled unannounced into his room. Apart from being extremely rich, with a car and an interminable supply of gramophone records, Clark shared Connolly's liking for good food and drink; he had a nimble wit and could tell very funny stories, but a certain shyness and reserve and neatness of demeanour were sometimes mistaken for priggishness.

*

After a trip to Cambridge to see old school friends, including Dadie Rylands, Connolly left for Spain in early April. His mother, who had recently taken a flat nearby, in St George's Square, saw him off at Victoria; he was seasick on the Channel ferry, and after changing trains in Paris he headed towards the Spanish border. Money was short, but he managed to travel part of the way without paying the fare. This time he managed to cross the Pyrenees on foot despite a heavy fall of snow, eventually emerging on the Spanish side of the frontier via a dripping tunnel that ran through the mountains. He made his way to Saragossa, and then through a landscape of gorges and cliffs to Teruel, and down to the sea at Valencia, where the air was scented with orange blossom and the almond trees were in bloom. From there he travelled on to Benidorm and Alicante, with its 'nice harbour and air of refined holiday-making'. The Spaniards might be 'ugly, garrulous, rasping and unattractive', but Elche, with its background of blue mountains and palm trees and a railway line 'like a forgotten outpost in a tropical forest', seemed like an intimation of Arcadia:

> I walked in the palms when it was dark and their black stems showed straight and fine against the dark blue sky while the moon rose and the clear light faded behind the mountains and the stars looked as if they were fused and I heard the water running silently and the frogs croaking and the wind stirring the branches with their faint strange smell – and I thought of you

he told Bobbie Longden, who was being a dutiful nephew in some unglamorous English watering-place and worrying about a reprobate uncle, an ex-colonel with a DSO and an inveterate sponger who had agreed, to his family's relief, to emigrate for ever to California but had cashed in the ticket and was living unashamedly off the proceeds. Thoughts of Bobbie did not prevent Connolly from taking an interest in the 'veiled women of Mojacar'. Dinner was the main meal of the day, eaten in a rustic *posada* with an earth floor, and surrounded by goats and cats and lugubrious old women and unshaven elderly men spitting on the floor. Not surprisingly, 'I waver between hunger and diarrhoea', and before long he was home again and banging on Mollie's front door in Pimlico.

Diarrhoea was rampant three months later in Greece, during the summer vacation of 1924, combined this time with a rheumatic shoulder, much sweating and a high temperature in Crete: all of them were dutifully reported to a worried Bobbie Longden. Connolly arrived in Athens via Istanbul, and was bored and lonely until he met Ernst Buschor, the Head of the German School of Archaeology in Athens and a world authority on Greek vases, and a colleague of his named Woodward. Woodward turned out to be the 'worst kind of pompous, worldly, well-meaning usher', but Buschor seemed entirely admirable, 'ageless, attractive, frightfully brilliant, frightfully industrious, Spartan, and always laughing, like one of the first Franciscans'. Connolly had an introduction to Buschor from J.D. Beazley, a don at Christ Church and the leading authority on Greek vase paintings who was soon to become the Professor of Classical Archaeology at Oxford, and the two academics took him to the National Museum to inspect the vases and the statues, one of which looked disconcertingly like Bobbie Longden. Greek art, Connolly told Noël Blakiston, was 'the greatest thing in the world – almost – the Parthenon is so shattering that it made me weep which I don't usually do under these circumstances.' He preferred early Greek sculpture to that of the classical period, thought the Greek temple 'far the most spiritual and perfect form of building', and – after inspecting Hayia Sophia in Istanbul, and the mosaics in a monastery in the mountains where he spent the night – was, like his contemporary Robert Byron, much taken with Byzantium. Nor was Buschor's influence restricted to artifacts: Connolly was impressed by his apparent austerity, as a result of which he was 'trying to become independent of material things like food and comfort etc'.

From Piraeus he took a boat to Crete, where he spent four days, and made himself known to Sir Arthur Evans, then hard at work excavating the Minoan palace at Knossos. Sir Arthur's long-serving assistant, Duncan Mackenzie ('I'll tell Sir Arthur you're here') was an 'untidy old fossil', but the famous archaeologist proved to be a 'terrifying little man, v. old, 73, and

v. lively'. He offered his visitor a choice of Chablis or Burgundy, and after lunch he showed him some newly-excavated frescoes, including some 'baboons picking flowers off rocks' and a 'row of red-legged partridges'. Safely back on the mainland, Connolly visited Delphi before boarding a ship for Brindisi. The Mediterranean seemed aswarm with returning emigrants, bringing with them Brooklyn accents and undesirable American habits: 'vulgarity reigns everywhere', an unwholesome combination of 'straw hats, suspenders, bars, sweat, football and Mr Eugenides'. Nor was his alma mater – and Messrs Clark, Balfour and Bowra in particular – immune from heat-induced dyspepsia: 'I hate Oxford people, K and his dogmatism and heartiness, Patrick all puffy physically and mentally, a blown strawberry, Maurice uncouth in his love and savage in his hate.'

In Brindisi he got hold of two bits of red-figure vase to give to Beazley on his return, before making his way north to Ravenna, Milan and the Alps. From Courmayeur he walked round Mont Blanc to Sligger's chalet, taking refuge from a thunder-storm in a shelter 8,000 feet up in the snow. Although he assured Blakiston that 'this is the earthly paradise', life in the chalet seems to have been a particularly dismal affair: Sligger spent his time playing spillikins and dreaming vain dreams of converting Connolly to Rome, an undergraduate called Tommy Barnard did nothing but knit, Mynors was waspish, and even Bobbie Longden was found wanting. 'I find Bobbie rather tiresome,' Connolly confided to Blakiston:

> – he is so very florid and worships his own comfort, arranging cushions for about 5 minutes before sitting down and always swinging golf clubs about and chortling and guffawing from his arm-chair – he has very little idealism and is rather self-satisfied and tepid. I miss your seriousness and way of moralising from things you see which he hasn't and you have – he is rather spoilt by social life of the naval regatta kind and very insular and critical of foreigners and travelling – he is bound to comfort and food and tennis and an intelligent interest in things – while I want fanaticism with good manners, seriousness, and the sacrifice of what one thinks good for what one thinks better.

Despite such reservations, which anticipated in a more personalised form Connolly's intense dislike, some ten years later, for golf-loving, bridge-playing middlebrows whose favourite authors were P.G. Wodehouse and 'Jolly Jack' Priestley, Longden's early departure left them all in tears, or so Sligger assured Patrick Balfour. Connolly filled in his remaining days doing pole jumps and hurling assegais, and, after celebrating his twenty-first in dreary vein, he made his excuses and left.

Although Sligger fondly believed that his young charge was heading for the wholesome green hills of Umbria, Connolly had a different destination in mind. Northern Italy, he felt, had none of the romance of Spain or Sicily. He disliked Siena and the country round; Orvieto was even worse, 'less spinstered but more depressing'; life began to look up a little in Viterbo, which felt more Spanish. In Naples he was approached by a beautiful page boy who murmured in his ear and made him feel like some 'vile old man': this was not their first encounter, for back in the spring he had stopped in Naples on his way out to Istanbul and lunched at this same hotel, and – or so he told Balfour, who was interested in such matters – 'he came and spoke and people stared and I took no notice and now he has his revenge – in white ducks and wistful divinity'. To restore his spirits, he lashed out on half a bottle of wine and a cigar after dinner; money was again short and matters were made worse when he mistakenly paid a taxi-driver five pounds instead of five shillings.

From Naples he made his way south to Calabria and the impoverished heel of Italy. Taranto was 'a most Ionian city, full of delicate colours and warm grace'; the narrow streets seemed to be peopled almost entirely by small boys walking arm-in-arm and sailors on leave, 'lovely Eritreans in baggy white trousers and blue sashes and tassels to their fezzes'. He dined in a little restaurant on the shore, went to the cinema with a thirteen-year-old boy from his hotel, and – in search of relics from the Ancient World – was sent to see a VD doctor who doubled up as a dealer in antiquities, and was thoughtfully pushed to the head of the queue by the tarts and pimps awaiting treatment. Cotrone proved a dirty and dispiriting town, with 'bits of decaying fish in the streets'; from there he walked through a dismal landscape of barren hills and moth-eaten palm trees to the Capo di Colonna, where the houses had been emptied by malaria, the fields were full of thistles, and the column itself consisted of a 'lonely grey doric column supporting a broken capital'. It all seemed a long way from Ancient Greece or the scenes described by Norman Douglas, and it was with some relief that he crossed to Messina in Sicily, noting 'the violet sea and the ferry crowded and mandolins and mouth-organs and people dancing'. He was filthy, his glands were swollen, he had a huge boil on his face which had to be lanced, and he worried that he might have picked up the plague. But Taormina was full of Greek-looking young men holding hands, 'so like my conception of Gorgias'; he wished, he told Longden, that the two of them and Noël Blakiston had grown up by the Mediterranean ('I do not think it is too late to get Hellenised'), and was understandably disappointed to get a letter from Longden claiming that English food, scenery and hotels were the best in the world. Travelling third-class, he made his way slowly home via

Milan, Basle and Paris. In Paris he mistook a West African civil servant for a Fellow of All Souls; he turned out to be a friend of King-Farlow, and kindly allowed him to take a much-needed bath in his club before boarding the boat train. The Blakistons had invited him to stay at the rectory in Kirkby-on-Bain, and a 'muffled autochthonous Apollo' in the form of Noël Blakiston was waiting to greet him off the train: 'Could Odysseus have found a better home-coming?'

Noël Blakiston went up to Magdalene, Cambridge, that October, and over the next few years he was to play an ever larger rôle in Connolly's life. Although at Eton Connolly had been irritated by Blakiston's rather priggish religiosity, part of him shared his friend's idealism, regarding 'worldliness' as the ultimate vulgarity; and if Buschor had infused him with 'a proper contempt of the world', Blakiston encouraged a momentary rejection of hedonism in favour of 'cloistered virtue'. 'I think you are entirely right in your contempt of food and raiment and sport and golf, bridge and tennis and learning that masquerades as thought and habit and confidence and all that cause them,' he told his younger friend; and their desire to retreat from the world on to a higher, more ethereal plane was inflamed by their mutual admiration for Walter Pater's 'imaginary portrait' of the seventeenth-century Dutchman Sebastian van Storck. A young man suffering from 'a certain lack of robustness', van Storck had retreated up a winding staircase, and spent his days alone in his room, thinking difficult, rarefied thoughts and discarding all earthly distractions and attachments in pursuit of a 'calm, intellectual indifference' and a 'cold and dispassionate detachment from all that is most attractive to ordinary minds'. This pallid, reclusive figure exercised a curious fascination over the two young men, and his *obiter dicta* were constantly evoked in Connolly's correspondence.

Back at Balliol, Connolly strove to dedicate himself to the 'vita Sebastiana'; Oxford still seemed 'very limiting', and he found himself 'fighting a losing battle with autumn who has already driven me into lines of quietness and sober thinking and will soon drive me into listlessness and scepticism and general depression and futility. Damp afternoons of endlessly chiming bells are very wearying I find.' He had neglected his study of the English constitution, but Kenneth Bell had been perfectly pleasant about it 'so now I do 1688 onwards which is dull but not so antagonistic to classical ideals as the Middle Ages.' Bobbie Longden was proving 'florid and bustling and rather brusque in his judgements but superb when calmer, and he finds daylight intercourse rather an ordeal for he fusses and I chafe'; temporary relief was at hand when, towards the end of October, Noël Blakiston came over from Cambridge for the weekend, meeting Connolly's friends, dining at the Spread Eagle in Thame, and listening to Kenneth Clark's gramophone. 'N. was fairly quiet, presentable and attractive,' his host noted:

> He liked everyone he ought to and was attracted by the complete absence of any standards of good and evil in dons and people and by the grace and intensity of their existence... I gave him some harsh words about his selfishness to me and others and his sloppy, laboured cogitations about God. I dressed him in a jumper and tie that suited him and was rewarded by getting agony from such a lovely back, long, lithe, yellow, broad at the shoulders and tapering...

Sligger was much taken by their visitor, but was commensurately angry with Connolly, who, despite massive infusions of Sebastianism, had succumbed to the lure of gossip and been caught out spreading 'bad blood'. 'I agree with you about no slander but I think one must be fairly fugitive and cloistered to avoid it,' Connolly confessed, adding that some people – and Bowra in particular – 'make me nearly always succumb.' In Blakiston's absence, Mynors was the next best antidote, and although Longden was 'very ineffectual and bustling and terribly limited by property and conventions', he was 'fonder of him than anyone because he is warm and affectionate and loyal'.

A month later, and Sebastianism was still under heavy siege, for 'everywhere malice reigns. Slander seems the keynote of existence, and only in absolute seclusion, fugitive and cloistered, does salvation lie.' Hopes of a lasting friendship with Professor Beazley had been thwarted by the formidable Mrs Beazley, who was said to have been dug up in a Greek pot in Anatolia, and Sligger was feeling wounded by some uncalled-for criticism of the Deity; consolation was to be had from reading Milton, and planning a return trip to the less worldly and corrupted cloisters of Cambridge.

The first part of the Christmas vacation was spent at the Lock House, and returning there after three years proved a far more lurid ordeal than anything Oxford could offer. Connolly had agreed to 'cope' with the Major, who had taken to drinking a bottle of port a day, and was busying himself with a paper on 'snails as carriers of disease' when not 'tasting innumerable kinds of cider and fussing and losing his temper'. 'It was very ghostly coming back here after three years,' Connolly told Blakiston:

> – the taxi creeping through thick white fog, bumping over holes in the neglected road and crashing against overhanging branches in the unkempt

> avenue. My father hobbled out to argue with the taxi-driver whose face was bleeding from branches and we sat down to dinner together. We have no servants but a soldier and his wife rent our cottage and the wife cooks and makes beds. There is absolute silence but for my father who has a typewriter in the drawing-room and clears his throat and makes body noises and swears at intervals. He gets rather drunk and fuddled then he becomes maudlin or irritable and says the same thing several times with long pauses between each word. His speech grows thick and laboured and he failed dismally to say 'a new species from Mauritius' last night.

To Longden he reported that he had given up all attempts to be friends with the Major, who insisted that 'I am the master in this house' and complained bitterly when his son came back from the butcher having spent five shillings on a duck rather than 4/6 on two plovers. 'It was horrible to hear him talking drunkenly to himself last night with indescribable vulgarity, him in the dining-room and me in the drawing-room,' Connolly told Roger Mynors, whom he had last seen gazing admiringly at his photograph on the mantelpiece of his room in Balliol: 'His slow, sinister limping or laboured thick words nearly drive me mad.' Nor were conditions at the Lock House propitious for Sebastianesque contemplation of the verities:

> We live very squalidly with a shortage of sheets and towels and table cloths and boot polish and toilet paper and knives and soap. My hands always seem dirty and my feet always wet, nothing is tidied and disorder accumulates. Meals are very bleak and seem as if eaten in an empty railway station, waiting for a train.

Not surprisingly, Connolly spent a good deal of time hurling assegais and going for long runs along the Basingstoke Canal. Nor was other company to hand: apart from the old soldier and his wife, the only visitors were a man who came to tune the piano, and another who inspected the Major's bees.

Consolation of a kind was to be had from writing long letters to friends, teasing out the intricacies of 'the most important thing', to whit personal relations. 'The chief snag in our relations,' Connolly told Blakiston,

> seems not to be that I find you boring or you me humourless (my God that rankles) but that you object to me taking your arm etc which makes me think you don't like me – especially as you seem only to do it to annoy – I am not promiscuous but I can't be loyal to an icicle and so I stick to Bobbie who is very loyal and very constant.

Connolly assured Bobbie Longden that Blakiston's refusal to play the game, or to make allowances for his friend's particular qualities ('I am not a normal person, I can be normal at a pinch but have always been accepted as rather a phenomenom, and you often affect a rather brutal common sense in the hope of refusing to observe that I have a temperament') was due to his being dreadfully self-centred and lacking in notions of personal loyalty. Longden's own role seems increasingly akin to some devoted family retriever gazing sadly out at friskier competition: 'Poverty and stupidity have largely contributed to his originality and charm.... I think I am about his only friend but not according to my standards a real one.'

Real friend or not, Connolly was soon writing to Blakiston urging him to come and stay at the Lock House, preferably when his mother was there as well. Although there were no books in the house other than the works of Ernest Thompson Seton, he had brought with him Plato, Milton, Yeats and Proust. Not even this reading list was enough to lure Blakiston down from Lincolnshire, and Connolly was left feeling ever more irritated by the Major:

> My father has repeated after an interval of two minutes 'Expect you sometimes get a tune running in your head that blocks out everything else, like this one,' (sings) – Me, hopefully, 'It's called "What'll I do?"' My father, 'Thank you.' If he makes the remark and sings the tune a third time and asks me the name, I think I shall collapse (he has gone to pick it out on the piano) – it is so awful, Noël, to see one's flesh and blood behave like this and wonder if I shall get drunk and incoherent and permanently lame and noisy in my digestion in twenty years time (my father thinks he has invented that tune, and is writing it down)...

Music was a particular source of contention between father and son. Connolly liked to play his gramophone record of César Franck's Symphony, but the Major thought it a 'beastly noise' and insisted on typing throughout; and then, to make matters worse, replaced selections from *Boris Godunov* with 'When Irish Eyes are Smiling'. All this coincided with Connolly losing his best assegai in a pond and twisting his ankle out running and listening to a lecture from the Major on the importance of hunting; Christmas with both parents turned out to be a 'dismal' affair, and after it was over Mollie shipped her husband back to the Naval & Military Hotel rather than be left in the house with him by herself – the Major fought to 'conceal his joy under an air of martyrdom' – while their son, equally relieved, made his way to Reading railway station.

Sligger had taken a cottage at Minehead on the Somerset coast, where a select party was to join him for a reading holiday. Blakiston had declined his invitation, preferring to visit A.C. Benson in Rye before going on to various dances in London, and the party now consisted of Sligger, Connolly, Maurice Bowra and a good-looking Anglo-Irish undergraduate from Balliol called Piers Synnott. Described by Sligger as a 'gilded popinjay' and by Connolly as 'the Narcissus of the Balliol baths', Synnott had a powerful effect on the more susceptible members of his Oxford circle. Patrick Balfour was very taken with him, but of more immediate concern was the fact that Bowra had become quite infatuated. The Dean of Wadham was in fine and witty form – 'he really is a very great man, and a very good one too,' Connolly told Longden – but his passion was unreciprocated, and his efforts to woo the unresponsive Synnott laid him open to ridicule and humiliation. Connolly, who confessed to finding the older man's courtship 'nauseating', described how Bowra sang interminable music-hall songs, badly but with a good deal of confidence, in the hope that this would somehow ingratiate him, but Synnott responded with schoolboy abuse, ostentatiously picking his nose and whistling out of tune and telling his admirer to 'Shut up, your feet smell' – at which the Dean laughed 'inordinately' and continued to press his case. 'I think Maurice's slavery is rather bad for him,' Connolly informed Balfour after Synnott had ridiculed the Dean's noisy mastication, and told him to 'Take it away' when an arm had been flung about his neck; and when the snubs became too much to bear, Sligger – whose sole contribution so far had been to sing the praises of Noël Blakiston and make unflattering jokes about women – took his fellow-don, by now a 'broken man', for restorative walks in the country. Every now and then the worm would turn, and the Dean would accuse Synnott of being 'vain, hard, stupid, vulgar, selfish, lecherous and worldly' – unjust epithets according to Connolly, who found Synnott 'brave and loyal and charming, very fresh and serious-minded and very sympathetic and fine', as well as having a 'lovely athletic body and agreeable dissolute ways': but the body, of course, was at the root of the problem, since it held the unhappy Dean 'in thrall'.

Connolly kept aloof from these goings-on as much as he could, working in his bedroom in the morning, running six or seven miles in his Greek sandals in the afternoon, and writing long letters to his friends after dark. After a week, the two older men returned to Oxford, and Connolly and Synnott stayed on by themselves. Life without Bowra was 'incredibly peaceful', and the two young men enjoyed an indolent bachelor existence, idling about in their dressing-gowns till midday, when they had a bath, and walking and talking together. For Synnott, the Dean's departure must have been an unutterable relief: life with Bowra had been a 'surging sea' of crises and dramas, he told Balfour, and although Sligger had been quite useless throughout, never waking from slumber when the amorous storm finally broke, Connolly had done wonders in making peace between them. That was all very well, but the hapless youth now became the subject of further intrigue. 'Dear Patrick, I want to be frank with you,' Connolly wrote to Balfour, '– would you mind awfully if I slept with him?' He missed bodily contact with Longden, and 'could weep with loneliness when the wind howls and the rain beats upon the window'. He found Synnott attractive enough, though 'Of course I haven't done anything about it and I don't think he finds me attractive (he has been picking his nose and eating it for the last ten minutes)': would Balfour write at once and tell him if he'd rather he refrained, since he had no desire to make a conquest or continue the affair once they were back in Oxford.

Luckily for all concerned, Connolly decided not to try his luck: a day or two later he told Balfour that he regretted having written as he had, since he no longer wanted to sleep with Synnott, and worried that, had he done so, Longden might feel free to go off with other people. Complicating his emotional life still further was something best avoided: he had been discussing the vexed question of Longden versus Blakiston with Sligger, who was in favour of the younger man ousting his rival. 'If I slept with Noël and sucked Bobbie off I would probably like the former better,' he confided in Balfour, who seemed to provoke plain speaking while not remaining immune to the kind of obfuscation to which Connolly seemed prone when discussing schoolboy and undergraduate romance: '... that is the form my *Ποθος* [lust] takes because it has got entirely mystical and that gesture is something I have never done to anyone nor RPL and therefore absolute and also sacramental and religious – it makes my teeth chatter to think of it – I find myself hoping almost that RPL will sleep with someone or do something that I may demand it as compensation! Instead of overwhelming me in a blinding vision of fire and whiteness...'

One obvious way out of this impasse – or morass – of lust, frustration, infatuation and platonic idealism was to follow Blakiston's example and cultivate the opposite sex. 'Our friendship seems to be able to subsist on a purely intellectual basis and therefore with a gratifying freedom from jealousy,' he wrote to Blakiston from Minehead, 'and if you are going to care for women, as you have often implied, the less I want any other aid to reality than intellect and fondness the better – but I am afraid women if they begin by absorbing the physical side end by absorbing both – I find by ceasing to regard you at all physically it does not lessen my affection or interest, it has just become a habit of mine to regard you so – only it takes time to break a habit...' In the meantime, he told Synnott,

> I don't think I have ever been happier than in our last week at Minehead, partly because of the security, partly because you were so kind, but chiefly

> because it is for me an unblemished episode of pure romance, one of the only times one can have realised an ideal and proved that the Greek life or one aspect of what we consider the Greek life to have been not only can be realised sometimes but when realised is more superb and more ideal than ever.

Such classical allusions cut little ice, however, with the Dean. Connolly's own short-lived infatuation with Piers Synnott, and his observation of Bowra's behaviour during the reading party, took a heavy toll on his friendship with the Dean, who regarded him thereafter with a degree of wary resentment: so much so that it was only towards the ends of their lives that the two men became true friends again. Some months later, Bowra revealed that in Patrick Balfour's rooms he had read all the letters Connolly had written from Minehead, and 'enjoyed them a lot, though I cut a figure of fun'. Understandably embarrassed, Connolly explained that the letter in which he had described the Dean's elephantine wooing technique had been written 'in a fit of spleen when you were singing music hall songs'. But the harm had been done. Bowra felt that Connolly had set out to hurt him, and he told Balfour that he should have no compunction about showing Synnott Connolly's letters – and 'I shouldn't worry about being too loyal to Cyril. He shows all our letters to everyone, even Brian Howard and probably Sligger.' But even if Connolly was in disgrace, 'I must write what I have always felt too embarrassed to say, and thank you for behaving so inconceivably well towards me, Patrick, at times when I have behaved bloodily to you . . .'

Shortly after leaving Oxford, Connolly recorded in verse the mutual suspicion that set in after Minehead:

> How many geese has Maurice cooked
> The time I've been away?
> Why only one, but that's been done
> To last till judgement day.
> And whose was that? O Piers, Piers,
> Why do you turn away?
> Dear Cyril, we haven't met for years
> Sufficient unto the day . . .

*

* At about the same time Bowra himself resorted to sub-Yeatsian, mildly scatological verse when attempting to recapture the youthful Connolly, but All Souls – his literary executors – will not give permission for it to be reproduced. A pity, since it is far removed from the later emollience of his *Memoirs*, and forms a neat counterpart to Connolly's own equally unflattering verse.

In March the Lock House was let, but not before Noël Blakiston had at long last come to stay; after which, Connolly set out once again for Spain. He travelled over to France with Blakiston, whom he left at Boulogne 'with an adorable small boy in an enormous car' – the small boy was tutored by Blakiston and his brother Jack on alternate vacations from Cambridge – before taking the train south to Segovia, and on into Andalucia. He arrived at the Royal Hotel Washington Irving in Granada in a parlous condition: he had a cold, the Major had failed to forward £15 as promised, and his luggage had gone astray, leaving him with nothing to wear except a plus-fours suit and a pair of grey Oxford bags 'which whenever I wear I am greeted with mocking laughter and cries of "*Señor de Pantalones*", which becomes rather depressing.' The hotel itself was 'full of goatish faces', and not for the last time he was deeply depressed by the 'incredible bloodiness of the English abroad', and their 'stupidity, complacency and bad manners'. But among the goatish faces was 'a party which I am sure must be the Sitwells, which is rather thrilling'. It was indeed the Sitwells, and this was – in retrospect at least – a momentous meeting: for the Sitwells were the first members of the fashionable literary world whom Connolly had encountered, and apart from enjoying a long friendship with Osbert in particular, he was to become a firm and, towards the end of her life, increasingly isolated champion of Edith's poetry. Edith, he told Piers Synnott, was 'rather terrifying, a kind of Ottoline', but the two brothers were 'witty, cultured and kind', even if Osbert did look 'rather bloated'. A friendship was struck up, and the woes of the solitary traveller were soon forgotten.

Back in London, he dined with the Major at the Naval & Military Hotel, and was dispirited by his 'malignant leer' and his 'spotty face and huge windblown stomach'. Describing these distressing scenes to Blakiston – whom he had met in Avignon on his way home – he assured his friend that 'there is no longer any question of my liking Bobbie more than you', since 'you have the qualities that I try to attribute to Bobbie, freshness, cold pastoral, exploring...' Nor did Oxford seem much of an improvement on the Naval & Military Hotel as he and his friends gathered for their final term:

> Oxford is just bloody, work is intolerable, there only remains to waste time – one's parents' money, one's own time. Romance is dead in this self-conscious city and I do not want experience of which I have had enough or knowledge which puffs me up, but only romance, I mean the knowledge that one is using mind, heart and body worthily enough to satisfy one's conscience of what is beautiful and true.

Romance and bathos were all too often juxtaposed, as when he compared Blakiston with Tessa in *The Constant Nymph* ('especially eating dry bread and Perrier for dinner'), or listened to the Dean of Wadham describe how during the war an 'incredibly lovely young Prussian nobleman' had fallen out of an aeroplane into the British lines, and was so touched by the way in which the Dean-to-be had offered him drinks and stroked his hair that he had, on an impulse, given his captor his boots; nor did he have any better luck with a novel, which made slow progress and seemed 'rather bad and self-conscious'. The Major threatened to descend on Oxford to eat Lobster Newburg, a prospect which filled his son with dread; Roger Mynors had taken up beer-drinking and rolled a barrel of the stuff across a college lawn with Denis Dannreuther, a sight so dreadful that Connolly was compelled to pull down the blinds in his room; Bobbie Longden took up cricket; despite his disavowals from Minehead, Piers Synnott remained an attractive proposition and a kindred spirit, but one who wanted to be a friend and no more. 'What worries me is that you should want to recover Passion,' Synnott told him, adding 'Shall I come and say goodnight and no more at midnight? Will you take an unprejudiced and unerotic lunch next Thursday here?'

And, of course, money remained a perpetual problem – made worse by the fact that although Oxford tradesmen were more than happy to allow their 'young gentlemen' to pay for almost everything on tick, bills had to be settled in the end, sometimes months or even years after the undergraduate in question had left the university for ever: as Evelyn Waugh recalled, 'There was no need to pay on the nail for clothes, books, tobacco or wine', while Peter Quennell remembered how all the undergraduates of his day were 'extremely lavish spenders', most of whom 'went down leaving many bills unpaid'. Looking back on his Oxford generation years later, Connolly characterised them as 'highly successful social climbers' for whom 'clothes were an intoxication. Waisted suits by Lesley & Roberts, white waistcoats from Hawes & Curtis with only a narrow white strap at the back, silk monogrammed shirts in cardboard boxes, top hats, opera hats, Oxford bags...' Not surprisingly, he failed to pay his subscription to OUDS, and was hauled over the coals by the college authorities on account of his debts; after he had run up bills of some £200, an enormous sum in those days, Sligger – as generous with his money as he was with his time and affection – took his finances in hand, lending him the odd tenner, never repaid. The Major proved a good deal less co-operative, and Sligger had to dip into his reserves once again when the bank threatened him with a summons. Or, as Connolly put it in a competent imitation of Housman:

When days are long and sunny
The flower of youth is blown
We waste our parents' money
And time that is our own.

The days grow dark and colder
Beyond the summer's prime
We, before time is older,
Are old before our time.

To try to dispel his worries and his melancholy, he went on long solitary walks and paddled his canoe, sometimes for hours on end; and he spent more of his time with younger undergraduates, including Henry Yorke, Anthony Powell, Penderel Moon, who later joined the ICS and became an authority on the history of India, and – until he was eventually sent down for having an affair with a married woman – the alarmingly precocious Peter Quennell, of whom Alec Douglas-Home once enquired 'What sort of a fellow is Quennell? Is he quite decent or something like Harold Acton?' Although they were contemporaries at Balliol, Quennell was two years younger than Connolly; and, like him, he found Oxford boring and dispiriting. He too was already a formidable presence: 'I had thought Brian Howard precocious, until I met Peter Quennell,' Harold Acton recalled: 'He was discriminating to a degree that killed appreciation: everything froze at his touch.' He was, Acton went on, 'skinny and narrow-chested with a piping voice, high shoulders and a dancing gait . . . His thin straw hair was carefully combed like a bang over his forehead, and the moth eyebrows had been brushed upwards – perhaps in imitation of Edward Marsh's'; over the next half century he was to weave in and out of Connolly's life, half envied and half derided, part rival and part friend.

By now Connolly's time at Oxford was nearly over, and Schools were upon him. To Blakiston he confessed that he hadn't looked at half the books he should have read for his finals, and such Oxford notebooks as survive are filled with the names of his friends rather than with details of the manorial system or thoughts on 'Otto the Great as Holy Roman Emperor'; anticipating the worst, he told William le Fanu that he wasn't worried about the results, since 'long ago I decided to make myself an educated man rather than let other people make me an historian and I have no wish to linger in Oxford.' The finals themselves seemed 'like a death struggle between style, intelligence and plausibility and a stern unknown board of examiners . . . It is like a cat playing with a mouse, just as I feel secure and playful a great paw knocks me down with "Outlines of Constitutional History from 1307".' He took time off in mid-exams to drink ginger beer on Brill with 'Bobbie who was very hot, Sligger who was very incurious, Maurice who is gone on Piers again, and Piers who was very nice' and kissed him goodnight; and after it was all over he invited Kenneth Bell, Humphrey Sumner and Bobbie Longden to a celebratory lunch in his rooms. According to Evelyn Waugh, most of his friends went down with bad degrees or no degrees at all, and Connolly was no exception. Among those who gained firsts in history that year were Roger Makins, the future diplomat, and a clutch of embryo historians that included Denis Brogan, K.B. McFarlane and A.L. Rowse, who noted in his autobiography that Graham Greene had got a second, while among the thirds were 'the surprising name of the Brackenbury Scholar at Balliol, C.V. Connolly, and Lord Dunglass.'

'How horrible. I am so sorry about the third,' Roy Harrod wrote from Christ Church: 'The examiners must be somewhat to blame, aren't they? You and others always told me that you hadn't worked. But I can't help feeling that they ought to have put you one higher up.' Wise and considerate in academic matters, if not in affairs of the heart, Bowra was among the first to extend a consoling hand: Connolly was not to worry 'about that absurd history school', for 'no one ever thought you cared for history or for technical success in it. So if you do feel humiliation, Cyril, please put it away and realise that it is totally irrelevant to you and your life.' Bowra's only concern was that 'Sligger may be nasty to you' as a result, but such fears were unjustified.* 'Oxford remains a bad dream for me,' Connolly wrote the following year to Denis Dannreuther, who went on to become a Fellow of All Souls and a barrister, and was soon to drop out of his life: but now the dream was over, and the future looked blank indeed.

* Bowra also pointed out that gaining a third 'means Queen's won't give you money'. Laming Travelling Fellowships at The Queen's College, Oxford, were designed for those considering a career in the diplomatic service. Although Connolly was to claim in *The Missing Diplomats* that as a young man he had been attracted by the idea of a job in the Foreign Office, there is no convincing evidence to this effect; nor does Queen's have any record of his having applied for such a Fellowship – unlike his contemporary Claud Cockburn, who became a Laming Fellow.

NINE

In Limbo

Like generations of freshly-fledged graduates before and since, Connolly was now faced with the age-old problem of what to do next. Oxford had provided him with a bad degree, a liking for Milton and Proust, some passionate friendships, a litter of unpaid bills, and a vague, familiar feeling that he ought to be a writer; and its Appointments Committee hurried forward with inappropriate suggestions. 'You *must* bestir yourself in trying to find work,' the Major had warned him before he took his finals, adding that he and Mollie had no intention of supporting him after he left Oxford, and enclosing a memo on Colonial Appointments – among them 'several things you would like', such as being an administrative officer in Kenya, starting at £300 a year; and over the next year the Appointments Committee kept up a steady flow of ideas, including details ('as requested') of positions with the Asiatic Petroleum Company and British American Tobacco, an opening as a trainee rubber-planter in Malaya ('if the assistant could play games so much the better'), and helping out a Mrs Prideaux-Brune of Knightsbridge, who was looking for a tutor to prepare her son for life at his prep school. Nor was the Major alone in urging his son to put in a week of 'solid hunting for a job': Sligger bustled about in the background, providing a reference for Guinness the brewers, writing on his behalf to Barrington-Ward on the *Observer* and the editor of the *Manchester Guardian*, and urging his sceptical young protégé to look to the Deity for support: 'Don't let yourself be too much influenced by the apparently sceptical and indifferent world about you,' he wrote: 'Don't let yourself think that because the thought of God and the effort to get into relation with him and to hold his hand is a comfort that therefore it is insincere . . .' Connolly told Patrick Balfour that he had a fairly clear idea of what Sligger would say were he there in person:

> Remember, Cyril, that you must be of use in the world. There are a fearful lot of dragons to be licked and fair ladies to be rescued, knights errant are badly wanted everywhere, men with sound heads and warm hearts, and you might do a lot – I don't for the life of me know in what position.

'Well, the great fight must begin soon,' the real Sligger wrote, with not a word said about knights errant or damsels in distress: 'the fight for your job, and all our forces must be mobilised – I'll do what I can and you must do your part as keenly as you can, and use all the advantages you have.' Testimonials poured from his pen. 'Mr Cyril Connolly of this college, who has asked me for a testimonial, is a man of unusual ability,' he informed To Whom It May Concern:

> He was a scholar at Eton and Balliol and his failure to get good Honours Class at Oxford was due mainly to the fact that he worked at things which interested him rather than at the subjects of his examination. He has a wide knowledge of many topics, especially of English literature, and has travelled in many parts of Europe. He would be *particularly* good for a fairly able boy reading for a scholarship. He would also be very useful as a tutor-companion for a boy travelling abroad. I need hardly say that Mr Connolly is a gentleman of high character and perfectly trustworthy.

Among the by-products of Sligger's endeavours were interviews with John Buchan and Henry Newbolt. Although Connolly told Balfour that he was busy reading Buchan in the long grass in between playing tennis and motoring with his mother and a cousin, neither author was of the kind one would associate him with, then or later; but Sligger had persuaded them to interest themselves in his literary career. He was asked to bring some samples of his work, including some poems and a couple of letters to Bobbie Longden, presumably unposted; the two grandees pronounced the letters to be 'very vivid and interesting', and it was agreed that were he to write some travel pieces, Buchan, in his capacity as a director of Nelson's, would try to get them published.

With that out of the way, Connolly and Bobbie Longden travelled down to Cornwall, where they explored the estuaries and inlets of the south coast; after which he went on to Bath, where Granny Connolly crammed him with food and fussed around him, and a visit to the Abbey provoked 'a mild dose of ancestor-worship'. He read *Wuthering Heights* for the first time and, back in London, took one of his Quenington cousins to dinner at the Berkeley because her red hair and the shape of her head reminded him of Bobbie Longden; besides which, he wanted to see if he could remember how to talk to a woman. While in London he bumped into Brian Howard, and together they 'scoured' the Embankment: they had no luck, he told Bowra, though they did bump into Eddie Sackville-West and Philip Ritchie – both homosexuals, and both presumably doing a bit of 'scouring' themselves.

Though no longer an undergraduate, Connolly was still on Sligger's guest list for the Chalet, and he was asked if he would like to bring Blakiston with him for the first part of the holiday. No sooner had they arrived than Connolly wished he had taken Bobbie Longden instead: 'Dependence does not suit Noël, who became mawkish, obtuse and clinging, and got terribly on my nerves. I would have given anything to be quarrelling with Bobbie instead.' And although he had told Blakiston that the Chalet was 'the nearest approach to Milton's Eden going', this particular holiday turned out to be unusually fraught, and its emotional reverberations were picked up as far away as Oxford, doing further damage to his relations with Bowra, who instantly suspected him of making 'bad blood'. 'The dearth of good talk is almost as oppressive as that of good food,' Connolly told the Dean. He decided he loathed the Alps; Roger Mynors seemed interested only in drinking beer; and, worst of all, Blakiston and Piers Synnott seemed far too keen on one another. Blakiston, he claimed, had made the first move; despite Blakiston's 'wistful and lecherous appeal', he was fairly certain that the romance had been restricted to poetry-reading, damming streams together, and a certain amount of kissing. The combination of mawkishness and stream-damming proved too much for Connolly. 'Bobbie stands alone and supreme for me,' he told the Dean:

> After being with him and Noël I know how much better I like him than HNB though we quarrel an enormous amount. Though superficially complacent and hearty, his inner self, though dwindling slowly, remains the finest character I know and his physical appearance can still destroy every atom of my peace of mind and leave me weak and exhausted at the very thought of it.

Longden, in the meantime, was installed in Ye Wells Hotel in Llandrindrod Wells with his eighty-year-old Aunt Emily; and from there he wrote to his friend, expressing polite interest in the 'Noël-Piers idyll', urging him not to treat Sligger like a prep-school master, and asking him to 'bury a token for me either on the ledge or by the Oxus and we will dig it up next year.' Longden's letter had an electric effect, in that Connolly made Blakiston choose between himself and Synnott,

> which he did with general sublimation and nobility on the part of all three of us though Noël and I had another, less magnanimous, quarrel the next day when I found that he had protracted the 'come let us kiss and part' through several sittings after he had made his choice. Noël wept a great deal and said he was a whore ... Piers found consolation in religion and

> literature ... Noël and I recovered most of our former intimacy. He is a born bitch, a dark Dadie of the sonnets.

Trying to work out who was ahead in the favour stakes – one contender surging ahead, only to fall quickly back and be overtaken by his rival, or even a rank outsider – is baffling enough for the outsider, and even Connolly sometimes lost track of the field: 'I got mixed up in my relations with Noël and Bobbie owing to identifying them with Tessa and Florence in *The Constant Nymph*,' he told a school friend who had written him an envious note apropos Blakiston ('How beautifully brown, how lasciviously languid he must be under a southern sun'). He hastened to assure Bowra that he had no designs on Synnott, and that he had 'never tried to make bad blood between you', but neither party seemed convinced by his protestations, or by his account of events at the Chalet. Synnott felt he had been the pawn in some private feud, in which Blakiston was the hapless victim. 'He treated Noël (who is terribly devoted to him) so shamefully, both at the Chalet, and still more after it,' he told Balfour:

> just because he knows the man is 'safe' for him, and again because he does not provide as much as Bobbie. Cyril makes him play second fiddle and treats him like dirt. Abominably, full of spite and deliberate cruelty. On Noël that is wicked, though it might do Bobbie good. You may as well take it Cyril's account of the Chalet is all wrong. The real meaning of it all is that Cyril was being bloody to Noël and used me incidentally.

The qualities inherent in a letter written 'after the Cyrillic mood', Synnott decided, were that it should be '(i) left lying about (ii) unfinished (iii) unposted (iv) untrue'.

Nor was Connolly any more warmly regarded in Oxford – except by Sligger, who continued to write references and lobby on his behalf, to such an extent that 'I feel I have watched over you at times like an old hen – hoping the chick was really a young eagle.' 'Your going away has made Oxford very different. "Egypt was glad at their departure: for they were afraid of them" – there is a certain amount of that, of course,' Roger Mynors informed him; and another Oxford friend told him that although Mynors always spoke kindly about him, others – including Bowra and Kenneth Clark – 'have nothing but spiteful and malicious things to say of you' as a result of the 'deliberate disclosure' of his letter to Balfour about the unhappy scenes at Minehead: all of which showed 'how dangerous it is to have a character as strongly influential as yours, for you know you have amazing power and no one can apparently forgive it to you.' Doubtless this undercurrent of hostility exacerbated Connolly's long-standing dislike of Oxford, and over the years his visits were to become ever more reluctant and infrequent. He did, however, remain on good if distant terms with Kenneth Bell, with whom he dined in All Souls the following year.

In the meantime, Connolly went from the Chalet to Bordeaux, where he stayed at the Hôtel du Chapon Fin, and met up with Blakiston's elder brother, Jack, who shared a room with Noël in Magdalene and went on to become the Librarian at Winchester. Jack was, Connolly told Bowra, 'extremely good value, nicer than Noël in some ways, very upright and intolerant and paederastic'. Unlike his younger brother, he had not been to Eton, so his relationship with Connolly was less freighted down by old associations: 'our relationship will always be interesting because it will represent the extent to which friendship can be carried without romance,' Connolly once informed him. In his letters at least, he adopted, a bluff, no-nonsense tone with his brother's friend, which may well have come as a relief to someone already accustomed to people tiptoeing carefully round him, never quite certain of his mood and fearful of provoking an unnerving display of boredom, silence or disdain. 'De Musset indeed!' Jack once exclaimed, apropos Connolly's reading matter: 'Why don't you try to do a little *reading* some time?'; or again he complained that 'There is nothing to read until your masterpiece appears. Hurry up, or I shall complain to John Buchan about you.' They visited Spain and Portugal together in the autumn of 1925: 'I never thought I could get on so well travelling with anyone,' Connolly wrote from a rain-swept St George's Square, pining to be back among the 'fruit and wine and boys' of southern Spain. Jack told Connolly that he was having problems with Symonds's *Problems of Greek Ethics* since the author failed to distinguish between love between two men and love between a man and a boy, 'and so far I have only fallen in love with boys': but this may have been a passing phase, for the following summer an embarrassed Jack confessed to having fallen in love with the mother of some boys he was tutoring – 'Don't mind me falling in love with a woman (the affection is returned) because I think of you a lot always.'

Back in London, where he stayed with his mother in St George's Square, Connolly was struck down by the terrible gloom that often afflicts those who have left university and find every prospect vile. Sligger, he told Blakiston, seemed determined to push him into journalism, the career which, above all others, seemed 'the most precarious and possibly the most degrading'. Momentary relief was provided by Bobbie Longden, who came to London for two days, staying at the Langham Hotel: both men enjoyed his visit a great deal, though towards the end Longden was taken ill at the Zoo, collapsing over dinner in an 'agony of indigestion' and taking to his bed with a hot-water bottle and a plentiful supply of bicarbonate of soda.

His health restored, Longden returned to Oxford – although Bowra was to refer, unkindly, to his being 'weighted down with scholarships which should have been given to infinitely poorer, infinitely nicer people', he had won a Prize Fellowship at Magdalen, to be followed by a Craven Fellowship for his work on the Roman Empire under Trajan – and Connolly was left wondering what to do next. From Bath Granny Connolly wrote to her 'darling Spratkins' to say how 'awfully sad and anxious' she felt about his future: to try to make his life a little easier she had given the Major £200, on the understanding that this should go towards his son's 'allowance'. Later that same month she wrote again to say she had settled his account with his tailor, so that he wouldn't have to start his new career with that particular albatross about his neck, but two years later the kindly old lady was still picking up the tabs – in that case, a debt of £11 still outstanding to Tom Brown, the Eton tailors. Nor did tradesmen desperate for their money restrict their invoicing to the family circle: the following April Jack Blakiston, blunt as ever, asked Connolly if he could please 'pay some of your Oxford bills because my people naturally don't like them coming rather often to Kirkby.'

And then, in October, Connolly found himself a job in Jamaica through Gabbitas & Thring, tutoring 'the world's bloodiest boy', and about to board ship at Avonmouth with the boy and his 'elegant cock-eyed mother'. He sailed at the beginning of November – in the nick of time, he told Mynors, given the 'enormous bills' he had run up in London, though luckily he had 'put £5 on Masked Marvel and so saved a crisis'. The Major must have heaved a sigh of relief as the SS *Pantuca* cast off and headed down the Bristol Channel, but hardly had his son stepped ashore than he had sent him details of a job with the Overseas Services of the Anglo-South American Bank, adding that while he was in Jamaica he might do well to make enquiries about the 'status of bank clerks in South America': he realised that Connolly didn't particularly 'relish' this kind of work, but it could well prove 'less hackneyed and routine than that of a bank clerk in another business'. If that didn't appeal, he should seriously consider getting another job in Jamaica once his tutorship expired, rather than 'loaf about' back in England. A solicitor had been on to him about yet another Halls Bros bill, and if Connolly had any other debts he should consider selling some shares to pay them off. All in all, 'I am more than disappointed at your behaviour during the past year,' the Major concluded: 'Knowing that you had these huge bills for battels and clothes on your hands you should have saved up every possible farthing of the money I sent you' instead of frittering it away on 'useless travelling'.

In an emollient PS, the Major wondered whether the Da Costas – the family for whom Connolly was working as a tutor – were in any way related to S.J. Da Costa, a well-known shell-collector who had died in 1908. Be that as it may, Mr Da Costa was a 'yellow little man and the whole family are Jews though one must not say so. They are supposed to be the richest people in Jamaica ...' Mr Da Costa was quiet and kind, but his wife was Connolly's favourite; as for their son Charles, 'he is quite affectionate and humorous but that is about all I can say for him. He is incredibly selfish, greedy and conceited, old for his age in the most unpleasant way and young in the nastiest too ...' In due course Connolly became fonder of his charge; and when, in 1966, he revisited the island, Charles wrote to him about the 'exquisite moment of nostalgia' aroused by his reappearance. He died only months before his former tutor, and his son wrote to say how profound an influence Connolly had had on his father, and how his 'memories of you were always affectionate'.

The Da Costas lived in 'a fashionable suburb which looks like the garden of Eden – greenness in every direction to green mountains on one side and a lagoon on the other'.* When not tutoring or sitting on the verandah writing to his friends – humming-birds hovering over his head – he rode and ran and swam and danced and played tennis and read Valéry and Rimbaud, in editions urgently posted from England, for the Da Costa library was alarmingly bare. He found half-caste boys a good deal more attractive than their 'overrated' black compatriots ('black people are rather difficult to stomach'). 'I have given up all attempts to conform to the Maurice creed,' he informed Synnott, and

> the result is that I have enjoyed three months of perfect chastity as no woman seems able to arouse the slightest sensation of sex or passion in me, only I find them soothing, decorative and amiable while the men here are dull and squalid and the perpetual spicy breezes and eternal sunshine make any strong feeling quite impossible beyond a mild loneliness on moonlit evenings and the anguish of remembering Eden when the rain falls long.

To Blakiston he confessed that 'I have never felt so chaste in my life and I am perfectly content with dancing and drinking lime squashes and talking idly in cool rocking-chairs.' He became adept at the tango and, despite his disclaimers, enjoyed some mild flirtations with the local girls. '*Je suis porté à*

* 'You would never have thought so many tennis courts could have been got into Eden,' he told Jack Blakiston.

la triste conclusion que je vous aime, pas passionement, ni même à la folie, mais assurement je vous aime,' he told a girl called Dorothy: '*Mais j'ai decidé au même temps que vous me trouveriez gauche, maladroit et laide.*' Nor did such feelings of inadequacy prevent him from breaking into verse: '*Dorothée de Lauriston, divine Dorothée/Dieu m'a mis en exil aux lieux ou vous fûtes née...*' He missed England dreadfully, sending Blakiston detailed instructions about London shops and restaurants, pining for the 'real greenness, buildings of Bath, something solid and not as alien as I thought: Marvell's England, too good to fight for, with all the charm and sober melancholy of Bobbie.' But if Bobbie seemed, from this side of the Atlantic, 'the finest and friendliest person I know and the best critic and highest symbol in my Platonic scale', it was of Blakiston that his narrator dreamt in one of the many fictional false starts that he abandoned and carefully kept over the next ten years or so:

> Simon awoke: for a moment he was fuddled with dreams, always these nightmares of the English tropics, of West Country rivers that disappeared in steaming everglades or metallic brightness of thin-scented mangroves, and always buried in them Noël, Noël and the unwilling heirs of this intemperate Eden.

Christmas 1925 was spent in Montego Bay, at the other end of the island; at a New Year's party a few days later he told a Miss Robinson that he had booked a table for two, but 'you needn't dance with me all the time, of course'. But always his thoughts returned to his friends and home: to Blakiston, 'remote and mysterious and gifted with perpetual boyhood', longing for whom 'I live in an anguish of wild impatience or wistful sorrow'; to Freddie Harmer, 'the classic side of *l'esprit moderne*'; to Synnott, 'the grave gay young man of the Renaissance'; to Sligger, 'the beneficent god, the father of all this', who, still cherishing vain hopes of effecting a conversion, had written to say that he hoped his former pupil would 'slip into a church to say a bit of a prayer as you used to do in the Chalet': evidently he never got a reply, since Patrick Balfour warned Connolly that Sligger was feeling bruised by his protégé's 'base ingratitude'; to Granny Connolly in Bath who, Sligger-like, hoped that her grandson would make his Communion at Christmas and enclosed some uplifting extracts from St Thomas à Kempis and Sir Thomas Browne; to 'home and family, both delapidated, but Mummy and the Lock House both comforting and real.' 'I try to find romance but get tired of someone as soon as they call me Cyril. I don't think I will ever be able to fall in love – for thine is the Kingdom,' he told Blakiston – for whom he provided, on another occasion, a detailed critique of *The Constant Nymph*, rounded off with Martial's best-known line ('*Nec tecum possum vivere, nec sine te*'). As well as providing images of Eden and of exile, Jamaica drove him to verse, much of it leadenly antique –

...I to return
Again to exile, the gradual death
Begun on the ship's side and all the load
Of sorrow as the outpost English lights
Fade from the fool in the stern, and tears obscure
The last pale sighs of home...

– some of it imitation Eliot –

Between the conception
And the creation
Between the emotion
And the response
Falls the shadow.
  Life is very long

– and the best of it, as ever, lyrical and formal:

O wasted youth among the isles
That faithless Caribbean surge
And dark interminable miles
Of vexed Atlantic would submerge

In living death beneath the palms
Return while still the spirit grieves
For sorrows that no sun embalms
And smell of woodsmoke over leaves...

And then, in early April, it was all over, and Connolly was heading back across the Atlantic aboard a Fyffe's banana boat, with the Headmaster of Winchester to keep him company.

Hardly had he set foot in England than the General Strike broke out, and he enrolled as a special constable, leaving his mother's flat at dawn in order to guard deserted buildings and moving the crowds along at Marble Arch, 'which was better fun'. He was about to be promoted to Scotland Yard when the strike was called off. 'Sorry if I have lost caste through strike activities,' he confessed to Synnott, but 'there was little else to do in London and we had not laid in enough coal to exist here.' 'Here' was the Lock House, where he longed to be, and as soon as he could he hurried down there and spent his days riding and reading Milton. He was increasingly convinced that salvation lay in art in general, and literature in particular: although Jamaica had been 'perfect hell', it had restored his sense of independence, and 'if I have learned anything in Jamaica it is a renewed ability to talk to myself, which I suppose is on the way to writing for oneself, presumably as it robs me of my perpetual sterility and imitation.'

Anxious to advance his literary career, he answered an advertisement in *The Times* as secretary to a 'literary man', and found himself being interviewed by 'the most awful old satyr who seems anxious to have me. He looks like an old toad and knows all literatures. I think he's a satanist and shan't go if I can possibly help it.' A Corvoesque figure in dusty clerical dress, Montague Summers was – according to David Garnett, who had come across him after joining Francis Meynell and Vera Mendel as a partner in the Nonesuch Press in 1923 –

> short and fat, his greasy hair was plastered in black or greying ripples to a big skull and hung in curls over the back of his dog-collar. His nose was small but rapacious, his cheeks smooth as bladders of lard. But his most disagreeable feature was his mouth: small, cruel and sharklike, with no modelling to the lips, if lips they were. His voice and manner were unctuous.

Although he thought him a 'monster', Garnett eventually became quite fond of the old brute: but Sligger, after some busy enquiries, warned Connolly that Summers was 'an unpleasant man who had scent and paint and that sort of thing and was very unpopular in College and went away'. Sligger needn't have worried: Connolly had already decided against, but not before encapsulating the incident in appropriate blank verse:

Cardinal: And what is Connolly's profession now?
Antonio: My Lord, apprentice to a sorcerer,
A fruity unfrocked cleric of the Nineties
Like an old toad that carries in his head
The jewel of literature, a puffy satyr
That blends his Romish ritual with the filth
Scrawled on Pompeian pavements . . .

With no job in prospect, he poured out in letters to Noël Blakiston his thoughts on poetry and life, on Gray and Collins and Crabbe and Flecker, along with a torrent of his own verses, all of them tinged with autumnal melancholy:

Since friendship haunts Arcadian fields
And love is but a rural child
And every fruit the summer yields
Now sheds its blossom on the wild

Forsake the town and come with me
To where the weedy Liris flows
No fairer woods did Daphnis see
And Eden knew no lovelier rose...

He visited his Quenington cousins and played in a jazz band in the village hall, went to the Russian Ballet, planned an epic work set in Ancient Britain, to be written jointly with Blakiston in Miltonic blank verse, and – with Sligger, Roger Mynors and Dom David Knowles, the future authority on mediaeval monasticism, and another habitué of the Chalet – spent some days at Downside Abbey, mugging up on early English history and feeling glad to be out of a sulphurous London. And then, some time towards the end of June, he was given an *entrée* – and with it a job – that was to have a profound effect on his future, introducing him to literary London and the literary life, influencing his ideas about the role and the duties of the writer, and reinforcing his abhorrence of journalism.

'Has Bobbie or Sligger spoken to you about Pearsall Smith?' Kenneth Clark asked him:

> He, though a worldly old gossip, is not disreputable and goatish like Summers. He wants a secretary, or rather he wants to keep some young man from journalism, and in return the young man is to do various odd jobs of scholarship – look up passages in seventeenth- and eighteenth-century authors, mainly in quest of philological queries... You would find him a trifle pedantic and very much the slave of polite civilisation.

Although Clark went on to warn Connolly that Pearsall Smith was 'rather looking for the steady second-rater, and you certainly don't fit that,' Connolly appeared to have no qualms about accepting the post. A sigh of relief went up from his family. From Bath, Granny Connolly wrote to say that it seemed 'just the thing for you, to give you the best of chances in the "world of letters"... I hope you won't drop your silly old granny when you are a celebrated author!'; the Major expressed pleasure in the fact that Pearsall Smith was reputed to be fond of a game of chess, and went on to suggest that he – the Major – should look after his son's income, 'provided you promise not to turn up *any* more bills.'

This seemed improbable to say the least; but before Connolly embarked on his new career he found time to make his annual visit to the Chalet. Sligger had filled the place with Wykehamists from New College, and only asked Connolly at the last minute: the party included John Sparrow, the future Warden of All Souls, whom Connolly found 'intelligent and nice and also makes rather a convenient butt', and Jack McDougall, who went on to work at Chatto & Windus – from where, in the early 1930s, he discussed the possibility of Connolly editing a book of parodies – and later at Chapman & Hall, where he looked after Evelyn Waugh's interests. Connolly enjoyed himself enormously. 'Ultra-hearty and affable,' he played hockey, cricket and bridge, took part in charades in Sligger's honour, and even joined in part-songs; he was spared the high emotions and incestuous intrigues of earlier Chalet holidays, and 'the complete absence of envy and intensity is very refreshing'. 'One of the most profound effects of Jamaica has been to cause me to forget all the reasons why one hated people,' he told Synnott: 'I seem to be through with love, lust, hate and personalities for the time being.' He planned to cultivate a detached 'Childe Roland' attitude, treating people as means rather than ends, presenting himself simply as an entertainer, 'unsexed and affable'. Looking back to his time at Oxford, he seemed a 'creature repugnant to the verge of insanity'; as for Bowra, 'I am so impregnated with Maurice that the consciousness of his hostility warps my outlook as much as his friendship did – I mean I can only see myself through his eyes now as an uncouth menial at Oxford, a deceitful bitch in vacations.' Though he was 'still susceptible to passing fancies' and enjoyed 'having someone decorative about the place' – by which he meant a male someone – he was beginning to like women more than he had, even if (or so he assured Piers Synnott) he still found them 'sexually appalling'. He could no longer associate Noël Blakiston with sex, and although Bobbie Longden would 'probably destroy me in a minute', he never wrote, and was seldom in his thoughts. In the meantime, Sligger was encouraging him to find a publisher for his journals, and had written to say that they would be shown to T.S. Eliot 'with a view to getting me work on his paper'; he hoped to hear from Osbert Sitwell about some poems he had sent him; and before leaving London he had gone to a party at which Mary Pickford and Douglas Fairbanks had been fellow-guests with E.M. Forster and Lytton Strachey. New worlds were opening up, and the literary life was beckoning.

TEN

Uncle Baldhead and the Affable Hawk

Years later, looking back over his life for the benefit of Texan book-lovers, Connolly suggested that, as a young man, he had spent a good deal of intellectual and emotional energy on the hunt for a 'replacement father'. This seemed a bit harsh on the Major who, though bibulous, peppery and peremptory, was at least available and happy – perhaps too happy – to assume his parental responsibilities; be that as it may, the first 'replacement father' he itemised was Maurice Bowra at Oxford, and now two further candidates were to present themselves in the avuncular shapes of Logan Pearsall Smith and Desmond MacCarthy. Though very different from each other, both men had much in common with their brilliant protégé, in temperament, attitudes, strength and weaknesses; and, as is the way with avuncular or tutorial figures, both loomed large in his life for a while before withdrawing into the wings, where they observed his progress with pride and affection, tempered at times by a certain disapproval and a slightly bruised sense of having been discarded in favour of younger and more contemporary friends.

Born in 1865, Logan Pearsall Smith came from a family of rich Philadelphia Quakers, whose fortune was based on glass: a good deal of 'thee-ing' and 'thou-ing' went on in the family home, and his parents spent much time evangelising in England – at least until Mr Pearsall Smith was involved in a scandal as a result of his taking too literally St Paul's command to 'salute one another with a holy kiss'.* After Harvard, Logan had come on to Balliol, graduating in 1891 with a second-class degree; and although America provided him with a welcome source of unearned income, he spent the rest of his life in England, which he regarded as his spiritual home, with occasional forays to France and Italy. He was an authority on seventeenth-century divines like Jeremy Taylor and John Donne: he had several brief

* According to the family biographer, Robert Pearsall Smith put into practice a curious doctrine whereby a female subject of his ministrations 'felt it her duty to ask him to stand naked before her'. A warm, unstable character who shared his son's manic-depression, Robert tried his hand as a publisher before joining the Whitall-Tatum glass factory. His wife, Hannah, was a Whitall; the Pearsall Smiths had made their money from a cemetery on Laurel Hill.

volumes to his credit, but prided himself above all on his talents as an aphorist; his best known work, *Trivia*, published in 1902, consisted of a series of highly-wrought epigrams which affected to disdain worldly concerns from an Olympian height but reflected, rather, their author's fearful withdrawal from them. 'The pleasure of giving to fine phrases a finer polish is the only pleasure of which the Soul never wearies', he once wrote, whilst Connolly – who shared, and was much influenced by, Pearsall Smith's epigrammatic proclivities, his tendency to recycle the same ideas and images again and again, and his literary perfectionism – told Blakiston that 'he is the complete craftsman in writing and takes days over sentences which in any case always contain four or five sentences stolen from the past'; but whereas Connolly's aphorisms had vigour and originality, Pearsall Smith's own writings – though 'strained off drop by drop, through the muslin of a super-sensitive critical sense' – had the musty, inanimate quality of something sheltered from too much life.*

According to Robert Gathorne-Hardy – who met Pearsall Smith in 1928 while working in an antiquarian bookshop, helped him with the bibliography of his selection of Jeremy Taylor's writings, and eventually succeeded Connolly as his assistant-cum-secretary-cum-protégé – Pearsall Smith was

> a largish man with a stoop that disguised his height; it wasn't so much that he appeared fat, as that his weight seemed too much for his strength. His back and shoulders and legs were curved; his neck appeared crushed down by his head against his shoulders. His spectacles rested on a long and pointed nose (the nose so faithfully exaggerated in Max's caricature); his hat was straight on his head, the grey hair showing beneath it; his clothes were nondescript and expensively respectable. It might have been a well-to-do clergyman who chose not to wear his clerical collar.

John Russell, who got to know him later in life, and was another of the young men whom Pearsall Smith took under his wing, remembered him as 'a tall man, with big heavy bones and, if such a thing may be conceived, a commanding stoop'; he had a 'face of antique grandeur' which, in conversation, 'assumed a kind of snapping animation which perhaps momentarily reminded one of a turtle or a tortoise.' To Kenneth Clark he seemed more like a stork, or some ungainly wading fowl: 'His tall frame, hunched up, with head thrust forward like a bird, was balanced unsteadily on vestigial legs which seemed to have lost their sense of direction through long disuse.'

* Musty or not, 'poor Logan' – as Henry James called him – was a recognised authority on the correct use of English. His *Words and Idioms* was published in 1925, and he was invited to sit on the BBC's pronunciation committee. He had become a British citizen in 1913.

Virginia Woolf, who shared the Stracheys' disdain for Logan as being 'so trivial, smart and snobbish', noted that 'He is a very well brushed, bright-eyed, rosy-cheeked man, seemingly entirely satisfied with life, which he appears to have mastered; visiting each of its flowers, like a bee. These flowers he keeps stored in his waistcoat pocket: lines from Jeremy Taylor, Carlyle, Lamb & Co.'

Though kind and well-meaning, Pearsall Smith was not an easy man to get on with; he was possessive, touchy and easily wounded. 'I don't want respect, treat me with affectionate derision,' he would tell his friends, after which he would take a masochistic, guilt-inducing delight in listing slights incurred and offences taken. Like Connolly at Eton, he used 'worldly' as a pejorative, and affected to concern himself only with art and beauty, yet he was an avid if credulous gossip, for whom 'friendly malice' was 'the most delicious and enduring of all ties'; he claimed to despise fame and success, and spent much of his life in bed, polishing his aphorisms, yet he was a snob and a name-dropper, loved luxury and comfort, and took an almost sadistic delight in playing 'cat and mouse with a succession of young men who hoped to succeed to his bachelor inheritance'. He could be a witty conversationalist, he was generous to his fellow-writers, and like Connolly he was a nimble mimic, adept at elaborating intricate fantasies about the lives of his friends ('*Do* so and so for me,' Henry James used to beg); but he was also easily bored, could be extremely rude ('Oh my God, this is the greatest bore in the world') and had more than a 'touch of the ogre' about him.

And yet, for all his affectations, he comes across as a rather melancholy figure – and he was to become more so as the years went by. Julia Strachey, who was related to the Pearsall Smiths through her mother, recalled how as a child, 'When Uncle Logan was in his glory he appeared to me the wittiest, handsomest and most stimulating man on earth.' He 'would be radiant as he entertained his friends', and yet 'with only myself and Aunty Loo for company, you wouldn't have recognised Logan – this stranger who shuffled stiffly into the dining-room to join us, with drooping shoulders and dead face, who went around the table with the closed, insulated expression of a sleepwalker . . .' Years later, she learned that her uncle was in fact a manic depressive – a condition that steadily worsened as he grew older. According to Kenneth Clark, 'At the height of his euphoria he really did become a gobbling old clown; at the bottom of his depression he could not put up with human company and retired to his room to read'; caught on the upswing, however, he was 'one of the most enchanting companions I have ever known. Then he would gradually ascend to euphoria and one wouldn't know where to look.' One place not to look was in the garden of his next-door neighbour in Chelsea: when in manic mood he was given, according to

Gathorne-Hardy, to ghastly practical jokes such as buying dead cats and hurling them over the garden wall;* after which, as the pendulum swung in the opposite direction, he would retreat into 'long, dark, sullen months of dullness'.

Pearsall Smith divided his time between Chelsea, where he 'enjoyed the company of Desmond MacCarthy and a number of sharp-tongued spinsters of independent means' – MacCarthy's daughters referred to him as 'uncle Baldhead' – and Big Chilling, a Tudor-beamed mansion overlooking the Solent. He shared his house in St Leonard's Terrace, overlooking the grounds of the Chelsea Hospital, with his sister Alys, Julia Strachey's Auntie Loo, who acted as the housekeeper, painting a thin blue line two inches from the bottom of the bath to mark the maximum permissible depth, and making sure, in her niece's words, that 'the steam from the banana soufflés and American waffles in maple syrup, of which he was so fond, came wafting through the house.' Alys, who was younger than her brother, had been unhappily married to Bertrand Russell, who eventually deserted her in the most brutal way. Her older sister, Mary, had married Bernard Berenson, whose companion, Nicky Mariano, confessed to being 'almost disappointed' at finding Alys 'looking so placid and cheerful, quite unlike a woman with a great tragedy behind her'; like the rest of the family, she was 'big and handsome with fine regular features', and appeared to have 'made almost a profession of being good'. Waffles and maple syrup were not the only odours to greet the visitor to St Leonard's Terrace: according to John Russell, Pearsall Smith had 'contrived to saturate the tall, narrow-waisted, inconvenient house with the lingering, badger-like smell of foxed leather and powdering-ink; and one could find one's way, by nose alone, to the little room on the second floor where Logan would sit, like Faustus in his study, with folio and inkhorn at his side.' On the walls of this book-lined retreat were a sepia drawing by Corot and a painting of sailing ships at sea; there was a small hearth-rug designed by Duncan Grant, a needle-work fire-screen embroidered by Alys, and from the window one looked out through the plane trees to Wren's Chelsea Hospital and the chimneys of Battersea power station. As for Big Chilling, it was 'a small Tudor farmhouse made habitable by added windows, lawns, peach trees and bathrooms, and it stands a field away from the Solent and very close to the corner where it joins Southampton Water.' The trees in the garden were 'frizzled by the prevailing wind', and from the upstairs windows one had views of the New

* His non-manic jokes were equally elaborate and unfunny. The best-known involved the pretence that the artist Hilda Trevelyan had been kidnapped by bandits and kept in a cave: a 'rescue fund' was set up, and the names of its eminent contributors printed in an accompanying pamphlet. Connolly contributed 6*d* and was awarded an OBE for his pains.

Forest in one direction, of Cowes and Osborne House on the Isle of Wight in the other, and of the yachts and liners making their way across the Solent and up Southampton Water.

The young men who came to work for Pearsall Smith found themselves, in Gathorne-Hardy's words, 'in a position for which there is no regular term; I was not what could properly be called a secretary, nor, in the professional sense of the word, a companion; what I was then settling down to seems to me, looking back, a sort of perpetual apprenticeship. Logan was just as much my instructor as my employer; I was both pupil and assistant.' They were encouraged to emulate his perfectionism, his fascination with words, his disdain for journalism and popular success, and to cultivate, as he did, the role of the spectator rather than the active participant. This passivity was to include the emotions as well. 'He disclaimed all first-hand acquaintance with the passions,' and once wrote – in tones more timid than world-weary, as intended – that 'the act of copulation is an unstable basis upon which to build a life'; he regarded marriage as fatal to a writer's chances of remaining true to his art – a theme that, together with the perils of journalism, was to resurface in more memorable form in *Enemies of Promise* – and only continued to employ his young men on the understanding that they didn't get married or try to write a best-seller. Indeed, the two were in his mind inextricably interwoven: leisure, a precondition of good writing, was incompatible with domesticity, and 'young authors who get married are bound to ruin their talents by writing for money.' 'How do you pronounce the word g-i-r-l?' he once asked a rarely-encountered sample of the breed. 'And how do *you* pronounce it?' she counter-attacked, so giving him the opportunity to deliver his *coup de grâce*: 'I never do.'

According to John Russell, the position of secretary-cum-assistant 'was not really workable over any great length of time', since Logan 'at once exacted and despised an absolute compliance with his wishes'. Like an old-fashioned bachelor schoolmaster, he 'required his pupil to practise a kind of affectionate defiance; the disciple had also to suggest that somewhere within himself was a strain of irreducible delinquency.' For the time being at least, Connolly was happy enough to play the part of the delinquent schoolboy when occasion demanded: writing facetious reports from Miss Agatha Warsash, Principal, Chilling Home for Backward and Difficult Boys, provided good training for his skill as a parodist and reviewer of middle-brow novels; and the old gentleman, duly gratified no doubt, bestowed upon him the persona of Joe Congothly, a Borstal boy in the making, 'to whom I stand in the position of guardian, and who is to me of considerable anxiety and care' – so much so that he wondered whether 'frequent bodily chastisement is advisable in his case?'

Pearsall Smith paid Connolly £8 a week, a sum that was due whether he was in attendance or away on his travels. He was given the run of Big Chilling: he could invite his friends to stay and make use of all the facilities, including a well-stocked library, a gramophone, a small sailing-boat, and Mr and Mrs Cave, the butler and housekeeper. Pearsall Smith seldom appeared before lunchtime, so Connolly had the mornings to himself, sailing or going on runs or hurling assegais; he had a large bedroom under the eaves; and when it was wet or storm-bound the two men would play chess for hours on end, or listen to concerts on the wireless, or talk together, before settling down to one of Mrs Cave's 'very passable' meals. Very often Connolly was the only person in the house, apart from the Caves. 'The worst thing so far has been the gong which I have to ring at the end of each course,' he told his new friend Molly MacCarthy, the wife of Desmond:

> Mrs Cave is deaf and the penetrating din which I am terrified to make at all has to be done several times with intervals of misunderstanding while the kitchen door opens and shuts despondently and I seem to make no sound while in my end of the house I feel more rude, exacting, noisy and imperious with each fruitless shattering of the silence.

The gong apart, he went on, he liked 'the steady drip, Middlemarch country, and the distant bell buoy': with its 'woods and greenness and briars and dusty nettles and tired pigeons and midges hovering above the sycamore leaves', Big Chilling was, like the Lock House – which, his mother informed him the following spring, would have to be sold: she hated the idea but a Colonel Pennythorn was insistent – a 'Mariana house'.

As for his employer, he was, or so Connolly assured Blakiston in early August 1926, shortly after starting work, 'courteous, sympathetic, serious and amusing though vain as authors are'. Some ten days later he was finding him 'very adequate, witty and sympathetic but rather bleak and scrupulous at the same time', while to Piers Synnott he described him as a 'blithe old Chinaman with a kind of bleakness that delays always those excessive confidences that ruin friendship'. Pearsall Smith, for his part, was very taken with his new protégé. 'God knows how much I enjoy your company,' he told him: he found himself laughing out loud whenever he thought of his letters. Unwisely, perhaps, but with typical generosity, he told him to 'Let me know if you want any of what is called the "wherewithal".' Such an offer was too hard to resist. Connolly's finances were as parlous as ever. The Major and Granny Connolly were still sorting out tailors' bills from Oxford; the Metropolitan House in Jamaica had threatened him with a solicitor's letter if he failed to settle debts of £17 15*s* 6*d*; he still owed money to Sligger, who, mercifully, decided against telling the Major about the £10 outstanding 'in the interest of the Republic of Letters!' Before long Pearsall Smith was lending Connolly the odd fiver or tenner, and bailing him out on his travels; on one occasion a man arrived from Gosport to serve a writ, expressing deep disappointment when he was told that his victim had fled overseas, and Pearsall Smith deducted the £40 owing from Connolly's future wages.

According to Kenneth Clark, Pearsall Smith had 'always dreamed of meeting a young man who would be like himself when he first went to Balliol, talented, devoted to literature and yet without direction', and although Clark felt that Connolly 'had no need of instruction from Logan, whether as a literary critic or a stylist', Pearsall Smith was anxious, above all, that his protégé should make the best possible use of his time. 'That you should be at work and writing is all I ask – there is no hurry for immediate results – the world must wait. I should never like to say how many years I spent in writing *Trivia* – I believe in the long delays of art and the nine-years-pondered lay,' he told his young friend: but what exactly Connolly should be writing, and indeed whether it was possible to write in quite such a vacuum, was another matter altogether. Sligger busied himself trying to interest publishers in a 'black book', though what it contained, and how they reacted to it, remains unclear; Pearsall Smith and Kenneth Clark jointly suggested a life of James Thomson, the eighteenth-century poet, and a biography of Swift was mooted; Desmond MacCarthy, who doubled up as a reader for Heinemann, wondered about his writing a travel book for them; T.S. Eliot was said to be 'much struck with my promise and eager to meet me': but actually getting down to it, to writing a full-length novel or that elusive travel book was a very different matter to knocking out long letters to Noël Blakiston or reports from Agatha Warsash. 'I write quite a lot and soon I think I will do it quite well, only I am bored by finishing things and don't want to publish till I have done something quite good; it is also rather pleasant to be a dark horse beside a mossy stone,' he told Patrick Balfour, adding that he had finished two stories, which he would be submitting to *The Dial.* (Neither was published nor, it may be, even submitted.) 'Dies Irae' – the typed-up text of which was amended by his mentor – was an abstract, philosophical discussion between Ecclesiastes, Aristippus, Po Chui and a Pearsall Smith-like sage called Arnold, which 'ends in consternation when they discover they have eternal life'; the other, 'Imaginary Portrait' was, in an indirect way, about Julia Strachey, whom Connolly had yet to meet, and was written at Big Chilling between tea and dinner one Sunday in November 1926. The story takes place on a dreary Sunday afternoon in November. The rain drums against the window-panes, the wind howls off the sea, and

Tristram, the narrator, can't get down to his writing. He opens a desk drawer and comes across a file marked 'Julia's Reports', and as he reads what her teachers have to say about her he is not only filled with angry indignation, but finds himself falling in love with this unknown girl, with her serious face, elegant hands, pale, grey-green eyes, long nose and grave looks reminiscent of the famous portrait of Beatrice d'Este. 'She must be grown-up by now,' he reflects,

> half-sensuous, half-intellectual, still probably untidy and unpunctual, elegant, casual, offhand, unruffled, quiet-voiced and cold, beautiful at certain moments and always interesting, vain perhaps but with the vanity of Narcissus, the self-absorbed internal brooding, the placid and remote egotism that would drive a lover to desperation...

As for love itself, it was, Tristram concludes, 'that grave of the implicit, that dismal leak in the artist's independence, whither all his peace of mind went flowing like water down a sink.'

The notion of love as a contagion – with women increasingly supplanting men as the source of the infection – much preoccupied Connolly at this time, and his musings on the subject were, in terms of his own life, both descriptive and prophetic. 'Love,' he told Blakiston, 'is a painful but not a dignified malady, I think, like piles;' and later in the same letter he discussed his own vulnerability to an irresistible face:

> When then the just man falls in love his friends should comfort him as best they can, and unite with him in deploring the unfortunate state into which through no fault of his own he has fallen – but when he does it again and again or when he comes to glory in his weakness or boast of his successes, when his malady is quartan, tertian and irremediable in its vehemence they must abandon him to his creature, let him take it home and put it in his house and place a ring on its finger to distinguish it from his friends till the lapse of years brings him suppliant to their doors again.

The only answer to such turbulences, he suggested, was to try to put such people firmly out of mind and cultivate a Sebastianesque detachment – though by now Sebastian had been replaced by, or subsumed into, 'Spinseban', the ingredients of which were Sebastian himself, Spinoza, and the contemporary philosopher Santayana, whom Pearsall Smith considered 'the greatest living writer and the happiest man and the most clarifying intelligence he knew'.

Both Pearsall Smith and his close friends Desmond and Molly MacCarthy had elaborate private vocabularies – Pearsall Smith's ungainly neologisms included 'swimgloat' ('an eagle-hurried rapture into high society after which it isn't easy to find one's feet'), 'cramthroating' ('one's friends with books') and 'sheepgoating' (separating one from the other)* – to which Connolly in time became an intimate, adding some suggestions of his own, such as 'genji' for 'enterprising amorous niceness'; and in his own writings, and in his letters to his friends, he continued to elaborate, as he had since his school-days at Eton, a complicated personal mythology, drawn largely from the classics, many features of which – like the shrimp in the rock pool, or Narcissus gazing at his own reflection, or Aeneas's helmsman, Palinurus, who fell overboard while asleep at the tiller and was drowned – were to recur again and again in his writings. The sense of loss and exile, and the urge to withdraw in the face of life's futility, were as potent as ever, though increasingly under siege from a countervailing greed for experience, and a desire to flee the nest and sample the wider world. His restless love of travel was, he felt, the direct consequence of his expulsion from Eden. 'The loss of Eden,' he told Molly MacCarthy, 'has inspired all Adam's sons to travel: Eden is the place where one can be alone, sanctuary. Remembering Eden is being sad because of exile. The nicest woods one knows remind one of Eden which all travel sets out to find.' And 'no sanctity' was to be found in unEdenic places like the Alps, which had no consolatory traditions of art and literature. An equally pervasive image was that of Narcissus, a Blakiston-like figure who 'expresses the absorption of the adolescent in himself, his body and mind, and his pool becomes the whole world of art and imitation, where he seeks for his more perfect watery image, which his own tears may sometimes destroy.' 'I am chiefly occupied in trying to fix Narcissus on paper but he eludes me with either a pose of artificial elegance or a boring and exasperating sincerity like a schoolboy,' he told Piers Synnott, though elsewhere he managed to pin him down – not very helpfully – with the aid of verse:

Hard by the wood Narcissus lies
The grass is long and cool
And brown as honey are the eyes
Within the forest pool...

Literary and mythological personages, each freighted with private meaning, were herded together for the enlightenment or bafflement of his friends:

* 'Milver' was Pearsall Smith's word for the kind of job then occupied by Connolly, and later by Robert Gathorne-Hardy: he was, apparently, disappointed that it never entered the language.

to the same letter to Molly MacCarthy in which he described his misadventures with the gong he added a long, arcane PS:

> Orpheus in Thrace, Childe Roland, Heathcliff, the rider in the Listeners, le prince d'Aquitaine à la tour abolie & the man in Rimbaud's Chanson de la plus haute tour & Arnaut in the Purgatorio & Ugolino & Moeris in the Eclogue seem the same person or rather a chain of symbols for the same passion for discarding everything from a sense of futility rather than a conviction of a mission, listless adventurers unable to escape themselves, while Eve in Eden, Mariana, the Sleeping Beauty, *O quam te memorem virgo*, Ophelia and possibly Solveg are the feminine counterpart passively futile rather than actively and anyhow equally solitary except for their encircling trees (Orpheus & Co really link on to the water tragedies, Narcissus, Hylas, Lycaon etc). Faulty mysticism but underived. Where the goat is tethered O that way madness lies!

At this stage in his life at least, Connolly thought Pearsall Smith's *Trivia* 'supreme', and his mentor's aphoristic approach bore fruit – never picked, though Anthony Powell, then at Duckworth, may have seen something of them – in what seems, in retrospect, a very early prototype of *The Unquiet Grave*. It was written, he tells us in his foreword, 'purely to teach myself to write for my own edification and not for someone else's – a pretty hard job as a matter of fact as there was a lot of self-consciousness to be got rid of...' It was, he went on,

> rather the expression of myself, of myself and by myself, than a work written for posterity. The sort of book most authors end their literary careers with, a *Trivia*, a craftsman's handbook, a collection of tropes and felicities, few quotations and much criticism, views on life with observations from nature and poetry both grave and gay – in fine a meal of savouries, and for that cause perhaps somewhat hard to stomach.

'There is no idea that lacks a name and cannot be made recognisable by a myth of antiquity,' he tells us, and after mentioning Oedipus, Tiresias, Phaeton and Adonis, he moves on to 'the drowned man, Lycaon or Palinurus, who revives in Ferdinand Prince of Naples, Philebas the Phoenician, Bateau Ivre, le Jeune Tarantine – these seek a watery obscurity, or have it thrust upon them...' Although music, while giving much pleasure, was 'comparatively irrelevant to the needs of my nature', it too could symbolise or embody the notions that obsessed him. Ravel's 'Aprés Midi d'un Faune' remained 'the best expression of the over-ripeness of afternoon, and of the forlorn regret of youth that has discovered excess, and learnt to be weary and know not why, and to yield for yielding's sake to inaction and gloom, and to the morbid destruction of what is beautiful, in the hope of finding what is new.' The same composer's 'Belle au Bois Dormant' symbolised the 'distress and solitude of Eden', just as a much earlier musician, Orpheus, embodied 'the strange and mystic retirement, the fatal, fated sense of isolation which often affects one; the need of vanishing, of preparing to dispense with life while we still have it.' As in *The Unquiet Grave*, he was cloaking an accurate account of feelings common to us all – in this case, the rather morbid self-pity and self-regard of a protracted late adolescence – with a confusing and, some might feel, redundant mythology: but what is of interest here, for the literary historian at least, is the way in which he was toying with the themes and images that would eventually find their way into print some eighteen years later. As for Palinurus, his future *alter ego*, 'it is interesting to note that the tragedy of most literary drownings is that they usually take place in a calm sea... the race of the elements is less dramatic than their ironic indifference'; while to Molly MacCarthy – whose reactions, if any, to these sometimes baffling effusions is unrecorded – he suggested that 'Lycaon (the drowned man) is a summer man for he met his death in a calm sea and sank to the bottom very slowly and getting greener and greener as he went...'

All this suggests that, as a newly fashionable young literary man, he had been reading T.S. Eliot and Sir James Frazer, whose *The Golden Bough* was much admired at the time. Whether either author would have recommended himself to the MacCarthys is open to doubt. Desmond and Molly MacCarthy lived in Wellington Square, off the King's Road and a couple of minutes' walk from St Leonard's Terrace; and although MacCarthy was a member of the Bloomsbury circle, he and Pearsall Smith seemed to embody, in their tastes and attitudes as well as geographically, the literary world of Chelsea as opposed to that of Bloomsbury – more conservative and traditional and belle-lettrist, less austere and intellectual and avant-garde. In August 1926 Desmond MacCarthy came to stay at Big Chilling, and Connolly took to him at once. He was, he told Blakiston, 'a very good man indeed – wise, humorous and kindly with a complete inability to finish anything he sets out to do and a pathetic belief that he is going to do so'. MacCarthy was to prove another 'replacement father', and for a while he and Molly provided the young Connolly with a substitute family as well, both in Wellington Square and at Shulbrede, their house in Sussex. Like Pearsall Smith, MacCarthy was to play an important part in shaping Connolly's career; like Pearsall Smith, he had much in common with his protégé, though his failings were far more obvious, and as eagerly confessed.

Both men had Irish names and, though born and bred in England, were, often to their irritation, taken to be Irishmen; both were Etonians; both were to make their livings, at some stage, as regular book reviewers for the *Sunday Times*, a way of life they both relied upon and resented; both failed to produce the books they (and their admirers) felt they had inside them, though MacCarthy's dereliction was by far the graver; both were fond of high society and good living, though MacCarthy was more bibulous; both had inherited from Bloomsbury a disconcerting habit of putting the telephone down at the end of a conversation without saying 'goodbye'; both were generous, improvident and extravagant, with the result that richer friends – Sibyl Colefax in MacCarthy's case – had to organise whip-rounds or make discreet contributions to the funds; both, in later life, would be seized by occasional spasms of self-pity when faced with all they felt they had failed to achieve, MacCarthy lying in the boiling baths he loved so much repeating over and over again 'My life, my life', while Connolly, at much the same age, was stranded in bed, sucking the sheets and groaning 'Poor Cyril' like a melancholic mantra.

Desmond MacCarthy had been born in 1877. At Trinity, Cambridge, he had become a friend of G.E. Moore, Bertrand Russell, Lytton Strachey and the Trevelyan brothers, but unlike many intellectuals and literary men he was an affable, sociable figure who enjoyed the company of, and interested himself in, an enormously wide and varied range of people. He had started life as a journalist in 1903, and – as a man without private means – had kept himself precariously by his pen ever since, apart from a spell in Naval Intelligence during the First World War. He became the drama critic of the *New Statesman* in 1917 and its literary editor three years later, contributing a weekly essay as well under the pseudonym of 'Affable Hawk'. He was generous in his encouragement of younger writers, giving them books to review and urging them to get on with their own – he had a soft spot for the relatively hard-up, like Peter Quennell, who was taken on as a reviewer in preference to Harold Acton, who looked (and was) too rich – but found it impossible to practise what he preached. Novels surged through his head ('Henry has fallen in love on the platform of Paddington Station and is just passing Sutton Seeds on his way to Eton') and a great biography of John Donne was pondered but somehow never embarked upon, set aside for a review or a piece of journalism or a long, convivial talk or a literary gathering. Lytton Strachey thought him 'incapable of pulling himself together', while Virginia Woolf doubted whether

> he possesses any faults as a friend, save that his friendship is so often sunk under a cloud of vagueness, a sort of drifting vapour composed of times &

> seasons separates us & effectively prevents us from meeting... This arises from a consciousness which I find imaginative and attractive that things don't altogether *matter*. Somehow he's fundamentally sceptical. Yet which of us, after all, takes more trouble to do the sort of kindnesses that come his way? Who is more tolerant, more appreciative, more understanding of human nature? It goes without saying that he is not a heroic character. He finds pleasure too pleasant, cushions too soft, dallying too seductive...

According to Gerald Brenan, who, like everyone else, was extremely fond of MacCarthy,

> Desmond simply did not have in him the stuff of a writer. As a talker, however, it was very different, for his conversation was the most entrancing I have ever listened to. To begin with, he had the air of being completely relaxed and at ease in company. He could talk to anyone and, what was more difficult, make them talk back.

He was, Brenan thought, the best raconteur he ever knew, matched only by Compton Mackenzie. 'Discursive rather than witty', he had no difficulties in charming his listeners, was direct and forthright in his opinions and intolerant of what he considered pretentious or obscure, including much modern writing, and had the advantage of a beautiful voice and impeccable timing: Frances Partridge remembered how he 'used his voice like a musician'. In person he was small and neat and dapper, a bow-tied hawk 'whose feathers were often somewhat ruffled': he and Molly together reminded Frances Partridge of 'a pair of china birds on the chimney-piece, partly because they were more complementary than alike, and both sharply observant as all birds are.'

Molly was the daughter of Frank Warre-Cornish, a well-known Eton housemaster. Though self-effacing and modest, it was generally agreed that she was a better writer than her more voluble husband, and whereas Desmond's books consisted of nothing more than reprinted essays and reviews, she was the author of a much-admired autobiography, *A Nineteenth-Century Childhood*. Her relations included Thackeray and Leslie Stephen, the father of Virginia Woolf and Vanessa Bell. She was, in Gerald Brenan's words, 'a plump, warm-hearted, motherly woman who lived in a cloud of vagueness and indecision, out of which she would emerge in short, erratic flights of wit and fancy which ended, like a hedge sparrow's song, suddenly.' From her thirties onwards she became increasingly deaf, and both Brenan and Frances Partridge recall her disconcerting habit of unplugging her hearing-aid when bored. She seemed quite happy to let her husband do most of the talking, and before long Connolly was noting how 'Desmond's voice rises up authoritatively through the scullery ceiling and the familiar rise and fall proclaims inaudibly the literary topic of the week to the cook and children'. Fond as Connolly always would be of Desmond MacCarthy, Molly was, for the time being at least, his particular confidante. 'Molly and I have formed a diehard secret society,' he told Blakiston: '. . . it is non-political and based on admiration for the last century and the better parts of the preceding one.' He relished her 'emancipation and a vein of divine madness', and much admired her autobiography, with its evocation of Eton life. 'I regard you definitely as an ally,' he told her: '. . . Noël and Jack, Bobbie Longden, Desmond and Molly, Cyril's friends.'

Braving Pearsall Smith's disapproval, MacCarthy asked Connolly to try his hand at an anonymous book review for the *New Statesman* of a work by the French writer Paul Morand, and professed himself well pleased with the result; so embarking his protégé on a lifetime of reviewing, and a connection with the *New Statesman* that was to last, on and off, through to the 1940s. It was not until the following year that Connolly began to review regularly for the magazine, and to see his name in print, but the Major was swift to exploit his son's literary connections to advance his chosen cause. Was this the book MacCarthy had in mind, he wondered, enclosing details of a new study of the snail? If so, he would be delighted to review it, though the pages he had read so far seemed 'full of imperfection'.

Both Pearsall Smith and MacCarthy were lavish with advice for the young writer starting to make his way in the world. 'Mind you,' MacCarthy would say, 'this is all the advice I have never been able to follow, but it is the best'; while Pearsall Smith explained that 'Desmond and I have all this vast vocabulary of exhortation, Desmond especially, that we have been storing up for years and never had an occasion to use'. Such avuncular attentions were more than welcome, but a 'replacement father' from an earlier incarnation was, it seemed, still in unforgiving vein. That December, by which time Connolly had temporarily abandoned Big Chilling's howling south-westers for the calm of St Leonard's Terrace, he encountered Maurice Bowra in Wellington Square. Bowra, he learned afterwards from Pearsall Smith, had 'moved heaven and earth to stop them receiving me but was confuted – no friend like an old friend!' 'I hear you have begun an offensive against me again. Can't you manage to leave me alone for a moment, for, after all, it must be nine months since we met,' Connolly wrote to the Dean: 'I realise that to you absence and failure are unforgivable, but I am neither wholly absent, nor completely failing.' Bowra must have felt bad about having inveighed against Connolly as forcefully as he had, for the following month he wrote to Molly to apologise for his 'unguarded and thoughtless talk' about him: he meant what he had said, but it referred to the past, and he was ashamed at having tried to prejudice his host and hostess against their new friend. But, as far as Connolly was concerned, the damage was done. Some years later, in one of the sketches he wrote under the name of 'Alpdodger' – mercifully unpublished, from the Dean's point of view – he provided a lethal portrait of Bowra as a timid provincial snob, not dissimilar to that provided by Evelyn Waugh in the form of Mr Samgrass in *Brideshead Revisited*. A 'little round man', 'Mr Bogey' 'stands on the pavement in an ulster, a very bitter ambitious man, he is thinking about Blenheim and how to stop other professors going there.' 'I see the sun through the gates of Trinity,' Mr Bogey writes,

> I see a peer's heir on the grass. I see other dons in ulsters, taller than me, desiccated, middle-aged, low-born, and I dislike them for reminding me of my appearance, of who I am. I can't bear my contemporaries or my equals, though I have to keep on the right side of those who can elect me Professor of Greek. My taste in literature is vulgar and rhetorical. I can't write, but nobody knows it. I propose to earls' daughters after going to stay with their brothers. I have a right to the good things of the world. I am a magnificent talker, a wit who cauterises everyone, myself included, and then asks the most sympathetic listener to stay behind and shows him my tender little Jew's heart sewn on my sleeve. Intellectually I am content, I have no money worries, but socially and sexually I plot revenge and aim above my station. My pupils leave and go to London. They steal a march on me. I cannot follow, for my success in London rests on my apparent devotion to this provincial town . . .

*

Despite his new friends, and the unpleasantness with Bowra, Connolly was far from turning his back on the past. Freddie Harmer asked him to join him on his travels in Eastern Europe, and they agreed to meet in Vienna. Mrs Da Costa, with whom he had dined in Aix-les-Bains on his way back from the Chalet in July, had written to suggest that he might like to meet her in Biarritz, but he decided against since 'I am not very much in favour of romances with pupils' mothers which seem to me rather drearily banal and Gallican'; he was more tempted by a quick trip to south-west France to see Blakiston, who was bored and unhappy in his vacation job as a tutor, but a meeting proved impossible, and he made his way instead to Paris and on to Vienna. From there he and Harmer – 'whose face seems permanently red and rather large, vacant and moon-like' – took a train to Budapest; after which they took a boat down the Danube, travelling on from Bucharest to Constanza on the Black Sea. This particular stage of their journey bore fruit in the ill-fated form of a guide book to the Balkans, of which a mere three pages survive, full of advice on where to eat in Budapest ('Go to the Astoria, where the food is excellent, and sturgeon can be tasted for the last time. Here the head waiter is dignified beyond all words, he has served in London at the Langham, is handsome and polished, and a mine of information on things Hungarian. Do not attempt to tip him'); and in a story called 'The Sisters Good', in which two young Englishmen who had been at school together find themselves in a Danubian town. They go to a night-club called the Kakadu – Rupert, who speaks German, helpfully explains to Miles, the Connolly figure, that this means 'cockatoo' – where the manager, a 'deplorable fellow', tells them that if, as Englishmen, they fancy any of the girls at the bar, they have only to ask. For this piece of impertinence he is put in his place with a 'prefect's stare'. Among the acts on stage are two towering blondes in white tie and tails called the Sisters Good. 'There was something sexually disturbing about the way they manipulated their long legs, a freeness in the crotch, a parade of pear-shaped behinds, a comradely gruffness of voice. Miles and Rupert experienced a pang of piercing sadness together with a fearful itching sensation of frustration and desire,' and after the two girls have marched off playing saxophones, they take up the manager on his offer. The two girls, Brenda and Barbara, join the young men, summon up champagne at 350 kroners a bottle, and talk in a homesick way about London life, about Jack Hulbert and Mrs Meyrick and Freddy Lonsdale, about lunch at the Berkeley and supper at Ciro's and the difference between Oxford and Cambridge boys and 'Did someone mention another bottle? Shall us? Let's!' The sisters, who lived in either Norbury or Norwood, 'knew peers and racing men, actors, actresses, even pansy chorus boys, but no dons or retired house-masters, no civil servants, respectable hostesses, debs, artists, politicians or writers though they had been to the Chelsea Arts Ball and seen Augustus John. They had not heard of Lytton Strachey or the Sitwells...' Eventually they take to the dance floor, clasping their partners ever more tightly; and 'When they returned to their tables Miles and Rupert had each taken a resolution. Somehow they would shake off the other and lose their virginity...' After such excitements, the two young men took a boat from Istanbul, stopping at Athens – where they dined with Connolly's old hero Buschor, the authority on Greek vases – Corfu, Brindisi and Venice, and so home to London.

Harmer, who came to stay at Big Chilling, momentarily reviving an old infatuation despite the moonlike features, was not, of course, the only figure from the past with whom Connolly kept in touch. Noël Blakiston also came to stay, and was visited in Cambridge in turn; their meetings were less frequent than in the past – in December Connolly worked out that 'since leaving Eton only 108 days in 1640 have been spent with Noël that is only 6 per cent of your time in the last 4½ years' – but although Connolly was often dismissive about him behind his back, he retained a particular place in his affections. He kept Blakiston's letters in a blue ginger jar in his room at Big Chilling; he thought back with a terrible nostalgia to the days they had spent together at the Lock House or at Lulworth Cove, and the Palinuran notebook was 'all curiously saturated with you and the Lock House in the early summer – we have done what Bobbie and I could never do – forged an Eden for ourselves to be alone.' He longed for them to be able to travel together, for Blakiston to 'comfort me with apples, stay me with flagons', for 'I miss you with grief in the afternoon and joy in the evening. You block the world of my imagination and nothing else finds room.' And yet they seemed 'to swerve away from frankness as if we had accorded each other the preciousness of an illusion rather than the security of a friend... We do not want to fall in love. We both want to live together and write books but dare not face our capacity to do so and rather than you should be hurt or I shocked we both willingly bury our heads in sand.'

The book that Connolly wanted to write above all others would be based on his friendships at Eton. Desperate to recreate a prelapsarian world, he badgered his friends for memories and – most importantly of all – for the return of old letters, the raw material from which he would work. Denis Dannreuther had written to him in Jamaica to say that he would be happy to comply; back in England, he sifted through them at Big Chilling, finding in them the only record of Blakiston's first two terms, and regretting that Terence Beddard had not taken comparable care. He would like, he told Dannreuther, to 'use the letters to make a vast corpus of all my correspondence with voluminous notes so that one might at least be reminded of what adolescence was really like and also preserve a fairly adequate likeness of a lost society'; and to Blakiston he wrote that the letters he had been re-reading were 'confident and natural and there is a tang about them that seems lacking in everything I have written since leaving Eton. I would be afraid to be so flippant or so serious now.' He pored over the correspondence between Thomas Gray, Richard West, Horace Walpole and Thomas Ashton, four eighteenth-century Etonians whose passionate friendships and equally passionate regrets at being expelled from Eden seemed to mirror and anticipate his own. Alone in Big Chilling, the rain drumming against the window-panes, 'I worship the Past – our Past – and like some great festival of the mediaeval church the services drag on: the lonely vigils of the memory, the great sacramental visions, the veneration of holy relics and the symbolic monotony of ritual...' Although he was 'appalled to find that the past, which I thought I possessed so glibly, is really lost beyond all hope of animation,' old friends with whom he had lost touch or who had moved into very different worlds – like Jacky O'Dwyer, who had gone on to Woolwich and become a regular soldier – could be preserved in literary amber, eternally young in memory if not in fact. 'He must be alive somewhere now but can hardly be said from our point of view to live,' he told Blakiston: 'the fact of his spiritual death is enough to make his old self entirely one's own possession.' As for his own mortality, 'I don't think I shall die at present but I think there is hardly any time of day when I should really mind dying – I feel I have lived such a lot already that there would be hardly any kind of experience I had been deprived of, only quantity.' The sense of the best of life being over, of the remainder as an inevitable anti-climax and falling-off, was as pervasive as ever: sometimes – or so he claimed – he longed for death, and 'naturally it was the romantic sense of climax that demanded it, the fear of bathos and a vaguer apprehension of a squalid old age and a certain literary pessimism and sceptical despair...'

Plans were made to enshrine such Sebastianesque thoughts in *The Athanasian*, a magazine that was to be compiled by Connolly and the Blakiston brothers and produced, hand-written, in a single issue of one copy (the print-run having dropped from the initial four or five). Writing to Molly MacCarthy, Connolly had defined 'Athanasian' – together with other private terms, like 'Orphic', 'Childe Roland', 'Heathcliff' and 'cold pastoral' – as 'relying entirely on your own judgement and being taken for granted in your company', though in the preface to the 'Athanasian creed' which he sent Noël Blakiston he suggested that 'Truth is revealed by grace, not experience', which would seem a rather different matter. The magazine was to include poetry, stories, love letters, 'a young girl's meditations on homosexuality' and 'our ex-cathedra dictums on various subjects'. Among these were the 'Ten Tripes': the editors' particular animadversions included 'Alps, arguments, intellectuals, anti-intellectuals, civics, Chippendale, gossip, going to Chartres, modern French prose, Sundays'; Kenneth Clark had suggested Chippendale, and 'civics' was the work of a new friend, David Garnett, then running his bookshop in Gerrard Street with Francis Birrell. A current – and future – obsession was also proposed for inclusion: 'Don't you think a feature of *The Athanasian* must be a bibliography of Orpheus, Hylas, Narcissus and the Drowned Man?' Connolly asked Blakiston: '...thus Lycaon (*Iliad* 18) is the first drowned man, then there are sundry in the anthology, then comes Palinurus who fulfils the main condition of being drowned in a calm sea.'

Not surprisingly, this improbable precursor of *Horizon* never found its way into print (or script), though the three editors continued to use the word as if denoting membership of a secret society. It sounds on the face of it a fairly juvenile enterprise, though whether it was any more infantile than Uncle Baldhead's 'Handbook of the "Down with Cyril Society"' is open to doubt. Consisting of pages stapled together, and again restricted to a print-run of one, this peculiar publication was just the kind of thing small children produce in emulation of a book. The back cover carries the words 'To be published shortly – MAXIMS OF THE ANTI-LOGAN LEAGUE (by CVC)', plus some disrespectful scribblings by its recipient, noting train times and where he was supposed to be meeting David Garnett; within are personalised aphorisms, replete with a sad self-pity assuming an urbane disguise ('There is more happiness on the other side of baldness than Cyril can possibly imagine' and 'Cyril would be a perfect friend if he loved perfection; but if he loved perfection, where would I come in?'). 'I am delighted to learn that the Chilling experiment has proved propitious,' its compiler wrote to its dedicatee in November 1926: 'I have had many misgivings, for the test seemed a severe one; and when the west wind howled about our urban chimneys I often thought of you meeting its unimpeded blast, and feared that it might shake your resolution as it shakes the walls of Chilling.'

In fact, much of that winter was spent in London. He went to the play of *The Constant Nymph*, writing an extended critique to Blakiston, and met its author, Margaret Kennedy, but 'could not fathom her much'; he was introduced to Arthur Waley, and decided that he didn't hold with the Sitwells ('Edith is tedious, humourless and combative, Osbert advertises, Sachie is remote'); the Major, who had five papers on snails ready for the press, including one on snails in Italian Somaliland, enquired after his well-being as a fellow-writer, and tried in vain to lure him back to Alassio with the promise of 'one of the prettiest girls (of her type of beauty) I have ever seen as a playmate'; safely ensconced under the urban chimneys of St Leonard's Terrace, he fell into what was to become a familiar and lifelong routine – 'I lie late in bed to make the mornings shorter – the days begin with the dusk, I think' – and was overcome, as he so often would be, by the dullness and the melancholy of London: 'This Debussy weather is very disturbing, like the Unquiet Grave.' He got to know Maurice Baring, a friend of the MacCarthys who proved 'much nicer than his novels' and fed him on 'pre-war vodka and caviare sandwiches', and he abandoned pâté in favour of tropical fruit, 'an old failing of mine', buying bags-full of muscat-flavoured lychees and filling cinema ash-trays with discarded skin and stones.* He enjoyed being independent, he told Patrick Balfour, who was

* He may have been influenced by Molly MacCarthy, who had 'identified a fondness for pâté de foie gras with a distaste for women, and has been begging me to give it up.'

working as a trainee journalist in Glasgow, and thought he was probably rather nicer than he had been at Oxford; he had 'renounced the academic and all its ways & don't mind what view I hold on anything as long as it's my own', spent his spare time reading Latin and eighteenth-century verse, and felt congenitally restless. As far as travel was concerned, 'I don't feel that it is an end in itself or the basis of any real aesthetic, it is just one's peculiarity to find it hard to keep still, homeless since the loss of Eden.'

Connolly's urge to travel was indulged in February 1927, when he set off to Spain with Pearsall Smith. He enjoyed travelling with his patron, he told Blakiston, were it not that he 'talks too much'; and he found it hard to adjust to the fact that, for once, he was travelling as a rich man, and spent a good deal of time trying to persuade the old man not to spend money unnecessarily or take rooms with baths. From Paris they took the Sud Express to Bordeaux, where he relished the 'green Poussin woods and golden sunshine of Entre Deux Mers and the lovely rivers and the solidarity of this town with its respectable houses and cobbled quays', dined at the Chapon Fin and visited Montaigne's castle. He was thrilled to be in Spain again, which 'we (you, me, Jack) so much assume that it is the best country that one forgets how hard it is to explain why'; they visited Avila, Toledo, and Madrid before taking the train down to Andalucia, where they took in Cordoba and Seville and went to a bull-fight in Malaga. At some stage the older man left for Italy, where he would be staying with the Berensons; Connolly was to rejoin him later, but in the meantime he decided to revisit North Africa. Tangier was full of glaring English officers and their sour-looking wives and even more repellent French bourgeois families ('I have been anti-French for some time and am always surprised to confirm it'), all of whom he compared unfavourably with the Spanish; to cheer himself up he drank Blakiston's health in champagne before moving on to Fez, where he had a good shave in the Jewish quarter and an alarming dream – a recurrent nightmare – in which he had stayed on an extra year at Eton and had been 'forgotten, outworn and generally unwanted by a generation that knew not Joseph'. On board ship for Naples, he was racked by another nightmare in which Blakiston – back at Eton once more – had taken up rugger, and went off to play in a match without addressing a word to his old friend. No doubt it came as a relief, as arranged, to meet Bobbie Longden in Rome. Longden was still riding high, but not for very much longer. Although Connolly had confided to Molly MacCarthy that Longden was 'about my only equal', and to Balfour that 'Bobbie will make a superb equal & they are so very hard to find', before long he was scribbling on the envelope of a letter from his equal that 'his prose smells of mice'; and although Longden was to write of how 'I feel now more than ever that we forged a friendship, during those years, which I anyhow can never have with anyone else... I want your conversation, your jokes, your impulses, your expression, all the subtleties which are alchemy to friendship,' the two men had begun to drift apart. For the time being, though, Connolly had promised to write his guide book to the Balkans for his old friend, who would shortly be continuing his academic researches in Greece.

From Rome, he and Longden travelled up to Florence to stay with Kenneth Clark. Clark had gone to work with Bernard Berenson in the spring of 1926: he had disliked him a great deal at their first meeting, finding him intolerably arrogant, and had been surprised when the great man had asked him, on the spur of the moment, to help him prepare a new edition of his *Florentine Drawings*; and now he was back again, with his wife Jane, and had taken a house in Settignano. Earlier in the year Connolly had confessed to 'nursing a secret heresy' in finding K. Clark a 'crashing bore'; but even if Clark did get 'a bit garrulous and dogmatic before set of sun', he enjoyed his company a great deal, and was very taken with Jane. He found sightseeing with Clark a positive pleasure, and when they weren't trudging round the galleries he amused himself hurling assegais and getting on with the Balkan guide book. Early in April, however, a cloud appeared on the horizon in the form of Maurice Bowra, who was coming out to stay with the Clarks together with John Sparrow: apparently Connolly had become the Dean's *idée fixe*, and evasive action would have to be taken when they arrived. In the meantime, however, the Clarks took Connolly and Longden out to I Tatti to be introduced to the Berensons. Connolly was very taken with Mary Berenson, whom he thought 'the nicest person there, large and broad and homely in a Chaucerian way', but was less impressed by the sage himself. Over dinner Berenson attacked Connolly for admiring *The Seven Pillars of Wisdom* and *The Waste Land*, with such ardour that even Pearsall Smith, who hated Eliot's work, was driven to defend him. Uncle Baldhead was, Connolly told Blakiston, very 'sprightly and rebellious', but according to Clark Berenson had a low opinion of his brother-in-law, stirring restlessly in his seat when he attempted a funny story and muttering 'Dear me, what a smutty old clown Logan is becoming.' Some days later, Connolly was still unreconciled to 'B.B.': 'I haven't much taken to him, he talks the whole time and downs everybody else, and though he has enormous and universal knowledge and is excessively stimulating, half his remarks are preposterously conceited and the other half entirely insincere.' He was annoyed at the excessive deference shown to the diminutive art historian, the company hanging on his every word while grumbling behind his back: 'nothing is ever allowed to upset him, conversations at meals are deftly turned, contradiction is extinct, and the visitors return to scoff after they have come to pray.' Connolly's own defiance apparently paid off, and in the most gratifying way: Berenson, he learned, had not only taken against Messrs Bowra and Sparrow – it was generally agreed that a return visit by the Dean was out of the question – but had enjoyed Connolly's company so much that he was invited to stay at I Tatti. Understandably enough, Connolly felt suddenly warmer towards his host, who was now 'capable of fine, lucid and inspiring talk when he can be made to realise that his audience deserve it'. Once installed at I Tatti, he finalised with Noël Blakiston the arrangements for a journey they had planned to make to Sicily together, working out elaborate timetables and reminding his friend that 'we will want our brown suits for wear in the evenings.'

The trip which Connolly and Blakiston made to Sicily marked the climax and the conclusion of a particular phase in their lives; or, as Connolly wrote to his old friend some thirty-six years later, 'The Sicilian expedition ends the age of romantic friendship because it was so perfect that it could not go forward unless we lived together like Kyrle Leng and Bob Gathorne-Hardy or Ricketts and Shannon, but then we weren't homosexual...' Alone and homeward-bound in Vienna, he found himself convulsed by melancholy and the sense of an era ending. 'I am in for a bad backwash after Sicily like an elderly man who has suddenly lost his job,' he wrote to Blakiston. 'Half the thrill of Girgenti came in its echoes of Eton and ourselves when young,' he went on, and he thanked his friend for coming with him and so 'contributing to the most sustained ecstasy of my life...I don't think I shall ever be able to travel with anyone else again.' He must have written in similar vein to Pearsall Smith, eliciting thoughtful consolation:

> I am sorry that your woe has descended on you, but that is the price which you pay for your ecstasy, and it is a price which I am sure you are not unwilling to pay. Yours is a life of dizzy heights and deep abysses – I envy it in a way, for it is a life of that poignant reality which is the stuff of art; but my serene and pleased indifference, the 'constant mood of my calm thoughts', suits best my temperament and my years.

Fortified by these sage reflections, Connolly travelled home via Prague, Dresden and Rotterdam, where he boarded the Gravesend boat 'with a Conrad crew of 14 niggers who drank and fought upon the rough North Sea'.

*

Connolly's slow transition from the world of Eton and Oxford to that of literary London, from male romantic friendships to an active interest in the opposite sex, was recalled some years later by his *alter ego*, Alpdodger. Alpdodger – a 'very conservative young man', whose every act was 'faintly duplicated and blurred by the insincerity of adolescence' – returns from the Continent, eager to fall in love and to escape from 'the shadow of the settlement at Oxford, which stretches for at least two years over departing alumni and makes them gauche, retrospective and austerely misogynous for as long as it can.' He is watched over by three wise men, and indeed 'never was a budding writer so coddled, so born in the purple, so grateful to his benefactors or so anxious to please them.' Albanus gives Alpdodger books to read and sage advice ('Polish, always polish, constantly removing little awkwardnesses'); Santry gives him books to review, and yet more advice ('Read, never stop reading, be alert, be prolific in your idleness, don't become a miserable hack like me'); Drino – Maurice Baring in real life – 'made fewer appearances, but such as they were made him seem more romantic and enchanting, he left little jokes and vanished into a fairy existence of his own.' 'All three wrote prolifically,' he went on:

> Albanus polished away at his long paragraphs till one wanted to open a window as if a mouse had died somewhere in them. His was an old man's style, and his sentences seemed a slow ascent with a comma or semi-colon at every corner, like a bench, where one could rest a moment and get one's breath and admire the view. Santry wrote hurriedly for a living, vividly and suavely with many fumblings and repetitions except when he was able completely to transfer a page or two from an article he had written on the same subject a few years before.

Back from Rotterdam, Alpdodger quickly falls into his old routine – playing chess with Albanus, dining with Susan Santry, who exudes a 'lunar wisdom', reviewing a batch of travel books, and helping Santry out with the daily round of Grub Street life:

> 'There's always an extra quarter of an hour,' Santry used to say and he would teach Alpdodger how to take last-minute articles direct to the compositors, how to correct page proofs, how to sell enormous review copies to the big bookshops and take old novels in a sack to a man near Waterloo Bridge.

Santry has a daughter, Juliet, aged seventeen, with a 'small dark oval face, a habit of being convinced by everybody, and an exquisite diction, like a fountain in the dark'; and indeed, the MacCarthys had a daughter too, called Rachel, of whom Connolly became extremely fond. Rachel, who later married Lord David Cecil, was, according to the young Richard Kennedy, then serving his apprenticeship with Leonard and Virginia Woolf at the Hogarth Press, 'the most beautiful girl with a smooth glossy head like a seagull'; and although Connolly never fell in love with her – that was to be reserved for her cousin Racy, the daughter of Admiral Sir William Fisher – it may well be that, like Juliet in the Alpdodger version, she provided 'the earliest intimations of the love motif – the love of patriotic Alpdodger for the English rose, that culminates in the ballad of the sea lord's daughter'. Though 'trembling on the brink of love or dislike because she attracts me yet somehow by compulsion of habit against my will,' Connolly regarded 'the MacCarthys' quiet and rather old-fashioned daughter' – Gerald Brenan's epithets – as essentially a friend: they went riding together in Richmond Park and for long walks in Hyde Park; and sometimes he took her out to dinner, a source of future controversy. Best of all, he liked to join the family at Shulbrede, 'the house I have long worshipped and with the family I like best in the world'; and later he remembered

> Early autumn in the woods at Shulbrede – white mist from the valley hanging heavy in the air, Rachel dark-eyed, silent, watching me, Molly blinking and purring by the log fire, Dermod [Rachel's brother] away at Midhurst, bicycling away alone through the dew-damp lanes, into the same mist that creeps over the roses, drowning the smell of woodsmoke with the dank odour of earth and hedgeweeds. Cruel and lovely season, my enemy, my own.

Connolly was bracing himself, unconsciously perhaps, for the onslaught of what he would years later describe as the 'barbarian invasions', the irruption of women into his life; and he was becoming increasingly impatient with much that he had hitherto held dear. He was lonely in London, and Molly MacCarthy was 'the only person who understands anything'; he was beginning to find Pearsall Smith 'rather awful', for the old man had 'to have everything cut and dried till one wishes one had never said it, I can't bring myself to write to him and his mail is growing querulous'; he had to write about Sterne for the *New Statesman* – his first signed review – but found him unreadable; he went down to Oxford, and seemed to Piers Synnott to be 'malicious, boring and boastful. He repeated everything three times and even then it did not appear worth listening to'; after Sicily his letters to Blakiston, though still affectionate, grew cooler and less frequent. Peter Quennell, on the other hand, provided company better suited to a more worldly frame of mind. Since leaving Oxford under a cloud, Quennell had been making his way in London literary life, and, like Connolly, he was one of Desmond MacCarthy's bright young reviewers on the *New Statesman*. As would always be the case, Connolly viewed his old Oxford acquaintance with a complicated mixture of affection and disdain, envy and a diminishing admiration. 'Five minutes with Quennell turns the world like cream in a thunderstorm. Ugh!' he wrote to Patrick Balfour in May 1927, but a couple of months later he reported that 'I have rather come round to Peter, he is so intelligent and so unfortunate and has that kind of acute sensibility which once one has tasted one cannot do without, like a drug.' Quennell used to entertain his girl friends in a flat belonging to Harold Acton, complete with a Chinese servant, and Connolly would sometimes visit him there; one of the girl friends was Nancy Stallybrass, Quennell's first wife, and among those whom Connolly later held responsible for the success of the barbarian invasions.

In July 1927 Connolly toured Normandy with his mother before going on to the Chalet for the last time. In Rouen he felt a sudden longing to see Patrick Balfour, 'even to Ποθος', and scratched 'dear Patrick' on a church wall; it was raining in Houlgate, where they were almost the only guests in a vast hotel with 250 rooms, and he spent the days reading Pindar and Propertius and talking to 'burnished waiters'; and his francophobia was as strong as ever. 'Jesus Christ the French are bloody,' he told Balfour. Theirs was a country of 'mercenary women, sentimental men, corpse-faced children and slag-heap landscapes':

> *Tripe à la mode de Caen*
> French *à la mode de Tooting*
> No wonder my mind dwells on
> A luxury suiting.

From Normandy he went on to the Chalet. Although Sligger told Blakiston that, 'apart from complaining of feeling old', Connolly had been on 'excellent form', Connolly himself thought it a 'foul chalet', and told Molly MacCarthy that he wished he had heeded her advice and kept away. Apart from Roger Mynors, none of the old regulars was in attendance: his fellow-guests, 'a drear lot', included a youth called Markham, who was plain and spotty, wore plus-fours and smoked a pipe ('I can't stand Rugbeians'), and another called Renwick, endowed with 'suet voice, droop eyes and lollop jaw'. Sligger got annoyed with Connolly for sticking the stamps on a letter crooked, and before long they were locked in argument about the Romantic poets, for whom Connolly had long nurtured an abhorrence, claiming that if one liked Milton there was no need to read the Romantics, that he rated Blake far more highly than Keats, and that he would far sooner read Crabbe and Collins than Shelley and Wordsworth: 'I did not pretend that they were better only I thought if one was romantic oneself one could infuse a formal poetry with it and not require to read the poets where it is over-expressed.' 'Don't listen to him, he's jaded,' an anxious Sligger told his charges. He had had enough of dons, Connolly decided: 'O this academic world from which I have always felt estranged, fond of school and hating schoolmasters, fond of learning and made sad by talk of it, is it purely vanity and envy or a deeper antagonism?' In tones oddly prophetic of the poets of the following decade, he confided to his notebook that from now on he wanted to 'sort with comrades that face the beam of day'; was this, and his impatience for action, a sign that he was growing up at last, he wondered? Should he perhaps try to interest himself in politics?

Familiar scenes reminded him of the past, and he buried a baccy tin containing a suitable Greek epigram near a ledge where Longden used to sit and read; but his thoughts were with more recent friends. He longed for news of the Clarks and the MacCarthys; an absence of letters from Molly and Rachel and Balfour stirred ancient worries, never far below the surface and easily aroused, of being unwanted or rejected or forgotten or unloved; a lack of confidence that made him demand high standards of his friends, for in the words of a new friend, Gerald Brenan, 'Since he suffered from perpetual doubts as to whether he was really loved, he would impose severe tests on them. Yet if they satisfied these tests, he might turn away from them, for his love, at least where girls were concerned, fed upon his uncertainty.' He wanted to be helping Desmond MacCarthy in Grub Street, and he worried that Pearsall Smith would try to incarcerate him in Big Chilling; Pearsall Smith, he decided, 'has welcomed disillusion without a nature capable to rise above it, he has been too timid with life to be really afraid and he has had to borrow his philosophy of disillusion as he has had to borrow his analysis of experience.' Most damning of all, 'He went through life like a person who puts on his cork jacket on the first day of the voyage and sits in a lifeboat till the end.'

Connolly kept very much to himself at the Chalet, brooding on a novel – provisionally entitled *Green Ending* – which opened at Gabbitas & Thring and described the misadventures of a young man, recently down from Oxford, who is sent out to the colonies but deserts ship in Gibraltar and ends by committing a murder. Its theme, he told Molly MacCarthy, 'is really the misfortunes that befall someone who is only periodically alive and spends the rest of the time in an imaginative torpor'. To Blakiston he confessed that he found it impossible to invent characters or think of a plot, and that 'when I start to write I become vain, affected and facetious'. As an aspiring novelist he suffered from 'the curse of one's creative intelligence being always so many years younger than the critical'; and although he would dream for the rest of his life of becoming a novelist, and publish not many years later, he never felt at home with the genre, or overcame the problems he had diagnosed.

Pondering unwritten novels was nothing new; what was very different was his sudden, yearning interest in the opposite sex. On the train down to the Chalet he had met a friend of Jane Clark's called Alix, and he found it impossible to get her out of his mind. Alix Kilroy was working at the Board of Trade; she had been travelling with her mother – when first spotted, the two women were embracing in their apartment, prompting Connolly to assume, unchivalrously, that they were a lesbian couple – and the young man liked her at once, taking particular pleasure in the way in which she referred to the Chalet as though it were 'a comic old contraption like the leech-gatherer'.* 'It is both difficult and curious to find oneself suddenly estranged from the male sex and plunged into joy and bewilderment by all encounters with the other', her new admirer confided to his diary. He wrote to Molly MacCarthy to ask whether he could ever be attractive to women, and how he could please them. And, as if this weren't enough, he began to chew over the notion of marriage. Respect, he informed his journal, was the basis of marriage; respect was incompatible with passion; since he was both 'passionate and lustful', it followed that 'unless I marry someone like that the privation of these desires will lead to ultimate infidelity'. Musing deeply on these unfamiliar questions, he made his way home from the Chalet to see what the future would bring.

* Known to the world at large as 'Bay', she remained with the Board of Trade, holding the post of Under-Secretary from 1946 to 1955. She was made a DBE in 1949, three years after she had become the third of Sir Francis Meynell's three wives.

ELEVEN

Yeoman's Row and the Sea Lord's Daughter

Connolly returned to England via Paris in late July 1927. Eager to get on with his new life, and to put behind him the irritations of the Chalet and all it stood for, he was so glad to be back that not even a ghastly lunch on the Dover boat could dampen his spirits. 'Oh, the superb wretchedness of English food, how many foreigners has it daunted, and what a subtle glow of nationality one feels in ordering a dish that one knows will be bad and being able to eat it! The French do not understand cooking, only good cooking – that is where we score,' he confided to his journal. The morning after his arrival he hurried round to see Desmond MacCarthy in Wellington Square. MacCarthy told him that, as a young man, he had been as idle as Connolly was now, and that the result of so much indolence had been to make him ill; undeterred by his youthful bad example, he was discovered lying in bed groaning 'Oh dear, Oh dear,' and contemplating a breakfast of gentleman's relish, chocolate biscuits and Bath Olivers. Leaving his mentor to do battle with the balance of the day, Connolly went on to play squash with Kenneth Clark at Prince's Club, wait in the rain outside the Board of Trade in the hope of catching sight of Alix Kilroy, and take a first look at No 25a Yeoman's Row, a minute maisonette off the Brompton Road which after some hesitation he had agreed to share with Patrick Balfour, and into which he would move on a fairly full-time basis at the end of the following month.

Balfour had been serving his apprenticeship as a journalist on the *Glasgow Weekly Despatch*, and had now found himself a job as a gossip columnist with a London newspaper. 'That'll be the end of him, he'll be a butterfly,' Sligger told Connolly when he learned of Balfour's appointment as 'Mr Gossip' on the *Daily Sketch*, adding that he would inevitably become 'that hard thing, a man about town':* but Sligger's views could be safely discarded, and Connolly's own reactions had been much more positive. He liked the idea of their sharing a flat. 'We will grumble together in the autumn evenings and take huge haystacks of review copies off to sell in a

* He may also, in his capacity as a gossip columnist, have provided the original for the Earl of Balcairn in Waugh's *Vile Bodies*.

wheelbarrow through the green November fog,' he told Balfour; and a month later he confirmed his enthusiasm, adding that although Dadie Rylands had a room to let, this would mean living in Bloomsbury, in part of Vanessa Bell's house. He was keen to have a Persian cat and a gramophone; and given the very different lives they led, and their differing tastes in friends – as befitted a gossip columnist, Balfour was eager to move in Society – 'we must decide on a system of "no apologies" for our guests.' Connolly worried that Balfour's friends would be too social and too high-living, and Balfour shared some of his anxieties. It was essential, he wrote, that Connolly should have a room of his own, so that he could have friends like Blakiston and Longden to stay, just as he might want to invite, say, Christopher Sykes or 'my boys from school'; but if Connolly felt that the problems presented by his own conviviality were insuperable, they should abandon the idea. Evidently Connolly decided to run the risk, and in July Balfour wrote again to say that he had taken Yeoman's Row, paying a rent of six guineas a week, and had engaged a cook, Mrs Egg, for a further 25 shillings a week. 'We'll have a rule that we never have champagne for dinner parties,' he went on: 'I am so sick of it, and so is everybody. Nice Burgundies instead.' He had already alerted his future flat-mate to the possibility of his having an affair with a Mrs Peel, on the grounds that 'one must have an affair with a woman to complete one's experience'; and Balfour's 'womanising' – however half-hearted – was to aggravate Connolly's own feelings of inadequacy and uncertainty in such matters.

They did not move in until September, but Connolly was very taken with his future home. Yeoman's Row was a cul-de-sac, almost opposite Brompton Square and the Brompton Oratory – a part of the world for which, he told Molly MacCarthy, he felt an ancient fondness from the days when he had lived with his parents in the square, and which in those days combined slumminess with upper middle-class opulence. No 25 was a red-brick Edwardian terrace house, the most elegant and evident feature of which was a tall-round-headed studio window with leaded mullions and a touch of *art nouveau* about it. Behind this window was a large hall-cum-studio with a black-and-white chequered floor, which would double up as Balfour's bedroom; the other rooms included a galleried dining-cum-sitting-room, and an upstairs sitting-room, which looked on to a small garden at the back and was to be Connolly's bedroom. He was particularly taken with its 'quaint staircase, and the black high chairs and tables in the sitting-room' – the chairs had a leathery, Spanish look to them – and although the Lock House was unable to provide any towels, he was sure he could lay his hands on vases and eiderdowns.'

Until then though, he had been 'banished to *work* alone – to Chilling'; but although he was reading two or three books a day in his rustic solitude, not a great deal of actual writing was being done. 'Solitude confirms me in my faults, sloth, untidiness, abstraction, morbid imaginings, and scornful arrogance,' the exile confessed; while to Molly he admitted that 'Nearly all my happiness here is dependent on the grossest physical pleasures, lying in a hot bath or hearing the gong go, reading in bed on a windy night or walking down the path on a fine one.' He spent more time than he should stroking the cat or gazing out of the window; he longed to have other people to talk to, and even missed playing chess with Uncle Baldhead; after dinner he danced by himself to the gramophone; he found it impossible to get to sleep until two or three in the morning, and then was racked by nightmares; he began to suffer 'book nausea', hemmed in as he was by reading matter and 'a litter of inky papers that lie about like tea leaves in a sink'. Loneliness and failure to get on with various literary projects were bad for the morale and the self-esteem, and yet Chilling in mid-summer was to inspire one of those tiny, brilliant shards on which so much of his finest writing is found, a perfect justification – to posterity at least – for hours of indolence, in a way that the self-conscious, stiff little fragments of fiction never were:

> Perfect summer's day, which seems the flower of all the summer days in history and makes England incomparably richer than Greece. Went out after dinner and walked down to the shore, where the cat followed me. There were some men cutting up a log of driftwood. The sky was rose and the sea pale green, and though the hills of the Island and the lights of Fawley were clear, there was a thick mist on the shore, through which the men at the timber loomed large as I walked along with the cat over the pebbles. Came back and called up an owl. Bonfires on the air, horses in the mist, the boy scouts singing and their tents glowing in the dark. The black cat very lovely on the garden wall, and the light in a bedroom window shining out over the fields.

Green Endings made slow progress before petering out altogether, but he was beginning to make his mark as a reviewer. His first signed review had appeared on 25 June. MacCarthy had sent him the seven volumes of the Oxford Collected Sterne: ploughing through them had proved an arduous business, exciting complaints of unreadability, but the review itself displayed all the qualities that were to distinguish him thereafter as a reviewer – wit, elegance, a gift for the vivid and arresting turn of phrase, and a down-to-earth, commonsensical note far removed from academic abstractions or the equally arcane philosophisings to which his own letters and journals were prone. He drew on his lethally accurate understanding of human nature to pin-point 'the terrible flaw that dominates Sterne's sensibility, the habit of luxuriating in emotion he thinks creditable, that turns his sympathy to self-congratulation and sets a smirk on all his tenderness', and already his tone was wonderfully assured:

> The tempo of *Tristram Shandy*, for instance, must be the slowest of any book on record, and reminds one at times of the youthful occupation of seeing how slowly one can ride a bicycle; yet such is Sterne's mastery, his ease and grace, that one is always upheld by a verbal expectancy, slow though the action moves he will always keep his balance and soon accelerate till there follows a perfect flow of words that ends often with a phrase that rings like a pebble on a frozen pond.

The opportunity to fling pebbles of his own in public places was immeasurably enhanced when, that August, MacCarthy asked him if he would like to become one of the *New Statesman*'s regular novel-reviewers. It was, as he soon realised, an onerous undertaking; he would be on a fortnightly rota, and MacCarthy would send him as many as fourteen new novels from which to make his choice. After confessing his doubts to his journal – as a highbrow, he would have to find himself praising, or trying to praise, middlebrow novels, he found it hard to be punctual and reliable, and he would have to keep on reasonable terms with Peter Quennell – he decided to accept, and his first contribution appeared in early September. Among the many long-forgotten works he surveyed was *The Hotel* by Elizabeth Bowen; she was to become a lifelong friend, whose work Connolly always referred to warmly in print while admitting in private that he had difficulties in getting through to the end.

MacCarthy wrote to say that he was delighted with his piece: he urged him to get copy in earlier so as to be able to see it in proof, and had some stylistic reservations: 'A good many of your sentences were obscure and it took me the best part of an hour to clear up the obscurities, for it is very difficult to alter other people's script and preserve exactly what they intended to say... Do keep an eye on your long, draggle-tailed sentences and use full-stops more frequently.' But MacCarthy's overall enthusiasm for his new protégé was entirely justified. As George Orwell later pointed out, reviewing fiction on a regular basis is a difficult balancing act, involving a certain suspension of disbelief or standards, in that even the most austere and scrupulous critic may, in his anxiety to find something good in that week's offerings, tend to compromise and be far kinder than he might be in civilian life; or, as Connolly put it after a year's hard labour,

> The great difficulty in reviewing novels is to maintain a double standard – one to judge novels as fiction, and the other as literature. Luckily very few

novels pretend to be literature, but when they do it is necessary sometimes to slate them by one rule and praise them by another.

No one, apart from Orwell, has written better than Connolly about this dilemma facing the reviewer, and in his pieces for the *New Statesman* – regular for the next two years or so, increasingly intermittent thereafter – he combined a rueful account of the reviewer's lot with a lethal eye for the clichés and the banalities and the sad absurdities of the run-of-the-mill novel. From early on he was a forthright and courageous reviewer, warm in his praise but ready to criticise if criticism seemed in order, whatever the writer's reputation or literary allegiance; but although he is remembered as an early champion of writers like Waugh and Hemingway, and as an enthusiastic champion of the Modern Movement, much of the fascination of his pre-war work lies in the insights it provides into the dreams and aspirations of the period as reflected in middlebrow fiction.

Within a very short time, a certain sad cynicism had set in, mitigated and made palatable by comicality and often ferocious wit. 'To read all these books is to be brought face-to-face with the tragedy of the worthy,' he wrote in October, after grappling with new offerings from, among others, Elinor Glyn and Forrest Reid: 'They are all books that it is worth while to have written if there did not happen always to have been something written on the same lines that was better.' Not surprisingly, the reviewer himself was invariably overcome by 'the feeling of obscure guilt that comes after a day spent in this thankless task of drowning other people's kittens.' Most English novels, he decided, and especially those written by women, tended to be autobiographical, and as such blighted by those 'dark spots where the mildew of childhood dreams and school friendships has laid its shadowy web', for 'to write an autobiographical novel is to live on capital, hence only permissible when, like Proust, you know you will not live to write about anything else.' Nor was he afraid to exercise his gift for epigram or paradox: 'The love of life is often not an indication of vitality but the reverse, just as it is the languid vultures that collect round the red meat and the bull that feeds quietly on grass' or 'There is a growing superstition that "real life" is only to be found among clerks and typists; that the deep stream of human experience coils and eddies swiftest round the people for whom is intended every invention, like the film or the feuilleton, that purveys life to those who do not live it.'

Before long Connolly was capitalising on the world-weariness of the seasoned book-reviewer, combining disillusion with a sprightly, sardonic zest. 'By an ever-deepening pile of volumes, a wilder enthusiasm in the publishers' blurbs, and the livelier iris that colours the gay wrappers of the love stories, the reviewer learns to greet the spring,' he wrote; and later he informed his readers of how

> Twice a year, in the spring and in the autumn, the harsh lonely croaking of the novel-reviewer becomes unnaturally loud. There may have been a time when writers were intimidated by this, but now they know better, and continue unperturbed to turn out what is expected of them, sustained by two fallacies: that every human being is capable of writing one good novel out of his own experience, and that everyone who has written one good novel can go on effortlessly producing others. The first object of a reviewer is to get people to write better, and in the present state of the novel, to prevent a great many people from writing them at all.

One novelist whose latest offering was deemed a disappointment was Margaret Kennedy, of *Constant Nymph* celebrity – by a curious irony, this lachrymose tale had owed much of its success to a rave review by the *New Statesman*'s editor, Clifford Sharp, who wrote his editorials with the aid of a pint of whisky and reviewed the odd novel as light relief – but still harsher words were reserved for other contemporaries. Godfrey Winn was pronounced to have 'that rare gift, the pure typist temperament'; to read the concluding volume of Galsworthy's 'Forsyte Saga' was 'to enter a world in which people move who must once, one gathers from their chance allusions, have been human beings. Like paintings on Sicilian carts, like marionettes, the characters recall some buried legend of man's doings.' Nor were friends exempt from his derision. Harold Acton's *Humdrum*, reviewed in the same batch as Evelyn Waugh's first novel, 'reads like a painstaking attempt to satirise modern life by a Chinaman who has been reading *Punch*' – 'such was the treatment I had learned to expect from literary friends,' Acton commented in his memoirs.* By contrast, the humour of *Decline and Fall* 'is of that subtle, metallic kind which, more than anything else, seems a product of this generation. A delicious cynicism runs through the book': this led to a meeting with the novelist and his first wife, Evelyn Gardner, in their tiny terraced house in Islington.

Radclyffe Hall's *The Well of Loneliness* – a novel about lesbianism which became a *cause célèbre* – was, Connolly decided, a 'long, tedious and absolutely humourless book', provoking in its reviewer some thoughts of his own on the subject of 'inversion':

* Relations between the two men became extremely cool as a result – 'Well, my dear, it is *mainly* directed against Connolly,' Acton reportedly told Evelyn Waugh, apropos his first volume of autobiography – but they were eventually reconciled when Connolly and his third wife, Deirdre, visited La Pietra, Acton's house outside Florence.

> It is presumably a plea for greater tolerance, but the world is perfectly prepared to tolerate the invert, if the invert will only make concessions to the world. Most of us are resigned to the doctrine of homosexuals, that they alone possess all the greatest heroes and all the finest feelings, but it is surely preposterous that they should claim a right, not only to the mark of Cain, but to the martyr's crown... Homosexuality is, after all, as rich in comedy as in tragedy, and it is time it was emancipated from the aura of distinguished damnation and religious martyrdom that surrounds its so fiercely aggressive apologists.

Not everything incurred ridicule or damnation, however. Gide's *The Counterfeiters* struck a sympathetic chord in that, like the eighteenth-century poets whom Connolly so admired, it was 'romantic in outlook, classical in style', a hybrid quality that was common among English writers but rare among the French, and it prompted the reviewer to some familiar reflections: 'the hybrid is perpetually haunted by a conviction of exile, his spirit is expended in homesickness, his intellect in trying to discover what is his home. This central loneliness, this native hue of indecision, causes the hybrid to cling desperately to all societies that are at ease in the world...' Arnold Bennett was awarded a pat on the back, for the catholicity of his taste if not for his novels, for

> He is one of the few famous novelists of the last generation that have not entirely lost the respect of youth. This partly because he has resisted the sclerosis of the imagination which drives elderly novelists into the last Tory refuges of English society, so that while Mr Galsworthy and Mr Walpole are borne down the stream of time, humped anxiously on slabs of property like eskimo dogs marooned by the thaw on crumbling pack-ice, Mr Bennett is appreciating Proust and Joyce, and even inducing other people to do so too.

A more obvious champion of the Modern Movement, Wyndham Lewis, was less kindly treated. Of *The Wild Body* Connolly wrote that 'perfect laughter casteth out fear': it was a novel that appealed to those 'who find hair coming out and corpulence coming on', and the author's 'mature and clotted sentences, his prickly and torrid sensibility... drive the reader to mop his brow perpetually as he perspires in the sullen combustible atmosphere of Mr Lewis's highly mannered prose.' 'Once more our English rogue elephant has broken loose, goring and rooting after his favourite quarry, the jungle folk of Montparnasse,' Connolly continued some six months later, reviewing *The Childermass*; but he went on to compare Lewis favourably with 'the majority of our living writers, whose only talent is the galvanic virtuosity by which they are enabled to walk and talk years after their heads have been cut off.' Even better was Hemingway's *Men Without Women*, for here 'We at once enter the front line of modern literary warfare. We are face-to-face with the largest and wildest of the game that Mr Wyndham Lewis chivvies through the warrens of the Rive Gauche, and with the only one of its fauna on whose tail he has tried to place a pinch of commendatory salt.' Combining 'ferocious virility' with a dash of 'strong silent sentimentality', Hemingway 'remains easily the ablest of the wild band of Americans in Europe... at present he is more of a dark horse than a white hope, but his book makes a good test of one's own capacity to appreciate modernity.'

As is always the case, the Waughs and the Hemingways were exceptional items, eagerly seized upon as relief from the 'worthy second-rate', from the genteel 'collection of sincere and respectable balderdash which any young man or young woman who has read too well and loved unwisely is at liberty to create'. Publishers would continue to 'place their dead babies on the critic's doorstep', while the novelists themselves 'dish up yet another pale replica of *Sinister Street* and call it *While Greasy Jane* or *A Young Man's Fancy* according to sex... What can you expect from a slug but a slug track?' Blighted by gentlemanliness and gentility, the English novel seemed doomed 'unless some kind of contraception is practised at the start'; in the meantime, 'It is the inefficiency of these slop writers, stupidly churning out emotions that have already been better expressed, in a dumb replica of the language that was used to express them, that really infuriates the reviewer...'

*

Urging middlebrow novelists to practise some form of birth control was all very well, but Connolly's own attempts at reproduction seemed all too easily doomed to failure – even when, as with *A Partial Guide to the Balkans*, the book had actually been completed, albeit at minimal length. Bobbie Longden, its dedicatee, showed it to David Knowles, who told its author that it was 'the most remarkable and delightful travel book I've read', but Anthony Powell, who had expressed interest in seeing it for Duckworth, turned it down on the grounds that at a mere 25,000 words it was far too short, as well as being insufficiently detailed to succeed as a guide book: 'I liked best the discussion passages in the Handbook, about sulking, traveller's loneliness, friendship and so on,' he wrote, before suggesting that Connolly might like to consider publishing a collection of essays with the firm. Connolly felt it deserved to be rejected, and although he was well aware of its faults he couldn't face the drudgery of putting matters right; but when he remembered that David Garnett was a partner of Francis and Vera Meynell at the Nonesuch Press, he re-submitted the book to him. In the middle of August Garnett wrote to say that he was 'delighted' with it, and that he would like to post the typescript to Francis Meynell, who – appropriately – was on holiday in Dalmatia. A long silence then fell, broken when Garnett wrote to say that although he was still 'tremendously enthusiastic' and thought Connolly 'an enchanting, most amusing and very good writer', one of the other partners was opposed to taking it on, and to break the deadlock it had been decided to submit it to an outside reader; after which another long silence ensued. Connolly approached his old friend from St Cyprian's, Cecil Beaton, about the possibility of his designing the jacket for his 'psychological travel book'; Beaton found it 'odd that a person so devastatingly intellectual should give the impression of so little aesthetic sense. He falters when talking of pictures'; an opinion supported in later years by the painter John Craxton. Garnett, in the meantime, found himself caught between promises rashly made to an author and the opposition of his colleagues. He apologised for 'neglecting you shamefully', but he had been frightfully busy: 'I feel sure that I shall fix up publishing the handbook either with us (for a most favourable report was made on it by an independent reader) or if this should fail with Chatto'; he had hopes that Viking might publish it in the States, but in the meantime perhaps they could meet for lunch to discuss possible revisions? Some three weeks later Garnett sent a contract for the book, expressing the hope in his covering letter that Connolly was hard at work on the revisions, and that once these were out of the way he would press ahead with his book on Spain. Another long silence fell, broken in late January, 1928, by a note to the effect that they were worried about possible libel; and then, on the last day of February, Connolly was sent a cheque for £30. There was no great hurry to publish the guide, Garnett told his author: it might be wiser to wait until the novel had been finished and publish that first, since – keen as they were on it – the guide was unlikely to sell in vast quantities, and the important thing was to do as well as possible with the first book. The advance should be set against whichever came first. He would be very interested to see the diary which Pearsall Smith had encouraged Connolly to write, and he wondered what had happened to the typescript of the guide: had its author lost it by any chance? And with that the *Guide to the Balkans* – all but three pages of it – disappeared for ever.*

* Over thirty years later, when he was playing around with the possibility of writing a second volume of autobiography, Connolly tried to track it down, and asked Sir Francis Meynell if he remembered anything about it. 'I am shocked to think that it was accepted and then (on what seems a flimsy excuse) turned down,' Meynell replied; but he could shed no light on the matter, and the firm's files had been destroyed during the war.

The guide, like *Green Endings* and the travel book on Spain and the diary and innumerable opening pages of novels, vanished into oblivion or incompletion, but in the autumn of 1927 publication in book form had been achieved at last. Desmond MacCarthy, writing as 'Presto', had agreed to provide the verses to accompany some scissor-cuts of historical tableaux by Ada Steiner, to be published by the Medici Society under the title *Mirror of Fashion*. MacCarthy was running late as usual and asked Connolly if he would help him out, paying him £5 and a supper at Kettner's in exchange for his labours. Coinciding with his earliest contributions to the *New Statesman*, it was, Connolly wrote, 'my introduction, to Logan's horror, to the spoils of journalism', and it consisted of a Prologue and two of the twelve stanzas that followed. One can see why Pearsall Smith might not have been best pleased.

In days of old, when art was young
And poetry was always sung
  And men believed in glory
The pictures that they used to make
Were all of Hereward the Wake –
Or good King Alfred's burning cake
  In fact they told a story.

But now that art has found its own
The stories are not often shown
  That lie concealed and furtive;
Enough the pattern on a plate,
Enough a pencil and a slate,
Enough the goldfish in the Tate –
  A plot were self-assertive.

And so I add a rhyme or two
They are not good, they are not true,
  They are an old contraption;
And though they may assist the eye
They will not do to reckon by.
They are umbrellas when it's dry –
  The best film needs no caption . . .

That same year Connolly also contributed a piece, entitled 'Urban Summer', to *The New Forget-Me-Not: A Calendar*, published by Cobden-Sanderson, which had been devised by Kenneth Rae, an Oxford friend, and included among its contributors J.C. Squire, Hilaire Belloc, Vita Sackville-West, Max Beerbohm, Harold Nicolson, Edmund Blunden, Raymond Mortimer, Hugh

Walpole, Rose Macaulay, Clive Bell, Ronald Knox and Lord Berners. It had been devised, Connolly claimed, to 'find material for Rex Whistler and give pleasure to his fashionable friends'; as was its successor, *The New Keepsake*, which was published four years later and boasted an equally eminent list of contributors – including Connolly, whose essay 'The Art of Travel' elaborated on the delights of travelling alone in Spain.

*

With every day that passed, Connolly became more interested in women. He continued for a while to suffer acute 'Alix mania', haunting the Board of Trade in the hope of spotting her leaving work, and to his diary he confessed that she had taught him what his better half desired in a woman. The Alix-like ideal was 'based on the qualities I wish I had, not on those I've got, and requires chastity while I am lustful, common sense while I am intellectual, and humour where I am narrow.' Highbrow women, he decided, 'are exactly what one doesn't want, all their education does is deprive them of their own judgement and supply them with a bigoted devotion to Bloomsbury's. One does not need someone who has read Proust and despises anyone who hasn't but someone who would call it nonsense if they thought it so . . .' Before long he would be taking a rather different line about women who had or hadn't read Proust, but in the meantime, like a vast army of Englishmen before and since, and ex-public schoolboys in particular, he made a distinction between the kind of girls one lusted after, and the decent types one admired and eventually married. Rachel was 'prudent' and Alix had 'something fine and sisterly about her'; but neither prudence nor sisterliness seemed terribly sinful or exciting, and, like many men of his generation, he indulged (or pretended to indulge) his carnal appetites with a touch of low life.

Shortly after his return from the Chalet, Connolly bumped into an impecunious school friend, and during an evening they spent together he tried to persuade him to divulge 'where he found his women'; and from him he learned of a woman called Chica, who lived in South London. Over the next few months Connolly was to spend long hours patrolling parts of London – Whitechapel, Wapping, Rotherhithe, Limehouse and the rest – that must have seemed even poorer and more alarming than their modern equivalents; and now, 'with a sense of dream-like fatality', he made his way over the river to Lambeth to visit Chica in Charnwood Street. Children were playing in the road outside in the 'glaucous twilight', and Connolly felt like a character out of *Sinister Street*; after dining in an Italian restaurant in the Brixton Road off sole, champagne and a cigar, he returned to Chica's drab little room, where they were joined by her friend Peggy and discussed the pros and cons of boys and women. Chica had dark red hair and a very white skin; like many another traveller in exotic places, he 'couldn't help feeling that these people at grips with love and poverty and death had a real simplicity and dignity which made me proud to be their companion and I seemed to learn more from them than from anyone in Chelsea or Bloomsbury.' He was, he told his diary, glad to have spent the night there; next morning he woke exhausted, but still able to relish the 'squalor, remoteness and proximity' of it all. Connolly once claimed that, instead of paying off his debts, he had spent all the money he had raised from the sale of the first editions he had amassed at Oxford – he had already embarked on his career as a book-collector – on a woman; in his journals he recorded some vigorous anecdotes by London prostitutes – many of them employees of the notorious 'Mrs Fitz' – and in one of his unfinished stories a young man makes a narrow escape after a tart has turned nasty over some sums outstanding, and summoned her ponce to her aid.

Connolly moved into Yeoman's Row in September 1927. Pearsall Smith affected to feel shy at seeing his protégé in his new surroundings and fearful of meeting Balfour ('I hope he will like me and treat me well'), while Connolly's own reactions to London living were wildly volatile, swinging from elation to depression within a matter of days, and reflecting his ambivalence about England and the English, and the vagaries of literary life. On bad days he loathed 'this fag end London', thought literature a 'dead form' ('Avoid literary people, they go round and round like water running out of a bath, dregs that can never forgive each other'), and vowed, like many a writer before him, to give it all up:

> Damn life, damn love, damn literature! In other words, damn journalism! Live out of London, drop journalism – yet to quit one made impossible by loneliness, the other by finance. Make £1000 a year, make pots of money out of a novel! Too soft for journalism, too rough for literature, I should be wretched abroad, bored in the country – what can one do?

On good days, though,

> I am just twenty-four and dangerously happy. For once I feel ambitious and desire and believe in my chances of fame. I want to give lavishly to everyone, to enrich life as it is enriching me – granted but the vitality to enjoy life, I will give it everything that has made it enjoyed.

At times like these Yeoman's Row seemed as close to Paradise as Big Chilling on that luminous summer evening:

> I get happier and happier, autumn intoxicates me, so does London, so does Yeoman's Row and the slum children and the evenings spent *à l'ombre des jeunes filles en fleur*... the sun shines through my window, the air is fresh and cold, and the bell rings to take me down, to lunch alone off beer and a cold partridge, before going for a walk in the park.

Shortage of money remained a problem, however, and within a few weeks of moving in he was worrying about the cost of Yeoman's Row, turning off lights and struggling to economise; when gloom set in he missed Shulbrede and even Big Chilling, and found Balfour a 'cold, unsympathetic and estranged' companion who tried to patronise him: 'Being a householder has turned his head, becoming a womaniser has chilled his heart.'

One answer to Balfour's temporary womanising was to join him, and together they laid siege to the *jeunes filles en fleur* – Molly MacCarthy's two nieces, Ros and Racy, the daughters of the formidable Admiral Sir William Fisher, the brother of H.A.L. Fisher, the liberal historian and Warden of New College, Oxford. Before long Connolly had persuaded himself that he was '*madly* in love' with Racy, a 'fair-haired, Grecian, English' beauty who was to loom large in his private mythology as the first great female love of his life. She also provided, in the autumn of 1927, an elegant centre-piece for a vivid evocation of Yeoman's Row and the life he led there:

> Brown and gold – brown curtains and chairs of Yeoman's Row, gold tiles in the fire, the green leaves through the lattice windows, then yellow leaves, then black stems of trees. The lights of Brompton Road, the newsboys outside the tube station as I come back from the *New Statesman* to the gramophone, the warm light, the evening paper and a late tea. Drinking with Patrick on idle Sunday mornings, going to the Film Society, dinners alone at the Ivy, theatres alone in the cold fog. When I say suddenly 'autumn', I first see nothing but brown and gold, then I see three pictures rolled into one, the brown fur rug on my sofa, the two gold cushions, R.'s brown dress against them, her golden face and hair, a glimpse of the trees through the drawn curtain, a wild excitement in the air – still brown and gold the picture changes, a cold wet afternoon by Battersea Bridge, R., slim, golden, slant-eyed, in boy's felt hat and brown jumper, looking down the road and tapping with one foot on the kerb – the swirl of the grey autumnal river, the wet Embankment, the waiting figure against the trees of the park, her marsh-green eyes and yellow hair. Windy twilight on the Fulham Road, the roar of buses, the November dusk, walking away from Elm Park Gardens [where the Fisher sisters lived] in the eddy of fast-falling leaves from plane and elm crushed close on the wind-swept pavement: swirl of the Debussy quartet matching the

> wide curve of the road and the depression in my heart: walking on this windy evening, the lamps just lit and wet with rain, alone along the broad street, brown streets with lights of gold.

The following February both sisters came to a party given in Yeoman's Row by Noël Blakiston's future fiancée, Georgiana Russell. Racy, who 'glowed' with happiness – or so Connolly assured her cousin Rachel – held his hand throughout: 'I have never known anything like it, it seemed like daylight after a tunnel and my youth spouted up like a fountain and Racy balanced on top like a coloured ball.' Ros told Balfour that she didn't see how her sister could possibly marry anyone else, and that their mother, Cecilia, had promised not to interfere with her daughters' choices of husbands. Both girls agreed that they had enjoyed the party more than anything else in their lives.

It proved a lull before the storm, a last glimpse of paradise before summary expulsion; for the following weekend Connolly learned that 'Racy and I are at all costs not to meet again'. Molly, it seems, had told Cecilia Fisher that both her daughters' admirers were 'upside-down' men (i.e. homosexuals), and that

> I had wept and confessed the most horrible things to her (an absolute lie) and wasn't fit for Ros and Racy to know and Cecilia told the admiral and he has forbidden Ros and Racy to write to us, to see us, to get letters from us or ever to have anything to do with us again. Molly must be off her head. It isn't true in the first place, and if it was, it is inconceivably unfair to repeat it.

Ros had written to say that she didn't mind her admirer's reputed past, but that they couldn't disobey the admiral; Connolly, who had 'sobbed myself awake every morning', had sent Racy a frantic letter, and done his best to enrol the support of Rachel and her father, whose obvious duty it was to 'square the admiral'. None of this had borne fruit, but after briefly contemplating the Foreign Legion, Connolly told Rachel that, in order to keep Racy, he would not only sacrifice 'literature and liberty' and concentrate exclusively on journalism, but look around for a regular job as well – indeed, Bob Boothby had, over dinner, offered him £1000 a year as his secretary, but was unable to put his suggestion into immediate effect.

Desperate to understand why Molly, whom he had thought of as one of his closest friends, should have so turned against him, Connolly wondered whether she worried that for Racy to fall in love with him would invariably result in her being 'as wretched as her and Philip (since I can't persuade her that I am not a fairy).' A contemporary of Connolly's at Oxford, and at one stage Lytton Strachey's lover, Philip Ritchie was a brilliant homosexual with whom both Maurice Bowra and, more recently, Molly MacCarthy had fallen hopelessly in love. A year or two earlier Connolly had asked Bowra to make 'good blood' with Ritchie, who had become his 'strongest fancy figure', in a purely intellectual sense; when he learned of Ritchie's death in September 1927 he dropped Molly a commiserative note, while to his diary he confessed that

> Philip's death has given me a nasty jolt – it is the first time that someone who has played a serious though slight part in my own life has actually died, someone whom my greatest friends have loved, someone I would like to have slept with... though he never read anything and never wrote he always seemed to me the most complete intellectual and the quintessence of what was most Oxford. I sympathise with Maurice more than Molly for the latter had a silly mainly physical love affair and to Maurice he was a confessor and an ideal and his death must seem a kind of treachery.

No doubt the admiral would have been unamused to see his daughter engaged to a penniless literary man, let alone one with a real or reputed homosexual past, and it may be that Molly had been temporarily deranged by Philip Ritchie's death; but there is no doubt that she had turned against Connolly, or that their friendship was over. 'The only person I have ever met in the large and varied community to which we belong whom I consider crude enough to be described as Bogus is Cyril Connolly,' she wrote: she despised him for his relentless self-pity – 'he simply seems to me a little ass now' – but above all she hated the fact that he was 'mean with his own money and extravagant with everyone else's'. Though the most generous of hosts and giver of presents, Connolly – at least when young – was thought of as something of a sponger, the kind of man who left the room when the bill was presented, or shamelessly pushed it across the table in the direction of his lunching companion. Frances Partridge had noted in her diary that

> Cyril Connolly has been told by someone how badly he behaves about money, and indeed he used to take poor Rachel out to restaurants, order the most exquisite dishes, and then suddenly find he had forgotten his wallet. Now he takes every opportunity of paying for Rachel in public, saying in his flat voice 'Oh no, I'll pay, or Desmond will be complaining.'

Although he told Desmond MacCarthy that he had behaved 'magnificently' towards him over the whole Racy business, his kindly mentor felt obliged to ventilate the vexed question of money, and Connolly's social standing in general. Some months after it was all over, he wrote him a 'painful letter', which made its recipient feel 'hot and cold' whenever he re-read it. 'I'm not as bad as you make out,' he told his old friend,

> – I'm not a *scheming* cadger, but as to being an opportunist you are painfully right. I'm not disloyal about my friends either, within the margin that conversation allows. I have had a *pariah* sense in a way ever since the Fisher incident last year, a feeling of being a Cain at war with respectable people – not a strong sense, that would be self-dramatising, but *au fond* a vague feeling that all was not for me.

As for not paying his way in restaurants,

> Actually whenever I do have money I usually spend it on my friends, even with the grabbed three pounds I spent quite a lot on giving someone luncheon and then lent him some more – but that side of anyone is always less observed and makes one feel 'Well, I've spent enough on other people, now they can spend some on me.'

He couldn't disguise the fact that he was extremely cross with Molly, but whenever he saw Desmond he realised with a pang 'how many things there were we couldn't talk about and how I should probably never see you with Molly and Rachel again and take down your conversation in my notebooks.' MacCarthy's reply must have given him some of the reassurance he sought. 'You can depend on me (and others) to fight your battles behind your back,' the older man wrote:

> You have power and grace of mind which can triumph over criticism and detraction. You have no idea how quickly the attitude of gossips will change if you determine on independence and guard against those habits into which fascinating hard-up people slip. And out of your wounds and your capacity for every kind of enjoyment will come something which will lead to triumphant recognition – sooner or later. You have the intellectual daring necessary as well as the indispensable power of perception. I believe in you, and I don't readily believe in people's gifts.

Connolly was to remain extremely fond of his old patron, but his former friendship with Molly never recovered. 'Molly seems to have told every mortal soul about my quarrel with her, really she has no dignity and no discretion,' he confided to his journals in July 1928; and although, for her part, Molly may sometimes have missed 'that nice feeling of "Cyril coming to tea presently" which I liked so much and am now regretting,' it seems unlikely that their paths crossed again until 1940, when Connolly was editing *Horizon* and Molly wrote to him about the possibility of Desmond's writing something for the magazine, and suggested that Connolly might like to visit them at their new home, Garrick's Villa in Hampton Court. 'Of course I do not regard you as an enemy and have not for at least ten years,' Connolly wrote back, writing a few days later to thank them both for a 'most *delicious* evening'. Three years later they were in touch again. 'I fear it is as a Rip Van Winkle that I appear before you,' Molly told him, before going on to say how touched she had been by his sending her his love in a letter to Desmond, for 'I feared you regarded me as a *life* enemy'; and after Desmond's death in 1952 she wrote to say how 'I can't thank you enough for your love of Desmond', and invited him down in an attempt to recover 'that delightful "Desmond feeling" that may be lost if there is no record of it'. But gratitude was tempered with dislike: she took grave offence over a particular sentence Connolly included in his affectionate, evocative introduction to *Memories*, a posthumous collection of MacCarthy's essays, complaining that 'That horrible Connolly is like Mr Hyde, how extraordinary it is that we have to submit to this beastly little fellow.'

As for Racy, the innocent instigator of this whole unhappy business, 'divinely English, unawakened, staid', she continued to haunt his imagination for a good many months after the admiral had issued his interdict. Two months after the door had been slammed in his face, he was still in love, though 'meanwhile I can get along very well on egotism, friendship and wenching'. From Paris he asked Patrick Balfour to tell the sisters, if he saw them, that 'I am writing and intending to live in an attic and obscurity.' He was thrilled to learn that Racy had met no one else, but 'wished she was older and had a will of her own': 'I would like to make sure that I wasn't only in love because she was not in love with me, and that one wouldn't get bored by reciprocation.' That same summer of 1928 hope momentarily flickered when Pearsall Smith's friend Bob Trevelyan reported that he had seen Cecilia Fisher in London; despite the admiral's embargo, she claimed to be very fond of her daughter's wayward admirer, and if only he had a regular job she would happily resume contact... He had been in love, Connolly confessed to Desmond MacCarthy, 'with one of those drone-bee passions in which one feels one has left all the best of oneself behind in them. I didn't love like a hero, but like a Maurice [Baring] hero. Timid, gauche, sentimental and when once cowed, cowed for ever – I am only just getting over the old-fashioned idea that women are either angels or tarts.' As time passed he became increasingly convinced that 'Racy's grave beauty and promise of exquisite dignity and repose are too good to be true in marriage – one doesn't go travelling with the Virgin Mary . . . I loved her with the ideally best of myself and the best one is, let alone the best one would like to be, doesn't have a chance.'

Years later, in his fifties, Connolly – who loved to revisit the scenes of his past, in an agony of pain and nostalgia – found himself, 'one blue summer twighlight', 'passing by a mews flat in Knightsbridge where two window boxes were in flower above a painted portico.' A young man stood on the doorstep, a baby in his arms; the door had been opened by 'a laughing girl in nothing but a bath-towel, silhouetted against the light in the hall-way'. Standing outside his old house in Yeoman's Row, Connolly was suddenly overcome by the past; he saw himself as he might have been in the young man with the baby, and Racy as the girl in the bath-towel, and

> Even after twenty-five years I cannot read the jottings of this vanished youth who bears my name without discomfort. Insecurity and the only-child's imagined need for love have stamped him and I remember every detail of his unhappy courtship; the two lovely sisters who captivated the newly-installed young bachelors, the marvellous promise of that autumn, the mischief-making false friend, the apprehensive mother and the furious father who so easily separated us.

Evelyn Waugh wrote expressing admiration for the piece, and in his reply Connolly said that he had returned all Racy's letters to her after they had been forbidden to see one another again, and that she had destroyed them when she married Mungo Buxton. He had seen her only once since then, at the wedding of David Cecil and Rachel MacCarthy; he had hoped to see her at Desmond MacCarthy's memorial service, but only her husband was there. But they did meet again after that: once when Racy and Mungo Buxton came to dinner, and once at Cranborne Chase, where Connolly was 'shirty' at first, affecting not to know her. Racy was, by her own admission, no great reader – as a young man, Connolly was amused by the fact that the only book she seemed to have read was called *Stumps* – but she came across 'One of My Londons' after it had been reprinted in *Previous Convictions* in the early 1960s, and claims to have been astonished to learn there of the strength of Connolly's feelings for her. She remembered him fondly as a friend, who took her to places like the Café Royal and – for all the slurs about his meanness – was generous when it came to footing the bill; and she continued to think of him whenever she heard the song 'Side by Side'.

In those innocent, far-off days when Racy had sat on his cushions in Yeoman's Row and he had walked her home through the dusk to Elm Park

Gardens, Connolly had drawn up a list of the pros and cons of marriage. The reasons against were that he was too poor, too jealous, unsure of his ability to be faithful, not keen on children, too fond of his independence, knew too little of life and women, and would find getting married so embarrassing that he would have to perform it in secret and then disappear to South America. On the other hand, he felt he could make a woman happy, and couldn't fulfil himself until he had done so; for all his worries about infidelity, he felt he was made for monogamy and the 'passion, equality and sane intimacy of married life'; despite appearances, he was not a real bohemian; a wife might make him finish the books he was writing; he saw marriage as an escape from claustrophobic cliques and the demands of Society; he could get over his jealousy, and economise, if married; with luck his wife would be prepared to wait before having any children; divorce was 'fairly easy' if things didn't work out; most improbably of all, perhaps, he saw himself as a home-loving creature who much preferred 'the romance of respectability to the romance of disrespectability; I do long to sit at breakfast with my wife with two newspapers and the marmalade between us . . .' All in all, the pros outweighed the cons; but the eventual object of his uxurious passion, the figure on the far side of the marmalade pot, would prove a good deal gamier than the beautiful sea lord's daughter.

TWELVE

A Young Beethoven with Spots

Connolly's brush with Admiral Fisher not only aggravated his sense of social insecurity, but it reinforced the instinctive dislike he shared with his contemporary, Evelyn Waugh, of the Old Men who ruled pre-war England, and who seemed to embody, together with cheery, beer-swilling middlebrows, with their plus-fours and golf clubs and Book Society Choices, all that was wrong with the country. But however much he may have felt himself to be a *pariah* among the Fishers and their friends, his social life was intermittently brisk, as befitted a flat-mate of Patrick Balfour, and he was getting to know many of the writers of the time. He saw quite a bit of Bob Boothby and Gladwyn Jebb, the future diplomat and British Ambassador to Paris, of the socialite Nina Seafield and Mary Borden's daughter, Joyce Turner, who later committed suicide; he met George Moore and Rosamond Lehmann, whose *Dusty Answer* he much admired; he attended a soirée at Lady Cunard's, where he experienced a 'snobbish thrill at sight of the Prince of Wales walking alone up the wide staircase and shaking hands with Maurice Baring and Diana Cooper at the top', and relished 'the lovely women, the vacant faces of the extroverts, the expression of envy on Clarence Marjoribanks and the incredible stupid air of luxurious abandon on Lady Cunard's face as she danced with the Prince of Wales'; Robert Byron wrote to ask whether he would contribute a story to a still-born 'Enquiry into Contemporary Values' which he and Brian Howard were planning, other hoped-for contributors to which included Henry Yorke and Tom Driberg. But by the end of March the combination of Racyitis and general gloom proved too much, and he made up his mind to go abroad. He had decided to flee London for a while, he told Balfour: he was suffering from persecution mania, exacerbated by the realisation that whenever Balfour gave a party there was never anyone he wanted to ask; he had no women friends, and envied Balfour his dissipation and his success with the ladies; at least he would be able to live cheaply for a time in Paris before going on to stay with the Berensons, whom he had re-met in London. To his diary he confessed a

> general sense of depression and disgust, with usual horror of literature. Last days in London characterised by financial needs, desperate anxiety to get abroad, and deepening passion for low life. Spent every evening exploring London; one should be able to live at least three lives concurrently, and heaven knows how many in rotation...

He arrived in Paris in early April, 1928. 'There is some very good low life there,' he told Noël Blakiston, 'particularly a place called the Bal Colonial where you get the full blast of *le charme nègre*.' In Paris he felt a 'real sense of release, and of life somehow beginning again', as well as a 'growing affection' for the city. Nor was he deprived of female company. 'Had a Moroccan, young and v. lovely, but very cold, competent and costly,' he confided to his journal. He also, or so he claimed, lived with a woman for the first time. She was called Olive, and was probably American; though never mentioned again, she boosted his self-esteem after the Racy débâcle, and 'it shows I can be loved by them, which is important'. He indulged in fantasies of living in a garret with a Spanish mistress, but 'instead I met Cecil Beaton'; he had lunch with Pearsall Smith at Foyot's; he went slumming in Belville and Menilmontant, touring the 'Apache' brothels in the boulevard de la Chapelle, where he posed as a journalist taking notes ('I am rather courageous at that kind of thing'), and the men stood at the bar glaring at the girls who glared angrily back at them. All in all, he decided that he needed to spend more time in the city; he could make use of its low life in a novel, and 'work off my surplus bohemianism'.

After such excitements, life at I Tatti seemed a very dull business. Berenson was 'rather boring except for one or two jokes', though he liked Mrs Berenson as much as before, and was very taken with Nicky Mariano. Piers Synnott was in attendance, 'very piano' and sporting two buttonholes in his jacket; the conversation was formal, the food rich rather than good, and 'my phobia of culture gets so much exercise'. He went to have tea with Percy Lubbock, the writer and authority on Eton life, but found that 'I don't really appreciate these Italianate English and Americans, their huge villas and gardens and rather precious manner'. Lady Colefax and Mrs Otto Kahn ('with £1500 a day!') were staying nearby, and he thought them 'greasy snobs', but he much enjoyed visiting the villa in which Mrs Keppel – an Edwardian beauty and the former mistress of Edward VII – had installed herself with a suitably raffish entourage that included Mrs Winston Churchill. The villa had an Edwardian feeling to it which Connolly found immensely congenial, redolent of gun-rooms and huge breakfasts and long hours spent poring over the English newspapers. Among Mrs Keppel's visitors were her daughter Violet Trefusis and her husband, 'an intelligent soldier, just back from Russia': Connolly took an immediate shine to Mrs Trefusis, whom he found 'very attractive, rather heavy and vicious-looking and the only person here who one feels is really modern.'* Even so, Connolly found he had Racy 'more on the brain than ever'; in losing her, he told Balfour,

> I've also lost the best of myself. I shall never be in love so youthfully and innocently again – I feel exiled from the Edwardian world and not hard-boiled enough to fit easily into the modern. With the really smart, the really Bohemian, or the really low one is not reminded of this respectable English Eden...

Notions of Eden – synonymous with 'Grace, Greenness and Security' – and the Fall, of homesickness and the restless search, through art and travel, for a physical and spiritual home, remained as pervasive as ever:

> All activity arising from distress arising from homesickness. The romantic's fondness for childhood and children and cats is his fondness for their state of grace; this transferred to fondness for his own childhood – which all romantics associate with grace and security – security also found in pneumatic bliss (bright star).

The lure of empty Eden, acknowledging as hopeless the search for retrieved grace, leads quickly to obscurity, listless renunciation and the love of Death.

> Hence all romantics are soft-boiled, because the background/keynote of every romantic is a religious sense. The romantic is a spoiled priest just as the prose writer is a spoilt poet...

Back at the Keppel villa, though, 'I am expected to entertain every pig-tailed creature that is towed up by aunt or mother, they seem to think I am a nymphomaniac'; and the humdrum realities of life intruded in the form of a

* He remained on friendly terms with Mrs Trefusis, later to achieve a certain notoriety as the lover of Vita Sackville-West. Peter Quennell used to tell a story of Connolly going to stay with her in Florence, in the Villa Ombrellino, sometime before the war. He brought with him a virulent flowered shirt, and the butler, assuming it to be night-wear, laid it out on the pillow. Mrs Trefusis showed a party of guests round the house, including Lady Hore-Belisha, whose husband, ultimately immortalised by the Belisha beacon, was the Minister of Transport. None of them failed to notice the flowered shirt on the pillow. Next morning, quite unsuspecting, Connolly appeared by the pool in the shirt, and was mortified when jokes were made about his wearing the same shirt in bed and by day. Back in London, he found an excuse to ring Lady Hore-Belisha's husband:
CC: 'By the way, please tell your wife that I don't wear my day shirts in bed.'
H-B: (frostily) 'I hardly think she would be interested.'

post-dated cheque sent off to Yeoman's Row – 'the best I can do' – to cover his share of the rent.

From Florence he took a train to Venice, which reminded him of the Oxford Canal, and so on to Yugoslavia by way of Trieste. In Zagreb, after visiting a 'cabaret', he took a girl into a vineyard, where they lay on the ground and kissed beneath the vines. From there he travelled on to Hungary, Vienna, Prague and Berlin, where he had arranged to meet Gladwyn Jebb. Through Jebb he met Harold Nicolson, who had recently been appointed Counsellor at the British Embassy. Nicolson was 'rather a big man, red face, nice hazel eyes, small mouth, moustache, looks absurdly young, dresses like any casual amateurish Englishman... Appears a *faux bonhomme*, but is not one really'; and although relations between the two men became, and were to remain, fairly fraught – from the beginning, Connolly thought the older man 'rather protean and slippery, the adaptable diplomatic manner' – Nicolson was elevated, for the time being at least, into his pantheon of heroes. 'I like him more than anyone I have met since Desmond and Maurice Baring,' he wrote:

> ... I like the way he does his work, managing everything with so little fuss, and so much perspicacity, and not being taken in by any of it all. Beautifully arranged life as a writer, a father, a gentleman, a husband, a friend, and a man of action. I observed all this after being told that he was a cad and that one could not trust him.

Nicolson's wife, Vita Sackville-West, hated Berlin and the diplomatic life and had decided to stay at home in England, and so Jebb and Connolly stayed with him in his flat in Brückenallee. Together with the composer and writer Lord Berners and Ivor Novello, the composer of musical comedies, they embarked on a 'dreary round' of homosexual night-clubs, at the end of which Connolly and Novello went out to supper together. Doubtless Jebb was relieved to miss the meal, since he had taken an instant dislike to Novello, whose advances to him were 'imperiously rebuffed'; but Connolly was rather taken with the little Welshman, and 'got on well with him by hauling my standards to half-mast and practising a little self-effacement'. The following day they were joined by Christopher Sykes, a friend of Balfour who was also attached to the Embassy and had recently returned from Persia.

'He is very clever, but a *sponge*, and a terrible mischief-maker; and the more dangerous because he knows how to make himself charming,' Eddie Sackville-West had warned Vita apropos her husband's visitor, but for the time being all was sweetness and light. 'Cyril came yesterday,' Nicolson wrote to his wife, at home in Long Barn:

> Like the young Beethoven with spots; and a good brow; and an unreliable voice. And he flattered your husband. He sat there toying with a fork and my vanity, turning them over in his stubby little hands. He tells fortunes. Palmistry. But the main point of him is that he thinks *Some People* an important book. *Important!* And it was just scribbled down as a joke...

Smoothing the path before him, Connolly had earlier told Jebb, who had passed it on to their host, that he thought Nicolson's *Some People* – which consists of light, amusing sketches from diplomatic and literary life – one of the three English novels written since 1900 that were actually worth reading, the others being Norman Douglas's *South Wind* and Aldous Huxley's *Antic Hay*; in his diary, however, he thought otherwise, deeming it a 'most unpleasant book' that might have been written 'by an undergraduate trying to combine Max Beerbohm and Aldous Huxley with a touch of Beverley Nichols'.

Jebb and Connolly had agreed to travel through Germany and Czechoslovakia together, and after saying goodbye to their host – who had just been joined by two young officers from the Blues in search of brothels and 'smutty cinema' – they set off in Jebb's blue Darracq for Dresden, Prague, Bavaria and the Rhineland, before parting company at Dusseldorf. As they trundled along they agreed that they were too good for whomever they fell in love with, and Connolly enjoyed a 'real sense of balmy convalescence and impending cure'; Jebb had restored his faith in friendship, and he longed to see again both Blakiston and Longden, but Longden in particular. In a night-club in Prague they found themselves consorting with Russian émigrées; Connolly seemed drawn to a particularly hideous woman, and when Jebb queried his choice he answered, very loudly, 'We needs must love the lowest when we see it!' So well did the two young men get on that they discussed the possibility of their sharing a flat together.

After leaving Jebb, Connolly made his way to Paris, where he took a room in the rue Delambre. Money remained a problem. In May Pearsall Smith wrote to say that he hated lending money, but would let Connolly have £5 on the understanding that it must be paid back; some weeks later, in response to a 'harrowing telegram' he sent a further £3, followed by another tenner to allow his prodigal secretary to come home. In the meantime, Connolly had written to say that the £3 wasn't enough, since he had to pay for his room as well as his travelling expenses; the *New Statesman* had failed to produce four guineas owing him, as a result of which he had been reduced to living off 'a bowl of porridge and a ham sandwich' for the last two days. At this stage in what turned out to be a long and lurid letter, the penitent (if aggrieved) man of letters handed over to his *alter ego*, Joe Congothly, whose tale of high living – addressed to 'Dear Governor' and written in a kind of pseudo-Cockney – made it clear that any shortage of funds was hardly to be wondered at. According to Congothly, he had walked from Montparnasse to the Opéra in the hope of cashing his benefactor's cheque. Barclay's Bank wouldn't honour it because it hadn't been crossed, and he was walking away feeling sorry for himself when he bumped into Evan Morgan, a rich socialite whose father, Lord Tredegar, had made a fortune from coal in South Wales. Morgan had invited him out to dinner, and after a swim in the Lido they had gone on to the Ritz for drinks. Drinks were followed by more drinks and a chance encounter with two English girls in the Café de la Paix. Somehow a Spanish night-club merged into its Russian equivalent and then an American restaurant, where Congothly met the two girls again. One of them claimed to be the only lesbian in Blackpool, prompting Congothly to a fine display of wit, worthy, he felt, of *Trivia* ('Do you know Lesbia, I said – Lesbia who? – Les'be a nice girl now'). A Jew called Cohen, who claimed to be a friend of Harold Nicolson's, then tried to seduce Congothly in a taxi, and had to be forcibly ejected. All this, Congothly explained, had cost him a fiver – and, to make matters worse, he had lost his silver cigarette case in Sylvia Beach's famous bookshop, Shakespeare & Company.

Momentary succour was to hand in the form of an officer on leave from the Indian Army who knew the Major, and bought him a 'damned good dinner', and a young American girl – a Bryn Mawr graduate and 'a lesbian like the rest of them' – who lent him 100 francs in exchange for his helping her to finish a poem she was trying to write. What with the lights and the drinks and the noise and, above all, the girls – 'O Jesus if you saw the girls,' Congothly told his patron, hardly the right man to try to enthuse on the subject, 'all laughing, God, and every bloody one with an easel and pen and all so bloody bad and so confident and happy' – England was going to seem 'flat as a baby's head and smooth as its bottom'.

Mara Andrews, the poetry-writing lesbian, was to play a pivotal role in Connolly's life, and her eventual suicide was noted in *The Unquiet Grave*. Connolly had met her first in the Select Bar in Montparnasse after returning, rather drunk, from dinner in a Russian restaurant. She had with her a red-haired friend called Helen Ashbury, whom he thought a bit dull; but he liked Mara for her 'frankness and sincerity, her boys' clothes and rather talented unhappiness', and took her to the Bal Nègre. He quizzed her in detail about her lesbianism, and found that 'she held much the same views as I held in my best period (Noël and Bobbie) as a fairy'. Although she pretended to be in love with an Austrian called Fredl – better known as the writer and editor Alfred Perles – her real love was for another eighteen-year-old called Jean Bakewell, who had been with them in Paris, and would be returning, but was in the meantime at home in Baltimore. Back in London, Connolly soon forgot 'the frail and passionate lesbians nobly misadventuring through love and literature and youth'; but their time would come round again.

*

On his way back to London, Connolly stopped off in Kent to stay with his new friends the Nicolsons – 'Harold and Vita are the perfect pair' – at Long Barn; afterwards he wrote her a long letter about her poem 'The Land', 'begging not to be considered a neo-Bloomsbury young man'. While staying with the Nicolsons he ventilated, with Balfour, his worries about whether he could, and should, stay on at Yeoman's Row. He was worried about money, didn't like being tied down, dreaded jeopardising their friendship, feared that Balfour would come to resent him: in short, 'Friendship, which survives separation, does not survive the small vexations which CVC's casualness and indigence will always bring on.' 'I believe too,' he went on, 'that our different choice of sex would in time begin to tell on us – through our corresponding choice of friends.' As for the possibility of sharing a flat with Gladwyn Jebb,

> Of course I shouldn't be so happy living with Gladwyn – he is rather obtuse and lacks most of the human emotions which make us have such fun at the Yeo. But he is good for me because he is not interested in comfort and is rich enough to get on without it – and I am afraid of him. We got on pretty well travelling but he is not a man one would expect to share a thrill of any kind . . .

As it was, nothing came of sharing a flat with Jebb, who got married instead and virtually dropped out of Connolly's life thereafter, briefly resurfacing over thirty years later to warn him against feeling tempted to admire 'that crook Philby'. In July Connolly wrote to say how relieved he was to learn that Balfour's new flat-mate was a bore, and that he was working on a novel in which he planned to 'glorify the Yeo'. The most obvious evidence of this is a fragment called 'The English Malady'. Miles, who writes speeches for politicians, shares a house with the Hon. Hugo Alcheapcharm, a gossip columnist, with whom he has been friends since Oxford ('both had been debagged on the same evening'). Both young men 'wore the stigma of their university, a facile, slightly shabby charm, a rather unscrupulous careerism and an opportune belief that there existed a short cut to every experience which only they knew how to take'. Miles is always in debt to the grasping Hugo; and although Hugo's father has come down in the world to such an extent that he has been reduced to living at 17a Montbretia Terrace, Bournemouth, his son is a relentless social climber. Most evenings Hugo has to go out for his work, but when he is at home he likes to fill the studio, with its 'fake musicians' gallery', with his grand friends; on such occasions he often asks Miles if he wouldn't mind spending the evening with an aged aunt. On the rare evenings they spend together, 'Hugo would fidget, strum on the piano, arrange his press cuttings and decide to go and see if there was anyone at the Café Anglais'. And although Hugo sees in Miles 'the first symptoms of a very unpleasant and infectious disease called Failure', the world that he inhabits seemed as predatory and exclusive as a 'tank of alligators'.

Connolly's feelings about Yeoman's Row mirrored his ambivalence about England in general. 'Back in England I feel nothing but an intense disgust at its stupidity,' he noted glumly in his journal: '... really it is the most deplorable country, Americanised without America's vitality, or America's variety of race'. Its only assets, it seemed, were 'the climate, the countryside, the children, the presence of a few kindred spirits in rebellion, the country houses, the fact that I speak the same language as its female population, that Robert Longden and Racy Fisher live there, that it is in easy reach of the Continent'. His vision of the England of the future was dispiritingly accurate. Saving the countryside would merely convert it into an open-air museum; under siege from the crowds and the semi-detacheds that were snaking their way out from the suburbs along the new arterial roads, soon 'England will be a slagheap city in a rubble field, stogged bottles in the stingy grass, burdock and peeled hoardings stretching down to a litter of boots and halves of empty grapefruit cast up by a bathwater ocean on an insanitary shore...'

Nor was London any better, at least for hard-up literary men:

> One really cannot love London. It is disappointing in every way. A foggy, dead-alive city, like a dying ant-heap. London was created for rich young men to shop in, dine in, ride in, get married in, go to theatres in, and die in as respected householders. It is a city for the unmarried upper class, not for the poor. Every artist and writer must feel a sense of inferiority in London unless he is (like Browning or Henry James) a romantic snob – or else fits into the Reynolds-Johnson tradition of Fleet Street, Garrick, good burgundy and golf. Arnold Bennett is the English Bohemian. Of course, there are Bohemians, but they have to be smart ones, otherwise they are afraid to show themselves; without a quartier, without cafés, their only chance is to get rich and fashionable and give cocktail parties...

Although on good days he still felt the old exhilaration, liking nothing better when in London than to 'run my fingers through the town's limp body, to caress the lax pulsating city as rashly, as apprehensively as a Greek might an Amazonian, or a small spry leopard', he pined for the lights and the cafés and the noise of Montparnasse. 'It is ghoulish to be poor in London,' he told Desmond MacCarthy, for 'London is like those old-fashioned prisons where one can have luxuries if you pay for them, and the poor prisoners not unnaturally batten on their friends.' He felt himself adrift between different worlds, in none of which he felt entirely at home – 'I can't really fit into smart Bohemia, I hate the metallic voguey London as much as the Mr Punch and *Tatler* London' – and all too often the city brought out his sense of being an outsider whom nobody really loved:

> It takes time for a young man to get used to London, as opposed to undergraduate friendships. One is used to spending whole days with one's friends and talking far into the night. The London friendship, with its brisk bouts of clique life over a luncheon table, its occasional accidental heart-to-hearters at a chance meeting in the street, appals and horrifies the young man who is used to walking into someone's room after breakfast and going away several hours after dinner. When I first came to London I was always convinced of a plot or a grievance when people walked out of my life for a few weeks...

One answer to this nostalgia for an undergraduate past was the company of old friends – and of Bobbie Longden in particular. This was in fact to prove his swan song, but its effects were as potent as ever; so much so that 'the main feature of this summer has lain in being with him – has been in lying with him'. In July Longden came down to stay at Big Chilling for a week, and for a few idyllic days it seemed as though the barbarian hordes had retreated and life had resumed its ancient savour. They breakfasted in their dressing-gowns and walked and sailed and swam and drove down the Meon Valley on a luminous summer evening that was to acquire the same glow in retrospect as his visit to the temples at Girgenti with Noël Blakiston the previous year; it was as though they were back at Eton, a 'perfect blend of warm Hellenic paganism, recollected boyhood, and original sinlessness'.

Early in August the two young men travelled steerage to Hamburg in the SS *Deutschland*, and then on by sleeper to Berlin to stay with Harold Nicolson. Nicolson had rented an apartment on the lake at Potsdam for the summer: it was extremely cramped and the landlord had failed to empty a brimming chamber-pot, which greeted Nicolson on his arrival, but Connolly found it luxurious, with boating and bathing to hand and Berlin within easy reach. The third guest was Raymond Mortimer, with whom years later Connolly was to share the honours as the *Sunday Times*'s two lead book reviewers, as umbilically linked in the minds of the reading public as Fortnum & Mason or Laurel and Hardy. A faun-like figure who combined waspishness with great kindness, 'Tray' Mortimer was nine years older than Connolly, and since leaving Balliol he had been making his way as a critic and reviewer; he was on good terms with Desmond MacCarthy, Harold Nicolson, Aldous Huxley and Eddie Sackville-West, and 'except for Philip Ritchie, was the only Oxonian to be accepted by Bloomsbury who thought him incurably "frivolous", with a frivolity of which they were secretly proud.' With his 'mass of black wiry hair' and his 'thin dark excitable face', he had a 'smile faintly reminiscent of Voltaire and a look, perhaps, of Locke' – appropriate comparisons, since he had a particular love of the eighteenth century, and of eighteenth-century France above all. Like Desmond MacCarthy, whom he would eventually succeed as literary editor of the *New Statesman*, he had difficulties in writing full-length books; but his own ambitions were modest, and he was not blighted by comparable feelings of regret. Years later Connolly wrote that Mortimer's 'younger self can best be pictured as entering a room, a little on tip-toe, like Horace Walpole, one hand extended, the other bearing a small present, an expression of slightly mocking cordiality on the face as he begins to describe his latest aesthetic adventure.' He was not, perhaps, the easiest of men to like on first acquaintance, and Nicolson reported to his wife that 'Cyril and Tray are very suspicious of each other, and stalk round each other with their hackles up like two poodles.' But such initial fencing was soon put behind them: Mortimer remembered that Connolly's 'talk and company proved even more delicious than I expected,' while a relieved Sligger was delighted to learn that 'my fears were groundless and that you and Raymond Mortimer got on like houses on fire'.

Apart from expeditions to Hamburg and Lübeck, most of the time was spent reading and discussing life and literature, with the three writers doing most of the talking and the future Headmaster of Wellington* keeping his thoughts to himself. Both Connolly and Nicolson wrote detailed accounts of their discussions, Connolly's in the form of a marvellously elegiac essay

* After teaching at Christ Church, Bobbie Longden was appointed Headmaster of Wellington; where, for reasons unknown, he seems to have taken against W.H. Auden. 'Thank you too for your harsh words about Bobbie Longden,' the poet wrote to Connolly shortly after publication of *Enemies of Promise* in 1938: 'That dishonest fascist shit has said that I shall never enter the grounds of Wellington College as long as he is the headmaster.' Longden was killed a year or two later when a German aeroplane, making its way home, unloaded its bombs over the school. According to A.J. Ayer, the Headmaster remained 'exposed like a good sea captain, until he had shepherded the boys into their shelters' – provoking from Robin Dundas, a fellow-Student of Christ Church, the unkind comment 'Late as usual'.

entitled 'Conversations in Berlin', which Desmond MacCarthy eventually published in his magazine *Life and Letters*, the first issue of which appeared in June 1928, with financial backing from Lord Esher. Connolly suggested that to have read Proust all through was a test of intelligence, 'something that would draw a definite line between Bloomsbury and Chelsea'; Nicolson thought this was nonsense, that whole armies of 'smart and stupid people' – Lady Gosford among them – had dutifully ploughed their way through Proust, and that it was quite wrong to equate culture with intelligence. Both Nicolson and Mortimer agreed that 'perfect intelligence was an absolutely free mind gifted with infinite curiosity, hence able to grasp and illuminate any non-technical subject'. Connolly replied that this was exactly what he lacked – 'Obscurity was my tonic, and I believed in and practised incuriosity. I hated well-informed people with fluent general knowledge and vivid curiosity about contemporary problems, they drove me to the Dark Ages.' He was, he said, 'only interested in that part of the present relevant to my imagination; for instance, I seldom went to a concert, but when I found a tune I liked I made it last as long as possible. I treated all the arts as a Narcissus pool; when I found no reflection I was absent-minded and bored.'

From there they went on to discuss daydreams. Mortimer said that, having no imagination, he never indulged; Connolly, on the other hand, 'brooded and vegetated for hours over the past, going over conversations and characteristics of people. I could sit for two or three hours chewing the cud or indulging in daydreams over the near future.' But according to Nicolson, Connolly confessed that most of his daydreams consisted of adventures in which, disguised as a sheikh and muffled in white scarves, he captured European tourists – sparing only Bobbie Longden, who was duly grateful; and with 'Bobbie so lately restored to me', Connolly felt – on one especially beautiful evening, when they dined by the water and 'two brown half-naked boys paddled by in a canoe, emerging like bronze savages out of the night, and disappearing as naturally into it again' – that, like his host, he had never been so happy before, and would probably never be as happy again.

From Berlin, Connolly travelled down to Villefranche in the South of France to spend eight days with General Spears and his wife, the novelist Mary Borden. The Spears' villa was a nucleus for the kind of London social life he most wanted to avoid: 'nothing memorable was said,' he couldn't avoid bumping into Godfrey Winn and disliked having to associate with Basil Bartlett, and although the Fisher family were holidaying further round the coast, he managed not to think about Racy. Greatly relieved to make his escape, he moved on to Barcelona, where he met Longden again and picked up a welcome £7 mailed out by Pearsall Smith. Spain seemed to him 'what drugs or women are to other people, an anguish, a *soif malsaine*, a kind of thrilling vice': they spent five weeks there together, bathing in rivers and sleeping rough, before returning dismally to London, to

> General dissatisfaction and distress... Unpleasant sense, not only of being just where I was this time last year, but of being practically just where I was the year before. As homeless, futureless, hopeless and unestablished as ever. Shall I live in Paris or the country? I am also less interested in literature, if anything, and not really interested in life, no sign either of the flow of natural high spirits that I had last year...

Once again, his life teetered uneasily between gloom and elation, high society and low life. Bob Boothby lent him his flat in Pall Mall in October, and Raymond Mortimer and Gladwyn Jebb mocked its decor; he drew up long lists of friends gained or lost or 'in storage'; he went to a grand party at Boulestin's at which the guests included Ethel Sands, Anna May Wong and Arnold Bennett, who told him he wrote 'damn well' ('I was speaking to Clifford Sharp* the other day and I said, tell me, who is this fellow C.C., who is he? Well there's nothing to tell, said Clifford Sharp, he's just C.C., he said, that's all. Well he writes damn well, I said, he knows as much as I do'); and Gerald Brenan introduced him to his friend Lily Connolly, an eighteen-year-old prostitute, a fascinating girl with 'a music hall style of wit' whose friends included a prostitute with a wooden leg and another who liked to dress up as an Edwardian governess with a pince-nez on her nose.† Brenan was then sharing a flat with another prostitute called Winny Stafford, with whom he lived on terms of chaste camaraderie; Connolly thought of him as someone who knew about life in the raw, and shared his fascination with the London underworld. In 'The English Malady', Miles goes to see his friend Beaton, a 'quiet priestly creature of military appearance' – Brenan had served in the First World War, and still sported a military moustache – in his rooms in Bloomsbury. Like Brenan, Beaton is fascinated by working-class girls on the game, and likes to take them home and listen to their refined turns of phrase ('You are a funny boy, fancy wanting to kiss me'),

* 'A massive man, red in the face, handsome, a glaring editorial chunk, full of drink' – V.S. Pritchett's words – Clifford Sharp was the legendary editor of the *New Statesman*, then housed in a rickety building next to a pub in Great Queen Street. With Sharp drunk for much of the time, the magazine was increasingly rudderless. Desmond MacCarthy had lost interest, and was devoting more and more of his time to *Life and Letters*: more often than not he was out of the office when the magazine was put to bed, and when Pritchett first visited the magazine in 1928 he was told that the literary editor hadn't been sighted for months.

† Another of Lily Connolly's admirers was the novelist Patrick Hamilton, who described her touchingly as the streetwalker Jenny in *Twenty Thousand Streets Under the Sky*.

but never actually sleeps with them. Miles – who hopes, in vain, that Beaton will find him a woman prepared to go to bed with him for nothing – is planning a picaresque novel about contemporary England: during his researches he encounters Mrs Plough, a madame who lies in bed with three overweight dogs ('Now I suppose you want a bit of fun, five guineas please and 'ere's a whisky-and-soda – now 'oo 'ave I got tonight? There's Billy, she's my clean 'ore . . .'), and a tart called June, whose Mayfair flat 'was of a kind he was beginning to know. A stuffy flat over a Mayfair garage, silk cushions, green sofa, gramophone, decanter and the telephone inside an elaborate doll.'

Nothing could have seemed farther removed from June's flat or Mrs Plough's bedroom than Sledmere, the Yorkshire country house in which Connolly spent the Christmas of 1928. It belonged to Sir Richard Sykes, the head of a Catholic family, whose younger brother, Christopher, Connolly had met in Berlin with Harold Nicolson earlier in the year. Sir Richard 'appealed to all the rake and Oppidan in me', and the snow-covered country and tobogganning and the bang of twelve-bores and draining glasses of port and brandy after dinner with men in red coats seemed wonderfully evocative of the 'grim rich game-pie England of eighteenth-century squires, yellow waistcoats, brown woods, top boots and leather gaiters'. Apart from his host, the others in the house included Christopher Sykes, his sisters Angela and Freya, and Freya's husband, a lawyer named Richard Elwes. Once again, Connolly's experiences were reflected in a fragment of fiction. Desperate to get away from Hugo for a day or two – early in November, Connolly had given up Pall Mall and briefly returned to Yeoman's Row – Miles goes to stay at Nonsuch, a country house in the North of England. As the train hurtles north, it begins to snow – much to Miles's relief, since he's terrified of horses, and hopes that the bad weather will put paid to any hunting or riding. The chauffeur who meets him off the train confirms that all the meets have been cancelled ('Too bad. I was looking forward to a day out'), and suggests some badger-digging instead. Nonsuch is a graceful Palladian house, and its inhabitants share a 'quality of great fairness of hair and complexion, a languid elegance, something immature and not quite grown up'. The butler relieves him of his rusty suitcase with a look of evident disdain, and when Miles goes up to his room he finds that his things have been laid out 'in such a way as to expose all the imperfections of his wardrobe'. Over dinner Miles conducts 'a silent guerrilla warfare' with his enemy the butler so as to persuade him to refill his glass with the excellent champagne on offer. The conversation turns to hunting, and Miles asks the two sisters whether they have read Anthony Powell's *From a View to a Death*, and whether it's true that horses are allergic to intellectuals. After dinner the men drink port round the dining-room table before rejoining the girls for a game of bridge; and as he lies in his four-poster bed that night, Miles realises that, for once, he feels entirely happy:

> The load of inferiority, the incipient persecution mania began to lift... He thought of his bedroom in London and Hugo's face when he seemed to be using too much geyser, he thought of Beaton's uncertain slumbers while Winnie danced, of the dogs' hairs on all the coverlets at Mrs Plough's, and he felt security, and slept.

Soon after his return from Sledmere in early January, Connolly left for Paris with Richard Sykes; and no sooner had he arrived than he set out to find Mara Andrews and the rest of her *petite bande*. In September Helen Ashbury had written to say that she was in London, and suggested a meeting. Balfour had opened the letter but Connolly, overcome by unnecessary shame at what she might or might not have said, had stuffed it unread in his pocket, and never got round to reading it until after he had moved into Bob Boothby's flat in Pall Mall. Eventually he got hold of Helen's address in Paris, and through her he made contact with Mara. Mara rang and left a message for him to ring back. When he did so, a husky voice – not Mara's – answered her phone ('You're welcome,' it said). Connolly explained that he was just about to leave for London from the Gare du Nord, but had enough time to rush round and say hello. He was met by Mara's mother, who took him upstairs, introduced him to Jean Bakewell, and left the two of them together. A whole new phase of his life had begun.

THIRTEEN

Jeannie

'A tall dark girl with a pale oval face, a slightly sullen expression and short boy's hair', Jean Bakewell had been born in August 1910, in a 'hideous green house' in Pittsburgh that overlooked an abandoned quarry now used as the city dump. Despite this inauspicious setting, her family was well-off on both sides: her father's family had made their fortune in steel in Pittsburgh; her mother, more grandly, was descended from Virginia plantation-owners, and through some Philadelphia connections she was related to Logan Pearsall Smith. According to a brief account of her early life which Jean scribbled on the virgin pages of one of Connolly's Oxford notebooks, supposedly given over to John Wyclif and the Peasants' Revolt, Mr Bakewell was a bad lot, sexually over-charged and given to drinking whisky from the bottle while driving at speed in an open car; but since the memoir seems obsessed with sex, and its author's early interest in masturbation and 'coprophagy', and reads as if written to shock and impress her new admirer, a certain scepticism may be in order. According to her lurid version of events, Jean's mother, who was pretty, flirtatious and, like her eldest daughter, a disastrously heavy drinker, derided her husband for his refusal to join up in 1917, presenting him with a bunch of white feathers as a mark of her disesteem; though passionate by nature, Mrs Bakewell 'didn't believe in fucking', and it may have been in revenge for the white feathers that her husband broke down the bedroom door and took her by force. The result was brother Tom, a sickly child and the youngest of three siblings – the middle one of whom, Annie, was 'amazingly attractive, small and pert with large liquid eyes', provoking spasms of jealous rage in her older sister, who as a child was 'untidy and conceited and most bad-tempered'.

Not surprisingly, perhaps, neither daughter had much time for their father – still less so since he was alleged to climb into bed with them 'and slightly toss us off. I saw his penis once. It was enormous . . .' No doubt they were mightily relieved when, in 1918, Mrs Bakewell divorced him on grounds of mental cruelty. The family then moved to California, where according to Jean further horrors lay in store in the traditional form of a man in a mackintosh, who offered the two girls a lift and then proceeded to whip out an object the colour and size of an aubergine ('I was very embarrassed and said I thought it was lovely'). Back in upper New York State, Mrs Bakewell married a distant cousin called Daniel List Warner, a mild, diminutive soul who came from an old Virginia family, and by the time her daughter met Connolly was living happily in the country at Woodbrook, near Baltimore.

In Jean's opinion, 'The family type is strong: black-haired, bad-tempered, reckless, near-sighted, gross, sensuous people'; but despite her early exposure to objects and situations best kept from little girls brought up as they had been by governesses and nursery maids, and the gaminess of her Bakewell blood, and despite the toll that would be taken in the years to come by drink and drugs and over-eating and high living, she was a woman who aroused – and still arouses – particular affection among those who knew her. She was a gregarious, lively, hospitable and kindly girl, whose broad features and pronounced cheek-bones and thick hair gave her the look of a genial Red Indian squaw. In his journal, Connolly recorded approvingly that she had 'short dark hair, green eyes and high cheek-bones, olive skin and a rather oriental appearance, like a young man from Indo-China'; she had a good figure and seemed refreshingly 'natural and pagan, almost without inhibitions and old world guilt'. And when he first knew her she was clad, almost invariably, in a navy blue skirt and sweater, a beret and a blue-and-white spotted handkerchief tied round her neck – a uniform that Connolly was to immortalise in the pages of *The Unquiet Grave*, that nostalgic wartime lament for the delights and pleasures of pre-war France, for the courtship of this fresh, spontaneous girl and long, idyllic days spent 'living for pleasure' with the wife he had loved and then lost.

Jean had, Connolly decided, 'all the good lesbian qualities – frankness, independence, masculinity and an interesting way of talking about women's faults and figures, hates anything tartish'; but although both Jean and Mara dabbled with the idea of being lesbians, in Jean's case at least it never quite rang true. Connolly liked to grill Mara on the subject, setting out his questions like an exam paper, the answers to be written alongside; she told him how she and Jean liked to lick their favourite foods off each other's breasts, and 'St Martin's apple jelly' in particular, but even though, for her part, she found women more physically exciting than men, she suspected that lesbianism might be a phase of adolescence, of the 'passionate friendship between young girls, "while still in a state of grace"'. Jean and Mara both dressed alike and called themselves, since zips were just coming into fashion, the 'Zipplings'; some months before Connolly got to know them, Mara – then back in Baltimore for the summer – announced that she had decided to become a 'boyle', an unfortunate choice of word that suggested 'not a lesbian but a girl who is boyish in a zippling way and comports herself as a "gentleman among women".' Boyles, she went on, would wear dark-blue berets, blue-and-white striped sweaters and dark blue skirts, carry canes and drink gin in a mannish way; they represented, perhaps, an intermediate stage, since 'after much thought, and some experimentation, I think I have no lesbian tendencies at all.'

Jean was then living with Mara and her mother on the Quai d'Anjou, on the Ile St Louis; and although Connolly would later take against Mara, telling Jean's mother that she had resented his taking Jean from her and tried to stir up mischief between them whenever Jean was away, since she was jealous of Jean getting married first, his initial reactions were entirely favourable. Mara was hardly a conventional beauty – according to Alpdodger she was

> tall with narrow hips and square shoulders, calves and thighs so long as to be ugly, big wrists and ankles, slender feet and hands. Her skin was white, she used no make-up, her eyes were dark and rather sunken, her face was neither beautiful nor ugly but fresh and interesting, the chin too square, the mouth too wide, the nose too bold, the brow too prominent, with an air of Velasquez' uglier sitters...

– but he was intrigued by the way she and her friends seemed to embody a spirit of spontaneity and raffishness and vigour very different to the chaste respectability of Elm Park Gardens. For Alpdodger, they seemed, in retrospect,

> a network of vivid and Elizabethan young people who not only loved adolescently and out of books, but were in reality also seduced and sometimes even aborted. Their feelings led them logically to action and an integrity deeper than chastity was the result. No social history, I suppose, will find them sufficiently important, those American girls who studied art in Paris in the ten years after the war. Yet their effect on those who knew them was incalculable. These frank, generous, confident beings, economically independent, socially free, had, when their youth and beauty were also taken into account, a kind of Amazonian splendour...

Much bantering went on among the Zipplings about how they had 'cocu'd' or cuckolded one another; and certainly in sexual matters Jean was a good deal more experienced than the respectable girls Connolly came across in London. According to Connolly, she was, in fact, pregnant when he met her: in 1968 he added a note to his journals pinning the blame on a champagne merchant who 'used perforated French letter as a ruse to get her pregnant and force marriage (financial gain). Afterwards threatened to shoot himself with empty revolver unless she married him.' She had an abortion shortly afterwards, but foolishly failed to keep a second, follow-up appointment; internal problems ensued, the melancholy result of which was that it proved impossible for her ever to have children*. Though titillated by her amorous past, Connolly was also extremely jealous. Later that summer Jean begged him not to keep criticising her about the 'Rosskam affair': she hadn't given her former lover a moment's thought since he dropped out of her life; she refused to feel ashamed of what she had done, and 'I have as much right as you to have affairs'. She told Connolly that Rosskam had offered to divorce his wife and marry her had she decided to go ahead and have the child: besides, 'What would you think of a nigger or semi-tart or real male tart? You would be even more unhappy I think.' Given Mara's views on the unhappy champagne merchant – '*Quand je pense à toi amoureuse de Rosskam, ça me fait tourner la tête. Quelle sâleté tu fais là-bas*' – it was 'piggy and right disloyal' of her new admirer to have discussed the whole business with her friend and, still worse, with Mrs Andrews: she was fed up with 'bothersome bitches' like Mrs Andrews, for 'all my life people have been trying to run me and I've been escaping them.'

All this lay in the immediate future; in the meantime, as we have seen, Connolly had been introduced to Jean on his way to the boat train at the Gare du Nord, and Mara's mother, however intrusive in other respects, had thoughtfully slipped away and left them to their own devices. They drank a good many *grogs americains*, and discussed what they were reading; she persuaded him to take a later train, confessed (when asked) that she was a lesbian, and revealed that although Mara had often described him to her, always in flattering terms, she had expected him to be rather 'more of a fairy'. Mara then returned, and they went out to lunch at the Crémaillière, which dragged on until late in the afternoon. Connolly decided to stay on another day, and had to borrow some money off Jean. That settled, they moved on to the Coupole, where they danced; in between dances, Connolly lodged another lesbian questionnaire with Mara, plus a note in which he asked her whether Jean was too lesbian to be kissed by a man. The answer was 'no', so he asked her out to dinner. Over the dinner table he passed her a note in which he asked her whether she would spend the night with him if he promised not to touch her. They booked into a hotel in the rue Delambre,

* Jean's abortion and its sad side-effects may have been something of a tall story, designed to impress her new admirer. According to Jean's close friend Freya Elwes, her sterility was caused by tubercular fallopian tubes, the result of a childhood illness; in which case, she would never have become pregnant in the first place, let alone had an abortion.

and climbed into bed. Connolly tried, without much success, to kiss her; but after a while she asked him to scratch her neck, and 'At that we fell. I had never slept with a young girl before. Jean was only eighteen, and seemed a lovely pagan from Tibullus or the Greek Anthology, with her youth, her passive and natural pleasure, her lovely boy's body, her uptilted elastic breasts.' It was a momentous occasion indeed, for – as Connolly told a friend years later – 'If my parents had arranged a teenage girl for me it would have saved years of frustration, when my loves were almost entirely for members of my own sex, never successful. I was virtually a virgin when I married Jeannie.' Next morning, feeling rather the worse for wear, they ate a large breakfast at the Dôme, Connolly borrowed another pound or two, and they made their way to the Gare du Nord and a tearful farewell.

After Paris, London seemed dull and cliquey and conventional; as an antidote, he went down to Wiltshire to stay with the sculptor Stephen Tomlin, who had recently married Julia Strachey. He thought Tomlin one of the most interesting people he had met in years: between them they decided that 'only expatriates were free, since it was not laws that hindered people's freedom but conventions.'* 'Well,' Julia Strachey reported to her great friend Frances Partridge, 'Cyril Connolly has been and gone. But not a word on the subject will you get out of me. Such a clever boy! But rather *plain* – don't you think? They *say* he is *most* talented – though somewhat impecunious. They tell such funny stories about him – I do think people are *beastly* about each other, don't you?'

Neither lunch at Boulestin's nor a short stint as the *New Statesman*'s theatre critic were enough to keep him in London, and one rainy evening he decided enough was enough, and took a train to Tilbury. He had a compartment to himself, so he lit a large cigar, put some fox-trots on the gramophone, and 'felt that at last I had become an interesting person again'. He arrived at Dunkirk in the freezing dark, and reached Paris at about half-past ten on a Sunday morning. After finding himself a hotel and having a shave, he hurried round to Jean, who was lying in bed in a dark-blue dressing-gown. They spent the day together, and in the evening he found himself 'dancing in the Bal Nègre, to the best jazz in Paris and the most awful collection of Martinique niggers'.

Through Jean and Mara, he got to know those members of Montparnasse bohemia with whom they were particularly friendly: among them Alfred Perles ('Fredl') and the Bessarabian painter Gregor Michonze, who re-

* Connolly was very taken by a story Arthur Waley told him about Tomlin. He had made a bust of David Garnett, which he left with Garnett's mother-in-law, Mrs Marshall. 'That's a rum-shaped bit of stone they've got at Mrs Marshall's,' the charwoman was reported as saying, 'and the joke of it is, it's a little like her son-in-law.'

surfaced intact as Rascasse in *The Rock Pool*, Connolly's novel about the melancholy dissipations of expatriates in the South of France. Fredl was then twenty-four: the future friend and biographer of Henry Miller, he lived in a cheap hotel, spent days in bed when unable to afford a meal, and – according to Alpdodger – was allowed by a friendly madame to gaze through a peephole at the goings-on in her brothel. Michonze had made his way from Vienna to Paris after fighting in the First World War, and had kept himself for a time by washing dishes; his hair had turned grey while he was still in his twenties, and with his 'wide forehead, protruding ears, heavy Jewish nose, large blue eyes, humped shoulders, fastidious mouth', he looked like someone out of a Hittite or Assyrian bas-relief. Like Rascasse, he talked a fluent 'wop American', and the 'fantastic fiery paintings' that hung in his bleak garret studio – most of which remained unsold – were surrealist affairs incorporating 'huge hands, hanging men, red protoplasm advancing down an empty road'. A less popular member of the circle was a Russian Jew called Alix, who ran a shirt shop, had a sister with four breasts, and features like those of 'a skinned calf's face in a butcher's window'.

A better-known though equally impoverished expatriate whom Connolly encountered at about this time, through Sylvia Beach, was the forty-two-year-old James Joyce, then living in the rue de Grenelle. Joyce was wearing a white cricketing blazer and blue trousers, and questioned his visitor in detail about his Vernon ancestors in Clontarf and their ownership of Brian Boru's sword – for, as he explained, 'I am afraid I am more interested in little things like that than in the problems of the solar system'. Connolly found him 'a quiet, sensitive, pedantic, tragic, and rather embarrassable man – a lot of the usher about him. He didn't put me at my ease, but I was frightened, and longed to know him better.' Joyce had recently published 'Anna Livia' – a section of what would eventually become *Finnegans Wake* – in Eugene Jolas's *avant garde* magazine *transition*, which was published in Paris; writing to Connolly some time later, Sylvia Beach told him that Joyce had asked her to let him know that 'the allusion to your family and birthplace in the current issue of *transition* is on page 213, line 9', before adding that 'the bulls will be a great bond between you and Hemingway if he is back here by the time you come to Paris.' She was quite wrong in assuming that Connolly shared Hemingway's enthusiasm for the bull-ring – far from it – but before long the two men met in her shop, and liked each other well enough; in the meantime, Connolly used 'Anna Livia' as the starting-point for 'The Position of Joyce', a long and laudatory essay on which he had started work, months earlier, while staying at I Tatti, and which appeared in the April issue of *Life and Letters*. Stuart Gilbert, a retired colonial civil servant who had abandoned his career in Ceylon to settle in Paris, where he was hard at work on his *magnum opus*, a pioneering work in which he elaborated on the parallels between *Ulysses* and the *Odyssey*, was worried in case Joyce, in a spasm of disloyalty or absent-mindedness, had passed on to Connolly his latest discovery, 'an analogy between A.L.P. [Anna Livia Plurabelle] and Nausicaa', so enabling this brash new enthusiast to claim all the credit via the improbable pages of *Life and Letters*: but his secret remained intact, and Connolly – whose enthusiasm for Joyce as a man and as a writer was to grow cooler over the years – was far too busy singing the praises of his new literary hero, and berating the English literary world which grew 'daily more bucolic and conservative' for their failure to render homage, to trouble himself with this particular point. Like Proust, he declared, Joyce was endowed with a quality seemingly absent in English writers – a 'Tragic Sense of Life', a conviction that 'life can only be appreciated, can only be lived even, if the intelligence is used to register all the beauty and all the intimacy which exist in ironic contrast to the unrelieved gloom of squalor and emptiness, mediocrity, disease and death.' The English language had become blighted by good taste, by whimsicality, by an ostrich-like refusal to reflect or adapt to the demotic, to the rhythms and patterns of the spoken word; nor was it 'able to profit, like American, from a rich background of polyglot slang'. Literary language had become debased and increasingly meaningless; 'the steady divorce of words from their significance owing to the literary exploitation of their melody detaching them from their meaning is perhaps the most serious cause of the break-up of poetical language today.'

Writers should emulate T.S. Eliot's readiness to deal with subjects 'hitherto considered unpoetical', writing in a way that combined simplicity with emotion and intelligence, while at the same time capitalising on 'the demotic English of our Tottenham Court Road civilisation'. 'Anna Livia' might prove a fake and a failure, but in terms of both language and subject-matter Joyce was prepared to be brave, to reflect the world as it was; and – remembering how his great novel had redeemed the boredom of I Tatti the previous spring – Connolly concluded his essay with a flourish which typically combined a dash of autobiography with a telling, recurrent obsession:

> for me any criticism of *Ulysses* will be affected by a wet morning in Florence, when in the empty library of a villa, with the smell of wood-smoke, the faint eaves-drip, I held the uncouth volume dazedly open in the big arm-chair – Narcissus with his pool before him.

*

With Joyce despatched to Desmond MacCarthy – whose only query was whether Joyce was 'adored' in France, or merely by the 'Anglo-American set' – Connolly and Jean set out on their travels. Before leaving he sent the *New Statesman* an admiring review of Ronald Firbank's Complete Novels – which, to his irritation, was lost in the post, along with an accompanying 'wail' in which he informed the literary editor that the latest bunch of novels he'd received were so ghastly that he planned to drop them into a Spanish river *en route* for the 'snows of Aragon'. It was snowing when they left Paris, and Jean was suffering from recurrent indigestion, later diagnosed as appendicitis. They made their way down into Spain, through places sanctified by his early youth: Huesca and Saragossa (where Jean jumped off the train and it went on without her) and Teruel and Valencia (where they made love five times in one afternoon) and Alicante, Benidorm, Murcia and Granada, where they booked into the Hotel Washington Irving. Sadly, they missed Gerald Brenan, who was now living a 'pre-Homeric existence' in the nearby village of Yegen, off 'rice and chicken instead of acorns'; he had been keen that together they should investigate a tribe of nomads who allegedly brought up their daughters to be prostitutes and launched them on their professional careers through the cafés of Algiers, and write up their findings in the *New Statesman*.

One of the problems of travelling alone with Jean was keeping the fact from her family. A degree of deception was called for, and Noël Blakiston – the most upright of men, and a reluctant dissembler – was enrolled as the alibi or fall-guy. From Freddie Harmer Connolly learned that Blakiston was unamused at having to pretend that he had been with them in Spain, and Connolly had to explain that naming him for the part had been intended as a compliment: after all, he had done a similar favour for Peter Quennell, pretending to enjoy imaginary evenings with Nancy Stallybrass. A month or two later, after Jean had returned to America for the summer, Connolly wrote to his old friend to make sure that he kept up the pretence ('Bless you for being so discreet'): Blakiston shouldn't be surprised if he got a letter from Jean in Baltimore, and sure enough she wrote to him from on board the SS *Rochambeau* asking him if he'd write her a letter, or simply send her a blank sheet of headed notepaper, so as to sustain the pretence that he had been with them all the time, for 'I'm afraid it will fall through if Cyril is always writing to me and you never are...'

Before long another elaborate deception was under way – with Peter Quennell and Nancy Stallybrass as co-conspirators, and the luckless Blakiston once again providing the cover. Despite his ambivalence about Quennell, at the beginning of the year Connolly had decided, momentarily, that 'in a sense he is my only friend', and that Quennell was 'my only contemporary interesting in himself and not because I choose to make him so'. On his return from Sledmere he had spent an evening with Quennell and Nancy Stallybrass, then newly-weds, and told them how 'I envied their married state and how debarred I felt from Eden'; and when, in April, Quennell suggested that he and Jean might like to join them at the Hôtel du Golfe in Ajaccio, he put the idea to Jean, who agreed with some reservations ('Peter has the drawback of Nancy. I can bear her if you can. What fun for Nancy to hate me as long as she can't do anything about it. I'm glad Peter doesn't'). Blakiston received his instructions on a postcard ('Can you – v. important, will write and say why – send a snap of yourself to the Hôtel de Noailles in Marseilles'); and on April the 19th, just as Quennell had given up all hope of their joining him, and had decided instead to spend the day writing an article on the terrace of his hotel, a car drew up on the drive before him:

> Inside Cyril and companion, Deadly Nightshade, an American girl, eighteen but looks younger, pallid, face like a piece of paper burnt at the edges and beginning to go speckly brown and black as pieces of paper do before they finally shrivel up and burst into flames, or (Stally says) a bluish sheet of badly printed Continental newspaper; an appearance I shall never quite grow accustomed to, but a nature that seems perfectly amiable.

Connolly and Jean, it seemed, had arrived in Ajaccio only that morning on a boat from Tangier, and had followed Quennell's 'trail of notes', hiring a car and chauffeur to speed them along.

That afternoon, while the women stayed behind, Connolly and Quennell explored a nearby estuary, getting soaked through in an attempt to ford the river mouth and annexing various islets in the name of the *New Statesman*. Next morning it was decided to make an expedition to Calvi, but the car broke down and Connolly and Jean went on by themselves: they booked into a large white hotel, where they were joined the following day by their friends. Connolly treated them all to dinner, and afterwards they danced in a café on the sea front. The day after the four friends were walking along the beach towards the Ile Rousse, Connolly and Quennell (unsuccessfully) playing ducks and drakes, when Jean suddenly announced that she was going to swim, and asked Quennell if he'd like to join her. He said he'd rather not, and was just straightening up after bending down to pick up a suitably flat pebble when he spotted Jean's 'dumpy, hirsute figure wading into the sea', stark naked. Stally – a former model who boasted 'a ravishing nut-brown skin, the complexion, as Peter says, of a fresh farm egg' – was overcome by ungenerous fury at the sight: 'Poor stumpy Jean,' her husband noted in his diary, '– to Stally a revelation of female ugliness.'

Staying in the hotel in Calvi had been expensive enough – Connolly's bill was 'stupendous' – but two days in the Ile Rousse took an even heavier toll. The most disastrous single item was lunch in a bar run by two homosexuals, one an American, the other a red-nosed Irishman. Champagne cocktails were followed by langoustes washed down by several bottles of vin rosé; and to make matters worse, the bar-owners, who were keen gamblers, then proceeded to fleece Connolly at dominoes and dice, adding insult to injury by calling Quennell 'old fellow'. By the time they had settled the bill they had no money left for the journey from Calvi to Nice. Connolly telegraphed for funds, but nothing happened; the bar-tender refused to cash any more cheques, and after spending their last 100 francs on lunch, Connolly and Jean limped back to Calvi, and somehow made their way back to the mainland.

Later that year, Quennell published his first full-length book, *Baudelaire and the Symbolists*, and Alpdodger was forced to endure 'the just torture of reading good work by a contemporary', as a result of which 'the usual splenetic torpor and solitude descends'. His jealousy did not pass unnoticed: Quennell wrote to him in Paris to say that he had heard from Stephen Tomlin that 'your references to me are not always as kind as mine to you. Am I irreparably identified with the siren motherland that you have thrust behind you? For alas she is a siren; Surrey calls you even in the heart of Montparnasse...' It was idiotic to quarrel, or for Connolly to harbour resentment, he went on, for 'I am still a few steps from the Hawthornden path to the everlasting bonfire – judging from the complete unsuccess of my book, quite a long way.'

From Paris, funds presumably restored, Connolly made his way to Berlin to stay with Harold Nicolson, arriving on the 11th of May and looking 'rather grubby'. He installed himself in Brückenallee, where he spent his time lying in bed till midday, talking till four in the afternoon, and then touring Berlin in the company of David Herbert, the twenty-year-old son of the Earl of Pembroke, who was there to learn German from a Captain Hauptmann, and Christopher Sykes, with whom Herbert was sharing a flat. Nicolson liked Sykes, but the younger man found his senior rather patronising; he was unwise enough to pass his views on to Connolly, who – according to Nicolson's biographer, James Lees-Milne – then passed them on to his host. As it was, however, Nicolson's ire was aimed at his lodger rather than his honorary attaché. 'Cyril is not perhaps the ideal guest,' he told Vita:

> He is terribly untidy in an irritating way. He leaves dirty handkerchiefs in the chairs and fountain pens (my fountain pens) open in books. Moreover

> it is rather a bore having a person who has *nothing* of his own – not a cigarette or a stamp. In fact the poverty of this colony is heart-rending. Christopher and David are both absolutely bust. But I really am firm about it, and won't take them to Pelzer's to eat plovers' eggs. In other ways, however, Cyril is a pleasant guest, easily amused and interesting about things. I don't trust him an inch and think he makes mischief. He is very thick with Violet Trefusis and I imagine he is very disloyal about me when with her.

Eventually Nicolson managed to winkle Connolly out of his flat and into the Adlon Hotel; since the Adlon was the smartest hotel in Berlin, Connolly then asked him to pay the bill, and called him a cad when he refused. Sensitive as ever to slights or disapproval, Connolly was all too well aware that he had been 'an awful nuisance in Berlin': he told Desmond MacCarthy that he had meant to leave far earlier and go to Big Chilling for June, but Pearsall Smith had written to say he couldn't since the drains were up, as a result of which he had lingered on for an extra month, overcome by 'paralysis of the will' and 'weakness, not deliberate cadging'. Nicolson's friend Leigh Ashton, the Keeper of the Department of Textiles at the Victoria and Albert, was especially outraged about Connolly's behaviour, albeit at second hand, but as Connolly assured a new friend, Enid Bagnold,

> It was Harold's affair, not Leigh's, and Harold has forgiven me. I'm not a canny sponge but am apt to be an irresponsible one. You probably heard that I was treacherous, malicious and idle as well. I am not the first though inclined to be the second, and fated to be the last . . .

Despite one 'memorable conversation', during the course of which Nicolson bent his mind to the vexed issue of 'why buggers were such snobs', and whether or not they were 'possessed of more vitality than womanisers' (it was agreed that they were), tempers must have frayed and harsh words been exchanged – so much so that Nicolson found himself apologising to Connolly for his bad behaviour:

> I don't think Leigh can have been saying disagreeable things about you, as he undertook not to. It is a bore the way people jabber, and in this case I suffer worse than you. I feel very ashamed of myself all round, and am inclined to agree with you that buggers always behave badly in the end . . . You see, what with David and having gone bust suddenly, and being unable to stand long evenings, I got badly on edge. I tried to make myself think that what annoyed me was your having so much time on your hands, such liberty etc., and then gibing me for my 'work fetish'. I felt

> that if it were not for this same 'work fetish' I should also be a wandering professional, instead of an amateur glued to his desk. But I fear that my bad behaviour was due to causes less noble than any conflict between work and play. I was jealous, I suppose – of your being young and free and so bloody clever – with all your future before you, and me merely with a Vanity Fair past...

'I behaved like a cad and I beg your pardon,' Nicolson went on: he denied having said 'filthy things' about his guest – if Connolly would like to read the letter he had written to Gladwyn Jebb he would realise that 'all I said was that you were sensitive and lazy'.

To his journal, Connolly confided that he had 'wasted exactly one month in Berlin, in stupid gregariousness and empty bummeling, only two or three interesting evenings, usually those without David, and hardly any memorable talk. All ended in persecution mania and resentment with Harold.' Light relief of a kind had been provided by plays written by Connolly specially for the occasion and performed, according to David Herbert, 'in Harold's apartment, in front of a most austere and distinguished audience, including the British Ambassador and his wife.' One of them had an oriental setting, and Connolly played a pimp, Christopher Sykes a carpet-seller and David Herbert a slave girl: in another Sykes played an Anglo-Indian colonel, Connolly his hideous wife, and David Herbert a tart; this too was performed in front of Sir Horace and Lady Rumbold, and although their reactions went unrecorded, Nicolson was apparently 'almost sick with laughter'.

From Berlin Connolly made his way to Paris, and a week later he returned to England via Dieppe and Newhaven. John Betjeman had moved into his old room in the 'Yeo' in March, so he was, in effect, homeless. 'Depressed at being back in England – countryside so dirty, sky and fields the colour of corrugated iron. Everybody so weak and knock-kneed, a race of little ferrets and blindworms,' he wrote; the crowds in Brighton, 'little ferrety robots squeaking round an empty bandstand', filled him with a glum despair ('Oh, the stupidity of the old regime and the silliness of its detractors! Yet for this Mr T.S. Eliot changes his brown passport for true blue!'). One bright spot, however, was staying with Enid Bagnold at North End House in Rottingdean, a few miles along the coast from Newhaven and dangerously close to Brighton's ferrety crowds. Married to the wasp-like martinet Sir Roderick Jones, then in charge of Reuter's, Enid Bagnold had been introduced to Connolly by Gladwyn Jebb. She had sent him a telegram in Dieppe asking him to come and stay; he had crossed on the night boat and had paced up and down the village green in Rottingdean until it was nine o'clock, and a reasonable time to ring her front-door bell. Knowing him to be broke, she had lent him £3 to help him on his way.* Although she was to remain rather intimidated by him – 'I fear the whip that flicks out of his talk' – they became close friends: later on he would prowl worryingly about her bookshelves looking for first editions, but in those early days she remembered best how 'when he went down to bathe with the children he would swim far out and turn back inshore, with his greenish seaweed hair coming down over his oddly tilted nose and looking like a sea-pug.' 'I heard good and bad,' she told her new friend: 'I heard the sort of things that villagers would have said of Rimbaud, after he had passed through the village. So you see I heard lots of bad. But it was a glowing sort of bad... You left me all a-prickle with laughter and excitement and curiosity.'

As an antidote to Brighton – if not to North End House, in which Burne-Jones had once lived – Connolly went down to Dorset with Peter Quennell. Desmond MacCarthy had asked to see something from his journal for *Life and Letters*, and their Dorset trip was to provide a fine conclusion, marvellously evocative of England between the wars, to 'England Not My England', which appeared in the issue of October 1929.

As ever, Connolly was racked by ambivalence, buffeted by alternating gusts of love and hate. Striding over the downs by Lulworth Cove, he felt a sudden 'moment of love for my country, just as we may suddenly prepare to forgive someone who has deceived us before the memory of their infidelities swarms in on us again'; but as they walked on he 'remembered not so much the beauty of the downs as the awfulness of the people who wrote about them: Kipling's thyme and dewponds, Belloc's beer and Chesterton's chalk, all the people writing poems at this moment for the *London Mercury*...' Lulworth Cove itself seemed blighted with all the detritus of the modern age, with charabancs and bungalows and tin shacks selling teas, and 'this England of ours' seemed a dead and alien affair, the celebrants of which embodied all that he most disliked about English writing and society:

> I thought of all the ardent bicyclists, the heroic coupleteers, the pipe-smoking, beer-swilling young men on reading parties. The brass-rubbers, the accomplished morris-dancers, the Innisfreeites, the Buchan-Baldwin-Masefield and Drinkwatermen, the Squires and Shanks and grim Dartmoor realists, the advanced tramp-lovers, and, of course, Mary Webb. I thought of everyone who was striding down the Wordsworth primrose path to the glorious goal of an O.M....

* Writing about her old friend in a special memorial issue of *Adam*, published in 1975, Enid Bagnold displayed an uncertain grasp of chronology: 'It was some time before the First World War that someone said to me: "There's a young man sitting over in Dieppe who has just enough money to cross and get to London. I think he'll amuse you..."'

To Noël Blakiston he confessed his dislike of 'respectability and conventionality in the English middle-class sense'. England seemed like a dying civilisation, 'going stuffy and comatose instead of collapsing beautifully like France . . . I really feel that the English country houses, like English music, painting, seasides, bright young people, or delicious people not so young, are all somehow side-tracked, irresistibly unvisited by the life-giving tide;' and as a writer – or an aspiring writer – he wanted to belong to his time, to reflect the world he lived in rather than an imaginary past preserved in social and linguistic aspic.

*

After his short stint as a drama critic – in early February he had reviewed R.C. Sherriff's *Journey's End*, comparing it unfavourably with J.R. Ackerley's *Prisoners of War* – Connolly had, as threatened, refused to take on any more novel-reviewing. Clifford Sharp tried to persuade him to change his mind, but he wouldn't be swayed: he told Sharp that he had signed a contract to write a novel of his own, and 'I have been hopelessly stuck since I have reviewed other people's as they put one off it so.' The contract he referred to was that with the Nonesuch Press, initially for the Balkan guide; but in Paris later that year, Connolly met Wren Howard, Jonathan Cape's business partner, who suggested that he should write a novel for them instead, delivering it in instalments and being paid on results. Connolly appreciated this firm approach, which seemed to promise rather more than Nonesuch's amiable *laisser-faire*, but the net effect was exactly the same.

In his letter to Sharp, Connolly suggested that, rather than review novels, he should contribute occasional 'middles' to the magazine – travel pieces, stories, sketches and so forth. As soon as he was back in England, in the early summer, he went to discuss the idea with Sharp, but little came of it. He was determined to spend the winter in Paris with Jean, but although Sharp urged him to try his hand at some sample pieces, he also insisted that Connolly should be available and in London, 'which seems absurd as I won't be wanted at the NS office and there won't be any books needed for it'. Nor was Connolly at all impressed with the magazine or its editor. 'I thought the *Statesman* very Grantchester and Fleet Street,' he told MacCarthy, who had resigned as literary editor and moved to the *Sunday Times* the previous June, though he continued to contribute his 'Affable Hawk' column for another year after that: 'Sharp seems to be breaking up, according to everyone. No more fine rages, but rather silky in conversation with that unpleasant foxy look of all solitary topers when they are thinking of an excuse to get one out of the room.' He was all too right about Clifford Sharp, whose drinking had now reached epic proportions. A difficult, lonely, arrogant man who hated uncertainty, cherished his prejudices (he particularly disliked Indians, the French, birth control and, Margaret Kennedy excepted, lady novelists), dreaded sentimentality and could only praise his staff behind their backs, he was given a year's leave in 1929 and replaced – permanently, as it turned out – by Kingsley Martin.* Nor was his the only familiar face to disappear. After Desmond MacCarthy's departure G.W. Stonier, who was to remain with the magazine for a good many years, occasionally reviewing films under the pseudonym of 'William Whitebait', was left in charge of the books pages. Although V.S. Pritchett thought Stonier the most talented man on the staff, 'a sharp and candid critic with an excellent eye for the delicate and bizarre', he was happier in a subordinate position, and was put briefly under Clennell Wilkinson, a drinking companion of Sharp's who wore 'the martyred look of a man whom God had heartlessly appointed to save the whisky business from bankruptcy', and then Ellis Roberts, a clerical-looking figure in a cloak and broad-brimmed hat. Roberts – who much later took over from MacCarthy as editor of *Life and Letters* – was duly sacked by Kingsley Martin; Maynard Keynes – who had joined the board when the *New Statesman* merged with the *Nation* in 1931 – then approached David Garnett, who claimed to enjoy the job but was thought to be both idle and incompetent. Kingsley Martin gave him six months leave to finish a novel; and eventually, at Harold Nicolson's suggestion, Raymond Mortimer was put in charge of the back pages, and order was restored at last.

But Connolly's growing dislike of the *New Statesman* was not simply a matter of ever-changing personnel: it mirrored his disenchantment with England in general, and the literary world in particular. The magazine seemed no more than an 'extremely competent, expert and philistine man in the street'; while to MacCarthy he wrote – apropos Sharp's suggestion – that

> I think it would be a hard job making the N.S. interesting against the editorial current anyhow. All English journalism seems to me archaic – good work in a dead form – but so out of touch with a post-war world, I think deliberately. People would rather read about *Punch* children in *Punch*, rambles round my books, bird sanctuaries, crossbills in Kenwood in the *New Statesman*... I think English letters are getting more and more conservative, more and more sulkily obsessed with the past. This

* Reviewing Edward Hyams's history of the *New Statesman* in 1963, Connolly recalled that 'I soon came up against Sharp, and I remember the terror of being sent for by him and entering his room to find his angry handsome bleary philistine face thrust at one. "Look here, Connolly, what the hell does this mean? Who the bloody hell is Valéry? Valery who? How much do you think our readers can stand?"'

> doesn't mean that I am now Joyce's pupil but that reading the *Statesman*, or the old governess *Nation* that goes dribbling on about education and liberal ideas, one gets a feeling of the complete effeteness of the two papers.

As an expatriate, he went on, it was possible to see things more clearly, to realise how

> the *Statesman* has become so *Fleet Street* – a mixture of xenophobia, common sense, man-in-the-street – but since fundamentally an Englishman and a Londoner, the man-in-the-street is the first to appreciate an anti-Proust, anti-Boney, 'Hey Musso' article, followed by septuagenarian goo about the long-tailed peequick nesting in an old pillar-box . . . the N. S. is a *joke* to a lot of people – or is getting one, like the *Mercury*.

'Disguise yourself as a weekly paper,' Alpdodger declared, and then proceeded to provide a lightning impression of its contents:

> Basle, Berne. Lausanne. Geneva. As we go to press there seems no sign of any improvement in the international situation. The stampede towards world chaos seems to complete the anomaly of, over the page, had the nations followed our advice in June 1927 we should not be the second-rate seedy under-dog non-conformist right-wing literary left-wing Labour that we are today. Over the page. On sharpening pencils. We must all of us, at some time, I think, have been inclined to drat all pencils and wished for some heaven-sent device to make them all undullable as well as indelible, there what do you think of that for two columns and a half. There's charm for you. Over the page. Once again the government neglected, over the page, I should be very unwilling to quarrel with a writer as distinguished as Mr Geoffrey Mannin, passion, the free play of intelligence, high craftsmanship, sincerity, over the page, shorter notices, publishers' announcements, Three Nuns Tobacco, the dregs of the bottle, gramophones, the City, motoring, reformed inns, bisexual hotels, Harris tweeds, homemade butter, why I became a Unitarian, epicures praise Sabrina's omelettes and waffles, bed-kitchenette in Bloomsbury available with Indian student and gas, full and final list of anal and oral infant schools. Gerald Heard. Gerald Bullett. Gerald Nicolson. Gerald Gould. St Matthew, St Macarthus, St Lucas and St John the Ervine.

With its derisive litany of long-forgotten literati – Gerald Gould, E.V. Lucas, St John Ervine and the rest – and its contempt for the whimsical, self-consciously charming *Times* fourth leader type of essay, and for the clichés of political and literary commentary, Alpdodger's summation amounted to an acute if one-sided flick through the pages of the *Statesman*; but book-reviewing, and novel-reviewing in particular, excited Connolly's especial bile – most memorably encapsulated in 'Ninety Years of Novel Reviewing', published by the *New Statesman* in August 1929. 'The reviewing of novels is the white man's grave of journalism,' he began: 'it corresponds, in letters, to building bridges in some impossible tropical climate. The work is gruelling, unhealthy, and ill-paid, and for each scant clearing made wearily among the springing vegetation the jungle overnight encroaches twice as far...' All the familiar symptoms came under his scrutiny: the short-lived excitement that even the most jaded reviewer feels when a virgin parcel of review copies is handed over by the postman; the inevitable tendency of most reviewers to 'go native', hailing as masterpieces works that will be forgotten in weeks, and welcoming 'each with cries of "genius!"'; 'the nerve strain and the nausea, the cynical hopelessness with which we strive to quench the indefatigable authors.' But,

> like the king at Nemi, the slayer shall himself be slain. Brave and agile, the reviewer enters the ring. He rushes blindly at the red wrappers. He disembowels a few old hacks. But his onsets eventually grow futile, his weapons are blunted, his words are stale. He may go under nobly, a Croker facing his Keats; he may simply wear out in praising or abusing – it matters not which – the never-ceasing flow of second-rate and worthy productions – but eventually the jungle claims him.

Nor was *Life and Letters* – which in format and contributors seems so evidently a precursor of his own *Horizon* – immune from his derision. It was, he decreed, 'august and readable as any late-Victorian arsewiper, and as daring and original as a new kind of Barley Water'. Its eclectic list of contributors included members of Connolly's own generation like Evelyn Waugh, Peter Quennell and Kenneth Clark – and, later, William Plomer, Dilys Powell and Antonia White – as well as members of Bloomsbury such as Virginia Woolf, E.M. Forster and Lytton Strachey, and a still older generation that included Hilaire Belloc, Max Beerbohm and even Thomas Hardy; but none of this prevented it from being a 'bitter disappointment, a heavily subsidised paper that could afford to experiment instead determined to pay its way by pleading to a respectable, moneyed and wholesomely English public that is frankly die-hard. The whole tone of the paper is that of a literary *Punch*...'

Similar criticisms were to be directed at *Horizon*, which shared much of its predecessor's eclecticism, particularly by Julian Symons. In the meantime, though, *Life and Letters* appealed to two worlds which Connolly found abhorrent: Chelsea, the abode of the cultivated public, for whom 'delicious, charming, exquisite, delightful, enchanting, delicious and delicious' were the highest terms of praise, whereas obscene books were dismissed as 'dreary and boring' and experimental ones as 'silly, childish and incomprehensible'; and Fleet Street, the home of the philistine and the 'plain man', whose arbiter of taste was Arnold Bennett, and who signified their approval with 'pretty good, jolly good, jolly good stuff, pretty remarkable, extraordinary, and very interesting', reserving 'pretty strong' and 'muck' for works that seemed beyond the pale.

'I hate the little London ménages, the Waughs, Murrays, Quennells type of existence – something so mousey about them,' Connolly told Patrick Balfour; but nothing is easier than to disapprove of a way of life while enjoying certain aspects of it to the full, and finding oneself part of the cliques and intrigues one abhors. Shortly before Jean left for America, Connolly became involved in a fracas involving the Sitwells and the composer William Walton. 'I must say Cyril dear it was scarcely tactful to attack the Sitwells to Willie of all people!' Peter Quennell reproached him: 'I am told that on his casting aspersions on your perfect normality you took off your coat and challenged him to *come outside* and fight to the death; with Constant in tears etc it must have been a very diverting evening.' 'Constant' was the composer Constant Lambert, who was rather keen on Jean, and his weeping had been induced by his asking her whether she liked what he was playing on the piano, and her expressing indifference. 'WW got tight and said you and I were Desmond's bumboys and only allowed to write for his papers as such,' Connolly replied, adding that the last thing he wanted to do was to upset Osbert Sitwell in particular.

Connolly's ambivalence – about England, and London, and the pleasures and pitfalls of the literary life – were reflected in his views of himself. Far from being a bohemian, he told Blakiston from the rustic calm of Sledmere, he was essentially a hybrid:

> I am governed by an alternate appetite for adventure and society. I must have somewhere to run away from and somewhere to come back to; I like the gossiping scheming clique life of London as much as I hate it, I enjoy the untartish dullness of country life as much as it bores me, I love and detest foreign countries. It is excessive love of one's country as much as hate of it that makes one live abroad.

While deriding its conventionality, he longed to be accepted in respectable society, to ride with the hounds while sympathising with the fox:

> I am too much of a snob to be a bohemian and much too fond, not only of security, but of a sense of respect and social power. I can't bear to be disapproved of by waiters, porters, hotel managers, hunting men, barbers, bank clerks, though I wouldn't mind writing anything that would annoy them – I can't bear to be unpopular though I enjoy being hated.

And to Desmond MacCarthy he confessed that

> I like and need affection and admiration, and yet I am always trying to wound others, polemically, while remaining infinitely vulnerable myself. As to my vulgar streak I agree it is inopportune to indulge it now, when I am poor, but on the whole I think it is valuable, there is so much unexploited beauty still in sheer hedonism, and the Bennett side I have is also a very good antidote to either becoming Bloomsbury or Squirey and Shanksy – I mean afraid of life, out of it, 'exploring from an arm-chair' in some gloomy little library.*

*

Before Jean returned to America in June, she and Connolly decided that they would get married; and although he was chary about the news becoming public property and the subject of gossip, family and close friends were informed. After promising that 'You will both find me an ideal mother-in-law,' his mother told him that she was sure something could be arranged with the Lock House if they would like to live there – an offer Connolly declined, on the grounds that they wanted to live in Paris and see as much of the world as they could before settling down. Rather dispiritingly, she warned him not to expect to feel the same for Jean as he had for Racy, who had been 'like your first glimpse of the tropics – even much more beautiful places can't stir you the same way.' Connolly affected to be unmoved by the simultaneous news, reported in the *Tatler*, of Racy's engagement to Mungo Buxton, a Norfolk landowner, and Noël Blakiston's to 'Giana' Russell, professing to feel merely a 'vague sense of waste and irony at the amount of affection and interest I had poured out on these two people,' while elsewhere he wrote 'So Racy is engaged, to a fresh young hearty. Whew! I felt – what a near shave – as the bomb burst harmlessly above my head, not even wounding me with a stray splinter.' Writing to

* Edward Shanks and J.C. 'Jack' Squire embodied in Connolly's mind all that was most frowsty and reactionary about London literary life. Shanks was a poet of the nature-loving 'Georgian' school; a keen cricketer and quaffer of ale, Squire was the editor of the *London Mercury*, a home from home for old-fashioned literary men. Connolly's Eton contemporary, Alan Pryce-Jones, the future editor of the *Times Literary Supplement*, was then serving his literary apprenticeship on the magazine.

Patrick Balfour, however, he indicated that, unsuitable as she might have been, Racy continued to embody some kind of unattainable ideal:

> I think I shall be very happy if I marry Jean but of course I don't feel the 'ideal' quality of love that I had for Racy. I've quarrelled with Jean and slept with her for one thing, so couldn't think of her in the same way as Racy whom I never argued with and almost never touched. The trouble with Jean is that we have all our friends in common, laziness, love of pleasure, extravagance, fondness for good food and drink, for travel, low life, long baths etc.

Jean, he went on, could 'never look reassuring to English women, though good with buggers etc', nor did she have any strong feelings about homosexuality. And 'I can't be sure how much the thought that she will one day have £15,000 may influence me...'

To Noël Blakiston – whom Freddie Harmer reported as being 'quite impossible since his engagement' – Connolly confessed that although he and Jean quarrelled a great deal, they were as easily reconciled; he found her 'almost entirely compatible', and 'like Giana she is masculine in mind and feminine in feeling... Of course at eighteen she is almost tiresomely young but also while it lasts refreshing and she is very mature and intelligent for that age.' Marrying an American gave him a 'feeling of release from the bogies of the old world'. Not long afterwards he wrote again to say how glad he was that Blakiston and his fiancée both liked Jean (as indeed they did). For his part, he liked her jokes, and 'She suits me perfectly because she is affectionate rather than passionate, fond of good food, good books and good films, good talk and good places, but essentially domestic and equable.' Quite apart from darning his socks, 'she has a natural taste for the first-rate rather than any restless intellectual pretensions, she never tries to be clever but her preferences are usually bright.' Jean, for her part, was often amazed at her fiancé's thoughtlessness, for 'I get very impatient with the ignorance of women – they're all so badly educated, and when I have to impart information I hate myself for doing it – I feel I ought to be with my intellectual equals instead of winning these easy triumphs.' Notions of male superiority jostled equally familiar fears of being constrained and compromised: 'Of course the trouble is that I'm emotionally homosexual still – I see red at the idea of infringement of my liberty by *la femme*... Every Englishman, don't you think, is really contemptuous of women – the sanctity of the smoking-room is always at the back of his mind.' Money, on the other hand, could always sweeten the pill, and as he assured his old friend, he wouldn't think of marrying Jean unless she had an allowance of £2000 a year.

Given the frailty of his own finances, Connolly was understandably anxious to keep the news of his engagement from Logan Pearsall Smith. Pearsall Smith had always made it clear that he expected his young men to remain unmarried, and although Connolly told Desmond MacCarthy that the old man would probably be relatively well-disposed to Jean on the grounds of her being a distant cousin, 'I don't think he would cut me out of his will for marrying but he will certainly cut me off the dole': quite apart from which he was anxious not to wound his patron's feelings, or leave him feeling deserted, for 'I'm really devoted to Logan, far fonder than of my parents.' As it turned out, breaking the news to the old man was less traumatic, emotionally and financially, than he had feared. Pearsall Smith's income had been hit hard by the Wall Street crash, and although he remained a man of independent means he now supplemented his funds by writing aphorisms for the *Morning Post* at 10*s* 6*d* a throw, paying his assistant a shilling for each accepted improvement ('Never judge a man by his umbrella – it may not be his' was one of his better-known efforts); and later in the year, when Connolly was back in Paris, Pearsall Smith – while simultaneously enclosing a cheque – wrote to say how much he hoped his protégé was getting 'lucrative work, or will soon be prosperously married, since I may not be able to go on helping you for long'. And earlier, much to Connolly's relief, he had written to say that 'I am sure you need to get married and won't be happy and settled till you do, and you seem to have found a delightful and congenial companion. That you won't have to support her is an added piece of luck.'

The fiercest – perhaps the only – opposition to Connolly's marrying Jean came from an unexpected quarter. Connolly had asked his old Eton friend Terence Beddard, now working in the City as a stockbroker, for advice, and Beddard had no intention of mincing his words. 'If you married Jeannie it would be completely disastrous for you both,' he wrote: 'she seemed almost more unsuited to matrimony than you are, and I can't say fairer than that.' He could see nothing whatsoever to be said in its favour – 'unless one admits a strong physical attraction which even you admit is not devastating, and a certain community of interests.' Physical attraction was anyhow short- lived – indeed, 'in your case you will almost have satisfied that side of it before you start... I can't think why you want to plunge into matrimony. You don't want children, nor a home of your own (cat, dog, carpet-slippers etc.), you won't want to cut yourself off from other women...' Connolly, he suggested, had no idea of the responsibilities marriage brought with it, or how it changed one's life. 'It's absurd to marry young on a vague impulse padded out with sexual attraction and a mutual preference for a good wine,' he concluded – adding, prophetically, that Connolly really ought to cut down on Jean's drinking: it was absurd for a girl of her age to down three or four cocktails before dinner. She looked really ill and, much as she prized her independence, needed to be looked after.

The subject of their correspondence was, in the meantime, on the far side of the Atlantic, camping in the Adirondacks (a matter, according to Connolly, of 'cocktail parties, aqua-planing and going over to Canada for drinks') and begging her fiancé – who was suffering from trench-mouth – to visit a dentist, since she wasn't keen to tie herself to a 'toothless sagging-jawed lover'. Connolly took himself down to Big Chilling, where he busied himself writing a guide to Spain for the Blakistons to take with them on their honeymoon in October. He worried about his honeymoon being discussed by the likes of Leigh Ashton – 'I can't be engaged you see unless Jean can get enough money out of her family, that's why it's so annoying to have Leigh talking away' – and he can't have been pleased when Balfour reported that his affair with Jean was well known, and that Maurice Bowra was 'retailing it as good gossip'; as late as October, Connolly was writing from Paris to tell Desmond MacCarthy that he was holding off from being officially engaged for as long as possible, and that

> All the pirate gang of London buggers will probably be malicious about it, headed by Maurice I should think, but with luck I shan't come across them, and though I'm not marrying for money at all they will be right in so far as I couldn't possibly marry without it. In any case, if people think I'm marrying a poor sweet girl for her money who's never heard of 'upside-down' people it will be much easier for her than if they said I'd been caught by an ambitious young American.

His monetary worries may have been partially assuaged by a letter from Jean in which she said that she had been to Pittsburgh to see her paternal grandmother, who would let her have 200 dollars a month; surely they should be able to manage on £10 a week, plus Connolly's five guineas from the *Statesman*? She went on to assure him that she didn't mind at all about Racy, and that she would eventually like them to have two or three children – but not until she was twenty-five at least, and they had done their travelling together. Quite how much money Jean's wealthy family would allow her was to become a recurrent and ever-varying element in her fiancé's correspondence over the next few months. Jean's mother wrote to say that she understood the newly-weds would need 750 dollars every three months, and that although providing this wouldn't be easy she would do what she could; later in the autumn Connolly confirmed that Mrs Warner had arranged for her former mother-in-law to fund Jean until she came into money from her side of the family, and although old Mrs Bakewell was difficult and autocratic they could expect to get some 12,000 dollars a year. In due course, when her mother's family money was available, Jean could expect something in the region of £6000 a year, an enormous sum of money. Quite how much Jean eventually received it is impossible to say – the following January, just before their marriage, Connolly told Blakiston that, come what may, Mrs Warner would let her daughter have £1000 a year – but whatever the sums they looked forward to a life of ease and luxury; there was much excited talk about honeymoons in Mexico or China, or living on an estuary in Devon or Cornwall in a house to be designed for them by le Corbusier, or buying a yacht and sailing round the Greek islands, with Bobbie Longden and Desmond MacCarthy on board as honoured guests.

In August, much to his irritation, Connolly had to move out of Big Chilling to make way for Mrs Berenson, plus two children and four grand-children. This was particularly annoying since Pearsall Smith had asked him to refuse any other invitations, which meant that he had turned down an invitation to join the Spearses on their yacht in the South of France; and now he found himself travelling instead to Dinard with his mother, which meant that he couldn't save any money or let Balfour have sums still owing on the Yeo. Dinard – the nearest point to Southampton – was a 'perfectly awful Balliol JCR sort of hole with appropriate mothers and sisters'; but despite the horrors of Normandy watering-places, and a persistent dislike of the natives – 'I think the French are a detestable nation, dishonest, dirty, sentimental and banal' – he found himself, once back in London, pining for Paris. 'I have a hatred for London, not a place to be poor in, I think in Paris one can,' he told Enid Bagnold. Jean had arranged to start a course at the Sorbonne in the autumn, and he was determined to 'spend my last months of celibacy in the sweet and melancholy atmosphere of artist life south of the river', in those cavernous mediaeval streets that lie between the Panthéon and the Seine. With the coming of autumn he felt – not for the last time – that promises might become reality: during the summer in Big Chilling he had become 'obsessed with autumn', and – installed in Paris in mid-September – he wrote of how 'Autumn is the season to which I am called like a vocation. In these first days of mist and feathery dusk, my mind begins to stir like a boat raised from the mud by the tide.'

Once settled in Paris, he informed Desmond MacCarthy, his courtship of Jean ran smoothly: he would meet her for lunch, after which they would spend the rest of the day, agreeably enough, visiting art galleries, attending fashion shows, going to concerts and films, eating out and dancing in night-clubs. When not with Jean he spent a good deal of time – more time than Wren Howard of Cape might have wished – exploring Paris with the aid of a map. He took a room in the Hôtel de Louisiane in the rue de Seine, right in the middle of the maze of streets that make up the Left Bank. 'I have a round bedroom with an eighteenth-century floor,' he told MacCarthy: 'The Louisiane is an old and buggy hotel. The goatherd still plays his pipes underneath it in the mornings' – and no doubt was playing still when Connolly, rising late, made his way to the Deux Magots on the corner of the boulevard St Germain, a café he was to revisit some fifteen years later, when it had achieved a different literary eminence. He bought himself books in Sylvia Beach's bookshop, where he met Aldous Huxley and Richard Aldington; his mother came over, and was much taken with Jean; although he had been too broke to return to England for the Blakistons' wedding, the newly-weds called on him on their way through on their honeymoon, and he was able to give them his fifteen-page guide to Spain – or, rather, to Granada and environs – with special reference to the trip he and Jean had made earlier in the year at which Blakiston had been a ghostly, reluctant presence: 'In mentioning me you may need a little tact, I don't think anybody really thought Jean and I were married but they treated us as if we were... It would be best to call her my *señora* and then take your line from them.' Much to his relief, Jean was very taken with Georgiana – a liking that was fully reciprocated.

It was in Paris in the autumn of 1929 that Connolly and Jean began to buy the unusual and exotic pets that were to become so distinctive a feature of their life together. They spent a good deal of time peering into the animal shops along the *quais*, and one day they decided to buy four young ferrets. They were dark-brown or tan in colour, and their names were Chica, Bianca, Paco and English Rose, a fat, rather pink animal that was larger than the others. To begin with they tore their new owners' hands to shreds, but before long they had become 'enchanting' pets, living off bread and milk and going for walks on collars and leads. They made little clicking noises, and spent a good deal of time leaping into the air and climbing the curtains. At night they slept in the same bed as their owners. Surprisingly, perhaps, for such an ardent animal-lover, Connolly bought two white mice in order to 'stage a gladiatorial show with the ferrets'. One of them was killed, 'dramatically', but the other escaped before being recaptured in a metal tube; a ferret was put in at each end, and the mouse was torn in two.

Not long after, Connolly bought Jean the first of the lemurs which, like the ferrets, were to haunt the pages of *The Unquiet Grave*. It was a kinkajou from Madagascar, with 'thick brown fur, monkey's body and hands, and a long pointed face with large brown eyes'. A timid, affectionate creature, much given to licking their ears with its tongue, it flew restlessly about the room, swinging off the furniture and the curtains: 'in restaurants it would snatch the spoon from one's hand and grow peevish, and everywhere it would make the most awful messes, it seemed just a machine for shitting and peeing, and had a genius for sitting where it shat.' Eventually it had to be traded in for a Brazilian marmoset, 'so small it could sit in an after-dinner coffee cup'; but it died of a mysterious ailment, and the ferrets were left to their own devices.

Still brooding sporadically on Racy, Connolly decided that

> if I am to marry, it's so much better I should marry someone as literary and bohemian as myself instead of a cultivated English rose who'd gentlemanise me into nothing or else drive me into exile by the correctness of her family . . . Think of the difference of not having to slave for her, not having stern father-in-law etc., of being an agile protective husband instead of a suppliant hiding a doggy and unconventional tail between a pair of English gentlemanly legs.

But that Christmas, while Jean stayed in Paris, he ventured north to Sledmere for a restorative draught of English upper-class life. He arrived at the station just as the Marquis of Londonderry was about to leave amidst 'immense bowings and scrapings', and he 'enjoyed the sense of class distinctions once again', being particularly struck by the servility of English railway porters compared with their French equivalents. Nor was Sledmere itself, with a butler and two footmen at the ready, lacking in an agreeable sense of luxury. 'The Eats are Swell,' he told Blakiston: they gorged themselves on huge meals of lobsters and pheasants washed down with first-class claret and, he told Jean in awe-struck tones, 'pâté is handed round as well as cheese.' Much time was devoted to charades, and the men fought each other with javelins, shields and fencing helmets, with Angela and Freya – who referred to their visitor as 'Beethoven' – acting as armour-bearers. Angela, who later married Connolly's friend 'Ran' Antrim, was the more outgoing of the two, and teased him about getting up late and smoking in the bath: he was tempted to ask the two sisters to join them on their post-marital yacht were it not for their being Catholics, 'which is a terrible bore'.

Wondering whom to invite on a tour of the Greek islands was all very well, but they had to get married first; and on 15 February 1930 the engaged couple boarded the SS *Bremen*, bound for New York. It was, Connolly told Balfour, 'perfectly bloody'. They travelled third-class, and Jean burst into tears when she was shown her cabin, and the old ladies with whom she was to share it; English Rose, more accustomed to eating raw eggs in Foyot's or the Bâteau Ivre, chattered its disapproval; life was only made tolerable by the fact that H.L. Mencken was on board and, as an old friend of Mrs

Warner, he invited them to join him in first-class for an occasional drink or meal. Nor was Connolly terribly taken with America: 'this is a bloody continent', and its inhabitants all 'bores or drunken bores', he informed Blakiston; it seemed a 'contemptible civilisation' after Europe, 'a world of money, jazz, motor-cars and speakeasies'.

Woodbrook was set in beech woods, overlooking a lake. Connolly was very taken with Jean's family: her mother was 'amusing and cultivated', her sister Annie, who was to become a lifelong friend, 'a sweet American rose', and Mr Warner a 'sweet, insignificant person'. Baltimore folk turned out to be Southern and horsey, eager for his views on English racehorses; the house was crammed with beautiful bits of furniture and valuable paintings, which 'we spend our spare time in surreptitiously valuing'; he was, he told Balfour, extremely comfortable but a bit bored, in that he had his own bathroom, a chauffeur was on hand to take them wherever they wanted to go, the food was excellent and the flow of drink unstoppable, but despite an electric laundry on the premises, there was 'no conversation, no intelligence of any kind except at bridge possibly'.

Timothy O'Connor, a contemporary and fellow-Colleger at Eton who was working in New York, had agreed to be the best man, and Anthony Russell, Georgiana Blakiston's brother, was roped in as an usher. 'You couldn't have picked a more inept best man,' a highly flattered O'Connor told him: luckily he had brought with him his tails from Eton, and he would probably come down on the bus from New York. As it turned out, he and Russell travelled down together by train, arriving in time for tea. Woodbrook, Russell told his mother, was right on the edge of the city, and had only been built within the last two or three years. The house was in a state of some confusion, with the result that 'one was always being burst in upon by a servant or someone by mistake': Russell himself was caught in the bath while changing for dinner, but before he could identify the intruder she had hurried away with a scream. Connolly, who seemed very on edge, insisted on their wearing white ties for dinner 'as a protest against American clothes'. After dinner the parson came round for a rehearsal of the wedding service, following which the younger generation went to dance in a 'road-house'.

The day of the wedding, 5 April, dawned warm and bright, but just as the three Englishmen were leaving for the hotel where lunch had been ordered, Connolly announced that he felt 'frightfully ill'. He drank some Bromo-Seltzer in a drug store, but that only made matters worse, and no sooner had he reached the hotel than he was violently sick – only to reappear moments later 'in great spirits'. Over lunch, Annie – who had never tried one before – found swallowing oysters an impossibility, and Connolly felt much improved after drinking a quantity of home-made wine (Prohibition was still in force). Congratulatory cables were read out, including one from Sligger and contributions in both Greek and Latin. Lunch over, they drove home for the wedding itself. Full evening dress was worn; Anthony Russell reported that 'Cyril, who has grown rather stout, managed to split most of his clothes but Timothy and I managed between us to fit him out with duplicates.' The wedding ceremony began at 6.30 and took place in the living-room, which had been emptied of its furniture to make room for flowers and a hundred or so guests. No sooner had the service ended than a 'crowd of coloured waiters in livery wearing white cotton gloves swarmed in with tables for supper'. They were headed by Emmanuel, the head waiter at the Baltimore, who looked exactly 'like John Sutro, only pitch black'. Champagne flowed, and Jean's brother Tom passed out and had to be locked in his room. As the meal was winding down, Connolly and Jean started the dancing, moving between the tables, while Emmanuel ladled out glasses of punch, making the brew more potent when there was a lull in the proceedings and diluting the mixture if matters threatened to get out of hand.

Jean's mother had offered to pay for the newly-weds to spend a week in New York before taking the *Mauretania* home on 10 April. They had dinner with Russell and O'Connor and then went on to see *Strictly Dishonourable*, a 'well-acted and funny play but decidedly what I think you call French', followed by a visit to the 'smartest speakeasy' in New York; Anthony Russell gave them lunch downtown, and showed them the Stock Exchange; Joseph Hergesheimer, a popular middlebrow novelist and a friend of Mrs Warner's, promised to introduce Connolly to the editor of *Vanity Fair*; the two of them were spotted walking hand-in-hand up a cavernous Manhattan street, like two small children adrift in a wood; and then, accompanied by English Rose and dragging with them Jean's 'fabulous trousseau, ermine coats etc.', it was time to board ship for the journey home. 'I came to America tourist third with a cheque for ten pounds, and I leave plus five hundred, a wife, a mandarin coat, a set of diamond studs, a stateroom and bath, and a decent box for the ferret,' Connolly informed Noël Blakiston, who was then moving into the house in Markham Square where he would live for the rest of his life. What more, indeed, could a young man want?

FOURTEEN

Living for Pleasure

Looking back at his life from the vantage-point of 1963, and a much-discussed, never embarked-upon second volume of autobiography, Connolly told Noël Blakiston that '1930 makes a real terminus and my life after that is an anti-climax'. Certainly the Barbarian Invasions had swept all before them, and Etonian friendships and all they had embodied were giving way to the worlds of literature and society; and yet his greatest achievements – writing *Enemies of Promise* and *The Unquiet Grave*, and editing *Horizon* – still lay before him, and he was embarking on a decade to which he would look back in later years with the same nostalgia and regret that he had hitherto reserved for the lost Edens of childhood and school. But, dauntingly, promise had to be transmuted into achievement, long letters to his friends, replete with youthful dreams and affectations, into the more prosaic matter of books and articles, innocence into experience; and, more than most, he found the transition a painful, sometimes agonising business, during the course of which he assumed his self-proclaimed and self-protective persona of the over-weight, indolent lover of pleasure, whose creative endeavours were blighted and undermined by the familiar cycle of sloth and procrastination, followed by agonies of guilt and remorse.

Back in England, the newly-weds moved restlessly about the country – from Bury Street, St James's, to Bath to Newton Ferrers to Big Chilling, to Swanage and to Oxford. Bury Street, St James, was the site of Rosa Lewis's louche and genially notorious Cavendish Hotel, widely patronised by raffish members of the upper classes. Its formidable proprietress had recently been immortalised as Lottie Crump in Evelyn Waugh's second novel, *Vile Bodies*; Christopher Sykes's sister, Freya Elwes, remembered visiting the Connollys in their room in the Cavendish with Evelyn Waugh shortly after the novel had been published, and how Waugh dived under the bed at the sound of approaching footsteps while the others sat in a row along it, their legs dangling down to shield their friend from Rosa's angry gaze.*

* She also remembered Rosa Lewis chasing the Connollys down the street, in vain pursuit of sums outstanding; and when, a few years later, her sister Angela married Ran Antrim, Connolly – already shamed in the church by his failure to turn up in tails – was further embarrassed (or so the story goes) by the unwelcome appearance of Rosa Lewis, who called out in a loud voice, ''Ere's the man wot owes me money. Bobbie, give 'im a writ.'

Despite his views on the French, Connolly and Jean decided to settle in France, and after visiting Bayonne and Biarritz they took a house called Les Lauriers Roses at Sanary, a few miles west of Toulon and on the other side of the bay from Bandol, another village much favoured by literary expatriates. 'All along the coast from Huxley Point and Castle Wharton to Cape Maugham, little colonies of angry giants had settled themselves,' Connolly wrote a year or two later in *The Rock Pool*: 'there were Campbell in Martigues, Aldington at Le Lavendou, anyone who could hold a pen in Saint Tropez, Arlen in Cannes, and, beyond, Monte Carlo and the Oppenheim country.' And now the Connollys were added to their numbers, moving into their new home early in July, intent on leading what Pearsall Smith, who came to stay in October, described as 'an ideal life, feasting on the essences of splendour'. Connolly had now decided that his real purpose in life was the 'rehabilitation of pleasure'. Money, he wrote in 'The Anonymous Voyage', was his favourite drug; the evangelists of his new religion were Catullus, Rochester, Dryden, Horace and Herrick, all of them redolent of 'the tragic pathos of Mozart and Watteau, that close pagan world of severe hedonistic discipline, of transient joys and pellucid sorrows'. 'A hedonist of first quality,' he went on, lining up the Major in his sights, 'can be recognised by his utter contempt for such occupational diseases as soldiering, sailoring, business or politics'; and, for the time being at least, he set his face against the 'committed' writing that was replacing the apolitical dandyism of the Twenties. The hedonist should avoid 'humanitarian' novels and exposés of poverty, disease, unemployment and the rest, for 'it is better to forget what one cannot alter.'

Connolly's cult of 'living for pleasure' and 'living for beauty' was to inspire some of his most eloquent nostalgia for the life he and Jean led together in the South of France, most famously in *The Unquiet Grave*:

> 'Living for beauty' – October on the Mediterranean; blue skies rinsed by the mistral, red and golden vine branches, wind-fretted waves chopping round the empty yachts; plane trees peeling; palms rearing up in their dingy underclothes; mud in the streets, and from doorways at night the smell of burning oil. On dark evenings I used to bicycle in to fetch our dinner, past the harbour with its bobbing launches and the bright cafés with their signs banging. At the local restaurant there would be one or two 'plats à emporter', to which I would add some wine, sausage and Gruyère cheese, a couple of 'Diplomates' to smoke and a new 'Detective' or a 'Chasseur Français'; then I would bowl back heavy-laden with the mistral behind me, a lemur buttoned up inside my jacket with his head sticking out.

Inherent in Connolly's philosophy of hedonism was the same romantic restlessness, the same unhedonistic tendency to enjoy life in anticipation or in retrospect rather than at the actual moment of its happening, that had earlier infused his visions of Eden:

> And 'living for beauty': in one lovely place always pining for another; with the perfect woman imagining one more perfect; with a bad book unfinished beginning a second, while the almond tree is in blossom, the grasshopper fat and the winter nights disquieted by the plock and gurgle of the sea...

Nor was such a life compatible with that of the artist. A year or two later, Alpdodger decided that 'a life of definite and studied materialism and a philosophy of appetite and cynicism, and a cult of sensual and senseless ease, are bad things for the artist. They narrow the imagination and dull the more delicate susceptibilities...' Alpdodger's creator was equally aware that creativity and the kind of hedonism he so lyrically extolled were not reconcilable: writing about D.H. Lawrence in his journal, he suggested that

> the real disadvantage of Lawrence is that the nearer one comes to his happy and intelligent paganism, the less one has to write about... A philosophy which satisfies man with his lot automatically destroys his imaginative desire to create a better world; a philosophy which encourages normal appetites provides normal satisfaction for the mood which leads to composition

– an argument he was to develop at greater length in an essay entitled 'Under Which King?', first published in *Life and Letters*, in which he mused on the incompatibility of the two elements in the magazine's title, and explored the paradoxes whereby most writers 'have not been passed fit for the business of living', while even the greatest literature has, in the very long term, only a limited life.

Such observations were almost certainly both genuine and self-serving, a realistic assessment which at the same time provided a justification and an excuse in advance for any failings on the part of their originator. And despite the new-found wealth which enabled him to indulge his hedonistic urges, the sudden acquisition of riches was as potent a daydream as the writer's life of lonely dedication. Like Alpdodger, he dreamed of winning

> £30,000 from the Grand National Sweepstake. I invest £25,000 at 5%, perhaps in Colombian 7% even, for they have never yet defaulted. With £1000 I buy up a Bentley, the large 8-litre tourer that goes 100 m.p.h. With another £1000 I finance my flight abroad, putting by the remaining three to rent and furnish a small Georgian house in London in the Fall. I go first to Foyot's Hotel in Paris, and book the little suite up the staircase,

> with the corridor looking onto the rue Condé. Then I go south, returning thin and brown . . .

And, sure enough, he had reassuring news about his physique, or so he informed his mother-in-law: 'The most important thing I have to say is how much *thinner* I am. I hate to think of you still picturing your son-in-law as one of those bloated young men that dine out a lot and work in museums in New York or London. I got so fat because Maryland cooking took me that way . . .' They made a point of not eating breakfast, he continued, and spent a good deal of time swimming and playing ping-pong; and 'Jean runs the house excellently though it only consists of one servant who goes away in the afternoon.' He was still toying with the idea of a yacht on which to ferry his friends round the Greek islands. Pearsall Smith wrote to say that he had been to see a yacht agent on his return; but in a later letter he urged caution ('I don't think you possess the qualities of a sea-dog, nor Jean of a sea-bitch'), after which no more was heard on the matter.

Visitors to Sanary included Jack Blakiston, who brought with him, as requested, Wyndham Lewis's *The Apes of God*, and asked his host if he could possibly pay back some money he'd lent him, since his bank was playing up; and Evelyn Waugh, who wrote afterwards to say how much he'd enjoyed meeting the Huxleys and inspecting the brothels in Toulon. The Connollys' encounters with two of their literary neighbours, Edith Wharton and Aldous Huxley, were to prove a good deal more traumatic. Mrs Wharton was of the same generation as Pearsall Smith: he regarded her as 'the social pinnacle of the two continents, and the meeting had to be carefully prepared with many letters telling us how to behave and what not to talk about.' In one of these letters Pearsall Smith told his protégé that Robert Gathorne-Hardy had inherited his mantle as secretary ('It would be fun if you would write him an anonymous letter, warning him against me as a merciless and well-known slave-driver, and saying that you have seen on the Riviera the wreck of his former secretary'), before going on to issue further instructions about Mrs Wharton; and in December the Connollys were finally invited to lunch at Ste Claire le Château. Robert Norton, Mrs Wharton's companion, was in attendance, and the other guests were Aldous and Maria Huxley:

> The Huxleys, with whom we were on terms of profound ambivalence, drove us over in their three-seater Bugatti. Jean and Maria Huxley were highly suspicious of each other, and Aldous was quite unaware that my deep admiration for him – which was responsible for us settling in Sanary – had curdled.
>
> We entered the dining-room like two opposing tennis teams before an already biased umpire (Aldous was an undisputed lunch champion.) The

> food was delicious. What eggs! But the conversation, except for some rallies from Aldous, hung fire. Unfortunately, it turned on differences between Americans and Europeans – and Jean mentioned that Americans had a different way of holding the fork, shifting it to the right hand. This was received by her hostess with blank incomprehension – and allowed by the Huxleys to go into the net. Forty-love. Bravely plunging, like Scott Fitzgerald on a similar occasion, Jean went on to say that many Americans addressed each other as 'Mr' on envelopes, not as 'Esq,' like the English. 'None that I know,' exclaimed Mrs Wharton, and awarded game to the Huxleys.

'We arrived in the shadow of greatness, while Mrs Wharton seemed in no doubt who mattered most,' Connolly remembered: 'She wrote and thanked Logan but next time invited the Huxleys without us.' Jean liked Mrs Wharton well enough, even if she was 'a bit elderly and Henry Jamesian', but, writing to Mary Berenson some days after this unhappy occasion, Nicky Mariano reported that 'Edith has had both couples here lately and liked Cyril but not as much as Huxley. She says that Cyril's wife is an awful lump but her descriptions of people are not always to be trusted especially if they are young and conceivably intimidated by her not always reassuring manner.'*

Although in fact the Connollys were invited again to Ste Claire le Château – they were grilled about Joyce and the Modern Movement – news of that disastrous first meal soon filtered back to St Leonard's Terrace. 'I feel you somewhat mismanaged that scene at Mrs Wharton's,' Pearsall Smith told him: ' – from what you say it is plain that she was *terrified* of you all – thought you regarded her as an old has-been and Mrs Humphry Ward, and that she put on, as she does to protect herself, her masque of wealth and worldliness. You ought to have made her drop it, which she would have done at a touch of understanding . . . Plainly I ought to have been there.' A month later, however, it appeared that 'you were a great success with Mrs Wharton. If she asks you to stay, remember she is a *demon* for tidiness, but the food makes it worthwhile.' The meals if not the tidiness would have appealed to her new neighbours – according to Kenneth Clark, 'the books snapped back into the shelves on an invisible elastic and the cushions were plumped into place by a footman the moment one got up from them' – but no further opportunities arose for sampling either.

Nor were relations with the Huxleys any happier: indeed, Pearsall Smith had made overtures on their behalf to Mrs Wharton simply because, despite

* The slight still rankled over thirty years later. Reviewing Nicky Mariano's account of her life with Berenson in the *Sunday Times* in 1966, Connolly told his readers that its 'only surrender to the modish cattiness of today occurs in the one reference to myself and my first wife: "An awful lump!" Who would know if I did not speak up that she was a beautiful Baltimore girl of nineteen.'

Connolly's admiration – 'overwhelming adoration', even – for the older writer, their friendship had failed to flourish as expected. Aldous and Maria Huxley had moved to Bandol in 1930, and were to remain in the Villa Huley until 1937, long after the Connollys had retreated back to England as 'failed expatriates'. Sybille Bedford, a frequent visitor to the Villa, remembers the country round as being still 'unspoilt, a classical landscape of hills, olives, vines': the Huxleys' villa stood on a 'slightly scruffy promontory', and although Huxley was enviably disciplined and hard-working, they received a steady stream of visitors, Raymond Mortimer and Eddy Sackville-West among them, whom they regaled with delicious meals of 'fried rabbit and zucchini flowers'. Huxley's witty, erudite, cynical novels had seemed the epitome of Twenties sophistication; both Huxley and Connolly were products of Eton and Balliol, and the older man's languid urbanity quite obliterated the memory of those distant days when as a severely short-sighted junior master, known as 'the Giraffe' on account of his height, he had been spotted groping his way up Eton High Street; it seemed like a literary friendship made in heaven, with Connolly cast in the role of acolyte, or apostolic successor. Or, as he put it years later, ' "Aldous!": that unique Christian name has reverberated through my life . . . I settled in Sanary to be near him and one of my happiest moments was when his red Bugatti first swung into the drive.'

And yet nothing seemed to go right between them. Part of the problem, according to Sybille Bedford, was that Connolly was far too familiar a figure, far too much like Huxley himself had been some ten years earlier, to be of much interest to the older man: 'Cyril may have reminded him of the attitudes of his younger self, which he was beginning to wish to slough off, aestheticism, pure art, the love of words; at thirty-eight Aldous at heart was no longer the literary dandy who had captured Cyril's generation.' Huxley's interests were already beginning to veer towards mysticism and religious experience; and despite Connolly's eloquent admiration for him, he appeared much to prefer the company of the Seabrooks, a conventional English couple who had come to live in the area. Nor were matters improved by the fact that Jean – whom Sybille Bedford remembers as endowed with 'slow, erotic charm, talented, witty in her own right, but wilful, lazy, prone to discontents, self-destructive' – disliked and resented Maria Huxley. Mrs Huxley was anxious to guard her husband against the time-wasting depredations of an endless stream of visitors, and whenever the Connollys called she would head them off with a raised forefinger and a whispered embargo ('*Aldous is working*') – with the result that 'years after Jean still spoke of the watchdog with bitterness'. And, to make matters worse, on those rare occasions when the Huxleys could be lured across to the Connollys' 'wind-battered house on the sea road east of Sanary',

The wedding of Matthew Connolly and Muriel Vernon. Aunt Tots is to the left of the picture; Harold Kemble on the far right.

Young Cyril in Corsica.

(*Right*) Connolly as 'Miggs' in *Barnaby Rudge*, December 1917.

(*Above and right*)
Connolly at Eton.

(*Below*) An Eton Field Day for the OTC, c.1920. Cyril Connolly is drinking from the flask whilst George Orwell is sitting on the log at the extreme left.

(*Right*)
Connolly and Bobbie Longden, walking round Mont Blanc in 1924.

(*Left*) Noël Blakiston.

(*Above*) Sligger Urquhart outside the Chalet.

(*Left*) Connolly and Richard Pares.

A group at the Chalet: the back row, standing, consists of Patrick Kinross, Basil Murray, Richard Pares, and Bobbie Longden. Connolly is sitting on the right.

Berlin, 1929. Left to right: Leigh Ashton, Alfred Beit, Gerry Wellington, Christopher Sykes, Connolly, David Herbert.

'L'Enfance de Palinure' by Christopher Sykes; Logan Pearsall Smith is the god-father.

L'Enfance de Palinure.

And when we're
bigger we'll write
ever such a nice
booksie wooksie
just like old
Logie Taughtums.

Xmas
1945.

To Cyril & Lys
with love from
Christopher
& Camilla.

(*Left*) Desmond and Molly MacCarthy

(*Below*) Jean and Connolly.

Connolly in Spain, covering the Civil War for the *New Statesman*.

A Tickerage gathering, taken by Joan Eyres-Monsell. Left to right, standing, are Patrick Kinross (barely visible), Constant Lambert, Dick Wyndham, Tom Driberg, Connolly and Stephen Spender. Jean is immediately below Constant Lambert, and Angela Culme-Seymour between Lambert and Wyndham. The bottom tier consists of Tony Hyndman, Mamaine Paget and John Rayner.

The Connollys; photographed by Barbara Ker-Symer in 1936.

> Neither she nor Aldous approved of their way of life; they did not see it as romantic or delicious. Eating your dinner with your fingers reading before the fire meant leaving grape skins and the skeletons of sardines between the pages. The ferrets stank; the lemur hopped upon the table and curled his exquisite little black hand around your brandy glass. Your *brandy glass* exactly: liqueurs after luncheon. The Connollys did like grand restaurants. And they would not descend to any disguising of their tastes. People, as I have said, tempered their behaviour to the Huxleys' standards; the Connollys were more irrepressible and to Jean it would not have occurred to make friends on anything but her own terms.*

'The Huxleys have added ten years to my life,' Connolly confided to his journal, while Jean told Jack Blakiston that he was much missed, since they now 'had nobody to hate the Huxleys with'; and, quite apart from the blow to his self-esteem, Huxley's industry and versatility – if not what he actually wrote – acted as a permanent reproach, and yet another reason for failing to get down to whatever great work surged through his head as he lay in bed of a morning. In an early draft of an autobiographical piece called 'Humane Killer', the narrator's endeavours to write are thwarted, in that 'whatever he attempted Aldous Huxley got in his way . . . He could nowhere find what the newspapers called an avenue unexplored without Huxley rising, like Etna, at the end of it'; and Alpdodger's efforts to put pen to paper were blighted by the mere thought of 'that human factory, whose siren blows at eight o'clock, whose evening hooter never seems to blow at all: book of stories, book of essays, novel, book of stories, poems, book of travel, novel, book of essays! How can I compete with him?' For a while, Connolly's erstwhile hero became, in literary terms at least, 'Private Enemy No 1', who 'does everything I want to a few years ahead of me, and bedraggles it all a little in the process, with more industry, more method, less talent and a horrible kind of hack-writer's fatigue.'†

* After reading a review by Connolly of a study of Huxley's work in the *Sunday Times* in 1972, Sybille Bedford, who was still working on her biography of Huxley, wrote to him to say

> I rather think you got it wrong about Aldous and Maria at Sanary. It wasn't because you and Jean were not clever enough for them, but because you were too clever. Clever in the same way Aldous had been as a young man, interested in the same books in the same way. This, in a kind of instinctive way, no longer interested Aldous. He wanted to stay away from his younger self. That is why he enjoyed seeing people like the Seabrooks, for instance, *terra incognita*.

† During the Thirties, Connolly turned against Huxley's writing as well, savaging *Point Counter Point* in the *New Statesman* and deriding Huxley's fictional world in one of his fiercest parodies, 'Told in Gath'. After the war, however, he was reconciled to the man and his work; interviewing Huxley for *Picture Post* in 1948, he recalled how, while living in Sanary, he developed 'an inferiority complex which prevented me from writing myself for, as I sat exhausted by idleness in front of my desk, I could hear, in my imagination, the tapping of the typewriter of this most prolific of contemporary authors drumming out across the opaline sea-dazzle of the little Mediterranean bay. I became a sort of mental poor relation.'

*

Looking back at those early years of Connolly's first marriage, Peter Quennell thought it his 'happiest and calmest' period, 'when, with a wife he loved and the series of cherished pets, including his splendid ring-tailed lemurs, he had settled down to "live for beauty".' His old friend, he remembered, had grown more solid as a result of his marriage; and,

> no longer a rebellious young romantic who rejected every commonplace worldly standard, he was now prepared to give the world its due. Not that he had quite abandoned his juvenile romanticism; the worldly-wise hedonist remained an imaginative perfectionist, dreaming of the perfect house he would buy in the perfect landscape, even – he had become a renowned gourmet – of the perfectly ordered and attended meal.

Quennell's abiding image was of 'Cyril heavily overcoated, bearing a load of books and magazines; Jean with a fox-faced, golden-eyed lemur wrapping its black-gloved hands around her neck – both a little stout, and neither inclined to hurry.' Despite Connolly's dreams of perfection, 'the bohemian disorder of their household was its only real drawback,' and squeamish visitors – in Sanary or London – may well have found their livestock unappealing at times. Quennell, reporting on what Huxley had told him, described how Jean would give the ferrets raw meat, and then wipe her fingers down the front of an embroidered Chinese house-coat; Georgiana Blakiston remembered the lemurs sitting on the lavatory seat in the Connollys' London flat, and warming their hands in front of the fire, and how shocked her mother was when their owners stole eggs from a bird's nest with which to feed them; Connolly himself told Noël Blakiston that they had acquired two new lemurs, 'young and dirty and clinging, and screaming all the time'. Two of them at least were immortalised in *The Unquiet Grave*: Whoopee, 'gentle and fearless', whom they bought in Marseilles along with an over-charged marmoset, and who chased large dogs and pulled their tails, rode around on the back of Connolly's bike, purred when stroked, and died after eating a poisoned fig put down for the rats; and Polyp, 'most gifted of lemurs', who – even though 'his manners were those of some spoiled young Maharajah, his intelligence not inferior, his heart all delicacy' – liked to brandish 'a black prickle-shaped penis' before 'one or two well-seasoned old ladies', and had a weakness for women, gin and muscat grapes. He died of pneumonia, and 'with him vanished the sea-purple cicada kingdom of calanque and stone pine and the concept of life as an arrogant private dream shared by two'. In due course the lemurs came to embody another vanished Eden, and to symbolise the dream of 'living for beauty':

> To have set foot in Lemuria is to have been close to the mysterious source of existence, to have known what it is to live wholly in the present, to soar through the green world four yards above the ground, to experience sun, warmth, love and pleasure as intolerably as we glimpse them in waking dreams, and to have heard that heart-rending cry of the lonely or abandoned which goes back to our primaeval dawn. Wild ghost faces from a lost continent who will soon be extinct...

Living for beauty was all very well but inevitably it proved a more expensive business than living by more conventional means – still more so since Connolly was proving a 'born host', and a generous one at that. Despite Jean's private income, money remained in short supply and, to make matters worse, debts from the past continued to haunt them. One of these concerned books to the value of £7 14*s* 2*d* – among them *To the Lighthouse*, works by Theocritus and Thomas Gray and books printed by Thomas Baskerville– bought three years earlier from Birrell and Garnett. A firm of debt-collectors was eventually employed to recover the money, and they in turn put their French agents on to the trail. In the end the balance was paid, via the London Association for the Protection of Trade, but only after a writ had been issued. Nor were Connolly's friends immune from the ramifications of debt: Patrick Balfour wrote to apologise for having given some institutional creditor their address despite Connolly's having begged him to keep them at bay; no doubt Balfour himself was still owed something, for he wrote later to say that 'I did not realise, when you asked me to stay, that your hospitality was intended as part payment of debt' rather than as an act of 'disinterested kindness'. It was inevitable, perhaps, that Mrs Warner was resorted to *in extremis*, sending Jean a Christmas bonus in the hope that 'it will get your car out of hock', or that Connolly's journal should be littered with freshly-minted aphorisms on poverty and its tribulations ('The artist is a member of the leisured classes who cannot pay for his leisure', 'Solvency is a fulltime job', 'The want of money renders insipid every joy that money cannot buy', and 'One can get richer by one's friends getting poorer').

Quite how long the Connollys remained at Les Lauriers Roses is unclear, though neither Mrs Wharton nor the Huxleys can have made them want to linger: 'We are both sick of Sanary,' Connolly told Jack Blakiston, adding that he was falling out of love with himself, and had reached the stage at which 'a romantic ceases to find himself romantic.' Much of 1931 was spent travelling: in Provence, in Normandy and Brittany in the company of Mrs Warner, in Spain, Morocco and Majorca, and to the Caernarvon Arms in Dulverton in Devon, a thatched farmhouse run by Mr and Mrs Webb (known as the 'Cobwebbs') and much favoured by literary folk where, according to Pearsall

Smith, Connolly tried his hand as an angler; and in November they took for four months No 10 Wilton Mews near Belgrave Square. The following month Connolly made a rare reappearance in the book pages of the *New Statesman*, his first for over two years, reviewing a collection of detective stories. He compared them favourably with most 'literary novels' on the grounds that they were the 'nearest approach to pure form in any work produced today' and because, with their insistence on accurate detail, 'in a hundred years our thrillers will have become text-books of social history, the most authentic chronicles of how we lived'. That said, 'There is something repugnant to me about this new class of detectives, they have no reticence, are no longer great gentlemen nor even well off,' he decided:

> They are bumptious, exhibitionist, Rugby-and-Balliol Broadcasting young men, virile male virgins, inquisitive, middle-brows, opportunists. They wear rough clothes, interesting ties and Bloomsbury black hats. They shovel poor Colonel Gore off the pavement and laugh at Beau Drummond's Three Nuns profile framed in the window of the 'Junior Sports Club' . . .

But despite this deterioration, detective stories remained 'the last repository of our passion for the countryside':

> Living in the South of France I began to pine for the English winter; in vain I turned to Georgian poets and lyric novelists of our unproductive soil. I received only a kind of nausea . . . I cured my homesickness, walking with Inspector French round the Mumbles, exploring Rochester with Thorndyke, going with Mr Fletcher to country towns till I could find my way in any of them to the doctor's pleasant Georgian house, the rectory, the spinster's cottage, the eccentric lawyer's office . . .

Connolly was not to resume regular book-reviewing until the spring of 1935, but in the meantime he tried his hand as an art critic. In October 1930, his successor at the Yeo, John Betjeman, went to work as an assistant editor of the *Architectural Review*, then flourishing under the eccentric supervision of Hubert de Cronin Hastings. Other members of staff included Hugh Casson and the architectural historian J.M. Richards; and before long Betjeman was commissioning articles from his Oxford friends – Peter Quennell, Christopher Hobhouse, Robert Byron and, later, Brian Howard, Evelyn Waugh, Patrick Balfour, John Sparrow, Alan Pryce-Jones and even W.H. Auden. Connolly, a relatively late arrival, provided his first contribution in the January 1932 issue. 'To be pitch-forked into art criticism without either the knowledge or the taste that distinguishes an art critic is a frightening thing,' he confessed: 'Like a new boy who arrives in the middle of a term, one adopts a brazen attitude, secretly keeping one's ears open for the jargon of the older boys, then timidly experimenting in the new slang.' He had, he admitted, been busily reading Roger Fry in order to prepare himself for the first task in hand – reviewing a collection of pots and furniture designed by, among others, Vanessa Bell and Duncan Grant. The following month he reviewed an exhibition of French paintings at Burlington House: Watteau provided the 'high spot', with one particular painting rendering

> what is most difficult of all sensations to portray without heaviness or sentimentality, the sadness of the moment, that fugitive distress of hedonism which falls imperceptibly, like a dew, from pleasure, and which, when apprehended, gives rise to the deepest, the most nearly tragic emotion admissible in the ancient world.

And if Eton had cast its shadow over his apologetic preamble to his first review, the spirit of Hugh Macnaghten and his pre-Raphaelite vision of the ancient world returned to haunt his evaluation of Epstein's water-colours: he praised Epstein for his semitic qualities, for 'no one is better equipped to rescue the Old Testament from the Anglican Church, to scrape off the accretions of Anglo-Hellenic good taste that generations of Etonian bishops have allowed to accumulate . . .'

Connolly's relations with John Betjeman were, and would remain, jovial, even facetious, and later in the decade he and Jeannie would often stay with the Betjemans in their house in Uffington; with his fellow-contributor, Evelyn Waugh, they were, and would remain, a good deal trickier and more ambivalent. The two men had much in common, and admired one another as stylists, but Waugh was unable to resist teasing and deriding the hapless Connolly. In October 1932 Christopher Sykes asked the Connollys to dinner, and Waugh's latest novel, *Black Mischief*, came up in the conversation. Not for the last time, Waugh had appropriated Connolly's surname for a character in his novel – in this case, an African general, whose lady friend was known as 'Black Bitch'. Connolly raved over the book, declaring it was the best thing Waugh had written, and when Jean brought up General Connolly and the Black Bitch he affected unconcern. Later on, however – according to Sykes – he expressed resentment on his own behalf and Jean's; and although, a couple of years later, he referred to Waugh as 'our valued friend – so mature and pithy and, religion apart, so frivolous', theirs remained a love-hate relationship, with Waugh the aggressor and Connolly the frequently squirming victim.

Both men were habitués of that snobbish, catty, time-wasting yet oddly beguiling world where bohemia and high society enmesh, and in one of his

Alpdodger pieces Connolly provided a withering account of what it was like to be yet another 'young man on the make, jealous of his rivals, desperately anxious to please, to believe in the people he is pleasing and yet miserably being reminded by every remark, every expression, of the horror this gathering of cultivated people inspires':

> A crowd of awful people whom one is supposed to like burst in suddenly. All the intellectually and socially elect who swim in smart Bohemia, whom one detests and daren't say so. Chelsea ladies with flower pieces and intimate little still-lifes of tables and sofas under their arms arrive for stale gossip and worse bridge, sleek levantines from the choicer museums, literary civil servants who set weekly competitions, literary hostesses who entertain literary generals who sign copies of their books for literary butlers, musical lions with scurf on their shoulders, tea-party tigers who ask searching questions ('How is Nobsplotch considered in America, where do the young rate him?'), people of taste and discrimination, fastidious people who go everywhere and listen to anything, delicious people scavenging for copy, the charming and talented Mrs Bryan Guinness [later Diana Mosley], with her large cowlike beauty and strident chatter, dragging her poetical little husband-attachment behind her, Miss Oglander, a goose but a dear goose, Lord Usher, David Cecil 'with his easy and informal manner and delightful and unforced sense of humour'. Mr Bogey is there, suspicious as a house detective, and the appalling Mitford family – the brother, like a male magnolia, leading a string of ever louder, ever fatter, ever more marriageable sisters – pretty little Mrs Quennell snooping up details of hats and dresses and determined not to let Peter stay too long, Lady Colefax, a middle-class puritan, a budding Maintenon, the most unlovable woman in the world, and Hope Johnstone, the canny little parasite, surely the most unlovable man. Roger Hinks titters after dowagers, with a perpetual dewdrop on his British Museum nose.* Young publishers in interesting black suits fix a grin on their faces and set rotating from customer to patron and back again their gentlemanly brown eyes. Bloomsbury intellectuals, scientific enlighteners of humanity in the cheap Sunday papers, wander round with that unemployed stoop, that hunched-up look that comes from carrying all the cares of the world; with large and crucified eyes they pretend not to have seen

* A contemporary of Connolly's, Roger Hinks was Assistant Keeper in the Department of Greek and Roman Antiquities at the British Museum from 1926 until 1939, when he had to resign, unfairly, following a scandal over the over-drastic cleaning of the Elgin Marbles: according to Francis King, Hinks decided one day that 'Those could do with a clean', and an underling set about them with 'the then equivalent of Harpic'; but the real damage was done by the wire brushes used. King thought Hinks, on form, 'one of the wittiest men I have known', but no love seems to have been lost between him and Connolly. Writing in his diary in November 1940, Hinks recorded how 'Joe Ackerley told me at lunch that after I had met him and Cyril Connolly the other day CC said, "He is my bitterest enemy"...'

each other, waiting for a chance to launch their respective monologues. Tea spoons rattle, tough young married couples roam acquisitively, the unattached men cry 'Wait a moment while I bring out my little blue book'...

He hated the smugness and the vulgarity of such gatherings, yet he went all the same for fear of being left out or disliked; in Alpdodger's case, at least, 'an acute interior loneliness drives him to society, and once there, with the natural tropism of a vain and egotistical creature, he turns his face to the sun, and uses his gifts for flattering others to solicit their admiration.' Or, the words of his *alter ego* Lincoln Croyle, the author of 'Humane Killer' and an imperfect anagram of his creator's name:

O Osbert, Father Osbert,
On whom the young men pray
A Sitwell voice, a Sitwell face
Bestow on me this day.

And teach me in society
To cleave to what is best
And jostle, ogle, push that I
May stink like all the rest.

In mellower mood, Connolly recalled 'the brilliant give-and-take of a smart luncheon party. Good talk: the delicious pleasure of explaining modern tendencies to a very great lady: conversation, the only thing worth living for – or so a few of us thought – that bright impermanent flower of the mind. London was full of it in the early Thirties – repartee, good food, great houses.'

Like most young couples, the Connollys were keen to have children, and spent time looking for suitable family houses. Despite Connolly's vainglorious boast to Mrs Warner, living for pleasure was bad for the waistline: both grew steadily stouter, but Jean's fatness was not simply a matter of overeating. She looked puffed-up even before Freya Elwes sent her to see her gynaecologist in the hope that he might be able to shed some light on her inability to conceive; she had to undergo an operation, as a result of which it was confirmed that it would be impossible for her ever to become pregnant. Early in 1933 Mollie Connolly wrote to Jean from South Africa to say how sorry she was; but it was surely better for Jean to have had the operation, and besides they had so much else to enjoy together. Jean grew fatter still after the operation, and the absence of children became a sore point – so much so that Georgiana Blakiston came to believe that Connolly's envy of their children contributed to a certain estrangement between the two couples, and that his well-known jibe about the 'pram in the hall' as the enemy of literary or artistic achievement may have been partly aimed in their direction. 'Giana and I no doubt have our labels now – complacent, domesticated, timid, hogwashy, English, ruled by the cowardice of conventions rather than the courage of convictions,' Noël Blakiston complained to his brother Jack: 'I am just generally exasperated by him laying down the law, and believe that the childless and moveable and independent are as likely to become bores as the fertile owners of homes dull and hogwashy.' Connolly had come to stay with Giana's parents, and had proved 'so boring that we went into corners of the garden to get away from his unceasing informing voice.' 'If I met him now for the first time I should find him an extraordinarily unattractive man,' Blakiston concluded – and as for his mother-in-law, she 'could not endure this little dago who walked on her flower-beds and called her Lady Vita.' In *Enemies of Promise*, in which the pram made its first appearance, Connolly was to include the 'clasping tares of domesticity' among the distractions that lay in wait to lure the young writer from the paths of dedicated virtue: a wife and a house and children not only cost money, the earning of which could all too easily involve hack work or distracting labour, but

> Children dissipate the longing for immortality which is the compensation of the childless writer's work. But it is not only a question of children or no children, there is a moment when the cult of home and happiness becomes harmful and domestic happiness one of those escapes from talent which we have deplored, for it replaces that necessary unhappiness without which writers perish. A writer is in danger of allowing his talent to dull who lets more than a year go past without finding himself in his rightful place of composition, the small single unluxurious 'retreat' of the twentieth century, the hotel bedroom.

Even if Jean's operation enabled Connolly to sidestep the particular snare of the pram in the hall, other enemies of promise were ready to take their toll; her health – and her drinking – still remained a problem. The following year she wrote to her mother to say that, since she was still feeling seedy and under the weather, she had been to see a consultant called Giebie-Cobb, who told her that her glands were 'disarranged' and that she had over-strained her heart, which was anyway of a 'nervous' disposition: he advised her to adopt a diet of fruit and veg., drink nothing but cider, go to bed by nine every evening and, ideally, live a quiet life in the country. Writing from the Easton Court Hotel in Chagford, in the heart of the cider country, Connolly told Elizabeth Bowen that following the doctor's regime in a country hotel was 'fairly easy, as the whole place is in bed by 10. After a few meals diet or total abstinence becomes second nature and there is really nobody one could conceivably want to have a drink with. She is very much better already.' Such optimism was almost certainly misplaced, for they were joined by Peter Quennell and his new wife, Marcelle, after which 'we maintain a happy balance between health and intoxication'. The two couples had dined together earlier in the year, during the course of which Marcelle had passed out and been put to bed. 'She is a fine girl,' Connolly had decided, 'the sexiest articulation, mouth like Betty Kemble's – a natural drunken Bohemian . . . she has several times woken up with strange men in bed and remembered nothing of what happened.' But now, in the Easton Court,

> Marcelle has entangled us with everyone in the hotel by the frankness of her speech and the freedom of her manners – we have any sitting-room we occupy immediately to ourselves. My conscience pricks me when I catch sad glances from elderly American ladies and others with whom we were on speaking terms before they came.

The Quennells subjected the old ladies to a 'constant stream of "fucks" and "bloodys" in a small and crowded dining-room', diverting them further with extended quarrels about where and how Marcelle had disposed of her sanitary towels.

After her initial operation, Connolly took Jean on holiday in Greece, in February 1933. In Athens they stayed at the Grande Bretagne, and after a few days they were relieved to bump into Brian Howard and his German boy friend, Toni Altmann, who had just been staying with Francis Turvill-Petre on Euboea:* Connolly had found Athens tedious and unattractive, 'a tenth-rate Turkish market town' transforming itself into a 'tenth-rate Californian suburb'. The food in the hotel was repellent, the whisky tasted of sawdust, there seemed little to do but read four-days-old copies of the Continental *Daily Mail* and watch 'heavily bearded' Athenian ladies escorting their equally bewhiskered daughters to lugubrious *thés dansants*. Variety was to hand in the form of an attempted *coup*. Elections had recently taken place, and it looked as though Venizelos, the long-lasting strong man of Greek politics, was about to be defeated. A general attempted a *coup d'état*; tanks moved into the streets; Connolly and his party were wandering about when the machine-guns opened up, and a man was gunned down in front of them, his brains spilling on to the pavement. Back in the Grande Bretagne, 'all was cheerfulness and commotion; everyone felt important and with a reason for living', and whisky and a gramophone were produced. Connolly wrote an account of what he had seen in the *New Statesman*, where it was published as 'Spring

* Turvill-Petre's bizarre homosexual establishment there was later described at length by Christopher Isherwood in his novel *Down There on a Visit* – in which Jean also makes an appearance, though at a later stage in her life.

Revolution', and, with calm restored, normal life resumed once more, and Brian Howard and Toni Altmann prowled the bars of Piraeus in search of sailors. The little party set out across the cold winter seas to Mount Athos and Salonika, and then overland to the Peloponnese, to Nauplia and Mycenae – where, years later, Connolly found that Brian Howard had written 'Shit. Prig' against his name in the visitors' book at the Belle Hélène Hotel.

By now they were pining for greenery, and for Portugal in particular. Connolly discovered that they could take a cargo boat from Piraeus to Seville, stopping off in Sicily *en route*: the crew was American, and Jello was eaten for pudding. It was agreed that the Connollys would pay for Toni Altmann, but that Brian Howard should repay his own fare as and when he could. Although Howard was no longer the golden youth of Eton and Oxford – drink, drugs and a general sense of hopelessness and drift were taking their toll – he still

> looked deliciously handsome and distinguished, and dressed with negligent charm in Mrs Stuart Richardson's shaggy Greek silk suits and tweeds, with a handkerchief knotted round his long neck. The enormous brown eyes in the long sad face could sparkle with malicious gaiety. He played his voice like a guitar. Both Jean and I were slightly infatuated with him . . .

Toni Altmann, on the other hand, looked like a wholesome English schoolboy, of whom 'I can't remember anything he said except "*Aber* Prian!" in permanent expostulation.'

They disembarked at Seville, after the cargo boat had picked its way up the Guadalquivir. From there they made their way to the Algarve, where Brian Howard built sand castles on the beach at Praia de Rocha, and a good deal of *vinho verde* was drained. Money was running low, and matters were made worse when Brian Howard took to visiting the casino at Estoril, where he lost all the money he already owed the Connollys and was reduced to writing out an enormous cheque on his mother's joint account. The Connollys were returning to England by sea, leaving the other two behind, and on their last day they all gathered in their favourite bar in Lisbon, where they were joined by another English couple, the Girouards. Connolly, Jean and Toni Altmann had three gin fizzes each, and the others two apiece, but they were charged for a good deal more. According to Jean's version of events, Dick Girouard ('a little rabbit usually') took umbrage at this and insisted on leaving at once, at which a chucker-out seized Connolly by the arm and was slapped in the face by Jean, a fight broke out, and they were all rushed to a police station with the exception of Brian Howard, who hid in a telephone box. In Connolly's account, written a good many years later, a porter prevented Jean from leaving, Brian Howard leapt to her defence and hit him, a fight broke out, and the revellers were carted off to prison and finger-printed. Either way, the British Embassy had to intervene before the Connollys could be released to make their way home.

England, by contrast, seemed 'inconceivably ugly, only a change from yellow brick and slate to red brick and slate to tell when one goes from a town to the country'. They went to stay at Prince's Hotel in Hove, from where Connolly wrote to Noël Blakiston to announce the arrival of two new lemurs and to ask him if he would send on a parcel of clothes, adding the cost of postage to the £5 already owed to his old friend. Jean told Mrs Warner that they were looking for a house in or near Brighton for the summer, with – ideally – a cottage attached in which to house the Major; and in June Enid Bagnold wrote to say how delighted she was to learn that they had rented Bayzehill House in Rottingdean – though 'Mind you pay, darlings, it will give me such a bad name if you don't...'

The weather in Rottingdean may not have been up to Sanary's standards, but the company of friends of their own age must have seemed like balm after Mrs Wharton and the Huxleys. Although Connolly apologised to Asquith's daughter, Princess Elizabeth Bibesco, for not sending her a written invitation to dinner at Bayzehill ('the moment I got back here the *horrible* inferiority of the country descended on us – it suddenly seemed impertinent to ask anybody to come sixty miles for dinner'), other friends seemed more than happy to make their way to the south coast – even if, as Alan Pryce-Jones discovered, there was always a danger of upsetting their host's newly-found expertise as a chooser of fine wines:

> Cyril picked me up at Brighton Station, and on the way stopped at a wine merchant's, saying he wanted to buy ingredients for a cup. On arrival I found Peter Quennell, John Strachey, Brian Howard and Eddie Gathorne-Hardy, Piers Synnott, later Under-Secretary at the Admiralty, and a young man of great physical beauty, Nigel Richards, a central figure in Cyril's subsequent novel, *The Rock Pool*. There were also a couple of lemurs, which frolicked up and down the curtains, in spite of, or because of, a chronic looseness of the bowel. All went well until dinner, when I was given a glassful of sweet foaming liquid out of a jug. I congratulated the host on his cup. 'It's not a cup,' he said. 'It's champagne.'*

* For Nigel Richards and his role in *The Rock Pool*, see p. 264. As for Piers Synnott, the object of so much emotional agonising in the past, a visit he made to the Connollys in Juan-les-Pins later that summer seems to have ended in tears: on his return to England, he wrote them a furious letter in which he said he couldn't bear having been mocked in front of 'outsiders' like Nigel Richards and Michonze, and although Jean had been kind, it was a case of 'Goodbye to you both, for God knows how long. It rests with you.'

Although the Connollys appear to have paid the rent on Bayzehill House, other aspects of their tenancy were sure to cause Enid Bagnold grief. That autumn a Mr Rhodes of Hickie Borman Grant, the letting agents, sent a long, reproachful letter to the Connollys in Cannes on the vexed matter of the state in which they had left the house after they moved out. 'I was,' he wrote,

> considerably surprised to find dirty marks all over the paint in many rooms, the brass work quite neglected, the steel fire-dogs in both the hall and drawing-room completely covered with rust as if no attempt had been made to clean them whatsoever. As evidence of how the place was left cigarette ash was found left in ash-trays in most of the rooms.

But worse was to come:

> What, however, is of a serious nature is the condition of the drawing-room. This surpasses anything that could reasonably be described as fair wear and tear. The carpet was badly stained in many places. Your butler reported to Mrs Edwards that it was the result of spilling coffee and port wine. There was also a small burn in the border of the carpet which looked as though it occurred through dropping a cigarette end or match. The fireplace and the whole wall above the fireplace are simply covered in smoke, and the stone-work quite black and the paint damaged and blistered . . .

A black lacquer table had been badly damaged, a sofa was 'absolutely past repair', a knob had been knocked off a valuable Chinese Chippendale chair, ink stains had damaged a brocade arm-chair and a gate-legged table, and various items of china had been smashed, including three white Worcester bowls belonging to a 'very old tea service'.

Nor was that the end of the story. Writing to Enid Bagnold from Cannes in September, Jean reported that cheques were bouncing, and 'I am afraid some poor grocer in Rottingdean is making the place hum with his anger.' Could Lady Jones use her influence to sort things out? Rather tactlessly, perhaps, she went on to enumerate the number and types of cocktail that they had drunk in Paris, and the nude and lesbian bars they'd frequented, before closing with a final plea for help ('Do ask Sir Roderick if he has a spare job to give it to Cyril').*

As well as drinking champagne with their friends and damaging the fixtures and fittings, they gave a certain amount of time at Rottingdean to

* Not surprisingly, perhaps, no job offer was forthcoming. Among those whom Sir Roderick did employ at Reuters in the 1930s were Ian Fleming and James Lees-Milne: Lees-Milne detested the little martinet, taking wicked revenge on his former boss in *Another Self*, possibly the funniest autobiography ever written.

amateur theatricals. Once again, Christopher Sykes was an eager participant. 'The play should be called *The King's Head* and have a song or two in it. You might be the king, we might make it part-Gilbert, part-fairy, part-detective story,' Connolly suggested, adding that 'Aunt Loo' – Alys Russell – might like to play the part of a dragon. Eddie Gathorne-Hardy came down with Julia Strachey to take part, and 'Julia and I had a high old laugh about the Cyril Coward-Connolly on the train back to London . . . Do make him produce a charade of *Cavalcade*.' Julia Strachey was equally enthusiastic: 'I can't tell you what an experience it was seeing Cyril and Chris Sykes perform in the evenings after dinner. It was the most staggeringly brilliant *tour de force* I've ever witnessed . . . You are certainly a remarkable couple.' She went on to suggest dinner, and wondered whom the Connollys might like to meet: 'Do you like Virginia and Leonard, I wonder? They are odd birds, however . . .'

As it turned out, this might not have been the most harmonious of dinner parties: for although, during the last fifteen years of his life, Connolly was to live in the same part of Sussex as Leonard Woolf, exchanging brief, rather formal notes about first editions of contemporary writers, Virginia Woolf had already taken an instant dislike to the young critic and all he stood for: 'Think if I died, and left as my only friends, Logan and that little pimp Connolly,' she wrote that same year to Vita Sackville-West. Nor was Connolly a fully committed admirer of her work. 'I would have given anything to have been approved of by her,' he confessed in old age, but in his journal of 1928 he had written of how 'She gets in my way, stopping the earths I wish to hide in, a female spider by whom I fear to be devoured.' His reservations about her writing were not simply a matter of unease or feeling vaguely threatened, however. She was not, he felt, a real novelist, in that she seemed to care little for her fellow-men: 'Her characters are lifeless anatomical slices, conceived all in the same mood, unreal creations of genteel despair.' Nor could he admire her that much as a writer of prose: he found her work marred by carelessness and a 'lush feminine Keatsian familiarity that comes from being sensually too at home in the world', an intoxication with words that led her, even in her essays, into clichés and easy tricks. And a year or two later, when he was trying to liberate himself from the mannerisms and the longueurs of the approved literary style in favour of a simpler, more demotic, less encumbered prose, he saw her, half-respectfully, half-resentfully, as the embodiment of all he was up against:

> The flavour of contemporary English literature was Virginia Woolf. She combined imagination of the kind that has always been pre-eminently *the* English heritage, with the style which, as the daughter of Leslie Stephen – who had married the daughter of Thackeray – was essentially the best to

> be obtained by attention to the great tradition of the Victorian upper middle class. She was the prima ballerina assoluta who had graduated from the severe, temperate, well-read and whimsical academy of Faringford, Onslow Gardens and Cheyne Walk. To be beyond her was heresy, to be behind was the duller, second rank of orthodoxy – and not for the first time the country was never happier than when governed by a queen.

Early in 1934, the Connollys – according to Virginia Woolf – 'gave a cocktail party to meet their lemurs to which I did not go.' After lingering in the South of France and Paris during the late summer and autumn of 1933, the Connollys had taken, in January, what proved to be their most permanent London address – 312A King's Road, in a flat above a shop and next to a Chinese restaurant called The Good Earth. They soon proved themselves assiduous party-givers, the flat resounding to the sound of flamenco music and the host – or so Stuart Hampshire recalled – looking like a 'Byronesque gangster' in a black leather jacket: according to Anthony Powell, their 'succession of cooks went up and down in quality, sometimes sharply. Whether the proprietor of a mobile coffee-stall got wind of this, one of these was parked every night in a strategic position opposite the house. There Cyril's guests would sometimes end the evening with a sausage roll or two.' An additional anxiety was provided by the lemurs, which occasionally escaped into neighbouring houses ('Oh Mr Connolly, please come and take your horrible mongoose away').

The Woolfs may have declined an invitation to the King's Road, but before long Virginia was to encounter her *bête noire* in person. Elizabeth Bowen was a mutual friend,* and she invited the Connollys to stay at Bowen's Court, her family home in Co. Cork; and after a bibulous dinner party at which the guests included Evelyn Waugh, Peter Quennell, Richard and Freya Elwes, Violet Hammersley, Joe Hergesheimer and Joan Eyres-Monsell – Connolly woke next morning with a fearful hangover, 'amiable, tipsy and Eyres-Monsell-conscious' – the Connollys boarded the SS *Washington*, bound for New York via Queenstown in Co. Cork, where they disembarked. Driving inland from Queenstown, Ireland seemed 'quite derelict, empty and down-at-heel', and Bowen's Court 'lovely but rather forlorn'. The following day Leonard and Virginia Woolf arrived – he a 'small spare intellectual Jew, she lovely, shy and virginal'. They seemed shocked by Jean's clothes, and Virginia asked her the meaning of 'unnatural vice' – 'I mean what do they

* Connolly and Elizabeth Bowen were introduced to one another at a party given by Ethel Sands, the American-born painter and hostess. During the late Twenties and early Thirties the party-loving Miss Sands, a friend of Logan Pearsall Smith's, widened her net to include younger writers, Connolly, Peter Quennell and Kenneth Clark among them. Connolly gave a party in 1943 to celebrate her seventieth birthday.

do?' – before moving on to mock the work of G.B. Stern, a prolific lady novelist of the time. Leonard Woolf reserved judgement on his fellow-guests, in print at least, but Virginia was scathing. 'We spent a night with the Bowens, where, to our horror, we found the Connollys,' she told Vanessa Bell: '– a less appetising pair I have never seen out of the Zoo, and the apes are considerably preferable to Cyril. She has the face of a gollywog and they brought the reek of Chelsea with them'; and to her diary she confided her distress at having to spend time with 'baboon Conolly [*sic*] and his gollywog slut wife'.

No doubt it was a relief when the Woolfs left next morning.* The Connollys then visited Mallow and Cork, and sat by the lake at Mitchelstown. The remains of Great-Aunt Anna's castle had been cleared away; trees had been felled, and the lake and its surroundings converted into a public garden. They walked by the Blackwater, inspected Spenser's castle and Raleigh's grove at Myrtle, and dined in Waterford before taking the boat home; and on his return Connolly wrote that he had

> absolutely outgrown Ireland, the climate Boeotian, the charm a nuisance, the West of all points of the compass the least suggestive, in fact nowhere in Ireland seems to have any *raison d'être*, any focus, the ruined demesnes along the valley of the Blackwater bear witness to an extinct society... Comparison with the Southern States of America – Faulkner etc but without the niggers, drink and tropics.

*

Writing as Lincoln Croyle at about this time, Connolly provided a neat self-portrait in which the ambivalences of his character were pin-pointed with typical precision:

> I have a reputation for being malicious, indiscreet and sadistic, and yet I am full of affection, geniality and sweetness. When I go out and get drunk I grow even more affectionate and genial and sweet, and even more and more, and then I don't remember very much – but when I wake up full of sweet thoughts in the morning, I know I have been malicious, indiscreet and sadistic. (I am indiscreet so as to add to my self-importance, malicious because I do not think people like me enough, sadistic because I play up to the masochist in me that way.)

* Five years later, Virginia Woolf's opinion of Connolly was still dismissive. Her reputation, she confided to her diary, was on the wane: she was considered 'second-rate, and likely, I think, to be discarded altogether. I think that's my public reputation at the moment. It is largely based on Cyril Connolly's cocktail criticism: a sheaf of feathers in the wind.'

Like Alpdodger, he saw himself as 'round-faced, protean, a person whose age and personality seem to vary within many years and extremes of time; a charlatan whose very charlatanism may only be a perfect disguise for genius...' Long hours that might have been spent writing were given over to listing the names of friends and enemies, or working out anagrams of these, or drawing up lists, like school reports, in which the women he knew were judged according to their various attributes, social, sexual, pulchritudinous and intellectual. He enjoyed, as he always would, inventing games, for 'the Thirties are going to be a paradise for the games-lover. During the last century it looked as though work had come to stay, but now happily most of us don't think it is so noble after all, and even those who still believe that a mysterious virtue lies in doing work of some kind all day are hard put to get any...' And although his own sartorial taste was often dubious – eccentric, perhaps – he bent his mind to designing a summer suiting for men, which Turnbull & Asser pronounced 'practicable':

> Navy-blue cashmere shorts and ditto trousers to be worn with crush or linen cream tunic, cut like private soldier's or Dutch stingah shiftah with large pockets, horn buttons, slit armpits and dark blue stiff collar, closed when formal or chilly, widely open otherwise. No shirt or tie needed, and cold taken less easily.

But the most enjoyable occupation of all was daydreaming – of a large private income or an unexpected windfall, of a house in Thurloe Square, with another abroad and a third in the country; and his favourite daydream of all, he confided to his journal, was to 'edit a monthly magazine entirely subsidised by self. Harmless title, deleterious contents'.

When not daydreaming or immersing himself in the eighteenth-century worlds of Horace Walpole, Henry Bolingbroke and Thomas Warton, he and Jean travelled, dined out and entertained their friends. They visited Sledmere, and Devon and Cornwall, where they stayed with new friends, Sir Robert and Lady Abdy; Robert Byron and Christopher Sykes were dined at Boulestin's on their return from Persia and Afghanistan, a journey soon to be recaptured in *The Road to Oxiana*; Peter Quennell remained precariously in favour, dispensing his belief that 'one should have a new house, new interests, new friends and a new lover every year and one would always be young', the practical effect of which was that 'all the little marriage-boats in the harbour rock uneasily as the back-wash of his new craft hits them'. Dinner parties in heaven were planned, the guests ranging from Tibullus and Catullus to Auden and Isherwood, via Rochester and Congreve; Anthony Powell and his wife Violet came to dinner, and 'He asked for my opinion on him and Evelyn. I said I thought Tony had more talent and Evelyn more vocation'; 1934 came to an end with a party attended by, among others, Joan Eyres-Monsell, Waugh, Henry and Dig Yorke, Patrick Balfour, Alan Pryce-Jones, Roy Harrod, Bunny Garnett, Kenneth Rae, John Sutro and the Elweses. A new friend was the young Welsh poet Dylan Thomas, then aged twenty and recently arrived in London. Early in 1935, the Connollys brought him to dinner with the Powells in their flat in Great Ormond Street and there followed an evening of 'perfectly normal drinking and talking, even if a great deal of both took place'. Connolly then gave a dinner for Thomas, attended by the Powells, Evelyn Waugh, Robert Byron, Desmond MacCarthy and several 'ladies representing fashion rather than literature'. Asked what he would like to drink, Thomas answered 'Anything that goes down my throat', at which a 'slight hush' fell on the proceedings; Desmond MacCarthy raised the subject of flagellation; and Waugh made an early escape, overcome by gloom when Jean suggested that the cherubic young poet looked much as he had at that age. Another promising young acquaintance was the poet David Gascoyne,* who travelled up from Twickenham to visit the Connollys; on one occasion they took him and Dylan Thomas on a day trip to Selsey, where they amused themselves throwing pebbles at bottles set up in the sand to represent such luminaries of the literary scene as John Lehmann, Michael Roberts, Edith Sitwell and Virginia Woolf.

Nor were old friends entirely neglected in favour of the new. Though no longer as central as before, Pearsall Smith remained a welcome figure in their lives, but his manic depression was becoming more extreme as he grew older, and with it a tendency to lash out at those who were closest to him. 'Tell Cyril he doesn't know good prose when he sees it,' he told Jean: 'His talk is the talk of a fox without a tail.'† In 1931 he told Connolly that he was selling Big Chilling on his doctor's advice; eighteen months later he wrote to say that 'You will find me sadly changed ... I have become the victim of a dreadful kind of masochistic vice, which makes my life a misery and is undermining my health.' One wonders what he made of Connolly's review of Jonathan Swift's letters to Sir William Temple, published in the *New Statesman* in February 1935. 'There can be nothing more galling for a young

* David Gascoyne was – with Roland Penrose, Herbert Read, Humphrey Jennings and others – one of the moving spirits behind the International Surrealist Exhibition, held in the New Burlington Galleries in June 1936; among those who came over from France to dignify the proceedings were André Breton, Paul Eluard and Salvador Dali, clad in a diving-suit. The show was greeted, predictably, with cries of outrage: according to Roland Penrose, Connolly and John Betjeman were among the few critics to take it seriously. Freya Elwes, who recalled how Connolly was 'very easily amused by things that were supposed to be serious' went along with the Connollys and Nancy Mitford; they were greeted at the door by a girl in a white communion dress, clutching a mannequin's leg with a mutton chop attached to one end.
† An epithet Connolly applied in due course to Julian Symons: see p. 358.

man than to find himself part of the scheme of auto-suggestion by which an old one justifies his existence,' he wrote; and his remarks about Swift's relationship with his patron were both heart-felt and lethal:

> It must have been too close an acquaintance with the style of Sir William Temple (a style essentially false, for it revealed not what he felt but what he would like to feel) that precipitated the prose of Swift into its rightful form, vigorous, mature, lucid and earthy... It is clear that he warmly admired and liked Temple at first and suffered agony from the slights which that spoiled and peevish mediocrity put upon him.

Another voice from the past was that of the Major. At first he had enjoyed warm relations with Jean, but the couple's money problems, and his reactions to them, were a source of mutual irritation. In 1930 the Major had been elected President of the Conchological Society of Great Britain, and in September the following year he gallantly invited Jean to accompany him to a reception at the Natural History Museum: he could guarantee her, he promised, lobsters, a band and the company of the famous. Invitations to Boulestin's and the Cheshire Cheese followed over the next year or two; but although the Lock House had finally been sold in April 1931, the Major's own finances left much to be desired. 'My little Mollie has been *very* ill again,' he wrote in September 1934: she might well have to have another operation – when or why the first one took place remains unclear – so it would help a great deal if Connolly could repay the £7 he'd borrowed from her allowance. The following winter Connolly wrote to his mother in South Africa, where she was living in a house on the other side of the road to that of General Brooke, to say that the Major was being very difficult, and that even Jean was fed up after all they had done for him. Jean's nursing-home bill for the previous year, plus alterations to the King's Road flat, had left them in straitened circumstances: the Major had offered to guarantee their overdraft to the extent of £100, but had then gone back on his word, saying that he intended to keep all his share certificates in a tin box under his bed in case Mollie needed money at short notice. Not only had he accused them both of extravagance ('I suppose because we gave him brandy when he came to dinner'), but he had even written to their bank manager on the subject; on top of which, he had then accused his son of being responsible for all his mother's wrinkles. In conclusion, however, Mollie might like to know that he had invested some spare cash she had sent him in a gold-edged tortoiseshell cigarette case and a dark green cape for Jean.

Connolly's finances were mercifully unaffected by a 5000-mile grand tour made that summer in the company of Mrs Warner – they were only prepared to travel with her on the understanding that she picked up all the bills. Her consumption of alcohol, never modest, had now reached epic proportions – so much so that she had to be carried off the boat train on a stretcher, dead drunk, when they met her at the Gare du Nord. Every evening she locked herself in her hotel room with a bottle of whisky, after which Jean would undress her and put her to bed, and 'most of the time she is half-drunk, very suspicious and unfriendly, terrified of everything.' From Paris they drove to north-east Spain, where the hotels were poor, and then on to the South of France, where a week was spent in Juan-les-Pins. A fortnight was then idled away at the Danieli in Venice; none of them felt well there, which was blamed on the drains. From there they motored on through Yugoslavia to Budapest, where they enjoyed the gypsy orchestras and the open-air swimming-pools, and 'the Prince of Wales was in our hotel carrying on in a very Ruritanian fashion with Mrs Simpson'. They then headed west, through Austria and Switzerland, to Paris, where, after drying out for a week in a clinic, Mrs Warner boarded the boat train, on her own two feet this time.

While in Paris, Connolly called on Jack Kahane, who would be publishing his novel *The Rock Pool* the following year, and a new acquaintance, the American writer Henry Miller. Brought together by a mutual friend, they met for dinner, and Miller's initial impressions were far from favourable. 'I thought you a goddamned snob,' he told Connolly later, 'a pretentious sort of cad, a cheap, wise-cracking bastard with an all-knowing air.' Eventually Miller got so 'fed-up' that he rose from the table and left. Nor was Connolly – playing the role, perhaps, of the reserved Englishman – any better pleased by the way the meal went. 'You remember that we got rather intimate, rather "personal" with you, and you were just a little surprised, a little irritated,' Miller recalled. 'You said you had accepted us and why in hell couldn't we accept you...' Despite this inauspicious start, they met again shortly afterwards, and this time Miller found Connolly a very 'different guy'. The third party, incidentally, and the man responsible for bringing them together, was Alfred Perles, by now working on the Paris edition of the *Chicago Tribune*. Eager to help his impoverished friend, he had commissioned Miller to write a long 'colour' piece for the newspaper, which had to be published under Perles's name. Connolly wrote to Perles to congratulate him on the piece and invite him out to lunch, but he felt unable to accept: since then they had enjoyed an occasional meal together, for

> Cyril was no pauper like most of my other friends; he was a fastidious gourmet who could well afford the *de luxe* eating places of Paris. It was always an experience to have a meal with him. Just to watch him consulting the *maître d'hôtel* and the *sommelier* was a treat. He knew the good things

money could buy and usually bought them. He would study a menu and a wine list very much as a general might study a map to plan his campaign.

Even so, Miller and Perles may well have assumed that the Connollys were richer than they were: after spending a night – and a small fortune – on the town together, Miller expressed a certain contrition ('Why did we feel so good about letting you spend all that money, Fred and I? Because we thought it was coming to you . . .').

Lives of writers all remind us
We can leave our wives at home
Go to places they can't find us
Frig and fuck till kingdom come.
Man of letters, ere we part
Tell me why you never fart?
Never fart? My dear Miss Blight,
I do not have to fart, I write

wrote 'Lincoln Croyle' in an early draft of 'Humane Killer'; while Alpdodger – looking back with almost masochistic regret to 'that awful moment when the drug of literature is first discovered, when Narcissus comes across the pool', and with regretful nostalgia to 'the life I did not lead, the artist's life in Paris' – not only wonders how and whether he is capable of spinning out 80,000 words, but is all too uneasily aware of the hazards facing the critic who tries to write: 'When one has to produce a book oneself, to pass the swimming test instead of being the waterman with the pole, how cold the ocean is, how big Geoffrey Mannin looks, and *The Good Companions*, and *Magnolia Street*!' For years now, Connolly had played the part of the artist and the writer without having a great deal to show for it beyond his book reviews: but the moment of truth was upon him, and Alpdodger's display of nerves was quite in order.

The Rock Pool – the subject of Connolly's discussions with Jack Kahane in Paris – was to form the centre-piece of a planned triptych of short novels; it was the only one of the three to be completed, and he worked on it sporadically throughout 1934. 'These stories are really three variations on a theme,' he announced, namely

> the influence of the sense of the past, the proverbial oldness of old England, on young writers who might have created something elsewhere. It would be possible to call them studies in snobbery, but the word has a connotation harsher than the romantic cult here described. It is a disease, if you like, which amiably destroys all that is real in a person and which may account for the presence in the dull ranks of our writers of so many rebels who have lain down their arms.

The three stories – 'Humane Killer', 'The English Malady' and *The Rock Pool* – were written in short bursts, with no great evidence, judging by the surviving drafts, of much regularity or concentration in their composition: each day's work, which might consist of five or six lines at most, was dated and initialled by a friend, probably Kenneth Rae. In June he appears to have been working on 'Humane Killer'* and 'The English Malady'; August was given over to *The Rock Pool*, and by October he was back with 'The English Malady'.

Whereas 'The English Malady' evoked Connolly's life in London in the late Twenties, 'Humane Killer' anticipated *The Unquiet Grave* in its nostalgia for the time he had spent with Jean in Paris, and *Enemies of Promise* in its obsession with the deficiencies of English prose and the need to create a more contemporary way of writing. 'Kenneth' is a twenty-four-year-old writer adrift in Paris. He lives in Montparnasse, and likes nothing better than to wander the streets, fearlessly exploring brothels and dark alleys and occasionally stopping to scribble in his notebook stray thoughts and quotations – a particular favourite being a quatrain from Tibullus which, years later, his creator translated as

> Ah Delia when my hour is nigh
> Be thou my feeling hand and eye,
> And range me on the burning bier
> And leave a kiss with every tear.

Whereas at school and at Oxford he had feigned literary emotions, making them seem more intense than they were – as Alpdodger put it, 'an artificial self-pity varying with as artificial a self-hate' – Kenneth is unhappily aware that he lacks any real experience from which to write: all he knows is that he wants to get away from 'literary' English, to escape what he sees as the deadening influence of Pater and Henry James. In search of a new style, he makes a point of regularly reading Eugene Jolas's *transition*, the standard-bearer of the *avant garde* and the experimental, but he has to admit to being 'secretly disappointed. There was so much adolescence in it and so much gibberish.' A more congenial temple of modernity – 'hidden, like a cache of dynamite in a solemn crypt' – was Miss Greville's bookshop. Miss Greville – Sylvia Beach, in other words – 'sat at her table in a brown coat, looking up with her quick dark eye like a thrush on its nest'; her shop was patronised by a 'thin stream of transient maniacs, and such few people of real talent as

* A shorter, very different version of 'Humane Killer' was eventually published by Alan Ross in the August 1973 *London Magazine*, which was given over to the celebration of Connolly's seventieth birthday.

existed at the time', among them 'the polished figure of Joyce, the swarthy face and broad shoulders of Hemingway'.

Miss Greville asks Kenneth what he is writing, and he tells her that he's hard at work on a story about a young man who suffers convulsive spasms while dropping off to sleep and is convinced he's about to die of a heart attack; as if this weren't bad enough, he picks up a girl who turns out to be an English nurse, and lies beside him all night describing the symptoms of septicaemia. To divert him from such unhappy matters, Miss Greville asks Kenneth if he would mind delivering a parcel to a customer, and he saunters off in the direction of the Ile St Louis, leaving behind him the narrow Left Bank streets described in 'the first chapter of *The Sun Also Rises*, which had first made him feel the moribund unreality of Balliol prose'.

The door is opened by a fair-haired girl in a white Shetland jumper, who 'had probably never cleaned her teeth less than four times a day nor ever worn a darned stocking', with whom Kenneth – 'a glorious example of English male virginity' – is soon hopelessly in love. Inside the house are another girl and her mother, and a young man mixing cocktails, a third rye, a third bourbon and a third 'lime-flower honey'; and Kenneth – used to

> the drawing-rooms of his relations, chintz-covered arm-chairs, flowers on the writing-table, photos of young men in uniform, watercolours and one or two indifferent miniatures on either side of the fireplace, the familiar swastika on leather Kiplings in the revolving bookcase, a corner cupboard with assorted china

– is given his first taste of American luxury. He is amazed, too, by the freedom of their conversation; and everything about the fair-haired girl 'had that delicious quality of luxury and waste, her rows and rows of shoes, the pots of powder, cream and scent, often evaporating and stopperless.' Through her he learns that Americans appear not to differentiate between highbrows and low- or middlebrows, with the result that there is not the great gulf set, as in England, between philistines and prigs. Although her literary criteria are fairly unsophisticated – books are either 'sweet' and 'simply adorable', or make her feel 'sick to the stomach' – she seems to share his tastes, and finds unreadable those writers whom he's reacting against.

Kenneth loathes long sentences, and has come to believe that 'All the false qualities in English prose derive from the essayist', with Addison, Lamb and a regiment of more recent arm-chair philosophers cast as the villains of the piece. The essayist was recognisable by his whimsicality, and by archaic, padding, fence-sitting turns of phrase like 'When all is said and done' or 'Show me the man who . . .' or 'Hardly of my own choosing'. He was marked by a 'frivolous egotism' whereby 'the author shows off his defects, his belongings – pipe, cat, carpet-slippers – his preferences – bad memory, capacity for losing things, absent-mindedness, ignorance of business and the hard way of the world, everything which might make the reader think he wrote for money'; and by a false or non-existent relationship between art and experience, which showed itself in those 'dodges by which the epicurean man of letters wrote about women, fighting, drink, sex and other direct and unliterary pleasures by substituting a prepared set of literary emotions'.

Equally wearisome was the intellectual style associated with Conrad, James and Pater – 'sentences full of hesitations and woolly profundities, as if nothing could be conveyed to the reader that was not subtle and difficult... that habit of endless mental mystification so tiresome in Proust'. Some recent writers, Huxley and Strachey among them, had evolved, as an alternative to the whimsical or academic styles, a 'faster, more metallic intellectual prose', smart, epigrammatic, replete with in-jokes and cunning references and latinate words and an 'attitude of ironic detachment which they were far from feeling'. All this would be elaborated at greater length in *Enemies of Promise*, in Connolly's celebrated distinction between the Mandarin and the Vernacular schools of prose; but in the meantime Kenneth had come to Paris – or so he assured Miss Greville – to learn and to practise the plain 'bald' style of Daniel Defoe and, presumably, Ernest Hemingway.

Neither 'Humane Killer' nor 'The English Malady' – like Alpdodger before them – was more than a dazzling fragment, shards from a bowl that remained maddeningly incomplete: but *The Rock Pool* was to be Connolly's first completed book, and the only full-length novel he ever wrote. According to Connolly's Introductory Letter, addressed to Peter Quennell, the novel was accepted by a London publisher, who then changed his mind, and subsequently rejected by a second firm, which returned the typescript with the offending passages heavily ringed. Faber & Faber was the first of these. 'I doubt if it can be published, at present, in England in any form, unless you can find a publisher willing to take the risk of imprisonment,' Geoffrey Faber wrote to Connolly in May 1935: 'This is not an exaggeration: the "Boy" and "Bessie Cotter" prosecutions are sufficient evidence. I think you are right in supposing that it could be done in America.'* The two rejections instilled in him a lifelong dislike and suspicion of London publishers, whom he characterised as 'culture-diffusionists', to be milked of their funds and

* London publishers had been unnerved by the successful prosecutions for obscene libel of James Hanley's *Boy* and Wallace Smith's *Bessie Cotter*. Connolly later told Barbara Skelton that Cobden Sanderson was the other firm involved, though The Hogarth Press has also been suggested (see p. 262). *The Rock Pool* was published in the United States by Scribner's, which – as Connolly never ceased to lament – sold a bare 300 copies.

treated with scant respect: he had already been bruised by his dealings with the Nonesuch Press, and 'we do not expect spring flowers to bloom in a black frost, and I think the chill wind that blows from English publishers, with their black suits and thin umbrellas, and their habit of beginning each sentence with "We are afraid", has nipped off more promising buds than it has strengthened.'

Salvation, albeit of an unorthodox kind, lay to hand in the form of an English publisher resident in Paris. Jack Kahane had been born in 1888 into a family of wealthy Manchester mill-owners. He worked in the family business for a while and fought in the First World War, after which he decided to settle in Paris, where he married Marcelle Eugene Girodias.* Though half-Irish and half-Jewish, he seemed to Alfred Perles the quintessential Englishman, sprucely turned out in a grey business suit with a carnation in his buttonhole, enjoying a bottle of Bass for lunch, and suffering from the occasional 'touch of halitosis'; he liked to live well – at one stage he owned seven bulldogs and fifty pairs of trousers – and since he enjoyed good writing and subverting the powers-that-be in his native land, he founded the Obelisk Press in 1931 in order to publish books that had been banned at home, *Boy* and *Bessie Cotter* among them, or were too *avant garde* for London tastes. He was friends with Joyce and Eugene Jolas, and wrote occasionally for *transition*; when, in the early days of the Obelisk Press, *risqué* novels were hard to come by, Kahane wrote them himself under the pseudonyms of Basil Carr and Cecil Barr, but before long he had published Frank Harris's *My Life and Loves*, followed by Henry Miller's *Tropic of Cancer*, Anaïs Nin's *House of Incest* and Lawrence Durrell's *The Black Book*, and the firm was forging ahead, its cellophane-wrapped offerings essential reading for the broad-minded and up-to-date Anglo-Saxon visitor to Paris.

Kahane had met Christopher Sykes – 'a tall bulky man with a beard and a stammer' – who suggested Connolly as a possible editor for a collection of letters from Henry James to Ralph Curtis. It wasn't the kind of book Obelisk would publish, but Kahane was anxious to help and got in touch with Sykes's friend, whom he remembered as 'a lovely talker, with a great appreciation of hospitality, and a robust interest in the finer facets of cooking'. Henry James's letters came to nothing, but

> Connolly whispered to me that he had written a book; it had been announced for publication by a very distinguished firm, the Hogarth Press, I think, but they had taken fright after *Bessie Cotter*. I at once

* Their son, Maurice Girodias, continued his father's publishing tradition under the imprint of the Olympia Press.

> offered to put it out. He sent the MS. It was as sweet a piece of writing as I have ever seen, the work of an exquisite, steeped in the classics, and in certain ways a model of impropriety. Its only fault was that it dealt with a period that was no longer of any interest – the raffish days of 1929 among the inhabitants of Montparnasse during their summer migration to the South of France. It was strange that it should date so much, in fact so much that it affected sales. But I did not mind, for I had the utmost pleasure in being responsible for a piece of such wit and distinction.

In later years, Kahane expressed a rueful chagrin at having published what seemed, when compared with some of the other titles on his list, so mild and unsalacious a work; nor has it stood the test of time anything like as well as Henry Miller's more robust accounts of expatriate debaucheries in France between the wars. Although the book still has its admirers, and although it has its redeeming moments of elegiac reflection, some of them pleasingly familiar ('The pain of watching beautiful young girls, the isolation of desire! They reminded him of the figures in one of those pictures by Watteau that are instinct with the beauty of the moment, the fugitive distress of hedonism, the sadness that falls like a dew from pleasure, as they stand, fixed in a moment of the dance, beneath the elm, beneath the garlanded urn'), it provides distressing evidence that Connolly was not a natural novelist; and that the mere act of assuming an extended fictional persona, however close to his own, had a curiously deadening, self-conscious effect on this most eloquent and passionate of writers. None of the characters comes alive; the dialogue is as stiff and awkward and unconvincing as that of a group of incompatible strangers, reluctantly introduced to one another and unlikely to take things any further; there is no sense of drama or involvement or interaction between its wooden-seeming puppets, and its ostensibly shocking subject-matter – bohemian life in the South of France, with its obligatory dashes of sex, drugs, drink and general dissipation – seems irremediably tame, lacking even the faintest whiff of brimstone or depravity.

In his Introductory Letter, Connolly described how his discovery while a schoolboy at Eton of the Loeb Classical Library – in which translations were printed alongside the original texts – had revolutionised his enjoyment of Horace and, later, Suetonius, Catullus, Martial, Juvenal and even Petronius Arbiter, and how the gist of their advice had been for youth to 'drink and make love to the best of its ability'; and the bohemian ex-pats he describes in *The Rock Pool* might well be regarded as the dispirited – and dispiriting – fag-end of hedonism and a pagan cult of pleasure. The Mediterranean they inhabit is very different from that which Connolly was to celebrate with such lyrical nostalgia in *The Unquiet Grave*, and its central character, Naylor, adrift in a world of tarts and gigolos and motor-car salesmen, finds himself understandably overcome by 'the intolerable melancholy, the dinginess, the corruption of that tainted inland sea':

> He felt the breath of centuries of wickedness and disillusion; how many civilisations had staled on that bright promontory! Sterile Phoenicians, commercial-minded Greeks, hysterical Russians, decayed English, drunken Americans, had mingled with the autochthonous gangsters – everything that was vulgar, acquisitive, piratical, and decadent in capitalism had united there, crooks, gigolos, gold-diggers and captains of industry through twenty-five centuries had sprayed their cupidity and bad taste over it.

A product of Winchester and Oxford, Naylor* is a young stockbroker who is also struggling to write a biography of Samuel Rogers, the early nineteenth-century banker-poet: what he would really like to write, though, is a picaresque novel about the lives of London prostitutes, but, like his creator, he finds himself blighted by the constraints of his background and education.

The inhabitants of Trou-sur-mer – itself based on Cagnes – include the Bessarabian painter Rascasse, a waif-like German girl called Toni, with whom the rather buttoned-up Naylor becomes hopelessly infatuated, a man in a kilt called Foster, and assorted riff-raff and hangers-on, all of whom spend a good deal of time discussing who is, or is not, a virgin. To the office-bound Naylor these inhabitants of the rock pool seem like 'beautiful cave-dwellers supporting in hieratic and traditional raggedness a dying religion', and as such they seem an enviable and increasingly desirable alternative to life in the City and brooding on Samuel Rogers. As the Pernod begins to take its toll, and Naylor succumbs to the faded allure of the rock pool, he comes to believe that 'he and Toni and Rascasse were "old souls", people who beneath their high spirits concealed a fundamental and Asiatic despair'; yet the world they inhabit seems, for all its loudly-proclaimed debauchery, remarkably innocent, almost prelapsarian, not least in the prevailing belief that 'There are so few wicked people in the world; the

* Nigel Richards, the original of Naylor, was a Wykehamist, an Oxford graduate – he got a first in History, and was a friend of Maurice Bowra's – and a stockbroker. His parents lived in Florence, and were friends of Harold Acton and Norman Douglas. He abandoned stockbroking to become a tea-planter in Burma, where his first wife, an alcoholic, fell overboard into a crocodile-infested river, and was eaten (or, as Norman Douglas used to cry, 'The crocs got her!'). Some time after publication of *The Rock Pool*, Connolly and Jean were having a drink in the Café Royal with Betty Fletcher-Mossop and Robin McDouall, the source of the above information, when Nigel Richards unexpectedly walked in: Connolly was, apparently, overcome with embarrassment, and blurted out 'My God, I thought you were dead!' Nigel Richards later married Betty Fletcher-Mossop; he joined the RAF and was shot down over Brunswick in 1943.

springs of vanity, fear, envy, cupidity and deceit, while sources of the general nastiness of human beings, do not make for moral evil on a grand scale.' Rascasse, for instance, is an amiable cove, whose attempts to speak some kind of Brooklynese ('Say' and 'Sure' and 'Gee, it's swell') collapse, disconcertingly, into the peevish tones of an indignant public schoolboy ('Thanks a lot for spoiling my last evening with her, sneaking her off to dinner like that'). The vapid-seeming Toni seems the ultimate free spirit to poor Naylor: more interestingly, perhaps, she was of a type that, as we have seen, had a disturbing effect on their joint creator:

> Her face had an extraordinary sweetness combined with a Mongolian beauty of bone. She had dark hair cut like a boy's and parted at the side, slanting grey eyes, a small nose, a mouth like a crushed blackberry, and minute pointed ears. She wore no make-up, but with her body of an archaic Dorian bronze and her little gypsy face, was the image of one of those dainty and heartless fauns with whom Georgian poets delighted to people the Oxford copses.

Despite his kilt, Foster is an altogether more familiar figure, with whom Naylor – eager to keep an obvious upstart in his place – is soon engaged in social fencing ('Do you know Wiltshire? What fun. It's my favourite county, though I only know the parts round Wilton and Longleat...'). Foster's vowels have a decidedly dubious ring to them, and Naylor presses home his advantage mercilessly, extracting from the wretched Foster the reluctant admission that he had not only been to an unglamorous Cambridge college, Sidney Sussex, but that he had been to a minor public school, in the form of Berkhamsted.* Flushed with triumph, Naylor feels he is living life to the full and seeing it in the raw: sexually emboldened after making love to a woman called Lola, he sees himself as an arch-seducer and ponders the possibility of having an affair with Mrs Foster so that 'finally the horrible truth would dawn on her husband – cuckolded by a WYKEHAMIST!'

Naylor now embraces the life of the rock pool with such enthusiasm – making love to all and sundry, patronising a brothel, hurling plates around, indulging in sessions of solitary drinking, making off without paying his taxi

* An unkind cut as far as the novel's dedicatee was concerned, since Peter Quennell – like Graham Greene, whose father had been its headmaster – had been to Berkhamsted, and spent a good deal of time regretting it hadn't been Eton instead. On the other hand, a minor character called Spedding – a City friend of Naylor's – *had* been to Winchester; as had his alleged original, John Sparrow. That same year Sparrow rose to the defence of A.E. Housman's poetry in the pages of the *New Statesman*, where Connolly had earlier launched a ferocious attack on his old hero. Sparrow and Connolly were never particularly close; nor is it certain whether Sparrow or Maurice Bowra was the originator of the much-quoted remark, 'The thing to remember about Cyril Connolly is that he is not as nice as he looks.'

fare – that its original inhabitants feel he's going too far, and he finds himself ostracised by bohemia. Even so, he can't bear the thought of going back to England: the mere thought of 'the BBC, the *Daily Express, Nash's Magazine*, Sloane Street' fills him with gloom and despair, and 'if sex and snobbery, at which he was a failure, were going out, he was no better fitted for the Communism and hope that were coming in', for

> He was, he supposed, still irretrievably committed to the central concept of the nineteen-twenties – futility, the problem of the clever young man and the dirty deal, of the sensitive clown, the Petroushka, done down and cut by his rival the Harlequin, the Moor, and finally, too late, turning into the Moor.

He ends on a suitably Connollyesque note, dreaming of an ideal house, Palladian by preference, where 'I shall cultivate obscurity and practise failure, so repulsive in others, in oneself of course the only dignified thing.'

In his Introductory Letter Connolly had, to some extent, disarmed the critics in advance by pointing out that his novel was dated in terms of its subject matter, in that the denizens of the rock pool were essentially ghosts from the 1920s, from the world as it was before the Great Crash, while Naylor himself was supposed to represent 'the last gasp, perhaps, of the *rentier* exhaustion'. But Desmond MacCarthy – who confessed in the *Sunday Times* to having read it twice already, with a third session imminent – felt it to be no more dated than the work of Eliot, Joyce, Huxley or Waugh; indeed, he thought it 'better art than *Antic Hay*' and 'more penetrating than the work of Mr Evelyn Waugh'. It was, he decided, 'the best account I have read of going to the dogs'; its theme was 'admirably and seriously handled', and the whole thing had been 'written with a peremptory, witty precision and a spirited, off-hand elegance extremely pleasing'. 'Dropping a donnish young man into this underworld of nancies, insolvent borrowers, drug-addicts, lesbians and the rest is the modern equivalent of sending a toff to the Wide Open Spaces, and Mr Connolly plays the traditional game with witty relish,' Desmond Hawkins* declared in the *Criterion*: '*The Rock Pool* is perhaps no more than a gay *jeu d'esprit*, but it has the maturity and poise that most modern English novels lack.' George Orwell, who had written to his old school friend earlier in the year, asking for news of the novel and expressing the hope that he might be able to review it, started his piece in the *New English Weekly* with high expectations ('As Mr Cyril Connolly is

* Desmond Hawkins was one of Connolly's fellow-novel reviewers on the *New Statesman*, reporting to G.W. Stonier. During the war, as a BBC producer, he initiated a series called 'The Writer in the Witness Box', to which both Connolly and Desmond MacCarthy contributed.

almost the only novel-reviewer in England who does not make me sick, I opened this, his first novel, with a lively interest'), and agreed that Connolly's treatment of his material was 'mature and skilful': what he objected to was the novel's subject-matter – partly because novels about artists' colonies in the South of France had been written about by the likes of Norman Douglas and Aldous Huxley 'a long time ago and probably better', and more importantly because he found it hard to stomach the fact that 'Mr Connolly rather admires the disgusting beasts he depicts, and certainly he prefers them to the polite and sheeplike Englishman.' Its author, he went on, 'seems to suggest that there are only two alternatives: lie in bed till four in the afternoon, drinking Pernod, or you will infallibly surrender to the gods of Success and become a London social-cum-literary backstairs crawler.' Although he had read only two books that year that interested him more – and none that amused him as much – 'I think he could write a better novel if he would concern himself with more ordinary people.' Writing to Henry Miller, Orwell admitted that although *The Rock Pool* had entertained him, 'I don't think a lot of it.' Miller, for his part, was rather more complimentary, at least when writing to the author. 'I swallowed yr book neat, in two draughts,' he told Connolly:

> Never would have believed it in you. To have put yrself down with such utter truthfulness seems to me positively heroic, considering, I mean, what yr background has been. As the bk progressed I began to howl with delight... It's amazing that a bk such as yrs shd not be gobbled up in England: it's the sort of bk England needs more and more.

Miller's strongest criticism was reserved for the French, as spoken by the locals: 'Such a French, *mon cher ami*, was never heard on land or sea.'* But perhaps this was only right and proper: the book had made him laugh so much, and touched him too, 'because you were so English all the time, and to be so thoroughly English is to be an idiot, at least in the world of reality.' Before too long, however, reality would begin to intrude, disrupting the Connollys' private lives and rumbling northwards from Spain: 'living for beauty' remained an ideal, and life's pleasures beckoned as alluringly as ever, but their 'fugitive distress' would become increasingly apparent.

* Connolly's French – like his love of food and wine, and his passion for collecting porcelain and silver – was a subject of unkind speculation among those anxious to find a great gulf set between alleged and actual expertise. According to Ludovic Kennedy, 'Maurice Cranston remembers Connolly in his cups admitting that for all his critical writings on French literature, he could hardly speak a word of French' – which is patent nonsense, not least because Connolly was never a heavy drinker. Connolly was cited to L.P. Hartley as a fluent French-speaker, with the qualification that he was 'very weak in verbs, for he has learned all his French from menus in which there are only nouns!' In fact he seems to have been a slow and careful speaker; for his rusty post-war French, see p. 392.

FIFTEEN

Mr Mossbross Goes to Spain

In a well-known passage from *Enemies of Promise*, Cyril Connolly characterised himself – endearingly, disarmingly and not entirely accurately – as a 'lazy, irresolute person, over-vain and over-modest, unsure in my judgements and unable to finish what I have begun'; and it was during these years that he developed the myth and the persona – half-rueful, half-defiant – of the writer of near-genius whose promise is betrayed not just by the snares and temptations that lie in the path of every young writer, but by his all-pervading sloth, with its corrosive corollaries of guilt and remorse. It was a subject, an affliction, to which he would endlessly return, so much so that his entire output might well be regarded as an extended meditation, essentially autobiographical, on the problems of being a writer. He could only write, he once declared, in the afternoon or – 'when I want to heighten the emotional value of what I'm writing' – in the evening, when if what he has written so far seems 'too flat or dry I tack on a luscious paragraph before going to bed'. But why, he asks, can he not write in the mornings, like most diligent and productive writers?

> Unfortunately, there is never very much of the morning for me, because I never go to bed at night. I try not to eat breakfast so as not to get any fatter. I have a glass of orange juice in bed. After that I stay in bed, reading the newspapers and then just reading. In winter I spend three-quarters of an hour in my bath, where I read faster than ever, and sometimes imagine having a slate beside me where I can write water-proof maxims. Then I go back to bed again and usually come down to a light lunch in a dressing-gown, still with a book, for I hate not to read while I'm eating. This leaves the afternoon for work and as it is also the time for going out or doing any of the things people do in the mornings, I tend only to write in it when I have to. And I would always rather talk than write. These words must be regarded as being like so many salmon, the few fine survivals of infinite accidents and hardships . . .

That Connolly remained over-addicted to long baths and lying in bed till mid-day – during the course of which he daydreamed away innumerable unwritten books, spluttering with laughter at his own jokes – is undeniable: but if what he saw as his major undertakings fell victim to procrastination, uncertainty and failure of nerve, hand-written pages soon petering out before being partially recycled, or ending their days as daydreams or conversational *tours de force*, he was far from slothful when it came to what he regarded as the altogether more humdrum business of writing reviews and journalistic pieces. His availability to literary editors depended to a large extent on where he happened to be, and long stretches of journalistic silence tended to coincide with equally long journeys round Europe, or spells in the South of France; but so industrious and so prolific was this allegedly slothful writer that for a time in the mid-Thirties he was not only reviewing as many as six or eight novels a fortnight for the *New Statesman*, and often reading or skimming more than he actually pronounced upon, but providing a similar weekly service for the *Daily Telegraph* as well as the occasional non-fiction review for the *Sunday Times*. It's hardly surprising perhaps that, in *Enemies of Promise*, he should have singled out journalism in general, and reviewing in particular, as the 'deadliest' of the temptations that await the aspiring writer, a 'whole-time job with a half-time salary, a job in which the best in him is generally expended on the mediocre in others', at the end of which the worn-out hack will be discarded in favour of some bright young aspirant for whom an identical fate awaits. Old friends of the veteran reviewer

> will talk about the current number of his magazine without mentioning anything by him in it, and ask what has happened to the brilliant guide book to the Balkans he wrote as an undergraduate, and why he doesn't try to do something like it again. He will be surprised and rather hurt when he meets people who have never heard of him, and suffer agonies when they deny him the position of a critic and confuse reviewing with the forms of journalism which he most detests. 'Now mind you don't publish anything about me!'

Even so, Connolly claimed, in another discarded passage from *Enemies of Promise*, that he had been lucky to have worked under two 'admirable' editors, presumably Desmond MacCarthy and Raymond Mortimer, who 'beside being personal friends have taken enormous pains to correct my faults and enlarge my opportunities so that often articles which have seemed good directly owe their goodness to their necessary comments and more necessary cutting, so that I am one of the few people who have probably won in the struggle with journalism. I have got more good out of it than it has got out of me . . .'

With money in relatively short supply, and a permanent London base in the King's Road flat, Connolly resumed regular reviewing for the *New Statesman* in the spring of 1935 after Raymond Mortimer had finally been made literary editor. 'To review some novels again after a lapse of several years might be an alarming experience,' he informed his readers, ' – but the novels are the same, the writers are the same, the same lovers hold hands on the front of the cover, and then men who were boys when I was a boy endorse each other on the jacket.' Although the occasional novel stood out – Isherwood's *Mr Norris Changes Trains* was 'extremely amusing and readable, a book one cannot put down', phrasing suggestive of an advanced case of reviewer's exhaustion, while of Hemingway he wrote that 'I can think of no other novelist living who unites to such purity of emotional content such mastery of form' – he soon found himself swamped by tidal waves of mediocrity.

'I was asked the other day why I inveighed against middlebrows since it would never lead to their writing any better,' he told his readers in August 1935, shortly before leaving on holiday without being able to find a single new novel he could bear to take with him:

> The reason is that I think the train of fiction is already hopelessly overcrowded, and that all the comfortable seats are occupied by people with third-class tickets. My mission is to evict them to make room for those few, sad, unappreciated vocational artists whose books are so much better and more entertaining.

English fiction, he declared, was blighted by 'three colossal, almost irremediable' flaws: 'thinness of material', 'poverty of style' and 'lack of power'. English life was, for the most part, 'without adventure or variety': most writers were drawn from the same 'mandarin' class, and their lives tended to follow an identical pattern of an uneventful childhood followed by public school, university, a job and bringing up children. The English writer was deprived of the raw material for more than one book, and – Connolly appeared to have forgotten that these same mandarins were ruling a large slice of the globe, and coming into contact with all manner of people – the unhappy fellow 'simply can't get at pugilists, gangsters, speakeasies, negroes, and even if he should he would find them absolutely without the force and colour of their American equivalents.' The etiolated English novelist, he went on, was condemned to write in the 'moderately intelligent, rather academic language of the mandarin class', and lacked a native equivalent to the tough, laconic and demotic *lingua franca* of American writers like Hemingway and Dashiell Hammett. Finally, English novels seemed to lack both maturity and 'intellectual power': whereas the Americans treated their readers as equals, communicating in a way that was 'natural, easy and unrepressed', 'English novels seem always to be written for superiors or inferiors, older or younger people, or for the opposite sex.' Of the novels he had reviewed that year, only Orwell's *Burmese Days* and *Mr Norris Changes Trains* had 'that decent and inspiring intimation of equality'. No doubt the climate was to blame, for 'there seems something in it that gelds and arranges all English writers, substituting timidity and caution for freedom and curiosity, hence all the flatness, dullness and feebleness of the novel – hence also, above all, the stagnation.' As for the reviewer, 'it is the quality of his nourishment that determines whether he is to be a reviewer or a hack. He may have every conceivable talent, but if he has only bad books to write about, he is doomed.' The three choices facing him were to become a cynic, churning out adequate uncritical copy; to go on struggling against mediocrity, and eventually be carried off; or to be blithely unaware of the problem, put in thirty or forty years' worth of reviewing, and end up 'bitterly hurt to find that they have long been the innocent dupe of publishers and the laughing-stock of the public.' Connolly's outburst provoked an indignant response from David Garnett, who charged him with writing 'snobbish and preposterous nonsense'. That was all very well, Connolly replied, but Garnett could afford to pick and choose the novels he read, whereas the unhappy reviewer spent most of his reading hours with bad books: 'Mr Garnett is the sleek drawing-room cat who dips his whiskers in the cream of the week's literature. Need he bristle so at the yowling, down in the area, of his unfortunate alley friend, who is choking over an ash-bin of fish-heads?'

Connolly's views on the average English novel complement, and were admittedly influenced by, those of Wyndham Lewis, whose 'The Taxi Cab Driver Test for Fiction', published in *Men Without Art* in 1934, ridiculed the opinions of Hugh Walpole and Arnold Bennett as well as the bland uniformity of most contemporary fiction, exposing Huxley's *Point Counter Point* – which Connolly also derided in print – as an outstanding example of middlebrow tosh disguised as something better.* Like Lewis, Connolly was extremely funny as well as splenetic, and reviewing bad fiction enabled him

* Despite their similarity of views, Wyndham Lewis disliked and disapproved of the younger man – an opinion shared by some of his admirers, such as Julian Symons and Geoffrey Grigson. Lewis once described to Symons how, some time in the Thirties, he was introduced in the Leicester Galleries to a 'well-known critic' – widely assumed to be Connolly – and how

> I put out my hand and something got hold of it, something slimy, and I looked down and, Symons, it was a marine growth, a marine growth that had got hold of my hand. No no, I said, no no, and I tried to pull my hand away but the growth had my hand, Symons, it had my hand and it wouldn't let go. I tell you I was really frightened, I had to pull hard to get my hand away from its suckers and I was very relieved to be able to manage it.

to give full rein to his wit and his sense of the absurd. Refusing to review any new novels was not the answer, he declared, since publishers would then withdraw their advertising and everyone would suffer: preferable alternatives would be for 'no new novels to be published for three years, their sale forbidden like that of plovers' eggs', and for their writing to be restricted to those over the age of thirty: banned subjects should include

> schools and universities, all homes with incomes of between three thousand and three hundred a year, words like Daddy, love, marriage, baby, birth, death, mother, buses, shops – I particularly dislike both the shopping expedition (She looked at her list, let me see, two bars of soap, three bars of chocolate, but already the huge store had overwhelmed her with its oriental mystery – it was an Arab bazaar, Eunice decided rapidly as she paused before a chinchilla mantilla. Seven yards of demi-rep the list continued) – and those horrible bus rides, when the stars are so close, and the young man treads on air (he was getting nearer, Pimlico was a forgotten dream, Fulham and West Brompton passed unheeded – supposing she should be out? 'Fares please,' shouted the conductor for the third time. 'Fourpenny to heaven,' he answered unthinkingly), and picnics, and going for walks, and conversations in pubs and all novels dealing with more than one generation or with any period before 1918 or with brilliant impoverished children in rectories...

Forbidden names included Hugo, Sebastian, Adrian, Chloe, Inez and Felicity; forbidden faces 'all young men with curly hair or remarkable eyes, all gaunt haggard thinkers' faces, all faunlike characters, anybody over six feet, or with any distinction whatever, and all women with a nape to their necks ("he loved the way her hair curled in the little hollow at the nape of her neck")'.

Most comical of all were Mr Mossbross, the Principal of Modelbrow College, and Felicity Arquebus, the blurb-writer's daughter, both of whom provided opportunities for the frustrated novelist in their creator, while at the same time enabling him to ridicule the world of the benign bestseller and the Book Society Choice. Mr Mossbross was a typical schoolmaster, with a touch of Mr Chips about him:

> And now for Mr Linklater's *Ripeness is All.*
> 'What are the characteristics of middlebrow satire?'
> 'Sanity, sir.'
> 'Not bad; MacDonnell?'
> 'Being Scotch, sir.'
> 'That's not funny; Collier?'

'Topicality.' 'Ribaldry.' 'Tolerance.'

'Don't all speak at once, one at a time – you, Agate?'

'Splendidly virile, robust, immensely readable, sir, a rousing bumper.'

'And you, Priestley?'

'Zest and gusto, sir, the high spirits of a clever man.'

'Very good, all of you, you avoided the trap. And you are quite right – for if you put irony, indignation, feeling – in short, wit – into this kind of thing you overdo it, like Swift, or merely irritate the public, like Joyce and Lawrence. You must be careful not to offend anybody. How are you going to manage? First: don't let your characters come to life – they must be types, you can abuse them freely. How do you create a type? You take a character and say he is a bridge bore or a golf bore or a colonel – and then whenever he appears he talks about bridge or golf or poetry or the army. Then you create a comic situation. You shut the poet and the colonel up in a lift, you put the bridge bore on the golf links, or you let loose a pig at the vicarage garden party, like Linklater here. And then you put in the satire.'

Felicity Arquebus, on the other hand, lived in Hampstead, where she moved in the arty set; her father, 'Dads', was a hard-working blurb-writer for Mr Goulash the publisher – himself not far removed from Victor Gollancz, perhaps – and Mrs Arquebus's favourite authors, housed in a glass-fronted bookcase, included 'Phyllis Bentley, Phyllis Bottome, Helen Waddell, Helen Simpson, G.B. Stern, Beverley Nichols, and Theodora Benson – and poetry, too, Humbert Wolfe of course, and some of the new writers who left one rather breathless, and whose books had lovely cold names like *Open the Sky* and *Armed October*.'*

Raymond Mortimer was to remain as the *New Statesman*'s literary editor until 1947, and Connolly found him very much a kindred spirit. Mortimer was widely agreed to be – in V.S. Pritchett's words – 'the most brilliant literary editor the magazine ever had': he exorcised the tradition of gentlemanliness and amateurishness to which Connolly objected, and the 'back pages' of the magazine, for which he was responsible, were held to complement perfectly Kingsley Martin's political (and polemical) first half. He was, Pritchett went on, 'a curious mixture of liberalism and ruthless intolerance, especially towards the literary puritanism growing up in Cambridge'; he'detested sloppy writing' and took immense trouble with his contributors, conducting the equivalent of a university tutorial to make sure that each

* Felicity – a graduate of the *New Statesman* – made three welcome reappearances in the autumn of 1937 in *Night and Day*, the short-lived periodical which Graham Greene edited as an English equivalent of the *New Yorker* (see p. 300).

sentence meant exactly what the writer had in mind. Looking back over their long association, Connolly remembered how 'as literary editor of the *New Statesman* he came to the rescue of many an uncertain young talent, finding ideas for one, reticence for another, commas for a third. There was no trouble he would not patiently take to make new writers more imaginative or more accurate, and the result was a very good paper.' Like any good editor, Mortimer realised the importance of varying the diet offered to contributors. In February 1936, for example, he asked Connolly if he would like to try his hand once more as a theatre-reviewer, and after warning his editor that he couldn't share Desmond MacCarthy's passion for the stage,* Connolly set out for the Westminster Theatre, where Rupert Doone was producing *The Dog Beneath the Skin* by Auden and Isherwood. 'The bareness of the stage reflected the poverty of the lines,' he decided. He was irritated by the 'didactic' choruses and the 'authentic rallying cries of homo-communism', and although Auden was 'the only real poet of any stature since Eliot', he was in danger – like so many writers of their generation – of subordinating art to politics: 'He may be a better man and will certainly be a happier man for trying to get in touch with the masses, but his work will suffer.' The difficulties of reconciling literature and ideology was a subject on which Connolly was to hold unfashionable views during the remaining years of the decade; in the meantime, although Mortimer tried him out as a film critic three years later, more congenial relief from the fictional round was afforded by a long piece for the magazine on what was to become a lifelong passion, the collecting of modern first editions, many of them written by friends; while a review of Marie Stopes's *Marriage in My Time* gave him an opportunity to air his own views on the subject ('I should like to add my recipe for married happiness. "Whenever you can, read at meals"'). And, for his part, Connolly liked to recommend up-and-coming young writers to Raymond Mortimer as potential reviewers. 'I think Grigson is intelligent, a good critic of poetry, and very much in the "advanced" movement,' he informed him; and in the same letter he also recommended the eighteen-year-old David Gascoyne, who had written a 'terrible but promising novel', though 'I don't know if he can write

* Connolly remained a reluctant and restless theatre-goer; and although he felt he should admire the experimental and the *avant-garde*, he secretly preferred the well-made middlebrow play. Deirdre Connolly remembers going with him and Ethel de Croisset to see *Les Nègres* in Paris. It was very hot, and Connolly stirred uneasily in his seat. At some stage the entire cast fell down, apparently dead, and muttering 'Thank God' Connolly rose from his seat and prepared to leave; at which the actors sprang to their feet and engaged in a frenzied dance, and a further hour of torment ensued. For Connolly in his sixties, at least, *One-way Pendulum* or *Beyond the Fringe* at the Theatre Royal in Brighton were vastly preferable to *Waiting for Godot* at the Royal Court. For Connolly's poor behaviour while watching Chekhov, see p. 375.

amusingly. *No young writer can write amusingly because they all admire Herbert Read.*'*

As we have seen, one answer to the Book Society Choice novel of the kind he so detested – Louis Golding, Francis Brett-Young, G.B. Stern, Humbert Wolfe and Hugh Walpole were among his particular subjects of derision – was to read detective stories instead. He admired laconic, tough Americans like Dashiell Hammett and, at the other end of the spectrum, he revealed an unexpectedly soft spot for Dornford Yates, perhaps because his heroes so enjoyed driving through Pyrenean France in large open cars:

> Sometimes, at great garden parties, literary luncheons or in the quiet of an exclusive gun-room, a laugh rings out. The sad formal faces relax for a moment and a smaller group is formed within the larger. They are admirers of Dornford Yates who have found each other out. We are badly organised, we know little about ourselves and next to nothing about our hero, but we appreciate fine writing when we come across it, and a wit that is ageless united to a courtesy that is extinct.

An opportunity to indulge his tastes and boost his earnings at the same time occurred when he was appointed one of the *Daily Telegraph*'s two regular reviewers of crime fiction in November 1935, replacing James Hilton of *Mr Chips* fame. His appointment was the work of Cyril Lakin, a dashing Welshman with a weakness for wide-lapelled suits, cocktail-shakers and playing golf in orange plus-fours. In 1929 Lakin had been appointed literary editor of the *Telegraph*, with Leonard Russell as his assistant, and among the younger writers from whom he commissioned reviews were C. Day Lewis and Rebecca West. Connolly was given a weekly spot on the Tuesday book page, doubling up with the crime novelist Francis Iles, who performed an identical chore on Fridays; and before long he was treating his weekly batch of thrillers with an affection denied to most conventional novels, as in his evocation of the E. Phillips Oppenheim type of Riviera whodunit:

> At this moment, high above the sauntering crowds, there are men putting papers away in the villa strong-room, Russian Grand Dukes laughing insolently over their hosts' priceless Courvoisier, beautiful women who suddenly clasp their hands round their neck crying 'My pearls – they're gone!' and butlers who, though they stay with the same family for more than two months, are feeling the irresistible and wonted shock, the

* Founded in 1933, Geoffrey Grigson's *New Verse* was a ferocious champion of, in particular, W.H. Auden. Grigson shared the uncharitable views of his mentor Wyndham Lewis about Connolly the man and Connolly the writer; and Connolly's antipathy to Herbert Read appears to have been reciprocated.

pleasure that never palls, of bringing in the whisky to a silent employer huddled over the writing-desk with a knife in his back.*

Connolly's reviewing for the *Telegraph* was not restricted to thrillers, however; and, with less space at his disposal and, perhaps, a less critical and sophisticated readership, he adopted a more emollient approach than that employed in the *Statesman*. He praised, with reservations, Lawrence Durrell's first novel, *Pied Piper of Lovers*; confessed, in words that his later self might well have disowned, that 'the advantages of having a French book accessible in good English, good print and good paper far outweigh the pleasures of reading the author in the original'; reproached Somerset Maugham for his belief that anecdotes were the essence of fiction (in later years he would write, often and defensively, in praise of a writer frequently dismissed as a middlebrow); announced that Evelyn Waugh's *Mr Loveday's Little Outing* confirmed his reputation as a 'fine writer and a deep satirist, and one of the few living writers to step directly into the great tradition of the English humorists'; pondered gravely on the transience of literary fame ('Galsworthy, Arnold Bennett, Lytton Strachey – who speaks of them now?'); and – reviewing the first issue of John Lehmann's hardback periodical, *New Writing* – wondered whether art and propaganda were compatible, and whether the left-wing writer couldn't serve his cause best by writing as well as possible rather than by explicit adherence to a party line.

Until 1936, when Lord Kemsley's *Sunday Times* split off from Lord Camrose's *Daily Telegraph*, both papers were jointly owned by the two Berry brothers; and from 1933 until 1936 Cyril Lakin was their shared literary editor. (After the separation he remained exclusively with the *Sunday Times* – as did Leonard Russell, who was to remain with the paper for the rest of his working life, together with his wife Dilys Powell, its long-serving film critic). For a brief period, before the divide, Connolly was reviewing sporadically for the *Sunday Times* as well as for its sister-paper and the *New Statesman*. In this, he found himself in uncongenial company, for whereas the *Telegraph* fielded Harold Nicolson as its lead reviewer, the

* Connolly's *Telegraph* thriller reviews, together with those of contemporaries like Francis Iles, Maurice Richardson and C. Day Lewis, were put to ingenious use in Cameron McCabe's sophisticated and original thriller, *The Face on the Cutting-Room Floor*, published by Victor Gollancz in 1937. The true identity of the author remained a mystery for many years, known only to close friends like Fredric Warburg: Julian Maclaren-Ross, for example, was convinced that this beautifully written, intricate novel was Connolly's own work, and was disappointed when, at their first meeting, Connolly assured him that it was not. The novel was reissued by Gollancz in 1974, prompted by admirers like Julian Symons and Frederic Raphael: McCabe was revealed to have been Ernst Bornemann, a young refugee from Germany who was working in the film business in the late 1930s. He eventually returned to Austria, becoming the Professor of Sexology at the University of Salzburg; in a melancholy twist worthy of his novel, he committed suicide in 1995 after his young wife had run off with another man.

Sunday Times's book pages – or, rather, such space as was left between gigantic publishers' advertisements, headed by those paid for by Victor Gollancz and Walter Hutchinson – were dominated by writers of the kind he derided in the *New Statesman*: Ralph Straus, G.B. Stern, Gerald Heard, Edward Shanks, Doreen Wallace and the Dean of Exeter among them. Connolly's reviews for the paper were, mercifully, restricted to one book at a time: these included T.S. Eliot's *Collected Poems* (never afraid, now or in the future, to criticise those he admired, he suggested that Pound had been a bad influence on Eliot's more recent work, encouraging him in the use of unassimilated quotations, and replacing the freshness of 'Prufrock' with a 'mystical but also rather muddy and disingenuous bardic quality'); and Hemingway's *Green Hills of Africa* which, while a first-rate contribution to the 'literature of big-game hunting', represented a falling-off from his earlier work.

All the same, the pages in Hemingway's book in which the Austrian Kandisky asks the narrator about the perils that lie in wait for the American writer ('Politics, women, drink, money, ambition. And the lack of politics, women, drink, money and ambition') may well have influenced *Enemies of Promise*; and the anxieties and the arguments that he would explore there were seldom far from his mind. 'Whom the gods wish to destroy they first call promising . . .' he told *New Statesman* readers, in words that would soon assume a more permanent form:

> When a writer is born among the Chatto islanders in the little-known Gollancz archipelago, a dirge is sung over his cradle: 'May he be dowered with the gift of unpresentability – some anti-social tic, drink, drugs, unbuttoning or a too great readiness to proceed to the extremes of malice; may he never support a family nor accept a regular income from a publisher nor join an advertising agency' . . .*

In an unpublished piece entitled 'Reviewers', he attributed the dismal state of contemporary fiction to the 'indigence' of authors, compelled to over-produce and dissipate their energies on journalism in order to earn a crust; to pressure from libraries and book societies, fearful of offending the canons of good taste or incurring the wrath of the censor; to the timidity of publishers, who combined caution in literary matters with the deleterious cult of the best-seller; and to the 'ox-like indifference' of the reading public. And yet the longing to write remained as strong as ever. 'I could write so

* The fate reserved for Peter Quennell, dismissed in Connolly's journal, under the heading 'Decay of Friends', as 'an advertising man, "smooth" ', together with Patrick Balfour, 'a Fleet Street tough'.

many books, instead I fritter everything away into articles,' 'Lincoln Croyle' confessed: he worried that 'he had made himself into that very English thing, a man of letters who wrote articles about writers', which were then reprinted as books of essays. Like his creator, Croyle was obsessed by the mechanics and the perils of the literary life: in a decade of ideological commitment – to socialism, to anti-fascism – 'the dilemmas of authors, the trends of modern literature interest me – the hardships of Chinese peasant women, bullfighters or Jews don't.' For Croyle at least,

> literature could not be too esoteric, too much in the hands of a priestly caste, nor could the beauties and mysteries of it be revealed except after a long initiate – as a reviewer he had to listen to his opinions of a book, which was valued at five pounds by his employer, be questioned by gramophone experts, taxi-drivers, aunts, friends, anyone who happened to read it. He sometimes thought that the function of middlebrows, the reason that Galsworthy, Walpole, Louis Golding and Peter Fleming were put into the world, was to divert the public taste from literature and feed it with an appropriate substitute.

Five guineas – rather than pounds – was indeed the weekly sum he earned from the *Statesman*: with the *Telegraph* and the *Sunday Times* added in he should, he told his mother, be earning around £50 a month in all.

The Rock Pool behind him, the urge to write at greater length could now be satisfied in part through parodies, an art at which Connolly excelled: 'Told in Gath', his lethal parody of Aldous Huxley's own fictional account of Ottoline Morrell's Garsington Manor, was first published in a collection entitled *Parody Party*, edited by Leonard Russell in 1936. Rather less demanding was the *New Statesman*'s weekly competition: readers were invited to send in parodies of particular authors or kinds of writing, and the winning results were printed a fortnight later. Although Raymond Mortimer and V.S. Pritchett were among the regular competition-setters and judges, Connolly was surprisingly diffident; but the competition he set (and examined) in November 1935 was of particular interest, in that it drew upon an interest and an enthusiasm which, like collecting modern first editions, was to become a permanent and much remarked-upon feature of his life. Readers were asked to evoke in chilling detail the worst kind of meal in an English hotel, taking particular care to describe the food itself, its presentation, the setting and the wine list. A fortnight later Connolly reported the results, and announced the names of the winner (Sir Harry d'Avigdor-Goldsmid) and the runner-up (Anthony Powell), both of whose contributions were printed. There had been disappointingly few entrants,

Connolly told his readers – proof in itself that few English people noticed what they ate. Through the competition he had hoped to draw attention to the 'mixture of ignorance, inefficiency and self-satisfaction which one comes across in English hotels, and also the extraordinary way in which people write about food in England.' The English, it seemed, could never be natural when writing about food, but clogged up their prose with quotations and anecdotes and literary references, so that 'there are cookery books in which one searches in vain among Shakespeare on herbs or Walton on syllabubs for the right way to poach an egg.' Among those responsible for this sorry state of affairs were the 'high priests' of the Wine and Food Society, who turned the business of eating into an increasingly 'inaccessible and esoteric' mystique.

The competition's winner was to become a lifelong friend and benefactor. A near-contemporary at Oxford, d'Avigdor-Goldsmid was extremely rich and, in fact, a keen member of the Wine and Food Society. After Connolly's death, he claimed that they met as a result of the competition; but since he dated the gastronomic tour of France which he then made with the Connollys to the period of the Stavisky affair – 1933 – he may not be entirely reliable. According to Sir Harry, the tour included 'pilgrimages to Illiers and to Pau for the Dornford Yates country' – Illiers was the original for Proust's Cambray, and, quite apart from Dornford Yates, Connolly's Aunt Mab lived at Pau – while Connolly's telegraphic account in his journals takes in Calais, Bordeaux, Irun, Saragossa and Paris as well. They were stoned by road-menders while crossing the Pyrenees, and – or so Sir Harry reported – Jean's digestion was not the equal of her husband's; and a further potential hazard for Jean took the form of Sir Harry's travelling companion, Betty Fletcher-Mossop. A year or two later, when his marriage had begun to unravel, Connolly dated its decline to this gastronomic tour. 'Miss Mossop', he claimed, tried to lure Connolly into her bed, but he felt unable to oblige.

That same year Connolly paid his first visit to Tickerage Mill, a house that was to loom large in his private mythology as a haven of good food, good wine, good company and welcome country air. 'The mill where I sometimes stay provides another cure for Angst,' he wrote of it in *The Unquiet Grave*:

> the red lane down through the Spanish chestnut wood, the apple trees on the lawn, the bees in the roof, the geese on the pond, the black sun-lit marsh marigolds, the wood-fires crackling in the low bedrooms, the creak of the cellar-door, and the recurrent monotonies of the silver-whispering weir – what could be more womb-like or reassuring? Yet always the anxious owner is flying from it as from the scene of a crime.

Tickerage's owner, Dick Wyndham, was a soldier turned writer, painter and patron of bohemia. A tall, square-jawed, impetuous, somewhat irascible figure, related to the Wyndhams of Petworth House, he had won an MC in the First World War, and had stayed on in the army after the war was over. Eventually he gave up soldiering, and took up painting instead, with Wyndham Lewis as his mentor; since then he had spent some time painting and photographing the Dinka tribesmen of the Sudan, and Connolly had written for the *Sunday Times* an admiring account of *The Gentle Savage*, his account of his adventures there. He bought Tickerage, a rather Tudor-beamy farmhouse near Uckfield in Sussex, in 1926: he was known to the locals as 'the Captain', to some others as 'Dick Whippington', since he was said to be keen on beating girls. Like Sir Harry, he was an enthusiastic member of the Wine and Food Society, which had been founded in 1933 by André Simon and A.J.A. Symons, and included among its members Peter Quennell, Tom Driberg, Sacheverell Sitwell and Patrick Balfour, as well as assorted dukes and Spanish grandees. According to Tom Driberg, Wyndham gave 'the best weekend parties I have ever attended' at Tickerage. A.J.A. Symons recalled a Society dinner there at which a lobster was 'not boiled at all but kept alive until needed, then killed by a knife through the head, cut in half and grilled', while Driberg – like Connolly – had particularly fond memories of Wyndham's cellar, and how, 'ranged on the sideboard and decanted well before dinner, would stand six or more magnums of château-bottled claret of the finest years.'

Whether Connolly's review led to a meeting remains unclear, but before long he too was delighting in the Tickerage regime of walks and croquet and all-night games and driving up the dead-straight drive in their host's Railton at ninety mph, and was celebrating 'the seven joys of Tickerage: when the car turns down the drive, when the gate clicks, when the soft-water tea appears, when the dining-room fire crackles, when the cork goes pop, when the ironstone soup tureen is put on the table, and the sound of the weir at night.' Among those whom Connolly encountered at Tickerage were Peter Quennell, Joan Eyres-Monsell and her future husband John Rayner, then a colleague of Tom Driberg's on the *Daily Express*.

Tickerage became more accessible to the Connollys when, in the early summer of 1936, he at last passed his driving test, 'which my psychological dread of examinations has prevented me taking for nearly a year, so one can use the roads of dear old arterial England again at last.' Connolly always took pleasure in cars and driving, and perhaps the most celebrated passage in *The Unquiet Grave* celebrated the delights of life behind the wheel ('Peeling off the kilometres to the tune of "Blue Skies", sizzling down the long black liquid reaches of Nationale Sept, the plane trees going sha-sha-sha through the open window, the windscreen yellowing with crushed midges, she with the Michelin beside me, a handkerchief binding her hair'); and Jean shared her husband's love of motoring, which he once listed – along with day-dreaming and reading – as one of the 'real drugs', which 'rot one through and through'. England's arterial roads were all very well, but what Connolly really enjoyed was setting out from Calais in his battleship-grey, seventeen-horsepower Armstrong-Siddeley sports saloon, with its dark-green leather seats. 'For once we are going to escape, we are going to do all the things we are ashamed of,' he wrote in an uncompleted essay on the pleasures of motoring. With a following wind he could reach a speed of eighty mph, but what he liked best was to settle down to a 'dreamy fifty-five over the N.1, for that is the speed at which I go best when talking and thinking of other things.' He was 'happiest on the N.7, on the black reaches of the way to the South, somewhere after Vienne, around Tain and Tournon, in the fields where the cicadas begin, and the Hermitage ripens, and the light becomes green and yellow behind the Cevennes. Valence, Montélimar, Pierrelatte, and, dear to geographers, the gap of Donzère . . . Here expectation is most intense, and reality most seducing, as the heart unwinds on the winding asphalt.' 'There are three good things in life,' he declared: 'to be writing a readable book, to be travelling south in winter with someone one's conscience permits one to love, and to enjoy a fine dinner with old friends.' Faced with the conflicting demands of journalism and literature, writing a readable book was a perennial problem; fine dinners with friends were expanding the slim youth of Eton and Oxford into the more corpulent figure of later years; reconciling his conscience with his choice of travelling companion was to place increasing strain on a marriage that was beginning to fray at the edges. Implausible plans to find work as a live-in couple, with Jean the cook and Connolly the butler, were hastily abandoned, as was the Betjemans' suggestion that they should come and live near them in the Vale of the White Horse. Connolly, in the mid-1930s, was both busy and adrift: he needed something other than the perils of the literary life and the pursuit of pleasure on which to focus his attentions; and – as it did for so many of his contemporaries – Spain, his old love, was to provide both an ideal and a distraction.

*

Connolly made his farewells as a regular fiction reviewer for the *New Statesman* in June 1936. A month later the Spanish Civil War broke out, and by November he was in Barcelona, supplementing the magazine's regular Spanish correspondent, Geoffrey Brereton. He crossed the border from France by train, and on entering Catalonia he became instantly aware of an 'extraordinary mixture of patriotic war fever and revolutionary faith', of 'an absolutely new and all-pervading sense of moral elevation'. Since Franco's insurrection, Spanish politics had become increasingly polarised, not simply between the Nationalists – a coalition of fascists, romantic royalists and traditional Catholics – and the more liberal-minded Republicans, but, very damagingly, within the Government side, where a secondary or subsidiary civil war would soon break out. Catalonia in general, and Barcelona in particular, was a bastion of Republicanism, within which left-wing groups were battling for supremacy, with increasing ferocity and ideological exclusivity: when Connolly made the first of his three visits they were still united against the common enemy, but before long the heady idealism of the early days would be replaced by vicious internal feuding. Connolly soon learned to distinguish between the various left-wing factions – the Socialists, the Communists (backed by Moscow), the Trotskyites of POUM (in whose militia George Orwell was fighting), the Anarchists and Catalan separatists among them. Whereas most foreign supporters of the Republican cause tended either to be Communist Party members or to support the recently-enunciated policy of a Popular Front, whereby Communists and moderate Socialists throughout Europe would shelve their differences and unite to combat fascism – at the same time taking an increasingly intolerant line towards rival or more radical left-wing tendencies – Connolly's own sympathies were with the Anarchists: anarchism of the Spanish variety should, he suggested, 'be an ideal not unsympathetic to the English, who have always honoured freedom and individual eccentricity and whose liberalism and whiggery might well have turned to something very similar had they been harassed for centuries, like the Spanish proletariat, by absolute monarchs, militant clergy, army dictatorships, and absentee landlords.'

Connolly shared the general idealism: 'The pervading sense of freedom, of intelligence, justice and companionship, the enormous upthrust in backward and penniless people of the desire for liberty and education, are things that have to be seen to be understood. It is as if the masses, the mob in fact, credited usually with instincts only of stupidity and persecution, should blossom into what is really a kind of flowering of humanity.' Elsewhere, however, he wrote of how much easier it was for members of the middle-class intelligentsia to identify with the cause of the workers in Spain rather than at home: in England they were divided by background and education, and he 'shared no common habits with the workers such as a liking for margarine, Woodbines and strong tea', whereas the Spanish workers seemed kindred spirits, 'so intelligent, so fearless', as well as being 'fond of wine and late nights, humorous, open-handed'. All the same, Connolly found himself, as an English journalist adrift in Republican Spain, an unpopular figure on account of the British and French policy of non-intervention, 'an arrangement by which every democracy is allowed to remain in the privacy of its own burrow, awaiting the visit of the stoats'. Unlike the Western democracies, the stoats were already deeply involved: Hitler and Mussolini were providing military support for Franco, while Stalin's backing for the Communist Party and the International Brigades would soon lead to the ruthless suppression of the Anarchists and the Trotskyites.

A month later, Connolly was back in Spain. By now Madrid was under siege by Franco's forces; the Republican government had been evacuated to Valencia, and Barcelona – itself under threat of bombardment – was overrun by refugees from the capital. Food was in short supply, and the atmosphere in the city was far more fraught and frightened than a month earlier. Years later, Connolly recalled how he had come across terrified people for the first time – 'bourgeois trembling for their lives, men whose hands shook, a group of mercenary pilots in a Barcelona hotel drinking in the evening before taking up their obsolete planes on doomed missions.' The walls were plastered with admonitory posters, anticipating those of wartime London ('*Les oreilles ennemies vous écoutent*'); the civil war within a civil war had broken out, and 'the war correspondents wandered with charmed lives through a blacked-out city while the anarchist cars tore through the Ramblas to pick up suspects and bear them off to the lonely execution grounds'. He attended a Kafkaesque popular tribunal – reminiscent, in retrospect, of the show trials then taking place in Russia – at which three ex-officers were tried on a charge of spying and condemned to death, his account of which was written for the *New Statesman* but never published; he observed 'the arms stacked in night-club cloakrooms, the party banners and slogans, the painted trains, the workers' processions'; together with half a million others, he attended the funeral of Durruti, an Anarchist leader who had been responsible for the murder of the Archbishop of Saragossa in 1923, and the attempted murder of King Alfonso the following year, and was variously regarded as a thug or a hero (and by Connolly as a 'rugged, lion-like man, possessed of natural intelligence and reckless courage'). From Barcelona he travelled down to Valencia, where – according to the historian Hugh Thomas, and to Connolly's almost certain relief – 'the population ate well throughout the war and visitors were often served with ten different *hors d'oeuvre* and ten courses.' Sitting in a music-hall with a 'sailor and his doctor friend', he found himself unhappily aware of 'the gravity of the Civil War for those to whom it is not the dawning of a new day, but the eclipse of an old one'; along with his fellow-correspondents, he was grilled by agents of the Comintern, and 'I remember pooh-poohing their absurd questions, like the significance in one's passport of an exit from Lisbon three years earlier, and reassuring a worried Spaniard with "*Lo que vale es la inocencia*" – sublimely priggish utterance.'

Writing on 'The Future in Spain' for the *New Statesman*, Connolly struck – from a Republican point of view – an unexpectedly optimistic note. 'It seems certain to me that, short of intervention on a scale so enormous as to obliterate the men, women and children on the Government side, the Government are bound to win,' he wrote: Franco's Moors were getting homesick, the coalition between the Anarchists and the Socialists was holding up, and 'it is now impossible for Franco to win except by committing, with German and Italian aid, an act which will prove intolerable to France and to England.' Power lay with the militia, whether Communist or Anarchist: Connolly's own money was on the Anarchists, but he was sympathetic too to the Trotskyites of POUM, a 'lively, intelligent but extremely intransigent body whose hostility to the Stalinites is putting them in an increasingly delicate position'. In Republican Spain, he went on, 'all is enthusiasm and fire'; once across the border in France, 'one renews acquaintance with the servile look and the extended palm'. He returned to England in the middle of the Abdication crisis, 'in time to take part in a witch hunt, observe the elders of the tribe conduct the tamasha, expel the guilty couple, make the country safe for mediocrity, humbug, cold feet and anaemia . . . '

Making his debut as the writer of the *Statesman*'s 'London Diary' in January 1937, Connolly set out his qualifications – or lack of qualifications – for the job. A diarist, he suggested, was expected to be 'alert, full of curiosity, active, topical and well-informed'; he, on the other hand, was

> none of these, being by nature incurious and slothful, with a tendency to hibernate in winter, not to get up till dark, leading in fact an obsessional life rather than an extrovert one, for I am a person whom certain ideas haunt for long periods, who reads and re-reads a certain book and then carries it about like an iodine bag. For the rest I am Anglo-Irish by extraction, continental in habits, thirty-three last September, and bear on my shoulders the round pyknic head of the manic-depressive without, as yet, giving way to the sterner symptoms.

He belonged, he continued, to 'one of the most non-political generations the world has ever seen': his generation at Oxford 'would no sooner have attended a political meeting than we would have gone to church, and we were greatly impressed, in a ninetyish way, by money and titles and the necessity of coming into closer contact with them.' He belonged to a generation for whom 'a bottle of champagne or a good suit had an almost mystical quality', while 'such action as was necessary in the life of reading, mutual criticism, aesthetic satisfaction and personal relationships for which we felt ordained was provided by foreign travel.' Realists like Kenneth Clark and Evelyn Waugh had quickly appreciated 'how entirely the kind of life they liked depended on close cooperation with the governing classes'; others – among whom Connolly included himself – wavered, and it was by these waverers, with their left-wing sympathies, that he was especially intrigued. They had, he suggested, been politicised entirely by foreign affairs, by the rise of Hitler, by Abyssinia, and – 'for the few remaining ivory-tower-holders' – by Spain. Some had become left-wing from expediency; for others, 'the consciousness of social injustice is a slowly-working poison';

> And then again there is the typically English band of psychological revolutionaries, people who adopt left-wing political formulas because they hate their fathers or were unhappy at their public schools or insulted at the Customs or lectured about sex. And the even more typically English band, and much larger, of aesthetic revolutionaries; people who hate England for romantic reasons, and consequently the class which rules it, which makes the Gold Flake and the Player's, the radio programmes and the Austin Sevens, the beauty spots, the residential districts, the camps and the cinemas, who select the Test teams and preside at Ascot; as if by removing them it would be possible to remove the whole cabbage-like deposit of complacency and stupidity from the English race or the unrest from the hearts of those who dislike it.

Connolly's cynical, unillusioned diagnosis of English middle-class revolutionaries upset one future friend and collaborator, whose left-wing commitment was more orthodox and more whole-hearted. 'It wasn't so much what Connolly said that depressed me as the feeling that the spirit in which he said it – a careless and profound and inexcusable cruelty – suddenly seemed almost universal,' Stephen Spender wrote to Christopher Isherwood:

> These people have a horrible way of making their own apprehensions seem the most *final* attitude of mind possible. Of course it is really their own passion to make their own attitude of mind seem fashionable. His *New Statesman* article is utterly destructive – and stupid, I believe.

Two months later, Spender and Connolly came face-to-face in Barcelona. They had first met after Connolly had reviewed Spender's critical book, *The*

Destructive Element, in the *Statesman* in 1935. He had thought it, though 'often awkwardly written, arid, inconsequent and hard to follow', an 'important book'; Spender was, he suggested, neglectful of apolitical writing, of art for art's sake, but he felt that in time he would distance himself from the revolutionary ideas of his friends and contemporaries. Some six years younger than Connolly, Spender had already made his mark as a poet and critic. In his autobiographical novel *Lions and Shadows*, Christopher Isherwood had described the nineteen-year-old 'Stephen Savage' as an 'immensely tall, shambling boy... with a great scarlet poppy face, wild frizzy hair, and eyes the violent colour of bluebells', and little had changed in the intervening years; another close friend, T.C. Worsley, remarked on the 'arresting prominence of his features which made his profile seem almost an exaggeration, like a long shadow of itself thrown on a wall by a candle,' and how Spender 'lived his ordinary everyday life at a dramatic pitch where the smallest personal details were as exacting as incidents from a murder film, and each of his daily encounters had the significance of a Great Occasion.' Spender had recently married Inez Pearn, and his former boyfriend, Tony Hyndman, had gone out to Spain to join the International Brigade; he had become a short-lived member of the Communist Party, and when its Secretary, Harry Pollitt, asked him if he would go out to Spain to investigate the mysterious disappearance of a Russian battleship, the *Komsomol*, and write up his findings in the *Daily Worker*, he leapt at the opportunity. His equally implausible fellow-sleuth was T.C. Worsley, a former schoolmaster and a keen cricketer, who went to work at the *New Statesman* as an assistant literary editor in 1937: his future colleague on the magazine, V.S. Pritchett, described him as being tall and thin, with the 'mottled complexion, schoolmaster's cold-looking glasses, girlish, violent gestures of the weak character'. After travelling through southern Spain and Morocco in search of the missing battleship, the two men returned, briefly, to Barcelona; and it was there that they came across Connolly, who was travelling with Jean and his friend Ran Antrim.

In *Behind the Battle*, a much-neglected masterpiece about his experiences during the Spanish Civil War – its publication in 1939 coincided, unhappily, with the outbreak of war – Worsley describes in comic detail their encounter with 'Derek Cranshaw' and Lord Antrim. Although Worsley was to become a particular friend of Jean's, as one of a group of homosexual men on whom she came to rely, and was to be a Sussex neighbour of Connolly's some thirty years later, he knew 'Cranshaw' only by reputation as one of the smart young men

> with expensive tastes, literary educations, witty minds, amusing manners and no inhibitions, who, in the 'twenties', justifiably cynical about the

world they lived in, had spent their time cultivating their taste on the Continent of Europe. It was before consciences were 'in'.

Cranshaw was 'small and fat, with a large perfectly round head and face and thick hair brushed back from the forehead; his nose was deeply depressed at the bridge and his features were set right into the face so he looked as if an amateur had scooped them out from a perfectly centric globe'. Cranshaw was keenly interested in the standard of food served at the Café Eustadi, where they met; and 'Something about them, whether it was their clothes, their manner, or the authoritative beckoning finger which summoned the waiter, marked them off from the other tables with their leather jerkins and Party scarves. One smelt a whiff of the Café Royal.' To Worsley's surprise, Cranshaw turned out to be extremely knowledgeable about the internecine feuding within the Republican movement, and sided vehemently with the Anarchists in their losing battle with the Communists, outwitting in argument an English Communist who accused them of deliberately sabotaging food supplies.*

Connolly spent three weeks in Spain on this particular trip, visiting Aragon, Catalonia, Valencia, Alicante and Murcia. At Isherwood's suggestion he looked up W.H. Auden in his hotel: the poet, who was working for a Government radio station, seemed thrilled to see them, and ordered up a bottle of Spanish champagne – 'a detail which delighted Isherwood, who said it would have convinced him that it was the real Auden and not some imposter.' They met Auden again in Barcelona, where he photographed Ran Antrim playing chess. Afterwards they went for a walk in the gardens at Monjuich, where Auden disappeared behind a bush for a pee; he was immediately arrested by two militia men, and was only released when Connolly produced a letter of recommendation from Harry Pollitt. Although Ran Antrim was given a 'terrible grilling' by the Communists in Valencia – it 'shook him very much as he had never been treated except as a peer before' – Harry Pollitt's letter ensured that Connolly's party was well looked after. Connolly was granted interviews with the Minister of Munitions, Marine and Air, as well as with Juan Garcia Oliver, the Anarchist Minister of Justice, who, despite his own violent record – he was said to have killed 253 men in his time – told his interrogator that anarchism aimed at 'eliminating the beast in man'. After one such interview, Worsley came

* In the unedited typescript of his book, Worsley charged 'Cranshaw' with 'sexing and dining himself across Spain' – presumably a reference to his earlier adventures with Peggy Bainbridge (see p. 295). This was removed before the book went to press: Connolly later pretended to have been deeply disappointed at this, since he had hoped to make a small fortune by suing Worsley and his publisher, Robert Hale.

across 'Cranshaw' sitting in a café giving an imitation of the minister in question. 'Cranshaw' then went on to play the part of Lord Antrim's butler, handing in his notice after seventeen years' loyal service ('But if your lordship insists on lecturing to the tenantry on Bolshevism, begging your pardon, it makes my position unten-unten – well, impossible...'); after which he announced that he had ordered a special dinner of 'Lobster Thermidor followed by Canard *à la presse*!'

Barcelona was, Connolly wrote to a friend, 'much more social than before' – 'Spender was there and Christina Hastings and an awful American called Muriel Draper and a man we all hated called Catlin and Basil Murray and a horde of journalists, English journalists, French deputies etc.'* But despite the jollifications, his report for the *New Statesman* struck a far gloomier note than those written on earlier visits. 'There have been considerable changes in the political, economic and military situations since I was there in December, and I should describe them as all for the worse,' he wrote. The major change, in line with Stalin's endorsement of the Popular Front, was 'the greatly increased power of the moderate elements in the Government backed up officially by the Communists, whose policy is to support a bourgeois democratic Spain against what they consider the premature revolutionary activities of the Anarchists and the POUM.' By advocating a policy of 'First win the war, then attend to the revolution', the Communists – though numerically weaker than the Anarchists – were tightening their grip on the Republican side; with left-wing groups apparently more intent on fighting one another than opposing Franco, 'it would be hard to find an atmosphere more full of envy, intrigue, rumour and muddle than that which exists at the moment in the capitals of Republican Spain.'

In *Enemies of Promise*, Connolly recalled how he had returned to England 'with a hopeless premonition of defeat', a septic throat, and 'the feeling we experience when we see a tired fox crossing a field with the hounds and the port-faced huntsman pounding after it'. He thought his readers had the right to the truth as he saw it, and so wrote what was seen – and attacked – as an unduly defeatist and dispiriting piece: he was right, as it turned out, though in a passage excised from the published version he confessed to mixed feelings:

> Looking back at the article now I do not think most people would see much the matter with it, all the same I would not have written it if I had

* Spender had returned to Spain, and was working for a Government broadcasting unit in Valencia; so too had T.C. Worsley, who was with an ambulance unit. Basil Murray was the son of Gilbert Murray: he and Peter Rodd, Nancy Mitford's future husband, were widely held to be the originals of Evelyn Waugh's Basil Seal.

> been myself today, for I realise how defeatism, being the congenital weakness of the left, is in itself an undesirable thing. I should have waited till my septic throat had disappeared and written something more constructive.

Malaga and Bilbao had just fallen to the Fascists, and the article 'made me immensely unpopular'. He had made himself unpopular before, in particular with his attacks on R.C. Sherriff's *Journey's End* and, after the poet's death in 1935, on the poetry of A.E. Housman: but 'literary unpopularity was very different from the political kind, from being called a coward, a Fascist, a stabber-in-the-back etc.'. Years later, reviewing David Caute's *Fellow-Travellers*, Connolly confessed that he had been a natural fellow-traveller himself until 'reason and scepticism gradually regained control of my excesses of good-will and optimism and closed the credibility gap'; following his *New Statesman* article, he had learned how, 'sitting round their tables at the Ivy or the Café Royal, the fellow-travellers could mount a very solid cold shoulder, and controlling, as they did, so many columns and corners in the Press, they put up a barrage of innuendo.'*

One man who didn't object to what Connolly had written was George Orwell, who wrote from Barcelona some four months later to say that he had been shot in the throat while fighting with the POUM militia, and would shortly be returning home. 'I was just reading one of your articles on Spain in a February *New Statesman*,' he went on. 'It is a credit to the *New Statesman* that it is the only paper, apart from a few obscure ones such as the *New Leader*, where any but the Communist viewpoint has ever got through.' (Presumably, given the views of – say – Lord Rothermere's *Daily Mail*, he was referring only to left-wing papers.) He thanked Connolly for letting the public know that he was planning to write a book about his experiences in Spain, and ended by extending a belated invitation ('A pity you didn't come up to our position and see me when you were in Aragon. I would have enjoyed giving you tea in a dug-out'). Although, as they later discovered, Connolly and Orwell had been living only a street or two apart in Paris in the winter of 1929, the two men got in touch for the first time since their schooldays after Connolly had reviewed *Burmese Days* in the *New Statesman* in July 1935. He had pronounced it an 'admirable novel'; 'it might have been

* Not all the criticism came from the Left, however. 'I remember reading in the *New Statesman* one of those warm-hearted little articles which used to appear in the early days of the Spanish civil war,' wrote Evelyn Waugh in *Robbery Under Law*, published in 1939: 'the author – Mr Cyril Connolly, I think – was describing his emotions when he crossed from capitalist France into the free, proletarian air of Catalonia; the particular mark, he said, of the Workers' State, was the elimination of the outstretched palm...' Waugh's mockery was aimed, of course, at Connolly's earlier articles, which found favour with the Left.

better if he had toned down the ferocious partiality of the Lawrence-Aldington school, but personally I liked it and recommend it to anyone who enjoys a spate of efficient indignation, graphic description, excellent narrative, and irony tempered with vitriol.' Connolly arranged with Raymond Mortimer for Orwell to be given some reviewing, and put him in touch with two mutual friends from Eton, Denis Dannreuther and Denys King-Farlow.* The following year Connolly reviewed *Keep the Aspidistra Flying* in the *Daily Telegraph*, together with *The Burning Cactus*, a collection of stories by Stephen Spender. It was, he decided, a 'savage and bitter book', and 'the truths which the author propounds are so disagreeable that one ends by dreading their mention.'† Orwell, as we have seen, then asked after, and reviewed, *The Rock Pool*; and when Connolly returned from France in May 1936 he wrote to his old friend to say he hoped he hadn't been disappointed by his review of *Aspidistra*, but 'I felt it needed more colour to relieve the gloom'. Anthony Powell, in the meantime, had suggested that the two of them should get together, and a month or two later Orwell gave Connolly dinner in his rooms in Islington. Orwell served up 'excellent' steak-and-chips: Connolly later recalled that

> his greeting was typical, a long but not unfriendly stare and his characteristic wheezy laugh. 'Well, Connolly, I can see that you've worn a good deal better than I have.' I could say nothing, for I was appalled by the ravaged grooves that ran down from cheek to chin. My fat cigar-smoking persona must have been a surprise to him.

Orwell's letter to Connolly about his *New Statesman* pieces on Spain remained unanswered until October 1937: Connolly had, he apologised, been travelling in the Balkans all summer, and had only just returned. Despite his earlier praise for the *Statesman*'s apparent readiness to print views other than those of the Communist Party and the Popular Front, Orwell had fallen foul of the ideological censors himself: he told Rayner Heppenstall how, in July, the magazine had asked him for an article on Spain, but had then turned it down when they discovered that it dealt with the suppression of POUM by the Communists; to sweeten the pill, they had then offered him Frank Borkenau's *The Spanish Cockpit* to review, only to

* Rather puzzlingly, Orwell told King-Farlow that 'without Connolly's help I don't think I would have got started as a writer when I got back from Burma' – in 1927.

† In those days, it seems, reviewers had few qualms about reviewing the same book twice, and Connolly returned to *Keep the Aspidistra Flying* in the *New Statesman*: it was, he wrote, 'a harrowing and stark account of poverty', written in 'clear and violent language, at times making the reader feel he is in a dentist's chair with the drill whirring . . .'

reject that too on the grounds that it ran counter to 'editorial policy'.* And, to make matters worse, Orwell's publisher, Victor Gollancz, an ardent supporter of the Popular Front, had given Orwell to understand that although he was happy to go on publishing his novels, he would not be bringing out *Homage to Catalonia*. In his belated reply, Connolly told Orwell that he would love to talk to him about Spain: he had been dispirited by the way POUM had been treated, for

> I suppose it was necessary that Government Spain should swing to the right in order to obtain more French and English support, but that doesn't alter the fact that they had to put down what was obviously a genuine revolutionary situation to do it. The moment one shows any anti-Communist feelings or shows any sympathy with Anarchist or Trotskyist down-and-outs who are far more interesting and also far more Spanish than the people who replace them, it gets increasingly hard to find a publisher or an editor who will print one.

He had, he went on, greatly enjoyed *The Road to Wigan Pier*, which he thought Orwell's best book so far; and 'If you have any difficulty about a publisher, I am sure Secker would jump at you. I know them if you want me to suggest it.' Frederic Warburg had bought Martin Secker's publishing firm the year before, and Secker & Warburg soon became known as 'the Trotskyist publishers' because of their readiness to publish non-Communist left-wing writers; Connolly's own connection there was almost certainly Warburg's partner, the languid Roger Senhouse, a well-heeled, aristocratic Old Etonian who translated from the French, was a friend of Stephen Spender and Harold Nicolson, and had been Lytton Strachey's last lover. Whether Connolly – as well as Fenner Brockway – put in a word for Orwell at Secker is something we may never know; either way, *Homage to Catalonia* was taken on by the new firm, which continued to publish Orwell for the rest of his writing life.

*

'The defeat of the Spanish republic shattered my faith in political action. I doubt if I have written a single political article since,' Connolly declared in 1969. Certainly he was far too aware of his own ambivalences, of his

* Kingsley Martin, while admitting that he 'probably under-estimated the Communist atrocities', remained unapologetic about having rejected Orwell's pieces: partly because he knew other papers would publish his work; partly because he felt that the war would be lost if run by the Anarchists – he admitted that they had been badly treated by the Communists, but since the Soviet Union was the only outside power providing support for the Republicans, he saw no alternative but to back them. Orwell's review of *The Spanish Cockpit* was indeed published, by Lady Rhondda's *Time and Tide*.

readiness to see virtue in often incompatible points of view, of his tendency to react against any one over-riding argument or interpretation of events, to be a good party man, or identify himself with any particular cause; and as a writer he was interested above all in style, in the writer's tone of voice, and viewed with unfashionable suspicion the notion, very prevalent in the late Thirties, that ideological correctness, and advancing the cause of the Party, should take precedence over all else.* He shared to the full his contemporaries' fear and hatred of fascism, but was more sceptical than many about the alleged virtues of Stalin's Russia, and equally sceptical about the idea that a writer could only fulfil himself and properly exploit his abilities by identifying with the working class and the policies of the Popular Front. In *Enemies of Promise* he included politics among the snares awaiting the young writer; and in a passage dropped from the published version he listed some of the alternatives facing the writer – conservative or right-wing views were precluded – while at the same time suggesting his own eclecticism and volatility, and his essential sympathy with a liberal, pluralistic point of view:

> He will support the Labour Party because it is the only left-wing party which is strong enough to take power constitutionally at any moment, it is the official opposition. He will support the Communist Party because they are more zealous, clear-headed and tactically efficient, and because Communism is based on an intellectual approach to the problems of the world as well as a moral and political one. He may deplore the Russian trials but realise that Western Communism could be very different from Russia... He may think that liberalism is an emotional luxury only made possible by the enjoyment of a liberal income, but he will respect the real devotion to ideals of freedom and justice in liberals, provided that their sense of property is not affected. He will appreciate the honesty of pacifists, the spiritual values of churchmen, the anarchist belief in human goodness...

This may seem, he continued, 'a tame and tightrope-walking attitude', but 'for a writer who is not a born politician but whose feelings are deeply involved it is more than adequate, it is the attitude, as far as I can judge, of Auden and Isherwood.' As far as his own beliefs were concerned, 'I am probably happiest with liberals for they share my interests and my education, but the social injustice beneath their intellectual freedom I cannot forget. In the same way I am romantically attached to anarchism, which is an extreme form of liberal-

* Interviewed by Richard Kershaw in 1968, Connolly confessed to having been, temperamentally at least, an anarchist when young: this was, he suggested, a reaction against the *Morning Post* conservatism of the Major. He was, he claimed, asked to stand as a socialist candidate against Sir Samuel Hoare in Chelsea.

ism.' His own theoretical antipathy to the ruling classes – and here he identified himself with the 'psychological revolutionaries', the diagnosis of whom had so upset Stephen Spender – he dated back, though not by name, to the Racy Fisher affair; it had been reinforced by the 'excesses of the Joynson-Hicks regime' – Joynson-Hicks had been a particularly censorious Home Secretary during the 1920s – and, later, by events in Abyssinia and Spain.

As a writer and a critic, Connolly felt increasingly uneasy about attempts to equate literary excellence with ideological purity. Reviewing *The Novel Today* – a survey undertaken by a Marxist critic, Philip Henderson – he noted Henderson's dismissal of Joyce, Lawrence and others on ideological grounds, but was quick to point out that those writers who were recommended for toeing the Party line were so dim as to be virtually unreadable. He was grateful for each new issue of John Lehmann's *New Writing* – and Lehmann, for his part, tried in vain to persuade him to contribute articles on Isherwood and Orwell – but worried that its propaganda quotient was too high: 'Literature is something which is just as good in ten years' time, propaganda is not, and the contrast is acute for many.' Contemplating *The Mind in Chains*, a collection of left-wing essays edited by C. Day Lewis, he suggested that most of its contributors almost certainly preferred reading 'reactionary' writers like Yeats and Eliot to long-serving socialists like Bernard Shaw: the book, he felt, would reassure anxious intelligentsia about life under socialism, except for a piece by Anthony Blunt on Art, 'which I don't think any painter can read without an apprehensive shudder, its conception of art under Communism not being very different from that obtaining under Fascism,' with the artist entirely subservient to the diktats of the Party. 'I hate Hitler and Mussolini,' he concluded,

> I am frightened of them, but that other chief with the long moustaches, who seems to me more and more like some great Roman Emperor – Tiberius perhaps – negotiating with his army, stamping out intrigues and guarding his empire from the Huns and Mongols, can we count on those who count on him?

'Being political is apt to become a full-time job,' he declared in *Enemies of Promise*, and he went on to quote two well-known lines from Auden's 'Spain', one of the great rallying cries of the idealistic left ('Today the expending of powers/ On the flat ephemeral pamphlet and the boring meeting'). 'Copies of his pamphlets are excessively rare,' Connolly sardonically observed; and earlier, in the *New Statesman*, he had pronounced the poem to be 'good medium Auden', while adding that 'the Marxian theory of history does not go very happily in verse, but the ending is very fine.'

SIXTEEN

Enemies of Promise

In *Enemies of Promise*, Connolly described how, cold-shouldered by the left-wing intelligentsia for what he had written about Spain, he fled abroad, not returning until the autumn of 1937; but it may well be that his motives for staying out of England had as much to do with the deterioration of his marriage, and anxiety to escape from the journalistic tread-mill, as with a not entirely convincing political martyrdom. The precarious state of the Connollys' marriage had various causes – among them Jean herself, Connolly's susceptibility to other women, frustration at his inability to get down to writing the books he felt he had inside him, and the chaotically self-indulgent life they led in the King's Road flat. Partly as a result of her operations, Jean had become very fat; she was fond – over-fond, in her husband's opinion – of parties and night-clubs and staying up all night, and was hopelessly disorganised at home; like her mother, she had become a very heavy drinker; and to Connolly's irritation she had become very friendly with, and chosen as her confidantes, a group of homosexuals who divided their time between London, Paris and the South of France, and included in their number such couples as Peter Watson and Denham Fouts, T.C. Worsley and his American boy friend Tony Bower, and Brian Howard and Toni Altmann. A.J. Ayer, who met the Connollys at about this time through Elizabeth Bowen – he had greatly admired Connolly's reports from Spain – remembered Jean as 'an untidy, large, easy-going, hospitable American, with a wit of her own', which indeed she was; but in her husband's opinion she wasted her time, and his, on 'drink, night life, tarts and Tonys'. 'Your role,' he told her, reprovingly, 'is to be a maternal friend – sexy too – to a hundred unhappy mice, pansies, glamour *fraus* and tired French businessmen'. If they were to remain together she must learn to think of him not simply as a fellow-hedonist, but 'as someone determined to become a great writer, sufficiently near to middle age to wish to gradually break himself of the habits of youth which end in tears if carried on from that period, with an absolute horror of footling, and footle-carriers, and weak enough to cling hard to any means of escape.'

My long dark lovely thinking one
Whose thinking days seem almost done
Whose talents rot on the night-club floor
Whom sloth and lust and pride devour
The little lie, the sawdust heart,
The easy joke, the postponed start,
And the one last drink before we start

he apostrophised her in an agonised 'Private Poem', the opening lines of which are 'Heart is a hole for hurting / Head is a pain for bearing', and its prophetic refrain 'All my America is ebbing away'. However irritated he might be by her inexhaustible 'footling', Connolly's love for Jean was never in doubt; and, like any old-fashioned, *Punch*-reading husband, he felt it incumbent upon him to set down her wifely duties on paper. A wife, he decreed, must live with and for her husband, not through him or against him. She must either have a career of her own, or help him in his, and she must try to follow him in his 'spiritual peregrinations'. Late hours and rival friends (i.e. friends who make similar demands on the wife as her husband) must go; a couple could only prosper if both worked or had a common cause – and entertaining was not a common cause.

Jean's footling may have been hard to take, but it coincided with sexual and emotional restlessness on her spouse's part. Looking back from the vantage point of 1939 on the seemingly inevitable collapse of their marriage – by which time the waters were muddier still – Connolly dated its decline to the first of the gastronomic tours he and Jean made with Sir Harry d'Avigdor-Goldsmid in 1936.* 'Miss Mossop' may not have had her way on that occasion, but Connolly was increasingly susceptible to the attractions of other women, whether innocent or intended. Among them was the quiet, elegant, willowy Joan Eyres-Monsell, often encountered at Tickerage or in the South of France, who was to become one of the people of whom Connolly became most fond, and of whom he spoke always with affection and respect. She was, he told Jean, a 'nice girl', who 'never bitched you'; but 'I was almost in love with her,' and when, in July 1939, she married John Rayner he declared that 'I couldn't be more miserable and I don't suppose I have ever been so unhappy before.' Rather more disruptive was an affair with Peggy Bainbridge, whom the Connollys met at Eden Roc, on the Riviera, in the summer of 1936: lying on the beach one day, they overheard a new arrival saying 'Well, this is better than Mar-gate isn-tit?', caught the

* On the second such tour, they were accompanied by Peter Quennell's second wife, Marcelle. A convivial, hard-drinking and very beautiful Belgian, she contributed in part to Connolly's portrait of 'Beulah' (see p. 296).

amused eye of a fellow-eavesdropper, and a friendship was struck up.* Peggy, who had recently left her husband, found the Connollys a 'refreshing change' from the Americans with whom she was staying; and when, in due course, she moved further round the coast with Nora Shawe-Taylor – whose cousin, Desmond, was the long-serving music critic of the *New Statesman* – Connolly wrote to her at the Cap d'Antibes.

The daughter of an Indian Army colonel, Peggy Bainbridge had a neat figure, curly fair hair, and violet eyes with long lashes. In a long, unpublished piece about a composite figure called Beulah, based partly on Peggy and partly on Peter Quennell's second wife, Marcelle, and named after Peggy's dachshund – Connolly wrote that she was then 'around thirty, tall in her smallness, with a very neat erect figure; one notices about her face a look of alertness, intelligence, good sense, and cupidity, all of which vanish into an occasional melting smile.' Beulah stood for 'the irresistible appeal of a certain kind of life, for all the possibilities and limitations which go with a certain set of privileges.' She was, Connolly suggested, a 'curfew girl' – the best of company before midnight, after which 'the glass fills and refills.' Peggy's first great love had been Ian Fleming, then at Sandhurst, but the romance had ended in tears. Peggy had then married an extremely rich young Guards officer called Emerson Bainbridge, whose family fortune derived from the Durham coal fields; an ardent Mosleyite, Bainbridge was an avid admirer of Hitler, decorating their house with plaster busts of the Führer and playing the *Horst Wessel Lied* non-stop on the gramophone. The final straw, as far as Peggy was concerned, was her husband's inviting his fellow-blackshirt William Joyce – later known as Lord Haw-Haw – to stay with them in Scotland, since when she had spent a good deal of time on the Continent.

Connolly found Peggy entertaining and attractive – so much so that he once told her how

> I walked up to Montparnasse thinking about you and over-excited myself so I went into a brothel and picked out the girl who looked most like you and rushed upstairs with her. No sooner was the door closed than I saw it

* Eden Roc and eavesdropping seem inextricably interlinked, as far as students of Connollyiana are concerned. As readers of *White Mischief* may remember, it was there, two years later, that Connolly overheard

> one of those never-to-be-forgotten voices, husky, yet metallic, almost strident, a voice of the period, a touch of Tallulah, or, if anyone remembers her, of Brenda Dean Paul. 'My God I hate men,' she was saying, 'I'd trust my dog more than any man. I'd tell my dog things I'd never tell a man.'

The speaker was June Carberry, later to be the principal witness at the trial of Sir Jock Delves Broughton for the murder of Lord Erroll in March 1941.

was no good and would not really make you nearer and so I paid her, put on my coat and rushed out again while she screamed '*Ce n'est pas correcte – soyez plus correcte, monsieur – je ne suis pas si laide . . .*'

It had been agreed that the Connollys and Mrs Warner would visit Budapest, and that the two women would travel there by train, and Connolly by car. He was keen to see more of Peggy, and to visit Kitzbühel, a fashionable skiing resort in the Austrian Tyrol, so he suggested that they should go there first; Peggy and Nora Shawe-Taylor set out in one car from Antibes, while Connolly and Jean's friend Tony Bower followed in another. Almost the first person they met in Kitzbühel was an embarrassed-looking Ian Fleming, taking time off from his duties as a stockbroker and 'having fun with the local Heidis and Lenis and Trudis'. The two men played bridge together, striking up a long-lasting if intermittent friendship – a year or two later Fleming tried to interest Connolly in starting another English equivalent to the *New Yorker*, following the closure of the short-lived *Night and Day* – but Connolly declined an invitation to picnic on top of a hay-waggon. Kitzbühel, to which he would often return, was to assume mythical status in his own mind as another symbol of lost love and happiness; he was to recall the 'smell of the sun-warmed pine needles', the ripe whortle-berries, lying in peat baths on rainy evenings, dancing at the Tiefenbrünner, the sun-warmed lake, buying lederhosen and dining with 'Peggy, Jennifer and the Paget twins',* and in *The Unquiet Grave* he elegised it with the same incantatory lamentation reserved for the Hôtel de la Louisiane or the Ile de Gavrinis ('Kitzbühler Horn, white roads, dark pines, and peat baths shared with darling Jean remind me of her. Tiefenbrünner's cold nights, lake with raft and lilies, O Kitzbühler Horn, help me and save me . . .').

From Kitzbühel Connolly, Tony Bower and Peggy set out along the length of Austria, making for the Hungarian border. They never reached their destination, however, for they were involved in a car crash, and Peggy's nose was broken; they stayed in the spa town of Badgastein while the car and Peggy's nose were seen to, and then headed back to London. Later that year Peggy accompanied Connolly on one of his trips to Spain for the *New Statesman*, and in the spring of 1937 they eventually visited

* Jennifer Fry, who later married Robert Heber-Percy and Alan Ross, was to become a life-long friend of Connolly's; Mamaine Paget was much admired by Edmund Wilson and later married Arthur Koestler, and her twin sister Celia worked briefly on *Horizon*. Recalling Kitzbühel from wartime London, the nostalgic Connolly seems to have conflated various visits: Peggy Strachey – as she later became – has no recollection of Jennifer Fry or the Paget twins being there on her one visit with Connolly, and when Celia Paget was there the following year Peter Watson and his lover Denham Fouts were in attendance.

Budapest together. But by then the romance was over; as well as being fond of Jean, Peggy had fallen in love with someone else, and the spark had gone out of the affair.

But Connolly's restless dissatisfaction was far from cured. Quite apart from the sad side-effects of Jean's operation – 'Horror upon horror. It made you fat, and it made the consciousness that you couldn't have children discontent the deep natural repose of our love. It was like cutting a ring of bark off a healthy tree' – his interest in other women, or so he told her later, was caused by the fact that (and here he dropped into the third person) he 'never had enough fucking. Except for tarts he had never been to bed with women when he met you. You were the first *equal* he went to bed with, who was like Bobbie, Noël, Freddie H. etc or even Patrick.' It was inevitable that he would have affairs 'to find out more about women, both as a man, and as a writer'.

Summoning up names that pre-dated the Barbarian Invasions was all very well, but – as Christopher Isherwood discovered when bicycling round Fontainebleau in the spring of 1937 with the Connollys, his German boy-friend, Heinz, and Tony Bower* – comparisons between homo- and hetero-sexual love could be invidious. 'I remember a coldness, only momentary however, between Cyril and Christopher,' he wrote in his third-person autobiography:

> Cyril had asked Christopher, in a tone which Christopher found patronising, how he felt about Heinz – the implication seeming to be that Cyril couldn't believe that an intelligent adult like Christopher could take such a relationship altogether seriously. To this Christopher replied casually but nastily: 'Oh, very much as you feel about Jean, I suppose.' Cyril obviously found this insulting, to Jean and to himself. But he couldn't very well say so.

Isherwood made a point of avoiding Etonians, 'as an article of his left-wing snobbery', but Connolly, like Brian Howard, was a rare exception. He admired the strength of his passions and the 'brilliant artifice of his wit':

* In his novel *Down There on a Visit*, Isherwood wrote of how the Tony Bower character's 'impudent, attractively comic face keeps breaking into grins, and his round blue eyes sparkle with a lit-up gaiety which is in its way courageous because he isn't as carefree as he tries to appear.' On this bicycling holiday, Isherwood recalled, the Connollys wrongly assumed Bower to be richer than he was because of his readiness to buy them expensive meals. Bower worked briefly on *Horizon* in 1940. He translated Camus's *The Rebel* – of which Connolly wrote 'I must confess that either I have softening of the brain or . . . this is one of the worst written and worst translated books to have come my way,' while adding that he wished he could like it 'one twentieth as much as I do its author and translator.' Tony Bower returned to America after the war, and was eventually murdered.

> His big face – flat blue eyes, tiny nose and double chin – looked as ageless as a Buddha's: but he was more of a pope than a Buddha, for he spoke with conscious authority – knew you historically in relation to the entire hierarchy of letters, past and present, and could assign you a place in it. You might lose that place later, of course. If you ever did, he would tell you so, blandly but brutally. He had a terrible phrase for such outcasts: 'Those whom the God has forsaken.'

Connolly may have seen himself, ruefully, as the embodiment of the 'Truly Weak Man' of *Lions and Shadows*, but Isherwood was understandably anxious to retain his admiration; in this he was not disappointed, and his affection was fully reciprocated.

Isherwood's other acceptable Etonian, Brian Howard, had, in the meantime fallen victim to Connolly the parodist at his funniest and most lethal, in 'Where Engels Fears to Tread', first published that year in Leonard Russell's collection of parodies, *Press Gang*. Ostensibly a review of *From Oscar to Stalin: A Progress* by Christian de Clavering, it charts, through the changing persona of de Clavering himself, the transition from the dandified, cosmopolitan aestheticism of the Twenties, redolent of Balkan Sobranies and Gertrude Stein and Diaghilev's Ballet Russe, to the world of the Left Book Club and the Popular Front, in which de Clavering (now transmogrified to Comrade Chris Clay) takes part in a left-wing march up St James's Street – spotting *en route* old school friends gazing out of the big bow window in White's – and spends his spare time reading poems like

> Come on Percy, my pillion-proud, be camber-conscious
> Cleave to the crown of the road

and

> M is for Marx
> and Movement of Masses
> and Massing of Arses
> and Clashing of Classes*

Best of all, though, are the school scenes – at Eton, of course – and in particular that in which de Clavering, inattentive at the back of the class, is caught out reading something unsuitable:

* Itself a parody, presumably, of Rex Warner's 'Hymn', the refrain of which reads

> Come then, companions. This is the spring of blood
> Heart's heyday, movement of masses, beginning of good.

'What is that book, de Clavering?'
'*Les Chansons de Bilitis*, sir.'
'And what is this lesson?'
'You have the advantage, sir.'
'What do you mean, boy?'
'Ah, sir, fair's fair. I told you what my book was. You must tell me what's your lesson.'
'Elementary geometry.'
'But it sounds fascinating! Then this delicious piece of celluloid nonsense is – I know, sir, don't tell me – a set-square?'
'I have been teaching it for twenty years, and never met with such impertinence.'
'Twenty years, and still at Elementary! Oh, sir, what a confession . . .'

'I don't think I have ever in my life read such a good parody as yours of Brian Howard,' John Betjeman wrote to its author: 'My God, it's almost too good.' Evelyn Waugh, on the other hand, was less admiring in the pages of *Night and Day*, to which both he and Connolly contributed.* He had, he said, greatly admired 'Told in Gath', but whereas Huxley was a well-known writer, Connolly had now chosen to 'devote his prodigious talent to a private joke . . . The object of his satire has for some years been a figure of fun in a tiny circle, but he is totally unknown to those whose adolescence does not happen to have coincided with his. A dozen readers in London, one in China, one in Gloucestershire, and possibly a handful in Spain, will revel in Mr Connolly's laying of this pathetic ghost.' Waugh himself was to portray poor Howard in *Put Out More Flags* and *Brideshead Revisited*; in his autobiography he referred in kindlier terms to Connolly's parody, as 'a brilliant pasquinade . . . which, incidentally, provides a leper's squint into Cyril's own life as an undergraduate.'†

* Edited by Graham Greene and John Marks, distributed by Chatto & Windus, and conceived as an English equivalent to the *New Yorker*, *Night and Day* ran from July to December 1937. Evelyn Waugh reviewed books, Graham Greene films, Elizabeth Bowen and Peter Fleming the theatre, Constant Lambert music, Osbert Lancaster art, Hugh Casson architecture and A.J.A. Symons wine and food. The Shirley Temple libel case was the ostensible cause of its demise, but in fact it had steadily been losing money, despite the excellence of its material and contributors.

† Seven years later, after Connolly had decided to include 'Where Engels Fears to Tread' in *The Condemned Playground*, his first collection of reviews and articles, he warned Brian Howard that Christian de Clavering was about to be resurrected. It was, he told him, 'sandwiched in between a lot of other parodies and I don't think it looks in the least personal. I still think it is essentially *kindly* and admiring and quite unlike Waugh's stuff.' Much of the piece was not about Howard, he added, 'and the whole thing is soaked in Firbankitis, which I had at the time.' 'It is not without faint trepidation that I look forward to it,' Howard replied: 'I admit, Cyril, to hoping that if Christian de Clavering is to appear, he will do so under a less resoundingly hintful name. I don't, I suppose, *really* mind, but now that Evelyn has almost stopped, after all these years, the approach of obscurity was so very delicious.' Shortly after *The Condemned Playground* was published, Maurice Richardson, who was carrying a copy, bumped into

Later that year Connolly found a larger and more alarming subject than Brian Howard on which to exercise his satirical gifts. He and Jean travelled through Nazi Germany; and if his initial reactions were couched in the comforting rhetoric of school – 'We are entering the larger of the two headmaster countries: the Head's picture is everywhere, and the question we must all ask is "Are we the sort of new boys the Head wants, the prefects want and the other boys want?"' he wrote, adding that he replied to the frontier guards' '*Heil Hitler*' with an evasive 'mumble-mumble' – a visit to the Nazis' infamous exhibition of supposedly 'Degenerate Art' in Munich, at which the work of modern painters was exhibited in a spirit of ridicule and loathing, provided the inspiration for a ferocious, even terrifying essay called 'Year Nine', published in the *New Statesman* the following January. It is set in Year IX of a new totalitarian regime headed by Our Leader, and the narrator and a woman friend spend part of Leaderday in the Arthouse, in which are to be found 'the ineffable misterpasses of our glorious culture, the pastermieces of titalitorian tra, the magnificent Leadersequence, the superstatues of Comradeship, Blatherhood and Botherly Love.' Unwisely, he goes down into the basement, which houses the 'stagnant rottenness called Degenerate Art, though only perfect Leadercourtesy could bestow the term Art on such Degeneration!' (The Leader himself is a painter, and holds strong views.) Here are to be found the works of Nacnud Tnarg and Ossapic and Ripep and Sutsugua Nhoj, who have the temerity to paint still lives and even 'illicit couples, depicted in *articulo amoris*, women who had never heard of the three Ks, whose so-called clothes were gaudy dish-rags, whose mouths were painted offal'. As a result of absent-mindedly annotating his catalogue, the narrator falls foul of the dread 'Stoop Traumas', and finds himself consigned to death and oblivion. It was a powerful broadside, and once again John Betjeman was almost ecstatic with admiration. 'I never realised what powers worthy of Swift you had,' he told Connolly: 'I always thought you the wittiest of writers we had, but I didn't know it was in you to make a picture of such ghastly horror as Year Nine. It has something of the Yahoo in it.'

Despite the imminence of the Anschluss, it must have been a relief to cross the frontier into Austria, where the Connollys attended the Salzburg Festival. Jennifer Fry had written to say that she would be there with, among others, Robert Byron: according to Isaiah Berlin, Connolly arrived looking ill-at-ease in lederhosen, while Elizabeth Bowen – who was there

Howard in Sloane Square: 'Brian was a bit downcast. "So he has put that in. Oh Lord!"' Swiftly rallying, Howard went on to review the book in the *New Statesman*, where he suggested that 'There is one review re-published here where Mr Connolly's considerable comic inventiveness is employed to perfection. "Where Engels Fears to Tread" deals with the imaginary autobiography of an Oxford aesthete of the 'twenties, and still makes me laugh almost aloud . . .'

with Berlin, Stuart Hampshire, Sean O'Faolain and Sally Graves – told William Plomer that

> Salzburg was great fun, and had some funny moments. The Connollys turned up, looking well in mountaineer get-ups. Our party didn't go into these, as we were all either too fat or too thin. The weather was heavenly and we drove about in fiacres. There was a good deal of conversation and eating, which I really did enjoy.

Writing as 'Our Continental Correspondent' in *Night and Day*, she reverted to the vexed topic of lederhosen:

> Articles of native dress are chiefly sold to the visitors. A good deal of excitement goes on before hotel mirrors during the final phases of dressing up. Few visitors, thus got up, look conspicuously ridiculous, though men conscious of pink hairless legs communicate their distress.

Christmas 1937 was spent at Tickerage in a cottage the Connollys rented from Dick Wyndham. Their guests and visitors included Stephen Spender and his wife, Inez Pearn; Peter Quennell and his dashing new girl friend, Glur, whom he would marry the following summer; Christopher Isherwood and Brian Howard, who spent the time dressing up as their mothers; Maurice Bowra and Audrey Beecham, to whom he was briefly engaged, much to the mirth (as he himself admitted) of the 'homintern';* and a slim, fair-haired, rather pink-and-white twenty-two-year-old called Diana, who had recently abandoned her studies at the Royal College of Music, and whom Connolly had met the previous month at a party given by John Heygate. Diana's boy friend had gone out to India to join the ICS, and before long Connolly had fallen heavily – and disruptively – in love.

*

* Audrey Beecham had been the heiress to a pharmaceutical fortune until her father lost all his money. A robust, boyish-looking Oxford graduate, she had lived for a while in Paris where she befriended Henry Miller, Lawrence Durrell and Anaïs Nin; she ran guns for the Anarchists during the Spanish Civil War, and only her hair-net betrayed her disguise as a man. When asked about his choice of *fiancée*, the Dean is said to have replied, ungallantly, 'Buggers can't be choosers.' He brought her to stay with the Connollys in the South of France the following summer; writing to thank his host, Bowra said he had much enjoyed the way Connolly had 'ragged Audrey for her more pompous and prefectorial opinions'. John Sutro – who thought Connolly '*au fond* a *mauvais sujet*' – reported that after Bowra had retired to bed 'Cyril systematically destroyed him with the girl': Sutro wasn't there, and may well have been passing on stale gossip, but Bowra told Connolly that, on her return to England, Audrey had decided that she was not, after all, cut out to be a don's wife. She appears to have remained on the Oxford scene, however: according to Dan Davin's biographer, she would sometimes arm-wrestle with the Oxford publisher in the Lamb and Flag in St Giles's. A published poet, she contributed several poems to *Horizon*. In the 1950s, she was appointed Warden of Nightingale Hall at Nottingham University.

Back in the summer, Mr Ragg – a patient and level-headed editor from Routledge & Kegan Paul, an eminent firm of London publishers – wrote to Connolly for news of various projects they had discussed together, including a collection of parodies, essays and travel pieces of the kind that would eventually materialise (for the same firm, but several years later) as *The Condemned Playground*. Replying from the South of France, Connolly thanked Mr Ragg for being 'very patient and long-suffering indeed'; he had been unable to get on with the collection of pieces, or a novel, or a book provisionally entitled *The Little Voice*, to be written jointly with Christopher Sykes (this was proving particularly elusive, since neither author ever seemed to be in England at the same time); but he would like to suggest abandoning the novel for 'a quite different kind of book which is half criticism and part biography, together with an appendix consisting of only about half a dozen articles of mine that I have had to reprint to show the development of my point of view'. The book was to be sub-titled 'How to live another ten years', and was provisionally entitled *Patent from Oblivion*, from Sir Thomas Browne's lines 'In vain do individuals hope for immortality, or any patent from oblivion, in preservations below the moon'; and it would concern itself with the problems involved in writing a book that would last ten years, and the obstacles that lay in its path. 'The trouble is that I am a perfectionist, and whenever I look at something I have already written or published I want to tear it up,' he told Ragg; to make matters worse, he was also very lazy, in that he was for ever postponing what he really wanted to write. He planned to come back to London, eschew journalism, and get on with his new project. Although he started writing what was to become *Enemies of Promise* in the South of France, Parts 1 and 2 were mostly written in Chelsea and in Paris, and the autobiographical third section in Chelsea and Cornwall.

Back in London in the autumn of 1937, Connolly declined Ragg's invitation to lunch, on the grounds that he didn't deserve it: 'I've had a very bad month and written hardly anything, chiefly because I've been out to lunch so much. As I read in the mornings and work in the afternoons these afternoons are more or less ruined if people come here or I go out and return full of cigars and brandy.' In November Mr Ragg offered him lunch once again, with Connolly paying for the claret if he failed to produce at least 10,000 words. Wisely, perhaps, Connolly declined and Ragg said how sorry he was, but 'if I can genuinely feel – and why shouldn't I? – that you will be hard at work writing, with possibly an interval for bread and cheese, then I suppose I must not grumble.' Some four months later he sent him a contract for the book, and three months after that Connolly posted the completed typescript from Cap d'Antibes, where Mrs Warner had taken a villa for the summer. Logan Pearsall Smith, he told his publisher, thought the autobiographical section, 'A Georgian Boyhood', a masterpiece; for his part, he was bored by the opening section, in which he defined and discussed the different schools of English prose, and had cut it back by half. In July he reported that he had been seeing a good deal of Somerset Maugham in the South of France, and wondered whether he should ask him for a quote; in August he was in touch from Bayonne, hoping that Ragg would forgive his 'dig at publishers' and promising return of the proofs; three weeks later the galleys were finally returned from Paris, with apologies for the mass of corrections, and a long list of people to whom copies might usefully be sent, among them Cecil Beaton, Desmond MacCarthy, Pearsall Smith, Osbert Sitwell, Kenneth Clark, J.M. Keynes, Maurice Baring, Raymond Mortimer, T.S. Eliot, Gladwyn Jebb, Elizabeth Bowen, Stephen Spender, John Hayward, James Agate, Lord Berners and E.M. Forster.

Finally published at the very end of 1938, *Enemies of Promise* is a curious, wonderfully original hybrid of a book, combining stylistic criticism, advice to aspiring authors and explanatory autobiography; it brings together many of his own private obsessions – in particular, the lost Edens of childhood and Eton – with views about writing and the literary life, and the perils that lie in wait for the writer, which he had been exploring in essays and reviews over the past few years, and which constitute both an apologia for what he saw as his own shortcomings and a shrewd insight into the mechanics of his trade. By turns funny, astute and elegiac, it is the work of a worldly aesthete for whom, in the last resort, the way things are written, the authorial tone of voice and use of language, are of more interest than what is being said. 'So much depends on style, this factor of which we are growing more and more suspicious,' he wrote: but

> although the tendency of criticism is to explain a writer either in terms of his sexual experience or his economic background, I still believe his technique remains the soundest base for a diagnosis, that it should be possible to learn as much about an author's income and sex-life from one paragraph of his writing as from his cheque-stubs and his love letters ... Critics who ignore style are liable to lump good and bad writers together in support of preconceived theories.*

* Connolly's defiant aestheticism may have run counter to the prevailing trend of left-wing, Marxist criticism, but detailed linguistic analysis was very much in the air. As it is, I.A. Richards receives two passing mentions, while William Empson's *Seven Types of Ambiguity*, published eight years earlier, is ignored altogether – a reflection, perhaps, of Connolly's lifelong suspicion of, and disdain for, academic literary critics.

Apart from his evocation of Eton and the much-quoted aphorism about there being 'no more sombre enemy of good art than the pram in the hall', perhaps the most famous feature of the book is his distinction in the opening section between Mandarin and Vernacular Prose. Mandarin prose – which had reached its apogee in writers like Pater and Henry James, and had recently enjoyed a revival at the hands of Huxley, Strachey and Virginia Woolf – was elaborate, allusive, rich in imagery and prone to subordinate clauses; at its best it was a marvellously civilised and subtle tool, at its worst – in the hands of the heirs of Addison and Lamb, professional essayists and *Times* fourth leader-writers – it was whimsical, archaic, long-winded and apt to confuse verbiage with profundity. Vernacular prose, which was now in the ascendant, was simpler, more direct and closer to the spoken word in terms of both structure and vocabulary, and was particularly associated with Hemingway in America, with older writers like Wells and Maugham, and with younger contemporaries like Orwell and Isherwood; at its best it was lucid, honest, intelligible and elegant, but its practitioners – fearful of affectation or the over-florid phrase – could all too easily sound flat, dull and disconcertingly alike. The ideal was to combine elements of both – like *Enemies of Promise* itself, perhaps. Making good use of his addiction to lists, Connolly separated modern writers between the two camps, with 'Dandies' hovering in between, and quoted from and juxtaposed their work in order to make his points: 'The pages of criticism to which I am most indebted,' he wrote in an early draft of his book, were Wyndham Lewis's 'The Taxi-Driver's Test for "Fiction" '; 'This form of criticism was in the air and not originated by Lewis, but his revival of it made a deep impression on me, for I saw it was the most congenial to my critical temperament.'

In order to write a work that would stand the test of time – ten years hardly seems ambitious, but novel-reviewing had made Connolly more cynical than he might otherwise have been, and he was always more aware than most that all but the greatest works would, in due course, be forgotten – the writer not only had to find an appropriate tone of voice, but negotiate the enemies of promise that lay waiting to ensnare even the most brilliant and idealistic. In Part Two, 'The Charlock's Shade', Connolly provides the aspirant writer with a primer-cum-cautionary tale which remains relevant and valuable over half a century later. In 'The Blighted Rye' he addressed the central problem of how to make a living as a writer, of which jobs were or were not compatible with writing (Peter Quennell's current profession, advertising, was especially inimical, since copywriting 'so resembles the composition of lyric poetry as to replace the process'), and the dangers posed by over-production and the publisher's insistence on the endless and damaging repetition of a trick once successfully performed. 'The Blue

Bugloss' – in which a young writer, Walter Savage Shelleyblake, is ensnared, corrupted and eventually discarded by Mr Vampire, the literary editor of *The Blue Bugloss* – warned of the temptations of journalism in general, and book-reviewing in particular: journalism had a quite different 'texture' from literature, in that it 'must obtain its full impact on the first reading'; it was

> loose, intimate, simple and striking; literature formal and compact, not simple and not immediately striking in its effects. Carelessness is not fatal to journalism nor are clichés, for the eye rests lightly on them. But what is intended to be read once can seldom be read more than once: a journalist has to accept the fact that his work, by its very todayness, is excluded from any share in tomorrow. Nothing dates like a sense of actuality than which there is nothing in journalism more valuable. A writer who takes up journalism abandons the slow tempo of literature for a faster one and the change will do him harm.

Connolly's insistence on the great gulf that was set between literature and journalism, and his dependence on literary journalism as a means of making ends meet, were to haunt and obsess him for the rest of his life; but the 'Thistles' of politics – the next on his list of temptations and distractions – were never that much of a problem as far as he was concerned, though he was well aware, from watching his contemporaries, of how they could easily develop into a full-time job, and how the apparent rightness of a cause could persuade a writer to confuse art with propaganda, uplifting slogans with the subtler insights of literature. Rather more applicable to his own case were the 'Poppies' of escapism, not in the crude sense of failing or refusing to face up to and write about the issues of the day, but in the more insidious sense of escaping from one's own talent, through drink or drugs or daydreaming or talk or adopting the life and mannerisms of a country squire, or simply proving unable to live up to early promise, that 'fatal word, half-bribe and half-threat'. Sloth – like daydreaming – was the form of escapism to which Connolly felt himself to be particularly prone: but 'Sloth in writers,' he suggested,

> is always a symptom of an acute inner conflict, especially that laziness which renders them incapable of doing the thing which they are most looking forward to. The conflict may or may not end in disaster, but their silence is better than the over-production which must so end and slothful writers such as Johnson, Coleridge, Greville, in spite of the nodding poppies of conversation, morphia and horse-racing, have more to their

credit than Macaulay, Trollope or Scott. To accuse writers of being idle is a mark of envy or stupidity ... Perfectionists are notoriously lazy and all true artistic indolence is deeply neurotic; a pain not a pleasure.

'The Charlock's Shade' stood for the distractions of sex and the 'clasping tares of domesticity', including the pram in the hall: quite apart from the demands which a family makes on authorial productivity, and the uncongenial work that has to be taken on in order to pay the weekly bills, domestic happiness was a problem in itself, for 'the fertility of the writer is often counterchecked by the happiness of the man'.

Last of all in Connolly's catalogue of snares were the 'Slimy Mallows' of success, whether social, professional or popular; and he ended this middle section by examining the different genres open to the writer – not surprisingly, perhaps, he sensed 'a return of emphasis to the autobiography over the novel in that it demands no fictional gifts from the writer' – and the ideal conditions under which one could practise one's trade. Rude health was undesirable, for

in 'this England where nobody is well', the healthy writer is communicating with a hostile audience. Most readers live in London; they are run-down, querulous, constipated, spot-ridden, stained with asphalt and nicotine and, as a result of sitting all day on a chair in a box, and eating too fast, slightly mad sufferers from indigestion.

Sex can all too easily be a substitute for creation, and 'a writer works best in an interval from an unhappy love affair'; as for the monetary aspects of his calling, 'Solvency is an essential. A writer suffering from financial difficulties is good only for short-term work.' 'Within his talent,' he concluded,

it is the duty of a writer to devote his energy to the search for truth, the truth that is always being clouded over by romantic words and ideas or obscured by actions and motives dictated by interest and fear ... A writer must be a lie-detector who exposes the fallacies in words and ideals before half the world is killed for them. It may even be necessary for the poet to erect a bomb-proof ivory tower from which he can continue to celebrate the beauty which the rest of mankind will be too guilty, hungry, angry or arid to remember ...

Thus far, *Enemies of Promise* had been a critical work-cum-primer to the literary life; in the final, autobiographical third of the book, Connolly set out his credentials by providing 'an analysis of the grounding in life and art which the critic received, of the ideas which formed him in youth; the education, the ideals, the disappointments from which are drawn his experience, the fashions he may unwittingly follow and the flaws he may conceal.' Connolly's only extended exercise in explicit autobiography, 'A Georgian Boyhood' is a small masterpiece, in which its author's wit, elegance, elegiac melancholy and honesty about his own motives and failings were displayed at their most eleoquent.

Enemies of Promise remains a brilliant oddity: uncategorisable, broken-backed, a summation of the ideas and arguments he had been setting out in essays and reviews over the previous ten years, a masterpiece that has long out-lived its ten-year span, and – in its very bittiness – triumphant proof that, in literary terms, Connolly was a sprinter rather than a marathon-runner, and none the worse for that. Like all deserving miniatures, it is beautifully framed: so beautifully that the opening and closing pages are perhaps the most haunting and evocative of all. 'This is the time of year when wars break out and when a broken glass betrays the woodland to the vindictive sun,' the book begins; after which he goes on to describe how and where he is writing – 'It is after lunch (omelette, Vichy, peaches) on a sultry day. Here is the plane tree with the table underneath it; a gramophone is playing in the next room' – until that moment when 'darkness falls, frogs croak, the martins bank and whistle over the terrace and the slanting hours during which I can be entrusted with a pen grow threatening with night.' Written in the year of Munich, the book's concluding words bring us back, appropriately, to Connolly himself,

> whom ill-famed Coventry bore, a mother of bicycles whom England enlightened and Ireland deluded, round-faced, irritable, sun-loving, a man as old as his Redeemer, meditating at this time of year when wars break out, when Europe trembles and dictators thunder, inglorious under the plane.

'This curious effusion was begun, it appears, after luncheon on a hot day in the South of France,' *The Times Literary Supplement* remarked, before going on to refer to its creator as 'an able, acute and often entertaining critic'. Writing in the *New Statesman*, David Garnett advised readers to start at the back, with 'A Georgian Boyhood', not only because it was 'essential to an appreciation of what is printed first', but because

> It differs from almost all accounts of schooldays that I can remember in combining exact memory with intellectual detachment and lack of sentimentality. Connolly has forgotten nothing and he tells all, but without a

> trace of heat, of self-love or self-pity. Perhaps in another ten or fifteen years' time he will be able to see the years which followed in the same wintry focus. The end of *Enemies of Promise* may prove to be the beginning of a truly great biography.*

Connolly, Garnett went on, 'has perfect self-knowledge and is honest. He may be taken in by all sorts of charlatans but never by himself.'

Evelyn Waugh, on the other hand, was more interested in Connolly the literary diagnostician than Connolly the autobiographer. Criticism, he suggested, was an art in itself, albeit of a rare kind, and 'The only man under forty who shows any signs of reaching, or indeed, of seeking, this altitude is Mr Cyril Connolly.' But his book, 'full as it is of phrase after phrase of lapidary form, of delicious exercises in parody, of good narrative, of luminous metaphors, and once at any rate – in the passages describing the nightmare of the man of promise – of haunting originality', was 'structurally jerry-built'. He wasn't persuaded that the three sections hung together, and felt that the author came 'very near to dishonesty in the way he fakes the transition between these elements and attempts to pass them off as the expansion of a single theme.' Nor was Connolly prepared to make 'the extra effort which would have helped him to attain his avowed object of writing a durable book'; despite authorial strictures, clichés and lapses into illiteracy abounded.

More serious, in Waugh's eyes, was Connolly's tendency to see 'recent literary history, not in terms of various people employing and exploring their talents in their own ways, but as a series of "movements", sappings, bombings and encirclements, of party racketeering and jerry-mandering', and his own career, 'which some of us might envy and all of us honour', as 'a struggle against intrigue and oppression'. Connolly's interest in literary politicking and his sense of persecution might well reflect 'the Irish in him perhaps' – taunting Connolly on account of his alleged Irishness was to become a recurrent motif as far as Waugh was concerned – but, more importantly, it reflected the fact that

> in all he admires and all that strikes him as significant, whether for praise or blame, there is a single common quality – the lack of masculinity. Petronius, Gide, Firbank, Wilde... the names succeed one another of

* 'This reversion to public school memories is a conspicuous and curious feature of the recent writing of the English,' Edmund Wilson suggested some years later in *Europe without Baedeker*: 'confronted by the coming catastrophe', they had tended to 'creep back into the womb of the public schools – see the memories of Isherwood and Connolly and the earlier poems of Auden – of which they gave a rather equivocal account, inspired partly by a childish nostalgia and partly by an impulse... to blame the schools for their own inadequacies and for everything that was wrong with England.'

> living and dead writers, all, or almost all, simpering and sidling across the stage with the gait of the great new British music hall joke.

According to Waugh, these 'epicene' writers liked to see themselves as 'outcasts'; they were by definition left-wing, rendered 'hysterical' by the fear of fascism, itself 'the most insidious of all the enemies of promise'. Connolly himself was torn between a desire to live well and be appreciated by English society, and a revolutionary, modish desire to destroy that same society: it was to be hoped that 'one day he will escape from the café chatter, meet some of the people, whom he now fears as traitors, who are engaged in the practical work of government and think out for himself what Fascism means.' It was unlikely that England would become either Fascist or Communist, but 'if anything is calculated to provoke the development which none desire, and Mr Connolly dreads almost neurotically, it is the behaviour of his young friends in the Communist Party.'

Waugh's disdain for fashionable literati was shared by Q.D. Leavis: belatedly reviewing *Enemies of Promise* in *Scrutiny*, she saw its author as symptomatic of lightweight, self-serving metropolitan literary life. 'Mr Conolly's [*sic*] list of who's who in modern literature, his choice of the hopes for English literature and those whom he thinks are reviving imaginative writing, has to be read to be believed,' she pronounced apropos Orwell, Isherwood and Auden;* as for the autobiographical section,

> The information he unconsciously gives about the relation between knowing the right people and getting accepted in advance of production as a literary value is even more useful than the analysis he consciously makes of the stultifying effects of an exclusively classical education conducted in an exclusively upper-class and male establishment.

Connolly was, she conceded, 'an exceptionally able and bright-minded member of our higher journalism'; but that in itself was faint praise, for he inhabited a world in which 'elegant unemployables' and 'inane pretentious young men who had known one another at public school' – where, as often as not, they were remembered for 'feline charm or a sensual mouth and long eye-lashes' – advanced each other's causes for no good reasons

* The Leavises, it will be remembered, had put their money on Ronald Bottrall, a figure now remembered solely on that account. Ten years after *Enemies of Promise* was published, F.R. Leavis spoke slightingly of Auden in 'The Progress of Poetry'; he went on to attack the 'currency-values of Metropolitan Literary Society and the associated University milieux' as embodied in Connolly's *Horizon*, and to ridicule John Hayward's *Prose Literature since 1939*, published for the British Council, for praising Connolly and *The Unquiet Grave* while taking a dig at the 'minority group' of intellectuals led by the Leavises.

whatsoever. It was all very well for Connolly to praise Spender's study of Henry James in *The Destructive Element*, but 'I suppose it is because instead of knowing Mr Spender personally I have been reading Henry James's novels for fifteen years that the only way in which his study affected me was as a botched-up piece of journalism by somebody who not only had no capacity for examining James's novels critically but who had not even read them with ordinary care or intelligence.'*

Another of the Leavises' *bêtes noires*, W.H. Auden, wrote to Connolly from Birmingham to

> congratulate you on a brilliant and also solid and moving book. I have been rather annoyed by the reviews which have praised the autobiography and carefully ignored the criticism. As both Eliot and Edmund Wilson are Americans, I think *Enemies of Promise* is the best English book of criticism since the war, and more than Eliot or Wilson you really write about writing in the only way which is interesting to anyone except academics, as a real occupation like banking or fucking, with all its attendant boredom, excitement and terror...

Somerset Maugham also wrote to thank Connolly for having a copy sent to him; he had noticed that he appeared in the book, and 'since I know that you are one of the carping and acrimonious ones I have a notion that it is more prudent to thank you before I have read it.' In fact Connolly was – and would remain, somewhat defiantly – an admirer of Maugham, whom he considered a fine practitioner of Vernacular prose: 'We are still on speaking terms,' Maugham told him a week later, though he was daunted by Connolly's ambition of combining the virtues of the Mandarin and the Vernacular ('If I understand you your aim is to combine the grandeur of Sir Thomas Browne with the snappishness of Hemingway, and if that is so I beg respectfully to suggest that you have got your work cut out').

In December Connolly sent Mr Ragg a mass of corrections to be incorporated in a reprint; and he added that although a Mr Cohen of the Cresset Press had written to ask if he could commission a full-length autobiography, he would far sooner write another book for Routledge. He had another novel in mind; and Mr Ragg soon found himself heading a long list of publishers who, over the next thirty years, commissioned and paid advances for books

* George Orwell, that model of rectitude, provided irrefutable evidence of metropolitan corruption when he told Connolly that he had asked Secker to send him a copy of *Homage to Catalonia*, and wondered whether he could see a copy of *Enemies of Promise* in due course: he might well be able to review it for the *New English Weekly*, and perhaps *Time and Tide* as well; it was, he went on, a case of 'You scratch my back, I'll scratch yours.' In the event, neither reviewed the other's book.

that never emerged from the chrysalis of daydreams, and scribbled lists of contents and chapter headings. Like so many of his successors, he began by being firm and sensible, pointing out that Connolly had already received a £75 advance on another novel, as well as £25 on *The Little Voice*: 'I feel we ought not to make things too easy for you and therefore encourage your well-known slothfulness: on the other hand, we want to make things sufficiently easy for you to encourage you to work,' he wrote, after which he went on to suggest a further advance of £200, to be set against all earnings from the novel and future earnings from *Enemies of Promise*. 'Now I understand why you suddenly fired at me the question "Of course you are terribly lazy, aren't you?" which I answered "Yes" to merely out of politeness, not realising that I had fallen into a trap,' Connolly replied: he had, he pointed out, worked very hard indeed on *Enemies of Promise*, revising it twice in typescript and twice in proof as well*, for 'Once I get going, I am not lazy at all.' As for payment of the advance, he would like to suggest £60 on signature of the contract and £30 a month between January and April 1939, with an output of 15,000 a month to be vouchsafed by an independent observer, and delivery at the end of May: 'I do not think thirty pounds a month will lead me into a life of such extravagance that my well-known predilection for yachting, real estate and stud-farming will be pandered to . . .'

In the meantime, Little, Brown had bought the American rights; Connolly told Mr Ragg that he had decided against Americanising the language and the examples of literary pitfalls, or providing too much background information about the more arcane aspects of English life: 'Where Eton words are unfamiliar, imagine them to mean anything that suggests the picturesque or barbaric, like native terms in a work of anthropology.' Some months later Mr Ragg informed him that the American edition had sold a mere 325 copies, but both Warner Brothers and Twentieth Century Fox had expressed interest in the film rights. 'I hope they make a wonderful film of *Enemies of Promise* with Shirley Temple as Promise and Ginger Rogers and Fred Astaire as Eton boys,' Connolly replied.

Had Mr Ragg got hold of an unpublished self-portrait, entitled 'Flight into Egypt' and written in the late Thirties, he might have felt even more worried about the sums he was shelling out. Addressing himself to the problems facing the modern hedonist, Connolly suggested that

> Having passed a great deal of time waiting for nothing very much in a shiftless kind of way, a victim of deep appetites, sudden enthusiasms and

* These revisions included substantial cuts – 23,000 words from Part One, 10,000 from Part Two, and 4,000 from the autobiography. 'Milton, Pope and a lot of other chappies' vanished altogether, along with 'all the political cracks, leftwingisms etc.,' he told Diana: 'I only wish I could get thin as easily.'

> crazes with their aftermath of brooding satiety, I feel qualified to speak of both positive and negative pleasures, and able to hand on a certain experience of them. Granted a little money, I have found the life of pleasure to be almost enough. That is my tragedy. Enough to give me very little time for anything else, but not enough to satisfy. Is it because one is bad at it? Not necessarily. It is because the times are not propitious to it; a life of pleasure to succeed requires certain sanctions that today do not exist, certain excesses that are not permitted. It is a life that must go always with the current and today must go sideways against it.

Unusually, perhaps, he had come to believe that the life of pleasure especially suited the English, 'For hedonism is a religion of sensation, and the English are a people with quite extraordinary depths of acute and violent feeling.' The key to all pleasure lay not in the mind but in the body, and unless it was 'sturdy, and responsive to all stimuli, and genuinely interested in the results, the whole idea of hedonism had better be abandoned.' Connolly himself had made a 'reasonable pact' with his body. His teeth were poor, but not getting any worse; although he would tolerate 'no nonsense about constipation – there I must insist on complete regularity', his intestines took their revenge through indigestion: 'Rage, anxiety, irritation, guilt, all these nervous insurrections, these breaches of our mutual trust, you may punish in the only way you know, by flatulence, barking your disapproval, or by a searing pain in the oesophagus.' Connolly's obliging body provided him 'with just that minimum of ill health without which, through the winter, it is impossible to work'; when his love affairs went well, it was expected, in a spirit of co-operation, to shed a pound or two, but 'when they go badly you must sympathise and not, as you did in Budapest, satirically raise a small hairy wen on the side of my nose.' As a result of this pact with his body,

> I have not spent a day in bed for the last three years. I wear no underclothes and very seldom a waistcoat, nor any pyjamas, yet seldom catch cold. I often stay indoors for several days or stay up all night in a nightclub and get nothing worse than a mild headache. I keep no medicines or drugs, though I sometimes enjoy a sodamint... I can motor from Turin to Kitzbühel in a day. Only the indigestion is always lurking, ready to appear with the slightest boredom or disappointment or even if I sit in a draught. I am passive and fatalistic when ill, and do not fear illness. The only thing I fear is cancer, for it usually attacks sanguine people...

As for the causes of his indigestion,

I have always been very greedy, and since I was delicate and often ill in childhood, my greatest greed is aroused by invalid foods – the egg, the grape, the pat of butter, the cutlet, the tangerine, and in those rare moments (dropping off to sleep, or waking up from a siesta) when childhood returns to me, its essence is held in some winter afternoon in Bath or London, the gas lit, the fire burning, myself playing by the fire with mines of matchboxes fired by trains of torn paper in the grate, and then the arrival of tea, my grandmother cutting the buttered toast into fingers, ready to dip into my three-and-a-half-minute eggs. Which tastes best, the first or the second? How much would we know about ourselves if we knew that.

Like most greedy people I went through a long period of over-eating, followed by a sophisticated period of foie-gras and other luxuries; now my natural appetite has been tempered by indigestion into the fine weapon of the gourmet. For I dislike equally all rich foods and all plain food badly cooked. As I have been frequently criticised for my fondness for food, especially by my left-wing friends, I take this opportunity of justification . . .

*

During the spring and early summer of 1938 Connolly began to see a good deal more of Diana, the girl who had been at Tickerage the previous Christmas and with whom he now declared himself to be in love. She shared a flat with another girl in Sloane Street, and had begun to take painting lessons at the Chelsea Polytechnic; although, as it turned out, they never lived together, Connolly told her that he was writing *Enemies of Promise* for her – Jean, he said, took little interest in his writing, and never encouraged him – and that the two of them should share a studio where he could write and she could paint. Diana, for her part, had a busy social life and a good many friends of her own age of whom, as she soon discovered, Connolly was intensely jealous.*

He was, as she soon discovered, possessive and demanding; she loved him, and delighted in his company, but they quarrelled dreadfully, and she

* Among these friends was the painter Robin Ironside. A close friend of Graham and Joan Eyres-Monsell and Maurice Bowra, he was then working as an Assistant Keeper at the Tate Gallery, which he left in 1945 in order to follow a precarious career as a painter, writer and stage designer. Despite his early jealousy, Connolly became extremely fond of Robin Ironside, who died in 1965 at the age of fifty-three. A gaunt, impecunious figure who dosed himself on Dr Collis Browne and wore, in lieu of conventional evening dress, tight black jeans, black espadrilles and the top of a suit dyed black, Ironside wrote about art for *Horizon*. He also wrote on Wilson Steer for a series on contemporary British painters edited during the war by Sir John Rothenstein; Rothenstein also asked Connolly to contribute, but nothing came of it.

came to resent his love of intrigue and conspiracy, and what she saw as a tendency to humiliate or drag down his women friends, alternating adoration with unnerving criticism of looks or clothes. 'You are quite right about me. I do spoil nice things; but I don't enjoy doing it, it makes me miserable. It is something to do with my mother, I am afraid,' Connolly once told her:

> You remind me of her because you are fastidious and delicate and vulnerable, and the same ancient injustice makes me cruel and scolding, and because I really know that I am to blame I try to heave it on to you. People like me have no right to the world of love, for they will not leave their arms in the cloak-room... And it tortures me to quarrel with you when I love you so much, and it is I who start the quarrels, and I want you to know I know it, and my vanity makes me behave worse than usual when I am jealous because I really do dislike competition, and not just say I do, and so I try to make myself *beneath* competition.

Because she was so much younger, he liked to educate her, to teach her things; she believed him when he told her that he loved her more than anyone else, and, being young, it took her time to realise that he was quite capable of being genuinely in love with two or even three women at once, making heartfelt protestations of love to their faces while grumbling and gossiping as soon as their backs were turned.

In the summer of 1938, Mrs Warner took a villa in Antibes, where the Connollys joined her: by now her drinking was so bad that she needed a full-time nurse to look after her. Among those who visited them there were Peter Quennell and Glur, recently married, Maurice Bowra, and Peggy Bainbridge and her new admirer. Diana, on the other hand, was still in London, where she was besieged with importunate telephone calls from Connolly, begging her to come out and join them and threatening to come back to London and abandon his guests if she failed to do so. Eventually, very reluctantly, she agreed to go.

Later that summer, after the guests had dispersed, Jean and her mother went on a slimming course at Brides-les-Bains in the French Alps. Jean had her glands examined, and was subjected to some 'ovarian injections'; both ladies lived off a diet of vegetables washed down with '*limonade purgative*', and spent their spare time walking and swimming. Connolly, in the meantime, was suffering from piles, and had taken his mother to Italy.

Back in London that autumn, Connolly found himself increasingly involved with 'Miss Busybee', as Peter Quennell called Diana. Connolly himself referred to her by the Greek letter 'delta' in his diaries – from which it soon became clear that he found himself caught between the rival demands of wife and girl friend. 'Δ situation very acute,' he confessed in mid-November: 'Δ reproaches me for not deciding anything definite,' while a friend warned him that Diana was not prepared to play second fiddle to Jean ('signed Δ the first fiddle if I may say so,' runs Miss Busybee's marginal comment). Travelling up from Tickerage a few days later, Raymond Mortimer told Connolly that few of his friends would condemn him if he decided to ditch Jean in favour of someone else – the Quennells were particularly sympathetic. A massive row with Jean over money 'marks the end of my jittery period about leaving her, and from now on I feel it inevitable, necessary and the beginning of a new life'; the following day Jean walked out in the middle of dinner, after which Connolly tried to cheer himself up by visiting the Blakistons in Markham Square, where 'Noël was very sweet.' A few days later, at lunch with Peter Quennell, the Connollys started rowing over Diana and money ('£30 of dressmakers' cheques'), and Jean walked out in a rage once again. The last day of November was blighted by 'rows and storms': Connolly had lunch with Diana in a pub on the Embankment, and came home to find Jean 'very gloomy and enraged – nobody loves her'. Dinner with Diana at the Café Royal was barely any better – the wine was rotten, Diana 'doubts if I can accept responsibility of fatherhood or indeed of earning my living' – and the battered lover trailed back to Chelsea and 'a long scene with Jean who yowls, scolds and beats the breast'. December began with Goronwy Rees and Rosamond Lehmann coming to dinner (both were drunk, and Jean in a 'pet'); the following morning was marred by the 'usual quarrels' – aggravated by Diana ringing in the middle – and when, that evening, the Blakistons and Alan Pryce-Jones came to dinner, their hostess 'yowled and wept'. The fact that Jeannie was spending so much of her time with her homosexual friends was a cause of further irritation, partly offset perhaps by 'homo dreams about giving myself to Raymond'.

Wretchedly aware of his own ambivalence, and very much in love with both women, Connolly havered like a barometric needle; although part of him longed to make a fresh start and a new life, the stronger part yearned, as it always would, for what had been lost, or was slipping away. It was, he confided to his notebook, hard to stop loving someone with whom one had lived for a good many years. The only way he could forget Jean when he was with Diana was by talking about neutral subjects – plane trees, for instance – and by concentrating his energies on his work, on social life of a suitably unfootling kind, and on remaining reasonably healthy, 'for good health establishes a kind of emotional autarky': for 'when I cease to love Jean I can be friends (or not be friends) with her – as with Peggy. While I love her, she can only rouse misery, anger or lust in me, and never happiness. To love her is madness, for it has made me wretched with her and with Δ.' Living with a pleasure-addict was intolerable, but for all that 'I love you more than anything in the world and am in love with you and can't bear to go to bed with anybody else'; he had, he told Jeannie on another occasion, fallen in love with a married woman, whose husband was

> a terrible shit, who was unfaithful to her and insulted her and got her down in every possible way. She is 24 or 25 and quite beautiful, tall, dark, with lustrous hair and lovely hazel eyes, a high forehead with a widow's peak and little ears. She has a nose like a Red Indian chief and a little mouth full of dazzling white teeth and delicate ears, and high cheekbones. Her voice is strong and sweet and restful...

She had, he continued, 'the most wonderful figure, long, powerful, with lovely ankles and thighs like pistons... it's like going to bed with a negress.'

Alternately buffeted by Miss Busybee's 'sad, gray, smudged face' and Jean's righteous fury, Connolly fled to Paris in the new year, where – or so he informed Mr Ragg – he found it impossible to work up interest in anything; all was 'dust and ashes'. A spell on the slopes at Megève soon rallied his spirits, however. He was, he decided, 'skiing mad', and happily spent whole days being hauled up the side of a mountain and flashing down again: 'If only there was no gap between the skiing and the swimming, one could stay thin all the year round.' The lease on the King's Road flat had expired, and Jean was thinking of taking a flat in Percy Street, off the Tottenham Court Road. Did they want to keep a place in London, Connolly asked her, and, if they did, would they then revert to 'entertaining on a dangerous scale'? As ever, he was worried about money: they owed back rent on the King's Road flat, and on Dick Wyndham's cottage, and he bent his mind to the uncongenial business of working out a monthly budget: if they saved on the £10 a month they were currently spending on clothes, plus a pound at the hairdresser's, they should then try to set aside £18 for rent, £6 for a servant, £6 for 'services', £3 for laundry, £2 for the cleaners, £20 for food and entertaining, £10 for wine and £20 each for pocket money; Ran Antrim – who had kindly offered to guarantee Jean's overdraft – could be repaid from the proceeds of one article a month for the *New Statesman*.

Despite such connubial plans, the Connollys were to spend the first nine months of 1939 boxing and coxing between France and England, each alternating with the other and seldom coinciding. Diana was as much in evidence as ever, and although Connolly warned Jean that he had no wish to share another house with her unless she could learn to run it properly without being permanently in debt, his own finances left much to be desired.

He travelled down to the South of France in April with the writer Humphrey Hare, and from Cassis he wrote (signing off as 'M. Connolly, Major') to say that he was down to his last twenty francs, and was being persecuted by restaurant- and hotel-owners waving unpaid bills; to make matters worse, his car had broken down, and he urgently needed £50 to get it repaired and pay off his debts.

Luckily Mrs Warner – by now suffering from a mild form of *delirium tremens* – was not planning to come to Europe that year: he had asked Mr Ragg (in vain) whether he couldn't tap into the Little, Brown advance for *Enemies of Promise*, but in the meantime 'if you write to Momma and ask for the customary clothes money she sends when she doesn't come abroad perhaps you will be all right.' Miss Busybee had given notice, and their affair was at an end, he assured her: he had had an 'awful dream of you tromping me with the Duke of Kent', followed by another, equally distressing, in which Sir John Simon had fallen for Jean, who had thoughtfully prepared for him 'a beautiful White Paper on Liberia, with coloured pictures of the coloured folk and pedigrees of some of the most aristocratic families showing their descent from the English peerage'. Cassis was empty apart from 'a platoon of lesbians, with a grey-haired commander'; Connolly found himself playing endless games of chess, while the political situation left him feeling 'very pacifist and Trotskyite'.

A diversion lay to hand in the form of Janetta Woolley, a pretty and companionable seventeen-year-old, whom he had offered to drive from Quimper in Brittany to rejoin her mother in Cassis. Janetta, who was to become a lifelong friend, had met Connolly through her older half-sister, Angela Culme-Seymour, who was then living in Cheyne Walk with Patrick Balfour, to whom she was later married. Angela had warned Janetta, who was only sixteen at the time, that she had 'the two ugliest people in London coming for lunch': Janetta thought poor Jean ugly and fat indeed, but she liked Connolly a good deal, and he subsequently asked her to the occasional party as well as introducing her to his 'best friend', Noël Blakiston, whom she liked, but found reserved and hard to talk to.

'I hope you'll have fun with Janetta, but don't get too involved,' Jean advised her husband: 'I feel Jan [Janetta's mother] has some plan up her sleeve, that you'll be good for her daughter, or something.' No doubt Connolly, susceptible as ever, fell half in love with his elegant travelling companion, finding her company a relief from the warring demands of wife and mistress. In *The Unquiet Grave* he was to mythologise her as one of the three or four people he had loved 'who seem utterly set apart from the others in my life; angelic, ageless creatures, more alive than the living, embalmed perpetually in their all-devouring myth', but when writing to

Jean he expressed suitably avuncular reservations. Janetta, he informed her, 'is really very sweet though disagreeable in the mornings and only coming to life at sunset . . . I don't think in the *least* in love with me, though anxious to collar me as a scoop, and annoy Angela.' He enjoyed her company 'since she suits my "second adolescence" – but you can't help being very boring at seventeen.' All the same, he found her 'a very sweet and passionate traveller' who 'sits in a pile of maps beside me and directs in silence, by waves of the hand, like a conductor with an orchestra. We grind along atrocious roads, occasionally catching sight of *route nationale* warnings, but always going across them and disappearing into the virgin forest.' As they trundled slowly south, Connolly took pains to educate his companion, and got her to quiz him about France from his guide books. His French, as she remembered, was good but slow and pedantic; at some stage in the journey she offended him by saying she couldn't remember seeing Jean sober.

At Carnac they inspected some megalithic remains, after which they rowed out to the uninhabited Ile de Gavrinis, which was covered with asphodels and contained the grave of a Celtic prince. In *The Unquiet Grave* Connolly idealised this as an interlude of calm perfection before they headed south, to where the Furies were waiting and 'happiness is thrown away'; he recalled Janetta's 'sad grave gem-like beauty', and how 'in black cloak with fair hair and Ingres profile appeared romantic love which I grasped and was not brave enough to hold.' Less romantically, Connolly was arrested a day or two later in Tulle, while he was being shaved in a barber's shop, and accused of abducting a minor. The local Chief of Police asked for proof that Mrs Woolley had agreed to her daughter's travelling with Connolly; he advised them to leave town at once, and 'for the rest of the trip, over the Massif Central for three days, we led the life of the hunted, never stopping anywhere where we saw a man in uniform, entering hotels like burglars . . . I suffer rather from having to enter hotels and book rooms with Janetta in her corduroys. We look like Rimbaud and Verlaine arriving, and I imagine people saying "Why she's only a child, how *could* he!", which makes me feel guiltier still and mumble.'

After they had reached the South of France, Connolly and Janetta visited the Luberon together and travelled around with the Quennells; Janetta wore a French soldier's cape and carried her belongings in a red spotted handkerchief. By now Jean was in Paris and, according to Peter Quennell, Connolly telephoned her incessantly, receiving the invariable answer '*Madame n'est pas rentrée . . . Non, monsieur, Madame ne répond pas*;' after which 'we watched him descend the staircase hollow-eyed and woebegone, to spread around him an atmosphere of nervous gloom that slowly overcame our spirits.' Diana had no desire to take part in such expeditions, preferring to remain in Cassis; and when, in due course, Janetta left for Toulon with Humphrey Slater – a writer and veteran of the Spanish Civil War, whom she later married – Connolly joined her there.

In April Connolly drove along the coast to Perpignan, and visited a camp for Republican refugees from Spain at Argelès. Nancy Mitford was there with her husband, Peter Rodd, arranging for families to be shipped to Mexico: Connolly noted how 'Darling is running the English help for the refugees with Peter Rodd, who is very histrionic and bossy, and the usual bunch of hysterical women,' all of whom appeared to be displaying 'the intrigue and spite associated with the left when made prefects.' He re-met a Mexican anarchist who had fought in the Asturias rising, ferried refugees around the camp, and drove up to the frontier, where 'a few filthy soldiers let their rifles off over my head.' Writing to Mr Ragg on his return, he claimed that visiting the camps had provided him with invaluable raw material for his novel, in which a group of friends who had been at Oxford together in the 1920s were to be 'gradually split up by political ideas or by the increasing intensity of their ruling passions', the whole adding up to 'a picture of weakness, or rather of the struggle of weak people to stop being weak'; and although 'the international situation makes it very difficult to write the sort of book I have planned,' he was forging steadily ahead.*

Writing from Porquerolles the following month, Connolly told Jean – who was then living in Jermyn Street – that he was worried about Diana's health, since she seemed to become thinner by the day; Jean, for her part, reported that she too was losing weight at the rate of five pounds a week, and felt exhausted by her diet; she was struggling to pay off their Tickerage debts, and, far from spending her time in night-clubs, was going to bed at seven each evening. But if Jean appeared to be getting a grip on her life, she was sceptical about her husband's achievements since they had gone their separate ways: 'I thought you were leaving me to be with Diana because she makes you work and is good for you – but you don't seem to be with her or working.' From Jermyn Street she moved into Rossetti House, a red-brick block of flats at the bottom of Flood Street, off the Chelsea Embankment; and although she claimed to be down to her last £6, she decided to join her husband and the Quennells on holiday in Italy. According to Quennell, the holiday was 'calamitous', and Connolly returned to England before it was over, leaving Jean and their two companions behind. She had had enough of the Quennells, she wrote from Menton: 'PQ' was 'tiresome and cross all day and tipsy and nervous', and they had terrible rows which ended with him

* Later in the year he wrote to Mr Ragg from Glenarm, Ran Antrim's house in Ulster, to say that the novel had been abandoned.

shouting 'No no no no no . . .' Broke once again, Jean had to borrow money from Tony Bower. Both her husband and Diana were, she suggested, 'playing at *la grande passion* and afraid of burning your fingers': even if he gave her up for good, she needed time to regain her equilibrium, and wouldn't want him back right away.

Connolly too had had enough of the Quennells, for the time being at least, though for rather different reasons. Casting around for others to blame, he saw them as 'champion trouble-makers' as far as his marriage was concerned, and 'PQ' as his 'evil genius'. As early as March that year – or so Freya Elwes told him – they had been urging Jean to leave him; it was hardly surprising that Brian Howard should have been heard spreading the rumour that the Connollys were on the verge of divorce. Another temporary villain was his future backer and collaborator on *Horizon*, Peter Watson, whom he had first met a couple of years earlier with Jean in Kitzbühel: guilty and embattled, Connolly saw him as a malign influence, and was furious with him for suggesting that he had ruined Jean's life ('What a bugger he is').

Early in July Connolly booked into the Royal Court Hotel in Sloane Square. He felt 'really dotty', he told Jean, by now in St Tropez: he couldn't sleep a wink – his room was next to a lavatory, and he was kept awake all night by the tearing of paper and the pulling of chains – and everything seemed 'unreal and insane'. London was 'defeating me utterly'; he had fantasies of taking a tramp steamer to Bali, and dreamed one night of rescuing Jean from a lesbian night-club. Diana had taken a bottle of brandy to the Major, who poured out his grievances about how seldom the younger Connollys came to see him, and what a bad daughter-in-law Jean had been; lying awake in his hotel room, his unhappy son glimpsed 'vistas of guilt and poverty ahead, becoming a Betjeman for a more haggard Penelope' or, alternatively, turning 'into a Desmond, with perpetual London ill health, much hack work and little money, and all the countries we were going to see I shall never see.' The bank manager was making threatening noises; despite abstaining from lunch, 'the fat is rolling back'; his literary nerve was shaken, and he wondered how he could compete with the new generation of bright young men who were writing for the *New Statesman*; and although Patrick Balfour was urging him to try living with Diana for a year as a trial run, he missed Jean's voice and good company, and, inevitably perhaps, he had some reservations about her rival. He worried about Diana's 'Nancy Quennellish manner with people', and tended to forget how 'forgetful and vague and inefficient' she could be; and although, for her part, Diana had said that she was willing to live with him whether he was married or not, she couldn't face the prospect of telling her parents. As sleepless night followed sleepless night, each preceded by doses of 'veganin and homoseltzers and barley-water, all useless' – he was suffering as well from a paralysed arm, a thumping heart, unfocused vision and a throbbing lump on the end of his nose – 'poor self-destructive Cyril' brooded interminably on what had gone wrong with his marriage. 'What has our marriage to show?' he asked: 'We have no home, and very few real friends, hundreds of acquaintances.' Their only discoveries were Tony Bower and Nigel Richards, and 'the fault for this I see as inherent in the adolescent nature of our love. A religion in which I am Jesus, you my Magdalene. You jealously worship me, but with faith not works, and the cathedral gets dirtier. I funk becoming mere man or accepting you as independent woman. We have both done our growing elsewhere.' A day or two later he returned to the subject. 'I do feel that marriage is a bond, almost a mystical one, and something that lovers and old friends can't supply,' he told Jean: 'I feel extremely angry with Peter Watson and his claptrap about women and ruined lives, and I regret more than I can say that you made a decision surrounded by him and other people.' She must realise that he was now a changed man. Both of them must bring a new seriousness to their domestic arrangements, the source of all friction between them. He was no longer interested in entertaining, and required 'nothing more than a nice room to work in and see a few friends, and a guaranteed light breakfast and light luncheon, with laundry fairly regular.'

This was all very well, but although he had had no difficulty in giving up Janetta – here he dropped into the third person – to give up Diana '(and he is bad at giving up people) would be the most terrible operation of his life, and if he were to do so he might become permanently old and bitter, like all the other reclaimed husbands who have had to drop their bone and come to heel.' For the time being at least he could no more abandon Diana than 'you could give up night life and jaggers'. Given his evident ambivalence, Connolly suggested that they postpone a decision till the following month, when they would meet in Dieppe and talk things over. Evidently his indecision was not good enough for Diana, for Connolly wrote again two days later to say that she was very upset and 'wishes to leave me for the country on Friday and not see me again'. On 20 July he reported 'a ray of light at last': he felt he could give up Miss Busybee – who, after all, had her painting, and other admirers as well – but only if Jean renounced 'jaggers and night life and scolding me and being "uncontrollable"'. 'I want to be free and poor and serious, to see the world, not Great Turnstile,* be like Lawrence, Maugham, not PQ': why didn't Jean get Brassai or her friend Peter Rose

* The passageway off High Holborn which now housed the *New Statesman*.

Pulham, the fashion photographer, to teach her photography, so that she could provide the illustrations for a travel book – on Mexico, perhaps? – that would constitute 'a leftist answer to old Waugh etc'? 'I have broken free from the appeal of money, comfort, glamour and playboys,' he announced: 'We must be serious. We must live as if the world was going to end – and we must see serious people, it's no good being serious over frivolous people.' Most of their friends were not worth 'the paper we don't write to them on'; even the lemurs must be set aside.

'Only a fresh continent can help me obliterate the accusing face of D,' he declared; and an annotated letter from him to Diana, written later in the year on the back of a printer's contract for the first issue of *Horizon*, suggests that many of the accusations he levelled against Jean were directed at Diana as well, and that she not only had the measure of her man but was well able to look after herself. 'I wish you would not employ so many feminine weapons,' he began, for 'nothing is easier, when you know me, than to produce a state of neurotic anxiety in me by walking out and breaking a date, and when you have produced it you can be confident that I will not be able to work or do anything important till it is relieved.' He accused Diana of sulking, refusing to answer his questions and treating him like a parent. If she was unfaithful to him in future she should bear in mind the injury inflicted on his vanity and trust ('*Thanks for the info. You ought to know*,' was Diana's marginal comment) and try to show him, as the injured party, that she loved him all the same ('*How, when you groan, scream and disbelieve every word I say?*'). She should be tactful when confessing an infidelity, and not simply blurt it out, and 'when being unfaithful go outside your spouse's circle of friends' ('*Why should I? You don't*'). Diana – and here the Jean-like accusations began – spent an hour every day simply making up her face ('*or sitting in a bath*'): 'the hours spent in dressing, window-shopping, eating, cinemas, being late for things etc should not exceed those spent in reading, working, music, pictures, nor should the hours spent in "seeing people" be more than the rest put together, if a creative life is being considered' ('*I agree. When are you going to start?*'). Peter Watson – now cited as a friend, rather than castigated as a disruptive influence – thought it very hard for couples to remain together in London ('*We are not, and never have been, a couple. We are a trio*'). 'And before you reproach me again with Janetta, remember that you did write and give me permission' ('*I never reproached*').

As a change from louche life in London, Connolly went in August to stay with Ran Antrim and his wife Angela – Christopher Sykes's sister – at Glenarm in County Antrim; his fellow-guests were Christopher Sykes and Freya Elwes ('mine and Jean's greatest friends respectively'), Richard Elwes and Robert Byron. 'Ulster is more hideous, wet and dull than ever,' Connolly told Jean, who was by now in Paris.* The house smelt of boiled cabbage, and exuded the 'usual Sykes atmosphere of solidarity and decay', while the womenfolk were 'individually sweet, but together such a lump of sterling bourgeois England'. Golf provided an unexpected diversion, played with Richard Elwes and the antiquarian bookseller Greville Worthington, who 'says I am a natural player'. According to Freya Elwes, 'Cyril developed a most remarkable style and often made championship shots ending up with one leg in the air in a sort of arabesque'; he told Jean that 'when I have a difficult putt to make I say "Jean" and it goes down. When I say "Jean Jean" by mistake I get an erection.' Such excitements were all too fleeting: 'Life here is dull, heavy, spiritless; beneath a veneer of gaiety I eat too much and fat advances inexorably.'

He was, he told Jean, 'pierced by memories of better days – the whortleberries and posies of Kitzbühel when we were just getting to know Peter Wattie.' Diana, he said, was feeling bitter and ill-used, but 'how can I love an exquisite little Arab pony when I am used to titanic struggles with my big black intractable mare?' He had, he knew, given Diana a raw deal, but she was 'compensation for King's Road blues. Take away the King's Road, and you take away the need for compensation.' Self-pity and remorse were seldom far beneath the surface:

> When I think of this time a year ago when I had a wife who loved me – I used to telephone her every evening to Brides, if you remember – and a girl who loved me, and a good book in the press and a house and a library and a car; and now my wife sits in the Flore and won't see me, my girl starves away and won't see me, no book even started, no house, no books, the car bill mounting up and nothing in the world but three suitcases...

Money remained short: could Jean look out the brown notebooks in which he had written *Enemies of Promise*, since Ran Antrim had offered him a tenner for them? He still dreamed of a new start, of visiting Mexico or going to Poland with Ran, but war seemed inevitable – 'I find the German-Soviet Pact very funny, and enjoy the bewilderment of the Communists and the despair of the capitalists' – and Jean must decide where she was going to spend it; for his part, he planned to 'try to get an interesting job, avoiding London till the air raids blow over'. In the meantime, he longed for their meeting in Dieppe, or Newhaven if needs be; they would make a new life together, and 'I will dance with you, drink with you, jagger you, pansy you and try to make up for what you give up and you must try to make up by intelligence and sex life for

* Relief was provided by a trip to Dublin to visit Connolly's cousin Mona Oulton, now living in Clontarf Castle. Mona, Connolly reported, was 'very dotty', and Mr Oulton 'did the honours like a well-fed vampire showing people round a cemetery'.

what I give up.' 'I would far rather you made your hobby looking after me than taking photographs,' he informed her: 'I offer you the major role, the only role, in my dream,' as well as 'fidelity, devotion, appreciation, entertainment, love, care, and the job of looking after me as a wife should.' He yearned to be faithful, to break free of the cycle of 'drinking, flirting – flirting, fucking – fucking, affair – affair, tragedy, and all the lies too'.

Notwithstanding his offer, Jean was rather more cautious about the prospects of reconciliation. 'I'm not ready to come back to you yet,' she wrote from Paris: 'I haven't recovered from loving you and hating you and suffering and trying not to think about it and despising myself.' She didn't want to become involved with other people, but needed time 'to convalesce from the sickness of love . . . My feelings for you were very complicated and morbid, and I want to get them clearer.' Her doctor had put her on a slimming course which involved taking five different pills three times a day after meals, the effect of which was to make her irritable and emotional. She found herself resenting Diana more and more – she hated having to pass her flat in Sloane Street – and couldn't bear telling people that she and her husband were leading separate lives. This was made worse by there being so many English friends in Paris, including Glur Quennell, who was working as a model, and Sonia Brownell, who was introduced to her at the Café Flore by Mark Culme-Seymour and seemed 'pretty and rather nice, I thought, but dull'. 'You say Jean *prefers* the Flore to your company,' Peter Quennell wrote to his old friend,

> but – after all – what she likes is not the Flore or its inhabitants but the comparative freedom from the sort of emotional wear-and-tear she has undergone during the last two or three years – before you entered on *your* tragic period and were still the successfully poised circus rider. Incidentally I understand from Glur that Jean is really and truly bored with Peter Rose Pulham: so you need have no alarms on that front.*

* 'Shabby humped elegant Pulham', as Dylan Thomas once described him, was a fashionable photographer, working for *Harper's Bazaar* in Paris and London. Nancy Mitford, who was photographed by him in 1930, thought him an 'odious youth'. Theodora Fitzgibbon, who first met him at the Café Flore in 1938, and later fell madly in love with him, vividly evoked him as

> a large man with a beautifully shaped head: his hair, which was dark brown, inclined to chestnut at the sides, started high on his forehead, and was worn long enough to curl gently in the nape of his neck . . . [He had] a prominent nose, under which was a well-trimmed, long, silky moustache, a well-shaped full mouth, and the most extraordinary eyes. They were deep reddish-brown, very large, but set slightly slanting in his face. Their expression was one of sleepy amusement. The eyebrows followed the shape of the eyes, and did not come down at the corners, so that they gave him a curiously Mephistophelian look. He was beautifully dressed in a dark striped suit, cream silk shirt, a buttonhole and, I think, a monocle hung round his neck.

When, the following year, she met him again in Paris, his suit was frayed, the monocle had vanished, and his hair and moustache were in need of a trim. Jean saw quite a bit of him at the time but – or so she assured her husband – never slept with him. Be that as it may, Pulham – together with Messrs Quennell and Watson – may have contributed to Connolly's momentary desire 'never to see anyone called Peter again'.

Despite all Connolly's pleadings, Jean had been too badly bruised, and had decided that, much as she loved him, they should go their separate ways. 'I'm sorry you've had such a miserable time,' Tony Bower told her; and then – referring to her decision to part – 'I suppose it is the most sensible thing to do, particularly as you never wrote a truer word than that it was like parturition. I shall not say anything *at all* so that if it gets about it will be nothing to do with me.' Connolly still insisted on their meeting in one of the two Channel ports. 'Without your help, advice, love and enthusiasm I am a mutilated person, a genius without a career,' he told her; and she needed him quite as much as he needed her, for without him she was deteriorating and becoming tough and embittered, and he couldn't bear to 'hear you talked about as a helpless, charming drug addict'. If, after seeing him again, she decided that she would rather continue with her 'selfish and independent' life, she should go back to America and start divorce proceedings; but he prayed she would not, for 'I am conscious of great powers which I can't release till I have some love, some peace and some security in my life, and those only you can give.' He arranged to meet her in Newhaven; and, after turning down the offer of a trip to the West of Ireland, he returned to London from Glenarm, collected some money from the *New Statesman*, and set off for Newhaven. He waited for three hours, but there was no sign of Jean on the ferry; went back to London, where a telegram was waiting; returned to Newhaven, but still there was no sign of her. Once he'd recovered from his anger, he took the boat train to Paris, where he joined Jean, Graham Eyres-Monsell and Peter Rose Pulham for cocktails in the Ritz Bar. Jean was looking 'very sweet and melting. Bar like a steam-room, usual collection of black-suited gigolos, pansies and women with expensive hair. Graham's broad back and pouting little voice, which I imitate, duck to water . . .' From Paris they set off for Dieppe on the day before war broke out. 'Dieppe was full of hope for me,' Connolly told Jean later, and as soon as they got back to London he went round to see Diana and talk it all over. Diana, for her part, had soon come to realise that their lofty ideal of living together as 'artists' was a fantasy, and that, for all the 'footling', Jean was just as 'right' for Connolly as she was. She was reluctant to cause any more domestic misery, and, fond as she was of her admirer, she would have been happy to back off and not see him again; but whenever she suggested this he reacted with such anguish that she gave in and continued the affair. Looking back on their relationship years later, she realised that, quite apart from his urge to be in love with two people simultaneously, he liked, as she put it, 'to keep the pot boiling and present a picture of himself as being fought over when, in fact, each of the two was trying (and eventually succeeding) to get away.' Once again, though, Connolly had presumed too much. Shortly after their return, Jean went north to stay at Sledmere, from where she wrote urging him not to join her: the food was disgusting, there were no servants, no booze and only Turkish cigarettes to hand, and, besides, if Diana 'makes you comfortable, if she is an agreeable person and loves you, if you love her as you are very near to doing, she might be the right wife for you.' She urged him to 'think of the times I have let you down, of my laziness and irresponsibility and selfishness and temper and discomfort.' He seemed to think it was up to her to bridge the gulf between them, whereas she thought it was up to him: 'We love each other but find it impossible to live together.'

Connolly's simultaneous passion for Diana was far from over, but she was temporarily removed from the fray later that month when a taxi in which she and Connolly were travelling up Sloane Street was rammed by an army lorry in the blackout. Diana's pelvis was broken and she was taken to St George's Hospital, where she remained for the next six weeks. Connolly visited her there every day, and was equally solicitous after she had been moved to a nursing-home near Amersham. She had to give up her art lessons at the Chelsea Polytechnic, and from now on she would concentrate on her writing, and her poems in particular.

Years later, Connolly told of how, in the months leading up to the outbreak of war, he had come to shudder at the sight of 'Chamberlain and his umbrella, his disapproving stiff collars, Halifax's camel face on its long neck, Sir John Simon, Lord Runciman, Horace Wilson': his views were 'those of the *New Statesman* and the *News Chronicle*: I bled with Masaryk and Benes, had faith in Litvinov.' Apolitical as he was, he seems to have had few doubts about the need to stand up to Hitler, or the inevitability of war, but 'I remember very well how disconcerted I was as an ardent anti-appeaser, when Richard Jennings in the London Column of the *Daily Mirror* took the logical step of urging all young men to join up and get into khaki'; Hitler may have been a nightmare, but 'we were not prepared to face the fact (familiar to the men of Munich) that he was actually longing for battle, nor that we would have to fight ourselves.' Quite apart from being at the upper end of the age scale, Connolly – unlike Evelyn Waugh or even John Betjeman – had no intention of joining up: he managed to find Peter Watson a job driving a Red Cross van, but Nancy Mitford reported, in mid-September, that she had seen the 'Scallywags' – Connolly and Jean – at Patrick Balfour's, and that 'they were full of pop. He of course is looking for a job of a non-military character.' The newly-formed Ministry of Information – which was to provide a welcome haven for writers, publishers, dons and other unmartial types – seemed the obvious place, but everyone was knocking on that particular door. He was lunching with Gerald Barry, who might be able to find something on the *News Chronicle*, and he would pull what strings he could with Harold Nicolson, Roger Fulford, Gladwyn Jebb and Sir Roderick Jones. A note of urgency had been introduced by the bank manager, who had subjected them both to a further wigging – 'Mrs Connolly seems to move from place to place – has no idea of the trouble she gives' – and he needed some money to buy a suit for job interviews, 'and a bicycle for running away'.

Although another year would pass before the Blitz began, air-raid warnings had become a familiar feature of London life. Connolly found himself squeezing into an air-raid shelter in Sloane Square with 'horrible old colonels and stiff upper lips of both sexes', though life was rather different a few hundred yards up the King's Road, in Markham Square, where Noël Blakiston gave him a guided tour of the shelter in his garden, 'complete with anti-gas blanket, anti-gas suit for Noël, tin helmet, mustard gas treatment etc. I couldn't stay in it for a second.' Further evidence of war was provided by the gradual drifting back of English expatriates from France. T.C. Worsley and Tony Bower were back in England, and so too was a gloomy Peter Watson, who had left his flat in the rue du Bac, with its Picassos and de Chiricos, in the care of a dubious Rumanian, and had travelled to the Channel, minus his luggage, on a crowded troop train: had Jean and Denham Fouts only exerted themselves more, he told Connolly, they'd all be on their way to Mexico or Bali by now, putting the war behind them. Peter Rose Pulham was reported as looking on as the others left, clad in a 'dirty white coat and corduroy trousers with a hole in the knee', finally quitting Paris as the Germans entered the city and bicycling the length of France to Bordeaux and a passage home. Brian Howard and Toni Altmann lingered on in Bandol until the following February, when they made their escape from Marseille on board a cargo ship: according to rumour, Howard spent much of the journey in the coal bunker, arriving in England covered in coal-dust but still – according to Harold Acton, who had himself recently returned from China – flaunting 'the same air of masochistic ease, the same elaborate charm which was apt to turn vicious after a number of drinks'.

However 'full of pop' the Connollys might have seemed at a party, resolving their apparent incompatibilities was proving predictably elusive. In October they moved temporarily into the maisonette in Yeoman's Row which Connolly had shared a decade earlier with Patrick Balfour. It had been smartly decorated and appeared to have come up in the world in the intervening years: 'You must come and see us here, in these rooms which seem haunted by the ghosts of an older civilisation,' the 'extinct volcano' wrote to John Betjeman, his successor at the 'Yeo'. By now Connolly was busy setting up *Horizon*, the first issue of which appeared in January 1940: 'The life I want,' he told Jean, 'is to create something permanent in the flux. A foyer, a monogamous marriage, a baby, books, *Horizon – vivre bourgeoise-*

ment.' Jean was unamused by his suggestion that they should live apart, but she should have an affair with him. Another alternative was for them to get divorced and for him to marry Diana: at least he could have children that way, and they could 'jog along somehow as long as you don't cut my allowance off'. Not long after Diana's accident, Stephen Spender reported to Christopher Isherwood – who had left for America with Auden shortly before war broke out, much to the derision of Evelyn Waugh – that

> Cyril told me that Jeannie went out at seven o'clock on Sunday night to see friends round the corner, intending to return in a few minutes for dinner. While there she fell into a deep sleep, in the middle of drinking only one glass of whisky. Her host undressed her and put her to bed and she did not wake up until ten o'clock the next morning. He told me that since then she had been sleeping most of the day. The war seems to have the effect of making people who are weak in some way crack up. 'It pushes people over the edge whose health or sex or sanity are uncertain,' said Cyril.

Despite such hazards, Jean was – she told Connolly early in the New Year – enjoying her London life, and seeing a good deal of Raymond Mortimer, Tony Bower and Joan Rayner in particular.

Early in March, Jean went to stay near Upton-on-Severn with Coote Lygon, who was full of consoling words and sound advice. 'My poppet, we all consort with inferiors,' she told her guest when Jean raised the vexed subject of friends and footlers: quoting her back to Connolly, Jean cited Stephen Spender with Tony Hyndman and Peter Watson with Denham Fouts, and wondered, as an unkind after-thought, why he spent so much time with Tony Witherby, the genial young man whose family firm printed the first four issues of *Horizon*. From Upton Jean moved on to a hotel in Malvern Wells, where she took the waters in the alarming company of two rival prima donnas, Peter Watson's friend Denham Fouts and Charles Fry, a demonic figure who tended to become 'pedantic, irrational and sentimental' after his first gin of the day, and was a partner in the publishing firm of Batsford. Before long they were joined there by two other members of the firm, Sam Carr and Brian Cook,* and they discussed the

* A satanic figure with a voracious sexual appetite, for men and women, Charles Fry was described by John Betjeman as a 'phallus with a business sense'. Later in the war, James Lees-Milne recorded how 'I had to lunch with Charles Fry my publisher at the Park Lane Hotel. He was late, having just got up after some orgy *à trois* with whips etc. He is terribly depraved and related every detail, not questioning whether I wished to listen. In the middle of the narration I simply said, "Stop! Stop!" At the same table an officer was eating, and imbibing every word. I thought he gave me a crooked look for having spoilt his fun.' Sam Carr later became Chairman of Batsford; Brian Cook, the artist responsible for the firm's striking landscape jackets, metamorphosed into Brian Batsford MP.

possibility of Jean's going to work for the firm; but instead she borrowed some money off Sam Carr, and went bicycling in the Brecon Beacons with Denham Fouts instead. By now, though, she had decided to return to America. It would be better for both of them to part: she needed to get over her 'phobia' about living with him, and because he kept changing his mind she had no idea where she stood. 'Darling darling heart don't grieve, I love you and will write to you every week and will come back to you,' she wrote: he would be better off without her, and with Diana, though 'I hope it is not blackmail to say that it makes me cry to write this':

> You hate living alone and you have a wife who won't live with you, you like comfort and you have a wife who is lazy, inefficient and sluttish, you are an artist and intellectual and she is an intelligent dabbler of boundless conceit and little application from the fear of showing herself up, you don't trust her and she will not give in and give you the assurances you demand. In fact, you must stop carrying this millstone about.

It was in her interest, too, for them to part, for however long it had to be: 'I shall have to realise all over again the pain of losing you in order to avoid the pain of having you ruin my life.'

A month or two earlier, looking back on his life in the Thirties, Connolly had indulged in the kind of self-congratulatory daydream to which most writers are occasionally prone:

> Cyril Connolly's first novel, *The Rock Pool*, was described as having a touch of genius by Desmond MacCarthy, his book of criticism, *Enemies of Promise*, still smoulders away in the minds of many of its readers, and now comes the great trilogy of which neither his other books nor his years of work on the *New Statesman* or *Horizon* give any inkling. It is a writer finding himself and yet at the same time a man summing up all he knows about life at the age of thirty-five, and reaching through his chronicle of a man and three women, of London, Paris, Barcelona and Budapest, and of the most eventful decade ('29–'39) in history, the most profound conclusions of which his art is capable.

Much to Mr Ragg's disappointment, no doubt, the masterpieces remained unwritten, matters of dream and speculation; the reality of life was all too intrusive, for both Connolly and Jean. 'It is beginning to sink in how very far I am going and for how very long,' Jean wrote from the Shelbourne Hotel in Dublin, where she and Denham Fouts had stopped off before boarding a liner for New York. As soon as she reached America she would start to plan her return; and after that 'it will be perfect and no more goings away . . . my dearest sweet stricken bull.'

O woman in our hour of ease
Unfaithful, cruel and hard to please
When war and desolation stalk
You jump a clipper to New York

was Connolly's summing-up. Once again, he had been deserted by a woman, only this time he had conspired to bring about all that he most dreaded. Jean's departure was to haunt him for the rest of his life, and inspire some of the most elegant and elegiac prose of the century; in the meantime, though, *Horizon* was in its infancy, and there was work to be done.

SEVENTEEN

New Horizons

Introducing a posthumous selection of poems, stories and essays culled from *Horizon*'s ten-year lifespan, Connolly wrote that the key to understanding the magazine's workings – and success – lay in the 'Bouvard-Pecuchet relationship between Peter Watson and myself. As Hardy, I emulated his despair, as Laurel he financed my optimism. He likes art to be slightly incomprehensible, while I fall an easy victim to political quacks and neurotic journalists; he is impressed by straw in the hair, I am taken in by fire in the belly: we were made to compromise.' Peter Watson was a very rich man indeed, and without his money, and his readiness to risk it, *Horizon* would never have taken off, let alone remained airborne for exactly a decade; but, as Connolly suggests, he was a good deal more than a mere moneybags, a rich young dilettante and patron with an interest in the arts. A literary magazine needs to be both unpredictable and dependable, innovative and familiar, bohemian in its readiness to embrace the new and untried, bourgeois in its routine reliability when it comes to such matters as typography, layout and regularity of publication. Connolly's editorial flair and intuition, his moodiness and his tendency to rush into things and then lose interest, were counterpointed by Watson's steadiness, approachability and level-headed common sense; and, most importantly of all – for a magazine with character must reflect the taste and attitudes of its editor – he was more than happy to remain in the shadows, and allow Connolly his head. 'All I want you to do is to put in exactly what you like as you know I think your judgement is better than anyone else's, you silly thing,' he once told his friend and collaborator: he might find it impossible to share – say – Connolly's urge to publish Evelyn Waugh's novella *The Loved One* in a single issue of the magazine, but 'if I am asked an opinion I shall try to be sincere. My opinion about something is *not* a prohibition and I really resent it being taken as one.' A proprietor who refuses to intervene on editorial matters is a rare and wonderful thing, and in this Connolly and the writers he espoused were unusually blessed; and, as if this weren't enough, 'Peter Wattie' was, by all accounts, an exceptionally likeable man, whose own melancholy and creative sterility were diluted by the support he gave to others. 'No one was more exploited,' Stephen Spender wrote after Watson's death in 1956, 'and yet, although this depressed him sometimes, he expected it and he could see beyond the motives of the exploiter to the person behind, with whom he continued to be infinitely patient and tender.'

The Watson family fortune was based on margarine. Peter Watson's grandfather had unwisely paid Maundy Gregory £30,000 for a peerage, which never came his way, but his son, Sir George, was the first baronet, and the Lord of the Manor of Sulhampstead Abbots in Hampshire. One of three children, Peter was born in 1908 and educated at Eton and St John's College, Oxford, from which he was sent down without a degree. A thin, sad-looking young man with an endearing smile and an unobtrusive manner, he was homosexual, with a liking for rough trade. Sir George retired from the Maypole Dairy Company in 1930, but Peter at least had no interest in following him into the family business. That same year, according to the ever-inventive Nancy Mitford – who referred to him as 'Hog' Watson after Lord Redesdale had answered the phone and told her that 'that hog Watson wants to talk to you' – he invested in a 'coral-coloured Rolls-Royce inlaid with gems and with *fur* seats'. Although involved with the stage-designer Oliver Messel, he also met Cecil Beaton, who fell hopelessly in love with this 'tall, gangling young man with the face of a charming cod-fish'. 'Of all my recently acquired friends, he was to strike the deepest and rarest chord of sympathy,' Beaton wrote: 'Peter's acute sensibility, subtlety of mind, wry sense of humour and mysterious qualities of charm made him unlike anyone I had known.' The following year the two young men visited America and Mexico together but, to Beaton's disappointment, their amorous encounters never got beyond pillow-fights and tickling. Back in England, Watson was taken up by Edith Sitwell, and painted as a knight in blue armour by their mutual friend Pavel Tchelitchew: 'I hear the new name for Pavlik's friend Mr Watson is "Trumpet Lips",' Miss Sitwell informed a correspondent. In the mid-Thirties he moved to Paris, where he built up a priceless collection of modern paintings in his curiously shabby flat in the rue du Bac. Jean and her friends were frequent visitors, and David Gascoyne remembers the Connollys spending New Year's Eve there in 1938, and the bohemian riff-raff drifting in and out. Watson shared his Paris apartment with the young American Denham Fouts, with whom he had earlier travelled in China and the Far East. Isherwood would later describe Fouts's fictional *alter ego* as 'the last of the professional tapettes' and 'the most expensive male prostitute in the world'; a drug-addict who had started life in a small town in Florida, and whose previous lovers had included Prince Paul of Greece, Fouts was the kind of vicious, unpredictable youth to whom the reserved and melancholy Watson seemed inevitably to be attracted. Isherwood recalled how Fouts's 'boyishly skinny' figure, with his 'strangely erect walk' was

> dressed like a boy in his teens, with an exaggerated air of innocence which he seemed to be daring us to challenge. His drab black suit, narrow-chested and without shoulder-padding, clean white shirt and plain black tie made him look as if he had just arrived in town from a strictly religious boarding-school.

He remembered too 'the lean, hungry-looking tanned face, the eyes which seemed to be set on different levels, as in a Picasso painting; the bitter, well-formed mouth. His handsome profile was bitterly sharp, like a knife-edge . . .'*

A spare, elegant figure, neat and tastefully clad – he liked to dress like an American, and was an early advocate of belt as opposed to braces – Watson had a sharp, pointed face and narrow eyes with black bags underneath; giving him the look of a benign and sensitive snake. Stephen Spender, who first met him in Paris at about this time, recalled how 'his despair, his cynicism, which went with his idealism, were gay and laughing, if rather bitter'; and Watson himself once reminded Brian Howard – by then deteriorating under the influence of drink, drugs, self-pity and despair – that he too had always been prone to depressions, and that 'I started life as moody, self-obsessed and bad-tempered; by an effort of will (the only quality which achieves *anything*, alas) I have tried to give myself a sunnier disposition.' Though 'generous, disinterested and good', Peter Watson was – in Spender's opinion – restricted by physical tiredness and his own (unpretentious) intellectual limitations, while his despair was induced by an innate craving for perfection that was inevitably disappointed. 'He was, as it were, essentially made for honeymoons and not for marriages,' Spender wrote after his friend's death: 'The best possible relationship with him was to be taken up by him very intensely for a few weeks, and then remain on his waiting-list for the rest of one's time.' Such fickleness may have been true of friends or lovers, but as far as *Horizon* was concerned, Watson was to prove the perfect patron; and the fact that his own interests lay more with modern painting than with literature, complementing rather than competing with those of his colleague, was all to the good.

* Gore Vidal remembered Fouts as being 'very pale, with dark lank Indian hair and blank dark eyes, usually half shut: he smoked opium, and the light hurt his eyes.' For a fuller account of this sinister but forceful figure, see Truman Capote's autobiographical novel, *Answered Prayers*, and *High Diver*, the autobiography of Connolly's friend the painter Michael Wishart. As we have seen, Fouts returned to America in 1940 with Jean; he spent the war as a conscientious objector in California, but later resurfaced in Paris (see p. 395).

The autumn of 1939 was not, on the face of it, the most propitious time to launch a literary magazine. T.S. Eliot had abandoned the *Criterion* in January, and two of the most influential poetry magazines – Geoffrey Grigson's acerbic *New Verse* and Julian Symons's *Twentieth-Century Verse* – had recently ceased publication. 'Grigson and I mourned through two or three lunches together fairly cheerfully, and talked about doing something, but I don't see that we can,' Symons informed Desmond Hawkins: 'The rise in the cost of paper, about 15 per cent now, will be prohibitive – really I think you may regard all verse magazines as dead if not buried.' But literary magazines, like publishing houses, pop up at the most unexpected moments, and Connolly was not the only prospective editor looking for a backer and a printer and paper and distribution in these early months of the war. Evelyn Waugh, Osbert Sitwell and David Cecil discussed setting up a magazine to be called, appositely, *Duration* and distributed by Waugh's father's firm of Chapman & Hall, but decided against when they learned from Patrick Balfour that *Horizon* was on the drawing-board. Both George Woodcock's *Now* and Tambimuttu's *Poetry (London)* were launched the following year; and so too was *Horizon's* best-known – and better selling – rival, John Lehmann's *Penguin New Writing*, the first issue of which was published by Allen Lane in December 1940.*

According to an account of *Horizon*'s origins which Connolly wrote for American subscribers in the autumn of 1940, he had first suggested to Peter Watson on a hot afternoon in a Paris boulevard in August 1939 that he should come back to England and start a new literary magazine. Watson had already been in touch with Lehmann and Stephen Spender about their plans for just such a magazine, and he told Connolly that he disliked living in England and would far rather start an art magazine in Paris; Connolly pointed out that Paris already had more than its share of these, whereas the demise of so many literary magazines in London made it all the more important to back a new one. The outbreak of war, and Peter Watson's reluctant removal to London, helped to tilt the balance in Connolly's direction; and when, at a party in

* A tall, gaunt, rather humourless figure with hawk-like features and cold blue eyes, Lehmann had succeeded Dadie Rylands as the Woolfs' assistant at the Hogarth Press in 1931, but had spent a good deal of time since then in Vienna. A literary polymath who divided his time between editing, publishing and his own writing, Lehmann was a brilliant, intuitive editor with a keen eye for new talent; he had greatly admired Desmond MacCarthy's *Life and Letters*, and the way in which it was impregnated with its editor's taste and personality, and 'spent hours brooding on how the magic worked'. In 1935 the first issue of *New Writing* was published, as a hardback periodical: the first three issues were distributed by the Bodley Head and the next three by Lawrence & Wishart, but it was taken over by the Hogarth Press after the Woolfs had invited Lehmann to join them as a partner in 1938. Among those to be published in *New Writing* were Orwell, Isherwood, T.C. Worsley and V.S. Pritchett. As early as 1935 Lehmann had talked to Allen Lane – then still at the Bodley Head, but on the verge of starting Penguin Books – about the possibility of bringing out a 128-page literary magazine in paperback; nothing came of these discussions until 1940.

Elizabeth Bowen's house, the subject was floated once more, Watson agreed to go ahead and provide the necessary backing. Connolly and Stephen Spender were to be the two editors of the new magazine – a seemingly harmless announcement which had immediate repercussions.

Connolly once wrote of Spender – of whom he was particularly fond – that he was a man divided: part of him was 'an inspired simpleton, a great big silly goose, a holy Russian idiot, large, generous, gullible, ignorant, affectionate, idealistic', while another part was 'shrewd, ambitious, aggressive and ruthless, a publicity-seeking intellectual full of administrative energy and rentier asperity'; and the two parts came into conflict, perhaps, over his divided loyalties between *Horizon* and *New Writing*. He and Isherwood had been brought in as joint editors of the sixth issue of *New Writing*, and he had been involved in Lehmann's discussions with Peter Watson about producing a paperback version; but once Watson had decided to finance *Horizon* instead, he was keen to involve Spender, whom he saw as a steadying influence on Connolly, less liable to lose interest suddenly and abandon ship. Spender claimed later that – so as not to inflame John Lehmann – his name was deliberately left off the *Horizon* notepaper; but it was certainly there in the early days, though he was never referred to as Connolly's co-editor on the title page of the magazine; and Lehmann worried that 'Stephen would represent, on the *Horizon* board, the policy that had made *New Writing*'s reputation', and that *Horizon* would 'make the position of a rival literary magazine untenable'. Virginia Woolf noted that a 'deadly feud' had broken out as a result of Spender's involvement with *Horizon*, with Lehmann anxious that the newcomer would lure away his best contributors, and referring to 'calamitous disagreements' between himself and Spender. Angry scenes ensued, with Lehmann's new secretary, John Lepper, acting as an intermediary. In the end, harmony was restored, with Spender nimbly shuttling between the two: although he loomed large as an influence on, and contributor to, the early issues of *Horizon* – most memorably in his 'September Journal' – his belief that such magazines had a political as well as a literary role to play was more congenial to Lehmann than to Connolly,* and whereas he remained a regular contributor to

* The difference in attitude between Connolly and Spender towards the war, and writers' reactions to it, was reflected in an annotated galley-proof of one of Connolly's 'Comments': Spender's marginal comments are printed in italic. 'The war has so far played but little part in the destinies of *Horizon*,' Connolly observed (*'except for Spender's "Journal"'*), and 'No contributor has yet expressed a wish to beat the Germans, or been provoked into writing about the blackout, the *Graf Spee* or Scapa Flow' (*'What about me? Also we've had several about barrage-balloons'*). Connolly's comments on the 'Chamberlain-complex of intellectuals' was '*awfully bad and politically naif*'; Connolly's co-editor was '*thoroughly against the discussion of all war aims at this level*', and '*having offended the Right, the Left, the Pacifists, the Foreign Office etc., you end up by offending Eliot and the Woolves . . .*'

Penguin New Writing, he was no longer effectively involved in the running of *Horizon* after the spring of 1941. And although Lehmann disapproved of Connolly's 'ivory tower' attitude, 'his view that the only thing writers could do while the war was going on was to concentrate on technique and shut their ears', the two magazines eventually settled down to a state of 'friendly rivalry'. Connolly would sometimes pass foreign writers in particular on to Lehmann ('Perhaps you would like a Turk for something?'); the 'friendly rival' would be spotted at the parties Lehmann gave in Carrington House, off Park Lane, 'surrounded by a circle of awe-struck devotees', and 'as the war became more embittered and destructive and shortage of supplies threatened us both, we began, I believe, to hold one another's editorial existence as almost sacred.'*

All this lay in the future; of more immediate concern was to find a printer, decide on a title, and make arrangements for distributing copies to subscribers and through the retail trade. A printer was to hand in the form of the twenty-four-year-old Anthony Witherby, whose family firm, H. & F. Witherby, had been founded in 1740, and combined printing with publishing books about birds; since 1905, the firm had produced a monthly magazine called *British Birds*, which gave them a certain expertise in the world of periodical publishing. Tony Witherby had joined the firm in 1935, learning every aspect of the business from the bottom up. It was agreed that he would design the page and choose the typeface, loosely following the style and layout of *Life and Letters*, and he entered into a formal agreement with Peter Watson, whereby he would be paid £35 an issue to produce 1000 copies at a published price of one shilling; he would deduct a 15 per cent commission from the proceeds before passing them on to the Proprietor, and be responsible for determining the terms of sale to the trade and to subscribers. John Piper designed the magazine's lettering cover, and the magazine's title, once decided upon, would be set in the exotically named Elephant Bold Italic.†

Finding a title for the new magazine was a hellishly hard business. *Equinox*, *Germinal*, *Capricorn*, *Western Review* and *Pharos* were chewed over and spat out. According to Stephen Spender, he first thought of

* Both magazines were held in high esteem, not only by the literati, but by men and women on active service: but in terms of sales, *Penguin New Writing* was a Goliath to *Horizon*'s David. Like its rival, *PNW* began life as a monthly, becoming a quarterly in 1942 as a result of paper shortages: the first issue sold 80,000 copies, at its most successful it sold 100,000 per issue, but when it perished in 1950 – the same year as *Horizon* – it was down to 25,000 copies. *Horizon*, on the other hand, started out with a sale of 3500 in January 1940, doubled that in February, reached its apogee in 1947 with sales of 10,000, and was still selling 9000 at the time of its closing issue.

† Tony Witherby printed the first four issues of *Horizon*, but the connection lapsed after he was called up; on his recommendation, the magazine was printed thereafter by Oliver Simon at the Curwen Press (q.v.).

'Horizon' while reading André Gide's journal, where the word kept cropping up; years later, when he suggested to Connolly that perhaps it had been his idea, his old collaborator 'looked at me quizzically and said, "If you go on remembering hard enough you'll find you remember every good idea we ever had, Stephen."' Towards the end of October, Spender had lunch with Geoffrey Grigson in the Café Royal, and although Grigson was full of helpful advice, and offered to let them have the use of his now-redundant *New Verse* subscription list, he was unimpressed by their choice of title, which 'suggests flatness, the flatness of the dead': there had been a good deal of mirth about it at a dinner party in Henley the night before, at which Betjeman and John Piper were among the guests, and indeed Betjeman himself had already written to say that he didn't think much of it, since 'I am sure you will find, somewhere around Red Lion Square, that a magazine called *Horizon* is already published by the Communist Nature Ramblers' Club'. 'We bow our heads,' Connolly told Spender: 'We accept Grigson's sneers, and thank him for them. But we might have pointed out that if *Horizon* is a dead title, *New Verse* is dead and done for. And if a metaphor is flat, nothing is so positively sickening in a title as the adjective "new".' But mutual animosity didn't prevent Grigson from passing on to *Horizon* some poems left over from *New Review* – or, indeed, from contributing himself to the opening issue, as did John Betjeman, who wrote to Connolly in typically facetious vein:

> We must all do our bit. *There's a war on, you know*. But if the best you can find to do is some highbrow paper with a communist-fellow poet, then take my advice and get a job with the Sussex Light. *There's a war on, you know*. And tell that fellow Peter Watson to strip off his 'artistic' poses and get down to some real work. Has he ever emptied latrines from the C/O into the GHQ, I wonder . . .

'How nice to hear of something opening, instead of shutting, and I feel in my bones that you will make a very good editor,' wrote Osbert Sitwell, who like Betjeman went in for jocular modes of address, calling Connolly 'Figlio Mio' or 'My dear Nipper' and signing off as 'The Dad' or 'Poppa' or 'The Governor'.

From his temporary quarters in Yeoman's Row, Connolly wrote to established writers of all ages and literary and political persuasions asking them to contribute to the new magazine. 'I note that Mr Connolly upbraids Leonard and Virginia Woolf for not writing for *Horizon*. Well, if you like to suggest a subject I'll certainly try,' Virginia Woolf wrote to Spender: but if Eliot, Forster and Virginia Woolf failed to come up with contributions, middlebrow writers of the kind that Connolly had spent so much of the decade deriding were more forthcoming. J.B. Priestley and Hugh Walpole offered articles for nothing, and Somerset Maugham sent a piece on detective stories which Connolly eventually sent back on the grounds that it would do nothing to add to its author's reputation. Nor was Connolly too proud to bend the knee – or, in the case of Forster, tell a harmless fib – when writing to grandees of an older generation. 'I know you disapprove of literary dictatorships, but when I tell you that such lords of the Abinger Harvest as Mr R.C. Trevelyan, Mr E.M. Forster and Mr Logan Pearsall Smith have all consented to appear in its provincial contemporary, I feel you may be more willing to consider this appeal,' he suggested to Max Beerbohm, (an article by whom on Lytton Strachey he begged to be allowed to reprint). Beerbohm's article never appeared and, grateful as he was to the likes of Priestley and Walpole, the 'middlebrow' type of contributor was soon phased out; but some damage had been done, in that Connolly's eclecticism had opened *Horizon* to the charge – most vigorously articulated by Julian Symons – of being bland, belle-lettrist and lacking in conviction.

Towards the end of October, the two editors met in the Cumberland Hotel to compare notes about the contributions they had received. Writing to Betjeman from the 'Yeo', Connolly said that they had received 'a very good poem of Prokosch, as good as any modern poem I have read, a so-so de la Mare, a pleasing Norman Cameron, a rather dim K.J. Raine (for WOMEN readers), two MacNeice, one nice, one rhymed journalism.' Since the poems printed in the first issue included Auden's 'Crisis', MacNeice's 'Cushenden' and 'The British Museum Reading Room', and Betjeman's 'Upper Lambourne', he was probably right in thinking their prose contributions inferior to the poems, and he wondered whether a tendency to 'go somewhat middlebrow' – even to regress to the standards of Sir John Squire's *London Mercury*, another of the magazines that had recently gone out of business – might not reflect 'anxiety neurosis about saving Peter W. money by making paper pay and also perhaps net something for its unpaid editors.' Whatever Connolly's own reservations, *Horizon*'s advance publicity emphasised its

> editorial policy of concentrating on literary quality, both in well-known and unknown writers, and of disregarding both the feuds of the past and the inertia of the present in their effort to synthesize the aestheticism of the Twenties and the puritanism of the Thirties into something new and better.

The magazine existed, he told readers of the *New Statesman* in a half-page advertisement which incorporated a form for new subscribers, 'to help to free writers from journalism' – ironically, some of *Horizon*'s most memorable contributions, like Woodrow Wyatt's account of advancing across Normandy with the Guards Armoured Division, and Alan Moorehead on Belsen, were to consist of reportage of a very high order, and war reporting at that – and to encourage 'such unpopular forms as the poem, the critical essay, the intimate journal, and the long short story'. Quite when Connolly began to draw a salary from *Horizon* remains unclear – according to Spender, Peter Watson was irritated by his tendency to raid the petty cash in order to pay for a lunch – but for the time being he was anxious to point out that neither of the editors nor their secretary was paid a penny, and that far from inhabiting marble-lined offices, they worked out of the back room of a flat. Spender's marriage had recently broken up – Inez Pearn had run off with the poet Charles Madge – so he made his flat in Lansdowne Terrace, in Bloomsbury, available to *Horizon*, reserving only the bedroom to himself. Tony Witherby was lodging nearby with the painter Robert Buhler and his wife; and whenever Connolly rejected a poem which his colleague particularly admired, Spender would leap on his bike and work off his anger by pedalling furiously round the block.

Trying to keep track of the various assistants, secretaries and business managers who worked on *Horizon* is an impossibly complicated business. A pattern emerged in due course, but in the early days in particular much seems to have depended on who was available and what needed to be done, with various friends and acquaintances holding the fort until Connolly made his belated appearance, as often as not after noon. Bill Makins, the business manager, was an early appointment: Connolly had expected a sober Lowland Scot, but found himself working instead with a bearded Highlander in a kilt with an insatiable appetite for women, drink and publishing gossip.* The magazine's first secretary was Spender's friend Tony Hyndman, and thereafter a shifting population of either sex worked as secretaries-cum-editorial assistants-cum readers, among them Tony Bower, the novelist Anna Kavan, Celia Paget, and a good-looking young man called Michael Nelson, who had been expelled from Bryanston, where he had been a contemporary of Lucian Freud's, and attached himself to Peter Watson, who found him – in Spender's words – 'very ornamental'.†

* Makins – who doubled up as a literary agent – is most memorably described in Julian Maclaren-Ross's *Memoirs of the Forties*, the best and funniest account of bohemian literary life at the time. Makins later joined up, and temporarily renounced alcohol and tobacco; Maclaren-Ross was distressed to learn from his widow that he had been burned to death in a fire in Cairo, but shortly after the war had ended he found himself standing next to him at the bar of The Wheatsheaf in Fitzroy Street.

† Years later, Nelson published – anonymously – a *roman à clef* entitled *A Room in Chelsea Square*, in which *Horizon* was transmuted into a fashion magazine, and Connolly, Watson and Spender made caricature appearances. 'Ronnie Gras', the Connolly figure, has 'the physiognomy of an ape and a mind of the most intricate and delicate pattern'; like his original, he spends much of the morning in bed, feasting off bunches of grapes brought to him by adoring female acolytes.

But none had the glamour or the good looks or the grave, almost reverential devotion of the *Horizon* girls whom Evelyn Waugh and Nancy Mitford derided – and immortalised – in their novels and letters. In November Connolly wrote to Diana, still recuperating from her accident, to offer her a job as a reader ('remuneration will be nominal as I am afraid we cannot manage more than £90 an hour'), and she would, before long, decamp to Devon for a month with the rest of the staff; she worked on the magazine from the late spring of 1940 to the end of that year, and went on to contribute poems, stories and reviews to it. Janetta, now married to Humphrey Slater, was to make occasional appearances, shocking Evelyn Waugh – who kept his bowler firmly on his head as a protest against encroaching bohemia – by walking round the office in bare feet, so earning herself the soubriquet of 'Miss Bluefeet' and a place in his fictional pantheon: but the two longest-serving *Horizon* ladies were Lys Lubbock and Sonia Brownell; and of the two of them, Sonia Brownell most closely approximated to the ideal of a literary vestal virgin, and had by far the stronger impact on the magazine and its contents.

A forceful, good-looking girl with a leonine mane of fair hair and rounded features, Sonia Brownell had been born in India, the daughter of an army officer, and educated – more strictly than she might have wished – at the Convent of the Sacred Heart in Roehampton. Best remembered as Sonia Orwell – she married Orwell in University College Hospital, only days before he died – she continues to arouse strong feelings, both favourable and antipathetic; but even those who resented her pretentiousness, her proprietorial exclusivity towards those writers and artists whose cause she championed, and, as she grew older, her drunkenness and aggression, had to concede that she was generous, warm-hearted, hard-working, and tireless in promoting the welfare of her favourites. The painter William Coldstream had been her lover, and she had posed for several of the artists associated with the 'Euston Road' school; when she learned that Kenneth Clark had been prevented by his duties at the Ministry of Information from editing an 'art number' of *Horizon* devoted to modern British painters, she persuaded Spender that she should be allowed to do the job instead. Spender arranged for her to meet Connolly at the Café Royal; and although nothing came of the 'art number', the connection was made.* Throughout the war she

* Although – according to John Craxton – Peter Watson found their work abhorrent, she published a piece on the Euston Road school, which included Victor Pasmore, Coldstream and Claude Rogers, in the May 1941 *Horizon*. Connolly was happy enough to reproduce drawings and paintings by up-and-coming young artists like Francis Bacon, Lucian Freud and John Craxton in the magazine, and he could hardly prevent Peter Watson from commissioning articles by Robin Ironside, John Rothenstein and Herbert Read, but John Lehmann recalled how 'Cyril, over the port or brandy in the blacked-out drawing-room of the Athenaeum, was wont to complain about his inability to keep them under his control and the shudders the prose style of art critics and art enthusiasts gave him.'

worked as a clerk in a government office, only becoming full-time on *Horizon* when the war was over; her small flat in Percy Street was conveniently close, and she was a formidably fast and efficient typist, well able, in Connolly's absence, to deal with contributors, printers and, in the days of paper rationing, obtrusive government officials. Though grateful to her for the hard work she put in, Connolly had decidedly ambivalent feelings about her: he found her bossy and domineering and liked, behind her back, to charge her with lesbian leanings and an obscure desire to wreak revenge on the male sex. Such reservations were one-sided, however: according to Spender,

> Cyril fascinated her with his brilliance, funniness and non-stop need for sympathy. No one could enter more enthusiastically into the idea that he was the cause of creative genius personified, and frustrated, than Cyril. Understanding the many ways in which Cyril was misunderstood provided Sonia with a tremendous brief, which took up much time and energy. Understanding Cyril increased her pretentiousness, her lofty dismissal of all those whom he (and therefore she) considered inferior . . .

Peter Quennell used to tell a story of a drunken Dick Wyndham chasing Sonia into the fish-pond at Tickerage, and how she told her rescuer 'It isn't his trying to rape me that I mind, but that he doesn't seem to realise what Cyril stands for.'* But in Spender's view, Peter Watson – who represented no kind of sexual threat – was the real object of her adoration: 'Cyril always told me that when he went to the office of *Horizon*, if Sonia opened the door he always knew whether Peter was there; for if he was, Cyril only got thirty per cent of her smile, seventy per cent being reserved for Peter.'

Sonia's loyalty and diligence were matched only by those of Lys Lubbock – except that whereas Sonia was a formidable presence who made her views felt, Lys was generally regarded as a lightweight, a decorative flibbertigibbet with a silly, rather squeaky voice who did sterling work as a cook and housekeeper but couldn't be taken seriously where weightier matters were concerned. Waugh, who much preferred her to the other *Horizon* ladies, greatly admired her cooking and often asked his host if he couldn't borrow her occasionally. The daughter of an American father and an English mother, Lys Dunlap had been brought up in Montana. A slim, dark, graceful girl who did occasional work as a model, she had been briefly engaged to the poet Gavin Ewart; but since he had no job and no money, nothing came of this, and she married instead an actor called Ian Lubbock,

* According to Nancy Mitford, the rapist in question was John Heygate, who had run off with Waugh's first wife, Evelyn Gardner; but since she conveyed the information in a letter to Waugh, she may well be a tainted source.

the son of an Eton housemaster and a member of a family long associated with the school. She was keen on the idea of being bohemian and leading the literary life; and after her marriage had become unstitched she had an affair with Peter Quennell, who introduced her to Connolly. She and Connolly were to live together throughout the 1940s. 'David Herbert said you had plain new girl like small black pig ugh', Jeannie cabled from New York. Formally uneducated, Lys may well have been a good deal brighter and better read than was generally assumed, and although it was generally agreed that Connolly, like most of his friends, treated her like a slightly slow-witted skivvy, he loved her too in his tortured, ambivalent way; never more so than when, after some ten years together, she decided that the time had come for them to go their separate ways. Lys, for her part, seems to have been passionate about her mercurial admirer – even going so far as to change her surname to Connolly, as a result of which several friends assumed that they were married at last, and wrote to congratulate the happy couple – and was understandably bruised at being taken so long for granted.

*

One of the tasks Connolly was to set himself as editor of *Horizon* was composing 'Comment', a monthly editorial at the front of the magazine. Early in October 1939 he published in the *New Statesman* an article entitled 'The Ivory Shelter', which gave advance warning of the way his mind was working. Now that war had finally broken out, writers were 'less free' than ever before; it was no longer possible for them to emulate Auden and Isherwood and flee the country, and they were instead 'concentrated indefinitely on an island from which the sun is hourly receding'. The Nazi-Soviet Pact and the outbreak of war had had two beneficial side-effects on writers, in that they had been able to throw off both the 'burden of anti-Fascist activities' and the 'subtler burden of pro-Communist activities'. 'It is a quality of an artist to be more imaginative and more truthful than his fellow-men,' Connolly continued, but in recent years 'this greater sensibility and objectivity have wrecked themselves in political causes, and forced political realities on many who would have been stronger exempt from them.' Now that war had broken out, the fight against fascism could be left to the General Staff, and the best advice he could give his fellow-writers was 'keep off the war'. During the last war, so-called 'escapists' like Joyce, Firbank, Norman Douglas and Lytton Strachey had produced much of their finest work; war provided writers with the chance to look after their own interests, for 'the best modern war literature is pacifist and escapist, and either ignores the war, or condemns it, with the lapse of time.' Nostalgia, he concluded, would return as 'one of the soundest creative emotions, whether it is for the sun, or the snow, or the freedom which the democracies have had temporarily to discontinue. War is a tin can tied to the tail of civilisation; it is also an opportunity for the artist to give us nothing but the best, and to stop his ears.'

As yet the war was only a few days old, and another year would pass before German bombing raids brought it home to those writers and readers who hadn't joined up; but if Connolly's own nostalgia, his sense of being incarcerated in a grey and grim-seeming island, were more rarefied than some – and was to achieve its most lasting expression a few years later in *The Unquiet Grave* – his political disaffection was shared by many of those whose commitment had, until recently, been more whole-hearted and less sceptical than his. Although 'Communist energy is unimpeachable, their pretensions to being more right than other people would appear to be shattered'; and even if, following the announcement of the Nazi-Soviet Pact, left-wing writers like Spender and Lehmann still felt that their general position was correct, in that 'poets, and other creative artists, cannot, if they are to remain fully living people, if they are to fulfil their function as interpreters of their time to their own generation, fail to interest themselves in the meaning behind political ideas and political power,' writers should 'remain true to their different, highly specialised and difficult task' rather than try to 'turn themselves into half-baked and half-hearted politicians'.

> There can be little doubt that somewhere between the Munich sell-out of last September and the defeat of the Spanish Republicans early this year, a significant change began to develop in the attitude of the literary and artistic 'left'. There are signs, not merely of a bitter disillusionment about the real power and meaning of democracy in England, but also a bitter revulsion from all political platforms. Many young writers and artists seem to be feeling now that they put too much trust in parties and catchwords, and that a withdrawal is necessary in self-defence,

Lehmann had suggested in the *New Statesman* the day before war broke out – an attitude that was shared by Spender in 'How Shall We Be Saved?', his contribution to the first number of *Horizon*. Connolly's own loudly proclaimed indifference to politics and the progress of the war was to prove more ambivalent and more diluted than 'The Ivory Shelter' and his early 'Comments' might suggest, partly under the pressure of circumstances and partly as a result of some hostile criticism; but in these early months of the war he succeeded, not for the last time, in catching the mood of the moment. That moment was, he declared in his opening 'Comment',

> archaistic, conservative and irresponsible, for the war is separating culture from life and driving it back on itself, the impetus given by Left Wing politics is for the time exhausted, and however much we should like to have a paper that was revolutionary in opinions or original in technique, it is impossible to do so when there is a certain suspension of judgement and creative activity. The aim of *Horizon* is to give to writers a place to express themselves, and to readers the best writing we can obtain. Our standards are aesthetic, and our politics are in abeyance. This will not always be the case, because as events take shape the policy of artists and intellectuals will become clearer... At the moment civilisation is on the operating table and we sit in the waiting-room.

Finished copies of the first issue arrived from the printers in mid-December 1939. W.H. Smith had restricted their order to 250 copies – something of 'a blow', Connolly told Diana – but the *Listener* and the *New Statesman* had already run half-page announcements ('With an almost parental mixture of hope and anxiety *The New Statesman & Nation* wishes good luck to this new monthly'), Desmond MacCarthy wrote approvingly in the *Sunday Times*, and although he had failed to come up with a contribution, E.M. Forster made favourable mention of the new magazine over the wireless.* In addition to the poems already mentioned, it included a short story by H.E. Bates, topical pieces about the war and its effects by Herbert Read, J.B. Priestley and Spender, Geoffrey Grigson on new poetry, and 'The Ant Lion', one of Connolly's most admired essays, in which he contrasts the conflicting claims of art and life (and ultimately opts for art).

In his February 1940 'Comment', Connolly told his readers that although the first issue of the magazine had sold out in a week, it had been attacked for being middlebrow, Georgian and old-fashioned, and for printing J.B. Priestley and H.E. Bates rather than the modern equivalents of Eliot and Joyce; to which he could only reply that *Horizon*

> makes no more apology for Priestley's admirable essay, or Sir Hugh Walpole's revealing glimpse of Henry James, than it does for Orwell's analysis of Boys' papers or Auden's elegy on Freud which will appear in the next number. Names mean nothing. *Horizon* is not to be judged by its names but by the quality of its contents...

As for John Piper's lettering cover, it was not old-fashioned but out of fashion, in much the same way as good writing was out of fashion; and

* Forster did in fact contribute an essay on 'The New Disorder' to the December 1941 issue.

when, after four issues, it was time to find a new printer, Connolly turned to an appropriately traditional and first-rate practitioner in the form of Oliver Simon. Greatly admired in the trade both as a craftsman and for his theoretical writings on typography, Simon was a founder-member of the Fleuron Society and the Double Crown Club; a gastronome as well as a literary man, he had printed both *Life and Letters* and the journal of the Wine and Food Society, and in the middle of the war he was to be honoured with a grand dinner at L'Ecu de France, attended by – among others – Connolly, Peter Watson and Major Connolly's admirer, André Simon. He was a stickler for detail, and kept a ferocious eye out for possible libels and obscenities for which, as the printer, he could be held jointly responsible, protesting on more than one occasion that the Curwen Press could not possibly set some 'irresponsible and possibly mischievous article'; once, in the early days, Janetta, Peter Watson and Mary Keene (who later married the painter Matthew Smith) spent an entire day at the Press removing the word 'bugger' from 6,000 copies, and carefully writing in a replacement in Indian ink. Years later, Connolly remembered how Simon

> would enter the office about tea-time with a smile and a kind word for everyone, his pockets bulging with ornate borders and swelled rules, his friendly, fastidious, mildly inquisitive face suggesting some popular padre arriving at the canteen. But, the initial courtesies over, there would often follow an explosion, the rules and borders be flung aside, and an offending manuscript appear, covered with blue pencil marks – 'Nonsense, unthinkable gibberish. No printer would set this up' or 'Do you want us all to go to prison?' Worst were the ultimatums delivered in a quiet, breezy *dies irae* voice: 'If the pages are cut to sixty-four and there are no more illustrations, you have paper for just one more number . . .'

But when it came to the vexed matter of paper rations, Connolly had friends in high places: although Duff Cooper, the Minister of Information, was never a close friend or admirer, his Under Secretary, Harold Nicolson, was able to promote *Horizon*'s interests for as long as he was in the job; and by the time he left the worst was over.

At a planning meeting in September, Spender had 'pressed that there should be features on the subject of Culture and War, so that we should be able to keep a constant criticism of how broadcasting, publishing, music, art are going', while Peter Watson was firmly opposed to the idea that art could be divorced from its social context, but Connolly continued to elaborate his ideas about the incompatibility of war and writing in the months that lay ahead. In the same 'Comment' in which he defied his critics, he famously acclaimed the departure of Auden and Isherwood as 'the most important literary event since the outbreak of the Spanish War' and 'a symptom of the failure of social realism as an aesthetic doctrine'. A reaction against the 'committed' writing of the 1930s was both 'necessary and salutary', for

> it must be restated that writing is an art, that it is an end in itself as well as a means to an end, and that good writing, like all art, is capable of producing a deep and satisfying emotion in the reader whether it is about Mozart, the fate of Austria, or the habit of bees. Since the Marxist attack ten years ago this fact has been lost sight of, and it is our duty gradually to re-educate the peppery palates of our detractors to an appreciation of delicate poetry and fine prose.

One of the recurrent themes of his 'Comments' – which were to grow increasingly infrequent with the passing of time and the waning of his own interest – was the writer's relationship with society: initially with the war itself, and then – as the prospects of victory grew brighter – with the benign, all-providing state which *Horizon*, like Penguin Books and *Picture Post*, hoped and believed would be ushered in once hostilities were over. The artist, Connolly told his readers in April, sat holding out his begging-bowl 'in the shadow of the volcano'. 'Many people,' he went on,

> would accept the idea of a benevolent world socialism as their political aim, a world in which all the resources were available to its inhabitants, in which heat and fuel and food were as free as air, in which Marx's familiar definition of an ultimate civilisation, 'to each according to his needs, from each according to his ability', was made good. But this world does nothing for the spiritual life of humanity except to provide for all its inhabitants the material comfort and security which has hitherto provided the point of departure of the few.

In the meantime, though, 'the almond blossom is out, the sun shines, the streets look shabbier, and the war slowly permeates into our ways of living,' while 'the intellectuals recoil from the war as if it were a best-seller. They are enough ahead of their time to despise it, and yet they must realise that they nevertheless represent the culture that is being defended.' The war, he declared,

> is the enemy of creative activity, and writers and painters are wise and right to ignore it and to concentrate their talents on other subjects. Since they are politically impotent, they can use this time to develop at deeper

> emotional levels, or to improve their weapons by technical experiment, for they have been so long mobilised in various causes that they are losing the intellectual's greatest virtues: the desire to pursue the truth wherever it may lead, and the belief in the human mind as the supreme organ through which life can be apprehended, improved and intensified.

For one reader at least, Connolly's insistence that writers should turn their backs on the war was asking too much of those who were expected to risk their lives so that they should be free to do so. Whereas Connolly, as the editor of a magazine, was in a 'reserved' occupation and so exempt from the call-up, the writer and academic Goronwy Rees had voluntarily enrolled shortly after the outbreak of war, and was now serving as a second lieutenant in the Royal Welch Fusiliers; and he wrote from 35 Welsh Divisional HQ to say that although he had no desire to insist on writers taking up arms, yet

> the soldier has the right, in return for his blood and his life and his despair, for the crimes he must take on himself, to ask that those most qualified, by their sensibility, by their more lucid perception of values, by their release from belligerence, should comprehend, analyse, illuminate, commemorate, his sacrifice and his suffering and the horror to which he is condemned, to understand and reveal that even in war he is a human being and not a brute too ignoble for the artist's notice; most of all he has the right to ask this because the values which he, poor devil, dimly feels that he is called upon to defend are those without which the artist cannot live, and because the soldier will now fight for his dim comprehension as no man ever fought before. A million men, and more, will die and the artist will live and create; and apparently he is to accept the fruit of this sacrifice as a free gift and acknowledge no responsibility to the giver.

Rees's 'Letter from a Soldier' was a noble and eloquent piece of work and, much to his credit, Connolly printed it at the front of the July 1940 issue, occupying the space usually reserved for 'Comment', and publishing his answer at the far end of the magazine.* He conceded that 'we cannot afford the airy detachment of earlier numbers. We have walked through the tiger-house, speculating on the power and ferocity of the beasts, and looked up to find the cage doors open'; but he still believed that writers would be better employed 'creating more culture as fast as they can', and that war remained

* Among those who wrote to congratulate Rees on his article was Guy Burgess (q.v.). In the second of his two volumes of autobiography, Rees recalled that 'at that time in England there was still a feeling that for an intellectual to be a soldier was in some way beneath his dignity and a waste of his talents . . . there was something immoral and absurd about being a soldier.'

the enemy of creative activity. He ended by taking another swipe at the blimpish, discredited elder statesmen – lovers of golf and P.G. Wodehouse to a man, no doubt – whose feeble-spirited connivance at the earlier aggression of Hitler, Mussolini and Franco had made war inevitable; in due course, he hoped, they would be replaced by a generation of technocrats and meritocrats, who would be more sympathetic to the claims of the artist, and share *Horizon*'s belief that 'the armies which defeat Hitler will be revolutionary armies, and the only thing which can defeat National Socialism is international socialism.' Connolly's socialism, never the sturdiest of growths, proved increasingly hard to reconcile with his libertarian fear of the tentacular, omnipotent state; after the German invasion of Russia in the summer of 1941, he announced that it was 'no longer possible for anyone to stand back and call the war an imperialist war', and – much to Evelyn Waugh's derision – joined Arthur Calder-Marshall, Bonamy Dobrée, Tom Harrisson, Arthur Koestler, Alun Lewis, George Orwell and Stephen Spender in producing a manifesto entitled 'Why not War Writers?', published in *Horizon*, in which they declared that 'Experience of two years of war has shown to writers that their function is to write a good book about the war *now*', and demanded that writers be given the same facilities as war artists and photographers.

During all this time, Connolly was learning the business of being a magazine editor. He was, Spender later suggested, a 'born editor', in that he 'took a vicarious pleasure in publishing the best works and the best writers as though they were by him, and he was bold in choosing things simply because of their content, without attempting to iron out faults of style which were idiosyncratic to their authors.' Peter Watson once remarked that Connolly was a brilliant editor 'because he's like a brothel-keeper, offering his writers to the public as though they were the girls, and himself carrying on a flirtation with them' – an analogy which Spender sustained in his autobiography:

> As an editor he was like a cook, producing with each new number a new dish with a new flavour. Sometimes the readers objected, finding it too light, too sweet, too lumpy or too stodgy, but he had somehow created in them a need to taste more. Or, to change the metaphor, he carried on a kind of editorial flirtation with his readers, so that they were all in some peculiar way admitted to his moods, his tastes, his whims, his fantasies, his generous giving of himself, combined with his temperamental coyness.

Looking back on his days at *Horizon*, Connolly himself wrote that

> Editing a magazine is a form of the good life; it is creating when the world is destroying, helping where it is hindering; being given once a month the opportunity to produce a perfect number and every month failing, and just when despair sets in, being presented with one more chance. Flop! the afternoon post falls on the carpet, the letter-box becomes a periscope on the outside world, encouragement arrives and fat subscriptions, letters from California and Brazil, contributions from all over the world...

'Are you certain that anyone will want to read it in twenty years?' he would ask Spender when considering whether or not to print a particular poem; for 'although Cyril was inconsistent, being energetic, enthusiastic, indolent, interested and bored by turns, he held his own views passionately and, on the whole, with judgement; and he faced adverse criticism with an equanimity which astonished me, as I knew him (in personal relationships, at any rate) to care greatly whether he was or wasn't liked.'

Ultimately, Spender conceded, 'the strength of *Horizon* lay not in its having any defined cultural or political policy, but in the vitality and idiosyncrasy of its editor. I, who started out with concern for planning post-war Britain, defending democracy, encouraging young writers and so forth, was disconcerted to find myself with an editor who showed little sense of responsibility about these things.' That was well said; but although *Horizon* was a mighty and noble achievement, both in itself and as a beacon of good writing and clear thinking, what strikes one most in retrospect is the editorial eclecticism, the mixture of old and young, traditional and mildly modernist. A.J.A. Symons, Osbert Sitwell and Logan Pearsall Smith rubbed shoulders with George Orwell and Henry Miller, Lawrence Binyon with Gavin Ewart, Dylan Thomas and Laurie Lee, Shane Leslie and Hugh Kingsmill with Clement Greenberg and Anna Kavan. Patrick White, Hugh Trevor-Roper, Noël Annan, Peter Ustinov and Michael Wharton made early appearances in its pages; space was given over to young artists like John Craxton and Victor Pasmore, and reclining figures by Henry Moore confronted the very first 'Comment' of all; Auden, Betjeman, MacNeice and Dylan Thomas published many of their best-known poems there, including Auden's 'The Fall of Rome', dedicated to its editor; topical items appeared from H.G. Wells, Richard Crossman, Roy Harrod and Mervyn Stockwood ('The Church and Reconstruction'). A ripple of excitement ran through the office when a genuine slice of working-class life, describing working in a coal-mine, was submitted and accepted – dimmed somewhat when it turned out that the author, Gully Mason, who was later killed in the Battle of Britain, was an old Etonian whose family owned the mine; 'Please tell me who is George Orwell? His article is *splendid*,' Peter Watson minuted

Connolly after the appearance of 'Boys' Weeklies' in March 1940,* though he went on to wish that Peter Quennell would abandon his rarefied *New Statesman* manner ('more guts needed'); a jubilant young fighter pilot, Rollo Woolley – Janetta's brother – scrawled 'MY STORY ACCEPTED IN HORIZON' over a full page of his diary, but was killed in North Africa shortly afterwards.

Finding new authors is one of the criteria by which a magazine editor is invariably judged, and Connolly was perhaps too respectful of existing reputations, too worried about what people might think, to run as many risks with new writers as – say – John Lehmann or, in more recent years, Alan Ross on the *London Magazine*. Two years after the war ended, Angus Wilson was encouraged by Robin Ironside to submit a short story entitled 'Mother's Sense of Fun', so initiating his writing career; but Connolly's finest discoveries were two oddities of genius, Denton Welch and Julian Maclaren-Ross, both of whom must be among the funniest and most vivid chroniclers of their time, and both of whom have suffered from being too eccentric and too uncategorisable, inhabiting lurid autobiographical landscapes, immediately recognisable as their own. A waspish, effeminate young painter, half-paralysed as a result of an accident, Welch published an unusual and highly comical memoir of Sickert in the August 1942 issue. Two years later *Horizon* published a story called 'When I was Thirteen', which prompted a four-page letter from Edith Sitwell in which she revealed that she and Osbert had 'laughed till they cried', and another from Hamish Hamilton asking if there was a book in the offing. The story gave a strong homosexual frisson, and when a reader wrote in to object, Connolly leapt to his author's defence, signing off with 'It seems to me that it is you who have deteriorated in the last four years, and not *Horizon*, for I can hardly imagine that the author of your letter can ever once have been the kind of reader whom we hoped to cater for.'

A legendary figure in post-war Soho and Fitzrovia, Julian Maclaren-Ross had spent much of the 1930s working as a vacuum-cleaner salesman in Bognor Regis. He had joined up in 1939, and his experiences as a conscript provided the raw material for two collections of stories, *The Stuff to Give the Troops* and *Better than a Kick in the Pants*. Early on in the war, Maclaren-Ross – who was permanently broke – sent *Horizon* a story entitled 'A Bit of a Smash in Madras'. He heard nothing, and eventually wrote to Connolly to ask for his story back, at which he received a postcard, written in Connolly's familiar green ink, which read 'Hold on, MS filed in error, just been found,

* Two issues later, Connolly printed an equally splendid response to Orwell's piece by Frank Richards, the creator of Billy Bunter. Orwell's other contributions to *Horizon* included 'The Art of Donald McGill', 'Raffles and Miss Blandish' and 'Politics and the English Language'.

now being read.' Shortly afterwards, Connolly wrote to say that they would like to publish his story, paying their usual rates of two guineas per thousand words. Connolly suggested that Maclaren-Ross might like to call in at the offices to discuss his writing, so he made his way to Lansdowne Terrace, 'a row of small smoky dun-brick houses built all alike, with big blank front windows facing a children's playground'.

Maclaren-Ross was a keen admirer of *Enemies of Promise*, and his only idea of what Connolly looked like was drawn from the frontispiece photograph of the black-jacketed Eton schoolboy, his top hat resting on protruding ears. As it was, the editor's 'face was round, plump and pale, his shoulders sloped from a short thick neck, and dark hair was fluffed thickly out behind the ears that no longer seemed to protrude. He had a short snub Irish nose and under shaggy brows his eyes, set far apart, looked both hooded and alert.' He walked 'as if with slippered feet though in fact he wore suede shoes', and he was dressed in 'the housemaster's outfit affected by many writers of the Thirties – tweed jacket, woollen tie, grey flannels baggy at the knee.' Connolly suggested that they should meet next day in the Café Royal, where he often held court. Bill Makins, with whom Maclaren-Ross had been out drinking the night before, had hinted that Connolly might not in fact publish some of his other stories; Maclaren-Ross was determined to have it out with him, but

> at sight of Connolly my resolve at once began to falter. He was in the upstairs bar as arranged, sitting on a sofa near the door with a bulging leather satchel beside him and galley proofs unfurled upon his knee. His round plump face looked mild enough and he even smiled as he saw me, nonetheless he was clearly not a man amenable to direct questioning (though fond of it himself), and he had a built-in resistance to such an approach.

No mention was made of the stories, but instead Connolly passed his companion a set of proofs of Maugham's article on detective stories, and asked him for his opinion. Maclaren-Ross read it, pronounced it to be good, and asked Connolly for his views:

> Connolly had folded up the galleys and was thrusting them deep into his satchel from which other proofs protruded. He succeeded at last in pulling the straps through the fastening buckles, the satchel by now at bursting point was rolled aside like an antagonist whom he had bound and gagged, and he settled himself more comfortably on the sofa. Only then did he reply.
>
> 'No,' he said. 'I don't think it's a good article.'

'You don't?' I echoed in dismay.

Benignly smiling, Connolly shook his head. 'In fact I've decided not to print it.'

'Not print it,' I gasped. 'But it's by Maugham!'

'I have the greatest respect for Maugham as a novelist,' Connolly said in his soft bland voice, 'and I don't say this is a *bad* article. It's good enough to be accepted for *Horizon*, but not quite good enough for me to publish.'*

In an unpublished memoir from 1942 entitled 'Dialogue between Ego and Superego', Connolly remarked on how 'as soon as I say anything I cease to believe it. I cannot make any statement without seeing its opposite reflected in my mind's eye.' If 'the real coward is a charmer, he ingratiates himself with everybody, he sees both sides of the question because he doesn't see one,' then

> editing a magazine is perhaps the only occupation in which my lack of belief in anything or anyone, and my ambivalence, my passionate belief in the BOTH, can be turned to advantage. In a writer this causes sterility, in an editor it is called 'readiness to give the other side a hearing'. I believe in God the Either, God the Or, and God the Holy Both.

This sense of ambivalence and detachment, so much commoner than the committed would have us believe, and seldom so honestly diagnosed, was something to which he would return a year or two later in an early draft of *The Unquiet Grave*, where – reflecting on those who for ever hover on the edge, observers rather than participants – he wrote that

> they will not kill, they will not compete, they will not boast, they will not join groups of more than six, they will not condemn, they are 'abandoners

* Maclaren-Ross's *Memoirs of the Forties* was published a quarter of a century later; like many of the best stories, this has been embellished by time and authorial licence. Stephen Spender told the same story, only the part of Maugham was played by an angry, bearded stranger who rushed up to a terrified Connolly in Venice after the war, accusing him of accepting but then failing to publish something he had written and eliciting the same response. On the fly-leaf of Anthony Hobson's copy of Maclaren-Ross's book Connolly wrote that

> I can remember almost nothing about these incidents. I am sure I did not have a bulging satchel, as I invented one for the imaginary self-portrait in *The Unquiet Grave*. I did once accept an article and tell the author that it was good enough to accept but not good enough to publish – but not Somerset Maugham, who sent me the detective story article for nothing and which I returned, saying I did not think it would add to his reputation (too frivolous for wartime). Maclaren-Ross was kept out of our offices as much as possible on account of his grand passion for Sonia, who was embarrassed by it.

He went on to deny wearing a 'housemaster's outfit' – 'in fact wore a tweed suit with silk tie'. Maclaren-Ross's hopeless passion for Sonia Brownell was shared by G.W. Stonier of the *New Statesman*, soon to achieve fame as the author of *Shaving Through the Blitz*; his pleasure at seeing his work in print was marred by his name being mis-spelt as 'Maclaryn' – a solecism perpetuated by Spender, who sent on to John Lehmann at *New Writing* some poems by Laurie Lee and W.R. Rodgers, and work by 'Maclaryn-Ross'.

> of revels, mute, contemplative', they are depressed by gossip, praise and success, they wait to be telephoned, they look sadder than they are, and they do not speak in public, or make use of their friends, or take revenge on their enemies. They do not lay down the law because they see, as a painter sees a complementary colour, outlined against any statement the shadow of its opposite.

Any worthwhile magazine will mirror the taste and the beliefs of its editor; and over its ten-year span *Horizon* reflected not just Connolly's passions and enthusiasms – some long-lasting, some ephemeral, most understandable, a few inexplicable – but his doubts, his uncertainties, his changeability, his liability to lose interest or be distracted; all those human weaknesses which proved so inimical to the writing of full-length works, but made him, as a miniaturist of the human heart, the most sympathetic and intuitive of writers as well as an outstanding editor.

*

In July 1940 Peter Watson rented from a relation of Michael Nelson a seaside house in Thurlstone, in South Devon, and he asked Connolly and Diana if they would like to join him there and work on the magazine away from London. The Beach House was an ugly bungalow, full of draughts and banging doors. Peter and Diana ran the place and did all the housework; apart from shrimping in the rock pools, his trousers rolled up to his knees, Connolly spent his days brooding on the sofa, nipping up to London, and watching the air raids lighting up the sky over Plymouth. 'I hear from Stephen that you are beginning to enjoy the spectacle of conflict and stand on the cliffs with the wind in your hair and shrapnel pattering down around you,' Peter Quennell wrote from London, addressing his old friend by Peter Watson's pet name for him of 'Squirrel', and passing his love on to 'darling Biz'. Visitors to Thurlstone included Janetta, Brian Howard and Tony Hyndman, and Michael Nelson and Lucian Freud came over from Dartington; with invasion rumours still doing the rounds, Connolly and the rest of the *Horizon* party were mistaken for German spies by the locals.*

* Earlier in the year, Connolly had been interrogated by a military policeman in the Randolph Hotel in Oxford. He was sitting alone in the lounge at half-past eleven at night, near a group of soldiers who were discussing the evacuation at Dunkirk. One of the officers thought Connolly was eavesdropping; he was unable to produce his identity card, and matters looked graver still when he revealed that not only had he an Irish name, but his passport had been issued in Austria in 1937. Producing a copy of *Horizon*, with his name on the title page, cut little ice – and still less so when it was shown to contain paintings of male nudes, albeit by Burne-Jones. Only when Connolly revealed that he had been to Eton, and was able to prove it as well, did his interrogators begin to thaw. Despite his dislike for the place, Connolly briefly contemplated moving the *Horizon* office to Oxford – which may explain his presence there.

No sooner had Connolly returned to London, after a month away, than it was Spender's turn to try his luck in the West Country. He was offered a job teaching at Blundell's, and was away for the whole of the winter term; but he decided that teaching was not for him, came back to London, and joined the National Fire Service, his fireman's uniform becoming a familiar sight on the wartime literary and social scene. From Blundell's he was in touch with John Lehmann about the possibility of his writing a monthly column on books for *Penguin New Writing*; and although he worried that *Horizon* might be unable to keep going without his active participation – 'Whereas Cyril is very hesitant, Peter wants to carry on', he reported in October 1940 – he began to withdraw from day-to-day involvement with the magazine. In the meantime, however, riding two editorial horses proved at times a complicated business ('Could you get me another copy of *The Thirties*, as I used *Horizon*'s copy for you,' he asked Lehmann, apropos Malcolm Muggeridge's book: 'I'll then send off this copy for *Horizon* to review...').

Teaching public schoolboys may have been uncongenial, but at least Spender was spared the onslaught of the Blitz, which began on 7 September and continued for the next fifty-seven nights. By now Connolly was living at Athenaeum Court, a block of service flats off Piccadilly. 'There is a little colony of chums at the Athenaeum Court – Cyril Connolly, Brian Howard, Peter Watson,' Nancy Mitford informed Violet Hammersley in November: 'Robert [Byron] says Cyril is happier than at any time in his life.' A month later she returned to the subject: 'Cyril, Hog Watson and many another lefty are avoiding military service by dint of being editors of a magazine which is a reserved occupation isn't it brilliant. Jeannie has fled to California but Cyril has managed to nab her 1200 a year and lives with a glamorous houri on the proceeds. How can they I mean the houris...' Earlier in the year a rather more reliable witness, George Orwell, had reported Connolly as forecasting widespread panic once the bombs began to fall, as well as moves to get intellectuals' police records destroyed by Scotland Yard, since it was well-known that Hitler would show no mercy to left-wing thinkers if his invasion plans succeeded. Orwell recorded

> sitting in Connolly's top-floor flat and watching the enormous fires beyond St Paul's, and the great plume of smoke from an oil drum somewhere down the river, and Hugh Slater sitting in the window and saying 'It's just like Madrid – quite nostalgic.' The only person suitably impressed was Connolly, who took us up on the roof and, after gazing for some time at the fire, said 'It's the end of capitalism. It's a judgement

on us.' I didn't feel this to be so, but was chiefly struck by the size and beauty of the flames.*

Bloomsbury was far from immune to the bombing: at one stage the office had to be closed for a fortnight, the Woolfs' flat in nearby Mecklenburgh Square was badly damaged, and Lys Lubbock recalled how a woman was killed in front of them, and her severed hand was found lying by the area railing.

Although Connolly did his weekly stint of fire-watching – Peter Quennell remembered him setting off for the roof 'carrying a case of cigars, a hot water bottle and a heavy tartan rug' – working in a reserved occupation and avoiding military service awoke in him a familiar blend of guilt and resentment. 'We don't know what our aims are yet / But take it from me they'll be high / And when the real show starts you bet / We'll all know how to die,' he had written, satirically, to Betjeman two months before the outbreak of war; and although he was anxious to point out that the life of a civilian in a city like London was every bit as hazardous and austere as that of the average serviceman, while lacking the compensatory glamour a uniform bestowed, the feelings of inadequacy remained. 'Cyril came here for the day and seemed very sadly out-of-touch and unchanged and rather old-fashioned. By old-fashioned I mean pre-war. I think he was depressed by not actually having any war work,' Georgiana Blakiston reported in August 1942 from Clandon Park in Surrey, where the Public Records Office – and with it the Blakiston family – had been re-housed for the duration; while Philip Toynbee – a young contributor to *Horizon* whom Connolly met from time to time in the Museum Tavern, off Great Russell Street – remembered going on a walking tour of Devon with Connolly and Lys, and Connolly chanting 'We don't like the sex war / We don't like the class war / We don't like the next war / We don't like the last war / WE DON'T LIKE THE WAR'. Connolly's feelings of guilt and resentment were brilliantly summarised in his celebrated 'Letter from a Civilian', published in the September 1944 *Horizon*, in which he thanked a pseudonymous contributor ('Victor')† for the camemberts he had kindly sent him from Normandy, before proceeding to compare the lot of the ground-down, sun-starved,

* 'Hugh' Slater was Janetta's husband Humphrey: a veteran of the Spanish Civil War, he was then serving with the Home Guard at Osterley.

† In fact the future MP Woodrow Wyatt, then serving with the Guards Armoured Division. 'When the tin arrived my first thought from the smell was *Quelle mauvaise plaisanterie*, as Madame du Deffand said when she felt Gibbon's face and thought it was his behind,' Connolly wrote: 'Finding it was from you reassured me and I opened it to find two *bien coulant* and quite wonderful camemberts...' As editor of the annual anthology, *English Story*, Wyatt published – among others – Denton Welch, William Sansom and Julian Maclaren-Ross.

under-nourished civilian, crunching along glass-bespattered streets, ration book in one hand, gas mask in the other, with the *réclame* and the exotic cheeses and the opportunities for travel afforded the man-at-arms. 'That it is brilliantly amusing you know very well, but it also says something that no one has said before and that I for one have ached to see said,' wrote Brian Howard, then serving, improbably, with the RAF, but soon to be discharged as physically below par.

Looking back on those years from old age, Connolly wrote that

> I spent nearly the whole war in London, from the great raids of September 1940 to the last doodlebugs and V2s. I waded through broken glass, brick dust, charred beams, unexploded bombs. I dined out many nights and seemed to lead a charmed life. I remember all the noises: tearing sheets, the Bofors guns like giants playing squash, the taxi-cry from street to street, the sweet smell of burned flesh; the sights – houses ripped apart, with a different stratum of civilisation exposed on every floor up to the servants' lavatory on the top; the hideous black or green cloth or Utility everything, moorhen or porpoise on the fishmonger's slab, the trains coming to a stop against the glare of burning streets, the whistles, the rumours, the wireless with the evening news like the angelus, the terrible tunes and dances, the anti-intellectualism ('After all, there *is* a war on').

Like John Lehmann, he inhabited

> the new symbolic city of the blackout, where one floundered about in the unaccustomed darkness of the streets, bumping into patrolling wardens or huddled strangers, hailing taxis that crept along learning their new element, admiring the gigantic criss-crossing arms of the searchlights as they lit up the sudden silver bellies of the far balloons or scurrying clouds on winter nights, and found new beauty, when it was fine and still, in the fall of moonlight on pavements and pillars and high window embrasures

– an effect most memorably caught by Connolly's friend Elizabeth Bowen. But Connolly being Connolly, humour kept breaking through. His immediate reaction to those who criticised *Horizon* for turning its back on the war was to commission an incongruous article by Major-General J.F.C. Fuller, a First World War tank expert with extremely right-wing views, which Connolly himself then followed up (and ridiculed) with an article in the *New Statesman* entitled 'What Will *He* Do Next?', in which he instructed those eager to do their bit against invading German hordes on how to build anti-tank traps with a spade and brown paper; and when, towards the end of the war, he told Harold Nicolson that he was frightened by the doodlebugs then raining down on London, Nicolson told him

> he ought to think of his dear ones at the front who are in far greater danger than he is. 'That wouldn't work with me, Harold. In the first place, I have no dear ones at the front. And in the second, I have observed with me that perfect fear casteth out love.'

*

Summing up at the end of his first year as editor, in his December 1940 'Comment', Connolly was blunt about the commercial difficulties facing *Horizon*: 'One of us, *Horizon* or its public, has failed the other,' he suggested, so 'let us have some recriminations.' There should be ten thousand people ready to pay a shilling for his magazine, but 'after a year still half of them are in hiding.' He then went on to list the specific difficulties he faced, including the 'Apathy of the Great' (the failure of Shaw, Gide, Eliot and the Woolfs to contribute), the 'Decay of the Reading Public' and the 'Collapse of Contributors': many of the young writers he hoped to attract as contributors were in the armed forces and 'too busy, too tired, too listless, or too much the victim of their own rude health to write a line', with the result that he had to fall back on journalists, pacifists, the elderly and the under-twenties. The editors themselves were, inevitably, liable to the 'faults of the amateur' – 'periods of intense energy, interspersed with long lulls of sloth', and straightforward 'errors of judgement': all of which had encouraged 'that body of permanent and implacable detractors without which any new magazine must feel lost and lonely':

> Most of these wicked godmothers, by a coincidence, have themselves had considerable experience of editing literary magazines. It must seem scarcely credible to them that a magazine as bad as *Horizon*, one in which incompetency vies with corruption, where the editors have not been on speaking terms for months, but sit sullenly burning manuscripts in different corners of the room, can come out at all.

The most eloquent – and persistent – of these 'wicked godmothers' was Julian Symons, later apostrophised by his victim as 'the fox without a tail' after he had resumed his attacks on *Horizon* as a 'neo-Georgian paper with modernist overtones'. Symons wrote to Connolly, accusing him of 'slackness and flippancy': the 'Comment' was, for the most part, vacillating, vapid and journalistic, and as for the editor's confession of sloth, it deserved 'no sympathy. No critic or poet who is not a good businessman should edit a literary paper.' Connolly annotated Symons's three-page letter and returned it to him; in his reply, Symons returned to the attack, deriding *Horizon* for its gentlemanly blandness and for publishing the likes of Priestley and Hugh Walpole, and urging him to make more use of writers like Graham Greene and V.S. Pritchett at the expense of Brian Howard. For the magazine to survive, he concluded, 'you will have to show much more energy, initiative and originality in the next twelve months than you have shown in the last twelve.'

But despite the odd dissenting voice – 'I find *Horizon* and all the things like it just a little collection of dried vomit. Better silence until we have the golden word to say than words and whispers and attitudes of this kind,' Lawrence Durrell observed to Henry Miller – reactions from the literary world were, on the whole, very favourable. Maynard Keynes congratulated the editor from Cambridge, and took out a subscription; V.S. Pritchett urged Gerald Brenan to follow his own example and submit material for publication; Christopher Isherwood received the first issue in California and confessed that 'it makes me homesick for what is, after all, my only real home'; Maurice Bowra suggested an idea for an article, adding that he had been spurred on by a re-reading of *Enemies of Promise*, so evocative of its author's 'seductive, cigar-like personality'; Pearsall Smith – rather surprisingly – congratulated his protégé on new discoveries like Maclaren-Ross and Gully Mason, and on 'the miracle of getting gold out of writers of trash like Priestley': he had persuaded several friends to take out subscriptions – Beatrice Webb among them – and would be contributing to *Horizon*'s 'begging bowl' for Antonia White.

First floated in the January 1941 issue, the 'begging bowl' reflected the editor's lifelong fascination with the economics of making a living as a writer, and put into effect an idea that originated in *Enemies of Promise*. It cost, he told his readers, £150 to produce 5000 copies of the magazine, and as a result 'We are unable to pay our contributors as much as we should like. If you particularly enjoy anything in *Horizon*, send the author a tip. Not more than one hundred pounds: that would be bad for his character. Not less than half-a-crown: that would be bad for yours.' Among the beneficiaries of this invidious scheme was Dylan Thomas, whose 'Deaths and Entrances' was published in that same issue, together with a 'Comment' wondering where the new generation of war poets was to be found. One such was Alun Lewis, whose 'All Day It Has Rained' earned him a miserly 3*s* 6*d* from the begging bowl: Lewis – who was later killed in action – visited the *Horizon* offices, but 'felt as if my khaki were too rough and my boots much too heavy to be near them.'

By now, though, *Horizon*'s attitude to the war had shifted slightly: the magazine, Connolly suggested, had 'always regarded the war as a necessary evil', yet he was now being attacked from the Left by those who, while sharing his contempt for Chamberlain, disapproved of his subsequent support for Churchill. 'There is no cartwheel in supporting Churchill rather than Chamberlain,' Connolly insisted:

> Whatever views we may all hold about a future society, it is clear that Churchill saved England from defeat more signally than any one man in history. He nearly saved France as well... even if we owe nothing to Churchill but his oratory, we owe him everything.

Supporting Churchill as a war leader didn't necessitate agreeing with him over India or the shape of post-war Britain, however: indeed,

> The only political movement in England today which possesses real dynamism, the dynamism to win the peace as well as the war, is that represented by the loosely joined progressive forces of Priestley, Hulton, Crossman, Harrisson, Foot, Owen, the *Daily Mirror*, *Sunday Express*, *Pictorial*, *News Chronicle* and so on.*

It was from there that 'our future government a democratic elite of the efficient' would come, and *Horizon* would give them its support; in the meantime, though, 'we must read one another or die'.

Connolly's own offerings could still be found sporadically in the pages of the *New Statesman*. He had put in a short stint as the magazine's film critic in the summer of 1939 – observing of the Gracie Fields phenomenon that English humour 'is really a synonym for fear, fear of life, fear of death, fear of anti-fascism, fear of sentiment, intelligence, sex, a cosy English fear of anything and everything' – and in December the following year he tried his hand again as an art critic. His review of some Augustus John drawings elicited a grateful note from the artist, who wondered whether *Horizon* might be interested in publishing extracts from his autobiography. *Horizon* was, not least because its publisher, Jonathan Cape, was prepared to waive a fee; and the interminable serialisation of *Chiaroscuro* began its stately progress, running to eighteen instalments between 1941 and 1949.

Earlier that same year, Connolly was commissioned to contribute to a series of topical pamphlets, published by Secker & Warburg under the generic title of Searchlight Books, and edited by Orwell and Tosco Fyvel:

* The publishing tycoon Edward Hulton and his Russian-born wife Nika saw a good deal of Connolly in the Forties and early Fifties, and he became an occasional contributor to *Picture Post*, of which Hulton was the proprietor. An occasional contributor to *Horizon*, Tom Harrisson was, with Charles Madge, the co-founder of Mass Observation.

the first titles appeared in early 1941, and included Orwell's 'The Lion and the Unicorn', Cassandra's 'The English at War' and T.C. Worsley's 'The End of the Old School Tie'.*

The series had to be discontinued after the Secker offices were badly damaged by a bomb, and much of the Searchlight stock destroyed – but not before Connolly, who had produced a brilliant two-page synopsis of his contribution, had pocketed half the advance (£15) before lapsing into silence. Fred Warburg's partner, Roger Senhouse, agreed to meet his defaulting author in the Reform Club, along with two other angry creditors, Raymond Mortimer and T.C. Worsley, who were equally indignant about his failure to deliver material promised to the *New Statesman*. It was a cold winter's evening, and as Senhouse helped his guest out of his fleecy camel-hair coat he felt a strong urge to hide it and refuse to disgorge it until Connolly came up with the promised material. As ever, Connolly got the better of his pursuers, employing a cunning blend of charm, ferocity and quick-wittedness. Senhouse knew that his opponent would become 'sulky and down-trodden' if he raised the subject of the missing Searchlight text too quickly, so he adopted a circuitous, bantering approach. When this failed to achieve anything, he became more direct, which had the effect of making him feel the guilty man: Connolly pointed out in aggrieved tones that he had given up a month's editing to work on the pamphlet; the fact that he had failed to write it was neither here nor there. The three inquisitors then noticed that Connolly's copy of the *Evening Standard* was covered with notes scribbled in his familiar green ink, which he was busy transferring into a notebook. He was, he explained, verifying quotations for one of his belated *New Statesman* articles; but when Mortimer suggested that these could be corrected on proof, Connolly brushed the idea aside with 'It's too long and boring', and, rather than continue a fruitless conversation, no more was said about the missing items.†

* Orwell and Cassandra both sold over 10,000 copies. Orwell's observation that pre-war England was 'ruled largely by the old and silly', and that power lay 'in the hands of irresponsible uncles and bed-ridden aunts' must have appealed to Connolly.

† Spender had earlier warned Senhouse that Connolly needed to be appreciated, and that one had to play his game his way; but he was, Senhouse noted, vulnerable and easily unnerved as well. Early on in the war, Senhouse arranged to meet Connolly at Chez Victor, one of his favourite Soho restaurants. Senhouse arrived late, only to find that, far from ordering up a preliminary drink and riffling through the menu, his guest was standing disconsolately on the street outside. Senhouse guessed at once what was wrong: Connolly, he suggested, had toiled up the steep staircase to the first-floor dining-room, only to find himself confronted by the austere, hawk-like features of J.R. Ackerley, radiating disapproval, and, unable to meet him in the eyes, had backed away down the stairs and into the street again. 'How did you know?' Connolly asked, his face lighting up with pleasure; and they made their way elsewhere. On another occasion, Senhouse noted the guilty look with which Connolly managed to pass a restaurant bill on to somebody else: more famously, Connolly is said to have waved aside a bill with 'I never ordered this. Take it away.'

A new departure which may have made inroads into editorial time was broadcasting over the radio. Connolly's brief stint as a film critic provoked a BBC internal memo suggesting his name as a possible contributor, and in August 1940 Desmond Hawkins asked him if he would join him in a discussion entitled 'The Writer in the Witness Box'; 'I had only two letters from my broadcast, both from professional lunatics (properly certified),' Connolly told his producer, Christopher Salmon. From now on Connolly's soft, oddly seductive tones could be heard now and then on the air, giving his views on James Joyce to Indian listeners (George Orwell was a Talks Assistant in the Indian Section), taking part in 'Any Questions' and, later, appearing with Professor Joad on 'The Brains Trust', and discussing Aragon and Claudel on the 'Spanish-American Service'. On one occasion he mounted a 'particularly wounding personal attack' on Stephen Spender: later he expressed amazement at his friend having taken offence, since his remarks had been 'only for India'.*

In the summer of 1941 Connolly visited Dublin, so escaping the blackouts and privations of wartime London. John Betjeman, who was working as the Press Attaché at the British embassy, arranged for him to lecture at the Royal Irish Academy, and introduced him to Irish writers and editors, including R.M. Smyllie of the *Irish Times*, Terence de Vere White and Patrick Kavanagh, as well as to President de Valera. In the 'Comment' which preceded the Irish issue of January 1942, which contained work by Frank O'Connor and Sean O'Faolain, and Kavanagh's long poem, 'The Great Hunger', Connolly wrote that returning from Ireland,

> with its lights and its crowds, its huge trees and cloudscapes, its shops full of food and newspapers full of nothing, and its wise ruler struggling with the insoluble problem of the future of small nations, is not unlike going back from Southern France to the Spanish war. The examination in the shed, the soldier with a revolver who goes through one's letters, the official with his questions, recall Port-Bou; the long, dark, shabby train with blacked-out windows or rifle-cluttered corridor carries one back to reality, to the five-year sentence in gregarious confinement which we are all serving.

* Some years later George Barnes, the Director of Talks on the Third Programme, was keen to use Connolly as a broadcaster 'not only because he should give an interesting talk in spite of an affected delivery, but because the fact that he has broadcast on the Third Programme will create interest in circles which are antipathetic to the BBC.' Connolly's talk on the Latin Elegiac Poets was, Barnes told him later, 'one of the best I have ever listened to . . . a model of what broadcasting can contribute to the stimulation of interest in an ancient civilisation.'

That September, International PEN held a conference in London attended by, among others, John Dos Passos and Thornton Wilder. Sibyl Colefax gave a dinner at the Dorchester, attended by important editors like Connolly and John Lehmann. Eager to do his bit, Connolly then offered Wilder dinner at the Ivy. A.J. Ayer, Philip Toynbee and Frank Pakenham thought they had been included in the party, but when they reached the restaurant they found Connolly – who was evidently expecting no one else – seated round a table with his guest and two girls from *Horizon*, so they sat down at an adjoining table and looked after themselves. Both groups rose to leave at about the same time, and as the rejects wandered off into the blackout, Toynbee made some unflattering remarks about their defaulting host. 'How boring you are being,' Ayer told him: 'If you want to be malicious about Cyril, the last word was said by Virginia Woolf: "I do not like that smarty-boots Connolly"' – at which a voice purred out of the darkness, 'Not so loud, Freddie, not so loud.'* As he edged his way towards his forties, Connolly was becoming a public figure, and a formidable presence as well.

* Although Philip Toynbee brought Ayer and Connolly together again, their friendship never fully recovered. Shortly after the liberation of Paris, the two men flew there together, in the company of the French painter Christian Bérard; and when Bérard qualified his admiration for *Horizon* by saying that it tended to be a bit too smart at times, Connolly agreed that 'One must at all costs avoid being a smarty-boots, mustn't one, Freddie?'

EIGHTEEN

Te Palinure Petens

In the spring of 1941, Connolly and Lys moved into a studio maisonette in Drayton Gardens, South Kensington, which they rented off Celia and Mamaine Paget, both of whom were nursing in different parts of London and living away from home. The studio room itself was tall and spacious, and a perfect setting for the reception that followed Stephen Spender's marriage to Natasha Litvin in April that year, attended by Sonia, Janetta, A.J. Ayer, Louis MacNeice, Guy Burgess and the architect Arno Goldfinger; but Drayton Gardens was best remembered for the furore aroused by Arthur Koestler's hair-net. Peter Quennell and Koestler had moved into the spare bedrooms, and according to Quennell

> an absurd quarrel presently broke out, followed by an irate correspondence, because I was alleged to have told a girl we both knew that in bed he wore a hair-net; and he protested that I had gravely injured his chances of securing her affections. 'Like every civilised Continental,' he said, he wore a hair-net only when he was going to the bath.

A veteran of Nazi Germany, Soviet Russia and the Spanish Civil War – where he had represented the *News Chronicle* and, at one stage, found himself awaiting execution in Malaga – Koestler had made his way to England in 1940 via a Vichy internment camp, a concentration camp in the South of France, and neutral Portugal; and after a short spell in Pentonville, he had dug trenches for the Pioneer Corps outside Cheltenham before receiving his discharge papers in 1942. Although their relationship was never easy,* he was quick to acknowledge his indebtedness to Connolly, who invited him to stay at Drayton Gardens on his return to London:

* 'I am not a friend of Koestler's,' Connolly once told Edmund Wilson:

> I endure him out of loyalty to literature. As a person I think he is insupportable (like Marx); as a writer he is perhaps only a journalist of genius, but I am afraid he is much more, a dynamo generating just the energy which the enlightened left had almost despaired of. Like everyone who talks of ethics all day long one could not trust him half an hour with one's wife, one's best friend, one's manuscripts or one's wine merchant – he'd lose them all. He burns with the envious paranoiac hunger of the Central European ant-heap, he despises everybody and can't conceal the fact when he is drunk, yet I believe he is probably one of the most powerful forces for good in the country.

> Cyril took me under his wing.... Instead of spending my time in loneliness and isolation like so many exiles, or confined to an émigré clique, I was welcomed into the *Horizon* crowd. I wouldn't say that I was exactly an outsider – more a strange bird on the periphery: but the important thing was that I felt at home.

Koestler had switched from writing in German to an equally fluent English: apart from signing the War Writers manifesto, his work for the magazine included 'The Yogi and the Commissar' and an essay about the myth that had grown up around Richard Hillary, the author of *The Last Enemy*. From early on in the war, Koestler had done all he could to alert his hosts to the realities of life under Nazi domination, while recognising that 'for an educated Englishman it is almost easier to imagine conditions of life under King Canute in this island than conditions of life in, say, contemporary Poland.' In the autumn of 1942, a Pole named Karsky gave him details of what was happening in the Nazi extermination camps, and Koestler made use of this in his novel *Arrivals and Departures*. Connolly agreed to print an extract in the October 1943 edition of *Horizon*; entitled 'The Mixed Transport', it described the sealed trains leaving for the East. A couple of months later he received an indignant letter on the subject from Osbert Sitwell. 'That really is a very wicked *Atrocities* number in *Horizon*,' Sitwell wrote: 'Is this rigmarole of Koestler's intended as fact or fiction?' His own experiences during the First World War – when German troops were alleged to have skewered Belgian babies on their bayonets – led him to believe that all such stories were gross exaggerations: Koestler was 'ill-advised' and 'blatantly impertinent', and he bet Connolly £5 that 'if you are alive ten years after the war has ended, you will truthfully and willingly admit that you have been hoodwinked and nose-led.' Once aroused, the 'Governor' returned to the subject in letter after bantering letter. Koestler – to whom Connolly had shown the correspondence – was understandably livid, and composed a scathing reply in which he accused Sitwell of being an 'accomplice by omission' to German atrocities; but he was reluctant to personalise the argument, and seemed happy to let Connolly answer for him in 'Comment'.*

Wilson agreed: Koestler, on a visit to America, had 'lived up in the most fantastic way to your description of him. But he carries obnoxiousness to a point where you realise that nobody can be as bad as that – if he were, he wouldn't behave so.'

* Koestler was grateful to Connolly for his support over this, but was less taken by his attitude towards the novelist Anna Kavan, who contributed to, and occasionally worked for, *Horizon* after her return to England from New Zealand in the spring of 1943. She was very much a protégé of Peter Watson: both were patients of a German émigré psychiatrist called Dr Karl Bluth, a friend of Brecht and Heidegger. Bluth was convinced that controlled doses of heroin were the only effective antidote to Anna Kavan's depressions, which had led her to make several suicide attempts; he had her registered as an addict, supervised her injections, and remained the source of her legally-acquired heroin until her death. She told Bluth that she found Connolly difficult to work for: Koestler, who was interested in both her work and her plight, reproached Connolly for retailing 'after-dinner stories in which you told with gusto about her last suicide attempt etc.'.

Drayton Gardens was only a temporary home, and in May 1942 Connolly and Lys rented two floors at 49 Bedford Square, letting a couple of rooms in the attic to Peter Quennell. Moving house had been a terrible business, Connolly told Lady Astor, and they were still living by candlelight: but before long they were comfortably installed – so much so that, as Quennell later recalled, 'Cyril's household, in these wartime surroundings, was a constant source of wonder. He kept the war at bay more effectively than any other man I knew.' When writing, or re-arranging the cut-up galleys of what would eventually become *The Unquiet Grave*, Connolly sat in a wide-armed wooden chair belonging to Peter Quennell, who had had it made in Japan when teaching at a university there in the early Thirties; a board was placed across the arms when an extra surface was needed. Roger Senhouse remembered that the rooms were 'furnished in much of the old King's Road style – the inlaid chairs, table etc.'; and, as in the King's Road days, animals were to hand, alarming the visitors and bringing comfort to their owner. Quennell recalled 'a lithe, beautifully spotted African genet, which had an awkward trick of refusing to relieve itself unless it was provided with a bowl of water'. Still more disconcerting was a 'white sulphur-crested cockatoo' which sat behind its master's throne; it flew at terrified strangers, but at Connolly's approach 'it would immediately sink to the ground, bubbling and gurgling an insensate song of love'. No doubt a rug was thrown over the bird-cage when one of Connolly's innumerable parties was taking place, such as that attended by Senhouse, together with Dick Wyndham, T.C. Worsley, Elizabeth Bowen, Raymond Mortimer, Diana Abdy, Janetta and Diana. Senhouse was handed a cigar by his host as he came through the door; Quennell was 'at the drinks, of course'; and Stephen Spender made an appearance in his fireman's uniform. Nor did Connolly stint his luncheon guests: ration book allowances were pooled, and Connolly would take his visitors out for a drink while Lys looked after the leg of lamb.

Peter Quennell's rooms in the attic offered, by contrast, a 'drab spectacle of bohemian laisser-faire'. He was working for the Ministry of Information, but although his office was a stone's throw from Bedford Square, in the Senate House of London University, he didn't see a great deal of Connolly and Lys since he was usually worn-out when he got back from work at seven in the evening. From the Ministry, he wrote to suggest that he should use Connolly's spare mattress, chest and towels in exchange for his china, glass and carpets, and agreed reluctantly that he should pay half the cleaner's wages even though he occupied far less space, 'Skeltie (whose permanence is always relative) or no Skeltie'. A pantherine *femme fatale* with a sinuous body, tawny skin, golden hair, high cheekbones under lynx-like eyes, and a manner that was unnervingly both humorous and malicious, taunting and farouche, Barbara Skelton was to play a major part in Connolly's life: but at this stage in her raffish, turbulent and seemingly insatiable amorous career she was dividing her favours between Peter Quennell in his attic rooms and the Polish artist Feliks Topolski.* Quennell – whose obsession with 'Skeltie', or 'Baby' as he called her, he would later compare to that of Hazlitt for the equally elusive and tantalising Sarah Walker – had first met Barbara Skelton during a bombing-raid, in which she displayed characteristic sang-froid; he had taken her to dine with Connolly on Christmas Eve 1941 and she had met his landlord again shortly afterwards, this time with a drunken Augustus John. 'Have had several grumpy meetings with Cyril on the stairs recently,' Barbara noted in her diary early in 1943, after she had been instrumental in removing a pouffe from his sitting-room and making off with it to the attic; all was soon forgiven, though, for a couple of months later she reported that she 'actually had a conversation with Cyril! And brewed him a cup of tea! (Worthy of note, I consider).' Before long Barbara Skelton left to work as a Foreign Office 'cipherine' in Egypt, but doubtless she had made an impression; shortly after moving into Bedford Square, Connolly went to stay with the Glenconners in Scotland, from where he reported that he had been sleeping very badly, racked by nightmares about Jean and the Major – who, to make matters worse, revealed that he had been having a long affair with 'Skeltie' ('Don't you understand, I've had 'em *all*, old boy – the lot of them').

Innocent of all such goings-on, the Major continued to lead his blameless life at the Naval & Military Hotel, meticulously providing the index for *Horizon* at five shillings an hour, treating himself to the occasional bottle of 'Algerian ink', sending his son postcards about where to find freshly-made mayonnaise, admiring Lys's cooking, and copying out recipes for kid and goat for André Simon. He translated a treatise on the wines of Burgundy, and set about reviewing the Wine and Food Society's Encyclopaedia with his customary thoroughness: the fish volume was riddled with omissions ('Fancy, no mention of *Calamares en sue tinto*'), though 'in sauces the only omission that strikes me is that of Gubbins's sauce for grills'. As Connolly grew older he became more sympathetic to the Major, introducing him to

* The two men came to blows over her one night in the Gargoyle Club, which had been opened before the war by David Tennant and was much patronised in the Forties and Fifties by writers, painters, socialites, publishers and assorted riff-raff – Philip Toynbee, Connolly, Francis Bacon, Lucian Freud, Raymond Carr, George Weidenfeld, Dylan Thomas, Nicholas Mosley and the actor Robert Newton among them. Quennell found Barbara Skelton sitting at a table with Topolski and John Davenport, and was so infuriated by the spectacle that he lunged at his rival. Topolski backed into the lift and made his escape, but not before he had pushed his far taller rival to the ground and ruffled his usually impeccable hair.

friends like Evelyn Waugh and Peter Quennell, and persuading Sir Harry d'Avigdor-Goldsmid and Lord Glenconner to provide him with financial advice;* and, of course, he shared his father's delight in the pleasures of the table. 'Lobsters he loved, and next to lobsters sex,' Rose Macaulay supposedly said of Connolly; and as well as crustaceans he loved fruit, and especially those – melons, grapes and so forth – which were hard to come by during the war and the years of post-war rationing. He yearned for the flavours of the south, for an almost unimaginable future when 'all the musky flasks of sugar and sunshine with their painted containers, oranges, pineapples, grapes and even avocado pears, return to the audience who had grown to love them.'

Looking back to the days when they lived under the same roof in Bedford Square, Peter Quennell wrote of Connolly that

> as he grew middle-aged, a circumference of double chins slowly encompassed his keen observant features. Though he liked to please, nobody, if the company were uncongenial, seemed less afraid of displeasing, and he would retreat into a deathly silence – a silence that could almost be felt, so strong was the effect it made, and such was the paralysing check it made on ordinary social gossip. Given an agreeable companion, however, preferably a sympathetic young woman or an appreciative older friend, he became a different character. The alert face appeared to absorb his jowls; his spider eyes would dance with fun and malice; and he might even execute one of his famous knock-about 'turns'.

The American author Frederick Prokosch met him at about this time at Lady Cunard's, and thought that whereas the pre-war Connolly had been 'playfully self-disparaging and bubblingly apologetic', he now looked 'older and flabbier, more pontifical. His face had grown puffy; his nose had shrunk to a mushroom. His eyes had grown shifty and his voice had grown circumspect, as though alarmed by the thought of an impending banality.' Whatever his linguistic circumspection, Connolly made fewer efforts as he grew older to disguise his feelings, whether of pleasure, amusement, bore-

* Years later, Connolly wrote of how, in his King's Road days, he had discussed with W.H. Auden his difficult relationship with the Major. Auden – then 'hard-edged and unmellowed, wanting the benevolence of his later years' – had urged him to take a tough line with the Major, so

> Shortly afterwards my father lunched with me in Soho, a treat he always enjoyed, and on the way back I stopped the taxi outside my door in Chelsea (he lived in South Kensington). He clearly expected to be invited in for a talk and a brandy but I bade him an abrupt farewell and gave the driver his address. Clutching his two thick cherrywood sticks with the rubber ferrules, his legs crossed, his feet in pumps, for owing to arthritis he could not stoop to do up laces, he fingered his grey moustache while a tear trickled down his cheek. I don't know which of us felt more unhappy.

dom or distress. He was easily moved to tears, of both pleasure and despair;* his charm alternated with rudeness, abruptly turning his back on those he thought boring or unimportant; his moodiness, his tendency to sulk and his fussiness over food made hostesses in particular desperate to win him round and put their best feet forward; his gift for friendship was combined with a passion for gossip and intrigue that made him seem at times faithless and two-faced, a disruptive mischief-maker redeemed by his originality and wit.

Although they would never lose touch, Connolly's feelings about his lodger – always ambivalent – were increasingly uncharitable. 'PQ as a goat,' he observed: 'His lechery, his omnivorous voracity, his pink and whiteness, his iron digestion, his dry destructive unsentimental goatish unappeasable hunger, scorching the earth all round him, with peaceful voice and mild blue eye.' Sexual and literary rivalry were combined with disdain, as though Quennell was his *alter ego*, embodying all that he most disliked in himself. 'It would be hard to find a character more horrible,' he went on,

> more selfish, more lecherous, more disloyal, more mean, more malicious, snobbish and cowardly. I have actively disliked him for the last five years and hated him for the last two, yet there he is, my parasite, always under the same roof, always owing money, the enemy observer who dines out on his anecdotes of my life, and turns the flattery on when he wants anything. What unites us then? Old associations, a little, and the Intelligence – that bond which holds minds together more firmly than families are held together by blood or interest. We hold the same intellectual rank, and are as bound to it as two people with the same language who dislike each other and meet in Siberia.

The fact that Quennell spoke the same language enabled him to go on writing for *Horizon* despite Peter Watson's reservations, and despite his appointment, in 1943, as editor of John Murray's *Cornhill* magazine which, old-fashioned as it was, could be seen as a potential rival; and Connolly's loyalty to him contributed to the humiliating fiasco of his brief spell as literary editor of the *Observer*.

* He was, quite literally, bored to tears at times. Stephen Spender remembered how, at a literary conference in Venice after the war, Connolly was seated next to a female journalist from the *Manchester Guardian*. After a while, Spender noticed tears streaming down Connolly's face; Connolly then rose from his seat, came round to where Spender was sitting, and begged him to change places, since he could stand the boredom no longer. Frustration over food was another source of tears. On another occasion, the two men were in a restaurant together, and Connolly ordered ptarmigan. When it arrived, it was half-cooked, and Connolly burst into tears. It was put back in the oven, reappearing some time later, apparently in cinders – so provoking another outburst.

'Did I tell you that Cyril Connolly is now Lit Ed of the *Observer* and is living in great style in Bedford Square, with two concubines – one to darn his socks, the other (Mrs Lubbock) to warm his extremities? As he is still on Jeannie's payroll and Peter Watson's, he is probably the richest of our friends still in a reserved occupation,' John Hayward informed Patrick Balfour, now Lord Kinross, in August 1942;* while Cecil Beaton – whose 'Libyan Diary' would soon be appearing in *Horizon* – chimed in with 'Cyril is now Lit Ed of the *Observer* and has nice little dinner parties (Galsworthian joint, parlour maid etc) and good wine and talk.' J.L. Garvin, the legendary editor of the *Observer*, had finally retired in February, leaving the twenty-nine-year-old David Astor in charge, with no editor and a tiny editorial team. Although he was on the staff of Mountbatten's Combined Operations Headquarters, based in Richmond Terrace off Whitehall, and could fully attend to the *Observer* only in his lunch-hours and at weekends, Astor set about remoulding the paper along more up-to-date lines. He removed the classified advertisements from the front page, replacing them with news items and even photographs; he began to nudge the paper away from its traditional conservatism in a leftwards direction; and he set out to enrol new writers, including Sebastian Haffner, Isaac Deutscher, John Strachey, Frank Pakenham and George Orwell, whose 'The Lion and the Unicorn' he had particularly admired. Astor met Orwell – and, later, Arthur Koestler – through Connolly, and in both his choice of writers and the kind of journalism he aimed for he was strongly influenced by *Horizon*, in that he greatly admired the free-standing, independent-minded essay as a journalistic form, and preferred to employ writers rather than professional journalists, at least as far as longer and more speculative contributions were concerned. All this boded well for the paper, and set the pattern for the years ahead, when writers like Koestler, Philip Toynbee and Harold Nicolson became regular contributors, but it didn't solve the immediate problem of who was to edit the paper on a day-to-day basis. Barbara Ward and Geoffrey Crowther both temporarily took the tiller in 1942; and then, in August, Ivor Brown – the long-serving drama critic, and an authority on Shakespeare – was appointed to the post, on the understanding that he would hold the fort until David Astor could fully enter into his inheritance. With that settled, Astor now

* The alleged sock-darner was Diana, who – at Connolly's request – returned to *Horizon* as a reader for a few months in 1942, when Lys was briefly called up on national service: far from being a resident concubine, she visited Bedford Square very occasionally to drop off typescripts. She had finally broken off her affair with Connolly in 1940, the year in which she met her future husband, whom she married in 1944: telling Connolly that it was over had provoked howls of misery and threats of suicide, but he continued to publish her in *Horizon*, and later recommended her work – without success – to Hamish Hamilton. Hayward's letter is an example of the way in which Connolly's every move provoked a flurry of gossip, often tendentious and inaccurate.

turned his attention to the cultural side of the paper, and he wrote to Connolly to ask if he would like to become its literary editor: quite apart from being 'the best writer of English going', he was – he assured him – the ideal man for the job. A salary of £800 a year was agreed, and Connolly looked forward to what would prove to be his first stint of regular salaried employment.

Unalarmed as yet by Atrocities, Osbert Sitwell wrote to congratulate him: he would have the field to himself since

> I am afraid Desmond is very bad at his *Sunday Times* – not, of course, that he isn't a discerning critic of *certain* books (I am sure he would be wonderful on, let us say, Andrew Lang, if anyone was interested in Andrew Lang): but in modern poetry he likes nothing except Hilaire Belloc's rather smutty poems, and his hedging becomes less exhilarating every day . . .

'Don't stand any nonsense from the Astors,' Sitwell concluded: prophetic advice, for within a short time of his arrival Lord Astor was writing to the new literary editor to say that reviewers must be picked with great care, and combine 'ability and character and high ideals': he was particularly worried in case A.L. Rowse proved a 'militant atheist', for 'I am firmly convinced that our great influence in the world is due to the fact that this country has given a definite place to religion and to free religion i.e. Protestantism at that.' Undaunted by this edict from on high, Connolly made it plain in his reply that he was not prepared to put up with such nonsense: he himself was an atheist, or at least an eighteenth-century deist, and he could discern no difference in behaviour between an English Protestant and an English atheist.

With that settled, Connolly bent his mind to the question of reviewers. The *Observer*'s regular team was redolent of Mr Mossbross, including as it did Frank Swinnerton, L.A.G. Strong, Arthur Bryant, Lord Elton, Edmund Blunden and Basil de Selincourt; and just as David Astor had enlivened the 'cultural' pages with new arrivals like Osbert Lancaster and Tom Harrisson, so Connolly – like any self-respecting literary editor – brought in his own candidates, to the detriment of the old guard, and Lord Astor's blood pressure. 'You'll have to bear with our limitations,' David Astor wrote to him from Richmond House: changes would have to be introduced slowly, but he hoped that, for his part, Connolly would be prepared to compromise, making 'tiresome concessions' if need be. Connolly started his own 'Books of the Day' column in November, and among the books he reviewed over the next few months were Raymond

Mortimer's *Channel Packet* – Mortimer wrote to say how bad he felt about asking him to review it, but '*in vino veritas*' – Bowra's *The Heritage of Symbolism*, and Vercors' short novel about the German Occupation of France, *Le Silence de la Mer*, which he described as a masterpiece and went on to translate for Macmillan, for publication the following year. The reviewers he brought to the paper included A.L. Rowse, Spender, Orwell, Maurice Richardson and Peter Quennell; and of these Quennell proved the only bone of contention. 'You'll think I've got a down on the elegant Quennell. But really I think his writing so consciously fastidious that it is becoming clownish... It seems compartmental and glossy and artificial and airless,' David Astor told him: nor did it in any way reflect the fact that there was a war on, which he saw as 'a sign of spinsterish insensitiveness and self-love. Of course, you're all inclined that way, you super-fine literary haberdashers...' 'I think you write the most disagreeable letters of anyone I know,' Connolly replied: 'if we are literary haberdashers, you are the customer we all dread.' He had no intention of dropping Quennell, who was in any case doing his bit at the Ministry of Information: 'I liked your one-sidedness, but don't get your teeth into me, I won't play.' Astor, in the meantime, had written to Quennell to say that although he would like Connolly to commission 'less specialised' reviews, he had not forbidden him to employ his friend, though 'I should add that I have told Cyril abruptly and plainly that I do not regard you and himself as arbiters of art who should be unquestioningly deferred to.'

Although Astor assured Connolly that 'I have chosen YOU to be the lit ed of the Obs – I safeguarded you in your tenure of the main space as chief reviewer,' relations between the two men deteriorated fast: 'I don't know if our relations permit me to forward the enclosed to you without causing offence,' Astor wrote when recommending a French author to *Horizon*. His mistake had been to become too intimate with Connolly before ascertaining whether they could in fact be friends – a misplaced intimacy that included inviting Connolly and Lys to stay on the Astor estate on Jura. 'Mr Quennell is gnashing his elegant teeth in harsh sayings about me,' but Quennell was not the only source of disagreement. The entire paper consisted of a mere six pages; Ivor Brown – whom Connolly despised as middle-aged, middle-brow and middle-class – was by background and inclination more interested in the literary side of the paper than in politics, though this didn't prevent him from spiking one of Orwell's reviews on political grounds; with too many chiefs jostling for position, Connolly's role was unclear and unthought-out, and constantly being eroded or intruded upon. Connolly soon made his feelings known, and in December he received a letter from Tom Jones, Lloyd George's old henchman and a well-known political fixer, and a board member of the *Observer*. Writing from Wales, Jones said how sorry he was to hear about Connolly's difficulties, and how much he wished he'd been in London to sort things out. The trouble was that too many appointments – Connolly's included – had been made too quickly; and, as far as the books pages were concerned, too many reviews had been commissioned and then not used, which had irritated Ivor Brown. Not long afterwards Jones wrote again to say how relieved he was to learn that Connolly and Ivor Brown had had a friendly talk, and that Connolly would continue to be associated with the paper, not just on its books pages. Early the following year Astor hoped that Connolly was no longer feeling bruised about the *Observer*, for 'it still needs you, and I hope you need it;' but Connolly was far from mollified, for in February Astor wrote 'You have just flown – so sorry. I hope you can equally appreciate why you have provoked me... You can attribute it to "philistinism" if you like. But you must not attribute it to ill will, unless you want to dismiss me as a friend. Which dismissal I would resist.'

Quite where and why Connolly had fled remains unclear; but although he continued to write occasional reviews for the paper until October 1944, his role as an employee came to a head, and an end, in August 1943. In December he had agreed to accept the 'altered status' of literary adviser and lead reviewer; but when, in due course, Astor brought in Donald Tyerman – later the editor of the *Economist* – to look after the political side of the paper, he felt once again under threat. Tyerman's appointment came as a relief to Ivor Brown, who remained the nominal editor, but was eager to involve himself more with books, as well as continuing as theatre critic, a post he had held since 1929; and he decided that J.C. Trewin should look after the arts pages, under his overall supervision. All this was too much for Connolly. The previous summer he had, much to his delight, been elected to White's;* he arranged to meet Astor there, and a stormy meeting ensued. Astor tried to persuade Connolly to restrict himself to writing articles and reviews; Connolly reminded him of earlier promises; Astor accused Connolly of an untruth; Connolly stormed out in a rage, leaving Astor alone in the enemy's club. Not to be done down, Astor wrote to say how angry he was at being accused of dishonesty. 'You seem to forget the remarks you have actually made, the manner you adopt. Or else you are

* The haunt of hard-living, hard-drinking, florid-faced adventurers and aristocrats – faced with the prospect of Peter Quennell's being elected a member, Waugh suggested it should be reserved for 'gamblers, lords and heroes' – White's was hardly a literary club; but it held for Connolly the same alarming allure as Pop or – some years later – the raffish inhabitants of Kenya's Happy Valley. He was proposed for membership by Dick Wyndham, and seconded by 'Ran' Antrim and Evelyn Waugh, according to whom it was 'the only club that has the coffee-house character – one goes there to talk to the other members, not to entertain strangers.'

particularly insensitive to other people's feelings, while being very sensitive in all that affects yourself,' he suggested. He was determined to remain patient in the face of Connolly's accusing him of being 'cynical, unscrupulous, power-seeking, uncouth and barbarous', and hostile to art and intellectuals, but 'I agree that we are bad for each other. I mean all that I have said and am deeply hurt by your egocentric and gross malice towards me.' The break was final, and Waugh was able to report home that Connolly had been sacked, and 'expects to be directed down the mines soon'.

'You must, I can well imagine, think me a weak editor and you may well think I should not have allowed your relations with David Astor to come between you and the paper,' Ivor Brown told Connolly the following month, after thanking him for the contributions he had made; and although Astor wrote to congratulate him on *The Unquiet Grave*, expressing a hope that they could now talk again, he remained something of a bogey-man for some years to come. Judging by the marginal notes, he featured, if not by name, as the sinister Leader – and Jon Kimche, one of his Young Turks on the *Observer*, as a Commissar – in an unpublished piece called 'Spring Assignment' which Connolly wrote in 1943, five years before Orwell's *1984*. Like Orwell, Connolly had been reading James Burnham's influential book *The Managerial Revolution*, according to which the world would eventually be divided into three super-states, and administered by internationally-minded technocrats and meritocrats; his story is set in the 1980s, and Europe, now re-named 'Centralia', is menaced by 'Westralia' (the Americas) on one side and, on the other, by 'Ostralia', 'where the Indo-Russo-Chinese are eaten up by managerial ambitions'. The Leader wants England to be a 'big termitary, one concrete hive of warriors, leaf-crunchers, spittle-mixers and poison-puffers', which must be 'purged and re-purged'; all three super-states are, in effect, 'the same thing, national socialist managerial bureaucracies'. It's hard to imagine anyone less suited to the part of the Leader than the tolerant, liberal-minded Astor, and Connolly's marginalia, rather than the story itself, reflect how bruised he was by his experiences at the *Observer*; but 'Spring Assignment' does reflect the way in which he was moving away from the managerial socialism of early 'Comments', and coming to see the omnipotent state, with its rules and regulations, and its well-meaning but deathly army of 'culture diffusionists' – a wide-ranging pejorative that took in 'pin-headed publishers', broadcasters and members of bodies like the British Council – as a threat to the ever-beleaguered 'artist', and yet another enemy of promise.

*

As his brush with the Astors made plain, Connolly at forty was a daunting presence, by no means always prepared to observe the social niceties. Alan Pryce-Jones – who observed of his Eton contemporary that 'either he sang for his supper or he sulked for it' – rented a farmhouse in Kent from Sir Harry d'Avigdor-Goldsmid for a time during the war, and recalled that his two most nerve-wracking guests were Patrick Kinross, who tended to swing back on fragile chairs and use unsuitable items of china as ashtrays, and Connolly, who, although there was a bathroom next door, 'regularly filled a chamber-pot and left it defiantly in the middle of the floor, for Thérèse or me to empty'. When taken to the theatre, he made little effort to disguise his impatience if he took against the play or the production: according to Peter Quennell, 'he soon began fidgeting so desperately, and uttering so many loud reproachful groans, that our neighbours protested and we were obliged to leave our seats halfway through the second act.' Julia Strachey went to see *Uncle Vanya* with Connolly and Lady Cunard in the spring of 1944. Lady Cunard provided a *sotto voce* running commentary throughout, and

> at the end, when Vanya weeps in the deserted lamplit room and says 'We must work – work – work – my dear, my darling,' Emerald creaked out loudly: 'What *is* this man's work, as a matter of fact?' and Cyril barked out 'Estate' and all the audience started to laugh and the play was ruined.

He was, and would remain, an enthusiastic gossip. Elizabeth Bowen met him for dinner that same year; he had a sore throat, but she noticed how 'when he began to say critical things about his friends his voice came back to him.'*

'In myself I recognise three beings,' Connolly wrote at about this time:

> the romantic melancholy outcast, who was once thin, wild-eyed, uncompromising, who likes southern scenery, flamenco-singing and passionate love, and still hopes to be a genius, and another, an eighteenth-century hedonist who enjoys food and conversation, convivial evenings with friends, motoring, luxury, architecture, attractive faces and the gossiping good sense of the world, and a third, an efficient twentieth-century left-wing intellectual who makes a good literary critic and would make a good political journalist, diplomatic correspondent, editor and publisher. The first of these has sabotaged any chance the other two might have of being happy, but not before they have mortally wounded him.

* Much depended on the time and the occasion, however: at a dinner given by Lady Colefax, attended by T.S. Eliot, Professor Joad, Edith Sitwell, Arthur Waley and Connolly, 'the pack of lions were so disconcerted by each other's presence that none of them spoke at all.'

And in an early draft of *The Unquiet Grave* he recorded, more explicitly than in the published version, his own sense of his literary worth:

> Intense emotion, half relief, half despair, at reading Sainte-Beuve's note-books, and finding 'This is Me'. This 'elegiac', as he called himself, who quotes my favourite line in Latin poetry as his, who sums up happiness as '*Lire Tibullus à la campagne avec une femme qu'on aime*,' who calls himself the '*dernier des délicats*', who has loved and suffered and been disillusioned and yet recognises love as the truest source of happiness, who criticises everything and everybody and is a better artist, and yet a weaker one, than any of the contemporaries whom he criticises, than Spender-Hugo, or Auden-Lamartine, or MacNeice-Musset, who loves the eighteenth century, who is never taken in, who knows that the wine of remorse is trodden from the grapes of pleasure, and who accepts both, who hates puritans and prigs and pedants...

Elsewhere in the same draft he wrote of how

> It is quite clear to me now that my destiny is to fight a rearguard battle for art and literature in this country against the politician, the culture-diffusionist, and victorious common man. I am to run an old-fashioned restaurant with sawdust on the floor, 'fine wines' and true cooking... I must be the last literary gent.

Horizon – that beleaguered redoubt of the literary gent – continued to offer eclectic fare, including contributions from Patrick and Antonia White. Spring 1943 was enlivened by a controversy over the merits (or demerits) of Alfred Wallis, the Cornish primitive painter, who had recently died. After an extract from his diary had appeared in the magazine, Evelyn Waugh wrote in, ridiculing those who took the old gentleman seriously as a painter and suggesting an annual Alfred Wallis Prize, to be awarded for the silliest contribution published that year in *Horizon*; Graham Greene promptly nominated Waugh as its first recipient for his 'little castrated letter'. At the end of the year a less facetious prize was offered for the best contribution of 1943, to be chosen by the readers; the winner was Arthur Koestler, for his piece on Richard Hillary.

With every month that passed, Connolly's nostalgia, and his restless desire to escape this 'grey little fey little island' of ration books and blackouts, grew greater. Earlier in the war he had revisited his old haunts in Chelsea, 'one of the last strongholds of the *haute bourgeoisie* where leisure, however ill earned, was seldom more agreeably and intelligently made use of', and –

finding it sadly battered by the Blitz, and the Old Church in ruins – described, like a latter-day Piranesi, how, 'when the sun shines on these sandy ruins and on the brown and blue men working there one expects to see goats, and a goat-herd in a burnous – *sirenes in delubris voluntatis* – pattering among them.' He commissioned a long-running series of articles, generically entitled 'Where Shall John Go Now?', in which writers evoked the pleasurable destinations that awaited the traveller once the war was over; but his own longings were focused on France. In 'French and English Cultural Relations' – published in June 1943, and one of the few pieces he contributed to the magazine under his own name – Connolly elaborated a view of France and the French that was to gain wide currency in the mid-Forties, when writers like Sartre and Camus began to be known on this side of the Channel, and reflected his own views about the place of the artist. Compared with other European countries, France had, over the past fifty years, produced an astonishing array of artists, writers and philosophers; and if, looking back to the last century, 'we compare Balzac and Flaubert to Dickens and Thackeray, Baudelaire to Tennyson, Sainte-Beuve to Hazlitt, we must lower our eyes. There is nothing to say; the Frenchmen are adults: beside them the English, for all their natural advantages, have not grown up.' In France – unlike in England – the artist was taken seriously, and left alone to get on with his work. Warming to his subject, Connolly told his readers how he dreamed of revisiting France: of disembarking at La Rochelle, and then driving down to the Dordogne – 'that beautiful temperate Romanesque corner of France where Montaigne came from, where in the Virgilian countryside white oxen move about the maize fields' – and then over the Massif Central before taking the N7, 'unwinding like a black liquorice stick through the plane trees', to St Tropez, where 'for several months I shall lie on the beach without moving, like a lump of driftwood'. Until then, he would do what he could to help French artists and writers; and one way of doing this – apart from publishing translations of French writers and poets, and articles on French literature by fellow-francophiles like Raymond Mortimer – was to publish original work in French under a joint *Horizon-La France Libre* imprint.* The first of these, Louis Aragon's *Le Crève-Coeur*, appeared in October 1942, and it was followed in due course by Sartre's *Huis Clos*, Aragon's *Les Yeux d'Elsa*, a selection of poems by Apollinaire, and work by Henri Michaux.

Writing in *Horizon* in November 1943, Arthur Koestler – who had lived and worked in France for much of the previous decade – heaped derision on

* Edited in South Kensington by André Labarthe and Raymond Aron, *La France Libre* was published by Hamish Hamilton; by 1943 it had a circulation of 43, 000. The monthly magazine *Fontaine* had a reciprocal distribution arrangement with *Horizon* and was edited from Algiers by Max–Pol Fouchet.

this outburst of francophilia, without actually naming *Horizon* or its editor. 'The people who administer literature in this country – literary editors, critics, essayists: the managerial class on Parnassus – have lately been affected by a new outbreak of that recurrent epidemic, the French "flu",' he wrote; for its victims, 'a single word like "*bouillabaisse*", "*crève-coeur*", "*patrie*" or "*midinette*" is enough to produce the most violent spasms: his eyes water, his heart contracts in bitter-sweet convulsions, his ductless glands swamp the bloodstream with adolescent raptures.' Sufferers became ecstatic at the mere mention of Métro stations: '*L'usage du cabinet est interdit pendant l'arrêt du train en gare*', for instance, 'sounds like the pure harmony of the spheres, especially if you have been cut off from the Continent for three years.' The works which Koestler thought especially over-rated, all dear to *Horizon* and its editor, were *Le Crève-Coeur*, André Gide's *Imaginary Interviews*, and *Le Silence de la Mer* – the story of a 'good' German officer suffering from verbal diarrhoea, who is billeted on a tongue-tied French family, which Koestler considered politically suspect and psychologically 'phoney'.

Undaunted by Koestler's mockery, Connolly continued to yearn for France, and to promote the works of French artists and writers. A further outlet for his francophilia was provided by the publisher Hamish Hamilton. Half-American, and a former Olympic oarsman, 'Jamie' Hamilton had set up his own firm in 1931 after running the London office of Harper & Row – the American boss of which, Cass Canfield, was his closest publishing associate in New York. Like many of the most successful literary publishers, he was an assiduous social climber, trawling – like Connolly – that tantalising world where Bohemia and Society intersect, to their mutual advantage; and he was in the process of building up an impressive list of authors, many of them French or American. 'I have a list of authors whom I should like to publish if a recurrence of the Black Death were to remove all my rivals, and this might form the basis of an interesting conversation,' he wrote to Connolly in January 1944, and before long he was in touch again, suggesting that he pay Connolly a retainer in return for tips about books and authors the firm might profitably publish. Connolly recommended works by, among others, Sartre and Camus, both of whom joined the Hamish Hamilton list; and in due course Hamilton and Cass Canfield jointly commissioned from him a study of Flaubert, paying an advance of £300 and with a delivery date of July 1945.

At much the same time as the Flaubert was signed up, Philip Toynbee – another francophile – found himself in newly-liberated Paris, waiting to meet Sartre at the Café Flore. 'The galleries are opening, the bookshops are anything but bare, the people are a thousand times more alive than London people,' he told Connolly; and writing in *Horizon* on 'The Literary Situation in France', he claimed that the literature produced in France during the war was 'incomparably and undeniably superior' to its English equivalent. This was music in Connolly's ears as he mourned the parlous state of the arts in England after five years of war. 'The State now sits by the bedside of literature like a policeman watching for a would-be suicide to recover consciousness,' he proclaimed. The State would do everything for the writer 'except allow him the leisure, privacy and freedom from which art is produced'; the French, on the other hand, were still fighting an 'ideological war', retaining a clarity of vision as a result of not being 'worn out by long hours, air raids and propaganda work'. Toynbee's article provoked a sharp rejoinder from John Lehmann, listing at length those books published in Britain during the war which he thought quite as good as anything fielded by the French.

Daydreaming of France inevitably brought Connolly back to lost love and the sensitive subject of Jean – not that she was ever far from his thoughts. 'Poor Cyril how he hankers after that dreadful Jeannie who is drinking herself to death in America,' Nancy Mitford briefed Diana Mosley. In an early draft of *The Unquiet Grave* Connolly wrote of how 'whatever I write about, read about, think about, if I continue long enough, I am brought back to the misery of my crisis of 1939 – all ends in futility and tears.' Leaving her husband enables a wife to be 'both sadist and masochist, to be strong when he implores her to stay, and to weep because she has decided to go. Women are different to men in that to break with the past and to mangle their men in the process fulfils a deep need in them'; and 'there is a way of leaving someone and yet not leaving them, hinting that one loves them and wants to come back and yet never coming back, and keeping up a smouldering decoy of affection.' 'A person who is left is always psychologically groggy,' he went on: 'Their ego is wounded at its most tender part and forced back on the appalling separations and rejections of infancy.'

Not long after her arrival in New York in the early summer of 1940, Jean had got in touch, at her husband's suggestion, with a young writer named Clement Greenberg, who had recently submitted to *Horizon* an article entitled 'Avant-Garde and Kitsch'. A Trotskyite then working for the US Customs, Greenberg was to become a regular contributor to *Horizon*, the art critic of the *Nation*, and, in due course, one of the most influential and highly regarded critics of his time, best known as the champion of Jackson Pollock and the New York School of painters; in the meantime, though, Jean reported him as being 'nice and intelligent but shamingly plain, gauche and inarticulate'. Installed in a flat in East 73rd Street, Jean told Connolly that she missed him, and England, a great deal, and was dispirited by the 'great boringness of everyone in America': both the *Nation* and *Partisan Review* were interested in the possibility of his writing for them, *Enemies of Promise* was 'practically a bible', and Connolly and Auden were among the 'top English exports'. She saw a fair amount of Auden, who allowed her to call him 'Wiz', of Benjamin Britten, then living in Brooklyn with 'Peter Pierce', and of Denham Fouts: they practised yoga together, Fouts specialising in sucking water up his anus. Jean then shared a flat with her sister Annie, the journalist Alannah Harper, and Sybille Bedford, who remembered her as being witty, domineering, very drunken, highly sexed and promiscuous. Before long she was deeply involved with Clement Greenberg, who found her work writing on art for the *Nation*; and when in due course Greenberg joined the US Army, she transferred her affections to Laurence Vail, a former husband of both Kay Boyle and Peggy Guggenheim and an elderly, bibulous remnant of American expatriate life in Paris in the 1920s. In *Down There on a Visit*, Christopher Isherwood – who saw quite a bit of Jean during the war years – described 'Ruthie' as a beaming, drunken 'animal person', who 'might just have emerged from a warm burrow under a hill':

> Ruthie's face is chalky white, with huge vermilion lips daubed on it. She is a big girl altogether; big hips, big bottom, big legs. I've seldom seen anyone look so placid, so wide open to visitors, so sleepy-slow. Her great beautiful gentle cow eyes have sculptured lids which make one think of an Asian bas relief – the carving of some giant goddess.

He had lunch with Jean, Tony Bower and Denham Fouts in Los Angeles in the summer of 1940. 'Jean is much thinner and really beautiful, with her big gentle cow eyes,' he confided to his diary: she and Fouts were nursing their hangovers, and 'steadily tanking up for the next blind'.

As she had always promised, Jeannie – or Mrs Warner, rather – continued to send her husband money throughout the war: 'I think about you a lot and will always care about you – so will my big loving Jeannie,' Mrs Warner greeted her son-in-law in the spring of 1941, signing off as 'Mawmee'. But none of this compensated for Jean's absence, and in the early summer of 1942 Connolly wrote her a desperate letter, begging her to return, and reminding her that she had agreed to come back once the danger of invasion had receded. He gave the letter to Brian Howard, who promised to pass it on to a sailor friend who was leaving that evening on a convoy heading for New York. Howard forgot, or deliberately failed, to pass the letter on; and, although he keenly denied it, he must have read it as well, for, as he passed Connolly's table in the White Tower a day or two later, he drunkenly bent down and whispered 'I am so tired of being respectable' – a phrase he could only have lifted from the missing letter. Connolly stamped out of the restaurant in a rage, and Howard was left pleading for forgiveness.

'Everything connected with Jean or D[iana] is excruciating – places, faces, sounds, smells, letters, phrases, words. Living in the present – the only escape – made possible by drugs, injections of work or pleasure,' Connolly confided to his notebook; and the early drafts of *The Unquiet Grave* are peppered with agonised and self-pitying aphorisms about women, and marriage, and the perils of love. 'In the sex war, thoughtlessness is the weapon of the male, vindictiveness of the female'; 'A man who is in love with two women is in hell four times: with one, with the other, with neither, with both'; 'All women are tarts, because a tart is a woman free to behave as she likes'; 'I am attracted to those women who combine mystery with the promise of the integrity which I myself lack'; and – reverting to a lifelong obsession – 'All men revenge themselves for their betrayal by their mothers, hitting out blindly to destroy the memory of the triple expulsion – from the sovereignty of the womb, from the sanctity of the breast, from the intoxication of the bed and the lap'. 'What I love is an air of the primitive, an aloofness – as when Janetta walked in carrying her baby,' he observed: '*Visite angoissante de J* who bewailed the loss of mother and brother while, looking at her, I bewailed the loss of wife and child.' While Janetta fed her baby at her breast, the sun shone in through the tall pier windows of Bedford Square, illuminating

> evenly the greed and innocence of childhood, the courage and misery of youth, and the sterile remorse and despair of middle age. Too late, too late. And yet it was all so difficult at the time, caught in the Jean-Diana scissors with Jan [Woolley] and H[umphrey] S[later] as obstacles, and the, at that time, infuriating adolescence, 'like a puppy with worms', of J herself.

'A face seen in the Tube can destroy our peace for the rest of the day,' Connolly once decreed; and there is no more romantic moment in *The Unquiet Grave* than that brief, highly-charged scene in which, one August evening in 1943, Connolly comes face-to-face with a sullen, corduroy-clad girl with bare legs and sandals outside Zwemmer's bookshop in the Charing Cross Road, follows her into the maze of streets that lead towards St Giles, and then loses her forever, a tantalising symbol of all that might have been ('*Oh toi que j'eusse aimé*'). Though unmentioned in Connolly's account, Peter Quennell was with him at the time, and remembered that the girl had a bandage round one ankle. Describing the scene afterwards to friends, Connolly was led to believe that she lived in Margaretta Terrace, in Chelsea.

'Faint with excitement, led by magical coincidences to whereabouts of Zwemmer girl, surrounded by her sacred signs of courage, liberty, poverty, beauty, spiritual potentialities,' he prowled the streets of Chelsea in the vain hope of seeing her again. 'What I feel for,' he wrote – building an elaborate edifice of speculation on so brief an encounter – 'is the feminine shadow of the self I might have been, the counterpart of the romantic artist who might have had the courage to accept poverty, and to reject society, for the sake of the development of a true personality, a revolutionary genius.'

Connolly was suffering to a heightened degree the familiar, restless dissatisfactions of middle age, which he dignified and popularised with the generic title of Angst. 'Perhaps the most painful angst is that arising from a sense of the waste of one's own time and ability, though poverty, debt, ill health and unrequited love are all causes': racked by the familiar demons of sloth, guilt and remorse, Palinurus – the pseudonym-cum-*döppelganger* he assumed for *The Unquiet Grave*'s author and protagonist – had been found 'particularly rich in all the essential mighthavebeens'. At his lowest moments, it seemed that

> The world is full of people that shine;
> I alone am dark.
> They look lively and self-assured;
> I alone, depressed.
> I seem unsettled as the ocean,
> Blown adrift, never brought to a stop.
> All men can be put to some use;
> I alone am intractable and boorish.
> But wherein I most am different from men
> Is that I prize no sustenance that comes not from the mother's breast.

All Connolly's obsessions came together in an extraordinary blend of anthology, autobiography and aphorisms, originally entitled *The Tomb of Palinurus* but eventually published as *The Unquiet Grave*. Connolly hid, unconvincingly, behind the mask of Palinurus, Aeneas's helmsman who fell asleep at the tiller, was washed overboard, and put to death by unfriendly natives; but despite Connolly's long infatuation with Palinurus and watery deaths, his relevance to the main text remains disconcertingly vague. According to the blurb of the original edition,

> *The Unquiet Grave* is a manuscript which was submitted anonymously to *Horizon* and which seemed by its nature unsuitable for publication in instalments but so unusual as to deserve printing by itself. 'Palinurus'

appears to be some kind of professional writer who has given us his mysterious case history; he sets out to write a masterpiece but instead is drawn nearly down to suicide. Then through a series of images from his past he mounts from despair to original calm...

Early in March 1943, Oliver Simon told Connolly that he had bought 'a fine new typeface', and that he would like to baptise it with *The Tomb of Palinurus*. Connolly was an editor's and a typesetter's nightmare, in that he continued to revise and rewrite until the very last minute – the long-suffering Hamish Hamilton described him as 'one of the most uncontrollable proof-correctors on record' – and the bitty, aphoristic nature of his new book was an open invitation to interminable reshuffling and recasting, much of it done with Sonia's help in Peter Quennell's Japanese chair: so much so that, after the original galleys had been cut to ribbons and re-pasted and heavily rewritten, Oliver Simon decided to cut his losses and start all over again. Since the entire book amounted to just over 100 pages, it was decided that *Horizon* itself should publish it in the first place. The French painter Jean Hugo provided a frontispiece, and the November 1944 issue of *Horizon* announced that Palinurus's work would be available from the Curwen Press, which had printed 500 copies in hardback at eighteen shillings, and 500 in paperback at fifteen shillings. Earlier in the year, Connolly had suggested to Hamish Hamilton that he might like to publish a trade edition: Hamilton had decided against – 'You write like an angel and think like a sage, but we are distressed by the bitterness and despair which pervade the book' – but in the light of the excellent reviews he changed his mind and decided to go ahead, publishing six months after the original edition; a wise decision, since the first impression sold some 3500 copies by the end of the year, when a reprint was put in hand, and it was to remain on the Hamilton backlist for many years to come.* In New York, the book was taken on by Cass Canfield. Connolly objected to their insistence on printing his name in brackets under 'Palinurus' on the title page, and wanted to drop the dedication to 'Pierre' (Peter Watson) in their edition; but it was too late to make any changes, and when the Harper edition appeared in December 1945, he pronounced himself very pleased with it. And although the Hamish Hamilton advance was to have been set against all earnings from the book, including the author's share of American rights, he managed to browbeat Hamish Hamilton into passing the American advance straight on to him, and not set it against the original advance: so setting a pattern whereby he

* A pleasing by-product of Hamish Hamilton's commitment to Connolly's work was the firm's reprinting of *The Rock Pool*, now available for the first time from a London publisher; both books were subsequently sold on to paperback houses.

managed, more than once, to wheedle money out of fearful or over-indulgent publishers before it was contractually due to him.

> As I waddle along in thick black overcoat and dark suit with a leather briefcase under my arm, I smile to think how this costume officially disguises the wild and storm-tossed figure of Palinurus; who knows that a poet is masquerading here as a whey-faced bureaucrat?

Palinurus asks; and *The Unquiet Grave* is, above all else, a perceptive, poignant self-portrait of a man in middle age, nostalgic for the past and fearful of the future, and racked by restlessness, ambivalence and doubt. 'Approaching forty, I am about to heave my carcass of vanity, boredom, guilt and remorse into another decade,' he warns us; he is consumed by a

> sense of total failure: not a writer but a ham actor whose performance is clotted with egotism; dust and ashes; 'brilliant' – that is, not worth doing. Never have I made that extra effort to live according to reality which alone makes good writing possible: hence the manic depressiveness of my work – which is either bright, cruel and superficial; or pessimistic; moth-eaten with self-pity.

Torn between the claims of science and magic, action and contemplation, a Taoist withdrawal from the world and the pleasures of the flesh, Palinurus embodies the spirit of dualism, of believing in contradictions and reconciling the irreconcilable; for

> When I consider what I believe, which I can only do by proceeding from what I do not believe, I seem in a minority of one – and yet I know that there are thousands like me: Liberals without a belief in progress, Democrats who despise their fellow-men, Pagans who still live by Christian morals, Intellectuals who cannot find the intellect sufficient – unsatisfied Materialists, we are as common as clay.

For Palinurus, as for so many romantics, 'Happiness is in the imagination. What we perform is always inferior to what we imagine; yet daydreaming brings guilt; there is no happiness except through freedom from Angst, and only creative work, communion with nature and helping others are angst-free.' Waking to 'apathy, sluggishness and morning tears', Palinurus – with the help of sleeping pills at night, benzedrine by day – summons up, in vain, 'a new pincer movement' against Angst and 'remorse about the past, guilt about the present, anxiety about the future'. His obesity is a mental state, induced by boredom, disappointment, greed and fear; and just as the poet lurks within the 'whey-faced bureaucrat', so – in the most famous of all Connolly's maxims – 'Imprisoned in every fat man a thin one is wildly signalling to be let out.' 'The more books we read, the sooner we perceive that the true function of a writer is to produce a masterpiece and that no other task is of any consequence,' runs the defiant opening sentence of the first of the book's three parts; and yet, 'consumed by the weed of non-attachment', the solitary artist is doomed to irrelevance and ultimate extinction in a world in which Communism and the 'uncomprehending tyranny of the Common Man' seem inevitable. Unable to subscribe to the tenets of formal religion, Palinurus seeks refuge in a kind of pantheistic resignation, in which contemplation of dream periods from the past – Augustan Rome, Paris and London in the eighteenth and early nineteenth centuries – is combined with a reintegration with nature and the rhythms of the seasons. Redemption could be achieved by the reconciliation of intellect and intuition, action and contemplation; and his examination of his own and the human predicament was enlivened by snippets of explicit autobiography, and made more exotic by those extensive quotations from French authors which Evelyn Waugh ridiculed on the grounds that adequate English equivalents were readily available.

Not long after publication, James Lees-Milne had lunch with Peter Watson at Brooks's. 'He said Cyril Connolly's book was too subjective to be first-rate, although Cyril considers it quite objective,' Lees-Milne recorded in his diary: 'It is the brilliant production of a disappointed, uncreative critic, approaching forty, who is frightfully ugly.' Osbert Sitwell – or so Edith assured its author – could talk of nothing but *The Unquiet Grave*, 'which he carries about with him from bedroom to writing-room, from writing-room to dining-room', and Nancy Mitford wrote to say that she was 'extremely touched & gratified at being sent the Grave & have been gobbling about it the whole evening & can't wait to begin again . . . It is really very much like talking to you, always a major pleasure.' From America, Jean was in touch to say how much she had loved it, 'but it makes me too sad to talk about . . . I think you are one of the few people whom self-pity or unhappiness develops rather than shuts in,' while Aldous Huxley suggested that 'There is a very distinctive flavour about its *Weltanschauung* – a flavour which might easily become contagious, so that, just as we now note something we can describe as Wertherism, say, or Byronism, future historians may discover lingering traces of Palinurmia.' Philip Toynbee read it in Brussels, and was overcome by 'rapture and despair' – sentiments shared, perhaps, by V.S. Pritchett:

> It has given me great pleasure, a pleasure pricked by envy. For you have brought off something remarkable, original and disturbing in self-portraiture, and you have written scores of words and images that stay in the mind. But all the qualities of your book are nothing compared with one thing: you sum up a period, you clear ground once and for all. You have this gift, I think, above anyone in our generation. And the attraction of it for me is that you provide a climate, a freshened climate, in which one can write.

Stephen Spender, on the other hand, had some reservations. He admired Palinurus's honesty, but thought him at times too self-pitying and self-indulgent: most Elizabethan and nineteenth-century writers had been extremely prolific, and 'whether the best way to write a masterpiece is to refuse to write anything else, seems very doubtful'. A new friend, Mary Campbell – whose husband, Robin, had written in *Horizon* about being a prisoner-of-war* – wondered, shrewdly, why Connolly had quoted Eliot to the effect that 'the progress of the artist is a continual self-sacrifice, a continual extinction of personality' when 'the whole of your book is exquisitely self-revelatory and in that capacity alone holds the attention, enchants the heart.' It was the introspective, autobiographical aspect of the book that appealed to Maurice Bowra as well:

> Your picture of yourself is wonderfully candid – I wish I knew how you did it – and moving. The particular crisis which you describe so poignantly is familiar to us all but no one but you would have faced up to it in this courageous way. I kept on finding your remarks about yourself painfully applicable to myself, and no doubt others will do the same.

Another friend from the Twenties, Bernard Berenson, expressed his delight that 'a young man who seemed to be but a jackanape and viveur should live to write a book like *The Unquiet Grave*, so passionately in earnest about the meaning of life, so originally too . . . No recent work of *belles lettres* has pleased me so much as yours.'†

'I never wrote you how good the book was,' Ernest Hemingway wrote from Cuba some three years later: 'I think it is one of the very best books I

* As a Commando officer serving in North Africa, Robin Campbell took part in an abortive attack on Rommel's villa in 1941: his commanding officer was killed (and awarded a posthumous VC), and one of Campbell's legs had to be amputated after he had been taken prisoner (he was awarded a DSO). Later it was learned that Rommel had vacated the villa several days earlier.

† It's hard to imagine that any letter gave Connolly as much pleasure as one from Dame Una Pope-Hennessy, who revealed that she had known some lemurs rather well as a child: indeed, they 'sat in W.S. Gilbert's hearth and seemed to understand what he said and to do what he told them.'

ever read, I am almost sure it will be a classic (whatever that means)... I can see why you were so happy when you had just written it and I met you in Paris.' Nor was this the only balm to flow from Hemingway's pen: 'I was so sorry that I was so ballsed up in the war the times we were together in London and Paris. I always get involved in wars but I admired the way you did not. It would be wrong for me not to fight but it was many times righter for you to do exactly as you did.'

Not all reactions were as favourable as these. Herbert Read – for whom *Horizon* seemed 'the last flicker of pre-war decadence, a post-Proustian inquest on a dead epoch' – told Douglas Cooper (one of Connolly's particular *bêtes noires*) that although Palinurus wrote well about the place of the artist in modern society, 'his moralisings on life in general are rather superficial, and clumsy in comparison with the quotations in which they are embedded. It is a fallacy to imagine that one enhances one's own jewels... by setting them in other people's gold.' 'The middle ranks in England have a certain validity and balance; it's the social snob culture levels that are so putrid – these Sitwells and Connollys (have you seen HIS latest),' Lawrence Durrell complained to Henry Miller: 'An imitation of you (and what an imitation). It will make you laugh yourself sick!... *Mea culpa*, he shrieks on every page, I am fat, slothful and snobbish – and then, appalled by such a piece of self-knowledge, quotes a page of Ste Beuve.'

The reviews themselves ranged from the ecstatic to the derisive. Writing in the *New Statesman*, Raymond Mortimer foretold 'writers hundreds of years hence poring over a twentieth-century classic entitled *The Unquiet Grave*, and admiring in it the mirror of their own preoccupations'; as well as being 'enchantingly clever', Palinurus 'betrays throughout a solicitude for the *mot juste* such as seldom harasses writers born in this century', and was 'above all conspicuous for the dire penetration of the gaze he turns upon himself.' 'Even without knowing his identity one could infer that the writer of this book is about forty, is inclined to stoutness, has lived much in Continental Europe, and has never done any real work,' Orwell suggested in the *Observer*:

> On almost every page this book exhibits that queer product of capitalist democracy, an inferiority complex resulting from a private income. The author wants his comforts and privileges, and is ashamed of wanting them: he feels he has a right to them, and yet feels certain that they are doomed to disappear.

The book was in essence 'a cry of despair from the *rentier* who feels that he has no right to exist, but also feels that he is a finer animal than the proletarian.'

Another trenchant critic, Edmund Wilson, was more favourably disposed. He was an admirer of *Horizon* and its editor and, visiting London in the spring of 1945, had discovered that 'in the literary and Left political worlds, almost everybody complained about it and him, but that everybody, at the same time, seemed in some degree dependent on them.' He had sensed that 'the magazine must have behind it a personality of some courage and distinction': now the editor had revealed himself, and the result was 'one of the books that has interested me most, as it is certainly one of the best written, that have come out of wartime England.'

Evelyn Waugh, on the other hand, was a good deal more ambivalent. 'What he writes about Christianity is such twaddle – real twaddle – no sense or interest, that it shakes me,' he informed Nancy Mitford: 'And he seems ashamed by the pleasant parts of himself – as a soft, sceptical old liver. I am shocked by the Grave. But I have only read six or seven pages . . . I think Cyril has lived too long with communist young ladies. He *must* spend more time in White's.' He eventually struggled through to the end, and set down his reactions in the *Tablet* under the title 'A Pilot All at Sea'. For a year now, he began, 'the literary ladies of the Dorchester Hotel have been talking about their "Angst" '; the book had been lavishly praised by Raymond Mortimer, Desmond MacCarthy, V.S. Pritchett and Elizabeth Bowen; and yet it seemed to him that Connolly's *pensées* were the 'raw material of literature', and that 'a great deal of valuable matter has here been prematurely put in the killing-bottle and pinned on the setting board.' *The Unquiet Grave*, he went on,

> suffers from the fact that his observations have not been able to influence each other and, faced with the heterogeneous and often contradictory nature of his jottings, he has sought a factitious unity by attempting an innocent and ingenious imposture, pretending to relate them to classical mythology to the great awe and perplexity of the literary ladies at the Dorchester Hotel.

The book was intended to be a self-portrait, and yet Palinurus seemed to exhibit three quite distinct personalities:

> First, there is a middle-aged gentleman in reduced circumstances. He has hallowed memories of his better days, of scholarship, young love satisfied, holidays in the sun, fruit, wine and exotic pets; a disappointed hedonist who put his trust in fine weather and cannot face the storm; a wistful, fretful figure, hampered by minor ailments and small bills, who, in the fogs of bomb-ruined Bloomsbury likes to imagine that in happier ages he would have been admitted to the intimacy of Petronius and Rochester.

Behind him trailed 'his disorderly Irish valet, a man of high comic abilities in whom high spirits alternate with black despair'. Master and drunken man make a good pair, but 'a horrible third has attached herself to the party, the flushed and impetuous figure of a woman novelist. She is a terror, rattling with clichés from Freud and Frazer and Marx... "When the present slaughter terminates," she begins, giving full rein to the tosh-horse whose hooves thunder through the penultimate passages.' But even if Palinurus has been 'duped and distracted by the chatter of psychoanalysts and socialists', the middle-aged gentleman 'writes with exquisite melody and precision; his lament for the lemurs and the final sentences of the book are as beautiful as any passages of modern English prose that I know; his occasional subdued, melancholy wit is enchanting.'*

But Waugh was far from done with Palinurus. Some eighteen months after first publication of *The Unquiet Grave*, Connolly described in a 'Comment' how, returning to England on the Golden Arrow, he had been overcome by 'what can only be described as a patriotic glow'. There was no black market in England; the cocktail bar on the train seemed 'a cheerful and ingenious affirmation of the right to pleasure'; the Labour Government's plans to decolonise India and Egypt amounted to 'one of the rare democratic actions of our time'. After approving the Government's planned educational and prison reforms, Connolly went on to list 'some major indications of a civilised society', including the abolition of the death penalty; model prisons; the abolition of slums; free light and heat, almost free clothing, food, transport and medical attention; 'vocations for all, not just work'; the abolition of censorship, phone-tapping, passports and identity cards; 'laws which deal with homosexuality, divorce, bigamy, abortion etc. to be based on intelligent humanism', with the same applying to bathing costumes and licensing laws; and no discrimination on the basis of 'colour, race, class or creed'.

Although no government could guarantee encouraging 'a passionate curiosity about art, science and the purpose of life', many of Connolly's desiderata remain on the agenda, and a few have been brought into effect: but they were guaranteed to incite Waugh to ridicule – still more so since he was still smarting over Edmund Wilson having criticised *Brideshead Revisited* in the *New Yorker* while admiring *The Unquiet Grave*.† Writing once again in

* 'Poor Smarting Smarty came to see me and said he hadn't meant to read the review but that wicked Raymond [Mortimer] told him it was most flattering and led him on,' Nancy Mitford reported to Evelyn Waugh.

† 'I think you over-praise Waugh, especially as you know Firbank,' Connolly wrote to Edmund Wilson: 'I thought *Brideshead* a terribly vulgar book, with a housemaid writing all the purple passages – though the satire is very good indeed at times.'

the *Tablet*, under the heading of 'Palinurus in Never-Never Land: or, the *Horizon* Blue-Print of Chaos', Waugh began by mentioning the popularity of *Horizon* among the armed forces during the war – even if much of what appeared there was nonsense, it was 'gentle, civilian nonsense which contrasted sweetly with the harsh nonsense of regimental orders' – before moving on to the vexed matter of its editor's socialism, and his recent editorial. 'It has been Palinurus's achievement,' he concluded,

> to produce a plan so full of internal contradictions that it epitomises the confusion of all his contemporaries. This plan is not the babbling of a secondary-school girl at a Youth Rally but the written words of the mature and respected leader of the English intellectuals. It is reassuring to know that the revelation came to him in what he, less than poetically, describes as a 'lyric contribution to the poetry of motion' – the new cocktail bar of the Golden Arrow train.

Connolly, Waugh reported, was refraining from reading his article rather than jeopardise their friendship; but in the end curiosity proved too strong, and Connolly wrote to his assailant to say that 'I thought you fought unfairly i.e. pretending not to know who Palinurus was so as to insult me, and making cracks about the Golden Arrow unseemly in a fellow-toper.' Waugh's very personalised distaste for *The Unquiet Grave* was to return and haunt its victim over a quarter of a century later. He had read it first while stationed at Ragusa, on the Dalmatian coast, and had annotated his copy with comments far harsher than any that appeared in print; and Connolly's unwitting discovery of these was to provide a melancholy coda to a friendship in which – on Waugh's part at least – affection, sadism and similarity were luridly interwoven.

NINETEEN

Paging Mr Smartiboots

Four months after Philip Toynbee had written from the Café Flore, Connolly at last realised his wartime dream and returned to France. Like many of his grander or more literary compatriots, Evelyn Waugh, Cecil Beaton, Peter Quennell, Randolph Churchill among them, he stayed with Duff and Diana Cooper at the newly-reopened British Embassy, which had swiftly become one of the centres of Paris social life for French and British alike. The Coopers, he told Lys, had been 'angelic'; what he had particularly enjoyed about his trip, he told Diana afterwards, was 'getting to know you and Duff, who has always frightened me before – but I see now that one has to stand one's ground, however frightened, and the storm blows over.' His host and hostess, on the other hand, were a good deal more grudging about their guest. Duff Cooper found him intensely irritating – some years later Nancy Mitford reported him as being 'undeservedly vicious' about Connolly, adding 'apoplectically' that Noël Coward was in any case a far better writer – while Lady Diana dismissed him as 'disgustingly ugly in a fat yet mean way. I don't derive any pleasure from his company.'

'We've had C. Conelly [*sic*] for three weeks in the house being fêted as tho he were Voltaire returned,' Diana Cooper informed Evelyn Waugh; and indeed Connolly found himself being endlessly entertained. Philippe de Rothschild* took him everywhere in his car and plied him with 'duchesses and champagne', and French writers seemed far more accessible than their English equivalents. At the Café Flore – where he recognised many of the waiters from before the war – he met Queneau, Paulhan, Genet and Simone de Beauvoir: Sonia Brownell had written from London urging him to read Sartre's '*Qu'est que la Littérature?*' in *Les Temps Modernes*, but although it was re-published in translation in *Horizon* some months later, its author had gone to America. Connolly lunched with Michaux and Eluard, got on well

* Connolly had got to know the Baron Philippe – owner of Château Mouton Rothschild – in London during the war. De Rothschild escaped from France via the Pyrenees and Portugal in 1940, and made his way to London and joined the Free French. Shortly after his arrival, according to Virginia Cowles, he was approached in the Hyde Park Hotel by a complete stranger, who thanked him (and his wine) for making life bearable during the Blitz. Connolly was the grateful stranger, and a friendship was struck up.

with Cocteau, and relished French writers' apparent interest in ideas and lack of pomposity: English literary life, on the other hand, 'is not a world of ideas but of personalities, a world of clubs and honours and ancestor-worship and engagement books, where a writer one wants to meet has to be hunted for several weeks until he is finally coralled at bay under some formidable mantelpiece'. Paris in the January snow seemed more like 'Petrograd' than the city of his youth; but despite a visit to a Gestapo execution chamber, London, by comparison, seemed 'utterly remote – a grey, sick wilderness on another planet, for in Paris the civilian virtues triumph – personal relations, adult-minded seriousness, aliveness, love of the arts. Literature is enormously important there and one sees how pervasive, though impalpable, have become the irritable lassitude, brain-fatigue, apathy and humdrummery of English writers.' The only fly in the ointment was his rusty French: he found himself struggling to keep up, 'very much the official *étranger de marque*, grinning, dumb, anxious to please': he longed to be able to think in French but, more often than not, had to reproach himself with '*Comme vous étiez bête ce soir!*'

Back in the 'grey, sick wilderness' – where the war was still going on – his francophilia remained as ardent as ever. James Lees-Milne found himself sitting next to him at the Etoile, and 'He said he came back from Paris two hours ago; that in Paris you felt the French were living, whereas in London you knew the English were dead. Poor English!' T.S. Eliot asked whether he should take a dinner-jacket when visiting Paris, and honoured the *Horizon* offices with his presence at a reading given by the left-wing poet Louis Aragon, which was further enlivened by a doodlebug flying over – according to John Lehmann, 'a frozen look began to come over the faces of the audience' as the poet read on, undisturbed – and by the late arrival of a drunken Philip Toynbee, who announced his presence by tripping over a crate of empties in the hall, and then proceeded to comment on the proceedings in a loud voice. A counter-attraction was provided by Nancy Mitford, who – Elizabeth Bowen recalled – 'distinguished herself by standing in the middle of the room and saying in her clear, high voice, "Of course, I think Aragon's marvellous – what a pity we haven't got any poets in this country!" Eliot and the others merely lowered their heads like tortoises and blinked.'

Even if, in Nancy Mitford's opinion, English poets weren't pulling their weight, *The Unquiet Grave* continued to attract plaudits, not least through a *Horizon* questionnaire, in which writers were asked to nominate the best book published in England during the war, and comment on the outlook for English literature and culture: both Elizabeth Bowen and Philip Toynbee voted for Palinurus, and were lavish in their praise. Their eulogies have in retrospect a somewhat melancholy flavour, in that Connolly's future full-length books, much admired as they often were, consisted of carefully arranged and selected reviews, essays and sketches rather than original works, the titles of which – *Previous Convictions*, *The Evening Colonnade* – combined the comical and the elegiac, the rueful and the defiant; and later that year Routledge brought out the first and best of these under the title of *The Condemned Playground*. Back in 1941 Mr Ragg had expressed enthusiasm about a collection of pieces, while regretting that Connolly hadn't found the time to trawl through back-numbers of the *New Statesman*: two years later Connolly announced that he – or, rather, Sonia and Diana, both of whom did the donkey-work – had put a collection together, bearing in mind Herbert Read's suggestion that the material should be arranged in three sections: literary essays, parodies (including 'Where Engels Fears to Tread', 'Told in Gath' and two tales of Felicity, the blurb-writer's daughter), and general pieces, among them reportage from Greece in 1933 and the Spanish Civil War. 'You say somewhere in one of those articles that you are a lyricist,' John Betjeman told him shortly after publication:

> I think you are. I think these short articles are just your medium – for you have a gift for parody which never goes on for too long and which less talented writers would expand into a book . . . No one would think that you in that huge coat and with no hat on your head and going off to Soho would notice everything as you do. I must say old boy *The Condemned Playground* makes me proud to know you.

Equally admiring was Edmund Wilson, writing in the *New Yorker*: when it came to literary matters, he felt, Connolly was 'not quite a first-rate critic', but 'these imaginary memoirs and parodies are in a vein distinct from anyone else's, and some of them are really terrific'.

Not long after the Aragon party, another was given – not, this time, by Connolly and Lys – for Edmund Wilson, who arrived in London in April 1945, and stayed for a month at the Hyde Park Hotel. A short, pugnacious figure, keen on the bottle and a tireless womaniser, Wilson occupied much the same kind of position in New York literary life as Connolly on this side of the Atlantic: he was an influential and much-admired reviewer and essayist, an early enthusiast for the Modern Movement, and a shrewd assessor of the literary stock market; and whereas most academic critics were notable for the narrowness of their range and interests, Wilson was remarkable for his readiness to tackle, combatively and with authority, subjects as diverse as the Russian Revolution, American Indians and the Dead Sea Scrolls – in much the same way as, in the years to come, Connolly would often prefer to review for the *Sunday Times* a book on African wildlife or deep-sea diving or a political assassination than more ostensibly 'literary' subjects. Both men scorned academic literary critics, Connolly more fearfully, Wilson with greater confidence; both longed to be novelists, but lacked the necessary gifts; only on the vexed subject of writing books did their apparent equivalence fall down. 'I wish I had your *grasp*,' Connolly once told the older man: 'I am really only a napkin-folder.' Connolly and V.S. Pritchett were the only English critics Wilson admired; he found Waugh patronising and condescending, and particularly disliked Maurice Bowra, whose supercilious manner seemed to embody all that he most despised in English literary life. He brought with him the proofs of his novel, *Memoirs of Hecate County*: Roger Senhouse had rejected it at Secker on the grounds of obscenity, and Wilson was looking for another English publisher.* At the party, according to John Lehmann, London's literary 'top brass' were on their best behaviour, with only a drunken Brian Howard lowering the tone, though 'the little man in the drab clothes who was the guest of honour lurked rather silently in corners, was difficult to draw out, and gave a distinct impression of displeasure.' But Wilson probably enjoyed himself more than appeared: back in America, he wrote to Mamaine Koestler to say how he felt 'a certain nostalgia for London – those nice little restaurants and Cyril Connolly and his champagne . . .'

Even if Connolly never wrote – or wanted to write – an English equivalent of Wilson's *To the Finland Station*, his political instincts were still fashionably left-wing, though leavened as ever by ambivalence. Writing his 'Comment' in the June issue of *Horizon*, he said that although the country owed its survival to Churchill, he would be voting Labour in the forthcoming election: since 'all human beings are sentenced to death . . . we are all entitled to the courtesies of the death cell, just as being all members of that most exclusive institution, the *club des vivants*, we are all privileged to enjoy the amenities of the spherical reading-room which is our world.' Sharing these amenities involved levelling up society, narrowing the gap which separated the rich and the poor, and making Britain part of a Europe free of passports and travel restrictions: both were more likely to come about

* *Hecate County* was not published in Britain until 1951, and Connolly reviewed it for the *Sunday Times*. Wilson was, he suggested, a critic of genius, but – like many before him – he had been seduced by dreams of writing the Great American Novel. 'Critics are generally considered inferior to novelists, they are not "creative" and are supposed to lack invention, imagination and narrative power,' he went on, combining – as he so often did – elements of rueful self-analysis with discussion of the book under review: 'But critics are generally bad novelists because they prefer books to people; they like ideas in the raw, and characters at one remove.' Wilson was hurt by what he considered a 'hideously bad review', and was particularly stung by Connolly's describing the narrator as a 'desiccated buffoon'; writing to Mamaine Koestler, he consoled himself with the thought that Connolly was jealous of his good sales.

under a socialist government, run by kindred spirits far removed from the ineffectual and misguided ruling class of the pre-war years.

A passport was still called for when, in July, Connolly returned to Paris with Peter Watson. They stayed in Watson's flat in the rue du Bac, and it was, Connolly told Lys, dreadfully depressing. There were no clean sheets or hot water, and he had to sleep on the sofa; the flat was 'very dilapidated and buggery', and, to make matters worse, it was 'heavily mined' with memories of his pre-war life with Jean: a spring of mistletoe which Jean and Denham Fouts had nailed up in Christmas 1938 was still there, and Jean's photograph by Man Ray was pinned to the bathroom wall.* Nor did Paris or the French seem anything like as exhilarating as they had back in January. Wandering round the 'bleached, tropical city', Connolly felt that the French had suffered a kind of collective nervous breakdown. The trains were dirty, there was nothing in the shops, the black market was booming, the locals were mistrustful; only some kind of 'European federation' could put things right. As always, Connolly's reactions were suffused with nostalgia and regret: what he missed above all were the tourists and the artists and the armies of American girls 'with their satchels and sketch-books, their exotic looks and wholesome voices' whom he remembered from before the war: but maybe such regrets were nothing more than 'middle-aged mumbling over the grave of youth?'

The only consolation lay in company, English as often as not – though he had drinks with Gide, and met the painters Jean Hugo and Balthus, 'a depressing and anal gentleman' whose work he came to admire greatly. He spent time with Stuart Hampshire and Raymond Mortimer and Christopher Sykes, who drove him round in his jeep; got drunk in a night-club with Freddy Ayer and Solly Zuckerman; and, not long before the poet's death, paid a visit to one of his literary heroes, Paul Valéry. Mischievous as ever, Nancy Mitford passed on to Evelyn Waugh a French friend's account of the meeting, suitably exaggerated to the detriment of Smartiboots:

> The French don't think SB knows their language at all and they could see it was dreadful torture to him to be in the same room with the master and not be able to understand one word he said. SB turned first one ear, then the other, but all in vain.

After scouring the *antiquaires* in search of items that might look well in his new London home, Connolly took the train for Switzerland, still

* Fouts too was back in Paris. He told Gore Vidal how he and Peter Watson took Connolly to a restaurant in the rue du Bac where 'he ordered a huge lunch – he's very fat and greedy, you know – and he ate it all up very fast and then he ordered a second lunch and ate that too. Then he fainted. The waiters carried him back and put him over there on the floor.' A good story, but improbable, alas.

accompanied by Peter Watson. Switzerland seemed a miracle of cleanliness and opulence. The shops brimmed over with cigars and citrus fruits; they ate breakfast on the balcony of their sumptuous hotel in Berne, swam in the lake at Thun, and stayed at Gstaad where, Peter Watson informed Brian Howard, they dined with duchesses and Connolly made a particular friend of a Guinness. In between swimming and socialising and luxuriating – 'one can't be an intellectual in this atmosphere where watches are discussed like old masters and where to swim is the most important daily question' – Connolly bought clothes and shoes for Lys, assured her that '*je t'adore à la folie*,' and worried that Woodrow Wyatt, recently elected a Labour MP and 'in the full flush of his political glory', might be getting too friendly with her. After a few days the cleanliness and the well-stocked shops began to pall, and a certain boredom set in. He wished he'd been in England for the elections, he told Lys: he was sad that the Liberals hadn't done better, but even so 'It will be so nice to be governed by intelligent and *quiet* people – not those horrible money-loving roistering anti-intellectual exhibitionists' who swelled the Tory ranks. He hoped that *Horizon* would have a part to play in creating a juster, more egalitarian Britain; but in the meantime, absence made the heart grow fonder and 'I love you so much I don't know when I have been so in love.'

Returning from the sunshine of Switzerland, London – seen from the air – was swathed in a 'vast thick cloud of sooty mucus', the capital of a worn and battered country in which wine, coal, domestic servants and the means of travelling abroad were all lamentably hard to come by.* Luckily Connolly had much to distract him from the dismal state of post-war Britain. Shortly before leaving for Paris, he and Lys had left Bedford Square for a house in Sussex Place, one of the white stuccoed Nash terraces that encircle Regent's Park. 'Connolly has moved from Bloomsbury to Regent's Park,' Waugh informed Patrick Kinross:

> He and Mrs Lubbock have imposed on a dead-end kid called, I think, Jacqueline, a former connection of yours, half-sister of Angela; she has bare feet like a camel, a face like Prod's, and a baby by a communist doctor. She has been induced to purchase a substantial mansion of which she is allowed the use of attics and basements while the Connollies squat on the three principal floors.†

* 'There is about London a certain flavor of Soviet Moscow,' Edmund Wilson observed: '. . . How empty, how sickish, how senseless everything suddenly seems the moment the war is over.'

† 'Prod' was Nancy Mitford's husband, Peter Rodd; the 'communist doctor' was Kenneth Sinclair-Loutit, by whom Janetta had a daughter.

Janetta (not 'Jacqueline') had, until recently, combined occasional work on *Horizon*, rejecting unwanted offerings, with her duties with the ARP. Sinclair-Loutit, whose name she had taken, was keen to marry her, and wrote from Belgrade, where he was stationed, urging her to join him there with their daughter: but she was reluctant to do so, not least because she had recently met, through Nico Henderson, a handsome young ex-RAF pilot called Robert Kee who had escaped from a German prisoner-of-war camp and was beginning to make his way as a writer.* Her close friends Ralph and Frances Partridge advised her against going to Yugoslavia; and she decided instead to take an entire house in Sussex Place on a twenty-year lease from the Crown Agents, paying £30 a quarter and sub-letting part to Connolly and Lys. Janetta lived on the ground floor, where she was joined by Robert Kee, and had the use of the third floor and the attic; Connolly and Lys had the use of the two first-floor rooms, opening up the connecting doors when they gave a party, and slept on the second floor; all four shared the basement, which consisted of a vast kitchen for Janetta's use, and a smaller kitchen-cum-dining-room in which Connolly served up what Waugh described as 'superb grub' at his dinner parties. Invariably there was a great deal of coming and going, which made Kee understandably irritable; the house had dry rot – a problem which Lucian Freud's architect father, Ernst, struggled in vain to remedy – and John Craxton provided a dash of colour by painting vivid allegorical scenes on the interconnecting doors.

That June, Frances Partridge visited Sussex Place, and was 'stunned by its grandeur and beauty'. Janetta's rooms looked fresh and bright, and opened on to the garden; and since Connolly was away, Frances was unable to resist stealing upstairs to take a look at the lodgers' quarters:

> Oh my lord what a contrast! I had seen these rooms empty and fallen in love with them. But instead of treating them in any way visually, as a painter his canvas, he has stuffed them with symbols of success and good living – massive dark furniture, side-boards groaning with decanters and silver coffee-pots, Sèvres porcelain, heavy brocade curtains, safe but dim pictures. I think the worse of him after seeing it.

'Cyril is now obsessed by porcelain and silver gilt and nauseated by books,' Waugh confided to his diary a couple of years later, followed soon after by

* Kee was, in fact, then working on his account of his experiences as a POW, *A Crowd is not Company*: originally and mistakenly published as a novel, it is one of the finest books to emerge from the Second World War.

'Cyril obsessed with French eighteenth-century *objets d'art*. "I want to make a mausoleum where I can lie surrounded by the finest works of the period where students will come to peer through a window at me and them".' Connolly never abandoned books as objects to read or collect, but as he failed to write them, collecting porcelain and silver and furniture and first editions, and prowling round expensive antique shops, became, perhaps, a kind of substitute: the only trouble was that his visual taste – as manifested in his taste in paintings, or in his curious liking for Hawaiian-type shirts, ablaze with palm trees and worn outside the trousers, and sinister-looking black lattice sandals – was inferior to his taste in writing; and, as Anthony Powell unkindly remembered, his real knowledge of (say) wine and porcelain seldom matched up to the grave enthusiasm he brought to bear upon them, so laying him open to mockery and the occasional harmless confidence trick.

*

One of Connolly's neighbours in Regent's Park was Elizabeth Bowen, and during the week of VE Day she wrote him a fan letter. He was, she suggested, one of those – like Churchill – to whom 'one owes something better than mere survival':

> I know that many of us owe you a lot, and I do certainly. *Horizon* has been most valuable of all as evidence of continuity; and you've done so much for this continuity in your person. Your parties had something more even than your and Lys's beautiful hospitality can account for, and something without which even intellectual happiness would be desperate: real spirit . . .*

One spokesman for wartime Britain who felt less well-disposed towards Connolly was Noël Coward; though admiring of *The Unquiet Grave*, he had harboured a grudge ever since Connolly heaped some well-turned derision on his autobiography in the *New Statesman* two years before the outbreak of war. In his play *Peace in Our Time*, first produced in 1947, Coward presupposed that Britain had been occupied by the Germans, and that among those on especially good terms with the local Gestapo was Chorley Bannister, the editor of a high-brow magazine called *Progress*. Bannister's conver-

* She also joined him and H.G. Wells in a letter to *The Times*, protesting against the possibility of the Government pulling down some of the Nash terraces. The houses were saved; but in his March 1949 'London Letter' for *Partisan Review*, Connolly noted that strip lighting and no curtains were all too often *de rigueur* now that the pre-war inhabitants had given way to dreaded civil servants.

sation is 'affected and inclined to be over-provocative. He is devoid of moral integrity and easily frightened. He can, however, be witty on occasions.' Towards the end of the play Bannister is savaged by a good egg called Janet, according to whom 'You babble a lot of snobbish nonsense about art and letters and truth and beauty. You consider yourselves to be far above such primitive emotions as love and hate and devotion to a cause...' Peter Quennell was incensed on his friend's behalf, but there is no evidence that Connolly saw the play, or was aware of the strong feelings he aroused in the Master's breast.

Among those who affected to share some of Coward's disdain for *Horizon*'s literary pretensions was, inevitably, Nancy Mitford. 'I've just had this month's Smarty's Own Mag & of course the great joke is that one does write better than all of them (not SB himself) because even when they quite *want* to be understood they can't be,' she told Waugh; she had asked Duff Cooper whether she shouldn't keep her back numbers for hospitals, but he said he couldn't see why 'you should *add* to their sufferings like that'. Waugh, for his part, must have been relieved to read the 'Comment' of December 1945, in which the editor promised to use fewer contributions by French authors now that French journals were more available on this side of the Channel. Connolly went on to say that he would continue to campaign against the death penalty and identity cards, and in favour of unfettered travel and 'our free-born privilege to use a false name once in a while'. His hope of a Labour government ushering in a more civilised society seemed doomed to frustration: not only had a 'socialist literature' failed to emerge, but the Government had done nothing to alleviate the writer's lot, forcing even the brightest and best into becoming 'culture diffusionists'. Connolly's obsession with the ways in which writers made – or failed to make – a living resurfaced in a *Horizon* authors' questionnaire, in which writers were asked how much they needed to live on, whether they could earn this through their writing, what occupation was most compatible with writing, whether the State should do more for writers, and what advice they would give young writers starting out. Those whose replies were printed in the magazine included Robert Graves, Rose Macaulay, George Orwell, V.S. Pritchett, John Betjeman, Stephen Spender, C. Day Lewis, Herbert Read and – from a younger generation – Maclaren-Ross, Laurie Lee, Dylan Thomas, Robert Kee, William Sansom and John Russell. For his part, Connolly suggested that for a writer to enjoy 'leisure and privacy, marry, buy books, travel and entertain his friends', he needed at least five pounds a day. Selling everything he wrote in America as well as Britain was 'the only dignified way of making more money without giving up more time'; a rich wife was the ideal secondary source of income, but the State should supplement private patronage, shelling out money to those starting out, and providing pensions, tax allowances, and the occasional year's holiday with pay.*

If earnings from American magazines and publishers were important to the writer, American subscribers were increasingly essential to *Horizon*; and it was to drum up American support, and gather material for an American number, that Connolly and Peter Watson set out for New York on board the *Franconia* in November 1946. Glimpsing the Nantucket light marked the end of a 'prep school voyage' characterised by 'dull dormitory life, brisk monotonous heavy meals, no drink, a constant scramble for chairs, endless pitching and tossing', redeemed only by 'the charm of my sweet Peter and by the total penetration of my being by the author of *Les Fleurs du Mal*'. As the ship docked, England seemed very remote, like 'a weekend cottage which one has abandoned with all the washing-up undone'. Peter Watson was staying in luxury at the Cumberland, Connolly less grandly at the Grosvenor, where he was met by W.H. Auden and Tony Bower: Auden, he noted, was 'charming though very battered-looking, more American-looking and much less self-conscious than in London'. Connolly's shopping-list included a Parker 51, a blue overcoat, socks, shoes, shirts and clothes for Lys: Hamish Hamilton warned Cass Canfield that his 'greatest material ambition' was to buy an American car and have it shipped home, and suggested that Harper might consider advancing him some more money to help him realise his dream. Connolly longed to eat lobsters and avocadoes, and no doubt he gratified these urges while lunching at the *New Yorker*, with his hero e.e. cummings, and with Canfield – who, or so he told Hamilton, was deliberately playing it cool, whereas Connolly's other American publishers, Macmillan, had overdone the hospitality, setting up innumerable useless appointments, to their visitor's irritation. Connolly's stock was high, and it was given a further boost by the influential critic Jacques Barzun of Columbia University: writing at length in *Atlantic Monthly*, he diagnosed and praised Connolly as a representative of modern sensibility. 'Cyril's triumphant tour here must be seen to be believed,' Peter Watson told Brian Howard: 'The Director of the Metropolitan had us to lunch and gave us a personally conducted tour of the Museum, and everything else is rather at that level. It's too much for me.' After such grandeur, Connolly welcomed the 'luxury of poverty' in Chester Kallman's bed-sitter, where he and Auden were treated to 'clam juice mixed with chicken broth, chops with

* Connolly was a firm believer in the symbiotic relationship between the upper-class patron and the middle-class writer or artist, between Society at its most intelligent and liberal-minded and Bohemia at its least farouche. As he put it in *Enemies of Promise*, 'It must be remembered that in fashionable society can be found warm-hearted people of delicate sensibility who form permanent relationships with artists which afford them ease and encouragement for the rest of their lives and provide them with sanctuary.'

a sauce and lima beans, lederkranz cheese and pumpernickel, dry California wine'. Auden spoke of the importance to the writer of anonymity, of escaping from the 'happy family at home'. Connolly wondered how life in a black slum, with a view of fire escapes, could be preferable to Regent's Park or the Ile St Louis; but walking back to Washington Square at two in the morning he bought some more e.e. cummings in an all-night second-hand bookshop – interviewed on the radio, he had described his religion as 'cummingsism' – and relished, for the first time, perhaps, 'that anonymous urban civilisation that Auden has chosen, and of which Baudelaire dreamed and despaired'. 'Seldom has a more harmless or profitable philosophy of life been evolved, a more resolute opponent of art, remorse and introspection, or one further removed from the futile European speculation about the Soul or the Past, the moping about sin and death, the clinging to moribund methods, ideals, relationships, the pangs of *ennui*,' he informed *Horizon* readers after meditating on the cheerful materialism of the American Way of Life: he found the shops and the restaurants and the bars an endless delight, all of which went

> to form an unforgettable picture of what a city ought to be: that is, continuously insolent and alive, a place where one can buy a book or meet a friend at any hour of the day or night, where every language is spoken and xenophobia almost unknown, where every purse and appetite is catered for . . . If Paris is the setting for romance, New York is the perfect city in which to get over one, to get over anything. Here the lost *douceur de vivre* is forgotten and the intoxication of living takes its place.

'I could never write a line in New York, what with the drink and the people, it is hard enough to *read* there,' he told Edmund Wilson: a 'glowing, blooming, stimulating material perfection' over-charged the mind, 'causing it to precipitate into wit and conversation those ideas which might be set into literature'. Once the visitor began to succumb to the allure of wit and wisecrack, 'it's time for flight, for dripping plane trees, the grizzling circle of hyper-critical friends, the fecund London inertia where nothing stirs but the soul.' Writing to Lys, he said he had resolved '(1) to withdraw from the world and the office and live for literature on my return (2) never to forget for one moment that Flaubert and Baudelaire are for me *the* ideal, the touchstone.'

No doubt Cass Canfield – who had, after all, commissioned a book on the subject, not one word of which had been written – rejoiced in his author's enthusiasm for Flaubert; in the meantime, he hurried through a 2500-copy reprint of *The Unquiet Grave* – it had, inconveniently, gone out of print just as Palinurus arrived in New York – and lent a sympathetic ear when Connolly told him that *Horizon* was taking up too much of his time and energy and would probably be abandoned by the end of the decade, and that he was thinking of moving into book publishing instead: perhaps, Canfield suggested to his colleague in London, the two firms should co-operate in backing Connolly Books? But before he could bend his mind to such matters, Connolly had taken a plane to California. From San Francisco he drove south, calling on Henry Miller at Big Sur, near Carmel. 'I felt I could live there if the Bohemians weren't so destructive,' he told Edmund Wilson; though Miller's 'romantic shack' was crammed with editions of Rimbaud, Miller told Lawrence Durrell that 'what he really came for, I think, was to see the last of the race of *otters*, which are off this coast. But he saw none – and showed his disappointment keenly.' He disliked Hollywood, but felt 'exquisitely refreshed' after meeting his former idol, Aldous Huxley. The year before, Connolly had reviewed Huxley's *Time Must Have a Stop* in the *New Statesman*, and declared that his fallen hero 'seems to have been born again'; and now, lunching with him in his home in the desert, 'I loved him again'. After lunch he fell asleep, dreamed that his host appeared to him in a blue light, and awoke 'with an extraordinary sense of serenity and consolation'. Huxley's reactions were less ecstatic: 'One likes him, *malgré tout*,' he told Christopher Isherwood.*

From Los Angeles he made his way to New Orleans, which he found disappointing, and so by train to New York and home. He liked America very much, he told Edmund Wilson, the proofs of whose novel he was showing to possible publishers and fearless printers, with no success so far: 'I have thought a lot about whether I would like to go and live in America,' but although he was attracted by the food, the climate and the friendliness of the inhabitants, he worried about the shortage of antique shops ('but perhaps one would want them less?'); and he could always see Auden, e.e. cummings and Wilson himself on their occasional trips to Europe. And, of course, America provided constant reminders of Jean, from whom he was now divorced, under American law at least. While in New York he had a

* Thereafter the two men kept in touch on Huxley's occasional trips to London. Connolly wrote a profile of his old mentor in *Picture Post* – he remarked on the 'radiance of serenity and loving kindness on his features' – and two years later they enjoyed a triangular lunch with Raymond Mortimer. 'Longevity is the revenge of talent upon genius,' Connolly remarked during the meal:

Aldous: Who said that?
Cyril: I.
Aldous: When?
Cyril: Now.
Aldous: Then I think we must all applaud.

nightmare about 'Jean who comes back as a puffy, corpse-like creature,' and before leaving for New York he had told Wilson that

> I have an American wife whom I still have the misfortune to love and as she has divorced me to marry another American, with a vastly ramified literary family, I have a great sense of inferiority about the continent – or rather ambivalence, since I feel superiority as well – and I naturally imagine that the customs officer at the pier head will say at once, 'So that's him – well, I don't blame her.'

He worried that he would 'come on Jean's traces everywhere, and I don't think I should be able to bear it': could Wilson find out 'if she is (a) officially divorced from me (b) actually married to him yet, and whether she is well and happy... Do tell me more about the marriage. I know the children make her v. happy and I have brought myself to acknowledge that she is in love with Vail.' The year before, Peter Watson had seen Jean in Paris with Denham Fouts; he had urged Connolly to get in touch with her, and was sure she was only interested in Laurence Vail as a makeshift. In New York, Tony Bower told Connolly that he was certain Jean wasn't in love with Vail; he wondered, too, why Connolly spent so much time there with Jean's sister Annie, being with whom filled him 'with a guilty melancholy and *tendresse*'. Connolly's reluctant separation from Jean was as complicated and as agonising as their pre-war parting, exercising to the full his powers of self-pity, ambivalence and nostalgia for all he had lost.

In October 1944 – according to a statement he later provided for his solicitors – Connolly had written to Jean to say that unless she returned to him within three months he would institute divorce proceedings; by now she was living in New York with Laurence Vail and his two children by Peggy Guggenheim, and some five months later she wrote back to say that she was in love with Vail, and couldn't come back. From Switzerland Connolly wrote to Lys to say that he couldn't bear to be away from her – he felt as though he had been cut in half – and that he was thinking of getting a divorce from Jean; would she make sure that Tony Bower didn't leave England to return to the States without seeing Connolly's solicitor, Craig MacFarlane, as 'his evidence may be invaluable'? Three months later MacFarlane suggested that his client should institute divorce proceedings; but in the meantime Jean had cabled from Reno, Nevada, to say that she intended to start unilateral proceedings. MacFarlane pointed out that a Reno divorce wouldn't apply in Britain: there should be no difficulty in proving her adultery in the States, but if extra evidence was needed they could cite her adultery in England as well, shortly before she left in 1940;

quite what this consisted of remains unclear. But despite his assurances to Lys, Connolly was reluctant to go through with even a Reno divorce. Jean cabled again in November, begging him to sign the necessary papers; a few days later she wrote to say that she would happily get divorced twice over if needs be: she had stayed in Reno quite long enough, and wanted to be shot of it ('I don't look forward to a Christmas spent in company with other lonely souls in the bar of the Riverside to the clash and clatter of slot machines and the click of the roulette wheel'). 'Think you are making greatest mistake of your life and can't connive. What is three months anyway, I waited here for five years,' Connolly cabled back: 'Three months here like 300 elsewhere. Please let me out,' came Jean's reply. In a following letter she told him that she had learned to stand on her own two feet since leaving him – he had always made her feel unsure of herself. One particular episode from their parting had always rankled: 'When you were in love with Diana and came back and made love to me . . . you said she was more like your wife while I was your mistress. I was a poor wife, I know. But you hurt me in my heart and upset me in my body then and ever after.' As for Vail, 'he is not young, but he is not the burnt-out end of dreary candlesticks you seem to imagine.' 'Well,' she concluded, 'I loved you very much and I like you very much and I hope you will be happy with someone managing and pliable and much nicer than apeface Jeannie . . . You are a great successful man now. Not for you a middle-aged, poorish American expatriate on-the-town-girl, romantic, insufferable.'

Reno was all very well as far as the States were concerned – Jean's Nevada divorce came through in March 1946, and she married Laurence Vail that same day – but it was not until April 1948 that Connolly was granted a Decree Nisi, and was finally divorced from Jean on both sides of the Atlantic: the marriage was dissolved on grounds of desertion and adultery, with Clement Greenberg and Laurence Vail cited as co-respondents. Mrs Alannah Statlender (*née* Harper) provided a statement; Tom Driberg was asked if he could remember exactly when Connolly had first told him about Jean's affair with Greenberg (most probably, he thought, in the spring or summer of 1941). A year before the divorce came through, Greenberg wrote Connolly an extraordinary letter about Jean. She was, he suggested, 'a kind of praying mantis whom love consumes'; having known her so long, and from so young an age, Connolly probably failed to realise 'how utterly and absolutely destructive she is'. 'Heathen, idolatrous, carnal, Gentile', she was all that he had been warned against as a nicely brought-up Jewish boy. 'Everyone who is ever in love with Jean contracts a mother neurosis,' he suggested: she paralysed and destroyed the men in her life by playing a bogus motherly role, revenging herself on her father when they were finally reduced to pulp, 'helpless, prostrate and weepy'. Connolly would be destroyed if she returned to him, and was far better off without 'her fear of humiliation, her willingness to be humiliated, her vengefulness'. As for the hapless Vail, he was a nice, kind man in an advanced stage of alcoholism; he and Jean were drinking more than ever, and gradually fading out together . . .

With the divorces coming through, Jean's drunken decline continued apace. The painter Michael Wishart saw a good deal of her in Paris during the last years of her life, and remembered her as being 'wonderful company, especially during the first stops on our endlessly exploitative club crawls, but by the time I knew her the ravishing had become the ravaged.' Wishart shared Peter Watson's infatuation with Jean's constant companion, Denham Fouts, who eventually died of a heroin overdose while sitting on the lavatory. One evening Wishart and Jeannie came home to find him naked, with a hypodermic dangling from his bleeding arm: though extremely drunk herself, Jeannie sloshed water over him, and brought him round.

In May 1947, Jeannie was admitted to hospital in Paris for a minor operation; and afterwards she and her mother – who had recently had a stroke – went to recuperate in Laurence Vail's chalet at Megève in the French Alps, where Connolly had been ski-ing before the war. He and Lys paid them a visit, and he saw Jean again for the first time since 1940. She was thinner and younger-looking than expected. After lunch with Vail and his children, Connolly and Jean walked alone into the village. She cried, and as they passed the church she told him that she often stopped off there: it was, he later surmised, 'perhaps a way of telling me that she was often bored'. He saw her again in Paris in November 1948: she was with all her old friends from before the war, Joan Rayner, Graham Eyres-Monsell and Jennifer Fry among them, and although Connolly later claimed that he enjoyed the occasional clandestine meeting with Jeannie in London, it was thought unwise to allow him to lunch with her alone, and her sister Annie came along as a chaperone.

In July 1950, Annie Davis sent Connolly a telegram to say that Jean had died, without much pain, after a week's illness. She had meant more to him than any other woman, and her loss – which he continued to feel for the rest of his life – coincided not just with the end of *Horizon* and the beginning of his necessary enslavement to the books pages of the *Sunday Times*, but with the effective abandonment of any real attempt to produce those full-length masterpieces of which he felt himself capable, and which provided him with his literary *raison d'être*. She haunted him in ways that were often macabre or bizarre. In 'Happy Deathbeds', Jonathan Brinkley – the over-weight, disappointed editor of a much-admired literary magazine – has a dream in which 'his first wife like a dark Greco-Roman ephebe was pointing at her new male genitals. "Look, darling, I've got something you'd like – a surprise!"'; and in 'Birds of America', Brinkley – losing weight, like his creator, at a health farm – comes across a nineteenth-century view of Baltimore, Jean's home town, in a book of Audubon's engravings, and has a sudden, morbid vision of

> the brown plump fore-arm, the narrow wrist, the very small but somehow stubby hand, so practical, self-indulgent and self-appealing, the blunt nails and the thin red scars where she had tried to cut her veins the last time he was unfaithful – the hand of his dead ex-wife which he knew once almost better than his own, now vaulted up and in a state of unimaginable decay.*

*

Jean's death was the greatest single severance from youth and its vanished Eden, but others had preceded it: starting with that of Logan Pearsall Smith, in March 1946. Over the last few years of his life, Pearsall Smith's manic depression had grown steadily worse. In 1938 he made a disastrous trip to Iceland with his secretary, Robert Gathorne-Hardy, during which pneumonia was succeeded by a spell of actual insanity; according to Gathorne-Hardy – who fell out with the old man not long before his death – he began to deteriorate in 1940, and had he not died, some five months after his eightieth birthday, he might have become an 'inescapable lunatic'. Lunatic or not, he remained in St Leonard's Terrace throughout the war, despite a bomb landing on the house. He quarrelled with those who tried to help him, including his long-suffering sister Alys, to whom he wrote messages on cheque stubs or sheets of lavatory paper; afraid to examine himself too closely, he blamed others for his shortcomings, and what had once seemed mildly malicious jokes became major grievances. He admired *Horizon* and was an occasional contributor to it; but his relations with his former protégé were marked, as ever, by guilt-inducing self-pity and a pretence of being somehow above the fray, inhabiting a rarefied empyrean of flawless syntax and perfectly modulated sentences. He liked to see himself as a roguishly subversive influence on his younger acolytes, undermining their regrettable attachment to worldly concerns and lightly rebuking them for their follies:

* There is no evidence that Jean ever tried to cut her wrists, but Brinkley's vision is a measure, perhaps, of the guilt and regret Connolly felt towards Jean. At the very end of his life, shortly before he was admitted to hospital for the last time, Connolly lay in bed with photographs of Jean propped up on the blankets around him.

early in the war he told Connolly that he had poisoned him by making him 'eat the gilded gingerbread of good writing'; he had Hugh Trevor-Roper in mind as his next victim, and suggested that 'it would be charity to warn the poor young man'. Not long afterwards he congratulated Connolly on mastering the colon, though 'the semi-colon you handle with less assurance, while your use of the apostrophe makes my flesh creep. True, you no longer write *it's* for *its*...' Connolly stood him up in the summer of 1944, and this unleashed a torrent of sarcasm:

> But in the serene, exalted, Olympian atmosphere of the stately homes of England, in which you weekend so gloriously, all Grub Street gossip can have but little interest. News that would be welcome in the intellectual circles of Noël Coward, of Sir Edward Marsh, of Ivor, I cannot aspire to provide. I am only a stepping-stone for your social Pilgrim's Progress...

'He who would free himself of shabby companions does well to shake them off in a gracious and gradual manner,' this 'dreary old nobody' went on, waxing eloquent with self-pity.

Such reproaches notwithstanding, Connolly joined Ethel Sands, Hugh Trevor-Roper and John Russell in sending his old mentor greetings on his eightieth birthday, and he reminded *Horizon* readers that he wrote 'English better than anyone now living'. But although Pearsall Smith continued to have moments of lucidity – when Connolly rang him the day before his death, he wanted to know all about George Orwell, whose writing he much admired – his melancholy and his misanthropy grew steadily worse. He turned Alys out of the house, and Gathorne-Hardy told Connolly that 'his ferocious cruelty during my last visit to him made me hate him so much that I was glad when he died.' For years, Pearsall Smith had used his will as a snare and a bait with which to entice and entangle his secretaries, but at the very end of his life he changed it once again and left everything to the writer John Russell, then in his twenties, who had worked for him for two hours a day for eight weeks after losing his job at the Admiralty.* 'How *dreadful* for you after all the promises he made you,' Mollie wrote to her son from South Africa; and Gathorne-Hardy wrote to say that, although neither of them were beneficiaries of the old man's will, he and Alys were keen that Connolly should have some of the old man's books. 'Civilisation will not lose by his death for it has his books, but his friends will all feel less civilised,' Connolly

* No sooner had Russell left Pearsall Smith's employment than he broke the old man's principal commandment and got married for the first time. An occasional contributor to *Horizon* and, later, a colleague on the *Sunday Times*, John Russell first met Connolly in Cambridge during the war: both had been to see one of Dadie Rylands's Shakespeare productions, and were fellow-guests of Victor and Barbara Rothschild.

wrote in the *New Statesman*, in an affectionate and graceful tribute to a man who had had a profound influence on his own career and his approach to literature. 'Two weeks before his death,' he wrote of his old mentor,

> a friend asked him half-jokingly if he had discovered any meaning in life. 'Yes,' he replied, 'there is a meaning, at least, for me, there is one thing that matters – to set a chime of words tinkling in the minds of a few fastidious people.'

Pearsall Smith may have been a substitute father, but a year later, in March 1947, Connolly's real father was found dead in his room at the Glendower Hotel in South Kensington, where he moved after a bomb had landed on the Naval & Military Hotel. For some reason Connolly had felt particularly depressed that morning, and had gone in to the *Horizon* offices earlier than usual; and it was there that he was rung with the news. He hurried round to the hotel, where his father was 'lying in bed on his right side with his face to the wall and seemed asleep except that his face looked very calm and distinguished. He wasn't wearing any pyjamas and the room was terribly cold.' A rug which Mollie had sent him was on the bed, but his shoulders were bare: it had been one of the coldest winters on record, there was a fuel shortage, and, Mollie told her son later, the Major not only refused to light the gas fire in his room, but had spurned her offer to send him a pair of pyjamas from South Africa. He had always wanted to die in his sleep, she went on, and she was convinced that his death had been caused by the coldness of his room.

A year or two earlier Mollie had expressed the hope that, for all the tribulations it brought in its wake, the Major wouldn't suddenly give up drinking: it could affect his heart, and 'with that lameness and pain I do not think he should give up anything that gives him comfort'. Not long after the war ended, Connolly persuaded his father to sell some furniture which had been kept in store, which raised some £300. The Major makes a brief appearance in an unpublished story from about this time – 'I'm just a little bit shabby, and a little bit noisy and insecure. I bear F for Failure like a brand that's hardly visible as yet, which will get more and more visible as I get older and show up red when I lose my temper. I can smell the cabbage odours of the hotel where I'm going to die' – but, or so Connolly reassured Mollie after his death, he began to enjoy life more towards the end: he liked writing and translating articles about food for André Simon, and enjoyed the new friends he met through his son. 'Dear brave old Daddy – it was a shock to hear he has gone,' Mollie wrote from South Africa: there was no way she could come back for the funeral or attend to the paperwork – General

Brooke's bronchitis and rheumatism were both playing up – but the Major's papers could be found in a box beside his bed, the key to which was in his waistcoat pocket. Would Connolly arrange for a gravestone in Bath Abbey cemetery, and send her the bill? And something would have to be done about his possessions – his microscope, for instance. 'He was very fond of you and very proud of you, though he may not have shown much of what he felt,' she went on; and indeed one is aware of a growing warmth between father and son in these final years, and a corresponding diminution of affection towards his absconding mother.

From Amélie-les-Bains in the Pyrenees, Aunt Tots asked if her nephew could very kindly look out for a silver shoe-horn with 'Betty' inscribed on the handle. 'He was so looking forward to coming to lunch with you and Lys next week – you were both a very High Light in his life,' she continued. What, she wondered, should be done with his collection of minerals? Should they be given to a Mrs Botley, since 'some of his happiest times' had been spent poring over them in her company? A rival claimant was Mrs 'Rusty' Payne, a girl in her early twenties who had worked with the Major on snails in the Natural History Museum: Connolly took against her – 'I think she is rather a grasping young lady' – after she had claimed that the Major had given *her* his microscope.

As Mollie had anticipated, the Major's will left nearly everything to her, even though his account at Lloyds Bank yielded only an overdraft of 6*s* 8*d*. But the Major's silver went to his son; on top of which – if we are to believe the vivid autobiographical sketches contained in 'Happy Deathbeds' – Connolly found himself the recipient of

> a vindictive eruption of trunks and boxes full of tram tickets, bus tickets, used envelopes, odd socks, old newspapers and theatre tickets – everything he had through a long life been too frightened to throw away. Cases of hideous objects resembling fossilised faeces, 'Not worth tuppence, old boy, but might come in useful some day.'

Equally dispiriting was the old man's funeral in Bath, attended by Connolly and Lys – clutching a sprig of mimosa ordered by Aunt Tots – and the infuriating 'Rusty' Payne. 'The snow fell thick and fast,' Connolly wrote in 'Happy Deathbeds', in which he appears as the magazine editor Jonathan Brinkley:

> The big Rolls from London gave one final discreet rattle and stopped on the hill. The sexton and his men helped the London drivers out with the coffin, the six of them shouldered it. 'A nice bit of elm,' the undertaker

> had called it: 'You could have pine, but you can't do better than a nice bit of elm.' A hundred pounds for as many miles, the last journey of Brinkley's father had been his only extravagance: a man who, though crippled with arthritis, would not buy an overcoat or stop a taxi which was going the wrong way as turning round added to the fare.

The clergyman had an irritating cockney accent, other funeral cortèges were pressing in behind, and the whole thing, Connolly told his mother, was 'like being left as a little boy at a new school I thought – such a final hopeless parting.' 'This cold spell knocks 'em off,' the sexton remarked as the coffin was lowered into the grave: 'Seventy-six years of fear and caution and loneliness and collecting and poverty and vintage port, fair play and bark worse than bite lay inside it, bitter with arthritis and alcohol.'

*

The funeral over, Connolly and Lys went to France, staying with Jean Hugo before moving on to Paris. Paris was, according to 'Comment', back to its pre-war self, with the Left Bank representing 'the final stronghold of free spirits against the Anglo-Saxon worship of money and respectability'. 'I hear Legionnaire Smartyboots is here – I die for him but evidently he doesn't die for me – too low-brow,' Nancy Mitford informed Evelyn Waugh. Lys came home ahead 'so that Connolly could entertain French intellectuals on her £75,' Nancy Mitford reported a few weeks later, though 'perhaps he agrees with Mr Bevin that taking your wife to Paris is like taking a ham sandwich to a banquet.'

After Paris, London seemed infinitely depressing. It was, Connolly told his readers,

> the largest, saddest and dirtiest of great cities, with its miles of unpainted, half-inhabited houses, its chopless chop-houses, its beerless pubs, its once vivid quarters losing all personality, its squares bereft of elegance, its dandies in exile, its antiques in America, its shops full of junk, bunk and tomorrow, its crowds mooning round the stained wicker of its cafeterias in their shabby raincoats, under a sky permanently dull and lowering like a dish cover.

As he rightly observed, the British inhabited

> a barren, humid, raw but densely over-populated group of islands, with an obsolete industrial plant, hideous but inadequate housing, a variety of

> unhealthy jungle possessions, vast international commitments, a falling birth-rate and a large class of infertile rentiers or over-specialised middlemen and brokers as our main capital.

Apathetic and careworn, the English suffered from 'undernourishment, lack of vitamins and sunshine, lack of hope, energy, leisure and spirit'.

One cause for celebration, however, was the award of the Order of Merit to T.S. Eliot. '*Cher Maître*,' Connolly wrote, 'In the name of *Horizon* I should like to tell you how deeply pleased we all are ...' Some six years earlier, after Virginia Woolf's suicide, Eliot had expressed his grave displeasure at *Horizon*'s failure to give him enough time to revise and correct the proofs of a tribute he had written, and this – combined with genuine admiration for the poet's work – may help to explain Connolly's eagerness to offer appropriate homage.* Another poet with cause for complaint – and that despite Connolly's heroic labours in raising money on his behalf – was Dylan Thomas. His poem 'Country Sleep', it seemed, contained 'something like *16* misprints', causing Margaret Taylor – wife of the historian A.J.P., and an ardent champion of Thomas – to write to *Horizon* to protest at the 'disgraceful way in which Dylan's poem has been offered to the public': it contained 'errors so crude, vulgar and nonsensical that the poem as it appears is quite ruined'. 'I hear on various occasions that *Horizon* is doomed to extinction,' Mrs Taylor concluded. 'If this is proved to be true, then utterly criminal artistic laziness and irresponsibility will have been the cause.'

Horizon's criminality proved no impediment to Evelyn Waugh's offering the magazine first publication rights in *The Loved One*, his novella about the Californian mortuary business. During the war he had allowed Connolly to publish an extract from *Work Suspended*, and although he liked nothing better than to ridicule the francophilia and the artistic pretensions of its staff, especially when writing to Nancy Mitford – 'I saw the inside of the *Horizon* office, full of horrible pictures collected by Watson & Lys & Miss Brownell working away with a dictionary translating some rot from the French' – he was more than happy to allow his work to appear there. 'I want it published entire,' he told Connolly in September 1947: 'That would mean devoting a whole issue to it. And I want it soon. These two stipulations may make the project unfeasible but I thought I would offer it to you first. I shall not want any payment other than your kind continuance of my

* The following year Eliot won the Nobel Prize for Literature. Connolly gave a celebratory party at Sussex Place, to which some seventy guests were invited: Connolly and John Hayward gave a joint rendition of 'Sweeney Agonistes', and Eliot followed by singing 'Under the Bamboo Tree'.

subscription.'* Twenty years later, when Connolly re-read Waugh's novella, he felt it tailed off through a 'failure of imagination', and displayed 'a certain brutality' on the part of its author – 'in my sixties I am less easily amused than when *The Loved One* appeared' – but at the time his reactions were a good deal more positive. 'Some days of anxiety about the safety of the MS of *The Loved One* – Cyril ill, his secretary incompetent, his colleague Watson mischievous, but in the end all right,' Waugh confided to his diary; and although Connolly told Enid Bagnold that he thought Waugh's story 'an immensely agreeable and readable piece of writing' rather than a masterpiece, his response to the author could hardly have been more enthusiastic: 'Est, est, est! as the bishop said! One of your very best, I think. I should be honoured to publish it.' He thought the American slang should be vetted, and although he wasn't worried about old ladies in England cancelling their subscriptions, he was concerned in case hostile reactions in America – US booksellers were taking 1500 of the proposed printing of 9000 copies – damaged *Horizon*'s market over there. It seemed a good idea to follow Waugh's suggestion and introduce the novella with some 'soft words' of his own. 'I anticipated ructions and one reason, apart from the predominant one of affection for yourself, for my seeking publication in *Horizon* was the confidence that its readers were tough stuff,' Waugh told him; and later he apologised for saying 'far too little about my debt to you for your patient and fruitful revising of *The Loved One*. You did it a whole world of good.'†

All this was gratifying, and deserved, but Waugh couldn't resist baiting and ridiculing his old friend. Connolly, for his part, wavered between a fearful eagerness to please, as though he were buying off his tormentor, and gruff spasms of defiance. Good wines and Lys's cooking invariably had a calming effect, with Connolly monitoring the proceedings like an over-anxious *maître d'*: 'Evelyn (unaware that I was watching him when he tasted the claret – and after a rather uninteresting *white* Haut Brion with the fish) raised his glass, sipped it, and nodded his head vigorously – and then took the rest. What more could one ask?' Sometimes, when Waugh's mischief-making had gone too far, the victim would bite back, or at least threaten retaliation: 'May I say that I have no intention of being provoked unless my affection for you is taxed beyond all bounds,' he wrote on learning that

* In the event, Connolly threw in some expensive architectural books as a bonus.

† By far the most pleasing reaction to *The Loved One* appeared in *Soviet Literature*. 'The stench of corruption emanates from Waugh's nauseating book,' it told its English-language readers in an article entitled 'English Decadents', devoted to *Horizon* and the writers associated with it: 'What is it about this gang of desperadoes that should so inflame Soviet wrath, and what kind of man is their leader?'

Randolph Churchill – egged on by Waugh – was brewing up trouble at White's.*

Writing from White's, Connolly told Waugh that he would love to replace Nancy Mitford as his 'pen pal', but lacked the necessary qualifications: he was not a professional diner-out, he failed to find 'other people's misfortunes uproariously funny', and the *Horizon* office was 'not the hub of the more literate landed gentry on their visits to London'. 'I was moved by your verdict that the misfortunes of your friends are not the proper subject for humour. I do not see how you can bear to go much into society if you feel this,' Waugh replied, scenting a weakness: to which Connolly retaliated by saying that he hadn't meant to sound priggish, but 'you have to have a basic security to laugh at other people's misfortunes. I always feel "There but for the grace of God" – or even "Your turn next."'

His turn came round all too soon when, a month after publication of *The Loved One*, he went to stay at a health farm in Tring, the cost of which was borne by the press magnate Edward Hulton. 'Did I tell you of Boots's stroke?' Waugh asked Nancy Mitford: 'His doctor sent him to Tring where he was strapped to his bed for three weeks and treated with enemas & synthetic orange juice. He lost 21 lbs. Well that is a lot for a shortish man. I think it will be the end of him.' 'Poor Cyril. Do you mean *another* seizure?' he questioned John Betjeman with undisguised relish: 'Well that is too much. If he has another seizure it is really all up with him.' Nancy Mitford fell upon the news with predictable glee –

> Awful about Smarty's stroke. I saw Osbert [Sitwell] and he said he put Cyril very high on the list of those who will have strokes – later at luncheon Lys disclosed that Cyril had had one in a train and I never had such winks as Osbert gave me. But as a lover of Smarty I feel sad about him, I thought he seemed wretched the night I dined alone with him

* He may well have been referring to the vexed issue of his conversion to the Roman Catholic Church. 'Osbert Lancaster, who asked me not to quote him, says that all Catholics are now assigned conversion targets,' Churchill told Evelyn Waugh:

> Penelope Betjeman is thought to be working on Lord Berners, while you have been given what most people consider the impossible assignment of Cyril Connolly. It is thought that your reconciliation with him has no other object than his conversion. Fred Birkenhead and I terrified Connolly with this prospect last night at the St James's Club. He vehemently denied that he was in any danger and stated that, since his return from France, he had been disgusted by the fact that nobody any longer talks of anything except religion. He had refused to allow a common friend to bring Lord Pakenham to his house for fear that he would discuss this odious topic. He makes an exception in your case and says that since you are a genius you are entitled to have your own opinions.
>
> He added that his greatest safeguard against conversion is the fact that, if he joined the Church of Rome, he could never look Maurice Bowra in the face again. I told him that you intended to mop up Bowra before Christmas as a preliminary operation and that you did not expect to achieve the overall strategic objective of the Connolly conversion before Spring.

and from Oxford Maurice Bowra wrote to enquire after his erstwhile protégé:

> What has happened to Connolly? Reports are various. (a) Stroke. Surely he is rather young for this? It opens up hideous prospects for all of us who are in the prime of life. (b) Heart attack. This need not trouble us and is much to be preferred. (c) Liver disease. Most probable of all after all those American parcels.

(According to the mockers, Connolly had made substantial inroads on the food parcels which arrived at the *Horizon* offices, sent from America by sympathetic well-wishers who had been moved by his accounts of post-war rationing, and destined for contributors as well as members of staff. 'I was told by somebody that Cyril, himself a deserving writer, was eating up all the stuff that was sent in response to this appeal,' Edmund Wilson observed: 'I asked Peter Watson about this, when I saw him in NY, and he answered: No – only the *foie gras*.')

The truth, of course, was altogether more prosaic. 'I have to go to a place called Tring to reduce my blood pressure which has been driven high by austerity, financial worries, *Horizon*'s difficulties and the ceding of valuable territory on the home front,' Connolly told Waugh (the concession of territory at Sussex Place was a by-product of Janetta's marrying Robert Kee in January 1948). The aim of the exercise was to lose weight, or at least to get back to what it had been before he went to America: 'My platonic idea of myself has always been of a personage much thinner than the armchair figure with whom you are familiar.' The treatment was successful in that he lost two stone, as well as having four teeth out,* but the whole experience, he told Enid Bagnold, was 'hell': he found it impossible to sleep, and the other inmates were ghastly ('I think the early Christians were probably just like the people at Tring'). In his sketch 'Birds of America', his *alter ego* Jonathan Brinkley – a publisher of about fifty who has come to hate books, eats interminable lunches, and drinks too much – books himself into a health farm, where he sweats the pounds away on a rubber sheet with a thick wool blanket on top, as well as undergoing osteopathy and enemas ('my exhaust pipe's a bit furred up'). As he lies there, desperate to escape, Brinkley thinks unhappily of how in recent years he has surrounded himself with 'some of the nastiest people in the world, people who drink entirely to corrupt and betray each other, cowards all searching for the formula that will kill in four

* Connolly's teeth were always a source of discomfort and ill health: his letters to Lys from about this time make frequent references to an abscess, presumably in the gums.

words, take a virginity, break up a marriage, ruin a talent.' But then, as the cure begins to take effect, he forgets all about them, and the dreams of youth return: wine merchants' bills and second-hand booksellers' catalogues drop away, and 'as the body gradually shed its load of unnecessary tissue, so the mind was rejuvenated and ancient adolescent ambitions awoke, a bicycling tour round romanesque churches, a canoe, and a tent by some green river.'

One way of realising these 'ancient adolescent ambitions' was to write a book about south-west France, the lush, green, rolling country that lay between the Massif Central and the Pyrenees, at the centre of which stood the Arcadian 'Magic Circle' evoked in *The Unquiet Grave*; and for this he turned once again to the patient duo of Hamish Hamilton and Cass Canfield. Hamilton had become a good friend, introducing him to his wine merchant and inviting him to grand, rather formal dinner parties; but Flaubert was still under contract, and not a word had been written. A false alarm to the effect that Enid Starkie was working on a similar book provided Connolly with momentary relief, but in April 1948 he told Hamilton that although Flaubert was the subject he wanted to write about above all else, he just couldn't get on with it. He had to get out of London, and the only way of doing so was to write a travel book. He must speak the language, and know something about the country in question; he had always wanted to write about Spain, but not while Franco was still in power, but south-west France would do as well. Combining travel, art and culture, drawing on writers as diverse as Ausonius and Dornford Yates, his book would celebrate 'all that is nicest about Europe'. In 'Happy Deathbeds', Jonathan Brinkley also dreams of writing just such a book, 'that perfect work of art – travel book in a sense, prose poem in another, evocation of vanished beauty and pristine freshness which formed a major defence of the guilty editor-publisher against the horrors of his conscience.' Like his creator, Brinkley sees the countryside of the Lot and the Dordogne as the ideal landscape, the embodiment of European civilisation, of all that he had dreamed of during the long years of bombings and blackouts: Aquitaine provided a glimpse of Eden, behind which 'lurked a further circle of perfection: the Roman province of that name in the great days of the fifth century, the golden decadence of Ausonius, the shining villas, the broad river, the city with its temples and foundations, the poetry, the scholarship, the long afternoon of the classical world.' He planned to go in June and again in October, he told Hamilton, and Dick Wyndham would come along to take the photographs: in exchange for an advance of £350 he would deliver 70,000 words by the end of the year. Amenable as ever, Hamilton consulted Cass Canfield, who proved willing to stump up £200 of the advance, noting at the same time that their elusive author had already moved the delivery date from December 1948 to the following April.

That spring, however, Dick Wyndham, on a journalistic assignment for the *Sunday Times* covering the Arab-Israeli War, was killed by a sniper in Palestine; and not only had Connolly lost his photographer, but Tickerage, that most convivial of refuges, was no longer a part of his life. In his will Wyndham left Connolly – who had long admired and envied the contents of his cellar – four hundred bottles of wine; and Connolly, for his part, mourned his dead friend in 'Happy Deathbeds', a poignant, bitter piece in which he lamented not just the death of individuals – the Major, Dick Wyndham – but the death of youthful dreams and ambitions, and the implacable passing of time. '*Dick*! The memory of his dead friend suffused him: the dead take with them their love for us and return it only in dreams until there is no one alive to love us and so we die and dream ourselves back through others,' he wrote:

> Brinkley recalled first the physical presence: a very tall man and very thin, but without any of a thin man's characteristics. He was what might be called a bad fifty, with a large brown open-air bald head, too burnt to be attractive, a little greying hair, a long crudely indented face with a projecting upper lip, mark of petulant sensuality, and an obstinate cleft chin; the eyes brown and dog-like, becoming slightly bloodshot with drink, immensely expressive.
>
> His body was untidy and gangling, a long sway back threw his stomach slightly forward, his legs kept crossing themselves when he walked, his long arms wandered outward. Appallingly dressed, usually in filthy flannel trousers with a Mosleyite black sweater and a ruined mackintosh, it was impossible to situate the immense charm which radiated from this uncouth old schoolboy . . .

'Incredibly handsome' as a young man, 'a Sargent drawing of the 1914 subaltern come to life', Wyndham had 'somehow camouflaged himself into middle age. His nails were always black, his fly buttons undone, his great nose like a blue lump of ice with hairs on it, his teeth yellow and irregu lar, his chin unshaven, his odour one of tarry anti-scurf preparations.' And yet this 'battered Bulldog Drummond', this 'Don Giovanni in rags' had a charm and a humour that Connolly found irresistible. He remembered how Wyndham

> was always accompanied, like a god or a saint, by certain properties. A tin of Egyptian cigarettes, often unopened, for his tobacconist delivered them

weekly to a long-standing order with which he could never keep up. A medicine bottle or so containing Valerian and other simple sedatives, an array of broken pencils and fouled biro pens bespeaking the artist and the journalist. A large shabby black notebook full of cryptic half-lines like '2.30 don't forget', 'Blue tie, toothbrush moustache, influential', 'Small breasts, tight bottom, free on Wednesdays', sandwiched with lawyers' letters and one or two unsubtle trout-flies – and, heaviest of all, a large silver flask containing some very good whisky with a little water, for a slow and regular flushing of the lively faculties . . .

'Dick is nothing without his home,' Connolly concluded, in a sad farewell to the last of his pre-war Edens:

> To know where he lives is to grasp his charm. A lane branches off from a Sussex road and descends steeply through fallen gates. We pass a large wood of Spanish chestnut redolent of bracken and stink fungus, an invisible stream descending through willow and dog-wood. Then we are at the door of the Mill. The car, a rakish Railton, with seats like hassocks reposing on rusty side-curtains, goes into a wooden garage. In the crisp night air the mill-race vibrates with rushing ecstasy. A latch is lifted, the luggage carried along a paved walk, we enter the magic abode. The latticed bedroom windows open to the monotonies of the weir, the paintings, the Chirico houses, the Bauchant flowers, are as we left them, the usual books are by the bed. Downstairs there are two rooms, a sitting-room, small, snug, well-heated, with rather feminine furniture, vellum-bound books damp with mildew, wax fruit, Victoriana, large paintings stuck with feathers, horse-hair, artificial jewels; across the hall is the dining-room with a big open fire and a long oak table where many decanters repose: cut-glass electuaries in which breathe their last the fabulous pre-phylloxeras. *Reverentia*! The food is always rustic and simple: some potted shrimps and fried sole – or perhaps stewed eel from the pond – washed down with delicious hock or chablis, then a boiled chicken or a rabbit pie to introduce the vista of clarets, 1924, 1920, 1906, 1899 – Margaux, Château d'Issan, Cheval Blanc, Ausone – which a stilton and celery usher out with a fanfare of Bath Olivers; and apples, nectarines, nuts with a '21 Yquem till the port is ready.

Appropriately enough, Dick Wyndham's replacement as Connolly's photographer was a fellow-veteran of those happy pre-war weekends at Tickerage. Joan Rayner was, Connolly told his mother, 'a person with whom I have almost everything in common – friends, tastes, intellectual interests – and very beautiful: tall, fair, slanting eyes, yellow skin.' Like her *alter ego* in 'Happy Deathbeds', Jane Sotheran, 'she had long legs, long ankles, toes like a Greek goddess, a neck that looked as if it had been artificially lengthened to support a princess's dowry of gold curtain rings and a face whose chief features were two enormous eyes of clouded violet blue, usually concealed behind dark glasses, a small fine nose, a slightly protruding lower lip, wrinkled brow and pelt of short blonde hair.' He had, he told Mollie, wanted to marry her after her marriage to John Rayner broke up, but she was always away, in Greece or Spain or Egypt: she was 'the one person who could have got me over Jean years earlier if we had better luck'. As if this weren't enough, she travelled light, had a private income, and always insisted on paying her own way. Back in 1940, she and Connolly had agreed, on the back of an envelope, to travel round the Mediterranean together once the war was over, and Hamish Hamilton's advance enabled them to test the waters.

In the early summer of 1948 Connolly set out alone for France. On the ferry from Dover he bumped into Louis MacNeice, 'who had just said, "What fun if Cyril were on board"'; in Paris he met Jean Hugo and Balthus (who said he wanted to paint him, since he had a perfect eighteenth-century face), Peter Watson and Sonia Brownell, and the twenty-three-year-old Truman Capote, whom he later published in *Horizon*. Merely being in France filled him with 'intoxication and delight'. He went to stay with Philippe de Rothschild at Mouton, and travelled down to the Spanish frontier; and he sent Lys a postcard of the Chapon Fin restaurant ('This is my spiritual home – last night it was Haut Brion '06 – and the staff remembers me as an undergraduate!') He then joined her in the South of France, staying with the Hultons and then with Somerset Maugham, where the Duke and Duchess of Windsor joined them for dinner. Shortly before Lys left for home, he was brought down by a combination of sinus trouble and diarrhoea: both, he thought, could well be psychosomatic, 'either a wild attempt to avoid meeting my fate, or guilt and remorse about Lys'. Early in August he said a guilty goodbye to Lys, adding the token words 'I wish you were coming too' and the rider – confined to his journal – 'which is what she has been doing for eight years while I kill time and writhe inwardly.' That done, he hurried off to meet 'this lovely sun-spirit, this heart of my heart's lights and liver, this divine sister-soothing girl, this Joan to end all Jeans'. In the days ahead, as they travelled over the bare mountains of the Massif Central and across to the Dordogne, Connolly 'fell very much in love' with his elegant companion, in her 'dark green cardigan and grey trousers, her camera slung over her shoulder and her golden hair bobbing as she walks, always a little fairer than you think, like the wind in a stubble-field'. They walked along trout-filled rivers and over bare limestone hills, and ate long lunches washed down with *marcs* and followed by a siesta; the Hôtel du Commerce, Millau, came to be 'numbered with the sacred places of the earth, with Delphi and the Dome of the Rock and 30 rue de Vaugirard'; they conducted a cave-wedding, interrupted by falling rocks and a party of boy scouts, and a poem he wrote her was 'proof of the total liberation of the Id from the thralls of *Horizon*'. 'Words fail to describe my hopeless passion for Joan,' he confided to his diary: 'She is Bobby, she is Racy, the sea-lord's daughter "with all Invergordon in her eyes", she is Diana with her aquarian justice and O such exquisite hands, she is Janetta with her golden skin and love of wild travel, she is Peggy with her evening brightness and sexiness and gourmandise...' 'With my lovely boy-girl beside me, like a casual, loving, decadent Eton athlete', he felt once again the pull of those archetypes that loomed so large in his amorous travails:

> If this was music I'd say that the great buried blonde-golden motif – the strain of Charles and Bobbie and Racy and Peggy and Diana and Janetta, which seemed with my failure with the last two to stop abruptly in face of the dark night motif of Noël, Jean and Lys – had surged up again...

Although their adventures were, in fact, innocent enough, both felt bad about those they had left behind. Joan sent reassuring telegrams to Patrick Leigh Fermor, whom she later married, and they decided the falling rocks in the cave must be the work of the cyclops 'Paddy-phemus'; Connolly hastened to reassure Lys that although 'Joan is a wonderful companion and our days are packed with pleasant incidents,' it was in the evenings that he missed Lys most. Their journey ended on the Atlantic coast. In a memoir of the French poet Olivier Larronde – whose work he had published in *Horizon*, with drawings by Lucian Freud – Connolly remembered 'climbing the Dune de Pyla, the highest in Europe, with a friend, and looking down on that fantastic mile upon mile of green pine forest... the Atlantic breaking as far as the eye can see on an endless emptiness of golden beaches.'

The year before Connolly had met, through Clarissa Churchill, a young American journalist called Rosamond or 'Peggy' Riley, who had recently been appointed the European features editor of *Vogue*. He had taken her out to an expensive dinner, and then on to the Gargoyle; and she in return had invited him to come and stay in the Dordogne the following summer, in a house she had taken with her future husband, a French journalist named Georges Bernier. Connolly arrived, alone, to stay for the weekend. No mention was made of his travelling-companion, but after a day or so he explained that he had to meet a photographer on a matter of business – and reappeared with Joan, whom he introduced with beaming, proprietorial pride. The weekend became three weeks; in the mornings Connolly lay in bed, surrounded by maps and Guides Bleus, working out where they should go, what they should see, and where they should eat, and as they drove around the lush, green country he tried out each restaurant in advance, dismissing the ill-favoured with 'It's *triste*' before moving on to the next.*

Joan was to remain one of Connolly's closest friends, loved, admired and respected, but although he published magazine articles on Bordeaux and the Dordogne, his book on South-West France remained quite as elusive as Flaubert: as Jonathan Brinkley admitted, 'Not one word had been written, though nearly a hundred thousand had been paid for. It was all in the Guide Bleu anyway, and the escape from guilt had become but another source of guilt, as is usual in the course of the disease.' Hamish Hamilton's wife, Yvonne, was given to understand that progress was being made, but – her husband informed Cass Canfield in January 1949 – this appeared to be 'the feminine equivalent of a pipe-dream'. Connolly then wrote a long, obfuscatory letter trying to describe the book he had in mind, but Hamilton – whose patience was beginning to wear thin at last – was unimpressed: 'I can just imagine either of us giving a pep talk to our travellers about "a novel which is not a novel and may contain some illustrations" – to sum up one of the most muddled letters I have ever received.' He would ask 'our friend Connolly' to send him some of the pages he had written – 'I happen to know that he has not written a line, so this should flick him on the raw.' Four months later there was still no sign of the book beyond another procrastinating letter, a copy of which was sent to New York:

> Quite fantastic, isn't it, in its disarming candour and its assumption that the artist is not affected by moral obligations? Imagine you or myself drawing my year's salary in advance and then writing to our firms to say that we prefer eating and drinking and making love and so don't propose to show up . . .
>
> P.S. 'Coming into *Horizon* all the time' actually consists of two hours a day in the afternoon. But if you rise at mid-day, this is quite early.

To which Canfield replied, rather more philosophically, that 'his reasons, sexual and alcoholic enjoyment, seem to be unassailable, and one cannot help admiring a man who is able to live on his friends indefinitely.'

* The Berniers – as they soon became – were to provide Connolly with a welcome and generous port of call in Paris in the post-war years of currency restrictions. A former diplomatic correspondent, Georges Bernier shared Connolly's love of the finer points of French food and culture. In 1955 the Berniers founded the bi-lingual magazine *L'Oeil*, which was devoted to art, architecture and design. Connolly wrote on German rococo in the first issue: other contributors included Herbert Read, Peter Quennell, Patrick Leigh Fermor, John Richardson, Connolly's *bête noire* Douglas Cooper, and John Russell – whom Peggy eventually married, after her divorce from Bernier.

As the decade drew to its close, Connolly's social life grew steadily grander, imposing greater strains on his waistline and digestive system. 'I'm not a socialist any more, by the way,' he told his mother, and his way of life was as far removed as possible from that associated with Sir Stafford Cripps. Champagne was served by waiters hired for the occasion of his Christmas 1948 party, attended by – among a good many others – Loelia Duchess of Westminster, Lady Rothermere, T.S. Eliot and Somerset Maugham; weekends might be spent with Lord Berners at Faringdon, or the d'Avigdor-Goldsmids, or Barbara Rothschild;* Evelyn Waugh reported a cocktail party he gave at which '100 bottles of champagne were drunk and two hams eaten'. James Lees-Milne – who had decided that 'Cyril is a lumpish, bad-mannered man' who seemed 'quite as bored with me as I was bored with him' – spotted him in a box at the Albert Hall looking 'like Rubens's Silenus': invited to dinner by Connolly and Lys – the other guests included Alan Ross and Alan Pryce-Jones – he noted how, once the meal was over, other guests 'dribbled in' for champagne afterwards, a mode of entertaining much favoured by his host and the people he knew.† As ever, Connolly resolved, without success, to take himself in hand: one particular set of Resolutions suggested that from now on he should restrict himself to cider, beer and red wine, and avoid spirits altogether; that the Ritz, White's before lunch, Wilton's (unless as a guest), most cocktail parties and expensive antique shops should be ruled Out of Bounds; that no cheques larger than £5 should be written without Lys's approval; that he should rise earlier, eat less, go to bed earlier and work more – 'reading, writing and the poetical life *always*'.

With the state conspicuously failing – in Connolly's eyes at least – to provide writers with the support they needed, and 'with the collapse of that highly cultivated well-to-do world bourgeoisie' who had once provided the avant-garde with its patrons and its audience, cultivating the rich was a reasonable end in itself, far preferable to diluting one's talents as a 'culture-diffusionist', 'selling culture for a living like the Aga Khan his bath water'. In one of the two 'London Letters' he wrote for the *Partisan Review* – he was standing in for George Orwell – Connolly noted how the writers he met at London literary parties, 'hugging a thimble of something warm and sweet with a recoil like nail polish remover', tended to be in their forties or over;

* Barbara Rothschild later married Rex Warner and the Greek Painter Niko Ghika; Connolly stayed several times at the Ghikas' house on Hydra, more often than not with Patrick Leigh Fermor and Joan Rayner.

† Lumpish or not, Lees-Milne remembered Connolly on that occasion as 'the most brilliant talker' he had ever listened to, though he surprised him by saying he had read no Trollope, no Dickens and only one novel by Jane Austen.

and how most of them combined writing with a job in publishing or the BBC or the British Council, the effect of which was 'gradually to extinguish the creative spark'. Demoralised by his failure to write the books he felt he had within him, unhappily aware of the encroachments of middle age, increasingly bored by *Horizon*, he was both sickened by, and central to, the time-wasting, incestuous, back-biting swirl of the literary merry-go-round. Nowhere was his disgust and his self-disgust more vividly displayed than in 'Happy Deathbeds', with its lethal pen-portraits of Brinkley, the editor and publisher, and of his assistant Elsa (Sonia Brownell) and his old friend Christopher Carritt (Peter Quennell). Brinkley spends much of his day playing the literary stock market, advancing reputations to visiting foreign publishers and pointing out the bright young writers to watch, and his evenings at literary parties attended by eager, jostling authors on the make and rapacious publishers like 'the tall grey-haired young Leishman with his cold blue vulture's eyes'. Brinkley has given up reading, collecting *objets d'art* instead, but Elsa still hurls herself into the literary fray, out-shouting her rivals at publishing parties, paying solemn, reverential obeisance to the genius of the moment, and, in bed at night, turning a few pages of *The When and the How: Studies in the Phenomenological Approach* before setting it aside in favour of *Leadguts, the Autobiography of a Killer*. Like his creator, Brinkley is a late arrival in the office – which, in the real world, had moved in June 1948 from Lansdowne Terrace to 53 Bedford Square, where, Connolly told his mother, they occupied 'two huge rooms on the first floor which Peter Watson has filled with the Picassos from his flat in Paris'* – and Elsa is adept at making him feel guilty about not coming in earlier:

> Elsa's voice on the telephone was sepulchral. It was her dreaded 'before coffee' voice, hollow as a walled-up toad. Brinkley wavered at the other end of the line but decided it was too late to hang up. 'I just wondered how you were,' which meant 'I have been alone for about half an hour and I can't stand it.'
>
> 'I can't talk yet. I haven't woken up properly. Lousy, I expect.'
>
> 'It's half-past twelve.'
>
> 'Goodness. Well, see you in the office this afternoon.'
>
> 'Oh you are coming in. Goody goody.'
>
> He hung up dismally. Of course he was coming in. What about the days she didn't come in? All those hangovers. Worsted as usual.

* According to Humphrey Slater – writing the *Partisan Review*'s 'London Letter' – *Horizon* only acquired the offices after a 'senior Cabinet Minister' had intervened.

To the melancholy Paul – Brinkley's partner – Elsa chatters away in a kind of schoolgirl French; despite her wholesome appearance and her 'blue archaic ox-eyes', she is dedicated to the sex war, revering men of genius and despising all the rest. 'I always regard Sonia as my unconscious enemy (unconscious because unaware of the strength of her lesbian drives – especially when reinforced by alcohol),' Connolly told Ann Gage many years later: she had damaged all his 'closest relationships', and since she was 'the enemy of the male principle, one has to have broken down to earn her pity.' But he had much to be grateful for: Sonia held the fort on his frequent travels abroad, dealing with contributors, hosing down an infuriated Oliver Simon – he had taken offence after she had objected to a 'bilious' yellow jacket, 'yelling that he'd just been reading Dostoevsky and wouldn't be pushed around any more' – and passing on gossip about Miss Temkin the production manager and Mr Harris the salesman, who had been drunk for a week after the birth of his second son.

Altogether more lurid was Connolly's portrayal of Christopher Carritt, a predatory rival where women were concerned, and a writer envied for his productivity but deplored as someone who had compromised his early gifts. A heavy drinker, a tireless womaniser and an avid social climber, hot in pursuit of dukes and hospitable country houses, Carritt rises late after a night of debauchery and gazes at himself in the mirror: 'His red hatchet face leered back at him, sandy eyebrows, cold china-blue eyes, goatish nose and chin, lips like blue thin elastic bands, skin of porous terracotta'. He dons his familiar uniform of dark suit, white shirt and black shoes, and sets off across the Park in the direction of a chemist's shop that caters for aristocratic roués, where he picks up a hangover mixture and a 'golden elixir' guaranteed to revive his sexual powers:

> His whole appearance by now had a brassy look, as if Byron had survived Missolonghi and gone in for old age on the boulevards. Hands in pockets of his dark overcoat (he called it great-coat now), black hat wedged over his face, all his hatches battened down for action, he bore down on the passers-by with an expression between a leer and a grimace according to the general prosperity and bedability of the person he confronted.

Once restored, he clocks in at his office, where he assumes the role of a vague and self-deprecating literary man, arranges lunch for two hours hence, eyes his secretary up and down and, without pausing, dictates a review of a new life of Lord Chesterfield, followed on by a recent thriller. Connolly's portrayal of his old friend as a sulphurous Regency rake who has seemingly succumbed to almost all the enemies of promise mirrors his own demoralisation and despair about the life he was leading, and the company he kept.

*

In November he escaped once again to Paris, where he met Jean, stayed with her sister Annie and her husband Bill Davis, and saw the Berniers and Sylvia Beach. 'I must say I *love* his company in spite of his terrible unscrupulousness,' Nancy Mitford told Violet Hammersley: Raymond Mortimer, who was also in Paris, was far sweeter, but less fun.* His only drawback was that he 'forms part of a *joyeuse bande de noctambules* and I can't stick the rest of the bande – a sort of bogus Gauguin with one leg called Campbell, Mary Dunn, Joan Rayner etc. *all very dirty* some disfigured by a taxi accident and covered in dried blood – you know, just what *one* doesn't care for.'

Back in London after a trip to Basle with Lys and the Davises, contentious issues such as who had been responsible for putting Quennell up for membership of White's (Evelyn Waugh and Randolph Churchill thought that Connolly had, at the very least, connived in the matter) and who had raided the drinks cupboard at Sussex Place and consumed some of Connolly's best claret (a drunken Philip Toynbee was generally agreed to be the guilty man) were overshadowed by the apparently inevitable dissolution of two mainstays of his life in the 1940s: his quasi-matrimonial relationship with Lys, and *Horizon* itself.

Being with Joan had made him realise that he just couldn't marry Lys, Connolly told his mother, although – or because – she was 'so devoted to me, and belongs to the everyday part of my life'. Lys's role in his life was equally unsatisfactory from her point of view as well. When she had changed her name to 'Connolly' by deed poll, many of their friends assumed they were married; part of Connolly went along with this, but he begged her not to talk about it, 'for part of me dreads it. I mean I am very frightened of myself & the adolescent libertarian strain in my character. Am I old enough?' Lys was very attractive and a good cook, but neither Connolly nor his friends seem to have taken her seriously: both intellectually and emotionally, she was seen as something of a lightweight, an invaluable domestic adjunct but not someone whose views were to be taken seriously, or who had the romantic allure of Connolly's great passions. 'Lys is very pretty and prattled of housewifely things like linoleum and dry rot,' Frances

* Mortimer, on the other hand, was better informed about the French, she thought: 'The English ignorance on French matters never ceases to astound . . . even the pundits like Harold Nicolson and Cyril don't really know as much as they pretend to. Raymond is another matter, he really does know.'

Partridge remembered: '... Cyril kept the conversation relentlessly on literary subjects, particularly his own writings, while Lys was untiring in her wifely deference – "Clever people like Cyril", or "Good talkers like Cyril" – but got little attention from him in return.' Nancy Mitford called poor Lys 'the mouse at bay'. 'Have you heard about the Mouse @ Bay?' she once asked Evelyn Waugh: 'Some other women were saying how the virility of men is in relation to the size of their noses & the M at B jumped out of her chair and said "It is quite untrue, Cyril has a *very* small nose."' According to Frances Partridge – who also noted how, 'with his long bobbed hair and smart South of France clothes', Connolly looked exactly like 'a china pug on a mantelpiece' – he tended to ignore Lys even when she was at her most gushingly nervous ('"Oh, that must have been wonderful, Cyril!"' or '"Oh, do you know Cyril was remembered by the waiter at the Chapon Fin who hadn't seen him for twenty years!"'), but occasionally – or so it was said – he could turn nasty. William Sansom recalled a dinner at which Lys 'sat upright and beautiful with one single feather in her hair and on her body oldish clothes done up with a sort of rope': no doubt her chatter must have proved particularly irritating, for at some stage Connolly 'led her from the table through enclosed doors, returned without her, saying "We were speaking too much, we had to be spoken to..."' Woodrow Wyatt claimed that Connolly sometimes beat her with a hairbrush, while Geoffrey Grigson – who detected a strain of cruelty in his dealings with women – recounted how Oliver Simon brought some proofs round to their flat, and overheard the sound of slapping and weeping: after a while Connolly came to the door in a silk dressing-gown and greeted his visitor with the words 'We have been naughty. We needed punishment. Ah, Oliver, the proofs. Good.'*

'Good (about Cyril and Lys),' Nancy Mitford told Waugh in June 1949, assuming – like many others – that they were now a married couple: 'I love Lys and she has grown bald in his service, it would be a horrid shame if he turned her off now.' As it was, it was Lys who did the turning, exciting from her outraged quasi-husband a spate of hysterical letters – adoring, accusatory, relentlessly self-pitying – in which he accused her of deserting him for other men, and ruining his life in the process. Lys had been provided with a foretaste of what was to come shortly after the end of the war, when she became briefly involved with a young Frenchman named Calmann-Lévy. Connolly's reaction, his fear of being deserted and his longing to be

* Since Grigson disliked Connolly intensely, and set the story in Russell rather than Bedford Square, its reliability may be open to doubt. Years later, Noël Annan recalled Connolly in the *Horizon* offices, playing the circus-master of London literary life: 'Round the ring pranced his young horses and a succession of young women answered with varying degrees of compliance. There was a sado-masochistic atmosphere in the *Horizon* office.'

comforted, was like that of a child whose plaything has been snatched away. He can't sleep, he wishes he was dead, he threatens to kill himself, he tells her that she is cowardly and cruel, that his life has no meaning without her; he lies in bed in tears, it hurts him to breathe, he can't sleep a wink; 'Oh please God do ring up – why are you driving me to feel resentment too – my trip to Paris ruined, *Horizon* a nightmare, our lunch together ruined' – in her eagerness to join that 'little termite' she had 'chucked' him for lunch twice, 'throwing me some horrible sardines in your zeal to be off'.

As it was, Calmann-Lévy posed no real threat, but as the decade ground to a close they began inexorably to drift apart, with Lys taking the initiative and Connolly loudly lamenting all that he had so long taken for granted, and was now slipping away from his grasp. Part of the problem was their failure to have a child – 'I am sure if you were to have a baby I would never look at anyone else' – part his assumption that 'leaving someone is much worse than being unfaithful', and that whereas there was no harm in his flirting or having affairs, for Lys to do likewise or, still worse, to decide to make a life of her own, was an outrage and a heresy. He was surrounded by beautiful and attractive women, many of whom he seemed half (or wholly) in love with, and all of whom he treated with a respect denied his common-law wife; and yet when, in the early summer of 1949, Lys left him in Sussex Place and went to stay in Florence, he reacted as though she had abandoned him for ever. 'I wish you wouldn't play about with my desertion complex,' he begged her: as a child, he 'used to pray "God *kill* Mummy God *kill* Daddy"' whenever they left him alone, and now she was making him go through all that again. Left by himself he couldn't be bothered to boil an egg, frittering the mornings away and drinking too much in the evenings. Sussex Place seemed miserably empty without Lys, and he found himself drifting aimlessly into Janetta's part of the house; her daughter imitated Lys trying to drive him out of the house ('Get up Cyril and go to your office. You're lazy. Now come along to the office with me'), and in return he threatened to bake her in a pie, so supplementing his meat rations and providing an alternative to the squid and gulls' eggs he offered his guests for dinner.

One way of offsetting his loneliness was to offer an empty room at Sussex Place to the painter Anne Dunn, the nineteen-year-old daughter of a wealthy Canadian banker, Sir James Dunn, and the future wife of the painters Michael Wishart and Rodrigo Moynihan. Anne was romantically involved with Lucian Freud, but although she thought Connolly terribly old, she liked the way he taught her things, and enjoyed dancing with him at the Gargoyle; he was a good and enthusiastic dancer, light on his feet, and looked like a piglet as he sprang about on tiptoe.* Not surprisingly, he found himself falling in love with Anne, though he assured Lys that this may have owed a lot to 'neurosis and alcohol', in that he sensed that she was unhappy, and they would sit together drinking in the evenings. As far as sex was concerned, 'I am afraid I am doomed to uncledom', while Lys's absence 'brings home to me continuously how completely I think of us both as belonging to each other & how much I love you body and soul.' That was all very well, but before long he was to become involved with an altogether more formidable and demanding figure, while Lys herself began to look elsewhere; and the life they had lived together would disintegrate amidst tears and anger and recriminations.

And yet, through all the hysteria and high emotion involved in their separation, Connolly retained a keen, self-lacerating sense of what he was like, and how he played with his own and other people's emotions. In 'Happy Deathbeds' – that key document for this period of his life – he wrote of how

> since a very early age those who entrusted him with their happiness had been most basely betrayed and driven to say intolerable things which he could never put out of his mind. 'Every grey hair your mother has, she owes to you.' 'You were my rock. For nine years I was faithful. I thought if I knew one man well enough I knew them all.' 'I am offering you the devotion of a lifetime.' 'You have the gift of destroying not only your own happiness but the happiness of all who love you' . . . His betrayals followed a seven-year cycle. He selected his victims and prepared them for sacrifice while pretending that they had selected him. And when he had forced them to desert him he became real to himself. He was like a faulty machine in which some malfunction led to the continual amputation of arms and legs in those who looked after it, because all the time it was really a machine precisely for amputating arms and legs. A safety razor for cutting throats. But the razor was a man and one who wanted above all to be kind. The guillotine had a conscience.

Like his creator, Brinkley was kind to animals and children: 'It was only in his central relationships that he struck through a dense fog of pity, guilt and hate . . . He was a machine for slowly breaking hearts.' What he omits to say is that no one's heart was more regularly broken than his own, or that the passions and miseries he underwent were no less genuine for being

* V.S. Pritchett spotted Connolly and Anne Dunn at the Gargoyle: 'He was quietly singing a long American song to her and also reciting his ballad "I'm the man who put the kibosh on the Kaiser" etc. which I believe has been his main piece of literary composition this year.'

simultaneously dependent on more than one object. Some twenty years later, his friend Anthony Hobson told Connolly that he would like, one day, to edit his letters. 'What would you do?' Connolly asked him: 'You'd find letters to two women threatening suicide, written within half an hour of each other, and then one to a third, written quarter of an hour later, asking her to lunch at the Ritz.'*

'For a long time after dinner the little sitting-room would spin round and round,' Connolly wrote in his elegiac farewell to those vanished weekends at Tickerage:

> Somehow people got to bed, the men going out to urinate on the lawn in the cool night air, the mill-race whispering, the owls hooting in the apple trees, the night-jar chugging in the wood. In the scented double beds the quarrelling couples smacked and copulated, collapsing into country sleep . . .

For Lys at least the quarrelling would soon be over; and the end of the decade marked the end of an era, for *Horizon* as well as its editor.

'I see Cyril's boom fading, *Horizon* losing subscribers, income-tax officials pressing him, inertia, luxury and an insane longing to collect rare things,' Waugh noted in his diary. Connolly's interest in *Horizon* had been flagging for some time now. His 'Comments' were increasingly sporadic; he had always said that ten years was time enough to give over to editing a magazine; he wanted, in theory at least, to get on with his own writing, and with a novel in particular. According to John Lehmann, he put it about in the autumn of 1949 that he was going to retire from editing for a year – '"Cyril must have a rest" was the theme of his helpers' – and Lady Rothermere told Malcolm Muggeridge that he intended to suspend publication for a year in order to concentrate on his own work, and that she was trying to persuade her husband to buy it. Nor was Rothermere the only possible purchaser. Connolly offered John Lehmann the magazine at a reduced rate over a bottle of champagne at the Athenaeum, though whether Peter Watson had been consulted is not revealed: Lehmann was tempted – he was having difficulties with Allen Lane over *Penguin New Writing*, which closed at about the same time as *Horizon* – but despite the modest sums involved, Purnell's, the printing firm that had recently undertaken to back his eponymous publishing firm, weren't interested, and nothing came of it. David Astor expressed interest in buying *Horizon*'s title and list of sub-

* Or, as a tearful Connolly once complained to Stephen Spender apropos his life with Jean and Diana before the war, 'It *is* hard – here have I been absolutely faithful to two women for a year, and they've *both* been unfaithful to me.'

scribers on behalf of the *Observer* and installing Alan Ross as editor: Connolly immediately, and unfairly, assumed that Ross had been plotting behind his back, for – as Ross later observed – 'someone else's interest would miraculously revive in him hitherto dormant passions', whether for women or a magazine. Nor did anything come of John Sutro's plans to rescue the ailing monthly: Connolly, Sutro and Kenneth Clark were to form an editorial board and choose a new editor, but although Connolly nominated Freddie Ayer, and Sutro Roy Harrod, that was as far as it went.

To the world at large, *Horizon* must have seemed as lively as ever, but in the November 1949 issue Connolly announced that the following month's issue would be a special number to mark the magazine's tenth anniversary, after which it would close down for a year, re-opening – if conditions improved – in December 1950. Although the circulation had remained static, he told his readers, printing costs were steadily rising, on top of which the lease was up in Bedford Square; but the real reasons for closure had more to do with his own frustration and disenchantment. Sales in England had fallen, and were only made up for in America; trying to publish a literary magazine was a thankless chore, given London's 'sterile, embittered, traditional literary society which has killed so many finer things than a review of literature and art'; it was becoming increasingly hard to persuade established writers to contribute, tempted as they were by writing for dollars or dissipating their energies on lectures or broadcasts. Above all, though, Connolly himself had grown stale, for

> to be an editor and also a writer is even more difficult than to be a publisher or a journalist and write oneself. An editor frays away his true personality in the banalities of good mixing, he washes his mind in other people's bath-water, he sacrifices his inner voice to the engagement book.

Looking back over the Forties, and *Horizon*'s reactions to it, in his concluding 'Comment', Connolly suggested that the decade had been marked by the 'desperate struggle of the modern movement, the struggle between man, betrayed by science, bereft of religion, deserted by the pleasant imaginings of humanism, and the blind fate of which he is now so expertly conscious', and he left his readers with a fine rhetorical flourish, worthy of Palinurus at his aphoristic best: 'it is closing time in the Gardens of the West and from now on an artist will be judged only by the resonance of his solitude or the quality of his despair.'

'We closed the long windows over Bedford Square, the telephone was taken, the furniture stored, the back numbers went into their cellar, the files rotted in the dust,' he wrote later: 'Only contributions continued to be delivered, like a suicide's milk.'* 'I enjoyed my funeral and obituaries... it is delicious not to have to meet any more authors or foreign journalists,' he told Evelyn Waugh: 'We have a little office in the spare room where Lys winds up payments and queries, requests for *The Loved One* etc.... Already my brain has expelled a huge wad of useless knowledge about unreadable modern writers, like an owl its pellet.'

One eminently readable modern writer who regretted the passing of *Horizon* was John Betjeman. 'I *must* tell you, even at the risk of appearing ridiculous, that the death of *Horizon* is like the death of a relation,' he wrote:

> You and Raymond M. and Peter Q., but particularly you and Raymond M., set me a standard. I always thought to myself 'What would Cyril think of this?' or 'This will puzzle old Raymond' and despite nerves and slight inferiority I would feel at the thought of how much French you knew, I also knew that you were an essential encouragement. In fact I think I was taken seriously first (and therefore took myself more seriously) after you had had the courage to print my poems in *Horizon*.

* The furnishings included an elaborate and very unusual chandelier, made by Giacometti, commissioned by Peter Watson, and now in the possession of John Craxton.

TWENTY

Oak Coffin

Looking back on his life in wartime London, Peter Quennell once wrote fondly of those whom he described as the 'Lost Girls' of the period, 'adventurous young women who flitted about London, alighting briefly here and there, and making the best of any random perch on which they happened to descend'; and of all these elusive, elegant figures, none was more tantalising, disruptive and widely resented than Barbara Skelton, last encountered living with Quennell in Connolly's attic in Bedford Square. The daughter of an unsuccessful soldier and a former Gaiety Girl, she had worked as a model for Schiaparelli before the war; affectionate, waspish and disconcertingly detached, she had lived, sometimes simultaneously, with a series of adoring admirers, flitting unconcernedly from one to another, raising blood pressures in the process, and leaving behind her a trail of devastation. Her first lover had been a middle-aged millionaire, a friend of her father's who seduced her in Brighton, and when war broke out she took up with a temperamental, kepi-wearing colonel in the Free French, a 'balding stocky man with a pale reptilian face': she much preferred fat, rather ugly men to conventional good looks, once citing Erich von Stroheim as her *beau idéal*. For Feliks Topolski she was 'the pivotal heroine of those days – her allure relying on the sphinxish muteness of her never-unriddled unpredictability married to an appropriate physique'; while his wartime rival Peter Quennell recalled her in his autobiography under the pseudonym of 'Julia':

> She might have had Eastern blood; there was something about her slightly slanted eyes, her prominent cheekbones, and smooth olive skin that suggested the youthful concubine of a legendary Mongol chieftain; while her narrow-waisted, rather wide-hipped body recalled the celestial dancing-girls I had once encountered at Angkor Wat ... She had an air of secret self-possession and, illuminating her face in rare flashes, a half-provocative, half-malicious smile.

'As feline in appearance as she later proved to be in character, she had the tantalising quality of needing a tamer, while something indefinable about her suggested that she was untameable,' Michael Wishart later wrote of her: her eyes, he went on, had the 'mysterious drowsy look of a baby panther. To catch her eyes was more or less to enter into a conspiracy.' She drove her admirers mad by her combination of elusiveness and volatility, blackly sulking one moment and laughing contagiously the next, bestowing and then as quickly withdrawing her favour; she was, according to Quennell, 'extraordinarily quick at detecting one's limitations and exposing one's pretensions, and always adroit at holding up a glass where one saw one's silliest face reflected . . . She had acquired a knack, perhaps half-unconscious, of distinguishing her lovers' weakest points, just as certain wasps, accustomed to paralyse their prey, know exactly where to sink their stings.'

Silent and farouche in company, a sullen presence exuding waves of boredom and disdain, 'Skeltie' was, in many ways, an alarming and formidable figure; but making her laugh was a far more effective antidote than conventional disapproval. She had a nimble wit and a highly developed sense of the absurd, and set great store on cleverness and humour. She would become in due course an extremely funny and ruthlessly observant writer, with a gift for the lethal, deflationary epithet, combining waspishness and affection in perfect proportions; and whereas the earnest, proprietorial, often rather pretentious young women who gathered round Connolly at *Horizon*, for all their literary airs, never set pen to paper, this new arrival – so frequently looked down upon as gauche, ill-educated, and frankly rather common, a mere model who was almost certainly out of her social and intellectual depth, and was only tolerated on account of her pantherine good looks – would, in due course, evoke him more fondly and more vividly than anyone else.

After sharing Peter Quennell's attic rooms in Bedford Square, Barbara Skelton enrolled, at Donald Maclean's suggestion, as a Foreign Office 'cipherine', and was sent out to Egypt, where she added the actor Anthony Steel and – notoriously – King Farouk to her list of lovers. She met Connolly again through their mutual friend Natalie Newhouse, a self-destructive girl who married the actor Robert Newton and eventually died of an overdose.* By now Connolly had been long installed in Sussex Place –

* Dick Wyndham's daughter, Joan, provides an unflattering portrait of Natalie Newhouse in her autobiography, *Anything Once*. She went on to describe how, one dreadful day, her father took her to dinner at Sussex Place. Lys, she remembered, was 'like some exquisite little oriental concubine'; the guests included Stephen Spender, Peter Quennell and Arthur Koestler, and

> everybody was being terribly bitchy about everybody else. It was like being in a nest of intellectual vipers. Nice Angela Thirkell was referred to as 'Arsenic and Old Lace', and everybody seemed to loathe poor Koestler and called him a phoney communist. As for Connolly, he was known as 'Squirrel'. When he went out of the room a young man leapt onto a stool and did a wicked impersonation of him and everybody screamed 'Oh darling, you've got Squirrel to a T.'

where Natalie occasionally stayed on her peregrinations round London – while Barbara divided her time between a flat in Queen Street, Mayfair, the rent of which was paid by John Sutro, and her tiny cottage in Elmstead, where the Kentish Downs run into the English Channel. Natalie Newhouse told her that Connolly was becoming bored with Lys; and when Barbara left for France with Peter Quennell in her new open-top Sunbeam Talbot, he hurried to join them in Paris. Barbara then went on to Geneva, where Sutro was expecting her: Connolly promptly booked into a hotel on the other side of the lake, from the bedroom window of which he could flash signals when 'Chuff' Sutro's back was turned. When Sutro flew back to London, Connolly took Barbara sight-seeing; they went their separate ways in Cannes, where Connolly met up with Lys, but when Barbara returned to London she learned that Lys had departed from Sussex Place, leaving Connolly on his own.

'She is the warmest and most efficient of wives and although I have obviously been trying to get rid of her for years, I may well have grown to rely on her permanent devotion to my comfort far more than I realise,' Connolly told Barbara; and Lys's 'desertion' was to provoke a torrent of tearful letters in which he told her again and again how much he loved and missed her, how miserable she had made him, and how he had only allowed himself to become involved with Barbara because Lys had rocked the boat first by encouraging her own admirers – 'dim little creatures' who included William Sansom ('an impotent mouthless epicene'), Tony Witherby ('a dwarf'), Jim Richards the architectural historian, and, most disruptive of all, a young man called Andrew, who was to assume almost demonic proportions in Connolly's private mythology. 'Oh I think you are a monster,' he told her:

> I long to die and be where you can't hurt me. I think you are a callous little wretch preaching to me about the 'best years of my life' etc. when you are doing everything to wreck it. I stood eight years of being bored by you and, in public, often excruciated, because I love you, and you can't take a few months of suffering without rushing off to humiliate me and avenge yourself.

He charged her with arrested development ('All I want is for you to grow up so that you can make me a better companion and are less of a shadow – it is just what happened to Jean'): even if 'our whole trouble was that we could not get rid of the child in you or the adolescent in me,' she should surely have realised where her duty and self-interest lay, for

> You are a person whose whole role is to be bound up in someone else's existence, you will never be as happy getting admiration as being in love

> and devoted yourself. If your devotion to me is the only original and interesting thing about you, there are many other people with looks and intelligence, hardly any with your good fortune to be absorbingly in love with one person for a very long time.

'The whole house was in mourning for his second wife,' he recalled in 'Happy Deathbeds':

> She had left him; he had got her to leave him; he loved her. Nothing more was sent to the laundry, no letters were answered, no china was bought, the bell rang, the telephone tinkled. The milk arrived on the doorstep, the bills for newspapers plopped through the letter-box, a man came with archaic implements to cut off the gas. The whole house was in mourning because in the game of mutual masochism, she had been hurt seriously and by leaving him had given him such offence that he could not ask her to come back.

But he did, incessantly and at length, adding for good measure long Freudian analyses of what was wrong with Lys, now bent – he was sure – on revenge and 'tit-for-tatting'; nor did it prevent him from pursuing Barbara with an equal and opposite ardour, or subjecting her to a comparable weight of psycho-analytical diagnosis ('the structure of our relationship is neurotic, that is to say it is based on a desire for an infinite love which it is not possible for two human beings to give each other – the result is a perpetual disappointment...') 'Boots has gone off with Miss Skeleton; both, apparently, in very cross mood,' Nancy Mitford informed Evelyn Waugh. They visited Wimbledon – the Queen was there, and Connolly spent more time peering into the royal box than watching the tennis – and in May 1950 they set off for Spain in the Sunbeam Talbot. Connolly suffered from diarrhoea; their hotel in Barcelona reminded him of the Naval & Military Hotel; they travelled round the coast to the French Riviera, where he swam and read (an easier business than before, now that he had been equipped with a pair of glasses) and worried about shortage of funds; he loved being driven in Barbara's car, but – or so he told Lys – he had never quarrelled as much with anyone before, and he found himself pining for the peace of White's and the grandeur of Nika Hulton's dining-room: or, as he informed his travelling companion, 'what should rise into a crescendo of loving and provide us with that "*adoration perpetuelle*" which we can only find together and which may well be the fundamental purpose of our lives (to make life out of our dream-wish) is jammed by these jealous scenes and quarrels which we are unable to make up, so that our energy is exhausted by neurotic tensions.' Lys's admirers were bad enough, but already his relationship with Barbara was blighted by jealousy, not least of Peter Quennell. 'PQ is determined to destroy our wonderful love-affair,' he told her:

> His vanity is involved in turning this, my only triumph over him, into defeat and you are making this easy for him because you are so subject to his influence that you swallow the ridicule (venom) in imperceptible doses. And I rise to all the baits out of my neurotic sense of insecurity...

Lys, in the meantime, was staying with Lauretta Hugo at Orthez, near the Pyrenees; one of her admirers, Jim Richards, was also there, and it had been agreed that Connolly would join her there after he and Barbara had gone their separate ways. According to Connolly's later, accusatory letters, Lys tried to put him off from coming ('*ne venez pas*'): this, he claimed, marked a watershed in their relations, and pushed him still further into Barbara's arms. Lys had used the Hugos' house as a 'base for fucking expeditions'; she was, he now realised, 'just like anybody else, vain, smug, self-righteous, vindictive – trying to revenge yourself on me, get some greens, and be in the right at the same time.' He went to Orthez all the same, and found it very dull; although he suspected Barbara of having gone off to Nice to join an unwholesome 'lawyer-sadist', he told Lys that she was 'quite wrong about her, she is neither pretty nor faded but gauche, strangely beautiful, best skin and figure I have seen, kind, sensitive, witty and brave and intelligent'. On the other hand, 'I feel very detached from Barbara and I hate her middle-brow friends and feel she will never get on with mine.' His attachment to her was not simply sexual, but

> a certain maternal sexuality in her satisfies at these moments my deserted little boy loneliness more than anything else does and while I am not writing I am more lonely than usual. My love for you is much deeper but the other is like a sun-ray lamp whose ten minutes have become very essential if only they wouldn't go on so long.

Connolly was not writing, and despite his new infatuation he was as demoralised as ever. 'I can't muster up the energy to think of going anywhere or doing anything. I have bought a tonic but can't find a tea-spoon; the iron lies rusting in the bottle instead of entering my bowel,' he told Evelyn Waugh. Just as he had with Jean, he blamed their friends and their way of life for Lys's departure, with Sonia Brownell and Peter Quennell cast in the role of villains, while Sybille Bedford and Kathleen Raine – in whose house in Paultons Square Lys had taken temporary refuge – were accused of encouraging her defection. Once again, his own dissatisfaction with himself took the form of lashing out at the bibulous, time-wasting forces of bohemia. 'I suddenly saw them through your eyes – smug, complacent, intellectually arrogant, jollying up with gin each other's pretensions based on nothing,' he told Waugh after spending a weekend with Philip Toynbee and his wife and Robin and Mary Campbell at Stokke, the Campbells' house in Wiltshire:

> It depressed me terribly and I couldn't sleep. At our age there is something very much the matter with us if we are not greatly upset by everyone. I realise I have found it convenient to pity everyone because it makes them touching and therefore likeable when of course one pities them because one pities oneself and one pities oneself so as to excuse oneself and while one is still excusing oneself one will suddenly be dead and nothing done.

'I expect I am bent on destroying myself because I cannot grapple with my own despair which is mounting all the time and because I need more than one maternal breast to fall back on,' he informed Lys. To Mary Campbell, on the other hand, he seemed a disruptive force, wilfully destructive of others as well as of himself. V.S. Pritchett, who met Connolly at Stokke on another occasion, told Gerald Brenan that Mary had come to dislike Connolly 'because he tells Robin he ought to live in Paris and have a lot of mistresses if he's going to paint, and not live in the country. Robin, who lives by copying others, wishes to emulate Cyril – at least, in everything except his sloth.'*

*

'Would you like to hear about Smartyboots only keep it a secret please. Well the smart old creature sent his mistress off to join Farouk and lived for quite a while here on what she managed to put up her knickers and remit,' wrote a breathless Nancy Mitford from Paris in the summer of 1950.† King Farouk had rung Barbara in Queen Street and asked her if she'd like to join him at

* Mary Campbell was not the only wife to find Connolly a subversive influence. Jacob Epstein's daughter, Kitty, married Lucian Freud in 1948: as a young wife and mother, she found the rather childless world in which Connolly then moved disconcertingly hostile to conventional domesticity, and Connolly himself, for all his charm, a disruptive and often hurtful presence.

† In a 'Memorandum for His Majesty' – carefully written up on the headed notepaper of Le Bar Basque in Saint Jean de Luz, but presumably never posted – Connolly told the King that his interview was designed to 'dispel the false impression created by press persecution in certain English papers'; he would submit the transcript to M. Tabet Pasha, and only after the King had approved it would he send it on to the *Daily Mail*, who had guaranteed not to 'tamper' with it, and were 'clearly more interested in the improvement of Anglo-Egyptian relations than in anything else.'

Paris Plage, at the southern end of France's Atlantic coastline. Connolly and Peter Quennell were with her when the royal summons came through, and after some brooding in the bath Connolly advised her to accept – and make sure that he and Quennell were invited to Egypt on the strength of it, as well as making enough money for a week in Biarritz. Barbara joined the royal party in La Baule. Farouk, whom she remembered as a slim young man, now looked like 'a huge sawdust teddy bear badly sewn at the joints'. Barbara managed, with difficulty, to smuggle out a letter to her 'Darling Wopsy': a 'coal-black eunuch' was permanently posted outside her room and followed her everywhere, and although 'the monarch is absolutely charming and has been exceedingly generous and sweet', she found the hysterical crowds shouting 'Vive le roi' almost unbearable, and 'a thousand times worse than modelling'. Connolly, in the meantime, had arrived in France on the strength of a commission from the *Daily Mail*, only to discover that the king flatly refused to be interviewed. Before long the royal cortège moved on to Biarritz; all the members of Farouk's party were kitted out in black berets, so Connolly donned an identical item of headgear and, as agreed with Barbara, positioned himself behind a table at the last café on the way out of La Baule, ostensibly reading a copy of *Le Monde*, in the hope that he would be mistaken for a missing member of the entourage and be swept along in its wake. But the royal party swept by unregarding, and he had to make his way to Biarritz under separate cover. Barbara lost money playing roulette but still managed to set enough aside to buy Connolly a pair of gold cuff-links; Farouk, generous as ever, gave her a gold cigarette-case, an emerald-encrusted ring and a hideously vulgar clip, and, having learned of Connolly's passion for exotic fruit, he sent her absent admirer some mangoes, and arranged for a crate of them to be delivered to Sussex Place via the Egyptian Embassy in London.

> Cyril very nearly died after eating six mangoes at a sitting, saying they were the best he had ever eaten, as though to justify his greed; but he managed to survive them, and we had a rather dismal journey back to Paris through the Dordogne part of France, stuffing a lot of the local *foie-gras* – which you didn't like, if you remember – at the Chapon Fin. We quarrelled incessantly all the way...

Barbara told the King, now back in Egypt. In Paris they went to a cocktail party given by Nancy Mitford, who complained that Barbara 'sat and read a book throughout': according to Barbara – still reporting on her adventures to her royal admirer – it consisted of four seedy English faces – two middle-aged toothless queers, one of whom asked me if I knew of a hotel that wouldn't be sticky if he took stray pick-ups back at night, I said it depended what he was in the habit of taking back and any hotel might draw the line at goats, for instance; there was a snooty duchess in widow's weeds, and a fourth unidentifiable. We drank vodka and took the hostess to dine afterwards. She is quite sweet and amusing.

'Sorry to hear about the scones, as am rather off fat men at the moment,' Barbara told Connolly not long after their return to a London 'agog with news of my visit to Biarritz'; but then, quite suddenly, they were secretly married on October the 5th, in the Registry Office in Elham, near Barbara's country cottage. 'No one knows about the wedding yet, in fact you are the first person to be notified,' Barbara informed the King. PC Wellington Boot – Barbara's friendly local policeman, who kept an eye on Oak Cottage in her absence – and a man off the street were the two witnesses; a bottle of champagne was then opened, and Connolly made polite conversation with PC Boot about the thick coats the badgers were growing in readiness for winter. That over, they went on to a pub before setting out for the dentist, where Barbara was late for her appointment.

If his letters to Lys were anything to go by – and with Connolly so much depended on whom he was addressing – the newly-weds, like the badgers, were preparing for a long winter. Consumed by regret for what he had lost, Connolly was full of plans to cut himself free from this new entanglement. His marriage, he decided, was 'the salutary mistake, the worst thing that happened to the pigeon and cured him finally of voyaging'. Barbara was 'so horrible' to him most of the time, but he had told her that he was still in love with Lys, and regretted leaving her: John Sutro was still waiting in the wings as far as Barbara was concerned, so it wasn't too late for them to go their separate ways, and he and Lys could get married as soon as his divorce came through ('in the meantime you would still be Mrs C as you were before'). Lys had got a job in the London office of the *New Yorker*; he had spent an hour on the pavement outside, watching her working and talking to her boss, but then the intrusive Andrew had come into the room, and everything was ruined. 'I am so terribly unhappy that I long to die – I wish I had the courage to kill myself – you are destroying me by refusing to see me,' he told her; his marriage was a 'tragedy', and he couldn't stop crying. He hadn't changed his will, despite his re-marriage, and he planned to dedicate his novel to Lys; if her love for him was still the 'mainspring' of her life, and they got back together, 'you will find me a much nicer and more reliable person than before and I know that I shall love you more than any one I have loved except for Jean . . .'*

Lys held firm against his begging requests to be allowed to see her again, for which he blamed her analyst; while to Hamish Hamilton, about whom he felt guilty in a different way, he confessed that he felt bad about deserting Lys and marrying Barbara – 'hence my general furtiveness and persecution mania'. He was suffering from fibrositis, palpitations and pains in his chest, and was re-admitted to the health farm at Tring for a further session of dieting and purges in November, so exciting Evelyn Waugh to a further frenzy of speculation. According to Waugh, Nika Hulton had given the happy couple a wedding breakfast, and

> after the first course Boots had a seizure, fell off his chair frothing and gasping, and was carried straight to a waiting van & whisked off to Tring where he spent the first fortnight of married life being starved and hosed and worse. He is now back in London enjoying a precarious tenancy of Sutro's flat in Curzon Street. Their total capital is £5 which Hulton gave him for tips at Tring, two sacks of sugar and a cottage in Kent . . .

Although for the time being the Connollys had the use of both Sussex Place and Queen Street, most of their time was spent in Oak Cottage. Elmstead is a remote hamlet, high up in that empty stretch of downland that lies between Canterbury and the English Channel. The 'Cott' itself was a tiny, free-standing cottage, two-up, two-down, with the two bedrooms separated by a low beam: it was mellow red-brick on the outside, with diamond-pane lattice windows (one of which, a dormer in the roof, glared down the front-garden path like an ever-open eye); at the back, where the roof swept low to the ground, the walls were covered with hanging-tiles. To the left of the front door was the sitting-room, with its open fireplace and cupboards on either side, Axminster carpet and chintz-covered sofa and chairs; to the right was a small dining-room, with a refectory table and high-backed chairs; out the back was a minute kitchen, and beyond that an outside lavatory, a garage and an outhouse, where intrepid guests – including Angus Wilson – could spend the night. Although Cecil Beaton expressed horror at the squalor in which he found his old school friend living, while Rosamond Lehmann made her excuses and left at the approach of night-fall, the Cott, with its symmetrical front garden and its air of Alison

* Once again, Connolly found himself plagued by 'awful thoughts of suicide'. 'I'm now sitting in the Ritz weeping in a corner,' he told Lys on one occasion: 'I talk aloud to myself all the time like a parrot – "Lys, Lys," "Kill yourself," "Poor Cyril," "Death" etc.' This particular letter ended 'I have no more wish to say nasty things as long as you don't scold me.'

Uttley snugness, looked like a Londoner's notion of paradise, and when life seemed good Connolly saw it as a '*clos de bonheur*', telling Lys that the ideal existence was to live quietly in the country, earning one's living as a book-reviewer, seeing very few people, listening to music on the Third Programme and pottering about in the garden; but when the post consisted of nothing but bills, and the bank threatened to cut off funds, and books remained unwritten, and a sea mist came in from the Channel, and the only company consisted of seagulls wheeling in the field beyond and PC Boot pushing his bicycle past the front gate, the Cott became 'Oak Coffin' in the village of 'Elmdeath' near 'Ashcan' in the county of Kent, and – pining for grander surroundings and walled gardens and an orchard – Connolly would get Barbara to drive him round estate agents' properties, and while away the days dreaming of life in some mellow manor house or eighteenth-century rectory he knew he could never afford. 'As to cottages, they are hell in winter,' he grumbled to Lys: 'Roofs leak, builders, plumbers and so on won't come, everything dies and ails in a garden unless it has constant attention, lamps have to be filled and eight buckets a day of coal and logs fetched from outhouses.' The water was never hot, the beds were unaired, and his particular early-morning chores consisted of emptying the pot and filling the coal buckets. Mrs Lea the cleaner was deaf and blind, restricting her comments to 'Bloody dark' when he first showed her round, and since her idea of housework consisted of moving the dirt from one place to another or smearing it more firmly in place, Barbara – a stickler for hygiene – found herself duplicating much of what had already been badly done; when the time came to clean their bedroom, Mrs Lea invariably asked of the bed-bound master of the house 'Are you getting up today, sir?' – adding, *sotto voce*, 'Slovenly bugger' – to which the only answer was a despairing groan.

When 'Hubby' – also referred to, fondly, as 'Pungle' or 'Pop' – was in a bad mood, Barbara found herself 'saddled with a slothful whale of a husband'; cramped together in a tiny cottage, sometimes not going out for days on end – shopping expeditions were restricted to once a week – they battled, as Connolly put it, like a couple of kangaroos. Connolly – who had put on weight, particularly about the jowls – would lie in bed, sucking the sheets and repeating over and over again 'Poor Cyril, poor Cyril' or, less kindly, 'Why don't you drop down dead? That's all I wish, that you'd drop down dead,' or wallow in the bath for hours on end, steam pouring out from under the door, muttering like a mantra, 'I wish I were dead' or 'a million miles from here...' Once out of bed or the bath, he would sit 'brooding like a furious fallen emperor', or potter about in carpet-slippers 'dusting his first editions and cluttering up the tables with cracked Sèvres and chipped faience', or listlessly polish the pieces of silver he had bought in Bond Street on his sporadic forays to London.*

From very early on in their marriage – when Barbara came across her husband lying naked on the bed, with a desperate look in his eye – Connolly claimed to feel trapped: but demoralisation and nagging financial worries could, to some extent, be offset by other interests, and by animals and plants in particular. Husband and wife shared a great love and understanding of animals, and their unusual and exotic livestock provided gossips like Evelyn Waugh and Ann Fleming with a new source of merriment. Perhaps their best-known pet was a coatimundi called Kupy, a racoon-like tree-dweller from South America with black prehensile fingers, a sharp, enquiring snout (also black) and a bushy striped tail. Kupy had been brought back from Uruguay by John Sutro, at Barbara's request: according to Barbara, it was such a nuisance on the flight from Montevideo that the other passengers begged Sutro to hurl it out of the window, and once installed at Oak Cottage it proved itself a fearful show-off – swinging from the beams, uprooting Connolly's carefully-nurtured shrubs and breaking his china, escaping into the fields beyond, and chasing the geese and guinea-fowl that had also come to live at the Cott. It insisted on sharing their bed, nipping Connolly in tender places if he objected to its presence: in Ann Fleming's version of events, Kupy was desperately in need of a mate – 'the house is full of unsatisfied women' was Barbara's comment on the proceedings – and, in its frustration, chased its master about the house, snarling and then biting his finger through to the bone.† Ann Fleming, the former Lady Rothermere, had come to live nearby with her new husband, Ian Fleming, in a house they rented from Noël Coward in St Margaret's Bay, on the coast between Deal and Dover; the Flemings provided a welcome injection of social life, on weekends at least, and one day Ann Fleming announced that she was bringing over a party of house guests to inspect the Connollys' new pet in its lair in the outside lavatory. Connolly busied himself polishing his silver tea service in readiness for a gathering that included Lady Diana Cooper, Patrick Leigh Fermor and Evelyn Waugh, who came clad in a particularly forceful set of tweeds, and had earlier expressed a keen desire to meet such a notorious 'penis-eater': much to the visitors' disappointment, Kupy behaved

* Those who wish to learn more about the Connollys' beleaguered life in Oak Cottage should read not only Barbara Skelton's two volumes of autobiography, but her short story 'Dorothy, Get Yourself Analysed' and – if they can find a copy – her novel *A Love Match*, which had to be withdrawn by its publisher, Alan Ross, after John Sutro had threatened a libel action (q.v.)

† According to Evelyn Waugh – or so Harold Acton recalled – Kupy was set to work as a servant, scouring the dishes with her tongue, bringing guests an early-morning cup of tea, and thoughtfully raising the blinds; her only drawback was a weakness for the bottle, as a result of which she had made inroads into Dick Wyndham's claret, and was liable to snatch guests' glasses from them at dinner and drain the contents.

impeccably, nor did the Connollys appear to be living in such squalor and discomfort as they had been led to believe.* In the end, though, Kupy became so fierce and wild that she had to be sent to a zoo in Ilfracombe; her place was taken by a lemur called Wirra, the gift of the *Sunday Times*, which purred and barked amiably enough, but shared Kupy's propensity for destroying Connolly's carefully cultivated shrubs.

'The Mayfair clubman has disappeared, and shrubs have replaced Sèvres,' Connolly informed Lys, ungallantly adding that his marriage was a matter of 'waking up from the nightmare *in* the nightmare': his only pleasure consisted of 'planting creepers on the cottage wall. "Fellow-prisoners," I address them.' On trips to London he spent his time 'plodding up Bond Street lethargically raising his trunk at all the *antiquaires*'; in Kent, he was similarly obsessed with his shrubs, tottering out of the kitchen with bucketsful of water and slopping the contents behind him. 'We are doing the whole garden from scratch and I have developed a violent interest in creepers and shrubs – visits to Kew, catalogues from nurserymen etc.,' he told Lys; while Ann Fleming reported him as having 'spent his all on tropical shrubs and is amazed they do not thrive, but he enjoys angst and it will no doubt please him to see the winter kill them one by one.'

Planting shrubs and sitting in a deck-chair in the sun in a pair of knee-length shorts and strolling about the garden stark naked were all very well, but creditors were pressing and bank managers had to be kept at bay;† so, in the autumn of 1950, Connolly embarked upon a routine that he was to rely upon, and resent, for the rest of his life, but which he was to undertake with a thoroughness, punctuality and assiduity that belied his self-proclaimed reputation as the embodiment of sloth. Leonard Russell asked him to become an occasional reviewer for the *Sunday Times*: he made his first appearance in September 1950, and he began as he meant to continue.

* A year or two later, the Connollys were visited in Oak Cottage by Jack Lambert of the *Sunday Times* and his wife Catherine. They took a taxi from the station, and were met at the garden gate by Connolly, wearing a cretonne shirt, green corduroy trousers and socks with holes in them. Barbara was waiting for them in the back garden; she was wearing breeches and a shirt undone to the navel, and looked like a 'beautiful witch'. Towards the end of the meal Connolly asked Barbara, 'Baby, can it come out yet?'; at which the coati sprang on to the table, upset the coffee cups, buried its nose in the sugar bowl and tore the back off Jack Lambert's camera. 'Baby, *do* something,' Connolly begged, so Barbara donned a pair of rubber gloves and hurled the offending animal into the guinea-fowl pen. Afterwards the ladies stayed outside, and Catherine asked her hostess whether she had any help in the garden: to which she replied 'I work on it three hours a day and I *loathe* it.' The men went upstairs – Lambert noticed how the ceilings were blackened with smoke from the oil lamps – and Lambert admired the view. 'I hate every yard of it from here to Folkestone,' Connolly replied.

† 'Goodness he is terrified and rightly so by poverty in middle age,' Evelyn Waugh told Nancy Mitford: '. . . Boots said: "I am going to become a waiter at a fashionable restaurant so as to humiliate & reproach my friends for their ingratitude." He saw a worried look, I suppose on my face & said: "Ah, I see now I have touched even your cold heart." So I said: "Well no Cyril it isn't quite that. I was thinking of your fingernails in the soup."'

Although academic critics liked to write him off as the quintessential metropolitan literary man – soft-headed, self-serving, eagerly indulging in mutual congratulation – one of Connolly's most admirable traits was his readiness to reprimand writers he admired, many of them his friends, if he thought their latest offering poor or disappointing: W.H. Auden and Evelyn Waugh were among those whose work he would berate in the *Sunday Times*, and in his opening review he dismissed Ernest Hemingway's *Across the River and Into the Trees* as 'lamentable', a 'romantic and adolescent' piece of writing impregnated with a 'false set of values'.

The *Sunday Times* was then owned by Lord Kemsley. 'I admired him and his family, tall dark folk with long legs and easy manners, and wanted to be approved by them,' Connolly wrote many years later, adding that the occasional congratulatory letter from his proprietor would leave him 'deliriously happy'. After the war Leonard Russell, the arts page editor, had been joined by J.W. ('Jack') Lambert, whom was to work closely with Connolly and his fellow book-reviewers; among those whom Russell took on were John Russell (art), Desmond Shawe-Taylor (music), and his wife, Dilys Powell (film). The book pages – which occupied one page of the paper's total of eight – were headed by Desmond MacCarthy and Raymond Mortimer, the two lead reviewers, and other contributors included G.M. Young, Ralph Straus, Arthur Bryant, Michael Sadleir, A.A. Milne, John Betjeman and A.L. Rowse. Connolly was an intermittent contributor to begin with: he provided one other review in 1950, and then fell silent until the following April, when he pronounced (favourably) on Stephen Spender's autobiography, *World Within World*. That month he was offered a fortnightly slot: and over the next twelve months he dismissed Edmund Wilson's *Memoirs of Hecate County* but dealt more kindly with his *Classics and Commercials*, suggested that Auden's *Nones* suffered from a 'tendency to whimsicality and sloppiness', to such an extent that 'stanzas are beginning to occur which, even written out in prose, would be rejected by the dimmest editor', and – in reviewing Konrad Lorenz's *King Solomon's Ring* – set a pattern whereby, far from restricting himself to 'literary' works, he made a point of keeping readers, and himself, abreast of popular science, and natural history in particular, reflecting his love of animals and his outrage at the ways in which men treated them.

In March 1952 it was announced on the books pages that Desmond MacCarthy was 'resting on medical advice', as a result of which Connolly became – as he was to remain for the rest of his life – a weekly reviewer, uneasily yet gratefully dependent on the £40 a week this brought him.* Ten

* Among those who were particularly keen to have Connolly writing full-time for the *Sunday Times* was his new neighbour in Kent, Ian Fleming, by now a figure of some influence on the paper. The two men had kept in touch since their embarrassing encounter in Kitzbühel: they had met from time to time

months earlier he had told Lys that he might in due course take over MacCarthy's column; and when, in June 1952, MacCarthy died, he stepped into his old mentor's shoes for the last time, sharing the lead reviews with Raymond Mortimer. Although Connolly's feelings for Molly had never fully recovered from the Racy Fisher affair, he had retained a soft spot for Desmond; and Desmond in turn had watched over his protégé's progress with affectionate concern. Connolly had been wrong, he once told him, to worry so about being 'outstripped' by the likes of Peter Quennell: his 'exceptionally protracted' youth had been turned to excellent account by Palinurus, and still greater triumphs lay in store if only he would 'now stop being so sorry for himself, so interested in himself', and use his imagination and his powers of observation to write about people and subjects outside himself. Writing to his old pupil in 1951, MacCarthy regretted not having seen him for so long; he himself had become an old man, but as far as Connolly was concerned *The Unquiet Grave* was a 'permanent contribution to the literature of introspection', and 'you need never lament over yourself as a literary failure, whatever else you may regret.' They met only once again after this, at a party given by Lord Camrose, and the news of MacCarthy's death – he had collapsed in Leonard Russell's cubby-hole while correcting proofs – came as a sad surprise. 'How terrible about Desmond,' Connolly told Jack Lambert: 'I only heard yesterday and thought how gay and distinguished he looked in the picture in Atticus.'

A year later, Connolly provided a prefatory portrait of MacCarthy for *Memories*, a posthumous collection of Desmond's pieces, published by Robert Kee's new firm of MacGibbon & Kee and carrying an Introduction by Raymond Mortimer. Connolly's account of his old friend was vivid, affectionate and acute, and equally well applied to himself. MacCarthy's voice – 'warm, friendly, independent and judicious, full of subtleties' – seemed to embody the 'tenor of humanism'; unlike the more austere kind of academic critic, he understood 'that the feelings of stupid people are as vulnerable as those of the intelligent', and he was always eager to engage his readers' sympathies

> before proceeding to an intellectual argument which might otherwise seem pretentious or alarming. Many of his talks and articles begin with some kind of pleasing social generalisation or an analogy that sets up a happy herd reaction, thus creating the intimacy in which his intellect

during the war, and although – according to his first biographer – Fleming would introduce Connolly to high-ranking officers with a muttered 'Look, General, this is Connolly, who publishes a perfectly ghastly magazine full of subversive rubbish written by a lot of long-haired conchies,' he had happily written on Jamaica for *Horizon*'s 'Where Shall John Go Now?' series.

> loved to operate. This is sometimes dismissed as 'the desire to please' by those in whom neither the means nor the ends are conspicuous.

MacCarthy too had been accused of sloth, yet his output had been greater than that of many apparently more productive writers – while sloth itself was 'the mark, in many artists, of a conflict between genius and talent, the broken surface water where two deep opposing currents battle'.

A paradoxical combination of sloth and conscientiousness – he was the kind of old-fashioned reviewer who did background reading where necessary – meant that little progress was made with his own writing. 'I always feel deeply sorry for writers who can't write, especially when they are as good as Boots,' Nancy Mitford told Waugh. V.S. Pritchett reported that Connolly was writing a novel with Mr Goldprick as its hero – 'it appears to be about the sex war and Peter Quennell' – while John Lehmann remembered his describing a 'new "internal daydream" technique' for the writing of novels: 'He confessed, however, to a snag: his imagination conjured up the scenes he intended so vividly, and they appeared so funny to him, that he just lay on the sofa and chuckled at the brilliant show his fancy was putting on for him. It was difficult, in these circumstances, to put anything down on paper.'

Quite what he was meant to be writing remained a mystery. P.H. Newby wrote from the BBC to ask whether he was really writing his autobiography; he told Lys that he was still at work on 'my Baudelaire-Flaubert book', as well as a long short story, 'a sort of *Loved One*', but then doubted whether he'd ever finish anything now, since his life was over and he was merely waiting for death; Hamish Hamilton was told that he had begun at John Craxton's instigation an 'Anglo-American comedy *à la* Congreve', as well as working on a novel, the writing of which had left him 'paralysed by my horror at discovering what I really think of Sonia – or what one half of me thinks of one half of her.' Despite the non-arrival of Flaubert and South-West France, both Hamish Hamilton and Cass Canfield were prepared to put up £25 each as an advance against Connolly's novel, whatever and whenever it might be, now that Routledge had agreed to release him from their option clause. 'I am pretty canny where Connolly is concerned,' Jamie Hamilton rashly assured his American partner; despite Connolly's twists and turns, they had achieved a 'temporary burial of the hatchet'. Once again, Messrs Hamilton and Canfield were to be disappointed in their wayward author. The novel, and the novella, remained as elusive as their creator: as Ian Fleming put it – after informing Connolly that his recently founded Queen Anne Press would be delighted to publish, with Hamilton's consent, a collectors' edition of the novella, restricting the edition to 500 copies and paying 150 guineas for the privilege – 'there remains the minor problem of actually writing the story.'* Many years were to pass before Hamish Hamilton finally conceded defeat, but Canfield was of sterner stuff: 'I give Connolly full credit for being one of the most charmingly devious literary gentlemen not actually behind bars,' he told a colleague, after Connolly had written to say that he had completed 30,000 words of a 'literary mystery story', and was nobly fending off the rival firm of Random House, who had offered him $3000 for the US rights.

Writing for newspapers and magazines was, for the most part, a far more remunerative business than writing books, and until the *Sunday Times* became a regular and reliable source of income – he finally joined the staff, thanks to Ian Fleming's intervention, in the spring of 1954, on a three-year contract – Connolly gladly accepted whatever came his way. He wrote on Bordeaux for *Harper's*; he interviewed Aldous Huxley and Somerset Maugham for *Picture Post*, who also despatched him and Barbara, quarrelling all the way, to Cornwall and the Scilly Isles to write a piece on 'Tropical Gardens of the West', with photographs by Humphrey Spender; he wrote travel pieces for Lord Kemsley's magazine *Go*, of which Leonard Russell was co-editor, and won £25 after entering one of its competitions in the name of Mrs Lea the charwoman. But the real money lay in writing for American magazines, and visions of wealth shimmered before his gaze when T.S. Matthews, an anglophile editor on *Time* magazine, commissioned him at the suggestion of V.S. Pritchett – who urged him not to pay anything in advance – to write a profile of Evelyn Waugh for $1000.

'I had an awful time the other day with Cyril Connolly who said he'd been commissioned to do a profile of you for *Time*. He kept on saying what a friend he was of yours till I asked God to save me from such friends,' Graham Greene informed the subject of Connolly's researches: to which Waugh replied that 'Cyril has many injuries to revenge. I can't blame him if he takes the opportunity, though I may have to horse-whip him on the steps of my club.' 'He approached me obsequiously with a series of fatuous psycho-analytical questions . . .' Waugh hastened to inform Nancy Mitford: 'I said: "On the day the article appears I shall horse-whip you on the steps of White's." He turned green white yellow and grey and said: "What will you pay me not to write it?"' Confirming some genealogical details, he suggested that 'you have little chance of your thousand bucks. The Americans have lost interest in me.' In this he was both right and wrong. Connolly received his thousand bucks – his suggestion that he might repay Hamish Hamilton

* Lord Kemsley set up the Queen Anne Press in 1950, with Fleming, Percy Muir and John Hayward as its three directors. The first book they commissioned was Patrick Leigh Fermor's *A Time to Keep Silence*, followed by Waugh's *The Holy Places*.

from the proceeds was soon forgotten – but T.S. Matthews left *Time*, and the piece was never printed; which was a pity, since Connolly on Waugh was both accurate and elegant. 'There are two of them, Evelyn Waugh the writer and "Evelyn" (to his friends) the man,' he suggested:

> They are not pronounced in quite the same way. 'I saw Evelyn,' is uttered with a meaning pause, for the speaker will have a story to tell. His audience conjures up a familiar vision of a short, stout, militant, brick-faced figure with a neat moustache, smiling at the final thrust he is about to deliver, his sharp eyes fixed on an opponent whose retreat he has pincered off by a glass of port in one hand and (except in Lent) a cigar which he brandishes in the other. Yet on such an occasion he may equally well have proved courteous, and warmly aglow with a faint melancholy all his own, his batteries masked, his inquisitorial curiosity benevolently muted, even though he will be tearing the departed victim to pieces a few minutes later; for certainly there lurks in Evelyn a demon of destruction.

Connolly's appraisal reflected the wary affection of one of Waugh's occasional victims. The two men had taken to trading peace offerings in the form of boxes of cigars, referred to as 'teats'; but if all seemed affable enough on that particular front, Nancy Mitford was readying a depth-charge of her own in the form of her novel *The Blessing*, published by Hamish Hamilton in the spring of 1951. Its central character, Ed Spain – otherwise known as the Captain – runs a theatre at which he stages *avant-garde* plays, preferably foreign. The Captain is short, lazy, fond of expensive French wines and prone to sulks; and he leaves the actual running of the theatre to a group of faithful and admiring young women, 'relentlessly highbrow', known as the Crew:

> They looked very much alike, and might have been a large family of sisters; their faces were partially hidden behind curtains of dusty, blonde hair, features more or less obscured from view, and they were dressed alike in duffle coats and short trousers, with bare feet, blue and rather large, loosely connected to unnaturally large ankles. Their demeanour was that of extreme sulkiness, and indeed they looked as if they might be on the verge of mutiny. But this appearance was quite misleading, the Captain had them well in hand; they hopped to it at the merest glance from him, emptying ash-trays and bringing more bottles off the ice.

'I don't want to hurt old Boot's feeling whom I love. He's really $\frac{1}{2}$ Boots $\frac{1}{2}$ Lehmann,' Nancy Mitford explained to Waugh. Hamish Hamilton worried about Connolly suing for libel if she made the similarities any closer: as it was, the Captain was 'flabby to the core. What about the guilty sun bathe while the matinee is on, and leaving everything to the Crew, who choose and produce the plays *and* see to the financial side *and* run his house (he can't even get his own breakfast when they go).'

'Bootikins won't speak to me, because of the Captain. What can I do to make it up? . . . Do try to pacify him for me – I love him,' the Captain's creator wailed to Waugh a year after publication. 'It seems,' she added later, 'he saw himself as one surrounded by the most beautiful and desirable women of our generation, and minded what I said about the Crew.' Eighteen months later she reported that she had been reconciled with her victim at last, at a dinner party in London. Connolly froze at the sight of his tormentor, refusing to say hello, but melted when – taking her cue from a remark Robert Helpmann had just made about Constant Lambert – she told him that he was the person whose company she most missed. Not long afterwards she asked Waugh if he had read Connolly's review of her *Madame de Pompadour*, in which 'he gets his own back for *The Blessing* without any hard knocks, or harder than I can take, which is clever.' Her period and subject matter were congenial to Connolly, and his review was generally favourable, but he warned his readers that 'Miss Mitford's outlook on life resembles that of a worldly schoolgirl. She admires money and birth and romantic love (provided it does not interfere with the first two), good food, fine clothes, "telling jokes", courage and loyalty, and has no use for intellectual problems or the lingering horrors of life.' It seemed a fair exchange.

That same spring in which *The Blessing* appeared, one of the Crew's originals went to live in New York, exciting in the Captain further spasms of misery, anger, accusation and nostalgia. Equipped by Connolly with a long list of names to look up, and firm instructions to be regularly psychoanalysed, preferably by a Freudian, Lys had taken a job at the *New Yorker*'s head office, and returned to the country in which she had grown up. 'I feel as if I had lost some mysterious essence of myself in losing you and will never be able to laugh again or write again,' Connolly told her. Overcome by nostalgia, he had walked down to Bedford Square and pondered on 'how much nicer we all were and more sincere and less corrupt: you, me, Sonia, the Toynbees, the Museum Tavern days . . .' His love for Lys was, he now realised, 'the uniquely important thing in my life'. His mother had written from New York to say that he could get a divorce from Barbara if he stayed there six months, and Lys came with him: but with the bank refusing to renew Ran Antrim's overdraft guarantee, and with no buyer in sight for Sussex Place, which was now on the market, he felt poorer than ever. After charging Lys with bad-mouthing him in New York, he claimed that he no longer cared what people thought of him, and that people and sex had been the two great time-wasters of his life: 'I hope people have lost their power to hurt me – I think all human relationships are impossible anyway and therefore not very interesting. I find places, plants, ideas, objects all much more rewarding.' Returning to London in a heatwave after visiting Bordeaux for *Go* magazine with Barbara, Janetta and Derek Jackson – whom Janetta would soon marry following the collapse of her marriage to Robert Kee* – he sent Lys a telegram from Heathrow, passing on Barbara's prediction that they would be married in three years' time; in the meantime, he urged Lys to investigate the possibility of his being invited to the States to give a series of lectures. Princeton expressed interest – Edmund Wilson had put his name forward, together with those of V.S. Pritchett, Erich Heller and Mario Praz – but nothing ever came of it, since Connolly was worried about losing his slot on the *Sunday Times* if he took too much time off.

That summer, Mollie Connolly made one of her rare reappearances from South Africa. 'She is a very saintly character, quite unlike me,' Connolly told Annie Davis, but most of the letters she had written her son over the past couple of years had been unashamedly earthbound, much concerned with her money worries and the modesty of her £60-a-month War Office pension, and urging him to chase Clement Robinson, the family solicitor, over the non-arrival of funds ('Do go and get on with it'). Mother and son visited the Major's grave in Bath Abbey, and travelled down to Petworth to see Aunt Tots, where he met an old Irish butler who remembered him as a boy, and referred to him as 'Mister Cyril'.

One way of improving the Connollys' finances – if not Mollie's – was to sell Sussex Place. When Barbara eventually quit Queen Street, they had made Sussex Place their London base. Philip Toynbee was an occasional lodger, and others who spent the odd night there included Robert Kee, Natalie Newhouse (once charged with appropriating the master bed for amorous goings-on) and a drunken Donald Maclean: but with Lys in America, and the Kees no longer a couple, and funds in short supply, it seemed pointless to keep on such a large and expensive house. To begin with Connolly hoped to get £4000, to be shared between the Kees, Lys and himself, but in the end they had to settle for a good deal less. Long letters were exchanged with Lys about the division of furniture and china and silver and pictures and household fittings ('Did I or did I not own the geyser

* Janetta was followed in due course – and two husbands later – by Barbara Skelton. A millionaire whose family fortune derived from the *News of the World*, Derek Jackson was a war hero, an amateur jockey good enough to ride in the Grand National, and Professor of Spectroscopy at Oxford. His first wife, Pamela, was one of the Mitford sisters, and he spent most of his time in France. Connolly thought him 'a truly awful man . . . an arch-boor compared to whom Bill Davis [q.v.] is a Stephen Tennant.'

for our bathroom?'), and those items of Connolly's that were not sold or divided with Lys were jammed into Oak Cottage. From now on the Connollys tended, on their flying visits to London, to stay with Sonia in her tiny flat in Percy Street, squeezing into her sagging double bed while she made herself scarce in another room.

Donald Maclean was a drinking companion of Philip Toynbee's – when Maclean was a Counsellor attached to the British Embassy in Cairo, the two men had gone on a drunken spree, smashing up a flat belonging to a woman who worked at the American Embassy – and although he had been made head of the Foreign Office's American Department, based in London, his increasingly erratic behaviour was of growing concern not just to his superiors and to MI5, who suspected him of Communist sympathies and had applied to the Foreign Secretary, Herbert Morrison, for permission to interview him, but to his controllers in Moscow as well. Dick White of MI5 had arranged for Maclean to be trailed by Special Branch men; his fellow-spy, Guy Burgess – recently returned from Washington – had asked Anthony Blunt to monitor the proceedings against him, so as to be able to take pre-emptive action if necessary. Night after night Maclean was carried home drunk from the Gargoyle: he had charged Goronwy Rees with being a fellow-agent ('I know all about you. You used to be one of us, but you ratted'), while to Janetta's half-brother, Mark Culme-Seymour, he drunkenly blurted out 'What would you do if I told you I was working for Uncle Joe? Well, I am. Go on and report me.' Told of this, Connolly replied that Maclean was testing his friendship, and that if it was true MI5 would certainly know all about it. One evening in mid-May, after the Connollys had returned to Sussex Place from a party given by Freddie Ayer, they were followed in by an extremely drunk Maclean, who hammered on the door and then stretched out in the hall under an overcoat, before being put to sleep in Robert Kee's bedroom. Ten days later, on 25 May 1951, Connolly bumped into Maclean in Charlotte Street, and although he thought him 'rather creased and yellow', he seemed genial and unconcerned: but that same evening Burgess and Maclean took the ferry from Southampton to St Malo and mysteriously vanished from sight, only resurfacing at a press conference in Moscow five years later.

Connolly's love of mystery and intrigue was instantly aroused, in much the same way as, years later, he was retrospectively gripped by the murder of Lord Erroll in Kenya; and still more so since – as in the Erroll case – he had some knowledge of those involved. Everyone was talking about their disappearance, he told Lys: Philip Toynbee was eager to prove Maclean 'innocent of any political motives', but 'most people suspect Communist activity and only the nicest or Philip believe in a general adolescent disappearing act.' What is certain is that Connolly knew a good deal more about the Cambridge spies – Anthony Blunt as well as Burgess and Maclean – than he was able to reveal in *The Missing Diplomats*, the booklet he published on the subject in the autumn of 1952.* He had known Maclean in the Thirties, when he was working for the Foreign Office and lived in Oakley Street, and remembered him as amiable but weak, like 'the clever, helpless youth in a Huxley novel, an outsize Cherubino intent on amorous experience but too shy and clumsy to succeed': Maclean had been a strong supporter of the Spanish Republic, and had disapproved of Connolly's sympathy with the Anarchists. Spain, and the role of the Anarchists, had also proved a bone of contention with the 'grubby, intemperate and promiscuous' Guy Burgess, then attached to the British Embassy in Paris, and affecting pro-German views, and 'in his reproaches I noticed the familiar priggish tones of the Marxist'. Stuart Hampshire recalled how, after he had praised *The Condemned Playground* in the *Spectator*, Burgess had reproached him for admiring Connolly, whom he dismissed as a 'lonely thinker'; and Connolly noted that although 'Sir Donald' – as he and Toynbee referred to Maclean – enjoyed *Horizon*, it was 'a blue rag to Burgess, a weak injection of culture into a society already dead'.

Nor, as it turned out, were Connolly's suspicions restricted to Burgess and Maclean. In the mid-Thirties, Guy Burgess – already a Communist agent – had tried to enrol Goronwy Rees as a 'sleeper', reporting back on the conversations on high table at All Souls; and he had let slip that one of his fellow-agents was the art historian Anthony Blunt, whom Rees – then doubling up as the assistant editor of the *Spectator* – employed as his art critic. Rees later became involved with Rosamond Lehmann – described by Connolly as 'the Alcazar of Toledo, an irreducible bastion of the bourgeoisie entirely surrounded by Communists' – and told her about Blunt, and no doubt she passed the information on. Connolly had singled out Blunt's contribution to *The Mind in Chains* for particular opprobrium, and in a letter to Connolly thanking him for publishing 'Letter from a Soldier' in *Horizon*, Rees wrote that 'I didn't mean your going to Spain was a concession to fashion; I meant that at times you had made concessions to the kind of views that Blunt and Burgess espoused'; and in his notes for *The Missing Diplomats* Connolly set out in schematic form the careers of not only Burgess and Maclean, but Anthony Blunt as well.

Connolly's musings on Burgess and Maclean were published first in two instalments in the *Sunday Times*, and then as a booklet, published by the

* Or – to quote his inscription in Ian Fleming's copy of *The Missing Diplomats* – 'Inside every third man is a fourth man – and more to come.'

Queen Anne Press with an introduction by Peter Quennell. He had, he wrote, been brooding over their disappearance for a year: unlike many others, he seemed to accept that they had probably been spies, and their treachery – and, later, that of Kim Philby – was to become one of those subjects, like the assassination of President Kennedy, in which he developed a sleuth-like interest, eagerly reviewing any book on the subject that came his way. As might be expected, he relied – accurately enough – on intuition, amateur psychology and knowledge of those involved to reach his conclusions. 'Politics begin in the nursery,' he suggested: '... Before we can hurt the fatherland, we must hate the father.' Both men were, he believed, starved of love: Burgess in particular was aware that the net was tightening round them, with the result that they had to take 'violent evasive action'.

Four years later, after the missing diplomats had reappeared in Moscow, Connolly reviewed a book about Burgess by their mutual friend Tom Driberg. His own short book, Connolly wrote, had given 'great offence': 'in a careful analysis the *New Statesman* pointed out that Burgess and Maclean had gone to Brest and been killed in a sailors' brawl. In the *Daily Telegraph* Goronwy Rees said of my assumption that they were alive and in Russia: "If Mr Connolly believes that he will believe anything." Now Mr Driberg explains that "Mr Connolly's fear of the real world around him" rendered my approach "incurably subjective".' 'I met with nothing but discouragement and evasions except among my own friends,' Connolly wrote years later, reviewing a book about Philby:

> One ambassador sent a personal message that Donald was incapable of doing anything dishonourable, another asked me on no account to mention Philby as it was so monstrously unfair that he should be incriminated merely for having put Burgess up in Washington, a third pleaded for a total blackout on Melinda Maclean, who had had to put up with so much already, and others were convinced that the diplomats had been kidnapped or gone to warn Russia, like Hess, for its own good, or been shanghaied in some waterfront dive in Brittany...

*

Another of Connolly's improbable obsessions, the world of underwater adventure, was given a chance to gratify itself when James Knapp-Fisher, an Eton contemporary and the managing director of Sidgwick & Jackson, asked if he'd be interested in translating Philippe Diol's *L'Aventure Sous Marine*. Connolly agreed to go ahead for a fee of £100; Knapp-Fisher asked him to deliver by April 1952, and set about arranging co-production with an American publisher. Warning signals were soon received, with Connolly complaining that Diol was boring and pedantic ('He is the first underwater schoolmaster') as well as proving incompatible with the demands of a weekly book review; deadline after deadline shot past, with Knapp-Fisher's letters becoming ever more desperate, until at last Connolly came clean and admitted that not a word had been translated. The American publisher, who had already printed the jackets, was incandescent with fury, no doubt at Knapp-Fisher's expense; and *L'Aventure Sous Marine* was finally published three years later, in a translation by Alan Ross.

Despite the continuing literary blockage, 1952 had got off to a good start, with Mollie sending her son a much-needed fiver, and the arrival in a delivery van of some long-awaited and unusual shrubs. Social life was given a welcome boost by the Flemings. The Connollys pronounced the Flemings' meals uneatable, but they provided a pleasing source of gossip and a haven for the likes of Peter Quennell and Noël Coward, both of whom appeared at Christmas lunch that year: Coward was incongruously clad in Tyrolean costume, while Barbara unkindly mocked Quennell's leather cabman's waistcoat, and a tendency to strike Byronic poses unbecoming in a red-faced man in his middle years. And once a week, after Connolly's review had been posted off, he and Barbara drove into Folkestone, ate a lunch of smoked salmon, grilled sole, ice-cream and fruit salad at the Grand Hotel, did some shopping and went to the cinema, and had dinner on the way home at the Rose and Crown in Elham.

A more exotic expedition consisted of ten days in Paris attending a cultural congress. Auden, MacNeice, Spender, Sonia Orwell, Peter Watson and Tony Bower were among their fellow-delegates, and not a great deal was involved beyond listening to speeches and passing the occasional resolution. Barbara glowered throughout, saying nothing and looking cross; she left two days before her spouse, who felt free to go on the town with Spender and Peter Watson and 'chase American flappers about. My first moment of irresponsibility since I became the anxious bread-winner, and all too brief.' Barbara's disconcerting silences had already impressed V.S. Pritchett, who found her 'a kind of cosy cat with her tail curled round her – thinking perhaps of Egypt'; Nancy Mitford reported that 'Everybody complains of his wife. She dined with a friend of mine, who had made great efforts both of food and company, and asked if she might eat her dinner alone on a sofa.' A new acquaintance, Kenneth Tynan – who visited Oak Cottage in order to write a profile of Connolly, and in due course replaced his old enemy Ivor Brown as the *Observer*'s drama critic – provided a vivid image of the Connolly ménage at this time: he recalled

> a draughty old Sunbeam Talbot being driven across country at breakneck speed in a rain-storm, Mrs Connolly furiously at the wheel, moodily grinding her teeth, and Connolly himself squatting in the back seat on what appeared to be a spare tyre and murmuring to me, in his fussy, tentative voice, 'By habit, of course, I am an Epicurean,' as the needle touched 70, the car lurched on a bend, and an ominous banging was heard, as I remember, from the neighbourhood of the back axle.

'You have no idea how dreadful life is as you get older,' Connolly told Lys –

> the cafard of the country, the boredom of London, the vanity of society, the falseness of friendship, the squalor of sex, the meaningless repetitiveness of everything, the longing for faith, the reinforcement of scepticism and disillusion instead – only the communion of a few great artists with each other keeps me alive

– though, he hastened to add, some nylon socks from New York would improve matters no end. 'I struggle feebly like a fly on a flypaper but I know I can never get free,' he told her later that year. He spent a weekend with Raymond Mortimer and Desmond Shawe-Taylor at Long Crichel, and 'longed to remain there for ever and become a King of the Queers'. In the summer he took 'a honeymoon with myself', relishing his own company in Kitzbühel and the Italian lakes, but no sooner had he set foot in England than 'I am back in my prison of boredom where I hate every blade of grass.'

'He has become quite humpty-dumpty-shaped, his egg head backed by a wild tangle of hair and merging necklessly into the larger egg of his body,' Frances Partridge noted, adding that Barbara seemed 'pretty but aggressively silent; she absolutely refused to be drawn into the conversation.' As he grew older, Connolly's taste in clothes grew odder, complementing his unusual looks, perhaps. On formal occasions he would look elegant in a pale grey chalk-striped suit; at home in Oak Cottage, Pungle might relax in a lumberjack's check shirt and knee-length white shorts, his equally white 'Chinese cooly's legs' protruding underneath. Waugh once asked him 'why he always wore such horrible clothes and he said it was to spite Molly MacCarthy who ruined his life 30 years ago by telling an admiral that he was a bugger.'

Waugh's half-bullying, half-affectionate relationship with Connolly was revived in September 1952, when *Men at Arms*, the first volume of his wartime trilogy, was published. Waugh inscribed his old friend's copy 'To Cyril, who kept the home fires burning'; Connolly – or so Ann Fleming reported in excited vein – was 'hopping mad' as a result, taking the inscription as a slight on his wartime activities. Mrs Fleming had lunched with him at the Grand Hotel in Folkestone, and the outraged dedicatee 'needed much soothing with slices of smoked salmon. Between every expensive swallow he muttered that if you were referring to his fire-watching it was libel.' According to Nancy Mitford, Connolly's anger could be felt as far afield as Venice, so Waugh felt a placatory word was called for. He was sorry if he had wounded him: '"Keep the Home Fires Burning" to me plainly meant what you so clearly expressed in a *Horizon* "Comment", thanking for a camembert cheese and saying very justly that the civilian had the worst of the war.' Despite his outrage, Connolly had reviewed *Men at Arms*, along with *The Old Man and the Sea*, but whereas he found Hemingway's novella a 'golden and perfect tale', he had his reservations about Waugh's latest offering. 'One raises the silver loving-cup expecting champagne, and receives a wallop of ale. Once we accept that it is beer, a chronicle rather than a novel, it is of its kind perfect,' he suggested: as befits a chronicle, perhaps, the author had failed to build up his characters, and must learn to be on his guard against 'the perishable nature of gregarious clowning'. To Waugh he wrote to apologise for confusing Apthorpe with Atwater, a character from *Work Suspended* whom he wrongly assumed to have strayed into the new book: he thought the novel too long, and found the whole business of Ritchie Hook decapitating a sentry and pickling his head implausible – but, that said, 'one has no room to review a book properly in the *Sunday Times* – only to send a rather long telegram about it.'

Although, according to Waugh's friend and biographer Christopher Sykes, 'Evelyn refused to see in Cyril Connolly a great literary critic and thinker, and persisted in regarding him as fraudulent in large part, he remained deeply disturbed by a hostile criticism from him,' and pined for his 'good opinion'. Sykes thought that Waugh's ambivalence towards Connolly concealed an almost 'amorous infatuation' with him: he recalled Waugh bursting into White's looking for Connolly and, on being told that he was having his hair cut nearby, rushing round to the barber's to sit with him; or, on another occasion, dining at the club with Father D'Arcy and Waugh, who vigorously demolished some recent review by Connolly before 'adding with a reflective sigh, "Heavens, how I love that man!"' In some curious way, each yearned for the other's company. 'I deeply wish that I saw you more often. Why are you always in such a bustle in White's, the last refuge of leisure. Is it because you have given up cigars?' (Waugh to Connolly); 'Of all the people I never see you are the one I most want to see. *Toujours plein d'amour et d'admiration*' (Connolly to Waugh). * And when, in the spring of

* Looking back on the two men, Anthony Powell suggested that both were 'always mesmerized by *beau monde* mystique, both in their different ways fundamentally ill at ease there, unless in a position to perform his own individual act, put on a turn in fact.'

1954, the *New Statesman* published an anonymous profile of Connolly, pointing out – *inter alia* – how the post-war revisions to *Enemies of Promise* had emphasised and expanded the grander and more aristocratic ingredients in his lineage, since 'like Yeats and Evelyn Waugh he is a snob in the grand and vulgar way in which only writers can be', Waugh felt 'moved by disgust' to write a letter of sympathy. In fact, John Raymond's profile was rather more flattering than the accompanying cartoon by Vicky, in which Connolly looks more like a malign Wagnerian dwarf than a distinguished man of letters, his embonpoint bulging beneath his double-breasted suit. There were three main strands to the Connolly legend, Raymond suggested: 'a fecund sloth, a devastating wit, and a streak of *terribilita* when confronted by trespassers or intruders'. With his fierce sense of the artist's privacy, and his distrust of ideologies and nostrums, 'he remains the sea-green incorruptible artist, one whose unremitting search for perfection as a writer is one of the half-dozen literary inspirations of our time.' Never an Establishment figure, for all his social pretensions, he was the kind of writer young men looked up to and modelled themselves upon; and 'storm-tossed Palinurus can look back on his first half-century with a briny satisfaction. As he has said of his spiritual master, Sainte-Beuve, he is a smaller man than many of his contemporaries, but an incomparably greater artist.' It's hard to believe that Connolly objected: but Waugh – stung to the quick by accusations of vulgar snobbery, perhaps – thought it 'as caddish as anything I have read in an English weekly', and hoped that Connolly would seek out its perpetrator and chastise him accordingly.*

Waugh was an all-too-familiar presence, but one of the *Horizon* authors whom Connolly never met was Denton Welch. As a young man he had been crippled when a car knocked him off his bicycle, and he died in December 1948. His boy friend, Eric Oliver, came to visit them at Oak Cottage: Barbara liked him a good deal, and they began an affair which was to drive Connolly wild with rage and jealousy. 'All right, I had a quick fuck with E.O. on the breakwater,' Barbara would tell him; and although jealousy provided a welcome boost to their own sex life, fearful rows ensued every time Barbara received another letter from her lover, with Connolly begging her not to see him any more and Barbara becoming 'very violent and

* Connolly was grateful for Waugh's support, but less bruised than he might have been. 'How typical of the *NS* to think it a fantasy and delusions of grandeur to have wanted in one's prize-winning schooldays to try for the Foreign Office . . . ' he wrote: 'It surprises me that they waste time on people like Spender and me – old hacks choking on piles of review copies . . . ' John Raymond later became a colleague on the *Sunday Times* book pages, acting as number three to Connolly and Raymond Mortimer. He had a brief fling with Barbara Skelton after she had divorced both Connolly and George Weidenfeld, and she recalled 'his pale podgy countenance like an oversize bum'. A brilliant reviewer who found it impossible to write books, his particular enemy of promise was the bottle.

hysterical'. 'For six months every row has been a row about E.O. and every breath of love been dispelled by him,' Connolly confided to his diary. He spent hours looking through old photographs of Jean, taking 'refuge in her company and in memories of youth and happiness':

> Saved from night of agony by reading J's early letters and diaries which I have never looked at for 20 years, intense reality of Jean and our early love, a breath of truth and passion and goodness from an extinct world, wild remorse for ever having lost it, at same time wave of happiness and sense of her protecting care...

None of this diluted his admiration for Denton Welch's work, however, and reviewing his *Journals* Connolly struck a suitably elegiac note: 'Like many artists he was mildly snobbish and thus fortunately aware of the magical and sombre poetry of the Fall of the most haunted of all houses of Usher, the aristocratic civilisation built up by the English over 200 years of plenty.' As middle age advanced remorselessly, he brooded over what seemed like the fag ends of civilised existence, and the vanished splendours of the past. Barbara recalled a dinner at the Hamish Hamiltons, during which her husband and Isaiah Berlin debated the ideal period in which to have lived – they happily settled on the late eighteenth and early nineteenth centuries, with Connolly postponing the moment of death so as to be able to read Flaubert and Baudelaire – and Connolly returned to the theme when reviewing a life of Samuel Rogers, the long-lived banker poet whose biography Naylor, in *The Rock Pool*, was supposedly writing: 'Few existences are more to be envied than those which savoured of the *douceur de vivre* of the high eighteenth century, the climate of the French Revolution, the phenomenon of Napoleon and the romantic revival. For a complete life I would add a whiff of Victorianism at the close.'

Writing to Lys in the spring of 1953, Connolly claimed that he was undergoing 'death by boredom – an ever-increasing death-wish as if one was following a beautiful woman'. He couldn't bear to see people or take any responsibility; writing his weekly column was all he could manage in the way of work; he was reading four or five books a day, and neither drank nor smoked; 'this room is my cell, this cottage my prison, you, Jean and death my only companions – *mort sur le champ d'ennui*.' Relief of a kind was provided by a dinner which Henry Green master-minded at the Trocadero in honour of John Lehmann. Purnell's, which had bought Lehmann's small and extremely distinguished publishing firm, had decided for financial reasons in the face of a good deal of indignation from the literary world to close down John Lehmann Ltd, and the dinner was both a protest and a commemoration. Among those present were E.M. Forster, William Plomer, J.R. Ackerley, Rosamond Lehmann, Laurie Lee and Alan Ross. According to V.S. Pritchett, it was 'an unspeakably flat, distinguished gathering', during the course of which T.S. Eliot 'got up and mumbled a sort of collect' over Lehmann, while Henry Green made 'a sort of Chamber of Commerce speech'. In his speech of thanks, Lehmann mentioned how, as a publisher, he had had to send out innumerable rejection-slips to discarded hopefuls: 'We all shuddered,' Spender recalled, 'Cyril putting on an expression as though he were stuffed with John's rejection slips.' Nor were the food and drink any better. The meal cost 18*s* 6*d* a head, and Walter Allen remembered that, towards the close, Connolly complained in a loud voice 'We've had the sixpennyworth. When do the eighteen shillings begin?' Spender recalled how

> Cyril got rather indignant because the waiter – through not having heard what he ordered – brought him the worst instead of the best wine on the list. After some altercation I heard Cyril say: 'Well, you can leave it if you like, but I won't drink it!' Like a child saying, 'So there!'

*

A lesser peril facing publishers – lesser, that is, than being closed down against their will, and then having to endure a dinner at the Trocadero – is losing authors to rival practitioners; and despite the advances and the undelivered manuscripts and the urbane dinner parties, Connolly took his next two books to a publisher other than Hamish Hamilton. Despairing of receiving any of the books they had commissioned, but anxious to recoup some of the money advanced against them, Hamilton and his colleague Roger Machell suggested, in June 1952, publishing a collection of reviews and articles culled from various sources, to be delivered to them by the end of July: a not unreasonable suggestion, since the pieces had already been published in magazines like *Go* and *World Review*,* and any new writing would simply consist of an introduction. Connolly wrote back in a state of great alarm: to make up 70,000 words he would have to write something new ('the nicest place I know'); Mr Knapp-Fisher wanted his money back, the dentist and the optician were both banging the desk, and the bank manager was rumbling in the background. What he would far sooner publish, he went on, were two books drawing on his work on *Horizon*: a collection of 'Comments', to be published under the title of *Ideas and Places*, and an

* *World Review* was published six times a year between 1951 and 1953 by the *Picture Post* tycoon Edward Hulton. In format, layout and contributors it anticipated *Encounter*; Connolly's contribution – published in the March 1952 issue – was entitled 'Farewell to Surrealism'.

anthology of the best work that had appeared in the magazine during its lifetime; he would be ready to surrender his passport to ensure that the work was done on time, though at the same time he wondered whether they might be prepared to advance him £75 to fund his honeymoon with himself in Kitzbühel and the Italian lakes, since he could always write a piece about it, to be included in *Ideas and Places* together with his *Picture Post* interviews. Neither Hamilton nor Machell felt that 'Comments' stood up to being reprinted in book form, and urged him to include instead reviews and essays written for the *Sunday Times*. Not long before, Connolly had written to J.B. Priestley – who had come up with a similar suggestion – to the effect that such pieces were too short to stand reprinting ('they would be like a meal of stuffed olives'): he worried that Hamish Hamilton had lost confidence in him, and wanted to publish such a collection simply in order to do him a good turn, and, once again, he floated – unpersuasively – the possibility of repaying the advances from the money received from *Time* magazine, making use of a post-dated cheque. Rather than pour good money after bad, Hamilton decided to cut his losses, and withdrew; and by the end of the year Mike Bessie – a colleague of Canfield's at Harper & Row – was in correspondence with Connolly's new publisher, George Weidenfeld of Weidenfeld & Nicolson, about the possibility of their acquiring American rights in *Ideas and Places* and its companion volume, *The Golden Horizon*.

Some sixteen years younger than Connolly, George Weidenfeld had arrived in England from Vienna in 1938, and was by way of establishing himself in the vanguard of that remarkable influx of Jewish émigrés from Central Europe – among them André Deutsch, Paul Hamlyn, Max Reinhardt, Walter Neurath and, the rogue elephant, Robert Maxwell – who were to have such an invigorating effect on British publishing in the post-war years. He had aroused Connolly's suspicions by founding a magazine called *Contact*, of which Philip Toynbee was nominally the literary editor, but it had not proved a threat to *Horizon*; and in 1948 he had set up in business as a book publisher in partnership with Harold Nicolson's son, Nigel. Weidenfeld had married a Sieff; the firm was launched on the strength of a bulk order for children's books from Marks & Spencer, but Weidenfeld was far happier consorting with literary, academic and political grandees than with children's librarians, and before long his list began to take on a rather more worldly and sophisticated flavour. Weidenfeld was eventually introduced to Connolly by their mutual friend Clarissa Churchill, who later married Anthony Eden, but relations got off to a rocky start when Weidenfeld, who had just returned from seeing some printers in Manchester, hurried round to a party in Sussex Place wearing a double-breasted brown suit. The other men were in dinner jackets, and 'Cyril greeted me with a limp hand-shake, raising his eyebrows to the brown suit. His measuring glance made me most uncomfortable and I felt that terrible English freeze which exudes when an unwelcome visitor joins a congenial circle.'

Despite this initial solecism, the two men began to see a fair amount of one another. Sonia Orwell had replaced Clarissa Churchill as an editor at Weidenfeld, and she persuaded her new employer to use her old boss as a literary mentor, performing much the same role as he had earlier for Hamish Hamilton. Weidenfeld found Connolly helpful and friendly, if a shade patronising; quite what advice was given remains unclear, but one by-product of this new friendship was Connolly's appearance, in the summer of 1953, on the Weidenfeld list. This was, Weidenfeld wrote later, the year in which the fledgling firm established itself, citing with particular gratitude Tito's memoirs, Isaiah Berlin's *The Hedgehog and the Fox* and *The Pleasure of Ruins* by Rose Macaulay, with whom Connolly shared a launch party.

'I love you for the genius I don't possess,' Raymond Mortimer told the author when *Ideas and Places* was published in May, while Mary McCarthy, when asked to provide a quote for the American edition, suggested that 'Cyril's writing has a sort of magical property that makes it fresher when you open it ten years later than it seemed when pristine; it's like some wonder-working saint growing younger in the tomb.' Despite those happy hours spent in the Museum Tavern, Philip Toynbee found it hard to drum up much nostalgia in the *Observer*. 'His collected "Comments" read badly just because they are collected, and thereby create the impression of a formidable, and formidably silly, body of opinion'; and – in a thrust which sorely wounded its victim – Toynbee intimated that those attitudes which Connolly seemed to embody were equally out-of-date: 'Hatred of England, an adulatory and snobbish love of France, embittered and boring connoisseurship of food and wine, an inaccurate and unsupported *laus temporis acti*, these are some of the errors of taste and judgement which can no longer give pleasure.' 'I thought Toynbee's review a monument of hypocrisy and ingratitude,' Connolly complained to Alan Ross.

Whereas *Ideas and Places* consisted of selected 'Comments' plus odd essays on, for example, Bordeaux and Logan Pearsall Smith, *The Golden Horizon* combined essays, poems and short stories which had first appeared in *Horizon*, with the editor himself providing a suitably elegiac introduction. A welcome tribute was received from Evelyn Waugh, who said he had no intention of passing his copy on to a maiden aunt: 'I always enjoyed the magazine & was grateful to you for printing my work in it, but there was an ugly accent – RAF pansy – which kept breaking in; not indeed from you, but from your artless colleagues... "Modern" has always had a pejorative sense in English. *Horizon* was the first (and first considerable) attempt to give it attraction.'*

That summer, V.S. Pritchett and his wife had the Connollys and the Campbells over to dinner. Connolly was in mellow mood. 'He coveted our house at once; wanted the trees, as if they were the first asparagus of the season: "How can you say I don't like life and that I despair, when I have that beautiful woman there for my wife. I am a collector of beautiful things, beautiful women," ' Pritchett reported back to Gerald Brenan in Spain. Brenan, in the meantime, had been introduced by Connolly to Bill and Annie Davis, who were then living in Madrid but would soon become neighbours of his – and play a far larger role in Connolly's life than hitherto. Earlier in the year, in February, Connolly and Barbara had travelled out to Spain, and they were met off the train at Madrid station by Bill Davis, clad in a dandyish grey overcoat and clutching a silver-topped cane. A New Yorker by origin, a snob and a social climber – he sent his son to Eton, and fought a long and successful campaign to become a member of White's – something of a bully and a drinking companion of Ernest Hemingway's, Bill Davis had the battered, coarse-grained, narrow-eyed features of a professional pugilist: he liked to correspond with Connolly about his collection of first editions, but was probably more at home talking about 'a good-looking natural cock-sucker (female)', and once admitted to Barbara that what he really enjoyed in life was farting in company, peeing on lavatory seats (preferably when women were about to use them), and blowing his nose into his fingers. He was generous, shared Connolly's interest in food and drink, and was keen on women. He referred to Annie – a placid, indolent, entirely amiable woman, who controlled the purse-strings – as his 'squaw', and was memorably described by Jonathan Gathorne-Hardy as a 'big, balding, shambling man, with a deep hoarse, mechanically indistinct voice, who walked with a slight slouch or list, as if holed below the water line.' Not to be outdone by Bill Davis's overcoat and cane, Connolly had included in his wardrobe a pair of virulent orange pyjamas with black piping and his initials stitched on the pocket, to be worn with a pair of scarlet slippers; and so equipped the little party – Bill and Annie, and the Connollys – drove south to Andalucia, where Connolly waxed indignant at the number of English tourists adrift in Torremolinos, relived the scenes of his youth with flamenco dancers in Cordoba, and visited Brenan, who evidently enjoyed meeting his 'sweetly smiling wife'.

Back in England, Connolly advised Brenan that he would find the Davises 'delightful neighbours'; and that summer Brenan informed him that the

* To Nancy Mitford, though, Waugh remarked that 'it is striking . . . how poor the contributions were.'

Davises had succeeded in buying La Consula, the house they had been after in La Churriana. Although he referred to 'Thurber-simple Annie' and 'big inarticulate Bill' as 'intellectual snobs' – which they almost certainly were, offering comfort and boundless hospitality in exchange for the company of the literate, the artistic and the well-connected – Brenan told Ralph Partridge that he was very taken with his new neighbours: 'His slow, droning voice is like a force of nature, soothing to the ear but difficult to understand. She is very nice to look at – a sort of human geranium.' Over the years, La Consula and its generous, bibulous owners were to provide Connolly with a kindly refuge, combining luxury, good food and a welcome breath of Mediterranean air, and Brenan noted that Connolly soon became its presiding genius, even in his absence: 'Every conversation comes back to him. Mrs Davis, a very simple, naïve woman, adores him and he writes to her in the kindest, most affectionate tones, like a brother. Bill Davis admires him, but is cynical. As for myself, I admire Cyril enormously, for his courage in always being himself.' And when, a year or two later, Kenneth Tynan and his first wife, Elaine Dundy, were invited to La Consula at Connolly's instigation, they noticed how, as the 'house writer and master of ceremonies', he 'would take charge of the table placements and see to it that certain guests were asked only to a swim before lunch, whereas others would qualify for lunch as well.' Nor could they fail to notice his bathing-costume, made from an 'unbecoming fake leopard-skin'.

La Consula had been built for a rich nineteenth-century Neapolitan, and Hemingway remembered it as 'a wonderful huge cool house with big rooms and esparto grass reed-plaited mats in the corridors and the rooms and every room was full of books and there were old maps on the walls and good pictures.' It was approached by a long gravel drive flanked with cypresses; to one side was a 'forested garden as lovely as the Botanico in Madrid', and the swimming-pool was fed by a mountain stream. There was a fire in every room at night; meals were eaten, as often as possible, at a long table on a verandah by candlelight, and were cooked over a charcoal grill. Bill Davis, according to Hemingway, 'loved good food and knew good food and where to get it better than anyone I had ever known', and Brenan recalled how 'great slabs of steak and fish, baskets of gamba and lobsters' would be grilled: 'the taps run with whisky and vodka. Drinking begins at eight, dinner at 10 or 10.30 and one staggers home at two . . .' In his profile, Tynan described Connolly as a 'baggy, besandalled Buddha, with a pink child's face, a receding fuzz of hair skirmishing across his scalp, and somewhat sour, blank eyes which express the resignation of one who envisaged himself in a sedan chair sucking on a hubble-bubble and was fobbed off with second-hand Sheraton and cigars'; but La Consula, at least, provided him with a glimpse

(*Above*) Lys Lubbock and (*left*) Janetta.

(*Previous page*) Connolly at the window of the *Horizon* office in Bedford Square.

(*Above*) Peter Quennell.

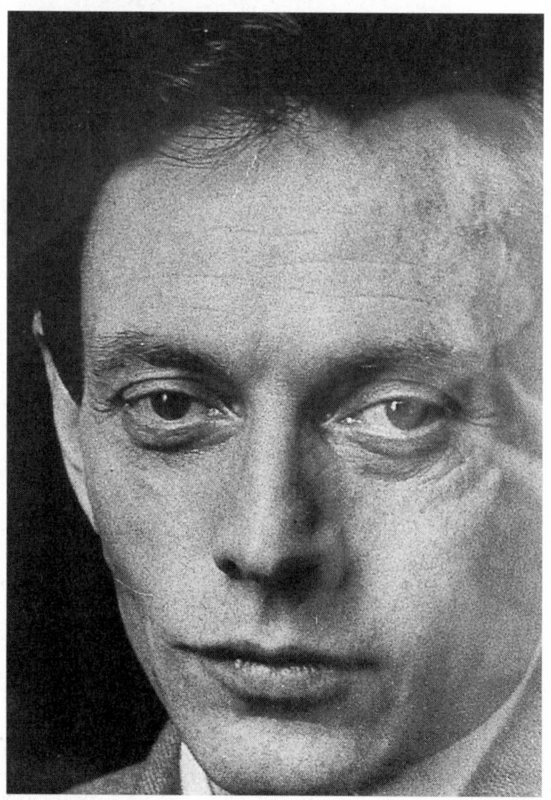

(*Left*) Peter Watson, by Cecil Beaton. On the back of his copy, Connolly wrote: 'Three dead men have I loved, and thou art last of the three.'

(*Right*) Connolly and Barbara Skelton, as taken by Alan Ross.

(*Below*) Sonia Brownell, Connolly and Lys Lubbock. The man in the middle remains a mystery.

On holiday in Hydra. Maurice Bowra is seated in the centre; Joan Leigh Fermor is by the chess-board; Patrick Leigh Fermor is behind Bowra's right shoulder, and Connolly behind his left.

Deirdre Connolly.

(*Left*) Connolly and Raymond Mortimer.

(*Below*) Connolly on a visit to the *Sunday Times*.

Connolly and Cressida,
by Richard Avedon.

Connolly, Deirdre and Cressida:
Bushey Lodge, 1961.

Connolly at home in Eastbourne: note the glass-fronted 'Controls'.

Some friends taken at the Glenconners' party for Cyril Connolly's seventieth birthday at the Savoy.

Robert Kee

Harry d'Avigdor-Goldsmid

Alan Ross

Ann Fleming

Bill Davis

Cecil Beaton

Connolly and Matthew, at home in Eastbourne.
Note the Augustus John portrait of Connolly above Matthew's head.

of the kind of life he relished and felt himself entitled to, a momentary glimpse of Eden from the wastelands of middle age.

Before long, the Davises would be offering Connolly consolation of a different kind; in the meantime, though, his new publisher suggested that he might like to join him on a grand tour of German music festivals. The Connollys flew to the South of France, where 'Pop' won 4000 francs on the lottery, so enabling them to stay at the Hôtel d'Angleterre in Nice. They saw *Figaro* in Aix, and lazed on the beach; after which Barbara made her way to Capri, Ischia and Rome, where she stayed with King Farouk (now deposed), while Connolly took a plane to Zurich, and so on to Bayreuth, Salzburg and Munich. He had been sad to leave Barbara behind – 'all we need is sunshine and a little money to reproduce the favourable conditions under which we met' – but before long he was deep into Wagner, 'gazing at fat women berating each other while the mind wanders further and further and the bottom itches on the hard seat.' It was boiling hot, and he had to wear a dinner jacket; listening to Wagner was a new experience, but Weidenfeld was impressed by Connolly's 'extraordinary capacity for intuiting the meaning of sounds'. In between acts (or operas) the two men lay in the sun and, emboldened by wine, discussed the state of Connolly's marriage. Weidenfeld had only met Barbara once, when he had shared a house with Peter Quennell in Park Village East, off Regent's Park, and they had taken an instant dislike to one another; and now, as Connolly lamented his lot, ungallantly wondering 'Why is there no knight in shining armour, no Siegfried, no Siegmund, no Lohengrin, to come and take her from me?', his companion – whose own marriage had recently come unstuck – murmured sympathetically but showed no interest in taking up the challenge.

Connolly found his new publisher likeable, intelligent and charming. 'He chases women and gets more and more Central European, which suits him, a chuff-like big businessman with wanton, bloodshot eyes and a bulging behind, always in a telephone booth, but there is the domed forehead and considerable intelligence and a soft spot for yours truly, whose fortune he proposes to make,' he told Barbara: he wasn't as nice as Jamie Hamilton, but was more highbrow and had more faith in him; besides which, the Hamiltons had become 'Princess Margaret mad – or failing her the Duchess of Buccleuch'.*

* This was all very well, but Connolly himself was far from immune from Princess Margaret mania, which seems to have struck down even the most cynical and level-headed. Barbara noted unkindly how, after they had received an invitation to a party given by Lord Rothermere at which the 'royal dwarf' would be present, 'Hubby' spent hours preening himself in front of the mirror, carefully removing surplus whiskers from nose and ears, and how, on arrival, he hurried away to the top table, leaving her stranded among assorted footmen and late arrivals. See also Ann Fleming's account of an over-charged Connolly confronting the Snowdons in Sardinia (p. 535).

The following month Connolly celebrated his fiftieth birthday. 'Fifty in September and for the rest of my life I shall never be sure of a cheque being returned,' he had lamented earlier in the year:

> Moved by old letters from Desmond and Logan, both showing faith in me as a writer which I don't possess myself. Irreparable sense of loss, disaster, a personality wreathed in mists, and consecrated to the dead. Dread and horror of all emotions – *les événements de 1950–1*: Lys, Jean, marriage, poverty. Ambition for 50th birthday: to have my silver out of pawn. Dreams now the most real events in my life, vivid harrowing encounters with Lys, Jean etc. . . .

To Barbara's horror, he planned to give a party for forty at the Ritz, but this was abandoned in favour of a far smaller gathering. Peter Watson, the first to be invited, couldn't make it, and neither could Graham Eyres-Monsell, so they were left with Sonia, Janetta and Robin Ironside. Barbara grumbled a good deal at the inclusion of Sonia, and objected keenly to her husband's choice of the menu and, in particular, the 'main course of partridge with, if you please, a salade niçoise'; it was, she declared, 'a thoroughly messy combination of dishes, the idea that Cyril is a "gourmet" being the greatest myth of the century, of course'. Early in October, Ann Fleming hosted an altogether grander 'official' birthday dinner in her London house. Barbara had flu and kept away: the dinner guests included Clarissa Churchill, the Campbells, Maurice Bowra and Peter Quennell, and they were joined for drinks afterwards by Alan Pryce-Jones, Cecil Beaton, Lucian Freud and his wife Caroline Blackwood, Francis Bacon, Stephen Spender, Ali Forbes, Freddie Ayer and Sonia Orwell and her new husband, Michael Pitt-Rivers. 'Cyril was radiant and feeling very warm-hearted at such a genuine display of affection. His heart and greed were equally overflowing at the tributes given to him,' Cecil Beaton confided to his diary.

Life at Oak Cottage remained as turbulent as ever. They celebrated their wedding anniversary with a row over the house-keeping: Connolly ended up by hurling *Gale Warning* by Dornford Yates at Barbara's head, and then ran upstairs muttering 'Bloody bitch, nagging shrew.' Some three months later, Edmund Wilson visited the happy couple with Jason and Barbara Epstein, who were on their honeymoon: Epstein, an editor at Doubleday, was keen to send Connolly to the South Seas to write a travel book, but was told that this was ruled out by the absence of second-hand bookshops.* Wilson thought

* Seven years later Epstein reissued *Enemies of Promise* as an Anchor paperback. Sub-titled 'An Autobiography of Ideas', it also included various essays, and was dedicated to Edmund Wilson. 'Do not despise the scrappiness of my book,' Connolly begged his American readers: 'I work best in scraps

that Barbara, single-handed, redeemed London literary life from 'the taint of homosexuality', but although 'she tried a little to vamp me by lingering glances from her brown long-lashed eyes', he found her hard to talk to: she ruled 'Hubby' with a rod of iron, he felt, reporting in awestruck tones how she had allegedly rapped an errant Quennell over the head with the heel of her shoe. As for their host, Wilson noted how 'like many wits and raconteurs, he never listens to anyone else's sallies or stories: his mind begins at once to wander, and when the other person has finished he gives a little nod and smile that indicate he has paid no attention.'

That same month the Connollys went to stay with the Campbells at Stokke; Freddie Ayer and Joan Rayner were their fellow-guests, and on their last evening Frances and Ralph Partridge came over from Ham Spray. Stokke was, according to Barbara, a 'vast unheated house like a boys' preparatory school': it was dirty, so cold that she had to keep her coat on at all times, the drinks before meals were in wretchedly short supply, and Robin Campbell – who evidently didn't care for the current Mrs Connolly – kept bursting into their bedroom, talking non-stop.* And, to make matters worse from Barbara's point of view, there was Joan – rich, well-bred, beautiful, clever, liked and admired by all, Connolly included. Unable to stand any more, Barbara invented a dentist's appointment, and asked to be woken at seven to catch an early train back to London. Unfortunately she took a couple of sleeping-pills, and was unable to struggle out of bed in time; the Campbells then drove them to the station for the next train, only for Barbara to realise that she'd left Kupy's basket behind. Connolly and Joan swept off to London together, while Barbara returned to Stokke to prepare herself for a third attempt: '"She's going on the 1.17, though," Robin said between clenched teeth.'

If Connolly's novel was becalmed, Barbara's sense of being an outsider, watching the antics of those about her with a sardonic, observant eye, was beginning to bear fruit. She was hard at work on her first novel, *A Young Girl's Touch*, which would be dedicated to her husband and published by George Weidenfeld, and looked back to her adventures in wartime London and Cairo. Connolly's encouragement was combined with irritation and an

and, besides, a little of me goes a long way.' Connolly marked his half-century – in America at least – by introducing a selection of *Great English Short Novels* for the Dial Press: by some curious editorial whim, these included Hazlitt's *Liber Amoris*, about which Connolly wrote in John Lehmann's *London Magazine*.

* Connolly's comments were equally unflattering. Stokke was, he told Waugh, 'a large Victorian small manor with mediaeval trimmings – a Maples minstrel gallery etc – furnished with that economy of which Mary is a past mistress: no stair-carpet but a few ancient dog droppings to relieve the bare boards at intervals. The walk from the drawing-room, where Robin is painting the carcass of a pig... to the kitchen, where they eat, involves passing a disused dining-room full of incubating chickens from which a smell proceeds guaranteed to give a frisson of which no gastronome has dreamed. One can just sit down without retching...'

understandable dash of envy or resentment: 'A lot of talk about helping me with the drivel, and then when it is produced a po-face, glares at each page for about ten minutes without saying a word, looking absolutely furious, and hands it back saying "It's perfectly all right."'

'I am terribly anxious to get out of this cottage as it is humiliating to be parked on one's wife, and am longing to find something of my own,' Connolly wrote to Annie Davis: could they lend him the money he needed to buy a 'Tennysonian rectory', with a library and a brick wall on which he could grow fruit? By doing so, he went on, 'you would be setting me free from a little of the cat-and-dog side of marriage and restoring my authority.' In addition to Kupy and the guinea-fowl, they now had two tame Chinese geese which followed them everywhere: he wished, though, that Barbara would have her 'tubes blown' before he became 'completely impotent', but 'she has a real dread of maternity'. Nor was Barbara any happier. 'I spend the whole time brooding on the selfish and slothful habits of my husband until I have worked myself up into a state of bitter hatred,' she confessed to her diary:

> I have nothing better to do than go over every word, look and deed of unpleasantness; every incident at every dinner party, his vileness in front of other people, his vileness alone, every nasty thing said, done, anticipated and threatened. And then I began to think how I could ever get away and lead my own life, doing the things I used to like doing either by myself or with someone congenial. Having decided that living with such a man is bad for me, that now I had become a crushed neurotic who had lost all self-confidence, I must get away . . .

Connolly would not give her a divorce, she went on, unless she was the guilty party, 'but why should I be guilty when I have done everything to make the marriage a success? I was even prepared to be faithful if I had not become so frustrated that it was physically impossible to be so any longer.' On a trip to Greece in June, Barbara found herself 'stricken with nymphomania'. As they made their way down the Adriatic by boat from Venice, she found herself irresistibly attracted to a retired sea captain, a 'stout, squat, mournful-eyed Greek with thick black cossack-like moustaches and a very commanding air'. She could, she confessed, 'think of nothing else but being crushed beneath his weight', but – much to her disappointment – his wife never left his side. She celebrated her thirty-eighth birthday in the Grande Bretagne Hotel in Athens, and Connolly gave her a Parker pen and a book on Mykonos inscribed 'To Baby, on her umpteenth birthday': it was too hot, everything stank of DDT, the food was repellent, Connolly irritated her by following her round in a dog-like fashion, exactly like John Sutro, and – worst of all – 'I feel man-mad wherever I go.'

The Connollys' marriage was subjected to a further battering when, in the summer of 1954, they travelled out to Italy, after the *Sunday Times* had asked him to write about the recent excavations at Herculaneum. Numbed with depression, Connolly lay groaning on his bed in the Albergo d'Inghilterra in Rome, while Barbara – or so he charged her – amused herself with a 'nigger'. 'I am glad he fulfilled a sexual want, sorry he did not prove the permanent attraction you are looking for – a prick with a bank balance,' he told her. He was shattered by her infidelity: 'I regarded our sex life as a sacred mystery' which she had defiled, and 'I was an alert and confident personality two days ago, now am a pathetic lunatic.' They travelled south to Naples, Paestum and Pompeii, where Barbara insisted on inspecting the frescoes usually withheld from female eyes; after which they went north again, to Florence, to stay with Bernard Berenson at I Tatti. Berenson was in forceful mood, denouncing Eliot as a humbug and Auden as no good, whilst reading Flaubert was 'like swimming in turtle soup'. Connolly's self-esteem received another jolt when Nicky Mariano said they had heard that he had become a heavy drinker, and extremely fat: this was an optical illusion, Berenson explained – Connolly's head was out of proportion, and if only he were a little taller, no one would think him fat. After such an onslaught, it must have been a relief to go and stay with Joan Rayner and Patrick Leigh Fermor in Niko Ghika's house on Hydra, together with Maurice Bowra.

That autumn, Lys Lubbock married Sigmund Koch, an academic teaching at Duke University in North Carolina, and another chapter of Connolly's life drew to a close. Lys had come over to England earlier in the year, and they had arranged to have lunch at the Etoile. 'You will find me a much sadder and wiser man,' Connolly warned her, adding that he often wondered whether he could bear to see her again: 'I think we are more likely to feel awkward and tongue-tied rather than burst into tears, but, as a precaution, let's make a pact not to talk about the past.' Nor were Lys and Jeannie the only past loves to whom he returned: writing on 'One of my Londons' in the January 1955 edition of *Encounter*, he remembered Racy Fisher and his youth in Yeoman's Row; the 'long-buried voice or gesture loom, adumbrating relentlessly the pangs of human loss – apprehension of beauty and awareness of loss – which constitute the sour-sweet juice of Time...'

Living not far away in Kent, in Saltwood Castle, was a friend from still further back, Kenneth Clark. 'We are tortured by the Clarks who are our neighbours and never seem to want to see us,' Connolly complained to Lys; but when Maurice Bowra came to stay, they were at last invited over. Bowra held forth at length, but Barbara was unimpressed by this booming mentor from thirty years before, finding him frivolous and trivial after Edmund Wilson or Berenson: Clark, on the other hand, she thought a cross between these two and Rudolph Valentino, and – or so Ann Fleming liked to imagine – Connolly was gloomily bracing himself for her becoming Lady Clark, if and when the post fell free. Nor was Connolly's melancholy dispersed by a trip to Egypt to write three articles for the *Sunday Times*. 'I have never been in a climate more unsuitable – endless coughing and spitting, and great struggle not to lose my voice altogether,' he told Barbara: it was far too hot, the dust at Abu Simbel made his nose bleed, and the only good things about Egypt were 'lemon squash, fried giant shrimps and seeing things with archaeologists'. He met Barbara in Rome on the way back, and only Elizabeth Bowen's presence in the same hotel provided momentary cheer. Back in England he walked out on Barbara for two days, but found the 'outside world so drab' that he soon came limping home. But then, quite suddenly, Barbara fell in love, and everything was changed.

TWENTY-ONE

E Arrivato Weidenfeld

The one sure thing about the brief, ill-fated relationship between Barbara Skelton and George Weidenfeld was that it was based, on both sides, on an intense if transient physical passion. Barbara became for a time utterly infatuated by her new lover, and found it impossible to keep away from him. Her affair with him destroyed her marriage, but it also destroyed the one relationship in her life to which she would look back in later years with genuine affection. For all their bickerings and unhappiness together, Connolly was the one great love of her life; and her recollections of him, in print and in person, combined mockery and an habitual waspishness with admiration, amusement and great fondness.

According to Barbara – who was always adept at wrong-footing the opposition – Connolly was really to blame for the whole thing. Much to her irritation – she had given him no encouragement, and found his persistence increasingly annoying – he had fallen in love with Lucian Freud's wife, Caroline Blackwood. 'I like lunching alone with her very much – she is now my only friend,' he informed Barbara; and when Barbara told him that in that case she'd better find a rival attraction of her own, he said he wouldn't mind provided he was a gentleman. One evening, in May 1955, John Sutro invited George Weidenfeld to dinner, followed by the theatre; and, since Mrs Sutro wasn't around, he asked Barbara if she would like to come along as well. After the theatre was over, they stopped off to pick up Barbara's coat before going on to a night-club: she brushed against Weidenfeld, and both were suddenly aware of an intense and mutual physical attraction. Connolly, who had spent the earlier part of the evening in a television studio, was already ensconced in the night-club: he was pleased, if surprised, to see his wife and his publisher getting on so well together, and when Barbara teased him about how well Weidenfeld danced, he told her that she ought to get to know him better.

Ever the dutiful wife, Barbara rang Weidenfeld early next morning, and invited him round to breakfast. He arrived to find her wearing a fur coat over her pyjamas, and breakfast was extended to midday; they then met again in Weidenfeld's house in Chester Square, only to be interrupted by the sudden arrival of Wagner's grand-daughter Friedelind.* Barbara told her husband that she had spent the odd night in Weidenfeld's spare room: he was surprised but unconcerned, only becoming suspicious when, the following month, he looked in her passport and discovered that, far from visiting a friend in Cornwall, she had spent two days in Paris. Later that month, on his way home from a party, Connolly found himself passing Weidenfeld's house in Chester Square. There was a light on in the bedroom, and

> at that moment his servant opened the front door, and the front door was open and the servant was standing there, and I was outside on the pavement, and I had a jealous impulse of rage and anxiety and walked in behind the servant. I said, 'Is Mr Weidenfeld in or not?' The servant said, 'I do not know. Would you like to go and see?' She knew me, because I had been there before. I walked up to the sitting-room which was in darkness. I started going on upstairs, and as I got near the bedroom I heard voices, and I heard my wife's laugh, and then I walked straight into the bedroom with the servant following, and they were lying on the bed together, and then he just stood up with nothing on but a dressing-gown, and she had her dress pulled up over her shoulders. I looked at them for a moment. I was sort of crazy for about two seconds. Then I turned straight round without saying anything and ran out of the house...

Next morning, a shattered Connolly took the early train down to Kent, picked up a few belongings, and returned to London, where he booked into a hotel. Oak Cottage looked like 'a paradise of which only we are unworthy: expelled from Eden by the Jewish snake'. A note from Barbara was waiting for him: she was terribly sorry for the pain she had caused him and for telling him so many lies, and bitterly regretted what had happened. 'It is not only that I am shattered by what I saw,' Connolly replied:

> I cannot stand the lies and deception, the needless separation and partings. Above all I cannot bear the malice and aggression underlying them. It is no good to say you lie to me because I mind things so, if you loved me you would not want to do the things I mind, and which all other lovers mind...

The only way to save their marriage was for her to give up her lover and return to him, and – if possible – for them to have a child. He was still

* The early stages of Weidenfeld's affair with Barbara had an appropriately Wagnerian flavour: Barbara recalled how her new admirer held her hand throughout the entire Ring Cycle; from that moment on, she tells us, Wagner was her favourite composer, and 'whenever I heard the Rhine maidens, I visualised a chorus of Sonia Orwells.'

'physically in love' with Barbara, and there was no way in which he could share her with another man. But 'it is obvious that what you really want is a *ménage à trois* with a town husband and a country one and alternate trips with each.' She was trying to 'recreate the PQ/Topolski situation' – to which the only solution was a divorce. Their home had become a 'torture chamber', but even so, 'better love in Oak Cottage than lust in Chester Square'.

But lust was in the ascendant, and despite Connolly's pleading, and Barbara's own guilt and misery, the affair had gained a torrid momentum of its own. Egged on by Topolski and John Sutro, Weidenfeld pressed keenly ahead, confident that he was in any event rescuing Barbara from an unhappy marriage; Barbara found him irresistible, wishing only that he had more hair on his back, and threatening to smear him with bone lotion to achieve the desired effect. Connolly stopped seeing and talking about Caroline Blackwood, claimed he never wanted to leave Oak Cottage, and seemed all at once the dutiful, loving husband: but before long he had confided in Ann Fleming, and the Connollys' marital problems were the talk of literary London, with mutual friends hurrying to take up positions on either side of the barricades. Sonia, Janetta and Joan Rayner were especially fierce in their condemnation of the intruder, while Peter Quennell and Freddie Ayer provided him with worldly consolation. 'Poor widowed Smartyboots – rather sad, isn't it, when he so loves to be the one that chucks,' Nancy Mitford told Evelyn Waugh, for whom 'Connolly's cuckolding is a great bore. I dined with him and he went on and on. The guilty couple are making rings round him.' Among Connolly's supporters, Weidenfeld assumed almost demonic proportions. 'There is certainly something mesmeric about him,' Lauretta Hugo suggested: 'Don't leave her and give W the chance of working on her. What a curse he is.' Sonia Orwell tried to act as an intermediary, but despite their professional association, she felt she could hardly bear to speak to her employer. 'You are the only one of us who really understands what love is about,' she told Connolly: he was quite wrong to think that everyone was jeering at him; there was a great deal of sympathy for him, and he must sit tight and see it through. Mollie Connolly, who had encountered the miscreant couple on one of her visits from South Africa, confessed that she felt quite faint when they left together. 'I think it is the last straw it should be your publisher,' she told her son, apparently overlooking her own abandonment of the Major: 'I thought that day in the Ritz it was unpardonable the way they went off together . . .' Only by divorcing Barbara would he be happy again: 'I think a lioness would have repaid you more – animals have not spite and deliberate cruelty,' she continued, before urging him to 'put her out of your mind and leave her to her present keeper.'

Early in July, Connolly went to stay with a new friend in Brussels, while Barbara went to St Tropez. Jewish by origin, but a devout Roman Catholic, Hansi Lambert was the widow of a Belgian banker, and extremely rich: more importantly, she was kind, level-headed, and unafraid to say what she thought, and over the next few years she would provide Connolly with much-needed advice and moral support, as well as a comfortable room and a welcome supply of large and delicious meals, the menu for which was sent up to his bedroom every morning with the breakfast. They went for long walks together, and he re-read Waugh's *A Handful of Dust*: he identified at once with Tony Last, and decided that it was 'the only book which understands the true horror of the withdrawal of affection in an affair from the innocent party.'* From Paris, Barbara wrote to say that although 'I really do love you more than I can ever anticipate,' she knew herself to be a 'great burden' to him, and needed her independence; she had no desire to resume their life at Oak Cottage, nor was she yet prepared to give up Weidenfeld. Connolly, for his part, was a good deal more dramatic. 'My life is really over without you, there is nothing left,' he informed her: 'I see Sutro and G.W. like the giants in the Rhinegold who take Freia away and leave the gods in darkness.' He threatened suicide – 'You will find my grave just as unquiet as I found Jean's' – while at the same time urging her to have a child by him: 'I don't suppose you realise how deeply sexed I am and how convulsively I have always felt about you in that way – often terrified of showing it to you,' and he would happily 'have injections, or live on garlic' if these would make her pregnancy more possible. As for Weidenfeld, his

> future is no concern of yours – he got on all right without you till the end of May, he will get on again. He is *au fond* a businessman and they are not worth loving because their business takes up most of their time: they cannot love whole-heartedly, and he will always be giving parties – it's no life for you . . .

From Brussels, Connolly made his way to St Tropez to join Barbara, John and Marjorie Davenport, and Michael Wishart and his wife, formerly Anne Dunn. They bickered ceaselessly, Connolly reproaching Barbara for wearing her 'angry despatch-rider's face', and then taking offence when she likened him to John Davenport in being 'a blame-shifter and neurotic shirker'. Connolly declared that they could get together again provided they had a

* He told Waugh that he was now old enough to see Brenda Last 'as a miserable victim of a *grande passion* and not as a fearful bitch'. 'You were really saying,' he went on, 'that in every marriage there comes a dreadful moment when husband or wife falls in love and discovers that whatever they felt when they married, it was not love. This new feeling justifies any deceit and cruelty and causes whoever experiences it to *hate* their partner so the marriage cannot go on even though the love affair must end in disaster.'

child, both agreed to be psycho-analysed, and were re- married in church. 'I love Cyril, that's certain, but cannot bear the rows and humiliations and bickers,' Barbara confided to her diary. She was also 'sick of the debts': all their money seemed to be wasted on taxis, expensive and indifferent meals and hotel rooms, on top of which 'three-quarters of the time at the cottage he lies on his back and moans.'

Whatever her feelings for her despairing husband, Barbara had agreed to accompany Weidenfeld to Switzerland and Austria, while Connolly went to stay with Joan Rayner and Patrick Leigh Fermor in Hydra. Before he left, he got in touch with his solicitor, Craig MacFarlane, who wrote to him about the possibility of employing enquiry agents to keep tabs on the absconding couple in Switzerland and provide evidence of further adultery: the fact that Connolly had slept with Barbara in St Tropez could be held as condoning her adultery, and were it to become known that she had had affairs before Weidenfeld, their position would be further weakened.

'I am really in the position of Lys at Orthez here: stricken in heart and ego, torpedoed, abandoned, unable to act, a bore and a nuisance,' he wrote from Hydra; but he swam and sunbathed and lost weight, and 'it is a great pleasure having Maurice [Bowra] here – a real friend.' He visited Poros with Patrick Leigh Fermor and Alan Moorehead, and read the Gospels for the first time in years. St John's Gospel was, he decided, 'an absolutely staggering document. It has really shaken my paganism, for I think there is much in it that could only be spoken by a god... On the other hand, I dislike everything else as much as ever e.g. God, Trinity, Virgin M etc.' – and the Resurrection 'seems terribly fishy'.* Far to the north, in Vienna, Barbara longed to be in Hydra too: she was fed up with cream cakes and a 'monotonous diet of veal or goulash with George saying "Very good" to everything', and the acts in the night clubs were so bad that even John Sutro could find employment there. And before the summer was out, husband and wife were indeed reunited, albeit on a different island. Christopher Sykes, now working at the BBC, had agreed to pay him £125 for a programme on Spain, and he was deep in discussions with the publisher Max Parrish about a short illustrated book on the country, with Bill Brandt providing the photographs: spending time together in Spain would 'give us a fresh start and new life', to begin which they made their way to Mallorca.

Barbara had gone to Spain on the condition that she gave up her lover, but no sooner were they back in England than the affair started up again, with Weidenfeld ringing the cottage and Barbara stealing off to meet him;

* Connolly put his new-found knowledge of the Bible to good use in the autumn. 'Last night,' Barbara recorded, 'Cyril read out the woman taken in adultery – "He that is without sin among you, let him first cast a stone at her. What a beautiful story." '

and Connolly felt more beleaguered than ever, on the literary as well as the domestic front. 'I hope it is not full of dreary digs at me,' he wrote to Waugh about *Officers and Gentlemen*, the second in the wartime trilogy.* It wasn't – the worst was yet to come – but Connolly felt disappointed all the same. 'I was not a great admirer of *Men at Arms*, and I had been looking forward to its successor to make amends,' he told the readers of the *Sunday Times*. He admired the opening scenes in the Blitz, and the Cretan disaster with which the book ended, but otherwise it suffered 'from a benign lethargy which renders it very slow reading'. The characters amounted to little more than 'a series of amiable cartoons': Waugh seemed to have lost his satirical edge, and 'we are therefore left with Mr Waugh's humour, which is gentle and anecdotal, depending largely on a simple use of exaggeration, schoolboyish jokes or military paradoxes.' Writing to Waugh after the review had appeared, Maurice Bowra suggested that the reviewer's domestic difficulties prevented him from seeing the novel as it really was: 'I think he had better settle down for life with the Lamberts in Brussels,' since they at least could provide him with the luxuries he craved. And although Waugh was worried by Connolly's imputation of 'benign lethargy', he too was well aware of his critic's parlous condition: 'I see his blue quivering face peer round the door at White's sometimes, but he scuttles away if – as there nearly always is – there is a hearty mob with me.' Barbara begged to be left on 'neutral ground' in order to think about her future and decide between husband and lover, but found it impossible to keep away: on one occasion she met Weidenfeld secretly in a pub before going on to lunch with her husband, Somerset Maugham, Alan Searle and Angus Wilson; he was wearing a new grey overcoat, looked slimmer, and 'with his alert stride and bright brown eyes – compared by some evil tongues to iron jelloids – I fell terribly in love.'

Still hoping for a child, Barbara was admitted into hospital in Canterbury in November for the removal of several fibroids from the mouth of her womb: 'Mary Campbell knows all about fibroids. When her cows get them they become so randy they're good for nothing and have to be shot!' Connolly told her. He drove her to Canterbury Hospital, and she remembered how she 'found his back view very touching, the uncombed hair round a bald patch on the pudding-basin head, his coat collar crumpled inward and when he turned towards me, his pale blue eyes had the pained expression of an injured child, not knowing what he had done to deserve such punishment.' Connolly booked into a nearby hotel for the next fortnight, while Barbara, from her hospital bed, fielded an unstoppable flow of flowers, telegrams and phone calls from his rival in London.

* 'I have Boots as a Corporal of Horse in the Blues, composing Palinurus during the Battle of Crete,' Waugh told Nancy Mitford; but the sinister Corporal-Major Ludovic was too unlike to give offence.

'I cannot imagine what this George can be like,' Barbara's mother told her unhappy son-in-law, who had taken to confiding in her: 'My youngest daughter, Brenda, said on the phone that he had a very foreign voice, which I should have thought would have put anyone off.' Far from it: John Sutro booked Barbara into the Westbury Hotel in Conduit Street for a dash of post-operative luxury, and when she arrived she found Weidenfeld already installed. They were joined there soon after by Connolly, after which Barbara went to stay with the Davises at La Consula, in the hope of somehow breaking the spell. 'Darling Cyril,' Barbara began a letter home:

> The Campbells have been very kind and sensible. Robin has done his utmost to keep me here, but it is really hopeless. The thing is, a quiet life makes me brood, although I love it here, just as at the cottage: you need to be in a whirl of activity to forget an obsession. I am still utterly miserable having to do what I do. After all, you have been indulging in your favourite pursuit (seeing people) which makes me feel cut off from you. If only you could accept my seeing W. from time to time until I sickened, but you cannot. Whatever happens, I don't want to be married to anyone but you . . .

Connolly, in the meantime, had written to Annie Davis to ask if he too could come and stay in January, for perhaps as long as two months: the *Sunday Times* were happy for him to send his reviews from Malaga, and 'you will have to treat me as a hopeless drug addict who is deprived of his heroin and be very sympathetic.' 'It is not very dignified for either of us to be in the position of waiting for your lust to be exhausted,' he told Barbara: 'I don't want to share you forever and be given the milk while another skims the cream.'

Barbara became increasingly restless at La Consula: Robin Campbell suggested that they hide her passport or kidnap her to prevent her escape, but after a fortnight she boarded a plane for Madrid. 'A terrible, terrible mistake, and I'm so ashamed of myself,' Barbara wrote to Robin Campbell: she had felt 'so dementedly depressed' in the middle of the night that she had rung Connolly – an act of 'weakness and selfishness' which 'gave him fresh hope'. She had then asked Weidenfeld to delay his arrival, the effect of which was to leave her

> in a worse state than ever, pacing and groaning like a mad woman so that someone in the next room began frenziedly beating on the wall. The boredom of the whole situation, and how sick of it everyone is . . . You were very kind and certainly did the best you could, but alas I can already hear the drum-beats of *E arrivato Weidenfeld* . . .

He had indeed, and when Connolly rang the hotel he was told that she was out:

> 'Gone to the Prado,' said Cyril to Robert [Kee]. 'I told her she must.' Then, as an afterthought, he asked the hotel receptionist: 'Is there a Mr Weidenfeld staying there?' 'Oh yes, sir, just arrived. Do you want to speak to him?' So Cyril has now posted off to Spain.*

Barbara and Weidenfeld spent a fractious Christmas together in Madrid, but after their return to London he resumed his bombardment, urging her to marry him and promising 'red roses red carpet a breakfast tray Sunday and real honest love'; and, unable to resist such blandishments, she moved into his house in Chester Square. Connolly, licking his wounds at La Consula, was understandably ill-tempered: 'He clamours for female company, but abuses his old friends like Janetta and Joan Rayner,' Mary Campbell reported: 'He got on splendidly with Gerald one evening, but after the next declared he was a fearful bore.' 'Hate is really all you can feel for me,' Connolly wrote to Barbara,

> and for two years now you have caused me more pain and harm than my worst enemy, you have broken my heart, belittled my work, destroyed my dignity and rendered me homeless, wifeless, an unwanted guest drifting about Europe . . .

But La Consula was balm to his spirits: 'I absolutely love it here and would like never to leave. It is everything I want in life – sun, trees, music, a drive every afternoon, good simple food, laughter, affection.'

In January, the Connollys were reunited in Tangier. They had dinner with Paul and Jane Bowles; Barbara smoked *kif* and fielded another onslaught of letters and telegrams, some businesslike (offering her a job as a reader with Weidenfeld & Nicolson), some of a more personal nature ('*I am very unhappy*'); an Arab boy told her that the only antidote to her infatuation was to have a verse from the Koran painted round her ankle, but – as Daphne Fielding remarked – 'First catch your ankle'. 'I am more in love with G. now than ever,' a distraught Barbara confessed in her journal: 'The only remedy is time. C. says I have been utterly destroyed by him, emotionally sapped, like an oiled gull, permanently drained.' She joined her lover in Gibraltar, while Connolly returned to La Consula; and after Weidenfeld had flown back to London, she met her husband again in Algeciras:

* Although Annie Davis would have relented, 'you have met your match in Bill.' Bill Davis was so furious about Barbara's defection that she was never invited to La Consula again.

> How I love them both, I think, as I see Cyril approaching the boat on the quay, his review book under one arm and looking so sun-tanned and sweet, wearing his food-spattered brown suede jacket that reeked of bad Tangiers cleaning. He grins. I grin back. I am relieved to note that he seems to be in a good humour, without bitterness and pleased to see me. He grins again, at the same time making a gesture of 'thumbs down', the famous gesture that Ann Fleming was supposed to have made at the prospect of our marrying. How can I possibly leave him? What on earth is one to do?

But, as they joined an interminable queue at Customs, Connolly's good humour evaporated. He refused to carry her luggage, stood about looking 'proud and puffy', and immediately asked her whether she had been to bed with her admirer. He would have to divorce her, he went on:

> Back at the hotel we go into luncheon. C. sits snarling and red in the face. Looking down at my wrist and seeing a new bracelet, he says, 'What a dreadful old woman you're going to be, covered in bangles and lonely.' He then shows me a letter from his lawyer advising him to carry on with the divorce . . .

He was tired of being a 'comic cuckold', he said; but for all his fierce words, they went on a sight-seeing spree together, to Ronda and Granada and Almuneca, bickering for much of the time and looking longingly at cottages for sale.

Reinstated in Chester Square, Barbara found living with Weidenfeld a 'lonely and barren' business. Despite his initial ardour, he had begun to equivocate and procrastinate; he worried about the effect a public divorce might have on his business; the heat seemed to have gone out of their affair, and Barbara found herself drifting back to her husband. But her divorce and re-marriage had acquired a momentum of their own, an apparent inevitability, despite Barbara's reservations and Weidenfeld's eagerness to leave things as they were. What 'really made the divorce inevitable,' Connolly wrote later, was the fact that Barbara

> was living with him in London when the case came up, although offering to leave. After the case I suggested that we tried to live together for six weeks, and that I would not make the decree absolute if she managed to give him up, but she became mistrustful and started seeing him clandestinely, whereupon I made it absolute.

'This never-ending searing grief of separation tears the guts out of me,' Connolly wrote to Evelyn Waugh: 'I am the one who is deprived of everything and the one person I lived for and was so proud of has been kidnapped from me.' On 27 March 1956 he was granted a divorce on the grounds of his wife's adultery, and a few days later he was writing to say that he had done a cruel thing to her, begged her forgiveness and enclosed six cheques of £20 each to cover her house-keeping. 'You will realise how much your friendships were spoiled by her,' a delighted Mollie wrote from South Africa: now that he was shot of her, he could concentrate his fire on Caroline Freud, for 'I think it is a foolish idea that you are like an uncle to Caroline. Lots of men of fifty really fall in love for the first time...'

That August, Stephen and Natasha Spender went to stay with Hansi Lambert in her chalet in Gstaad, and Connolly insisted on joining them there; he had brought his work with him, and 'all he wanted was kind faces and good food'. After three or four days he became bored and restless, brooding endlessly on Barbara and Weidenfeld. 'Cyril pretended to be interested in a detached sort or way in whether the marriage took place,' Spender recalled: 'Then one day a telegram arrived saying she was going to marry George on the following day, and sent Cyril all her love. After this we were all sunk into the awful maelstrom of Barbara's and Cyril's marriages, divorces and re-marriages.' The telegram was followed soon after by a letter. 'Darling darling Cyril,' wrote a seemingly distraught Barbara –

> Terrible news. I have signed up at Caxton Hall. The feeling of loneliness and dread, thinking of you as I did it, seems to indicate that I should not go through with it, and yet if I don't I am miserable; it seems to be something that *has* to be done. But the idea of being cut off from you makes me desperate, and I miss you terribly... Perhaps one can consider it an experiment that has to be carried out and got through... You don't need to feel you have lost me or been deserted, because far from it I feel closer to you than ever. But still, it might not happen even yet. But I had to write at once and tell you.

Connolly managed to ring Barbara from the chalet: she suggested that she should fly out to Gstaad at once, comparing her mission to that of Robert Menzies to Colonel Nasser, but it was agreed that Connolly would travel on to Ischia, where the Weidenfelds were taking their honeymoon. He was, Spender remembered, delighted to get away from Gstaad: no sooner had the train pulled out of the station than

> he gave a sigh of relief, said that anywhere was wonderful compared with Gstaad, that he hated being up in the mountains more than anything, that he could not work, that he could only play Scrabble, that there was

> something morbid and unhealthy about our life there, and that in Geneva he could again breathe the air of French civilisation.

Pondering on the moods and tribulations of his old friend and fellow-guest, Spender noted that whereas most people 'are to some extent kept going by a sense of minute obligations',

> with Cyril no such sense of day-to-day obligation exists. Therefore unless he is very positively enjoying himself, that is surrounded by all the circumstances of a children's outing or treat, he is in a state of disappointment. We did have one such treat: when Hansi took us to Berne to see the Paul Klee exhibition. But the two or three private collections we saw the next day did not come up to any of our expectations, and Cyril immediately became an object of pity to all of us.

As for his marital problems,

> what was evident was that Cyril's chief motive in his behaviour is simply dread of boredom. He was drifting back to Barbara because he had not got anyone else, and not having anyone else meant that he might have to spend days and nights alone. A kind of inertia has become so powerful that it is like a driving force with him . . . What causes him at any time real suffering is the failure even for a short while to be amused.

Barbara's marriage ceremony was, in the bridegroom's rueful words, 'a dismal affair, more like a wake than a wedding'. Barbara felt 'wretched and embarrassed' throughout, as though she was there 'under false pretences'; Weidenfeld's parents refused to attend, and a subdued party was given afterwards by Charles Clore, the property millionaire. Nor was the honeymoon in Ischia any happier, Barbara taking radioactive mud baths while – or so she alleged – her spouse lay on the sand in a pair of city trousers with the legs rolled up, buried under a pile of newspapers. Connolly, in the meantime, was staying at the other end of the island with Maurice Bowra and W.H. Auden, and Barbara at once wrote to him, suggesting how he might see her: 'This must be the ugliest spot on the island,' she told him – the food tasted of paraffin, it was 'fearfully noisy and full of ugly undistinguished people'. Auden informed Connolly that he – the poet – was a witch, and that he would bring Barbara back. In this he had a certain success. While on the island, 'Algeciras was revenged,' Connolly told Gerald Brenan: he might even have made Barbara pregnant, since (or so he reminded her) 'I was on top for a change and full of two weeks' radio-active semen.' 'I love you *more* than Jean because I have never fallen out of love with you, never been unfaithful, never treated you like a doormat,' he went on. He wanted to be a little boy again, and to 'worry over money, worry and guilt over Lys, or worry about having enough semen which the child thinks is taken out of his brain, hence weakens earning capacity.' The debilitating effect of sex on the brain was one of Connolly's pet obsessions, and so too was his yearning identification with childhood: sex was, to some degree, a case of 'the little boy who, in gratitude to his wonderful golden mother-sister-friend who saved him from despair, gives her his most cherished possession'.*

Life as a publisher's wife proved entirely uncongenial to Barbara. She claimed that she hated being woken every morning to the rustle of newspapers, was bored by Weidenfeld's business talk and tireless ambition, and refused to play the part of the compliant, charming publishing hostess, despite his begging her to 'Gush! Gush! You must be more gushing!'; he hated her cat, which peed in the grate and clawed the furniture, talked of the marriage lasting three years at most, and begged to be released at the end of that period – to which 'I chant "Until death do us part" and at once the distressed bird-face appears, nose beaky, mouth sucked in and eyes bulging, while he chews at his lower lip . . .' Connolly had moved into a flat in Chesham Place, not far from Chester Square, and on more than one occasion Barbara, on emerging into the street, was confronted by her ex-husband glaring balefully at her from the back of a taxi. She took to cooking him little meals, which she took round to Chesham Place; and when, in the autumn, Weidenfeld went to New York on a business trip, they began to see a good deal more of each other, going down to Oak Cottage so that Connolly could remove some of his possessions and arranging for Wirra the lemur to live with Gavin Maxwell. 'The last three months have been very unhappy except while he has been in America,' Connolly told Gerald Brenan:

> You assume that I am now the lover and she my mistress, W. becoming the furious husband, the whole thing having a Restoration comedy-French farce aspect, but it is not like that and remains more tragic, our broken marriage hanging like an uprooted tree in the air, profound habits of living, mutual understandings, shared thoughts torn apart or else putting out leaves as if nothing had happened. We love each other almost more than before, but I am much more lonely though less angry . . . I find life intolerably empty and flat; I have nowhere to live, no will-power, can't

* So upset was Connolly by Barbara's marrying Weidenfeld that he wrote – or at least drafted – a letter to the exiled King Farouk on the subject. Weidenfeld was, he told the king, 'a really odious little man' who had 'got a fearful hold' on Barbara. 'I am very unhappy, so if your Majesty would deign to allow me a word of sympathy you would cheer up your obedient humble servant . . .' In a PS he added 'I can tell you a little about the government's attitude to Suez, though I am sure you know it all already.'

> pack or unpack or make any sort of plan or work or concentrate – my weekly review and sending a few shirts to the laundry seem the most of which I am capable. Mostly I am just waiting for the telephone to ring.

As is so often the case, Connolly's misery and self-pity strained the loyalty and the patience of his friends. 'He is not a pleasant person & I do not know why you like him,' Ann Fleming confided to Evelyn Waugh: '. . . I chucked him because the October weather was too beautiful for self-pitying, whining, treachery and explanations.' As an occasional visitor to London, Edmund Wilson was pounced upon and subjected to the whole sad saga. He lunched with Connolly, Alan Ross and Barbara in the month she got married, and after noticing his host's restaurant technique – 'It is something to see Cyril examine a menu – will say "You have to be careful here not to get something too rich" – hesitates over sea food and wine, always anxiously enquires whether the fish he wants to order is really fresh' – he confessed himself ambivalent about his ex-wife. Whereas Lys had been a 'Shetland pony', Barbara 'was a lioness – her silvery hair and her green and feline eyes – her friends complained that she bit them, but then she would come back and rub against you, and you'd think she was a good lioness, that your friends might have been making passes at her.' But despite some mutual attraction, he still found her hard to talk to: 'there is no response in her face, a simple narcissistic mask, petrified by a fundamental sullenness. This is only occasionally diversified by gusts of flirtatious animation.' She seemed, he concluded, 'an empty and destructive girl, mischievous but not ever lethal on any very big scale'; whereas Connolly, for all his faults, 'has a wit and a distinctive, an innate cachet of the artist that none of his contemporaries (whom I know) has.'

*

Not surprisingly, Connolly's domestic tribulations compounded his writer's block. Edmund Wilson composed a clerihew on the subject –

> Cyril Connolly
> Behaves rather fonnily
> Whether folks are at peace or fighting
> He complains that it keeps him from writing

– and reported the hard-working W.H. Auden as being 'always full of moral indignation against Cyril Connolly, says he gets advances from publishers and doesn't deliver the goods – Wystan would like to flog him, only way to get him to work. Later, he was in favour of executing him, would like to perform the execution himself.'

One of the uncompleted works for which an advance had been paid was Connolly's literary detective story, now entitled 'Shade Those Laurels'. Connolly had once reproached Lys for showing Yvonne Hamilton 'the bit about Jamie' in New York, but since then he had switched publishers to Weidenfeld & Nicolson, who had offered him a contract for it, with an advance of £750. But although Barbara reported from Oak Cottage that her husband was hard at work on the novel, with only a hundred pages to go, 'Shade Those Laurels' was to prove a sad disappointment in terms of both quantity and quality: a mere 16,000 words or so hardly justified claims of near-completion, and the single extract that appeared in its author's lifetime provided further evidence that writing fiction was never his forte.* Nor did Connolly make great claims for it: 'Sir Mortimer Gussage is very light stuff – even so I can't finish it,' he once told Waugh '– it's a grey little wine from Luxembourg, about as far north as a grape will ripen, light, small, acid and without the staying power to become drinkable'. Stephen Kemble, a young literary journalist, is sent down to interview a grand old man of letters called Mortimer Gussage, recently knighted, in his country house. His fellow-guests include a dull dog of a publisher – according to Connolly's notes, an improbable combination of Jack Kahane and Rupert Hart-Davis – various acidulous literati and old cronies of Sir Mortimer's, a tongue-tied fruit farmer and his wife, and Sir Mortimer's daughter, who takes a shine to young Kemble; and although Sir Mortimer is found dead in bed next morning – hence the murder mystery – most of the opening section is taken up with a description of dinner: the placement is clarified with a circular diagram, the food and wines are spelt out in detail, and Sir Mortimer and his equally long-winded friends address each other in an implausible blend of affectation, waspishness, pedantry and French. Years later, in a discussion with Tom Rosenthal, Connolly explained that he intended to evoke the 'hammy', rather fraudulent literary world of Hampstead in the 1930s – by a neat twist, Sir Mortimer turns out to be a complete fake, a sonorous front-man whose writings were the work of a committee – and the country house setting is redolent of the old-fashioned thrillers he devoured at the time: but for all that, the writing is stiff and ungainly, lacking the sparkle, the wit and the elegance of his reviews, and the dinner guests remain so many tailors' dummies, spouting set-pieces and never coming to life. Connolly told Rosenthal that he was incapable of writing fiction because he was afraid of

* Connolly left a near-completed second episode, parts of a third, and notes for the rest. The novel was eventually – and skilfully – completed by his friend Peter Levi, who had once written to Connolly to say how much he had enjoyed reading the published extract on a train to Italy, and urged him to complete it.

other people, and had a horror of human contacts, of the human voice even. He found trying to describe human activities and master the mechanics of a novel utterly wearisome, and much preferred composing epigrams and maxims instead. 'Shade Those Laurels' proved once again the accuracy of his self-analysis.

'Shade Those Laurels' was published in the March 1956 issue of *Encounter*, of which Stephen Spender was the co-editor.* Leonard Rosoman provided a drawing of the bearded Sir Mortimer inspecting the exotic fruits in his conservatory; the piece was described as a 'diversion', and as a self-contained section of a novel which *Encounter* had hoped to publish in its entirety, 'but for various reasons that has not turned out to be feasible'. 'Of what is 'Shade Those Laurels' a parody?' John Davenport wondered in the *New Statesman*: 'A highbrow country-house thriller or of Mr Connolly himself?' 'An embarrassing piece of literary exhibitionism,' it was, perhaps, a reflection of 'our degenerate and middle-class society that a man of near-genius who might have communicated so much necessary and such potent pleasure should have turned himself into a sad figure murmuring meaningless words – Tibullus, Ausonius, Château Yquem and all the wretched rest of it.' Hamish Hamilton, on the other hand, wrote to say how much he and Roger Machell had enjoyed it, even if he did feel that too many characters had been hurried too quickly round the dining-room table, and that he would take great pleasure in contacting Weidenfeld to see how he felt about letting the rights go. Eager to build bridges with his old publisher, Connolly replied that he had got the rights back, though 'Perhaps I get too much on your nerves through my boorishness for us to resume relations?' He also urged Hamilton – successfully – to publish Gerald Brenan's *South from Granada*, which he had earlier recommended the author to send to Weidenfeld.

'Shade Those Laurels' marked the end of Connolly's ill-fated attempts to be a novelist; and a few months after its publication, in May 1956, another era closed with the death of Peter Watson. Though still active as a collector and patron of the arts – he had recently collaborated with Roland Penrose in setting up the Institute of Contemporary Arts – Watson was no longer the dapper figure of his youth. According to Cecil Beaton, he had become increasingly bohemian in appearance: he had taken to wearing 'awful mackintoshes', his hair stood on end, he no longer drove smart cars, and – as often as not – 'he would look like an old chicken, his complexion yellow; he had become very sloppy about shaving and generally had a few cuts about

* Spender asked if he could change the publisher's Christian name from 'Geoffrey', since this might give offence in All Souls, of which Sir Geoffrey Faber was a Fellow. Twenty years earlier, Sir Geoffrey had rejected *The Rock Pool*, and Connolly was not the man to forgo a grudge. But he changed the name all the same.

the face.' He relied less on charm than he had, but he still had a disarming smile; Beaton lunched with him at the ICA the day before he died, and remembered afterwards how he spoke 'with such gusto and intelligence'. Barbara thought him the most 'delightful' of Connolly's friends, even though 'he has become rather slouchy and shrivelled, with a bitter glint in his eye'. Watson was found dead in his bath in his flat in Rutland Gate. At the inquest his lover, Norman Fowler, admitted that they had had a row the night before, culminating in Watson's ordering him to bed; next morning the bathroom door was locked, and had to be broken down by a policeman. The coroner ruled out a verdict of suicide in favour of accidental death; and five days later a small party, including Connolly, Stephen and Natasha Spender, Roland Penrose and his wife Lee Miller, Graham Sutherland, Joan Rayner, Norman Fowler and the dead man's brother, Sir Norman Watson, gathered in the dismal red-brick chapel of a north London crematorium to say farewell. It was a bitter, windy afternoon: 'I noticed that Cyril Connolly was weeping, and I loved him for that,' Beaton noted in his diary.

*

Despite the tribulations of his private life, Connolly the book-reviewer continued to be both regular and reliable, and as he became more firmly entrenched he felt increasingly free to write about his favourite subjects from collecting porcelain to wild-life conservation. French literature remained a particular passion, and the subject-matter of Monica Sutherland's *La Fontaine* inspired him to flights unattained in 'Shade Those Laurels':

> Every few years I try to gatecrash a charmed society: with their plumed hats and tasselled canes, their embroidered coats and perfect manners, they loiter in some formal garden, lightly carrying their three hundred and fifty years – great Corneille, sombre Racine, honest Molière, Bossuet and Fenelon, La Bruyère and La Rochefoucauld, Madame de Sevigné, Boileau, Madame de Lafayette. The laughter vaporises as I steal up to them: '*Mais qui est ce malotru*?' There is a whisking of periwigs, an alignment of cold shoulders, a maxim raps out like a ball on a pin-table, followed by the tinkle of alexandrines: '*Retirons-nous*' (is it Racine speaking?) '*dans nos appartements.*'

But if his passions persisted, he was not averse to changing his mind in public. He had grown up, he once wrote, in a 'Keats-struck world'; as a schoolboy, he had been made to learn 'Ode to a Nightingale' by heart, and it had struck him as so much 'mawkish nonsense'. As an undergraduate he had shocked Sligger with his contempt for Keats and his contemporaries; but now, reviewing Herbert Read's *The True Voice of Feeling*, he suggested that the most useful advice one could offer a young writer was 'go back to the English Romantics', for they represented 'the summit of our literature, the last moment of universal greatness'.* The Victorians, on the other hand, remained beyond the pale: noting the revival of interest in Victorian art and architecture, he confessed that he had never recovered from his 'initial horror', and how, even now, 'I still catch a whiff of the gloom and the boredom, the puritanism and philistinism and snobbery and hypocrisy which hung about twentieth-century childhoods that were spent in too close a proximity to nineteenth-century surroundings.'

One motif that was to become more insistent with the years was a disdain – half-fearful, half-defiant – for academic literary critics. 'Mr Blackmur teaches at Princeton, he is a don, he writes to startle and impress; it would not do if he were too simple, or if what he wrote about was too simple. He is paid to seem above one's head,' he wrote apropos R.P. Blackmur's *Language as Gesture*. In the alien, ungainly world of academic lit. crit., 'one must be long-winded, profound and baffling to shore up the glorious cheese of modern literature so that it can continue to nourish so many mice'; and

> at the opposite end to the university critic or teacher of 'creative writing' is the literary journalist. He cannot afford to be obscure; he is not subsidised; he has to compress his views into a few hundred words, he must grade, explain and entertain all at once, and his work is immediately forgotten, totally ignored except for those who write in to correct a name or a date.

Remembering, perhaps, his own frustrated dreams of lecturing at Princeton, he suggested that they should swop places: 'He would acquire concision, I some depth.'

Connolly resented and deplored the way in which academic critics all tended to write about the same authors and the same books, for 'This means that a chain of authors who are considered central receives a proliferation of special studies while others, once dismissed, can never get back until some crotchety member of the literary establishment, like a goat eating his way through an orchard, browses on him out of perversity.' Equally irritating was the academic habit of emphasising the literary and intellectual influences on a writer's work to the exclusion of all else. 'What I dislike

* In a tribute to Connolly after his death, Stephen Spender suggested that 'he had the romantic feeling for the classical of an eighteenth-century man of sensibility,' but that 'he was not a nineteenth-century romantic because, although a perfectionist, he did not believe in human perfectibility.'

about Mr Kenner,' he pronounced – Hugh Kenner was the author of a 'clotted, over-written' commentary on T.S. Eliot –

> is the fatal atmosphere of the lecture-room, the subsidised incandescence which plays about his subject and ends by wearying us. Perhaps the easy life of Santa Barbara prevents him from grasping the key factor in Eliot's greatness as a poet which comes not from imitating Laforgue or digesting Bradley or from restoring neo-classicism to the moribund Georgians but from the deep awareness of personal unhappiness which, like Baudelaire's, breaks through the formal conventions of his verse.

He yearned for the 'unself-conscious, unsubsidised' critics of his youth, for Desmond MacCarthy and Lytton Strachey and Edmund Wilson and even the young F.R. Leavis, and abhorred a world in which 'a critic writes for other critics, as a physicist or philosopher writes for other physicists or philosophers, in the well-lighted penumbra of American college jails'. As ever, Connolly's disdain was vividly and memorably expressed: the subject – or victim – of a centenary tribute, 'Yeats appears like a dead bird covered by ants, each bearing off a thesis in its jaws.'

Abstract thought – as opposed to highly personalised musings on the human condition – was never one of Connolly's strong points, which may help to explain his admiration, shared by Philip Toynbee in the *Observer*, for that short-lived bestseller of English existentialism, Colin Wilson's *The Outsider*; as A.J. Ayer remarked, 'What originally led reviewers like Connolly and Toynbee astray was their unfamiliarity with abstract ideas combined with middle-class guilt provoked by the work of an autodidact.' Towards the end of his life, Connolly confessed that

> one of the bad moments in my life happened at Oxford when I started to read Greats and discovered that I had no head for philosophy – Berkeley, Kant, Descartes, Plato, the whole area known as metaphysics was completely over my head, or rather outside it. After a brief struggle I gave up and read history.

All his life, he continued, he had been dogged by this blank spot, so that 'every time I come across a word like "epistemological" I have to look it up.' And yet Connolly's own observations on human nature, with their beguiling mixture of poetic insight and common sense, wit and melancholy, speak to us more directly than many of the philosophers who left him feeling so baffled:

> I do not believe in original sin, but as a mythological statement of the human condition it seems poetically true. The fall, and the likelihood of falling, explains far more to me than the idea of progress and perfectibility; we have a bias to ruin, an itch for self-destruction; the moments of ecstasy are sometimes intolerable and must be blotted out.

*

Connolly's own 'bias to ruin' was, in the meantime, taking its toll. 'Malaise is a very polite word for the agony of boredom, loneliness, despair and separation which I feel most of the time,' he wrote to Hansi Lambert from La Consula. Although 'lethargy, sleeplessness, lack of energy' were its outward manifestations, 'I don't think it is a physical condition but a genuine "chasse spirituelle"... Sometimes the malady gets so bad that I try to clown myself out of it – that is when you find me good company.' Like a wounded animal, he wanted to 'creep off a good deal, chiefly to day-dream'. 'It was you and Debo who largely contributed to restoring my self-confidence by giving me a new scene and treating me as an intelligent and likeable person,' he told the Duke of Devonshire after he and Robert Kee had been to stay with the Duke and Duchess at Lismore in County Waterford in the spring of 1956. He had had no sex for eighteen months, he told Hansi Lambert, even though three women (all married) were in love with him; he worried about becoming impotent, but his ideal woman must have 'an almost Madonna-like tenderness and depth of purity', and few matched up to that. A friend had suggested – or so he informed Annie Davis – that he was mad in two respects: he didn't have a private income, and he wasted too much time chasing young girls ('no difference between me and Gerald'); as a result, 'I shall go for women of forty (they don't make unfavourable comparisons) AND play bridge for two hours a day at the club to supplement my income.'

Adrift in a sexual and emotional limbo, Connolly refused to take his own advice, and continued to concentrate his attentions on women far younger than himself. 'What you want is a lovely clean old man like me,' he told the novelist Elizabeth Jane Howard; the Spenders had suggested that they should see something of each other, but although Connolly might have enjoyed a rather public romance as a way of snapping back at Barbara, and although each enjoyed the other's company, their friendship was restricted to the occasional lunch or dinner. Much to her irritation, Caroline Freud – whose own marriage was coming unstuck – remained a particular favourite. 'You are a mirage of happiness which will always rise up to destroy my chance of any other,' he told her, in language that had a familiar ring; and –

here some nimble rewriting of history was called for – 'I helped Barbara to marry Weidenfeld so as to free myself for you.' Both of them wanted to settle down and have a child – and, after all, the difference between their ages was no greater than that between Porfirio Rubirosa and his fifth wife . . . Once again, jealous or disruptive friends were to blame for keeping them apart, among them Sonia, Janetta, Joan, Michael Wishart, Anne Wollheim, Ann Fleming and (not surprisingly) her husband, Lucian Freud. He urged her to get a divorce, and volunteered to be the co-respondent if one were needed. 'Cyril Connolly is hammering nails into the coffin of the Freud marriage,' Ann Fleming reported. Caroline disliked the way Connolly pestered her with notes suggesting assignations, and found tiresome his addiction to intrigue and romantic games; and when, on one occasion, Lucian Freud found him lurking outside his flat in Dean Street, hoping to catch a glimpse of Caroline, he rushed up to his wife's admirer and administered a sharp kick.

Nor was Caroline the only recipient of Connolly's romantic attentions. 'I really do love you,' he told the twenty-five-year-old Anne Gage, who had been chosen by both men as an intermediary-cum-confessor during the final stages of the Connolly-Skelton-Weidenfeld saga: once again, their relationship was entirely innocent, but she found him a kindly mentor who, though depressed by his own literary blockage, was anxious to help her with her own writing. He was jealous of the painter Rodrigo Moynihan, whom Ann Dunn married after her divorce from Michael Wishart, and took a proprietorial interest in her doings; he took a shine to Kenneth Tynan's American wife, Elaine Dundy, and encouraged her to write;* when Magouche Phillips – whom he had met first in New York in 1946, when she was married to the painter Arshile Gorky – suggested, facetiously, that perhaps they ought to get married, he told her that he'd like to find a rich American with children who was prepared to have some more; and when Alan Ross embarked on a brief affair with Barbara, who was still theoretically married to George Weidenfeld, he reacted as though he, and not his ex-publisher, was the outraged spouse. 'When will you realise that you destroy yourself by associating with anybody else but me, that I have got a really deep and luminous personality which can benefit, perhaps save you,' he asked her, adding, 'I hope this is your last birthday as a rudderless wreck floating on the high seas of lust and avarice'. 'I should have thought it obvious that I never

* Her first novel, *The Dud Avocado*, was a best-seller (Connolly unkindly suggested that it should have been called *The Dud Dundy*, by Elaine Avocado). A few years later, Dundy published *The Old Man and Me*, the heroine of which is a young American adrift in literary London. She falls in love with a stout, blue-eyed writer in his late fifties, besides whom all the young men in her life seem dull dogs indeed. He pores over menus in restaurants, has a passion for collecting antiques, and casts 'dazzling and worshipful glances' in her direction.

stopped loving her,' he scolded Alan Ross: he was deeply wounded by 'what seemed to me a betrayal of our friendship' – a betrayal that included plotting alibis with Barbara and engaging in all manner of 'James Bond stuff'. Connolly had earlier followed Barbara and Ross to Warwickshire, booked into the same hotel, and, maddened by jealousy and proprietorial indignation, rung Jennifer Ross to tell her what was going on. Ross was not prepared to put up with any more nonsense, and his reply was suitably blunt. 'At the relevant time she was married to, and separated from, someone else, and, by your own admission, of no interest to you whatsoever,' he told Connolly: the Bondian antics were designed to disinform Weidenfeld, and 'I can hardly have come between you and Barbara, since you were perfectly free to have each other if you had wanted it. Anyone who has had to do with either of you must be aware of the ambiguities of your relationship . . .'

Another friend and lover of Barbara's who fell foul of Connolly's possessive urges was the painter Michael Wishart. His marriage had recently become unstitched, and he invited Barbara to stay with him at Ramatuelle, in the South of France. This was bad enough as far as Connolly was concerned, but worse was to follow when they set out for Spain together. The booked into the Hotel Ritz in Madrid – the scene of Barbara's earlier rendezvous with Weidenfeld – and one morning Connolly suddenly materialised, unannounced and in proprietorial vein. He had just been robbed of £40, and seemed in a terrible state: he radiated a kind of 'frosty hostility' whenever Barbara straightened Michael Wishart's tie or kissed him on the mouth, but his temper improved when she began to complain, in her half-humorous, half-needling way, about the alleged shortcomings of her paramour. Bucked up no end by this, Connolly set himself up as their guide to the pleasures of Spain, hiring a car, accompanying them to Segovia, and going to some lengths to obtain tickets to watch a well-known *torero* who had recently come out of retirement.

La Consula continued to provide the most luxurious of refuges, with Connolly a presiding genius whose arrival was eagerly, if nervously, awaited. Ralph and Frances Partridge frequently coincided with these olympian descents, and she noted his doings with her familiar blend of sharpness, comicality and a certain resentful irritation. 'The much-heralded arrival of Cyril at the Consula took place yesterday. He drove up in a barouche pulled by a skeleton horse straight from the bull-ring,' she observed in the early spring of 1957. Over dinner she tried to humour him about a broadcast he had recently made,

> but when we moved to the sitting-room and collected round the fire, Cyril retired to a far corner of the room, flung himself back in a chair with his

face parallel to the ceiling and his eyes closed, and remained thus for the rest of the evening. (Janetta christened this his 'music position'.) She said afterwards that his excuse for this ostentatiously rude behaviour was that he was 'desperately miserable'.

'But what an extraordinary object he is becoming!' she remarked a few days later: 'With his great round head passing necklessly into his body; his torso clad in a flashy American beach shirt, ski-ing trousers and fur-lined boots, he looked like some strange species of synthetic man or Golem.'

Almost exactly a year later, Frances Partridge found Connolly in a better temper. 'Brilliantly amusing as well as a very genial host', he entertained them at a restaurant in the hills above Malaga: 'We sat at a long table on the balcony; a vase of flowers stood in front of us, and round it bulged the silhouette of the Master, haloed with tendrils of hair and backed by the sparkling sea far below in the harbour.' Connolly's genial mood was still in evidence a few days later, when they picnicked by a Moorish castle: 'Dressed in a spaceman's outfit, he lay on his back on the grass, relaxed and giggling at his own jokes and even at other people's.' A year later, and all was gloom once more: the Partridges were taken to see him as he lay ill in bed, and 'he motioned me to a chair with a royal gesture, lay with his large face in the pillow "in music position" and began talking about Robert and Janetta . . .'*

'I hate having to come back to England as I have nowhere to live – my life seems quite pointless there, whereas in Malaga I am part of a home,' Connolly told Jack Lambert of the *Sunday Times*. Back in London, Barbara was slowly disentangling herself from her disastrous second marriage. 'The only solution, I think, is to get another cat into the house INSTANTLY, *no matter what the breed!!!*' Barbara suggested in one of her reports on their continuing marital strife; but although it took them three years to get a divorce, she and Weidenfeld lived together as man and wife for a mere six months. In a neat display of marital tit-for-tat, Weidenfeld was granted a judicial separation on the grounds of her adultery with Connolly. Although the divorce was not finalised until September 1960 – Connolly was then cited as the co-respondent – the marriage was, in effect, over before it began:

* A highly unflattering account of Connolly during these years in limbo was provided by Daphne Fielding in her novel *The Adonis Garden*: according to Connolly's annotated copy of the novel, characters in the novel were based on, among others, Barbara, the Campbells, Gerald Brenan, the Partridges, Daphne Fielding and her future husband, Xan, and, of course, Connolly himself. Sheridan Cardew, who goes to stay in a cave in Spain, has a head like 'some great sea bird's egg, greenish and mottled. A faint smell of marsh gas exuded from his only country suit, almost identical in colour to his complexion . . .' Worried about becoming impotent, he pores over medical encyclopaedias; the object of his obsession, Pinky Fortescue, ridicules his gourmet tastes, and likes to catch him out by substituting margarine for butter. In the end Sheridan marries a 'pretty, tender blonde' of eighteen, and is last seen 'putting her through the Pygmalion treatment, combining guru with father-figure and demon lover'.

as Weidenfeld ruefully admitted in his autobiography, their brief, tormented relationship had been 'governed by alternating cycles of physical obsession, glimmers of hope, deep depression and profound guilt on both sides', and they parted with mutual relief. Gathering evidence against the guilty couple – Barbara and Connolly, this time round – was both farcical and painful. On the advice of his solicitors, after being alerted to what was going on by Caroline Frieud, Weidenfeld had employed a private detective to prove that Connolly had spent the weekend in Oak Cottage in the autumn of 1956, when Weidenfeld was in New York on business; the local greengrocer, the postman and – unkindest cut of all – the Connollys' gardener were persuaded to give evidence against them, as well as an unknown man who claimed to have seen the adulterous couple standing naked in the porch. So lurid were the rumours – including a story in the *Daily Mail* about Connolly's having spent the night in Barbara's flat, which he strenuously denied – and so worried was Connolly about adverse publicity that he was moved to write an explanatory and self-exculpatory letter to Jack Lambert: once again, he worried about his position on the paper, and hurried to assure the literary editor that there was no real evidence of adultery . . .

Connolly's nomadic existence could not continue for ever, and he began to look for houses out of London. He dreamed of buying Midford Castle, a 1770s Gothick house on the outskirts of Bath which, he claimed, had belonged to a relation of the Conolly of Castletown, but it was too expensive and he was, in any case, pipped to the post by a local hairdresser;* and then, one day in White's, he over-heard Lord Gage, a Sussex landowner, asking whether anyone might be interested in renting a farmhouse on his Firle estate, near Lewes, in exchange for a peppercorn rent. He and Barbara went down to inspect Bushey Lodge: she advised him about the decorations, but it was not a house in which she would ever live. Connolly was about to become a father at last, and in October 1959 he married, for the third and final time.

* The hairdresser was succeeded by the present occupants, Michael Briggs and his wife, the novelist Isobel Colegate. Connolly visited them there and inspected the Connolly armorial bearings: he wore, on his forefinger, a silver ring with the Connolly crest engraved upon it.

TWENTY-TWO

Bushey Lodge

Deirdre Craven, by now Mrs Connolly, was a tall, fresh-faced, whippet-thin girl in her late twenties, recently divorced and with two young children. With her fair hair and large blue eyes, she might well have stepped out of a painting by Romney, in Elena Wilson's opinion;* and her complicated family background somehow seemed to epitomise that surprisingly small, closely-knit, almost incestuous world where Society and Bohemia entwine, in which everyone appears to be related to or involved with everyone else, whether by kinship, marriage or looser, less permanent ties, and the looker-on is left feeling baffled by its intricate, circular networks and connections. It is a world in which Connolly had spent most of his adult life; he knew many of those involved, but since both Deirdre's parents had been married more than once, even he may have felt a momentary confusion.

Deirdre's paternal grandfather, Lord Craigavon, was the first Prime Minister of Northern Ireland, and part of her childhood had been spent in Ulster: Caroline Blackwood was a friend from those days, and they had attended dancing-classes together. Her father, Dennis Craig, known as 'Den', was an authority on the Turf, and combined business with authorship of a standard work on thoroughbred racehorses. He was twice married: firstly to Deirdre's mother, Aline, and – by the time his daughter married Cyril Connolly – to Joy Newton, whose brother, the actor Robert Newton, had been married to Barbara's friend Natalie Newhouse, Connolly's occasional lodger in Sussex Place. Joy's father, Algernon Newton, was a painter and a Royal Academician; her sister, Pauline, had earlier been married to Gilbert Murray's reprobate son, Basil, who was killed in the Spanish Civil War, but was now the wife of Sylvester Gates, a brilliant, extremely civilised lawyer and banker, and a friend of Connolly, Edmund Wilson and Isaiah Berlin. Joy had previously been married to Igor Vinogradoff and then to Roland Penrose's seafaring brother, Beakus: in the Thirties, Connolly and Jean had visited the Penroses at Lamb's Creek, their Georgian house in Cornwall, and Joy's daughter by Igor Vinogradoff, Tanya, later married the

* Edmund Wilson had married Elena Thornton – his fourth and final wife – in 1946.

scholar and bibliophile Anthony Hobson, a generous friend and (sporadically) the Boswell of Connolly's later years.

Although Deirdre was her father's only child, her extended family was made broader still by the fact that her famously beautiful mother married four times: to Dennis Craig, to Basil Murray, to Moray Maclaren of the BBC, and to Tom Hanbury, the scion of an immensely rich family of China merchants with property on the Italian Riviera as well as in London and the West Country.* Despite a shifting cast of step-fathers, Deirdre was brought up – conventionally, and very strictly – by her mother, dividing her time between London and the Cotswolds: and although she adored Den and the bohemian Newtons, and far preferred being with him, she was a law-abiding and unbohemian child, while her father, with his debts and his girl friends, was considered quite unsuitable to play the part of a parent. During the war Den had shared a flat in Cairo with Patrick Kinross, and it was through her father that Deirdre's world overlapped with that of her future husband: the two men had been near-contemporaries at Eton, and among Den's and Joy's friends were Patrick Leigh Fermor, Robin and Mary Campbell, Anne Dunn, Jennifer Ross, Henry Lamb, Anthony and Violet Powell and Robert Heber-Percy.

As a girl of nineteen, Deirdre had married a gentleman-farmer named Jonty Craven; they lived in Wiltshire, and had two children, Sarah and Simon. In the spring of 1956 Deirdre embarked on an affair with Alan Ross, during the middle of which she came up to London to stay with her step-sister – and step-cousin – Venetia Murray, the second daughter of Basil Murray and Pauline Newton. Venetia Murray shared a flat in South Kensington with her cousin Sally, Robert Newton's daughter, occupying the top two floors of a house belonging to Alan and Jennifer Ross, who spent most of their time at their house in Clayton, in the Sussex Downs; it was through Venetia that Deirdre had first met Alan Ross, and now she introduced her to Cyril Connolly as well. She told Deirdre that Connolly was coming round for a drink after dinner, and predicted – accurately – that he would take one look at Deirdre and say 'Goodness, you do look thin: why don't you come to the Milroy for some soup?' – the Milroy being a night-club much patronised by Connolly and his circle. Given his love of gossip and intrigue, Connolly knew all about Deirdre already, and was fascinated to meet her: they went to the Milroy and danced a great deal – Deirdre noting how light he was on his feet, bobbing about the floor like a cork – and talked even more, with Connolly pouring out his woes about Barbara and Weidenfeld. More than

* Readers with long memories may recall that Connolly enjoyed himself dancing with a Philippa Hanbury while staying with his parents in Alassio in December 1923.

two years were to elapse before a close, platonic friendship turned into an affair; but in the meantime they met and talked whenever Deirdre came up to London, with Connolly traipsing across Hyde Park to meet her train and see her off again.

After the discovery of her affair with Alan Ross, Deirdre went back to her husband; but the damage had been done, and in November 1958 she finally left home for good. By now she had begun her affair with Connolly, egged on by her step-mother Joy; Connolly used to stay with Joy in her cottage near Bath, and Bath Abbey provided a trysting-place. Although her affair with Ross was long over, it was he rather than Connolly – terrified of further bad publicity, and worried in case the rather puritanical Lord Kemsley sacked him from the *Sunday Times* following another public scandal – who was cited as the co-respondent in her subsequent divorce, after Jonty Craven's solicitor had dusted down a little-used item of divorce law known as 'revived adultery'. Understandably enough, Ross was unamused by the turn events had taken: though very fond of Connolly, he thought him a fearful moral coward, and a fierce exchange of letters ensued, followed by a temporary cooling in their friendship.

During all this time Connolly was still in limbo, dreaming of country houses but camping out in rented rooms in Chesham Place, near Belgrave Square, round the corner from where Barbara was now living in Lisle Street: all his possessions were in store except for his clothes and two treasured paintings – Lucian Freud's portrait of Caroline Blackwood, and Jean Hugo's frontispiece to *The Unquiet Grave*. From time to time he would meet Deirdre in a flat near Eaton Square belonging to Rupert Belville, a florid-looking White's Club acquaintance and a friend of the Davises, who had flown his own plane on the Nationalist side during the Spanish Civil War, and spent as much time as he could watching bull-fights; and, since it was impossible to stay at White's, which had no rooms of its own, the porter there recommended he take a service flat in Park Place, on the other side of St James's Street, a beige, net-curtained establishment with a uniformed porter in reception which Connolly used for a while after he had moved to Sussex, since it had the advantages of being discreet and a good deal cheaper than an equivalent hotel.

At the very beginning of their affair, Connolly had asked Deirdre whether she would have a child by him, and she said she would; but despite his hitherto frustrated yearnings after fatherhood, the realisation, about a year later, that she was pregnant threw him into a frenzy of anxiety. Ever since the end of his marriage to Barbara he had been free to flirt with and fantasise about all the attractive young women he knew, while at the same time indulging to the full his appetite for nostalgia, self-pity and remorse; but now, it seemed, unfamiliar obligations and responsibilities were intruding. Once again, Hansi Lambert was a source of bracing common sense. 'Even if you don't feel guilty, as you say, you cannot let this situation drift,' she told him:

> You must marry the poor girl as soon as you can and give her right away a feeling of protection and security. Don't try to hope for the best and leave her in a mess. If she really is the person you describe she must feel terribly unhappy and lost. You say you dread the ties of being loved and married but you forget that you have also been yearning for such ties . . . You are too intelligent and too old to play about with serious things.

And, later: 'Do give this girl a chance and don't behave like a little boy who cries every day "I want my Mama" . . . Can't you grow up and carry your cross bravely for a while? And work instead of lamenting and telephoning? Please try!'

Nor was Connolly the only one to be unnerved by his impending marriage. He broke the news to Barbara in a pub in Rye. 'Cyril (the final blow) tells me Deirdre is pregnant,' she noted in her diary: 'Awake in night sobbing.' Overcome by melancholy, her instinctive reaction was to sell Oak Cottage and escape from England; and, indeed, she was to spend the rest of her life abroad, in New York and later in Paris and the South of France. An entry in her diary from this time suggests that, like Deirdre, she understood exactly how his mind worked, how he combined a nostalgia for what was no longer his with a tendency – both benign and self-serving – to say identical things to two people at once, particularly women, and to tailor his remarks to please the recipient:

> After staying with C for a week he said he was sad to separate but Deirdre was due back. The day after she had been with him he rang me in the morning and said 'I missed you so much I could hardly be civil to her.' A week later it was my turn to spend the week at Bushey. The second day he rang Deirdre. I listened outside the door and heard him say 'I had such a disagreeable evening, I could hardly be civil to her' . . .

Connolly and Deirdre were married on 26 August 1959 – Barbara's birthday – at Mere, in Wiltshire, where Deirdre's paternal grandmother lived in the old rectory. Mere was ideal, in that it was considered too small and too remote to attract gossip-hungry journalists; the only witnesses were Stephen Spender – the male friend whom, in Deirdre's opinion, Connolly teased but loved the most, and could be the most hurt by – and Deirdre's eccentric Aunt Goll, who signed the register in invisible ink.* The following day Connolly left for Venice with his friend Ethel de Croisset and her mother in a chauffeur-driven car, with a pekinese in the spare seat. 'You should have come,' Ethel de Croisset told Deirdre on their return: 'We could have left the dog behind...'

For the first few months of their marriage, Connolly and Deirdre divided their time between Park Place and Sussex, camping out in the pantry at Bushey and cooking off a Baby Belling while they moved in and sorted out their possessions, and put the house in order. It was, Deirdre recalled, a 'supremely happy' time, and every now and then Connolly would open an Imperial Pint of champagne to celebrate their good luck or, when living out of packing cases became too oppressive, they would retire for the night to a turret room in the Grand Hotel in Eastbourne. Although the village of Firle lies under the foot of the Downs, Bushey Lodge was a mile or two to the north, on the far side of the Lewes to Eastbourne road. Set in flat farming country, and approached by a rough track that became waterlogged in wet weather, it was a square, stuccoed early nineteenth-century farmhouse, elegant but unpretentious, with outhouses all around in which cattle were housed and tractors stored; and for it they paid a peppercorn rent of £200 a year. 'I lived for nine years in a converted farmhouse whose yard and outbuildings were still in use,' Connolly wrote after he had finally abandoned country life for the orderly pavements of suburban Eastbourne:

> At first there were two gates and no cattle grids over a concrete track. It meant getting in and out of a car twice on every journey, sheer hell in winter. The lowing of deprived mothers, whose calves had been removed too soon biologically, though not too soon for their milk quota, poisoned our nights, the shouts of the farm-hands as they herded them in and out sounded like guards at Belsen, the rhythmic pattern of droppings beat like muffled drums on the winter air, the milk lorries shattered our rest...

Despite such raucous background noises, Bushey was, Anthony Hobson recalled, 'a delightful house, strongly marked by its tenant's personality', while Elizabeth Bowen told Deirdre that 'I don't know any house where more than yours and Cyril's one's brain and one's senses *and* one's heart all feel at their most alive, and most satisfied.' There was, she suggested on another occasion, 'a spell about your house. I love it with all my (I suppose) grown-up faculties, but also in the way I used to love places when I was a child: a sense of attachment.' It had been freshly re-painted and

* Connolly gave Deirdre as a wedding present a copy of *Ideas and Places* inscribed 'Tomorrow is my dancing day' and, at the foot of the page, 'A great love is a great doom'.

re-decorated by Barbara before Deirdre came to live there. There was an orchard to one side, and the garden had been newly planted by Connolly with old-fashioned roses and exotic plants; and inside the house each of the rooms had been painted in a vivid single colour. The kitchen was a bright clear yellow, and contained a huge dresser covered in blue and white china; the dining-room, with its freight of lovingly polished Georgian silver and gleaming glass, was burnt sienna, with a highly-polished brick floor underfoot; the sitting-room was scarlet, the library, with its cargo of cellophane-wrapped first editions firmly locked away in a glass-fronted book-case, pale blue, the hall and stairs apple-green, the porch French blue and the cloakroom purple. Upstairs there were five bedrooms and three bathrooms, painted in a variety of pinks, yellows and Etruscan reds, and a low, magical attic room, crammed with letters, proofs and discarded typescripts; and adjoining the house was a cottage containing a television room and what would become a playroom, and two bedrooms and a bathroom for the use of Portuguese maids provided by Mollie's jovial sister, Aunt Mabs, who lived in Portugal, and, later, the occasional *au pair* girl. Magouche Fielding remembered, above all, the smell of wax and flowers that pervaded the house, and Connolly's touching, pleased attempts to be domestic, laying the table and putting the silver away in its drawers; while John Betjeman told Deirdre how

> All in my mind's eye I see the warm contrasting colours of Bushey Lodge's rooms, the yellow blind and the purple passage to the view from Cyril's room and the drawing-room of those elms and willows blowing in the wind and the Downs beyond them and the knowledge that beyond the Downs is the sea . . .

Her son's life, Mollie wrote to Deirdre from South Africa, had been 'so sadly empty till he met you – of all the things that matter most'; and now, in his mid-fifties, he was leading a conventional domestic life for the first time and, for all the invariable grumblings on the side, enjoying it to the full.

As an only child himself, Connolly had spent his adult life in a curiously child-free world: but all that was changed in January 1960, when his daughter Cressida was born. She shared her father's rather elfin looks and, in due course, his quick wit, his way with words, and his teasing, mischievous smile; and although, in later years, he would pretend to complain about her being too bossy or too noisy or too talkative or too keen on boys and parties and 'so precociously like me', he saw in her at once a kindred spirit and an ally. He had never seen a new-born baby before, he told Barbara: 'When she smiles at me personally it is like being given a five-pound note,' and 'she certainly satisfies some profound instinct and I could not bear to lose her. She is, of course, not a patch on a lemur or a coati, so far...' Like any parent – and an elderly parent in particular – he tempered his delight in fatherhood with fear and anxiety about the future. 'She looks so much like me that I feel sorry for her instead of deriving happiness from it – will she escape the basic desolation?' he once wrote, and elsewhere he described how he once came into her playroom where 'she was having tea by herself, with cut-up pieces of cake, and swaying in her chair to the gramophone – one started to cry it was so perfect.' And although to Barbara he complained – as he felt in duty bound to – of 'squalling baby, nagging wife, bills and writs by every post', his friends remember the pleasure he took in his house, his family and his new-found domesticity, and how – a denizen of a world so different from anything he had known before, a paterfamilias at last – he would sit, very happily, surrounded by a sea of children's toys, hurrying through to the television room at the sound of the *Maigret* or *Perry Mason** theme music, eating salmon fishcakes off his knee in front of the screen while watching children's programmes and his beloved travelogues, and, in later years, listening to the Beatles' *Sergeant Pepper*. His own lonely childhood was reflected in a complete ignorance of games like 'pass the parcel', but he showed a surprising interest in the hardware of infancy, in prams, cots and the like; and although he was much older than the others, he was more than happy to have couples with young children of their own to stay for the weekend, among them Robert and Cynthia Kee, and Robin Campbell and his new wife Susan, whose book *Poor Cook* he reviewed in the *Sunday Times*. Nor were more familiar pleasures neglected: Deirdre was an excellent cook, and quickly discovered that the best antidote to a sulking fit or a tiring train journey back from London was a lobster or a leg of mutton.

To Barbara, on the other hand, he was loth to present himself as anything other than a henpecked, beleaguered failure, adrift in a 'desperate, lonely

* *Perry Mason* was a particular favourite, and provided the motif for one of Anthony Hobson's vivid vignettes of Connolly in later life. The Hobsons gave a dinner party at their house in Hampshire, attended by the Connollys and the writer James Stern and his wife. A facetious argument broke out, and Connolly began to impersonate the characters in an American court scene:

> *Connolly* (in falsetto American accent): '...objected to as irrelevant, tendentious and liable to prejudice the witness.'
> *Hobson* (interrupts): 'Objection. Mr Perry Mason is trying to lead the witness.'
> *Connolly* (placing red table-napkin on head, transforming himself into a hanging judge, and lifting the corner over his eyes): 'Objection over-ruled. Proceed, Mr Mason.'

'The effect,' Hobson concludes, 'was indescribably funny: the quickness of the action combined with his grotesque appearance – porcine jowls below scarlet wig...' Connolly's comic set-pieces – in which he often played several parts at once, alternating voices and accents as required – are notoriously hard to pin down in print, much to the frustration of those who remember them, but Anthony Hobson manages to recapture some of his fugitive art.

jungle of bleakness, shabbiness and failing powers'. Quite forgetting all they had endured together, he came to see her – to Deirdre's irritation – as the wronged embodiment of freedom and lost love. 'Every afternoon I go through a period of *cafard* and say Barbarabarbara all the time aloud. The rest of the time I haul my load of newspapers and straw around with me, like an ape at the zoo,' he told her. Lashing out at those nearest to him in moments of depression, boredom and self-pity was a familiar enough symptom, and so too were his rather half-hearted attempts to blame others for his own inadequacies and shortcomings, but as ever self-reproach was seldom far away. 'There is only one thing we can do in our predicaments, write our way out of them,' he went on: 'It is because we are disloyal to our gift that we are in this fix.' 'I sit through the marvellous early afternoons of early summer in the gloomy junk-room of the cottage fiddling with old bank statements, telegrams, corrected proofs or worthless articles – what a punishment,' he wrote on another occasion, with an almost masochistic satisfaction. In November 1961 Deirdre won care and control of her two eldest children, and from now on Sarah and Simon spent half their school holidays – eight weeks a year – at Bushey, and as much time as possible would be given over to them. Though he could be irritable if they ragged and fidgeted and whistled in the back of the car *en route* to Bondolfi's cake shop in Eastbourne or the panto in Brighton, Connolly got on well with his two step-children, addressing them as though they were adults, driving them about the country and showing an interest in what they were up to: he had a particularly soft spot for Sarah Craven, who shared his love of animals; towards Simon his feelings were, at first, ambivalent – even a male of prep. school age seemed somehow to be a threat – but such Freudian anxieties soon subsided. Yet even the most amiable children can be a trial to a man in his fifties, and in his moments of melancholy their presence made him feel 'more than ever caught on the flypaper' and 'a lodger in my own house, a kind of parasite':

> They bang around the house with guns etc. making a fearful noise and demanding D's attention so that I sit alone in my study most of the time unable to work and screaming with boredom and poverty and self-pity.

'I feel like Hereward the Wake reduced to a clump of rushes in the fens,' he told Barbara on another occasion: 'I cling to my bedroom and to the blue sitting-room downstairs, children's toys all over the floor of the red sitting-room, kitchen, playroom in cottage etc. . . . I skulk in my room and sign cheques.' Barbara by now was living in New York, working in a bookshop and as a dentist's receptionist, trying without any success to place articles by

Connolly with magazines like the *Saturday Evening Post*, consorting with other English visitors and expatriates such as the Tynans, John Russell and Caroline Blackwood, and about to embark on affairs with the cartoonist Charles Addams and Bob Silvers, the founder of the *New York Review of Books*; and when the angst was upon him, Connolly would brood about her and about Jean, poring over old letters and rearranging the past. For Deirdre, these spectres were, at times, too intrusive to be borne, and she would put her foot down:

> At the moment D. has whisked her [Cressida] off to Lewes after announcing that our marriage is finished as I obviously prefer you . . . she said that I was carrying your letter about in my wallet which I do because I can never remember your address. A Freudian lapse . . .

Such scenes were the stuff of gossip, the exception not the rule: for all the grumbling, Connolly was, almost certainly, happier than he had been for years; but because he drew his happiness from the humdrum and the everyday, it loomed less large than the occasional tantrum inherent in any marriage, or the loudly-proclaimed spasms of boredom or despair. He still tended to lie in bed for much of the morning, reading or writing, emerging at midday with, as often as not, blobs of shaving cream behind his ears; in the afternoon, if his review had been posted off, he might go shopping with Deirdre in Eastbourne, inspecting the 'white goods' – fridges, washing-machines and the like – in Bobby's department store, or potter round the antique shops in Alfriston with Deirdre's increasingly alcoholic mother, a heavy burden to whom he was unfailingly kind. In the evenings they might go to the theatre in Brighton to see *Beyond the Fringe* or N.F. Simpson's *One Way Pendulum*, to Glyndebourne (for whom he contributed programme notes in 1962) to see, ideally, *Der Rosenkavalier* or Stravinsky's *The Rake's Progress* or one of Mozart's operas; and, from time to time, Lord Drogheda would take them to the ballet in Covent Garden. Deirdre shared her husband's generous hospitality – it was generally agreed that Connolly was a far better host than guest – and they entertained, and were entertained by, their Sussex friends and neighbours: the 'Charleston Trio' of Vanessa Bell, Duncan Grant and Clive Bell, fellow-tenants of Lord Gage; Leonard Woolf, still living down the Ouse valley at Rodmell; Roland Penrose and Lee Miller, at whose house they might meet, for instance, Max Ernst; Ian Parsons of Chatto & Windus, and his wife Trekkie; and his old school friend, Denys King-Farlow, now retired from the oil business and living at Birling Gap; Cuthbert Worsley and William Plomer. In summer in particular, entertaining at Bushey was often idyllic: Anthony Hobson remembered the Connollys entertaining George and Mary Christie and Clive Bell and Duncan Grant with Bohle, a mixture of champagne, moselle and strawberries, which he claimed to have learned while staying with Harold Nicolson in Berlin in 1928. Peter Quennell, whose mother lived at Lewes, was a frequent visitor; they made regular weekend excursions to see Alan and Jennifer Ross in their house at Clayton, and the d'Avigdor-Goldsmids at Summerhill, where Rosie d'Avigdor-Goldsmid trimmed his hair with a pair of nail scissors and, on one occasion, he disgraced himself by stealing out and devouring the few ripe figs in the conservatory, and Maud Russell at Mottisfont, and Edward Rice at Danescourt, his house near Deal.* He had given up bridge as 'too time-wasting' but enjoyed a game of Scrabble; enjoyed trundling round the countryside in Deirdre's red Hillman Minx and, when in London, pretending to be a prospective buyer and sitting in the Rolls-Royces in Jack Barclay's showrooms in Berkeley Square; and, once a week, he would visit Mr Taylor the masseur in Hove and re-emerge looking pink and pleased, ready for whatever lay ahead.

*

Whatever his private agonies about work undone and potential untapped, Connolly's standing in the world of letters received a welcome boost when *Enemies of Promise* was among the earliest titles to be included in Penguin Modern Classics – though the pleasure was diluted by their getting his middle name wrong in the potted author biography ('Joseph' for 'Vernon'), and by their sticking a particularly unflattering photograph of him on the front cover. 'Greatly distressed by horrible picture on cover,' he telegrammed Allen Lane, and inscribed Anthony Hobson's copy with 'WANTED Kentish Joe. If you think you have seen this man, telephone Scotland Yard. PS "KJ" may be armed.' Nancy Mitford told Evelyn Waugh that she had recommended it to her sister, the Duchess of Devonshire: she liked to pretend the Duchess didn't like books without pictures, but 'luckily there is a very pretty one on the cover – Boots himself, looking as you once said like a miners' leader and unlike real life.' Despite the contretemps, Connolly signed a copy of the book for Allen Lane's private collection,† and

* A friend of the Gages', who wore brightly-coloured Chanel tweed suits, Edward Rice was one of the first farmers in England to grow peas commercially for Bird's Eye. His first wife was one of Lord Curzon's daughters; his second, Nolwen, was the daughter of Alice de Janzé, one of the key figures in the story surrounding the murder of Lord Erroll by which Connolly would soon become so fascinated, and later married Kenneth Clark. Rice's cousin, the economist Wynne Godley, described him as heartless if charming, a case of 'institutionalised selfishness'.

† Lane liked whenever possible to have a signed copy of each of the books published by his firm: signatures of authors who proved unco-operative or were unavailable were snipped from the bottom of letters and pasted into place.

Penguin soon made amends by including *The Rock Pool* in the same series. The rights were bought from Hamish Hamilton: since Connolly had unearned advances with his firm totalling £270, Hamilton was entitled to set these against the £300 offered by Penguin; but, anxious as ever to placate an eminent if unproductive author, he persuaded his fellow-directors that they should write off £170 of Connolly's debt, setting only £100 against the Penguin earnings. He continued, for some time at least, to tiptoe round Connolly, getting his secretary to ring with awkward questions ('Hope he doesn't sound too disagreeable,' he minuted an internal memo) and despatching a toy elephant and a stuffed bear for Cressida's birthday.

Equally flattering was an approach from what must have seemed, given their earlier disagreements, an unexpected quarter: David Astor, the editor of the *Observer*, wrote to say that he had 'taken literally' some remarks Connolly had made about the possibility of his leaving the *Sunday Times*, provided its main rival could offer him 'more agreeable working conditions'. Philip Toynbee, one of the paper's two lead book-reviewers, was keen on the idea of 'getting you out of the roller-shafts and giving you the full freedom to do what you want'. A month later Astor wrote again. He would like Connolly to join his paper as its lead reviewer: he would not be expected to review more than twenty-odd books a year, and would be given a free hand to write on broader cultural matters as well. They would be happy to send him to Africa, 'provided the expenses could be kept within reasonable bounds', and to try out a 'Connolly notebook-column': and for this they would not only 'treat you like a prince', but pay a salary of £2500 a year. Remembering, perhaps, their earlier falling-out, Connolly eventually declined, for in September 1960 Astor concluded the correspondence by saying that he was sad that his approach had come to nothing, but that Connolly was probably right under the circumstances.*

* Although Toynbee was keen that Connolly should join the *Observer*, the paper's other lead reviewer, Harold Nicolson, was *persona non grata* with his old friend from Berlin days. Three years earlier, in a travel book entitled *Journey to Java*, Nicolson had pondered on the fact that, though a disbeliever, Connolly had a strong sense of original sin. Nicolson found it hard to understand why he was quite so weighed down by feelings of guilt: 'True it is that on one occasion he filched three avocado pears from Willie Maugham's garden at Cap Ferrat, but this is not an episode that should weigh upon the conscience of a humanist.' Nicolson's remark touched a raw nerve. Connolly was staying with the Davises when the book appeared. 'It is warm and sunny by day, very windy, cold at night,' he told Jack Lambert: 'Fresh tangerines, water ices, avocadoes from the garden – not filched by me and never were – see *Journey to Java*. Shall I sue the old fart?' A year or two later, reviewing Robin Maugham's book about his uncle, Connolly returned to the subject, assuring his readers that he had done no more than retrieve an unripe windfall. Ann Fleming, of course, quickly latched on to the story. The Connollys, she told Evelyn Waugh, had come to lunch, together with Angus Wilson and Maugham himself. Maugham fell asleep over the lunch table, only waking at the pudding stage, when he refused to deny that Connolly had stolen the missing avocado, much to the delight of their hostess. 'I find it irresistible to bully Cyril,' she told Waugh: 'I don't love him like you do.'

Although, some three years later, Donald McLachlan, the editor of the *Sunday Telegraph*, invited Connolly to dinner to discuss his future plans, the *Sunday Times* retained his loyalty. As ever, money – or its absence – was an occasional source of friction. Ann Fleming recalled a visit to Bushey at which 'Connolly was radiating displeasure, looking most sulky and there was little talk: Connolly had been asking for a rise on the *Sunday Times* and Ian explaining Roy Thomson's attitude to literature and the unlikelihood of more cash.' Fleming must have held firm, informing Connolly that despite his ten-year stint on the paper forty guineas a week was an adequate wage, and he saw no reason to raise it to fifty. A year later, however, Leonard Russell got him an extra £250 a year, plus another £500 to cover any additional pieces – feature or travel articles – he might write. Three years on, and a further £250 was forthcoming; and in 1971 Harold Evans, the editor, wrote to say that he was increasing his salary to £4250 a year.

Connolly might have been invited to the French Embassy to meet General de Gaulle on his official visit to England – he thought him 'rather wonderful', and was much impressed by 'Bonny Johnny' Lehmann's chestful of medals – but, much to Ann Fleming's delight, the perfect occasion for a spot of Connolly-baiting was provided by the publication, in October 1961, of *Unconditional Surrender*, the concluding volume of Evelyn Waugh's wartime trilogy. A year earlier, Connolly had taken a dim view of Waugh's *A Tourist in Africa* – it was, he declared, 'the thinnest piece of book-making which Mr Waugh has undertaken . . . What a drubbing I would receive if I had written it' – but despite his earlier reservations the trilogy as a whole was 'unquestionably the finest novel to have come out of the war': he had re-read the two earlier volumes, he told their author, and realised now how much he had under-rated them. All this was well enough, but what touched Connolly on the raw, and set Mrs Fleming's tongue in motion, was the identification of Connolly – in his own mind, and in those of readers who knew or cared about such matters – with the figure of Everard Spruce, the petulant, pleasure-loving editor of a literary magazine named *Survival*, who surrounds himself with a gaggle of adoring hand-maidens, and spends as much time as he can attending parties, indulging his appetites and keeping his eyes firmly averted from the war. 'I am not surprised that Cyril is wounded by Evelyn's presentation of him in *Unconditional Surrender*,' Maurice Bowra told Ann Fleming: 'It is not very like him but sufficiently like him to be offensive. It is sad that Evelyn has such an urge to torture him. It must be a form of love.'

Eager, perhaps, to defuse the situation, Waugh hurried forward with a disclaimer. 'A mischievous woman in London tells me that you identify a character named "Spruce", in a book I lately sent you, with yourself,' he informed his victim:

> I hope this is pure mischief. If not, it is persecution mania. Just count the points of resemblance & difference between yourself & that character & see what the score is.
>
> There are of course asses in London, who don't understand the processes of the imagination, whose hobby it is to treat fiction as a gossip column... But what distresses me (if true) is that you should suppose I would publicly caricature a cherished friend.

And to Christopher Sykes he wrote, 'Gossip tells me that poor Boots has persecution mania thinking he is that editor. Silly ass.' Sykes was unconvinced – 'I try to think of Spruce as unBootsed but have not succeeded yet' – and Connolly himself remained unmollified. Although the two magazines seemed alarmingly alike, 'I did not get any strong feeling that Spruce was me': but then a mutual friend told him that she thought Spruce was based on him, and

> it was then that I began to mind a little, I think chiefly because *Horizon* had taken so much trouble about you and because I had been so pleased to publish 'My Father's House' in 1941 as well as 'The Loved One' etc. I felt you did not understand how much one loved doing *Horizon*, that it really seemed one had a chance every month to produce something perfect after the last imperfect one and that it was wonderful to be able to find out and publish what one thought was good when so much else was just destruction. You are like Nancy in *The Blessing* who thinks that parties and pretty secretaries are what editors really go in for!

'Don't let Mrs Fleming drive you to persecution mania. It is an aptitude of hers,' Waugh reassured his injured friend a day or two later:

> It is very proper that you should have proud memories of *Horizon*. It was the outstanding publication of its decade. I am greatly annoyed to see that two reviewers have attempted to identify it with my invention *Survival*. That magazine was the creature of the Ministry of Information. *Horizon*, of course, was Watson's benefaction. It is true that you had a semi-literate socialist colleague but he was not 'Spruce'; still less you. As for secretaries, Lys was beautifully neat and, as I remember her, Miss Brownell was quite presentable. Sometime later you had a barefooted landlady but (surely?) she had no part in *Horizon* and very little part in the delightful parties you gave. The whole identification is a fantasy.*

* The 'semi-literate socialist colleague' was the hapless Stephen Spender, a long-standing butt of Waugh's derision. Reviewing Spender's autobiography, *World Within World*, Waugh had written that 'to see him fumbling with our rich and delicate language is to experience all the horror of seeing a Sèvres vase in the hands of a chimpanzee.'

'I have told that mischievous London woman to look nearer her own hearth for "Spruce" and she is now busy identifying him with the editor of the *Cornhill*,' Waugh wrote a month or so later, in a vain attempt to divert attention from Connolly to Peter Quennell. But the damage had been done. 'I do not think posterity will ever believe in our friendship, any more than someone who looked me up in the index of your biography!' Connolly replied: 'It will take at least a dedication to put me in the clear!' But no dedication was forthcoming: Waugh died five years later, and the unkindest cuts of all were delivered from beyond the grave.

Waugh and Connolly – together with W.H. Auden, Edith Sitwell, Patrick Leigh Fermor, Angus Wilson and Christopher Sykes – were fellow-contributors to a series in the *Sunday Times*, later reprinted in book form, on the Seven Deadly Sins. The idea for the series was Ian Fleming's, and he and Leonard Russell originally asked Connolly to write on Sloth; but he asked if he could do Covetousness instead, and – unlike the others – he approached his particular sin by means of a short story. An altogether more animated affair than 'Shade Those Laurels', 'The Downfall of Jonathan Edax' tells the story of a passionate collector of first editions (preferably signed), silver and porcelain whose meanness and passion for the chase brings about his untimely end. Jonathan Edax has a small daughter and a wife who not only nags him for money but insists, against his will, on their investing in one of those childproof metal gates which parents position at the top of a flight of stairs to prevent toddlers from hurtling to their deaths. Such mundane concerns are of little interest to Edax, who prefers to spend his days poring over his first editions and wondering how he can add to their numbers: like his creator, he keeps them in a glass-fronted desk-cum-bookcase known as the 'Controls'. Edax is notoriously light-fingered when it comes to rare books and first editions, a charge which was often levelled against Connolly himself: the novelist Francis King has claimed that when Connolly was inspecting his bookshelves in Hove he asked his host for a glass of water, and while King was out of the room his visitor deftly removed a book from his shelves and slipped it into his briefcase, and Edax employs a similar technique while visiting the lovely Mrs Truslove, whose poet husband is away attending cultural congresses in south-east Asia. Mrs Truslove's china and silverware – and a hexagonal Queen Anne teapot in particular – add to her allure, made all the more potent when she thrusts upon him what turns out to be one of only three copies of a work by the nonagenarian late-Victorian poet Alberic Chute. Desperate to get Chute's signature before it's too late, Edax hurries up to Hampstead, finds the old man, 'with a nose like a tin-opener', lying in bed, 'his hands milking the coverlet', whips out his fountain pen, but leaves in a panic without his precious copy. Back home in Holland Park, he finds, to his fury, that Mrs Edax – defying his authority – has installed a childproof gate. The alluring Mrs Truslove rings, and suggests they run off together; driven wild by the thought of the hexagonal teapot, Edax bustles out of his room, takes a flying kick at the childproof gate, and hurtles down the stairs to his death...

It was widely assumed that Truslove, the globe-trotting poet, was based on Stephen Spender, and Edmund Wilson for one was unamused. 'It seems to me that the feeling of frustration and his envy of other writers who have done more work and made more money is having the effect on Cyril of making him overtly nasty about his friends in a way I have not noticed before,' he noted in his journal:

> ...Why that personal burlesque on the Spenders – Covetousness in the Deadly Sins series – in which he tried to make Stephen ridiculous and either violated or pretended to violate the confidences of Natasha about Stephen? He spoke of this and said that when Stephen had got wind of it, he had behaved as if he were threatening to sue Cyril for libel. 'He doesn't appear,' he said, as if this were justification. He must live more and more in a little self-centred world, self-indulgent and always managing to have a woman around to indulge him – does not want to hear other people talk, pretends polite but absent attention.

Connolly later claimed that Jonathan Edax was not a self-portrait, but a composite figure containing elements of Jack Kahane, A.J.A. Symons and the notorious literary forger T.J. Wise – and that, unlike Edax, he had welcomed the installation of a childproof gate at Bushey – but his passion for collecting exactly mirrored that of his creation. His library, and his modern first editions in particular, was both a source of delight and – as he explained to Warren Roberts of the University of Texas, who had enquired about the possibility of their acquiring his library and papers – an investment-cum-annuity as well: 'Since I have a wife and a small daughter my plan is to leave the library as complete as possible to be sold as some provision for them.'* He had begun collecting books while at Eton, and later recalled scouring the quayside stalls for early editions of the classics shortly before going up to Oxford. Fellow-bibliophiles at Oxford had included John Sparrow, Graham Pollard and his College contemporary 'Jake' Carter; he had run up hefty bills at Parker's and Blackwell's, buying up first editions of Eliot, the Sitwells, Huxley, Strachey, Forster and the productions of the Nonesuch Press, as well as seventeenth-century copies of Donne and Sir Thomas

* After his death his library and, later, his papers were sold to the University of Tulsa.

Browne, and editions printed by Bodoni and Baskerville, but money shortages forced him to sell the lot. In his fifties, he revived his old enthusiasm, poring over booksellers' catalogues, attending sales, ringing round to enquire after particular items missing from his collections. Like an elderly autograph-hound, he badgered writer friends and acquaintances to sign copies of their works: most of his surviving letters from T.S. Eliot consist of covering notes returning a freshly-inscribed copy, and on one occasion the poet was even persuaded to sign a Pullman ticket; he was driven wild with envy when Auden signed Anthony Hobson's copies of his works, and was distraught when Hobson discovered that a presentation copy to Jeannie of Auden's 'Three Songs for St Cecilia's Day' had already been sold; and Francis King recalled an uncomfortable occasion at the Royal College of Art involving E.M. Forster, who was not over-fond of Connolly. 'That wretched Cyril Connolly insists on coming here to see me,' Forster is said to have told King and Joe Ackerley, with whom he was lunching. Connolly arrived with a large pile of Forster's works tucked under one arm, and insisted that the old man should inscribe as well as sign them. This was not the kind of work Forster enjoyed at the best of times, but he dutifully 'scratched away with a weary politeness'. He then made a point of offering Connolly a single sherry – as opposed to a double bought for his friends – before bidding him a frosty farewell.*

Collectors like Anthony Hobson were happy to acquire the hand-written originals of his articles and reviews, and when creditors were pressing his manuscripts could always be sold: Jake Carter, who had earlier disposed of *The Unquiet Grave*, wrote from Sotheby's to say that he understood from Anthony Hobson – whose father had been, many years before, the firm's chairman – that *The Rock Pool* might be for sale; it was, and Connolly made £480 when it was included in a sale of modern autograph manuscripts. The Americans, in particular, were eager to buy – and not least well-endowed universities, like that at Austin, Texas, which saw the acquisition of libraries and literary papers as a means of attracting visiting scholars and acquiring academic *réclame*. One of Connolly's sprightliest correspondents – his excitable letters, ablaze with exclamation marks and written in a vast, rolling hand, were crammed with news of who was selling what and where – was a New Yorker named Jacob Schwartz, a former dentist who had settled in Brighton and was known by Connolly as 'the great extractor'. As well as being an antiquarian bookseller, Schwartz acted as a book agent for American universities, and he hurried to give Connolly the benefit of his wisdom.

* Asked what Cressida should be given as a christening present, Connolly is said to have replied, 'Cressida collects first editions.'

'Put on one side ALL the notebooks you have, abandoned work etc. as that is just what the Boys at the Universities seek,' he urged: 'No use their mouldering away in an attic. A new life for them and you . . .' Sure enough, Austin Texas was soon in touch, urging him to sell his papers and library *en bloc* rather than piecemeal: Connolly told Warren Roberts that he had acquired a 'violent aversion' to manuscripts while editing *Horizon*, and wouldn't mind disposing of those, but although he had a mass of letters from fellow-writers he wouldn't like it if they were flogging off his letters to them, and he felt he should hold back for the time being at least.

One friend who gave Connolly *carte blanche* to sell letters from him to Texas was Stephen Spender, but relations between the two were occasionally strained by Connolly's bibliomania. On one occasion Auden, who was staying with the Spenders, came home drunk after lunch with Connolly, and suggested to his host that they should jointly sign and present to Connolly his copy of Auden's *Poems 1928*, printed by Spender in an edition of a few copies: Auden's father had a copy, and he would make sure that Spender inherited this in due course. Very reluctantly, Spender agreed, and the signed copy was handed over; but no replacement copy ever materialised after the death of Dr Auden, and Auden himself appeared to have quite forgotten their agreement. And Spender's wife, Natasha, was deeply upset when she discovered that her husband had let Connolly have a book of his poems, together with some photographs tucked inside, which he had given her shortly before they were married. Spender wrote to Connolly to say that Natasha would never forgive either of them unless the book was returned, and offered him a far more valuable book in exchange, but Connolly was adamant. He could not possibly return the book, he told Spender: 'It was a spontaneous gift of yours, delightfully inscribed, and it is one of the half-dozen treasures in my collection.' The book had been in very poor condition when Spender gave it to him: he had had it rebound in black morocco (bill enclosed), and kept it behind glass with the other most precious items in his collection. All he could promise was that he would leave the book to Spender in his will; in fact he forgot – or failed – to do so, despite the fact that both Auden and Spender were witnesses to his will, but the book and the photographs were returned to the Spenders shortly after his death.

Not all Connolly's book-collecting was quite so fraught, though financial crises often intervened: George Sims, an antiquarian bookseller with whom he had frequent dealings, removed him from his mailing-list when he found waiting to be paid too nerve-wracking a business, reinstating him on receipt of a rueful letter of apology, or – at Schwartz's suggestion – accepting some manuscripts in lieu of a debt. And even if book-collecting did not always bring out the best in him, Connolly's humour was still poised to prick his own pretensions: he sometimes felt guilty about referring so frequently to first editions in his reviews, he told *Sunday Times* readers, and had come to dread reproachful letters of the kind that read

> I happen to be trying to bring up a family of thirteen on an income of £200 a year and was greatly impressed by Mr Connolly's advice to collect some books of verse in their dust-jackets 'when they make a fine showing' – I could not help wondering what sort of a showing Mr Connolly would make in *my* dust-jacket preparing breakfast for eleven (and two bottles) at five o'clock every morning . . . Mrs Dolly Pinprickle, Wuthering-on-Lea.

Despite his regular visits to Bertram Rota's shop, and his obsession with his library – 'It is the scarab's ball,' he told the Spenders – Connolly's urge to collect grew weaker as he grew older. 'Tapering off! That is how I answer questions about my book-collecting,' he wrote in 1967: 'The urge is waning: the desperate anxiety to corral all my favourite authors into the Ark where I can gloat on them at leisure even as they gloat on each other is a thing of the past. My wants list gets shorter and shorter.' 'It is sad to hear you say that your collection doesn't give you as much pleasure as it used to,' John Sparrow wrote from Oxford, where he was sorting out Maurice Bowra's library after the Warden's death in September 1971: but no doubt Connolly was gratified to learn that his old friend had left him an inscribed copy of Yeats's poems in his will.

Equally obsessive was Connolly's pursuit of china and silver. Collecting ceramics represented a 'wild goose chase' in which he happily indulged. The Major had been too thrifty to buy valuable items, and came to disapprove of his son's profligate obsession with Sèvres and Vincennes – an appetite that had been inflamed during the war, when his longing for colour and beauty 'could only be satisfied by objects, things which both by colour and shape and draftsmanship brought Europe closer'; and he had sought consolation then from the Wallace Collection, crammed as it was with objects from the French eighteenth century,* as well as from a china shop in King Street and an antique dealer in Grafton Street. Confronted by a Sotheby's catalogue, he always turned first to the sections dealing with china and silver; and he liked to imagine how, 'on a cold and wet afternoon as the dusk falls I shall climb the flight of steps with a tingle of excitement, pick up my catalogue and set off round the cases lit by the greens of Sèvres and Worcester or the blue of Chelsea and Vincennes that are like the luminous bed of the Mediterranean when all is cold and grey on top.'

* The Wallace Collection formed the subject of the second of Connolly's two contributions to the Berniers' magazine *L'Oeil.*

For all his ambivalence about his profession, Connolly was the quintessential journalist not only in his reliability about meeting deadlines or writing to length, but in the breadth of his general knowledge, in his knowing a little about a great many subjects without being an authority on any of them; and so it was, perhaps, with such genuine enthusiasms as book collecting, china, silver, food and wine, about all of which he was well-informed rather than expert. And those who disliked him, or were frightened of him, or resented his over-bearing or demanding ways, or had suffered from his wit or his sulks, or simply enjoyed teasing him, or laughing at him behind his back, were quick to seize on examples of ignorance or pretentiousness. 'Connolly loved the concept of being a scholar, dandy, bibliophil, gourmet, connoisseur,' Anthony Powell wrote of him:

> He knew more than the average about many things, but aspired to know all there was to be known about everything. This desire to lay down the law could result in howlers about such matters as marks on china or silver. Friends who produced (for attribution) a bottle of Australian champagne in a napkin were told it was Krug 1905 (or some such vintage); in consequence, losing their nerve and assuring Connolly that he was miraculously correct.

As far as wine was concerned, Anthony Powell recalled that 'he could talk convincingly on the subject, and I drank some of the best claret I have ever tasted in his house. At the same time I have seen him apparently altogether unaware that he was drinking something specially good. What was at fault was the claim to omniscience.' Annie Davis remembered how he raved over the bottle of Evian water she had left by his bed, 'and I hadn't the heart to tell him that I'd just filled it from the tap.' Nor were his other claims to expertise immune to criticism. Spender remembered Connolly proudly showing an expert a porcelain bowl with holes in the base, and how, after he had left, the expert plunged his head into his hands ('I should have told him – the bowl is valueless without the spoons to go into the holes').

Quite apart from kindness and good manners, it's unlikely that many were prepared to point out such errors of taste or judgement: for Connolly remained a formidable figure, one of those overwhelming characters – half-dreaded and resented, half-eagerly awaited, always the centre of attention – who demanded of others that they put their best feet forward, and whose moods determined the tenor of the occasion. 'His own personality, pervasive, mutable, is less easy to pinpoint than his writing. He was one of those individuals – a recognised genus – who seem to have been sent into the world to be talked about,' Powell suggested: '... Connolly's behaviour, love affairs, financial difficulties, employments or lack of them, all seemed matters of burning interest. He had, so to speak, taken the sins of the world on himself. Some rebelled, refusing to be drawn into the net of Cyril gossip. They were few in number, and perhaps missed something in life.' Among those who made sporadic and unsuccessful attempts at rebellion was Frances Partridge. 'I am expecting six or eight people to drinks – good God, and Cyril one of them!' she confided to her diary in the spring of 1962. Once again, she went out of her way to bend with the wind – as Powell noted, 'He was rarely at ease in an equal relationship' – and she did indeed survive:

> The arrival of the Master: at first a crossish baby expecting to find me alone and have a literary talk . . . I led him to my bookcase and shamelessly offered him baits to ingratiate him. He was soon on the floor, happy, with his fat legs splayed out and hair flying wildly; then his own jokes and embroidered fantasies brought twinkling geniality and he was busy signing my copy of *The Unquiet Grave*. My own tongue was tied – apart from the effort of materially seeing to my visitors' 'wants', I could *never* feel at ease with Cyril.

Even his detractors agreed that Connolly was extremely generous, taking a positive delight in bearing gifts and giving presents; but, as Powell observed, he 'could show himself less than grateful for generosity in others', and he liked to dictate the agenda, to give on his own terms. Much the same applied to his conversation. Later that year, when Connolly came for a drink with Frances Partridge, she found to her relief – no others being present – that 'guards were lowered, a sort of *rapport* established, and Cyril seemed at his ease with me as never before'; he had a gift for intimacy, for the close conversation *à deux*, but in larger gatherings he liked to dominate the proceedings, to indulge in the dazzling monologue, and would sulk if thwarted or in a bad mood, exuding what Jonathan Gathorne-Hardy memorably described as a kind of social 'nerve gas, slowly paralysing drawing-rooms and extinguishing entire dinner parties'. Preceded by a throaty chuckle and a flash from his pale blue eyes, and delivered in his soft, flat, slightly effete voice, his comic improvisations tended to start from an item of gossip, and become ever more fantastical and exaggerated in their elaboration, with Connolly playing the parts of the characters involved and acting out their personalities and accents. 'People forget what a great *humorist* he is,' John Betjeman observed to Alan Ross: 'His expression doesn't change and the funniest things come out when he goes into one of those soliloquising parodies.' Most of his friends found these bravura displays as dazzling and amusing as he must have hoped, though Stephen Spender confessed to finding them boring as often as not, citing Patrick Leigh Fermor as the only man brave enough to intervene at an early stage and stem the flow before it was too late.* 'Superlatively competitive, he had to give a one-man performance,' Powell remembered of him:

> Somebody else's anecdote or artefact was always a challenge. He was jealous, rather than envious: whatever was in question, he must always go one better. Unlike such good talkers as Constant Lambert or Maurice Bowra (anyway up to a point), Connolly had no great liking for being entertained by talk, and as a rule himself no flow of conversation. His flair was for the unexpected comment or elaborate set-piece.

In a more intimate conversation, and with women in particular, he had that seductive ability to charm by seeming to concentrate all his attention on the person he was talking to: to quote Powell again, 'he was a master of flattery; flattery of the best sort that can seem on the surface almost a form of detraction. There was undoubtedly something hypnotic about him.' Passionately interested in the doings of his friends, he was both a matchmaker and a mischief-maker, stitching couples together yet unable to resist unpicking his handiwork, loyal and disloyal all at once. V.S. Pritchett 'often thought of him in middle age as a phenomenal baby in a pram, his hands reaching out greedily for what he saw, especially when it was far beyond him, or, if he got it, delighted for a moment and then throwing it out and crying to get it back.' Frances Partridge noted how, if one put a foot wrong, 'he delights in showing disapproval. On the other hand if one is lucky enough to amuse him (I did once, though I can't remember how) he wrestles desperately to control his smile.' And his telephone manner could be equally disconcerting: Alan Ross relished the 'conspiratorial purr, a slightly effete throatiness' which he employed on the telephone, which he regarded as 'an instrument for the surreptitious transmitting and receiving of classified information' and made much use of, but noticed too his alarming habit – an inheritance of Bloomsbury, shared with Raymond Mortimer – of putting the phone down, sometimes in mid-sentence, without any of the conventional preliminaries of farewell.

'What, in short, was the point of Connolly?' wondered Anthony Powell, an astute if critical observer from Eton onwards: 'Why did people put up with frequent moroseness, gloom, open hostility? Why, if he were about in

* 'I don't think Stephen got it quite right,' Patrick Leigh Fermor suggests. 'I was a terrible gasbag and interrupter, and probably ruined what Cyril was saying; and as Cyril's utterances were not only brilliant but never repeated, it fills me with retrospective shame.'

the neighbourhood, did I always take steps to get hold of him?' His wit, his generosity, his tireless interest in the foibles of his friends, and of human nature, were an answer in themselves: but he could inspire dislike among those he thought of as his friends. Christopher Sykes, for instance, told Patrick Kinross of how he and his wife Camilla had come across Connolly at a dance given by the d'Avigdor-Goldsmids, and

> he was more odious than I have seen him in many a year. He was in his offensive ragging mood which was very amusing for the first twenty minutes but when it went on and on getting ruder and ruder it began to lose something in humour and just became embarrassing... With enormous generosity Cam and I brought him down a bottle of champ and a bucket of *foie gras*. Many jokes about keeping them to another day and by Jesu that's what the shit did. They did not reappear. To crown all (after a lot of whimpering about having to take his own car to the dance) when I asked Deirdre to dance he made a jealous scene!!! Everyone was mystified by his conduct till the truth dawned on us all. The other guests were Tony and Violet Powell and impotent Boots was of course devoured by jealousy of T's deserved success. In keeping with his revolting Irish sub-character he was *fawning* on Tony and getting even by being rude to Cam and me. He is revoltingly ungrown-up...

'About to be 59 on Monday 10th,' Connolly noted a couple of months after this unhappy encounter: 'My life only makes sense if from now on I concentrate entirely on becoming a great writer and so justifying all the waste and expenditure of emotion on people and places – my family will just have to put up with it.' That was fair enough, but the book he published that autumn, elegant as it was, seemed unlikely to attract the attention now being meted out to Powell's 'Dance to the Music of Time'. An American photographer, Jerome Zerbe, had compiled a portfolio of photographs of French eighteenth-century *pavillons*; and Connolly was commissioned by Hamish Hamilton and Macmillan New York to write an introduction. Though asked to deliver some 30,000 words, he eventually produced a third of that amount; but it was generally agreed that he had done a good job, for even if he lacked the architectural expertise, the period was one for which he felt an instinctive sympathy. The paintings of Watteau, the music of Mozart, the lost glories of Dresden moved him to tears by their beauty and their elegiac sense of autumnal transience, and in his introduction he combined this note of rhapsodic melancholy with a reaffirmation of his love of France. 'The French eighteenth century is a period we can literally live ourselves into,' he suggested:

> . . . It is a civilisation which contains everything we can desire except great literature. The seventeenth century and the nineteenth make up for that, but the one is too formal and remote, the other too chaotic and industrialised, to challenge our desirable haven: intellectually simmering, socially bland, aesthetically pleasing, with something about it of the large generous wholesomeness of France itself.

But another enthusiast for the period had her reservations. 'Cyril's book on the Pavillons is quite wild,' Nancy Mitford informed Waugh: 'Hardly one of the houses illustrated is a *pavillon*; nearly all are *hôtels particuliers* or *châteaux*. All very pretty however. He wrote and asked to dedicate it to me and then didn't – no explanation. What can this mean?'

None of this prevented Lord Adrian from asking Connolly if he would care to deliver the 1962–3 Clark Lectures at Trinity, Cambridge. He declined, but accepted an invitation for the weekend from the Provost of King's, Noël Annan. It was, Dadie Rylands remembers, rather a 'disastrous' occasion. Like many writers, Connolly preferred the company of men of action, of the raffish and the worldly, to academics, and Annan noticed how ill-at-ease he seemed among the dons at high table. Annan thoughtfully invited some more urbane figures for lunch the following day, Victor Rothschild and Jakie Astor among them, and his guest was himself once more.

Connolly's love of the eighteenth century had been indulged the year before, when he and Deirdre went to stay in Ireland with Desmond Guinness, the head of the Irish Georgian Society, and spent time examining the plasterwork in decaying Irish country houses and in Trinity College, Dublin; and in the summer of 1962 the two of them set out, courtesy of the *Sunday Times*, on a Grand Tour of France and Italy which gratified his passion for *trains de luxe*, railway timetables and station restaurants, and his liking for very grand, old-fashioned hotels, many of them recommended by the Davises. In Paris they had dinner with Sylvia Beach, lunch with Samuel Beckett, drinks with Schiaparelli, and a lunch-party given in their honour by Marie-Laure de Noailles, and were invited out by Susan Mary Patten, Mary McCarthy and Ethel de Croisset; in Florence they saw much of Harold Acton, lunched with Osbert Sitwell, and were given a lavish party by Violet Trefusis; in Rome they met the Leigh Fermors, Stephen Spender, Peter Quennell's ex-wife, Glur Dyson-Taylor, Jennifer Ross and Archie Colquhoun, the translator of *The Leopard*, with whom they travelled on to Sicily. They returned on the train via Zurich, 'muttering with Maecenas *Lubricos quate dentes* (shake out our last tooth) *vita dum superest bene est* (while one's alive all is well).'

Back from his travels, Connolly combined his love of adventure stories, his interest in espionage and his genius for parody in a brief addendum to the James Bond canon entitled 'Bond Strikes Camp'. Connolly had read the Bond novels, then at the height of their popularity, and seen some of the films as well, and had advised Fleming about vintage wines and the like; according to Fleming's first biographer, Fleming – who took his own work quite seriously – came home to their house in Victoria Square to find Connolly entertaining his wife's guests with readings from the novels, but when, over a dinner party, Connolly floated the idea of his writing a James Bond spoof, he encouraged him to go ahead. Bond (in Connolly's version) is asked by 'M' to undertake a particularly delicate mission: a visiting KGB general is known to have a penchant for men in drag, and Bond is ordered to pad himself out in a false bosom and a wig, and allow himself to be picked up by the lascivious brute. At the critical moment Bond, cornered by the general, seizes hold of his moustaches: they come away in his hands, only to reveal a lovelorn 'M', for whom recourse to such tricks seemed the only way of making Bond his own . . .

'Bond Strikes Camp' was first published in the *London Magazine*, where Alan Ross had taken over from John Lehmann the previous year, and Fleming took a keen interest in getting the details right, deluging Charles Osborne, the magazine's assistant editor, with small, Bond-like corrections ('Isn't "The Kitchen" in Lower Belgrave Mews, not Street?' and 'Please would you check the type of shrimp used in Eggs Omdurman'). Soon afterwards it appeared in an expensive limited edition, copies of which were sent to Bond's best-known admirer, President Kennedy, by Randolph Churchill and by Fleming himself. 'Imagine my delight when I got it home and found out what it was all about, because I am a second-to-none Fleming fan & have read all his books twice,' Christopher Isherwood wrote from California: 'As a matter of fact I think he had this coming to him. I have several times resented his attitude to the Minority to which I belong.' Only Edmund Wilson was unamused. His wife, Elena, had taken against Connolly after they had all lunched together at the Ritz, at Connolly's suggestion – she claimed that their host had allowed her husband to pick up the bill, and hadn't addressed a word to her – and Wilson had decided that Connolly combined 'a queer mixture of lordly courtesy with boorishness and infantilism'; and he thought that Connolly had written his spoof out of envy at Fleming's success, in order to 'expose him to himself – his "adolescent fantasies" – humiliate him, devastate him'. Judging by Fleming's evident interest in his literary step-child, Wilson was being super-sensitive on his behalf; and when, early in 1964, Fleming died, his widow wrote to Connolly to say that 'You did so much for him in these last months; he particularly enjoyed your company and lunching in Brighton. I am everlastingly grateful to you.' Connolly's reply, while disclaiming any pretensions to comfort – 'I wish I could say something to console you but, like Ian, I am too melancholy myself' – was oddly consoling in its bleak summation of all that Fleming had been spared:

> It seems to me that you have suffered in a particularly personal and traumatic form, in one fell swoop if you like, the process which is spun out for most of us in getting old – the awareness of being less and less wanted, desired, tolerated, and the being less able to want desire or tolerate although one's faculties of mind and heart are in their prime – and you have lost your husband, the half of yourself as it were, while most of us have to watch the loss inch by inch and cut by cut of all the warmth and intimacy on which we depend . . . old age is being flayed alive as the Frenchman said – and the areas of interest gradually restricted like being on a melting iceberg – and at the end nothing but death.

'Bond Strikes Camp' resurfaced at the end of 1963, when Hamish Hamilton published a collection of reviews, travel pieces and parodies under the title *Previous Convictions*. After a brief arrangement with a New York literary agent called Mrs Carleton Cole, who had negotiated the fee for *Pavillons* – 'or rather he calmly filled in the amount himself after a talk with Mrs Carleton Cole,' Hamilton memoed Roger Machell – Connolly had finally decided to entrust his affairs to a literary agent in the form of Deborah Rogers, then an employee of Ian Fleming's agent, Peter Janson-Smith, but soon to set up in business on her own. She took delivery of a large cardboard box crammed with tear-sheets from magazines, which she sorted out on the office floor before passing them on to the publishers. Relations between Connolly and his publisher became increasingly fraught as the book inched its way towards November publication. In the first place, Hamilton rejected – and then accepted – the facetious but entertaining blurb Connolly had written: 'After waiting in vain to be told that his friends were presenting him with a book for his sixtieth birthday, Cyril Connolly decided that the only course left was to prepare one for them,' the front flap began, while the masterly author biography concluded with details of the authorial coat-of-arms:

> ARMS: A nez, purpure, impaled upon a grindstone proper between two duns rampant,
> CREST: A hack in his element, hobbled.
> MOTTO: Filez sans payer.

Getting the proofs through in time was a nightmare of delays and last-minute alterations. At the end of August the proofs were sent off, with a request to return them within two weeks if they were to publish in time for the Christmas market. Connolly promptly disappeared to the South of France to stay with Anne Dunn and her husband, the painter Rodrigo Moynihan, after announcing, rather late in the day, that he wanted to write an Introduction. The proofs began to filter back in batches, but Connolly then decamped to Barcelona. 'Isn't this typical?' Hamilton noted, adding that they might have to abandon November publication – in which case, 'prepare for rage'. The final batch was returned, to the wrong address, at the end of September: there was still no sign of the Introduction, and throughout the first week of October the author, unrepentant, continued to fiddle about with his essays and alter their titles. Gritting his teeth, Machell informed him in late October that, alas, it was impossible at this stage to provide twelve copies with a blank dedication page – as it was, the book was dedicated to 'B.S.', much to Deirdre's distress – and regaled him with a cautionary tale about an author who had dedicated his book to his wife but insisted on one copy being left blank: the binder forgot to put it aside, with the result that all 5000 copies had to be unpacked...

'Secretly I am convinced that there is no happiness outside my prose and I want the world to know it,' Connolly wrote in his belated Introduction, while admitting that, in a book of this kind, 'the naked bones of reviewing cannot be concealed.' Regular reviewing for a Sunday paper had 'tempered my improvidence and widened my knowledge; it has respected my solitude and prevented *rigor mortis* setting in. Without the weekly stint I might have written longer and better – or dissipated my powers in false starts and frustration.' The book had been cunningly divided into four parts. 'The Visible World' included travel pieces (the 'Grand Tour' he had made with Deirdre, his trip to Egypt, Greece), musings on animals and plants and underwater exploration, the delights of rococo and collecting porcelain; 'The Grand Possessors' and 'The Modern Movement' were devoted to favourite authors, from Montaigne, Baudelaire, Flaubert and Proust to Denton Welch, Scott Fitzgerald and Dylan Thomas; 'Paging Mr Smartiboots' brought together James Bond and Jonathan Edax, the pleasures of the table with the elegiac nostalgia of 'One of my Londons'. And since almost everything Connolly ever wrote contained elements of autobiography, his claim that 'this book is so arranged that it builds up to a picture of the author; an ageing Narcissus complete with pool' was far more than a vain attempt to disguise a rag-bag of reviews as something other than it was, and impose a unity and a shape where none in fact existed.

All the same, there was nothing new in *Previous Convictions*, apart from the Introduction, just as there had been nothing new in any of the full-length books he had published since *The Unquiet Grave*. Well aware of his sensitivity on the subject, tactful friends hastened to reassure him. 'It is very much a book,' an over-anxious Elizabeth Bowen insisted: 'A whole, I mean, an entity in itself. The individual pieces enhance and throw light on and give an added significance to one another. Nothing you have ever written *is* ephemeral.' But Maurice Bowra's comfort had a colder edge: 'Though it is ghastly that you should have spent your life writing weekly articles, as articles they could not be better, and you have really done something to make an art of what was before and still is a most unpromising and limiting form.' Nigel Dennis, writing in the *Sunday Telegraph*, felt that Connolly had 'come to terms too easily with his Sunday stint. We must demand much more of him than he is prepared to give.' Connolly had claimed, in his Introduction, that if he had any gift it was for conveying his own enthusiasm for literature in general, and his favourite writers in particular, but the effect of this was to restrict himself to the past, averting his gaze from contemporary literature and concentrating instead on 'lemurs and gorillas'. This was a pity, Dennis thought: Connolly's essay on the horrors of British Railways food proved that he could be perfectly 'predatory', and it seemed a pity that he refused to sharpen his fangs on the present.

Writing in Connolly's own newspaper, Noël Annan – bearing in mind, perhaps, Connolly's unhappy experiences on high table – wondered why he was so ill-regarded by academics. He was, he decided, too well-read, too ready to ridicule 'what is trivial or smart or pretentious'; he loved pleasure, and because he was 'really more interested in what people are really like than by what they might be,' he was 'singularly lax in condemning people', which gave him a sympathy with failure, with those who found life hard. 'He does not think deeply, he thinks with agility. He does not bully or draw his reader after him by argument, he teases his reader to think for himself, by setting curious juxtapositions of ideas before him.' Connolly had been condemned by academia as a lightweight: the most lenient of judges, Annan condemned him to serve his sentence at the Cambridge University Press, 'sewing together quires of the reprinted edition of *Scrutiny*'.*

Annan's custodial motif was echoed in the *New Statesman* by Kingsley Amis, who suggested that few writers born after 1920 would award Connolly 'anything but a stiff sentence':

> Paid-up membership of the cultural Establishment, London literary-racketeering, engagement in weekly journalism (unlike all the rest of us, eh?), book-foistering, propaganda activities on behalf of abroad and its

* Nearly thirty years later Annan suggested that 'academic critics treated Connolly as if he were a hunting parson who had blundered into the Oriel Common Room when Newman and Keble were discussing the illapse of the Holy Ghost.'

> inhabitants, persistent dilettantism, capital lack of 'rigour' and 'moral preoccupation' – one can write out the charge-sheet with one's eyes shut.

Amis wrote not as an Angry Young Man or a puritanical provincial with Leavisite leanings, as Maurice Bowra consolingly suggested ('I suppose what Amis & Co dislike is the range of your pleasures, both intellectual and otherwise'), but as a disillusioned admirer of Connolly's earlier work. Though invariably disappointed by *Horizon* – 'the stuff was too old for me' – he had found *The Condemned Playground* 'full of wit and good sense', had fortified himself against army life with *Enemies of Promise*, and still thought *The Rock Pool* 'one of the four or five funniest novels of our time': but faced with the thinness of the material included in this new book, the imbalance of matter to style, he saw no alternative to 'sending him to the galleys'. Much of what Connolly had to say about writers was mere gossip and anecdote; and he subjected Connolly's well-known admiration for the poems of Edith Sitwell to the kind of ridicule that his subject had inflicted on middlebrow novelists thirty years before at the hands of Mr Mossbross ('Fire away then, Connolly.' 'Thank you, sir . . .')*

A similar sense of disappointment was voiced by Anthony Thwaite in the *Listener*. The new collection, he felt, lacked the sharpness of *The Condemned Playground*. This was partly caused by the brevity of the average book review, partly by a slackening in Connolly himself: either way, 'the result is either an elegant fumbling, as the tired muscles are flexed, or a smarty copywriting shorthand'. Too much of the book had 'a flavour of botched Wilde', with 'Bond Strikes Camp' as the one redeeming item: 'Here all Mr Connolly's formidable gifts as a disgruntled parodist combine in a performance which underlines what one finds boring or off-putting in the rest.' Far more welcome, no doubt, was a full-page review in the *Spectator* by a present admirer and future friend, the poet Peter Levi, for whom 'no one writing is capable of better prose' ('He can do in prose the equivalent of what Pope did in verse'): Levi's only regret was the exclusion of 'Shade Those Laurels', for 'that alone of his writings in the last ten years has been really great, in the same sense as *The Waste Land* and the later poems of Yeats. Can its rejection from the book mean that he may publish it complete? I can think of no other probable event in the literature of his generation by which mine would be a tenth so excited.' Malcolm

* Nor was Amis an admirer of Connolly the mimic: 'He thought talking in a fast squeal was enough for an imitation of David Cecil.' Three years earlier, Connolly – on one of his rare forays into contemporary literature – had declared Amis's *Take a Girl Like You* a disappointment after *Lucky Jim*: 'Let me now enunciate Connolly's second law (the first, you will remember, was that every non-fattening food is only palatable with a fattening complement). Literary success liberates the tensions generated by a hostile environment by removing the environment and so prepares the way for literary failure.'

Muggeridge, on the other hand, seemed reconciled to the non-appearance of future full-length books: 'A different Connolly with a different girth and different angsts (his word) and a larger, steadier income would not necessarily have been more productive. His lost masterpieces give a piquancy to his criticism, as childless women make the best baby-sitters and impotent men the most assiduous lovers.'

'The benignity of Cyril Connolly is alarming. I am totally relaxed with him, he has become warm, comfortable and cosy,' Ann Fleming reported shortly after the book's publication: the only 'little storm' had been caused by the dedication page, as a result of which Connolly had had to take Joan Leigh Fermor instead of Deirdre to Hamish Hamilton's publication dinner, protesting that 'The trouble with Deirdre is that she has no sense of history.' And yet the melancholy and the sense of failure were seldom far away. 'I wake with the death wish like a tumor,' he told Waugh, while to Bowra he wrote

> One is like a sandcastle whose flags and battlements are collapsing one by one –
>
> arthritic from finger to toe
> cancerous probably too
> and the last tooth beginning to go.
> I'm alive. That's enough. How are you?

And on the same scrap of paper on which he had scribbled, ten years earlier, his 'Ambition for 50th birthday', he now added, '*dix ans après*',

> Ambition for my 60th birthday – to have my silver out of pawn. Remorse over Midford Castle, failure to have saved both my capital and the Connolly park and woods, chapel etc. Realisation that I will never have a chance to own a house, that I live among strangers, am not allowed to cash any cheques. Endless money worry, endless hack work, not a real writer but an unsuccessful businessman. Unlovable, unloved. Weight increasing, energy dwindling, memory worse. At Midford one could have gone quietly mad in a dignified sort of way, with the Abbey cemetery at hand.

Momentary oblivion was provided by a sixtieth birthday party given by Lord and Lady Glenconner at their house in Swan Walk in Chelsea.*

* Connolly had met the Glenconners in 1941. Two years later he went to stay with Elizabeth Glenconner at Glen, their house near Edinburgh (where he was due to deliver the lecture reprinted as 'French and English Cultural Relations'). She remembers him walking miles across heather and through streams in a pair of sandals, and carrying her daughter Emma – later the novelist, Emma Tennant – when the going was too rough. She refused to bring him his breakfast in bed, and he inscribed her copy of *Enemies of Promise* with an appropriate aphorism by Brillat-Savarin: *Proposer à des obèses de se lever matin, c'est leur percer le coeur.*

Edmund Wilson went along with Elena, and found the 'usual jam of people' there, among them John Russell, Anthony Powell, John Betjeman and Sonia Orwell; and it was on the day after that Elena was ignored over lunch at the Ritz. Connolly's tendency, when in company, to indulge in monologues and ignore smaller fry had earlier been noted by Frances Partridge, a fellow-guest at a dinner given by Maud Russell and attended by Peter Quennell, the Connollys, Lennox Berkeley and his wife, Patrick Kinross, Boris Anrep and Baroness Budberg – though in this case there was some competition:

> The self-consciously 'good talkers' at the table were Peter Quennell and Cyril. Peter soon turned his back on Deirdre Connolly, by-passed the Budberg, and shouted across to Cyril at the opposite corner of the table. An answering sparkle and smile came back from Cyril – indeed, they talked to each other most of the evening and the wonder is that two such egotistical talkers will hear each other out enough to stimulate each other. Towards the end of the evening these two literary pundits came and sat each side of me – the poor slice of ham in their sandwich – on the sofa. The subject was literary of course (Desmond) and I felt their benevolence flooding down on me as from twin bedside lamps.

Neither Connolly's birthday not the publication of *Previous Convictions* had passed unnoticed in the *London Magazine*. Relations between Connolly and its editor might have been bedevilled by women, but they were alike in their editorial flair, their liking for gossip, and a tendency to embroider a prosaic truth with exaggerations bordering on fantasy; and Ross had an unqualified admiration for Connolly as a writer. He wrote, Ross once suggested,

> a prose that was more allusive, suggestive and elegant than perhaps anyone of his time; a prose at once reflective, wise and just. It may have been the prose of a man who was vulnerable, greedy, devious and susceptible to most vices, but in the last resort, perhaps because of all this and despite his own frequent depressions and disappointments, it was able miraculously to convey the excitement of reading and travelling, loving and looking, study and nature.

Simon Raven, a fellow-classicist, reconsidered *The Rock Pool* in the August 1963 issue of the magazine, and in December Gavin Ewart used *Previous Convictions* as a peg on which to hang a survey of Connolly's work and career. Connolly, he began,

> is one of those writers of whom one would not willingly miss a word. Just as it is impossible to imagine any music by Mozart being dull, one cannot picture anything written by Mr Connolly that would be boring, pompous or silly. One misses even the weekly reviewing at one's peril – not so much on account of the subject matter as of the originality of the mind at work.

Ewart then applied Connolly's famous criterion – 'the true function of a writer is to produce a masterpiece' – to his own work, memorably summarising *The Unquiet Grave* – his particular favourite – as 'the Great Missing War Poem of World War II'. Of more recent work, 'Shade Those Laurels' was highly rated ('This is a terrific super-Mandarin tour-de-force about a literary house party, ending with the death of the central character. Twenty-five pages fraught with uncontinuability'), while *Previous Convictions* was 'masterpiecewise, not really in the running. For mental stimulus and enjoyment, still a very safe bet.'*

In January, the Connollys went to stay with Philippe and Pauline de Rothschild at Mouton. Philippe had married his second wife, Pauline Potter, an American from Baltimore, in 1954; not only had she encouraged him to translate English seventeenth-century poets, and the works of Christopher Fry, but she had redecorated the château at Mouton. The Rothschilds' hospitality was legendary, combining lavishness with a scrupulous attention to detail. Guests' clothes were pressed and laid out every day; their host changed into a coloured dinner jacket and embroidered slippers for dinner; three different clarets were served at lunch and dinner, and the meal was rounded off with a thimbleful of iced Château Yquem. Cecil Beaton was a fellow-guest, and noticed how, despite his reputation, Connolly didn't over-indulge when faced with a dinner of curry-flavoured *moules*, quails, *pâté de foie* and sorbet, loyally praising the excellence of Deirdre's cooking and the products of Mr Rolph's fishmonger's shop in Seaford, and producing from his pocket a brown paper bag of Cox's Orange Pippins, bought before leaving Victoria Station.

* Ewart remarked on the similarity between Connolly's 'Imprisoned in every fat man a thin man is wildly signalling to be let out' and Orwell's 'Has it ever struck you that there's a thin man inside every fat man, just as they say there's a statue inside every block of stone?' *Coming up for Air* was published in 1939, but Connolly claimed that he had not read it when he wrote *The Unquiet Grave*: 'The expression was an old joke of mine and may have originated in a talk with him about our different physical conformities,' he explained in a Letter to the Editor. Not long after Ewart's article appeared, the two men met at Alan Ross's house. Half-flattered and half-irritated at not having been taken with sufficient gravity before – in his piece, Ewart remarked on how little had been written about Connolly and his work, despite the fact that 'Mr Connolly is Big Game' – Connolly invited Ewart to sit beside him, observing that he had never before been accused of plagiarism . . .

A month later, Connolly was off on his travels again, only this time far further afield – to the country which symbolised the lost Eden of childhood, lush and green and warm, the abode of wild animals and exotic fruit. 'Cyril Connolly has gone to his dying mother in Africa after a further rumpus with his wife for telling him he was too old to wear shorts,' Ann Fleming reported, inaccurate as ever (only Africa was true). Mollie had come to stay at Bushey on her last visit to England: a tiny, bird-like woman, she was irritatingly humble and self-effacing, complaining in a quiet voice and inducing spasms of guilt in son and daughter-in-law alike; she affected a rather fey humility ('Oh no, I wouldn't dream of staying with you'), but her effect on Connolly was alarming. 'After the first evening I was reduced to my childhood trauma – sulks, boredom, horror – inability to look her in the face, hardly able to speak, only to mutter from the floor,' he wrote: '. . . she brings back the vast boredom and oppression of my childhood and adolescence.' He couldn't bear her smell, or to touch her, and 'she won't stay put in the sitting-room but pops up wherever one is – kitchen or bedroom – with a little series of frets.' With his mother around, Connolly became a small child again; but her passion was for Cressida, to whom she was devoted. Now she was unwell, and Connolly persuaded the *Sunday Times* to commission some travel pieces so that he could visit her at home.

He flew out with Robert Heber-Percy, who happened to be on the same plane. The plane stopped at Brazzaville, where Connolly inhaled the 'heavenly tropical grass smell' of his childhood. George, the place where Mollie lived, was a 'paradise', with high blue mountains looming up behind, wide streets lined with oak trees, and citrus fruit, guavas and avocados growing in the gardens. Connolly booked into a hotel opposite his mother's house, and rented a Mini in which to drive himself around: 'I shed a load of guilt motherwise,' he wrote: 'It was the first time since heaven knows when that I had been alone with her without a woman of my own around the corner.' For years, he told his readers, he had held off visiting South Africa for political reasons: rather to his surprise, he particularly liked the Afrikaners, whom he found warm-hearted, humorous, well-mannered and less materialistic than their English-speaking compatriots. The climax of his trip was a visit to the Kruger National Park. Watching the animals, and his beloved elephants in particular, provided some kind of 'reconciliation, perhaps, with this estranged archetypal world of our childhood, a sense of harmony and reparation'; and – back in England – 'even now I am haunted by the sights and sounds of this earthly paradise.'

Earthly paradises are best enjoyed in silence, and Connolly wounded three South African admirers of his work who drove him round the Cape Peninsula by staring sullenly out of the car window and rebuffing all attempts at conversation.* In Cape Town, where he was very taken with the Cape Dutch architecture, he had an introduction, through Tanya Hobson, to Raymond Hoffenberg, a young doctor working in the black townships. The Hoffenbergs took him back to Wynberg, and arranged what turned out to be a disastrous meeting with Alan Paton: both were overcome by shyness, and conversation nudged its way forward 'like a train shunting in the Karoo'. Among the young writers he met were C.J. Driver, then in his mid-twenties, and Randolph Vigne, both of whom were eventually forced into exile. He introduced Driver to Alan Ross, who published some of his poems, and alerted Maurice Bowra to the plight of Vigne, a former student at Wadham, who was in political trouble with the Vorster regime.†

'It seems like a dream that you were here,' Mollie wrote to her son after his return to England: but they were never to meet again, for she died, peacefully enough, in July that year, and was buried opposite General Brooke. One effect of Mollie's death was a slight improvement in the Connolly finances. 'She had been saving up for years, and left me much more than I ever expected,' Connolly wrote: in due course the money he inherited would indeed enable him at long last to buy a house of his own – it included Mollie's wedding settlement of £4000, a similar sum from the sale of the house in George, and the family silver – but in the meantime the 'tax hounds' were circling, and Ran Antrim felt unable to comply with Coutts's request that he raise the overdraft guarantee to £2000. Connolly's finances remained a vexed and vexing matter, involving nimble footwork, sporadic sales of pictures and manuscripts, and the generosity of friends – Joan Leigh Fermor, Anne Dunn, Jennifer Ross and the d'Avigdor-Goldsmids among them – who were happy to help with school fees and keep the ark afloat.

Among these generous friends was Anthony Hobson, who arranged for the Connollys, including Deirdre's two elder children, to join his own family on holiday in Biarritz. 'I always feel very unreal in these family parties and creep off by myself,' Connolly told Barbara in New York, but little absenteeism was in evidence. He amused the children by pronouncing 'water bottle' with glottal stops for the 't's and quizzed them about the plants in the grounds of the Régina et du Golf Hotel, discussed Sonia Orwell and 'penis envy' after they had gone to bed, showed Anthony Hobson a grateful letter

* A few years later, Connolly found himself driving round southern Italy with Alan Ross and the painter Keith Vaughan, whom he had never met before. According to Ross, 'The pair of them sat in total silence in the back of my car, staring ahead or outwards like bodyguards, each incapable of small talk or making the first move. "What a nice person Keith is," Cyril typically remarked later, not having addressed a word to him for two weeks.'

† Sir Raymond Hoffenberg (as he became in due course) moved to England, and was eventually made President of Wolfson College, Oxford. The Hoffenbergs took the Connollys to see *Hair* shortly after it opened: Connolly loathed both the music and the nudity. C.J. Driver later became the Headmaster of Wellington, the linear descendant of Bobbie Longden.

recently received from T.S. Eliot ('I was particularly touched by the way in which you referred, in reviewing my *Collected Poems*, to my last dedicatory poem to my wife. You were the first sympathetic reader and critic to call attention to the unusual fact that I had at last written a poem of love and happiness'), and made an unexpected, if facetious, revelation round the hotel swimming-pool:

> I must tell you the change that has happened. I have been converted by Peter Levi to the Roman Church. He has laid on me the duty of giving up my books to the Church. They are being crated up now to be sent to the Brethren of St Ignatius, a lay brotherhood in Scotland, who are going to spare me the trouble of burning anything that is on the Index. The Sades I luckily burned myself first.

They had dinner at Biriatou, on the Spanish border, which Connolly had last visited during the Spanish Civil War with Dick Wyndham; and he took Deirdre to the Casino in Biarritz, where she won £30. On their way out they spotted the Duke and Duchess of Windsor going into the Café de Paris, and Connolly was keen to follow after: he had met them in Somerset Maugham's house in the South of France, and the Duchess had made polite noises about *Horizon*; he was sure she would remember him. Neither Connolly nor Anthony Hobson was wearing a tie, so he found a menswear shop and bought a black tie for himself and what looked like a Royal Engineers tie for his friend. Fully equipped, the four of them entered the Café de Paris and sat in a corner, but their arrival passed unnoticed. Afterwards they went on to a night-club. Connolly watched the young people dancing to the Beatles, and said he felt like von Aschenbach in *Death in Venice*: 'From now on,' he told them, 'one must expect these death associations to become more frequent.'*

Back in England, Hobson continued to note the paradoxes of his friend's behaviour – his social insecurity, his readiness, in conversation, to subordinate sentiment to a good story. He passed Connolly in St James's Street, and 'only the raising of his eyebrows a fraction, and an infinitesimal relaxation of his mouth, indicated that he had seen me.' Hobson, who was on his way to his club with a friend, was understandably surprised and a little hurt by this apparent snub; but Connolly, it transpired, was a good deal more agonised

* When Deirdre asked him for whom else he would buy a tie, he answered Eliot, Pound and Picasso. Despite his grateful letter, Eliot was something of a sore subject: Connolly told the Hobsons that he had invited Eliot and his wife to his 60th birthday party, but he had refused. The night before, John Betjeman and Elizabeth Cavendish had asked Eliot to dinner: again he had refused, but he had later asked them to dinner, but not the Connollys...

by their encounter. He had failed to acknowledge Hobson because 'I suffer from such insecurity . . . Anthony, though younger, is a father figure to me because of his position [at Sotheby's]: I was afraid he was with someone important and didn't want me to go into Boodle's.'* Despite his long devotion to Edith Sitwell, he was unable to resist the comical when discussing her recent death (' "Alan Ross killed her! He printed that piece on her in the *London Magazine*; when she read it she had a seizure and never recovered."); and when Hobson said he would like to collect anything by Connolly '*jusqu'à* your washing-bills', he came back with 'I think the easiest will be to send you our laundry.'

Washing-bills were all very well, but Connolly was in search of stronger meat. He had become obsessed with the idea of writing an autobiography, based on letters written at the time, which would take up where the 'Georgian Boyhood' section of *Enemies of Promise* left off, covering Oxford and the Twenties and ending with his marriage to Jean. As a young man he had asked his friends to return his letters to him, as if in preparation for a book of this kind; and now he began to get in touch once again with the friends of his youth. The most important single source of letters was Noël Blakiston. 'Shall we risk a meeting one day?' Connolly had asked him back in 1948, after turning down two of his old friend's short stories for *Horizon*: nothing had come of it – indeed, Georgiana Blakiston had snubbed Connolly at a party shortly after publication of her husband's first collection of stories on the grounds that he had deliberately ignored the book – but he got in touch with Blakiston at the Public Record Office after Cressida's birth, searching for information about his forebears. Friendly correspondence was resumed, Blakiston visited Bushey, and Connolly began poring over the letters he had written to his friend some forty years before.† The past came surging back, disruptive yet addictive. (An additional stimulus was provided by T.C. Worsley, who recommended anti-depressants as an antidote to writer's block: their only effect on Connolly was to make him clear his desk, rifling through family papers and letters from the past.) He longed for the arrival of each new batch of letters, the reading of which had become

* Connolly's sense of social insecurity was nothing new. Evelyn Waugh's old friend 'Coote' Lygon – one of the daughters of the 7th Earl Beauchamp – remembers Connolly and Jean coming to stay at Madresfield Court in the 1930s, and how mortified he was when the butler announced that 'There must have been some muddle at the station. There is only one suitcase for Mr and Mrs Connolly.' Jean, on the other hand, was quite unconcerned.

† One of Blakiston's short stories, 'Friends' describes the meeting, in a swimming-pool, of two old friends – one fat, the other thin – who haven't seen each other for years. Both make conventional noises of regret when the thin man reveals that he is leaving next day, but 'both of them, in their hearts, thought, what a good thing! For they were very old friends. They knew each other very well indeed. They knew that they could not bear to see each other for long. Each was to the other like a very good book, which was read at a receptive age and made an enormous impression.'

a 'drug'. 'I want to create a work of sustained delight in youth, friendship and the growth of minds,' he told Blakiston: it would be 'My life in some letters 1923–30', a transition summed up – or so he claimed – in one of those word games he so enjoyed ('PRIG/FRIG/FROG/FLOG/SLOG/SLOT/SLIT/SHIT'). Provisionally entitled 'At the Turn of the Twenties', and variously described as an 'erotodocumentary' or an 'erotobiography', the book would trace its hero's progress from 'College to office / play to work / men to women / friendship to passion / academic to avant garde / uncertainty to security'; its six sections would consist of 'Twilight of the Dons', '*Du Côté de Chez Logan*', 'The Thankless Mews', 'The Age of the Ziplings', 'The Watershed 1929 – Over the Hump' and 'The Birds of America', marking the shift from the passionate friendships of Eton and Oxford, which had reached their climax in the trip he and Blakiston had made to Sicily together, to the surrender of classical civilisation under the impact of the 'Barbarian Invasions'. He was grateful for Maurice Bowra's encouragement, 'but I lack the time and energy to hew the statue out of the block – I need six months' leisure and a better filing system.' He was thinking of two volumes, he told the Warden, one based around Noël Blakiston and Bobbie Longden, the other around Jean: he found himself falling in love with them all over again, especially with Bobbie Longden, 'but then one remembers all the boredoms and frustrations and surfeits as well.' 'At night,' he told Barbara, 'I litter my bed with old letters and retire into my youth.' Piers Synnott had promised to send some letters ('Next victim Freddie!'), though Adrian House of Collins informed him that Bobbie Longden had left instructions that Connolly's letters to him were to be burned were anything to happen to him. News of Connolly's plans soon leaked out to the world at large: Daphne Fielding told Waugh that Connolly was hard at work rounding up old letters, and that 'he is going to write a book around them and Patrick Kinross has suggested as a title "Promise of Enemies".'*

With the shape and the span of the book decided, and the letters to Blakiston helpfully to hand, the next move was to find a publisher. Chapman & Hall, then run by his Oxford contemporary Jack McDougall, was a possibility, but the presence of Waugh on the board was a hindrance; Ian Parsons of Chatto was a Sussex neighbour; he was fond of Adrian House, but 'I don't like the Top Brass at Collins'; as ever, Hamish Hamilton was poised in the wings, ready to offer a contract. But Connolly's most sustained discussions – sometimes held in the Starlit Room of the Grand Hotel in

* Connolly in the meantime had described her novel, *The Adonis Garden*, as 'a farrago of old cat'.

Brighton, one of his favourite venues – were with the poet William Plomer, another Sussex resident and, as Jonathan Cape's reader and literary adviser, the man responsible for spotting the potential of the James Bond novels. Writing to Connolly in June 1964, Plomer mentioned the rumour that he was writing an autobiography based on letters, and asked if Cape could be considered as a potential publisher. 'I am touched by your devotion to NB and by what seems to me a prevailing sadness in the letters,' he wrote after reading the material: the letters needed to be linked together with some kind of commentary or editorial glue, 'with the theme of your friendship with NB always central and predominant – as how could it not be.'* Apart from too many Greek and Latin quotations, and itineraries which read at times like a railway timetable, what worried Plomer most was 'too oppressive a sense of a remote private Oxford world with its own interests, jokes, gossip and matters taken for granted'. Connolly, for his part, was prepared to trim travel plans and classical quotes, but was anxious to retain the rather airless introspection in order to provide a greater contrast when the world of work and women broke through. In the meantime, Hamish Hamilton, who had learned of his discussions with Plomer, wrote in plaintive vein to ask why his firm hadn't been considered, and suggested joint publication with Cape ('I would hate it to be thought that you had deserted Mr Micawber').

As it was, neither Plomer nor Hamilton seem to have pursued the matter with much conviction, but others stepped forward to take their place, and Connolly continued to toy with the idea till his death. André Deutsch, who co-published Connolly's *The Modern Movement* with Hamish Hamilton in 1965, wrote to him earlier that year expressing the hope that he would one day write his autobiography.† Deborah Rogers replied that her client would very much like to write such a book for Deutsch; a contract was signed, with Deutsch paying £300 on signature, and it was also agreed that the firm would reissue *Enemies of Promise*, paying a further advance of £500 (it is still in print with them). Though a particularly shrewd and, in monetary terms, cautious publisher, Deutsch agreed to pay a further £150 at the end of 1972, after learning that a young editor named Andrew Rossabi was going through the Blakiston letters. Nor had Connolly abandoned hope: although Dadie

* Connolly's letters to Blakiston were published after his death as *A Romantic Friendship* (1975). Blakiston's editing was, alas, perfunctory to a degree: no editorial glue was provided, characters were defined solely in terms of their Eton dates and whether or not they had been in College, and no attempt was made to provide translations of the Greek and Latin quotations.

† Deutsch's firm also distributed *Art and Literature*, a literary magazine published three times a year between 1964 and 1968. Its editorial offices were in Paris, and the board consisted of Anne Dunn, Rodrigo Moynihan, Sonia Orwell and the American poet John Ashbery. 'It is infuriating that something so delicious to look at, so deliciously printed, should be so full of such utter rubbish,' Connolly told the Hobsons, but he contributed to it pieces on Olivier Larronde, Brian Howard ('Brummel at Calais') and 'Fifty Years of Little Magazines'.

Rylands had written to his 'Dear Chum of Far Away and Long Ago' to say that he had no letters or photographs to contribute, Connolly told Bill Davis how eager he was to press ahead with 'Jean's mausoleum', and urged Annie to remember everything she could about their wedding.

Although Connolly's epistolary autobiography remained a chimera, his lifelong passion for lists, for ranking friends and books and lovers in order of preference, in the manner of a school report, was combined with his love of literature in a curious little book entitled *The Modern Movement 1880–1950*. It consisted of a chronological listing of the hundred 'key' books which, in Connolly's opinion, had influenced, or constituted, the 'Modern Movement'; each entry was accompanied by a brief resumé-cum-critique and supplemented with a detailed if erratic bibliography, the work of a professional librarian, and the book was published as part of Deutsch's Grafton Library, a series normally reserved for the dustier reaches of librarianship. Once again, getting the book into production proved a nightmare. 'Cyril is doing the maddening thing he *always* does, namely disappearing to the South of France two days before the proofs reach us,' Max Martyn, Hamilton's production director, told Deutsch: 'This is one of the most troublesome books I have handled for some time.' Overcome by feelings of self-disgust, Connolly couldn't bear to read the proofs, and asked David Pryce-Jones to look them over for him; but since the main text, which occupied just over 90 pages in the published version, consisted of short self-contained items, the opportunities for altering on proof were limitless, and it was hardly surprising that revised galleys were needed before moving on to page proofs. Deborah Rogers blenched when Connolly showed her the first set of galleys, in which titles had been removed or replaced at the last minute, but somehow it found its way into print. The book was dedicated to Maurice Bowra, a gesture which, the dedicatee told him, 'fills me with delight and pride and gratitude'. 'I can't tell you how impressed I am by yr book ... Your summaries of the books are *masterly*,' John Betjeman wrote to him:

> You know, it's worth your having stuck to criticism and weekly journalism as you have, just because of this book. Without the painful training journalism is, you would never have been able to write so concisely and clearly and *readably*. But behind all that, there's your calm, uncompromising honest judgement. Oh, you dear old thing ...

But for all Betjeman's warm words, Connolly dreaded the critics' reactions. 'I tried to encourage him,' Anthony Hobson noted in his diary: ' "The book," I said, judiciously, meaning it of course nicely, "will be in a way the fruit of forty years' reviewing." "That's what they'll all say," Cyril snapped.' Much was made by the reviewers of Connolly's decision to include only books written in languages he could read – French and English, in other words – and to exclude translations and works of history or philosophy: a guide to the 'modern' which included John Betjeman and Evelyn Waugh at the expense of Pasternak or Kafka seemed, inevitably, a shade eccentric. Philip Toynbee in the *Observer* was far kinder than most:

> Mr Connolly's choice is both eccentric and severe. His language is as vivid and personal as ever. His book is not only brilliant but delightful. *The Modern Movement* reveals the heart and mind of a man who is a dandy but not a lightweight; of a lover of good books who knows that good books do more than entertain us; of an aesthete with a tragic sense of life; in short, of an amateur in the old and best sense of the word.

For several critics, though, Connolly's book was a mildly embarrassing joke or a kind of party game. Writing in the *Spectator*, John Davenport – after noting correctly that 'all Mr Connolly's best writing has been to a large extent autobiographical' – suggested that this particular offering shouldn't be taken too seriously, though 'it provides a splendid foundation for a house-party game or a weekend competition.' The *TLS*'s reviewer felt that 'what Mr Connolly has written is not a list: it is a Bloomsbury ghost story, a book of reminiscence, a restatement of old faiths': trying to be both a guide and a personal statement, 'it will be torn to shreds by any non-English critic, and the reputation of English criticism – particularly non-academic criticism – with it.' Anthony Powell berated his school-fellow for excluding languages he couldn't read, and charged him with 'preaching his own private literary religion rather than examining all the miracles available'; Karl Miller, in the *New Statesman*, while conceding that the book was 'affectionate, provocative and entertaining', referred to 'Mr Connolly's parlour-game' as a kind of 'Desert Island Books', and – more seriously – queried the inclusion of works like *Goodbye to All That* and *Animal Farm* which, though good in themselves, seemed to have little to do with the Modern Movement as such. But the most damning critique of all was provided by Frank Kermode, the epitome (one imagines) of the kind of academic critic Connolly most feared, and most affected to disdain. The book was 'light, bright, superficially stylish': it was also, Kermode suggested, badly written, lacking in intellectual rigour, and crammed with elementary howlers ('Little Gitting' for 'Little Gidding', 'The *calm* of evening, Lissadell' for the *light*, and so on). Connolly's accompanying comments were 'deplorable'; and as for defining modernism, 'his book will add confusion where there is enough already.'

Altogether less contentious was an exhibition at the National Book League that autumn of 'Treasures from Private Libraries in England'. Lenders included the Queen and the Dukes of Devonshire and Wellington, and Anthony Hobson persuaded one of the organisers to approach Connolly about his collection of first editions. He happily obliged, and his treasured books were reverentially laid out in a glass case under the title 'Homage to the Twenties'. That August Hobson had taken their two families to Annecy. They played Scrabble in the evenings, and made a foursome at tennis. Unconventionally clad in matching Hawaiian shirt and shorts, white socks and brown shoes, Connolly proved unexpectedly good on the court, 'with a twisted, idiosyncratic but wickedly effective service'. Deirdre complained that he tended to steal her shots, but 'Cyril wouldn't bend; he was looking particularly Sheridanish in his Hawaiian outfit, like a malevolent Niebelung.' Connolly was supposed to be editing for Alan Ross the diaries of Harry Crosby, the American poet and publisher who had committed suicide in 1929,* and he told them that he would have liked, above all, to belong to the *haute bohème* of Paris in the late 1920s; and they went to see a survivor from that world, Laurence Vail, at his chalet in Megève. Now aged seventy-four, Vail looked – according to Hobson – like 'a little old bird', with a 'small head, big beak, a tuft of white hair sticking up at the back, green corduroy jacket and white corduroy trousers.' '"He doesn't look as if he could have taken someone's wife away, does he?" Cyril said afterwards'; but he found the memory of his last visit there, to see Jean not long before she died, 'almost unbearably painful'. But the half-pleasurable melancholy induced by the past was more than made up for by the pleasures of family and home. As Cressida grew older, he enjoyed her company more and more – while remaining uncomfortably aware that she knew all too well the workings of his mind. She was precociously keen on dancing, boys and buying clothes, and had no compunction about making her presence felt. 'We intend to unite against the bullying of Cressida,' her father told Barbara: every now and then she would appear with a scrap of paper and say 'Here's your cheque for a million pounds today, Daddy, now be good and don't spend it.'

Despite the poor reception of *The Modern Movement*, Connolly found himself attracting an increased amount of attention. He was interviewed on the radio by Tom Rosenthal, and on television by Jonathan Miller in a series entitled 'Doubts and Certainties'; he became a regular participant in a

* Despite a vigorous correspondence with Harry Crosby's widow, Caresse, nothing ever came of the edited diaries. Equally abortive was a plan for Connolly to provide a 5000-word introduction plus captions for a book of photographs by Gisèle Freund of James Joyce, his family and friends in Paris in the 1920s: the contract between author and photographer was cancelled in March 1964, and Connolly was paid $275 for the work he had done. Ed Victor, a young editorial director at Jonathan Cape, tried to revive the idea of Connolly introducing a book of photographs – this time of 'classic authors' – but to no avail.

televised literary quiz called 'Take It or Leave It', devised by Brigid Brophy and chaired by Melvyn Bragg, who found him courteous, funny and extremely competent;* he took part in radio tributes to – among others – Evelyn Waugh and T.S. Eliot; he made his choice of 'Desert Island Discs', selecting – *inter alia* – 'Malagueña', some Hungarian gypsy music, and extracts from *Pelléas et Mélisande*, *The Rake's Progress* and *The Marriage of Figaro*, and nominating *A la recherche du temps perdu* as his book and a 'foam-rubber sleeping-bag' as his luxury item; he took part in a television programme about George Orwell and was filmed lying back on the grass on Beachy Head together with Malcolm Muggeridge, their white hair blowing in the wind; he lunched at *Private Eye*. In the *New Statesman* Weekend Competition, Kingsley Amis suggested 'the usual prizes' for a dinner-party conversation between Connolly and one of his favourite authors: he declared most entries 'disappointing', but the runner-up was the American biographer and critic Richard Ellmann, who the following month wrote a long and thoughtful review of *Previous Convictions* in *Encounter*. 'No other contemporary writer has made so ebullient a career out of being dispirited,' he suggested, and he ended with the most inspiriting of tributes:

> A major virtue of Connolly's prose can be stated negatively: it does not bore us, it does not flatter, it parades no pomposities. The mandarin dialect blends subtly with the vernacular. This voice so civilised and undeceived, so convivial for all its bleak awareness, is one of the ornaments – baroque verging on rococo – of contemporary criticism, as well as one of the few solaces of Sunday morning in London.

Two years later, in January 1966, Connolly was the subject of another long re-evaluation in *Encounter*, this time by John Wain. ' "Why are so many people in England down on Cyril Connolly?" Edmund Wilson asked me, really wanting to know, when I first met him in 1957,' his piece began: Connolly 'must be reckoned our most successful literary columnist', yet his 'work *does* tend, in England, to be dismissed with a patronising judgement, often by people who are obviously nothing like as sensitive, witty, and

* The make-up worn by those appearing on television was far thicker and more glutinous then than now: Melvyn Bragg remembers that Connolly often refused to have it removed after the show was over, since he enjoyed the idea of appearing in his make-up on the commuter train home. He remembers, too, how Connolly lost his self-consciousness about his looks when appearing on television; and how encouraging he was to a young writer, taking Bragg into Brown's Hotel lobby after bumping into him in Piccadilly in order to discuss his new novel, *A Hired Man*. (Angus Wilson was a fellow-panellist on one occasion, and although Connolly had a low opinion of his later work, he brought copies of his books into the studio for signature.) Connolly also befriended the television reporter Richard Kershaw after the break-up of his marriage to Venetia Murray, recommending him as a reviewer to Jack Lambert and agreeing to take part in a full-length television interview with him.

informed as he is, and there must be some reason for it.' One reason for this, Wain suggested, was that Connolly liked to portray himself as a reluctant critic, a 'Failed Writer' who had become a critic *faute de mieux*; and this self-deprecating attitude was unlikely to go down well with important professionals like Dr Leavis or the American New Critics, for whom criticism was a skill and a craft in itself, and one that called for no apologies.* And, to make matters worse, he was – like Lord David Cecil – 'popular and admired among people who are the enemies of genuine discrimination and hard thinking'. Connolly was enjoyed because he 'makes epigrams and comes out with dashing judgements', and he was also rather slapdash. His obsession with the obstacles that stand in the way of the writer 'is a more serious theme than his detractors allow', and in *The Unquiet Grave* 'the problems of the writer are seen as part of the whole predicament of modern man, the argument goes much deeper, and the passion which infuses the whole book raises it to the level of a work of real literary art':

> The book has a genuinely tragic element because the author convinces us of his passionate belief in art and also of his despair, his conviction that the world has wandered away from health and sanity and therefore necessarily from art, which demands both vision and confidence.

Dr Leavis and Connolly were 'generally supposed to represent the two opposite poles in contemporary English criticism', yet Leavis shared Connolly's suspicion of the modern world, and 'would surely agree that "the true function of a writer is to produce a masterpiece".' The difference between the two 'is that the one says it with a tear, the other with a frown'. Both men tended to turn their backs on what was being written at the present time: Leavis simply refused to read modern writers, whereas Connolly 'evidently makes it a policy to avoid reviewing any but the most marginal books'. His spiritual homes were in the past, and on the shores of the Mediterranean, but 'these notes on Mr Connolly are not intended as an obituary. He may seem, at present, to have withdrawn from anything like an active struggle to maintain quality; but he has energy, and knowledge, and above all he has generosity. He may yet surprise us.'

*

* One academic who was surprised and displeased by Connolly was Mario Praz, author of the highly esteemed *The Romantic Agony* and the Professor of English at Rome University. Connolly had observed of his most recent work, *The House of Life*, that 'alas Professor Praz's book might be retitled "The House of Death-in-Life" – for it is one of the dullest I have ever read; it has a bravura of boredom, an audacity of *ennui* that makes one hardly believe one's eyes.' Praz was understandably unamused, and wrote to his assailant in *ad hominem* terms:

Deirdre's son Simon was now at Eton, and – or so he assured Noël Blakiston – Connolly dreaded having to revisit his old school, for the first time since he had called in there with André Gide: *Enemies of Promise* had not gone down well with more conventional Etonians, and he half-expected some furious beak to summon him into his study for a wigging or worse. Drue Heinz made available her house near Ascot and, greatly daring, Connolly made his way to Eton, with Deirdre beside him to lend moral support. Much to his relief, nothing untoward happened; and for the remainder of Simon Craven's time at the school the Connollys made an annual visit on St Andrew's Day, in November – the Fourth of June was reserved for Simon's father, Jonty Craven – staying at the Old House Hotel in Windsor. Connolly was invited, by Fram Dinshaw, then a boy at the school, to address the Literary Society;* he contributed an article on the *Eton Candle* to a short-lived school magazine; and he proudly posed for photographs with Simon, resplendent in a shimmering Pop waistcoat.

He ventured rather further afield in the spring of 1966, when the *Sunday Times* sent him to Jamaica and the Bahamas. Deirdre, who disliked flying and the heat, stayed at home; Connolly, who liked to get away from England in the winter, found himself, once again, nervous in the air, clutching an improving volume – the sayings of Marcus Aurelius – in case he should be called upon to meet his Maker. In Jamaica he stayed with his former pupil, Charles Da Costa, who remembered his old tutor with fondness; in Nassau he ran out of reading matter and had to fight his way through the only book in the house – *The Cult of Softness*, by the octogenarian Arnold Lunn, a sustained attack on the abolition of the death penalty, homosexual law reform and many of the other liberal causes that Connolly had espoused in person and in print.

Connolly's liberal sympathies were perfectly compatible with royal infatuation, and he was suitably flattered when Princess Margaret sought him out at a party given for a book of photographs by Lord Snowdon: 'I felt like a large dog trying to amuse someone who may not be a dog-lover,' he told the Hobsons. After dreaming that the Princess had given him a castle, he

---

Suppose you had written a book about all the menus of your gastronomic tours through which you have dulled your brain: would I have enjoyed it? Decidedly not...

No doubt you would have wallowed in a psychoanalytical autobiography, and I have disappointed you. But you have disappointed me. Who would have thought that the author of *The Unquiet Grave* would have descended to such journalese as the cheap oxymoron 'fulminating cliché'?

Once at a PEN Congress in Vienna I saw you nearly crying about nothing (some disappointing dish, I think). I imagine what an amount of tears you must have shed in consequence of the uncongenial task to which my book has put you. I am sorry.

* It was, Fram Dinshaw remembers, a cold, raw day, and Connolly was shivering when they met; later he insisted that he was trembling, as though he was still under some ancient Etonian interdiction.

met her again in the summer of 1967, when he and Maurice Bowra replaced Roy Jenkins and his family as Ann Fleming's house-guests in Sardinia. The Snowdons and the Aga Khan came to stay nearby, with the result that – as Ann Fleming explained to the Duchess of Devonshire – 'Cyril made fearfully restless by vicinity of Snowdons, saying not to meet them was like being in Garden of Eden without seeing God! Local tycoon then called and invited me to dine with "Margaret and Tony". Cyril distraught!' The problem was explained to the tycoon, and Ann Fleming was allowed to bring her house-guests with her. She then invited the tycoon and the Snowdons back, and Connolly's excitement rose to fever pitch:

> Next morning Cyril rises at 11.30 and asks what I have ordered special for lunch, I say nothing since I can only communicate with Italians in deaf and dumb language, he scowls and says did I notice what the Princess drank last night, I say no, he says it was white wine and martinis and may he go to the hotel for the right stuff. I say yes, and have to pay enormous bill . . .

The lunch was a great success, and afterwards Bowra entertained them with a selection of First World War songs while Connolly joined the Princess in the swimming-pool, 'Cyril looking like a blissful hippo!' But life seemed very dull thereafter: 'It would be OK without Cyril who complains of mosquitoes, food and climate, and only wants royalty and money; now he has met the Snowdons he dreams of being invited on the Aga's yacht saying wistfully "But if I was, I might be expected to act charades on water-skis!" '

Connolly combined high life in Sardinia with a trip to Rapallo to meet Ezra Pound, for whose work he had acquired a belated passion. 'I now regard my failure to have met Yeats or even Pound and profited by their company as one of the worst mistakes in a lifetime hung with them,' he had recently complained to Maurice Bowra, and now the *Sunday Times* was offering him the chance to put things right; his self-confidence was boosted by the fact that Olga Rudge, Pound's mistress, had recently informed Faber & Faber – his publishers – that Connolly was the one person to whom he would entrust a new selection of his work. Connolly later recalled the poet as a 'serenely happy old man', conjuring up fond memories of their eating fish soup and risotto at Torcello and rabbit in an open-air restaurant above Rapallo: more immediately, though, he was unnerved by the old man's disconcerting silences and cold blue eyes, a discomfiture which inspired him to a fine flight of self-laceration:

> When we met he held my hand for a long time and fixed me with this penetrating gaze while I felt layers of ugliness and insincerity peeling off

> like an onion revealing even deeper layers of ugliness and insincerity within. In another moment I felt sure the ultimate 'nada' would be reached and the onion dissolve on the floor. My whole face was by now one hideous simper (I am an eye-evader at the best of times), and I withdrew my hand and turned away...

The simpering over, and the onion itself again, he read Pound his *London Magazine* essay on 'The Breakthrough in Modern Verse', in which the poet's key role in the making of modern poetry was vividly set forth. Back in Sussex, he corresponded vigorously with 'Mr Pound' and Olga Rudge about signed copies and first editions and the meaning of 'Mauberley', took up the cause of Pound's poetical protégé Basil Bunting – reviewing *Briggflatts* enthusiastically and vainly urging its claims when a Duff Cooper Prize judge – and elaborated his new variation on a familiar excuse:

> If only I had met you when I was at Eton and Oxford – in an hotel in Granada like I met the Sitwells, or in Montparnasse like I met Sylvia Beach, Ernest Hemingway and Joyce – then I might have been a poet myself, instead of pulling the roller over the pitch once a week.

Two years later Connolly visited Pound again, in Venice, on his eighty-fourth birthday: he had hoped to bring Deirdre and Cressida with him, but Deirdre's mother was unwell, and he went alone. Pound seemed younger and less depressed than before, but he was even more silent, and all the conversation was channelled through Olga Rudge. Pound asked his visitor to translate some Virgil for him, staring through his 'mild blue eyes' while Connolly – after getting off to a flying start – ground to a halt on the word *patulae*, and then began to flounder. Mercifully, lunch intervened, but the whole business proved something of an ordeal: writing to Olga Rudge on his return, Connolly apologised for having written so much about himself in his *Sunday Times* article, but 'I couldn't remember enough of what EP said.'

Exhausting in a rather different way was a trip he made for the *Sunday Times* in the winter of 1967 to Kenya and Uganda. Seen from the air, the green lushness of Uganda seemed like an intimation of Eden; and after having his buttonhole confiscated at Entebbe Airport – the importation of plants was forbidden – he set off for the Queen Elizabeth Park, on the mountainous border with the Congo. Once again, he took particular pleasure in the elephants, noting how 'their droppings are like enormous *vol-au-vents*', while the 'hippos with their huge piggy faces and terrier ears are the pyknic's dream of supreme sensual fulfilment.' He visited Ruwenzori with its volcanoes and the Murchison Falls, and had a close shave with a bull elephant, before moving on to Nairobi. Mollie and General Brooke had spent some time in East Africa before settling in South Africa, and their ghosts were all about: he visited some white settlers in the Kakuru area, 'postmark of so many old letters from cousins and aunts growing roses while "Jim" went out to shoot the mamba, lioness, Nandi Bear or whatever it is that's mucking up the drive', dined at the Muthaiga Club, gave a farewell cocktail party to which only three people came, bumped into Billy Collins the publisher, who shared his passion for African wildlife, sweated horribly in Mombasa, and flew in a small plane to Tree Tops, the animal observatory where the Queen had learned of the death of her father. 'Most exhausting trip by Land Rover, launch, one-engined planes. Never more than two nights in one place and that only twice,' he told Jack Lambert. The germ was planted for his impending obsession with the murder of Lord Erroll and the decadent denizens of Happy Valley, but for the time being it was the animals that mattered most. 'The animals and the parks are like museums and churches to the traveller in Italy,' he declared: 'A day without them is a day wasted, and the further one gets from their innocent world of co-operation and wonder the more ordinary life becomes – a dull matter of politics, greed and business like everywhere else.'

Back in England, in the meantime, the Connollys had decided that the time had come to make a move from Bushey – Lord Gage wanted to use it for one of his farm managers, the noise of cattle was becoming too much, and so too was driving Cressida to school. This meant that Connolly was able to indulge in house-hunting, the most romantic pursuit of all; or, as Deirdre put it, taking him out in his pram. Probate of Mollie's will had been cleared at last, and they were in a position to buy a house of their own. Once again, they started with Georgian rectories, and worked their way down, with Connolly displaying a preference for Voysey houses and Edwardian golf clubs, with sandy soil and rhododendrons by the door; the house had to be large enough to house his library, and allow for the slamming of doors. 'All my life I have wanted passionately to own a house,' Connolly told his readers in a piece entitled 'Confessions of a House-hunter': 'I have never owned anything larger than a book-case. I have been house-hungry now for some forty years without setting eyes on a title-deed.'* The Isle of Wight, which he had gazed at from Big Chilling, and where Philip Toynbee had a

* Connolly's house-hunting – and the problems of paying for a dream house – inspired in him a limerick:

There once was an eminent thinca
Who set his proud heart on a finca
He bunged in a cheque
To the owner on speque
And the bank bunged it back with a stinca.

house, was favoured for a time; he dreamed of buying Lady Monckton's Jacobean rectory at Folkington, in the Downs behind Eastbourne; Ireland seemed attractive now that the Irish Government had exempted writers from income tax, and in the summer of 1968 they took Cressida and Simon on a motoring holiday in Cork and Kerry, the children writhing on the back seat *en route* to Elizabeth Bowen's house in Kinsale. But by then it was already too late. Schools and shops and quiet and the feel of a pavement underfoot were what really mattered now; and the move, when they finally made it, was – in terms of distance at least – a modest and local affair, to a place in which Connolly had spent some of his formative and, at times, unhappiest years.

TWENTY-THREE

Eastbourne Revisited

'The more I think of it,' John Betjeman had written to Connolly in the winter of 1967,

> the more sure I am that you should move into a seaside town and that the provincial town with schools, concerts, theatre, films and large enough to escape bores and small enough to find silence and country, is the right way of life left for us. Eastbourne for ever . . .

The following January Connolly had lunch with Anthony Hobson at Brooks's, and told him that he had bought No. 48, St John's Road, Eastbourne. 'All the visions of Nash *cottages ornées* have faded,' he told his host – adding, touchingly, that he could see the sea from the top-floor windows of his new home. Hobson's instinctive reaction was that Connolly would be a 'lion domesticated': but although many of his friends found it odd that he should have chosen to settle in a suburban street in a genteel seaside resort best known for its large contingent of maiden aunts subsisting on modest private incomes, Betjeman was, unsurprisingly, all in favour. 'If one wants quiet and fresh air and country near,' he wrote,

> your house in Eastbourne with its sloping garden down to trees at the back, cliffs and a chapel of ease on the other side of the road, those wide, comfortable well-built late Victorian rooms housing your books, are much better than pigging it in the country down rutty, muddy lanes and miles from a letter-box, a shop and schools for the children. Eastbourne is the right place for a man of letters.

No. 48 was – still is – a large, solid-looking mid-Victorian house built of brick and flint, with a touch of North Oxford *sur mer* about it. At one end of the street loomed the Downs, where sixty years before the young Connolly had gathered blackberries and puffed along on school runs; at the other twinkled the sea, bright blue in summer – Eastbourne claims to be the sunniest spot in England, sheltered by the great bulk of Beachy Head from the prevailing south-westerly winds – and a lugubrious grey when the sun went in. Although much of Eastbourne belonged to the Duke of Devonshire, the house had been bought for £14,000 out of Mollie's legacy from a Miss Sanderson of the wallpaper firm. John Craxton – who shared Betjeman's enthusiasm for Eastbourne – had suggested that they should buy the ugliest house they could find; but if No. 48 was no beauty, it was far from unattractive, as well as being the kind of roomy, light, well-proportioned house that is easy and pleasant to live in. It had more rooms than Bushey, including a conservatory to house Connolly's collection of exotic plants and, in due course, a vine laden with black grapes; spare bedrooms for when guests came to stay, and for Sarah and Simon in their school holidays; a comfortable sitting-room with, over the mantelpiece, a painting by Alexander Cozens, a gift from Jennifer Fry; and a library lit by a chandelier and crammed with reference books and manuscripts and the all-important, glass-fronted 'Controls': Anthony Hobson noted how 'first editions, half-hidden in cellophane bags to protect their fragile dust-wrappers, occupied shelves along two walls like a petrified forest.' The Connollys moved house in April 1968. 'It is a great trauma to have to uproot oneself and all one's belongings after nine years and move again,' Connolly told Leonard Russell, but 'Eastbourne is heaven.' Cressida was the one who seemed saddest to leave Bushey, but Connolly felt only 'the relief of getting away from the mud and the flies and the inaccessibility'; and he enjoyed the mundane chores of moving house, to the extent that even installing oil-fired central heating 'awakens perfectionism'. He liked Eastbourne's cake and tea shops, Bondolfi's in particular, and so too did Cressida; there was a first-class fruiterer nearby and some equally good china shops in which to browse, as well as some excellent second-hand bookshops; Brighton, with its theatre, was within striking distance, and Lewes provided a neutral ground on which to meet friends like Alan Ross; and, most importantly, the station was to hand for his weekly visits to London. Musing on the apparent incongruity of the 'Man of Pleasure' – as he often referred to his old friend – having settled in Eastbourne, Peter Quennell suspected that

> he welcomed the opportunity of leading yet again an interestingly difficult, though nicely balanced double life, shuttling between Eastbourne and London, and changing the *persona* he assumed en route, from the family man to the adventurous man-of-the-world as he approached Victoria Station, and back to the book-laden bread-winner when he caught the six o'clock train.

Connolly's London expeditions might include – say – lunch at White's or the grander kind of publisher's party,* but their *raison d'être* was strictly professional. Like any good journalist, he was utterly reliable about such matters as meeting deadlines and writing to length; and, like most journalists, he worked best to a deadline. He was, for the most part, scrupulous about doing his homework for his weekly review, reading an author's earlier works and some background material before putting pen to paper, but the actual writing tended to be crammed in at the very last minute. Every Tuesday afternoon his copy – written out by hand on sheets of blue Basildon Bond, or on White's headed paper – would be put on the train at Eastbourne station, met at Victoria by a man on a motor-bike, and whisked away to the *Sunday Times*, where Jack Lambert or one of his assistants – John Whitley or Michael Ratcliffe or Jon Peter – would improve his vestigial or non-existent punctuation before having it typed up by a secretary adept at deciphering his elegant, spidery scrawl, and sent down to the composing-room to be set up in galley proof. Early on in their relationship Jack Lambert, greatly daring, raised the possibility of making some minor alterations and was urged to go ahead, but despite this *carte blanche* his wrath could be terrible if changes were made of which he disapproved. 'I should like to know (1) who altered the first sentence of my review (2) why (3) why I was not consulted. I cannot possibly write if such liberties are to be taken,' he protested on one occasion: whoever was responsible had resorted to clichés 'which I would never use and which reflect the general soapy timidity of the other parts of the paper.' 'Who was responsible for inserting that blood-curdling grammatical howler into the first sentence of my review?' he demanded after 'two facts' had acquired a singular verb: 'the thought of what people must think of such carelessness quite ruined all my pleasure in what I felt was a good piece . . . I can only think the motive was SABOTAGE.'

Unless he happened to be abroad – in which case enormous ingenuity was expended in getting review copies to him, while his copy, scribbled on hotel notepaper, would often hitch a lift home with a returning traveller – Connolly regularly followed his copy into the *Sunday Times* on the day after its arrival, correcting his proofs, rewriting on galley and, if needs be, cutting lines and words to fit the space available.† Every Wednesday morning he traded in his comfortable country clothes for a merchant banker's

* Like that given by Jock Murray, to celebrate John Betjeman's knighthood, at 50 Albermarle Street, followed by dinner at White's given by Sir Harry d'Avigdor-Goldsmid: the guests included Connolly, Alan Pryce-Jones, Christopher Sykes, Patrick Kinross, Maurice Bowra, John Sparrow, Ran Antrim and Alan Ross.

† Lambert noted how sensitive he was to the sneers of academics and the envy of other literary journalists: if he had to cut, he tended – to Lambert's regret – to trim his own jokes, in case they 'should give ammunition to those jealous puritans only too eager to dismiss him as a fraud.'

chalk-striped or grey flannel double-breasted suit and, in winter, an overcoat and dark felt hat, and boarded the London train. After lunch at White's, perhaps, he would take the tube to Holborn and walk up the Gray's Inn Road to the *Sunday Times*'s offices. An incongruous figure in that bleak world of strip lighting and grey metal filing cabinets and functional furniture, he would – unless in one of his bad moods – greet the inhabitants of the books pages in a friendly manner, take his proofs to the corner of a spare desk, and settle down to work. His proofs dealt with in a suitably professional way – he seemed perfectly amenable to criticisms and suggestions – he would choose himself a new book for review by the following Tuesday: some diplomacy might be called for if he and Raymond Mortimer both wanted to review a book on eighteenth-century France, though Mortimer tended to be more conventionally 'literary', but while Lambert would sometimes try to steer a book in the direction of his star reviewer, the choice of next week's lead title was usually arrived upon rather than dictated. With business done, he would sometimes talk in general about books and writers, conducting a kind of *ad hoc* seminar as practised by Desmond MacCarthy and Raymond Mortimer on the old *New Statesman*; and, if in buoyant mood, mention of a particular friend or incident would – according to Jack Lambert – send him off into one of

> those celebrated cadenzas which, beginning with a crisp statement of (let us hope) fact, developed effortlessly into an emphatic imitation and so spiralled up into fantasy, slander piled on slander, a grain of truth expanding into a ballooning moon of fantasy, his thick body ducking and swinging, his rubber face creased with laughter, assuming identity after identity while remaining ever his own.

'I suppose what every journalist asks for is appreciation and security,' he wrote in 1972; and the *Sunday Times* provided both, as well as a welcome sense of continuity: 'fearful changes and catastrophes may have taken place in our private lives, death's make-up men pencil more wrinkles on our brow or sprinkle our heads with dusting powder, wives leave us, friends forsake us, children come and go, but the rooms on the fifth floor still bulge with new books, resound with jokes and greetings.' It might well be that 'my funeral, should it fall on a Tuesday, will be remarkable for a hand holding an article thrusting itself out of my coffin,' but even if he remained in harness to the very end,

> there are very few jobs like mine: I wish there were more – it keeps me still learning; it forces me to be just (so much harder than being merciful), it

> keeps me humble, for there is nothing I write that might not be used to light a fire a few hours later; when better writers are neglected I am groomed and cosseted; I love books, I am paid to read them; when people commiserate with me on my weekly grind I thank them but I know that without it the duns would long have been picking my bones.*

'Not generally considered a happy man, here I have found happiness,' he told his colleagues; and hardly had he moved into St John's Road before they provided him with 'one of the happiest weeks of my life' by sending him to Tanzania, which he had missed on his last East African trip. He was flown out as a guest of Swissair – travelling first-class – leaving on 2 May and returning nine days later. In Nairobi he seized the opportunity to learn more about his latest 'King Charles's Head' – the murder of Lord Erroll in 1941 – but, once again, his real passion was reserved for the wildlife, and for the scenery of north-west Tanzania. He met Ernest Hemingway's son Pat, then working as a game warden, flew into the Ngorogoro Crater, picnicked with George Schaller in Serengeti National Park, and dreamed that he was showing Princess Margaret round No. 48 ('"But why must we go in by the kitchen?" "Because it is the best room in the house, ma'am"').

In September he turned sixty-five: 'My birthday passed off with support from Joan, Maurice Bowra, Elizabeth Bowen. I am now officially senile.' One of the things that had given him most pleasure in these recent years had been the revival of his old friendship with Maurice Bowra. While living at Bushey, he had conquered his ancient aversion to Oxford, and dined with the Warden in Wadham. 'I felt like Adam re-admitted to Eden as an old lag,' he told his host: 'One reason I have kept away from Oxford is that I can't bear it unless I stay with you, and if I stay with you I am afraid I will get on your nerves.' He had even enjoyed strolling round Balliol with his old companion, and 'Perhaps we have forgiven each other.' They had, and Bowra added Bushey – and later No. 48 – to his annual peregrination, which included staying with the Clarks at Saltwood, with the Leigh Fermors in Greece, and with Isaiah Berlin in Portofino. Deirdre remembers him as an ideal guest, whose only unorthodox request was that they should stop the ticking of the grandfather clock for as long as he was with them.

One friendship was restored but, a year later, another hung in the balance. Anne Dunn was now living in Provence with her second husband, Rodrigo Moynihan; but although Connolly was far more jealous of Moynihan than he ever had been of Michael Wishart – and Moynihan, for his part, found Connolly a terrifying figure – the Connollys were frequent visitors to the

* What he really hated, though, was when well-meaning people asked 'Tell me, Mr Connolly, what are you *really* writing at the moment – I don't mean your newspaper pieces . . .'

Domaine de St. Estève, and more than once he spent his birthday there. There too was Barbara Skelton, who had now moved back from New York, and was living in a farmhouse at Grimaud, in the South of France, where Connolly had visited her on his way back from Sardinia two years before. Barbara had now written a novel, *A Love Match*, which not only included a vivid account of life in Oak Cottage with Connolly, lightly disguised as a French writer called Claude Boursin – 'all the Elmstead part is still so raw and near to me that I can't tell what effect it will have on someone else,' he told her – but also Provençal scenes set in the Domaine de St. Migraine, the denizens of which were ungratefully referred to as the 'Meal Tickets'. Alan Ross had agreed to publish the novel under his London Magazine Editions imprint, but Barbara sent it first to Connolly for his opinion.* He later told Anthony Hobson that he had hated it, but had passed it on to Ross without comment; either way, the Moynihans were unamused, and wrote angrily to Alan Ross about it, as did Stephen Spender. Connolly told Anne Dunn that what Barbara had written seemed fairly harmless – for his part, he was used to being 'lampooned, put into books and betrayed by my friends' – but he was held to be partly responsible, and he was accused of 'whitewashing' her libels by appearing to give the book his blessing. Harmony was eventually restored, and *A Love Match*'s brief outing was terminated when John Sutro threatened to sue both author and publisher; but he too seems to have held Connolly partly to blame, asking Roy Harrod to inform the Committee of the Beafsteak Club that he would instantly resign if Connolly were ever elected a member.†

Encouraging Barbara's writing was all very well – if hazardous at times – but little progress was made with his own. He introduced, for the Bodley Head, a selection of photographs by Bill Brandt, some of whose wartime work he had published in *Horizon*; he wrote a preface to a privately printed memoir of the d'Avigdor-Goldsmids' daughter, Sarah, who had drowned at the age of twenty-one; his translation of Jarry's play *Ubu Roi*, first published in *Horizon*, was included in a collection of 'Ubu' plays edited by Simon Watson Taylor for Methuen, and went on to earn him more in royalties than any of his other works: but all too often nothing was achieved. Penguin offered him £500 for a one-volume paperback of *Enemies of Promise* and *The*

* He was discovered by Deirdre lying on their four-poster bed, wrapped in a bath towel and reading the typescript. 'I am *so sick* of Babs being treated as though she were *Tolstoy*!' she cried, and hurled it out of the window into the snow-filled garden, the pages blowing into the next-door garden and lodging in the branches of trees. Connolly – or so it was said – failed to put the pages back in the right order, with the result that Barbara was faced with a hefty corrections bill from the printers.

† All in vain, it seems. Connolly was put up for membership of the Beefsteak the following year: he was proposed by Robin Fedden, seconded by Frank Giles and Charles Monteith, and elected in September 1971. In 1948 he had been proposed by Lord Antrim, but withdrew at his own request.

Condemned Playground provided he wrote a new 5000-word introduction, but weren't prepared to be palmed off with a piece he'd already written for the American reissue of *Enemies of Promise*; Ed Victor came down to Eastbourne to discuss the book of photographs, now devoted to expatriate writers and provisionally entitled *The Face of Genius*, but that was as far as it went; Macmillan New York added to his financial worries by demanding the return of a $2000 advance for a work mysteriously entitled 'Where Breath Must Breathe'. Most humiliating of all, perhaps, was his failure to deliver the introduction for a sequel to *Pavillons*, to be called *Pavilions of Europe*: it marked the end of his professional dealings with Hamish Hamilton, and seems to have brought the hapless photographer, Mr Zerbe, to the verge of bankruptcy and nervous exhaustion. Despite Connolly's assurances that the work was being done, tempers soon began to fray. 'As you rang off when I was in mid-sentence, I write to ask when we shall have the revised Zerbe script,' demanded a furious Hamilton, signing himself off with a curt 'yours' instead of the friendlier valedictions of days gone by. Shortly afterwards Jerome Zerbe wrote, reproachfully, to say that, as a result of Connolly's failure to deliver, Hamish Hamilton had decided not to go ahead, and Macmillan New York would almost certainly follow suit. He had visited thirteen countries at his own expense in search of pavilions, and spent a small fortune on buying film and having it processed; his doctor had warned him that a nervous breakdown was imminent; his only redress lay in suing his negligent collaborator for breach of contract. A sum of $25,000 was mentioned, but more in sorrow than anger: 'Why, oh why, didn't you do your share?' Connolly continued to promise Hamish Hamilton the introduction, but by now the iron had entered his adversary's soul, and he began to insist on repayment of the £450 advance. Unabashed, Connolly replied that he couldn't possibly repay the money, since 'I am overdrawn for ten times as much'; he would have to sell some of his possessions if Hamilton was adamant, but 'You did say "at my convenience", which I took to mean when I next received some money.'

Such insouciance displayed a certain nerve and dash, but the demoralisation that accompanies promises unkept and plans that come to nought was hard to keep at bay. 'The best one can say is that I am well paid – or only just well paid – for failing, and that I am allowed to express my true opinions,' he confided in a note to himself entitled 'Overwhelming sense of failure':* and elsewhere he observed that

* On one occasion, over drinks at Bushey, the journalist Tom Stacey suggested to his host that he could make a great deal of money by going on a lecture tour of America. 'You don't realise,' Connolly told him: 'My fundamental instinct is for failure.'

> It is a mark of failure in life to work harder as one grows older. A man of sixty who is not kept by someone else is a disgrace. My name was once a byword for idleness and sterility, but now one cannot pick up a newspaper without finding it. The prince of non-starters pulls the big roller up and down the pitch. I blame nobody but myself. I have had golden opportunities for leisure and thrown them all away and as a punishment for many years have been forced to earn my living. This narrows one's outlook and makes one hate any who escape it, for I must go on now till I drop. An inability to complete large projects prevents me from writing books, an impatience with my face and voice disbars me from radio and television, a dislike of the human animal keeps me from writing novels and plays, I have no talent for verse. I am lucky to survive, one of the few literary journalists or men of letters who is not in an institution.

Travel remained, as ever, an antidote to despair: to Cyprus for the *Sunday Times*, where the food was the only drawback; to Paris, revisiting the scenes of his youth for the benefit of his readers; to southern Greece to stay with the Leigh Fermors in the house they had built at Kardamyli, a by-product of which was an exchange of letters with his host, each outdoing the other in a fever of latinate puns and arcane references to long-forgotten figures from the classical and early Christian eras; to Provence, now blighted by motorways, oil refineries and industrial sprawl. A planned visit to Mexico had to be abandoned but – as if making up for lost exotica – he donned a pair of dark glasses for a party given by Barbara Ghika for Joan Leigh Fermor: he looked, he decided, a bit like King Farouk, displaying 'a touch of the tarboosh'. John Betjeman gave him a pair of trousers that had once belonged to Henry James, and – for the benefit of the visiting Hobsons – he modelled Lord Queensberry's white dinner jacket before breakfast. 'In this I feel invulnerable to all women,' he told them: 'In Henry James's trousers I feel invulnerable to other writers.'

But a far greater and more lasting pleasure was in store. Towards the end of 1969, Deirdre told her step-sister, Tanya Hobson, that she was pregnant: Connolly, it seemed, had been horrified at first, then delighted – and touchingly proud to be a prospective father in his late sixties. A baby boy was born the following April: it was decided that he should be called Matthew Vernon Connolly, and he was at once put down for Eton. Cressida was thrilled by the new arrival, and showed herself to be 'very maternal': John Betjeman, Anthony Hobson, Rosie d'Avigdor-Goldsmid, Sonia Orwell, Jennifer Ross, Lady Diana Cooper and – representing the younger generation – James Fox agreed to be god-parents:* Diana Cooper presented

* Ezra Pound was also approached, but Connolly's letter got lost in the post, and was eventually returned unopened. As he explained to Olga Rudge, a week before Matthew was born, Connolly had a dream in which Pound sent him a battered old hat-box containing a baby boy and a message that read 'I am sending you a *wunderkind*, his mental age is four.' Taking this as an omen, Connolly asked the poet if he

her godson with an engraved cup, on which the word 'Matthew' was missing a 't'. 'I am in a way envious, but I know that my genes are no good and that I would produce someone like Basil Murray,' Maurice Bowra wrote, adding that Wadham was about to go co-ed: 'I don't mind. I always feel that my life would have been happier if I had known any girls in my youth.' In his reply, Connolly said how overjoyed he was to have a son, though he worried about the cost of a nurse in addition to two char-women and the all-important Mr Rush, the 'boilerman/gardener' who doubled up as the signalman at Ripe crossing: in fact a Sussex neighbour, Lady Birley, had agreed to pay for a nurse for the first two months, but all the same 'I seem to be sunk in torpor all the time... I read less and less, concentrate less and less – am remembered only as a person who was at school with Orwell.'*

The notion of Connolly as a half-forgotten nonentity – never persuasive at the best of times – was belied by the army of friends who turned up at No. 48 for Matthew's christening: he had always had a genius for friendship, working hard to keep them in trim, and here was evidence of his success. Robert and Cynthia Kee travelled down from London with Robin and Susan Campbell, stopping *en route* for a picnic in Ashdown Forest: none had any idea of what a grand function awaited them, and they were amazed – and slightly disconcerted – to find the garden of No. 48 crammed with well-dressed figures clutching champagne glasses and slices of cake, and ranging from old friends like Ran Antrim and Elizabeth Bowen to Sidney Bernstein† and James Fox, clad in a banana-coloured suit. Afterwards, some eighty selected guests stayed on for a supper of egg mousse, salmon kedgeree and raspberry sorbet.

Although – like any harassed parent – Connolly complained that 'the baby is always howling, always hungry, always claiming attention,' and 'makes a noise like a Siamese cat shut in a cupboard', Matthew was his 'ray of sunshine' – 'adorable, beautiful and funny – and still in the pre-cliché stage when only laughter and gibberish pass his lips.' He would sit in the garden beside the baby's pram, watching Twinkle the guinea pig ('I love his black button eyes and neat parting and trusting independence'), and rub noses with his son, who made 'hak' noises, and seemed to embody a prelapsarian innocence: 'He has very pale yellow hair with a quiff on top,

would be a god-parent: he realised that Pound was unlikely to be able to attend the christening in person, but a message of some kind would be much appreciated ('I am sure Matthew would prefer a poem'). Apparently Pound was touched to have been asked.

* Or – as he put it on another occasion –

At Eton with Orwell, at Oxford with Waugh,
He was nobody after, and nothing before.

† The founder of Granada Television, Sidney Bernstein was anxious to promote Connolly's career as a TV performer, and liked to provide his would-be protégé with Krug champagne and expensive clarets.

huge blue eyes, rosebud mouth, domed forehead, snub nose – his smile is happiness without guile or apprehension.' 'I don't know what to do, seem incapable of action,' Connolly wrote some time later:

> – perhaps I love Matthew too much. I can't bear to miss a moment of his emergence as a person, walking, talking (still unintelligibly) – he loves to draw, trace patterns with his fingers, and above all he likes to eat; he does not kiss but butts with his head, is always cooing and smiling . . .

Among the occasional visitors to No. 48 – and the guests at the christening party – was Caroline Blackwood, now married to the American poet Robert Lowell. Connolly and Lowell greatly admired one another, and Caroline and Deirdre were childhood friends with daughters of the same age. Although Caroline remained 'a femme fatale with large green eyes, a waif-like creature who inspires romantic passion', she was – in emotional terms at least – a figure from the past, to be looked back on with a kind of sentimental nostalgia. So too was Barbara, though Connolly continued to write to her, regretting and rearranging their past, and Deirdre continued to regard her with a wary (and understandable) mixture of resentment and suspicion, seeming 'crushed and miserable' if he lunched too often with his ex-wife on her occasional visits to England. Reviewing Robert Graves's *Love Respelt*, Connolly remarked that whereas the notoriously susceptible poet apparently relished the idea of falling in love at the age of seventy, he could think of nothing worse than 'being dragged from one's books and home and siesta to watch windows, patrol pavements, demand explanations and counter-explanations, thrombosis at the telephone'; but although small children and a comfortable domesticity were inimical to 'extra-marital friendships', he was still vulnerable himself. Like many writers, he remained, in many ways, a child, demanding attention and love: children, however loved, were competition of a kind, particularly for a man so addicted to the notion of maternal love; and his occasional sense of being excluded, of being a stranger in his own home, may well have been heightened when Deirdre's garrulous, alcoholic mother came to stay, bringing with her twenty-five suitcases and an assortment of plastic bags. He was always kind to her, taking her round the antique shops, and thought her 'affectionate in a cat-like way and deeply frivolous': but he found her 'always smoking, always beefing, always yacking about herself' a heavy burden to bear.

> Yackety yack
> Yackety yack
> Fasten your ear-plugs
> Mother's back

he once wrote: towards the end of her life she came to stay almost every weekend – she had cancer of the throat, and her hospital couldn't provide radium treatment at weekends – and as her taxi drew up outside No. 48 Connolly would draw Deirdre aside and ask 'When's that woman going?'

Many years earlier, in 1957, Connolly had met, at a party, a tall, strong-featured woman with a mane of raven-black hair. Shelagh Ross-Skinner was then in her early twenties, and unmarried; he had sat down beside her and talked, and later they left the party and drove round the docks and Rotherhithe together before she dropped him back home in Chesham Place. The following day they met for lunch in a pub in Lowndes Square: he impressed her with his patience, his kindness and his wit, as well as with the number of sausages he ate. Connolly was then in an emotional limbo: things might have gone further, but Shelagh – unsure of what he really wanted – backed off and went to live in America. In 1963 she married a much older man named Arthur Levita; five years later she invited the Connollys to a party she was giving in London, and since it happened to be on a Wednesday, Connolly came to it after his session at the *Sunday Times*. He took to visiting her on his weekly trips to London for the paper, and they made several trips abroad together; arranging when and where to meet revived his love for secrecy and plotting and intrigue – stealing down the road from No. 48 to ring her from a phone box, making sure they were never seen in company together, discreetly liaising at London Airport. Although very few of his friends knew about Shelagh – the first person he told was Diana Campbell-Gray, an old friend from Yeoman's Row days who had been briefly married to Bob Boothby, and married Lord Gage after the death of his wife – Connolly was unable to resist that fatal, familiar urge to confess. 'I can't bear to hurt Deirdre, nor can I stand either her grief or her rages . . . and I am frightened of losing my home, children, possessions,' he admitted, yet for all that he refused to give Shelagh up, 'having unleashed what is obviously a "grande passion" for which one of course is grateful too.' Deirdre, also, wanted above all else to protect her family and children, dreading the break-up of another marriage while resenting the fact that Shelagh seemed to be getting life's treats – visits to art galleries and cinemas, holidays abroad – while she kept the fort at home. For six years her life was made a misery by Connolly's affair, and the fact of her being so much younger than her husband made the insult worse; at some stage Connolly had another telephone line installed, of which only Shelagh knew the number, and Deirdre came to dread the click of the receiver being put back on its stand at the sound of her approach. As for Shelagh, 'People say she is dull, but she is interested in Yours Truly, which is what Yours Truly wants,' Connolly is supposed to have told Sonia Orwell, but there was no doubting his affection for her: he enjoyed her company a great deal, and liked teaching her things and suggesting books she should read, and she had the additional advantage of being rich enough to pay for herself, but 'even at the best of times it's often only tea and oat cakes': Arthur Levita had throat cancer, and 'whenever I see S., we talk of nothing but what he can swallow, what she can do...'

From time to time Connolly and Shelagh would travel down on the train together from Victoria, ideally in a first-class carriage: she would get out at Lewes and go back to London, and he would travel on to Eastbourne. When Shelagh was with him, Connolly made it clear to his fellow-commuters that he expected to be left alone. Among them was a stockbroker named Tim Jones, who lived in an eighteenth-century rectory in Berwick, a mile or two down the road from Firle. Jones and his wife had been introduced to Connolly by Deirdre's old friend Veronica Keeling, the daughter of Alec Waugh, who brought him over for a drink: because Jones knew of – and shared – Connolly's interest in food and wine, he brought up some vintage champagne for the occasion, so he was somewhat disconcerted when his guest made no comment whatsoever, and left without saying thank you or goodbye. A day or two later, however, their invitation was returned, and a friendship struck up. The two men vied with one another over the meals they served and the wines with which they washed them down, though towards the end of his life Connolly gave up wine altogether, still raiding his cellar when guests arrived but leaving his glass untasted when visiting friends – much to the alarm of his hosts, who worried that their wine had met with his disapproval; and they greatly enjoyed an elaborate charade, aimed in part at their fellow-commuters, whereby Connolly – clad in one of his double-breasted suits from the Regent Dress Company, which sold off Savile Row suits which had been ordered but never collected – pretended to be another City man. 'Well, Timothy, what's been going on on 'Change,' he'd ask. 'Rubbers are flat,' Jones might well reply; and Connolly would counter with 'What about electricals, and Pifco in particular...?'

Already dependent on barbiturates, Deirdre's mother eventually took an overdose and killed herself. Peter Levi, by now a Jesuit priest, helped to officiate at the funeral, and on the way back to London Connolly suggested to Deirdre that, since he was going on to dinner with Shelagh, she might like to do the same with Peter. Nothing could have pleased her more, for – although her husband had yet to notice it – Deirdre had fallen in love with the handsome young poet and priest. Peter had admired Connolly's writing since his schooldays, but only met him – and Deirdre – in 1963, at a party given in All Souls by Alasdair Clayre. He had just come back from his first visit to Greece, and had nearly completed his training as a Jesuit at Heythrop College: but despite the imminence of his vows, he was – or so he wrote years later – bowled over by Deirdre when he saw her coming down the short flight of steps that led down into the room in which the party was being held. 'I recognised the love of my life,' he wrote: '... I thought simply and suddenly, there is the one woman I have met I could love for ever and might, if things had been otherwise, have married. But I was still determined to be an acceptable clergyman, and in that course I persisted for fifteen more years...' Deirdre, on the other hand, claims that she was the one who was struck down at first sight, that Peter seemed only interested in talking to his literary hero, and took no notice of her whatsoever. Either way, Peter soon became a regular visitor, at Bushey and then at No. 48; his mother lived in Eastbourne, and when he was ordained in 1964, the Connollys were invited to the service, and to the subsequent celebrations in the Cavendish Hotel. Connolly liked Peter well enough, and admired his poems – he was, he told Olga Rudge, 'a great friend; a young scholar of great beauty, ill-at-ease in the dogmatic straitjacket' – but he affected to resent the growing affection he and Deirdre evidently felt for one another, innocent as it was: listening to them discussing poetry downstairs long after he had gone up to bed, he would say, in the tones of an aggrieved husband, 'I don't know which is the stronger feeling – jealousy, or relief that she isn't talking to *me*!' but such displays of indignation helped to divert attention from his own affair with Shelagh and, with luck, dilute the offence it gave. Deirdre's love for Peter remained, as it had to, a private passion from which she could draw no public solace; nor did her loving Peter prevent her from loving Connolly as well, and minding dreadfully the unhappiness he caused her.

Connolly's addiction to intrigue and complications – and the games that went with them – took a less tendentious form in watching *Mastermind* and *University Challenge* on television, trying to work out the originals for the characters in Anthony Powell's 'Dance to the Music of Time',* and making anagrams out of people's names: Wystan Auden became 'A Nasty Unwed' and Kingsley Amis an 'Ink-Slimy Sage', though, more lyrically,

> Honeysuckle, gently twine
> Round her unattended shrine
> *Lonicera gratissima*
> Anagram of Caroline...

* Pamela Flitton – 'who is breathing some life at last into the orchestra' – was generally agreed to be Barbara. He decided against Lord Longford's claims to be Widmerpool; after toying with the alphabetical similarities of 'Weidenfeld' and 'Widmerpool', he settled instead on 'the really ruthless and sinister Douglas Cooper, who tortured German pilots in the war'.

Opportunities to review new books about the authorship of Shakespeare's Sonnets, or the Cambridge spies, or the assassination of President Kennedy and the inadequacies of the Warren Report, were eagerly seized upon – he once wrote that he felt for Kennedy an 'affection and admiration verging on idolatry', and that his murder 'came as an insupportable personal bereavement' – but the mystery that came to absorb him above all others was the murder of Lord Erroll. A member of the raffish, hard-living 'Happy Valley' set – rich, well-connected men and women who had gone out to Kenya to farm and drink and bed one another's spouses in an intricate gavotte – Erroll was shot dead in January 1941, and the mystery of who had murdered him had never been resolved: but a fellow-inhabitant of the Valley, Sir Jock Delves Broughton – whose wife, Diana, had been having an affair with Erroll – had been tried for the murder and acquitted. For years Connolly had been fascinated by the case: partly because so many of those involved were Etonians (Erroll had been a contemporary, and one of Connolly's earliest friends in College, Randall Delves Broughton, was a cousin of the accused man); partly because of its African setting, so redolent of his mother's restless moves about the continent; and partly because the Happy Valley set embodied, in James Fox's words, 'that longed-for and detested world of upper-class glamour', rekindling that ancient, fearful longing to be as one with the worldly, the sporting and the philistine which had driven him to join such apparently uncongenial organisations as Pop and White's Club.* Reading about the trial during the war, he noticed that one of the key witnesses was a Lady Carberry, whose distinctive tones he had once overheard while sunbathing at Eden Roc in the summer of 1938; but he then forgot about the case for nearly twenty years until, while staying at La Consula, he read a short account of the trial by Rupert Furneaux, and his interest was rekindled. While in Kenya in 1967, he had stayed with Jack Block, who owned a chain of hotels, and was one of the very few people who knew who he was;† and through the Blocks he met Lazarus Kaplan, who had acted as Broughton's solicitor, and a Prince Windischgraetz, who reported Broughton's doctor as saying that his patient had confessed to the murder before the trial, but then decided to plead not guilty. Block himself claimed that, after the trial, Broughton had said to the prosecuting counsel, 'Bad luck, old boy. I did it.'

Some two years later, the Connollys paid a visit to the Bridges, neighbours of theirs in Sussex. Dinah Bridge's twenty-four-year-old son, James

* Evelyn Waugh was equally fascinated by the Happy Valley set when he visited Kenya before the war.
† Sir Michael Blundell had a vague idea that he was perhaps the editor of *The Times*, while Pam Scott insisted on introducing him to a gathering of farmers as 'John O'Connor', unkindly comparing him after he left to a stuffed pillow, on account of his understandable silences.

Fox, was also there, and when Connolly discovered that he had worked as a journalist in Nairobi before joining the *Sunday Times*, he asked him what he knew about the Erroll murder.* Fox's editor on the *Sunday Times* Colour Magazine, the writer Francis Wyndham – step-brother of Dick – had long hoped to persuade Connolly to write for him, but worried about finding the right subject, and one that would enthuse him into writing at greater length than he had become used to; since Fox shared Connolly's interest in the Erroll affair, it was agreed that they should work together on a long investigative piece, to be published in the Christmas 1969 issue. This was just the kind of work Connolly relished and had pined for, and he flung himself into his researches with unslothlike energy – drawing up lists of suspects and elaborate timetables indicating who was where on the night of the murder, writing innumerable letters, reprimanding James Fox for not making best use of his mental card index system, interviewing over fifty people and insisting that he and his collaborator write up their notes immediately afterwards from 'Car park, Burgess Hill' or wherever; he filled entire exercise books and covered 'unpaid invoices, railway menus and errata slips' with his detailed observations, trailing through Eton School Lists and Debrett's, combining intuition with academic exactitude.† 'Christmas at Karen' was published under their joint names; Connolly wrote some 4000 words of it, two-thirds of the total. Francis Wyndham found him very easy to work with, and was amused by Connolly's delight in cloak-and-dagger intrigues, and by the self-deprecating enthusiasm with which he pretended to be a 'real' journalist. After the piece had appeared, both authors were deluged with letters from people who shared their interest in the case: several members of Lord Erroll's family complained to the Press Council – particular exception was taken to the use, on the front of the Colour Magazine, of a now-familiar photograph of the murdered man's head on a slab in the morgue, the bullet wounds all too evident – and Connolly had to defend their actions in a written submission to the Council. Although Connolly was worried about upsetting what James Fox referred to as the 'country house network', both men continued their researches after their article had appeared: Connolly became so involved that he woke the house with his nightmares on the subject, and the Starlit Room at the

* James Fox was then married to the niece of another Sussex friend and neighbour, the journalist Ali Forbes, who also rented a cottage on Lord Gage's estate. Fox had been to Eton, and cut a dashing and stylish figure; and Connolly felt for him the same kind of elder-brotherly affection that he had earlier felt for Alan Ross and Robert Kee.

† One notebook, typically, combines thoughts on the murder with diary entries on a holiday spent in Ischia (among those he met there were John Gielgud, Terence Rattigan and Sir William Walton), more anagrams, and the opening pages of a planned 'personal anthology' of poetry ('I include only what has appealed to me through its intensity and imaginative intelligence, and because my whole approach to life is personal . . .').

Metropole became a favoured meeting-place for comparing notes. After Connolly's death, James Fox used their findings as the starting-point for his best-selling book, *White Mischief* – in which he eventually concluded that, despite Connolly's initial reservations, Delves Broughton was indeed the guilty man.

Connolly's interest in the Erroll murder brought together many long-standing obsessions, and the world it evoked was full of oblique echoes from his own past. A more strident and – as it turned out – less welcome voice from the past made itself heard when, in May 1971, he was invited out to the University of Texas at Austin to open an exhibition of manuscripts and first editions entitled 'One Hundred Key Books', which was based on *The Modern Movement** and made use of the Harry H. Ransom Research Center's unrivalled collection of archival material. John Lehmann was in Austin as a Visiting Professor, and Connolly suggested that its organizer, Warren Roberts, should get in touch with him if they had difficulties deciphering his hand-writing. He also mentioned that 'there is also in Austin an old friend, a secretary of mine who typed many things for me as business manager of *Horizon*': presumably he was referring to Lys, for John Lehmann later remembered how keen Connolly had been to meet the wife of a university professor, a former 'acolyte' of his, without her husband knowing, and how he had rung to ask for his help in making contact with her. Lehmann also recalled the delight Connolly took in the exhibition, poring over the glass cases and re-examining the works of writers who, in many cases, had been his friends, and had been published by him. One item, though, lay in its case like a time bomb, waiting to be detonated. Casting modesty aside, Connolly had, before leaving England, begged the organisers to include *The Unquiet Grave*, even though it was not one of the 'Hundred Key Books' listed by him: 'Some find the U.G. a mere common-place book,' he told them, 'others see in it, with its three movements and epilogue, a "chasse spirituelle", a beautifully constructed and harmonious whole.' Some years earlier, the university had acquired Evelyn Waugh's library, complete with bookshelves, desk and armchair, so, anxious to oblige, the organisers included in the exhibition Waugh's copy of *The Unquiet Grave*, which Nancy Mitford had sent him in January 1945, when he was based at Ragusa, on the Dalmatian coast. Connolly noticed that Waugh had scribbled comments in the margin in a diabolical red ink and unwisely asked if he might examine it more closely.

* It had been published in New York by Atheneum, but was – needless to say – out of print there as well as in Britain.

Waugh's marginalia amounted to a more dismissive and contemptuous rehearsal of the review he went on to publish in the *Tablet*. 'Why should I be interested in this book?' he wrote across the title page:

> Because I have known Cyril more than twenty years and enjoy dining with him? Because, alone in Dubrovnik, I have not much else to occupy me? Rather because Cyril is the most typical man of my generation. There but for the grace of God, literally . . . He has the authentic lack of scholarship of my generation, he read Freud while getting a third in Greats, the authentic love of leisure and liberty and good living, the authentic romantic snobbery, the authentic waste-land despair, the authentic high gift of expression. Here he is in wartime, strait-jacketed by sloth, in Bloomsbury, thinking of Jean in the South of France, instead of Lys and sirens and official forms. Quite clear in his heart that the ills he suffers from are theological, with the vocabulary of the nonsense-philosophy he learned holding him back. The Irish boy, the immigrant, homesick, down-at-heel and ashamed, full of fun at the public house, a ready quotation on his lips, afraid of the bog priest, proud of his capers; the Irishman's deep-rooted belief that there are only two final realities – Hell and the USA.

Palinurus was an 'Irish corner boy' with a 'Belfast accent', who had been 'given a testament in the slums together with the bowl of soup. He has excreted the soup and is now excreting the testament': but although most of Connolly's errors were 'full and simply explained in the catechism' and reflected a lamentable 'ignorance of the doctrine of the Fall of Man', 'Cromwell will get you, Paddy.' Palinurus's views on religion were 'deplorable': he 'seems never to have learned anything of the Fall of Man. It is his failure to take in the original calamity which is the dead rot putrefying his will.' As in his review, Waugh conceded that the book 'grew very much better towards the end', but his summing-up on the final page can hardly have comforted his posthumous reader:

> Who was Palinurus? First the Irish immigrant, free from the tyranny of the bog-priest, astute enough to see through that cleric's more preposterous over-simplifications, haunted by his warnings of hell; Paddy in the new tyranny of factory system and Tammany Hall. Second, the hack highbrow turning out a weekly middle on Sainte-Beuve. Third the Brains Trust pundit laden with the jargon of psycho-analysis and economics. Fourthly, most monumentally, the drivelling woman novelist. Fifthly and finally the decadent poet, the dyspeptic epicure.

Waugh's annotations were far more revealing about himself than Connolly – his dislike of Irish Catholics was common among his English co-religionists, particularly converts, and the way in which Connolly combined, in fact, a very strong sense of original sin without the trappings and the consolations of theology was, arguably, a good deal more honest and more interesting than his own defiant dogmatism – but his victim was predictably upset. He was far too professional a journalist, though, to waste good material, however unwelcome, and in due course he published a rueful account of his experiences in Texas under the title 'Apotheosis in Austin'. Waugh had been the 'wicked godmother at my exhibition's christening,' he wrote, and 'what I minded most was the contempt which emerged from a writer for whom for twenty years (1923–43) I had looked upon as a friend.' Although Waugh's caricature of Connolly the Irishman was too absurd to be taken seriously, he particularly resented 'the assumption that I was a bog-trotting lapsed Catholic immigrant in fear of Hell Fire'. For the rest of his stay he had been obsessed by Waugh, seeing in his mind's eye 'the bloated, puffed-up face of my old club-mate, with the beady eyes red with wine and anger, a cigar jabbing as he went into the attack. A certain coarseness of heart, I thought, marred his work ...' 'Of course we all knew that though he was servile enough to our faces, he was beastly about us behind our backs,' Maurice Bowra wrote in consolation: 'He found it impossible to be generous and was really devoured by envy of almost everything ... One of his troubles was that he thought (knew?) that he was not a gentleman and he tried to get over this by snobbery of an almost absurd kind.' Christopher Isherwood wrote from California to say how moved he had been by Connolly's article ('the candour was beautiful'), while Sacheverell Sitwell was outraged by Waugh's 'horrible remarks' and concluded that he had been a 'venomous little creature'.*

Two months after he had written his letter, Maurice Bowra was dead. In a piece commissioned for the *Sunday Times* by Godfrey Smith, Connolly paid tribute to his old mentor. Bowra, he wrote, had 'saved me from despair' at

* Mercifully, the librarians at Austin didn't show their visitor the annotated copy of *The Unquiet Grave* that had belonged to Sir Ronald Storrs, the friend of T.E. Lawrence. 'Who has not met with this type?' Storrs asked on the flyleaf:

> Well, but not widely read. Vagabonds whose obscenities cannot be hid for long, but will out. Who live obscurely and degradingly, carrying home their food in pails, to rend it with their fingers, whose bed-fellows are monkeys, whose companions, ferrets. Who prate of a love of animals, yet who expose wild animals to cruelty and death for their own pleasure, who prate of beauty yet have not perceived it, who disgust always with faint allusions to obscene things, never having the courage to fell with the pole-axe strokes of undiluted filth. Who wrap up muddled thinking in a jargon of unnecessary and recondite words. Intellectual snobs, of one kidney with their reviewers. Many who read this book are charmed to know that they too have read the same books, have been to school also, and read Latin books, and French. They recognise the old school tie and hail it, forgetting that that tie can encircle the necks of swine as well as saints.

Oxford, 'a place where I had been unhappier than I had ever been before': the great tragedy of Bowra's life was that although he had 'the verbal gifts, the energy, the high romantic imagination to be a great poet', some 'intractable inhibition' held him back. They had last met, not long before the Warden's death, in his retirement flat in Oxford:

> He talked about his 'breathing troubles' as 'just one of the things one has to expect of old age' – and I said I put blindness, being totally bed-ridden and dropping dead as the worst, in that order. 'Dropping dead,' he boomed, 'has no terrors for me.'

Connolly, like the Warden, was another frustrated poet. 'My life would only make sense if I was a great (lyric) poet,' he once confessed; and in the last piece he wrote for the *Sunday Times*, 'Poetry – My First and Last Love', which was published after his death, he said that he had loved poetry since he was six, finding it 'harder to be without than any other branch of literature', and that of his twelve favourite writers all were poets except Petronius, Montaigne, Flaubert and Proust. In his fifties and sixties he spent a good deal of time writing and endlessly revising poems and translations, the best of which have epigrammatic intensity and an elegiac melancholy – like 'A Thought from Propertius' –

> Good news we bring the expectant generation
> Our banquet broke no bones: be this our due!
> So kiss me, love; enjoy our mortal station
> When all that you can give are still too few.
>
> As leaves that wither from a blackened ceiling
> And on the wine bowl's midnight ocean fume
> Are we who put our trust in this deep feeling
> Regardless of the hour which seals our doom.

or 'After Servasius', written for Alan Ross's fortieth birthday:

> Only the tears outlive the sperm
> Only the lies outsmart the tears
> Only the grave can foil the worm
> Only lost love defeat the years.
>
> The hearts we sailed lie beached forever
> By saltings of the Fisher King.

Time folds the island in the river,
Attenuates the golden ring.*

Connolly once summed himself up as

an artist he of character complex
money he loved and next to money sex
no roses culled he from the Muses' garden
neurosis gripped him in a vice of Auden.

To know that he had been denied access to the Muses' garden was a bitter pill to swallow, and the verses he wrote towards the end of his life have the angry, 'metallic' quality he detected in Bowra's satires on his friends, and are of more interest for the light they shed on his state of mind than as poems in themselves. But perhaps, as his juvenilia hinted, Connolly's modest talent as a poet was for light verse, of the kind he put to good effect when reviewing the Scott Fitzgerald-Maxwell Perkins correspondence:

We're back on the old Scott Circuit
  On a bender as big as the Ritz
Where Gerald is shaking a Murphy
  And Zelda is throwing a Fitz

The Ring is in the Lardner
  Calling Wilson 'Bunny'
And Perkins with his pardner
  Is picking up the money

All high on the old Scott Circuit
  While Ernest is boozing in Spain
Shall we ever get back to Nantucket
  And wear a tuxedo again?

*

'Emotionally, Cyril would never grow old,' Peter Quennell wrote of his old friend:

> Physically, however, he had suddenly begun to age. His once rotund face, the ample cheeks grown hollow, wore, now and then, an anxiously

* 'Please alter "ears" to "years" in line 4 – this misprint has *ruined* it for me,' Connolly wrote to Alan Ross after the poem had been printed with a missing 'y': the 'island in the river' was the Ile St Louis, the 'golden ring' 'Jean's wedding ring, which we sold . . .'

enquiring look; while thin strands of sparse, silvery hair floated round his massive cranium. He talked little, had nearly lost his appetite, and often left his glass of wine unfinished.

Never a heavy drinker, Connolly's consumption of wine was curbed and then extinguished by 'bad conscience and bad liver': 'left to myself (grim legacy) I would hardly drink at all and it is only for my guests that I descend to the cellar.' His renunciation of wine was among Nancy Mitford's causes for complaint when the Connollys visited her in Versailles in June 1972. They brought with them some plovers' eggs, which were wrongly assumed to be cooked, splattering everywhere when attempts were made to peel them; and then, to make matters worse, he refused to taste the bottle of Château Lafite she had bought for the occasion. 'The truth is that Cyril is not *sortable* & I shall never ask him here again,' she told Anthony Powell afterwards.

Despite the plovers' eggs, she was in touch again soon afterwards when they were both awarded the CBE: 'I was much pleased to be the companion of you and Harold A. as well as of the ghostly Empire. I'd never heard of CBE but I'm told it's a good sort and Christopher S[ykes] advised me to accept. I wish I could go with you and accept it.' Some years earlier, Bob Boothby had tried in vain to put Connolly's name forward for a knighthood; but knighthoods and the literary life sit uneasily together, and the lesser award seemed more appropriate. Equally gratifying – and a good deal more exclusive – was being made a Companion of Literature by the Royal Society of Literature: the number of Companions was restricted to ten, and had included Churchill, John Betjeman, Forster, Waugh, Elizabeth Bowen, Edith Sitwell, Compton Mackenzie and Somerset Maugham. 'I cannot remember a more farcical occasion,' Alan Ross wrote later of the award ceremony. R.A. Butler, the President of the RSL, was responsible for introducing the new Companions – Connolly's fellow-recipients were Lord David Cecil, Angus Wilson and L.P. Hartley – and presenting them with the appropriate scrolls; but to Ross he seemed 'curiously inept and seemingly almost gaga', praising Connolly as a well-known novelist (these included, apparently, *The Unquiet Grave*), mentioning Angus Wilson only as a translator of Zola, and using L.P. Hartley's novel *The Go Between* as a peg on which to hang a rambling anecdote about a horse on which he had once placed a bet. Hartley, who seemed equally *distrait*, headed off in the direction of the lavatory when his name was called, and had to be pointed back to the podium; presented at last with his scroll, he whipped out his fountain pen, assuming it to be a petition he had been called upon to sign.

'You must think me an almost continuous stretcher-case suffering an almost continuous tooth-ache of the heart, with a fatal self-consciousness, watching myself, watching myself,' Connolly told Raymond Mortimer: 'Underneath my yoke nothing is changed; a river of gaiety, irresponsibility, even talent, certainly affection, flows on beneath the accumulation of sticks, dead leaves, saliva...' But even if 'financial ruin stalks and senility and death,' the urge to travel remained as strong as ever. He pondered the possibilities of Ceylon, but eventually persuaded Godfrey Smith to send him to Senegal. He remembered meeting its poet-President, Léopold Senghor, at a Foreign Office reception; the food would almost certainly be better than in anglophone Africa, its National Park boasted a rare variety of eland, and he could hope to encounter 'the nearest wild elephants to Gray's Inn Road'. The journey out was a nightmare. He could just remember calling at Tenerife in a troopship en route for the Cape at the age of five, and anticipated an Arcadia of tropical fruit and flowers, bright sun and temperate climate, with blue mountains shimmering behind and masterpieces of Spanish baroque peeping through the palms: but Las Palmas was a hell-hole of concrete monstrosities lashed by rain, he had diarrhoea induced by aeroplane food, the restaurant he chose for dinner was crammed with raucous middle-aged Swedes tucking into tinned tomato soup, and the hotel in which he holed up for the night had stains on the carpet and a view of a concrete wall and a neon light. In Dakar he sampled such favourites as 'red-fleshed melons' and langoustes – 'Meat and all vegetables except asparagus tempt me less than shrimp or scallop, lobster or crab, above all Dublin Bay prawns,' he informed his readers – before hiring a car, plus driver, and setting off in search of his beloved animals. Tenerife seemed as hellish as ever on the way home; in Madrid he stayed at the Fenix Hotel, sat next to the bullfighter Dominguin in the Jockey Restaurant, and enjoyed some flamenco dancing in a night-club.

Rather more restful, perhaps, was a part-time job with Christie's, advising them about sales of first editions. David Bathurst suggested that he should receive a retainer of £1000 a year, in exchange for which he would come in once a week and have the use of a secretary. Connolly was delighted: he told Jake Carter of Sotheby's that he liked using his expertise to help writers make some extra money, in much the same way as he had helped them into print at *Horizon*. Before long he was busy organising a sale of MSS and first editions. Stephen Spender, William Sansom, Francis King, Robin Maugham, Harry d'Avigdor-Goldsmid, David Pryce-Jones, Ann Fleming and others contributed material from their shelves; Olga Rudge was asked about possible Pound material; Robert Graves regretted that he had got rid of most of his manuscripts, but continued their correspondence on how and why he and his newly-found 'Dear Cousin' were related ('we are linked with most intelligent Anglo-Irish families since 1575'). Most rewardingly of all, he got in touch with Barbara Bagenal, a friend of the Bloomsbury set who also lived in Sussex: she unearthed a mass of letters from both Woolfs to Saxon Sidney-Turner, those from Leonard fetching £1800, and those from Virginia, though fewer in number, an additional thousand. The sale took place in April 1973, and raised a total of £24,704. A year later Connolly sold some of his own first editions, including several inscribed copies from Evelyn Waugh for which he no longer felt his old fondness, raising £2327 in all.

Connolly was involved in a different kind of literary evaluation in the autumn of 1972, when he chaired the Booker Prize's panel of judges: his fellow-judges were Elizabeth Bowen and George Steiner. He had a particularly soft spot for Aidan Higgins's *Balcony of Europe*, which dealt with expatriate life in southern Spain, but neither of the others shared his enthusiasm: of those that made it to the short list, he preferred David Storey's *Passmore*, but Steiner won him round to John Berger's *G*. It was a controversial choice, made more so when the author announced that he was giving half his earnings to the Black Panthers. He also took part in a celebration of the work of Ezra Pound at the Mermaid Theatre, very similar to one held earlier, in which he also participated, in honour of Dylan Thomas.

W.H. Auden died in 1973, and shortly afterwards Spender asked Connolly if he would like to contribute to a collection of commemorative essays he was editing for Weidenfeld & Nicolson.* Despite Auden's disapproval of Connolly's sloth, and an awkward passage after Connolly asked Auden's companion, Chester Kallman, what it felt like 'to be Alice B. Toklas to Gertrude Stein' – 'I shan't rest until Cyril Connolly is either dead or in a lunatic asylum,' an outraged Auden was reported as saying – the two men had kept in touch on Auden's occasional visits to London: they appeared together on a television programme, with Spender and Isherwood, and they lunched with Tom Driberg at the Etoile, Auden seeming – as Connolly sadly noted – 'totally uninterested in my family'. At the end of his life, Auden returned to England, to a set of rooms in his old Oxford college, Christ Church, and – much to his surprise – Connolly came to the Encaenia at All Souls in 1972, at which he was made a Doctor of Letters (' "Why, Cyril, what on earth are you doing here?" "I came to find *you*," I

* He would, and he did, though the piece appeared after his death. The choice of publisher presented no problem: Connolly and Weidenfeld had met again in David Pryce-Jones's house; Barbara's name was never mentioned, and Connolly subsequently visited his old publisher in his house on Chelsea Embankment.

answered').* They never met again, for – as Connolly remarked in his memoir of Auden – 'the old are diminishing universes racing further and further apart, piling up space between them, unable to cope with even the simplest mechanics of meeting.'

Connolly's tributes to Auden and to Maurice Bowra were affectionate, evocative and admiring, but when he himself was written about he proved surprisingly thin-skinned. He had admired *A Life of My Own*, Gerald Brenan's first volume of memoirs, 'though I find much of it too painful as it brings back the boredom and frustration of my father-fighting childhood'. In his second volume, *Personal Record*, Brenan provided what would appear to be a sympathetic and perceptive account of a writer whom he described as being 'after Auden the most brilliant mind in contemporary English literature'. 'In his deeper layers,' Brenan wrote of his old friend, 'he is a romantic, but shot through with the sort of psychological realism that an Englishman can only acquire by reading and assimilating French literature.' He was a narcissist, 'filled with a love-hate for himself'; as 'one of Nature's Rothschilds' – a phrase Brenan remembered Connolly using about himself – he loved luxury and eating, especially 'sea food and exotic fruit, for greed is a normal compensation for not having been loved enough as a child.' His most 'productive gift,' in Brenan's opinion, was his curiosity. For years he had been 'a hero-worshipper in search of a hero', and 'I can think of no literary man who has shown himself more generous in praising his fellow-writers, whether they were his friends or not.' He was 'of course' selfish, putting 'his own comfort and convenience high and his intellectual needs above everything.' Often described as malicious he was not – 'though since malice is the occupational vice of wits, he can say things which if repeated would give pain to others. However, when his feelings are hurt, as they easily are, he can react viciously and wound back.'

Connolly was indeed lazy, Brenan went on, but 'he had his period, the late 'thirties and early 'forties, when he wrote chiefly as a recorder and analyst of literary trends, inspired perhaps by Edmund Wilson's *Axel's Castle*, but writing with greater brilliance...' Among his friends 'he has always stood out by his conversational powers,' yet – unlike Desmond MacCarthy – he was not a good conversationalist:

> He is a solo performer and his presence does not help the conversation to flow. Indeed it often blocks it. There he sits with his heavy, expressionless

* After Auden's memorial service, in Christ Church, Connolly was introduced by Peter Levi to Philip Larkin, a great admirer of his work, who remarked that 'It's like being asked if you'd like to meet Matthew Arnold.' One of Larkin's last published works was an enthusiastic Introduction to a paperback reissue of *The Condemned Playground*, which he once described as 'my sacred book'.

face exuding boredom, waiting, it would seem, for the witty remark from one of the company that did not come. For Cyril is like a child, utterly sunk in the mood of the moment and determined to impress it on everyone else.

All this was true enough, but, as Stephen Spender reminded Alan Ross, 'Cyril is funny – a great wit – but he has a limited enjoyment of the anecdotes in which people are being funny about him.' Brenan was certainly not trying to be funny at his expense, but he was unamused all the same. He had published Brenan in *Horizon*, and introduced him to the Davises, and recommended *South from Granada* to its publisher as well as providing it with its title and reviewing it, enthusiastically, in the *Sunday Times*, and was even now urging Alan Ross to print some of Brenan's poems in the *London Magazine*; and this was all the thanks he got. 'It seems to me quite outrageous that Gerald should be such a boiled owl as to offend someone like yourself,' wrote Brenan's old friend Frances Partridge, and the owl himself was keen to calm things down. He gathered from Janetta that Connolly was hurt by what he had written, and was particularly upset at being accused of indolence. Not unreasonably, Brenan claimed that he had not presented Connolly in a bad light. 'Your strong changing moods and so forth are things that fascinate people about you – give you a distinction and originality that most writers lack... I said to myself "Cyril is so frank about himself that he will accept what I have said."' He especially liked Connolly's love of animals, and his 'gentleness and delicacy': knowing how easily bored Connolly was, he had not always felt at ease in his company, but 'you have an attitude to life and literature that appeals to me more strongly than that of any writer of our time and I would like to have been a closer friend of yours and known you better.' 'GB confuses the horror and embarrassment which he causes CC and others by his naive sexual boasting, which leaves them speechless,' Connolly remarked – which, given Brenan's futile passions for girls a third of his age was probably true enough, but a far from exhaustive explanation.

The Connollys revisited Geneva, Aix-les-Bains, Grenoble and Megève in the summer of 1973; he caught a bad summer 'flu on his return, which went to his chest. That particular corner of France was peopled by the ghosts of his youth – Sligger and Jean and the Chalet – but the present was all too insistent in 'horrible preparations for my seventieth birthday – I wish the papers had never heard of it – a public proclamation of senility when all one wants is to be left to enjoy life and literature while one still can.'

The largest, if not the grandest, of these birthday celebrations was organised by the *Sunday Times*. As well as donating a painting by Patrick

Procktor, it was decided to give some kind of party as well; and Frank Giles, the Foreign Editor, came up with the bright idea of giving this most eloquent and passionate of animal-lovers a birthday lunch at the London Zoo in Regent's Park. Solly Zuckerman, the Zoo's Director and an old acquaintance of Connolly's, reserved the Members' lawn and dining-room; but nothing was said to the Connollys, who only knew that something was in hand, but had no idea of what or where. Connolly was asked to draw up a guest list, and much time was spent, and much paper covered, on the invidious business of grading friends as though they were examination candidates, promoting some, demoting some, and dropping others altogether. It was thought a good idea to keep the 'politically-minded' together: these included Harold Evans, the editor of the *Sunday Times*, Sidney Bernstein, Sir Harry d'Avigdor-Goldsmid and Philippe de Rothschild, who flew from Denmark specially for the occasion. After much agonising and reshuffling of lists, Connolly wrote to Jack Lambert with suggestions of who might sit next to whom, and who were best kept apart – heading his letter, in facetious homage to Ian Fleming, 'Top Secret. For Your Eyes Only. Eat after Reading.' John Betjeman, for instance, 'doesn't like new faces'; for Anthony Powell, it was 'all grist to his mill'; John Lehmann had been at school with Noël Blakiston, who might otherwise feel adrift; Ali Forbes liked everyone, but was 'inclined to boast and name-drop'; Hamish Hamilton 'likes important people'; and as for the birthday boy, he 'likes *everyone* just this once'. As to the mysterious 'venue', 'Deirdre thinks it is either at 48 Bedford Square, 25 Sussex Place, converted for the occasion, or 10 Downing Street. I argue for some little-known but glamorous City hall – or some haunt of ancient peace like the former Vorticist room of the White Tower. As long as it is not the *Observer*.'

Connolly and Deirdre came up from Eastbourne on the morning of the birthday lunch, and Jack Lambert drove down from Gray's Inn Road in a large office car, picked them up from a hotel in Belgravia, and headed north on the mystery tour. Deirdre sat beside her husband in the back, clutching his hand, as one possibility after another flashed by and had to be discarded; and then, as they turned into Regent's Park, the truth dawned on them, and 'Cyril's face is glowing with a great beam that almost quenches the blazing sun . . .' It was a perfect late summer day, the roses were out in the paved garden where the reception was held, and, as the first arrivals, the Connollys prepared to receive their guests. 'Cyril looked calm, pretty as a celluloid cupid in a bath,' Cecil Beaton observed, noting too that John Betjeman's trousers were too short in the leg. After lunch, Harry Evans introduced Jack Lambert, who said how eagerly he and his colleagues awaited Connolly's visits to the office; Connolly then spoke, reliving his childhood, his schooldays and his early experiences of literary life, frequently referring to members of the audience as he went, and to his old friend Noël Blakiston in particular; and Betjeman concluded with a speech of thanks. 'Cyril looked like a pretty cherub and delivered himself of a soufflé of a speech only equalled in taste by the excellence of the food,' Diana Cooper told Jack Lambert, while Anthony Powell remarked that 'the claret was the best I have tasted in ages.' Writing to 'my precious Cyril', Raymond Mortimer said how flattered he had been to be placed at the guest-of-honour's right-hand (Kenneth Clark was to the left); for Betjeman, 'Cyril's seventieth was a glowing, golden, enlightening, elevating and fortifying occasion', while Hamish Hamilton observed 'What fun Cyril's speech was, with its recurring motif "I was the only child of an ill-assorted marriage."' As for Connolly – who, when lunch was over, led the party on a tour of the mammal house, later ringing the *Sunday Times* to say that he had somehow managed to lose Deirdre *en route* – he sent word to say 'how blissfully happy' he had been, with 'all my favourite people except Stephen, Maurice Bowra and Elizabeth Bowen'.

Spender's absence, at least, could be remedied a couple of months later, when the Glenconners gave Connolly a seventieth birthday dinner in the River Room at the Savoy. Ever the attentive host, Connolly – though increasingly frail, and almost blinded by cataracts – insisted on consulting Silvano Trompetto, the Savoy's head chef, about every detail of the menu, anxiously discussing food he would only pick at and wine he would never drink. The guests included the Powells, the Leigh Fermors, Ann Fleming, the Spenders, Raymond Mortimer, Alan Ross, Robert Kee and Cecil Beaton, 'looking like an old milkmaid with a floppy tie', according to David Pryce-Jones, for whom this seemed like 'a gathering of the Old Guard – and I, chosen by Cyril at the last minute, to fill a place, as though to be a survivor on a raft.'

Pryce-Jones's sense of an old order passing was reflected in Connolly's introduction and closing essay in *The Evening Colonnade*, a collection of travel pieces, essays and reviews published to coincide with his birthday. 'Is not my work compact of columns, in this case all that's left standing from some five hundred of them?' Connolly asked, after discussing the various titles, half-punning, half-rueful, he had considered for the book; and in the final item, 'A Voice from the Dead?' he found himself conversing with the shade of Logan Pearsall Smith and brooding, as he always had, on the transience of fame and literary reputation. Pearsall Smith is anxious to know which of his books is best remembered and how his reputation stands, and Connolly feels obliged to tell his old mentor that nobody reads him any longer, or Desmond MacCarthy, and that his books have been quite forgotten except by a few American PhD students researching 'the small fry around Henry James'. Pearsall Smith is roused to anger. 'You fling words like oblivion about too easily,' he tells his protégé:

> You pay lip-service to annihilation but do you know what it means? You apply it to everyone but yourself. I have noticed that you seem to think the dead form a kind of club, that a beaming reception committee representing all the right literary sets will be there to greet you. It's not like that – the death of writers is like so many candles going out all over the world. They gutter and fail and then there is nothing, nor does any communication exist between them. And writers die three times; first there is the bodily death which I will not go into, then the death of the personality as it becomes gradually distorted in the memory of the survivors, belittled by the littleness of the living, caricatured as you have caricatured me – then there is the death of their work as form and meaning evaporate like the frescoes on an Etruscan tomb. I'll give you a chime of words – *Qui nunc jacet horrida pulvis* – Who's now reduced to filthy dust – first me and soon you – *Qui nunc jacet horrida pulvis.*

All his adult life Connolly had been haunted by the ephemerality of even the greatest works of art, and still more so their creators: yet, reviewing the collection in the *Daily Telegraph*, Anthony Powell commented on the 'pervasiveness' of his personality, while observing that 'the more subjective Connolly's judgements, the better. If he falters, it is when he feels that he ought to toe the line.' He went on to refer to Connolly's sympathy for, and understanding of, American writers, feeling that he had, almost single-handedly, been responsible for Scott Fitzgerald's post-war reputation on this side of the Atlantic. Connolly's publishers, a new and short-lived firm called Bruce & Watson, gave a publication party at Brown's Hotel: according to the *Evening Standard*'s 'Londoner's Diary', the thirteen-year-old Cressida was the star of the evening, happily conversing with the likes of Edna O'Brien, Asa Briggs, Kingsley Amis, Leo Cooper, George Weidenfeld and Robin Maugham, a Sussex neighbour for whose novel *The Wrong People* Connolly had earlier written an introduction.*

Writing from Oxford to say that he wouldn't be able to make the launch party, John Sparrow told Connolly 'how much I have admired and enjoyed, for many years past, the things you write . . . You provide for me almost the

* One aspect of the book which deserved no celebration was the book's editing, which was shamingly sloppy and incompetent. So bad was it that Tony Godwin – a brilliant editor who had made his mark at Penguin (where he had taken on *Enemies of Promise* and *The Rock Pool* as Modern Classics) and Weidenfeld & Nicolson – wrote from New York to say that much as he would have liked to include *The Evening Colonnade* in his inaugural list at Harcourt Brace, he was unable to do so since the English edition was so riddled with mistakes that he would have to re-edit and re-set for the States.

only remaining reason for opening a Sunday newspaper'; while Angus Wilson wrote to say how eternally grateful he was to Connolly for starting him out as a writer on *Horizon*.* Public tributes came from Kenneth Clark in the *Sunday Times* – whose only reservation about Connolly the reviewer was that he was 'obstinately Mediterranean. He thinks the north begins at Hampstead' – and John Lehmann in the *Sunday Telegraph*, for whom *The Evening Colonnade* exemplified all Connolly's strengths and occasional weaknesses, in particular a 'desultoriness when he was bored' and too soft a spot for the 'in joke':

> But that is a small quibble beside my unchanging admiration for his style, for his unique flair (I call it that, though I know it to be the fruit of hard work and severe self-criticism), for avoiding the dead word or phrase, for throwing in the freshly apposite image, in fact for continually rejuvenating the language.

Interviewed by Simon Blow in the *Guardian* for his birthday, Connolly was half-defiant, half-apologetic about his reviewing and the lost masterpieces it might (or might not) have supplanted. 'It's destroyed me to a large extent. What survives of me are a few tufts on a fruit tree when I should have been a forest giant,' he suggested; and, apropos *Enemies of Promise*, 'I've fallen victim to everything I wrote then. I lack some quality whereby long books get written. I can't take people seriously enough and so I write parodies. But I would have been happiest as a poet; I've always been lyrical.' All this was true enough: but so too was his claim – paradoxically contradicting the tenets of a lifetime – that 'My journalism is literature.' And one alternative at least he had no regrets about:

> Many of my friends who went on to become dons felt I was a Puritan who hadn't made good. I should have been a repressed homosexual don and scholar, never getting into any sexual scandals because, of course, it would all be so beautifully repressed . . . 'My dear Connolly, I hope you're not going to take the primrose path of literature. Walter Pater went in for that and it only got him a bad name.' You had to justify your scholarship by becoming a Fellow and I didn't want that. I was too emotionally unstable.

In the *London Magazine*, Alan Ross marked Connolly's birthday with tributes from John Betjeman and Raymond Mortimer, and a long review of

* Wilson was less well-disposed than his letter suggested. Ten years earlier he had been bruised by Connolly's claiming that *The Wild Garden* – a collection of reprinted lectures – was 'one of the very few books I couldn't finish. I cracked at page 80': on reading that Connolly had, accurately, likened his looks to those of a sea-lion, he compared his tormentor's with those of a wart-hog.

The Evening Colonnade by a surprising – and belated – admirer. 'Strange to be reviewing old Connolly,' Roy Fuller told Ross: 'I've always thought of myself as somehow against him, but time heals all.' As a young man, Fuller wrote, he had shared the disdain felt by Geoffrey Grigson and his close friend Julian Symons for Connolly the critic, and for *Horizon*. In 'Fifty Years of Little Magazines', Connolly had once divided literary magazines into two kinds, the 'dynamic' and the 'eclectic'. Dynamic editors had a cause to fight, and ran their publications 'like a commando course where picked men are trained to assault the enemy position'; the eclectic editor – among whom Connolly included himself – 'is like an hotel proprietor whose rooms fill up every month with a different clientele.' For the young Fuller, *Horizon* had seemed 'too soft on eclecticism', and he was irritated by 'Comment's' endless worrying over the status of the artist during the war, and by its subsequent hostility to the Soviet Union; while Connolly himself had seemed 'to be speaking from an upbringing of aestheticism and privilege somewhat irrelevant and outdated', as well as carrying with him an unappealing whiff of 'booksiness'. During the past twenty years, however, Connolly seemed to have 'come into his own as a critic': and even if he was sometimes over-indulgent towards, say, the Sitwells or e.e. cummings – 'To find Cummings "far more rewarding than Wallace Stevens" is a critical judgement of such perverseness as to make one doubt whether the critic ought to be judging poetry at all' – he was more often capable of 'supreme and illuminating common-sense', as well as writing with both passion and insight about animals and Africa and writers who were also his friends. 'Through criticism (and that largely literary journalism) he has, against the odds, fulfilled himself to a greater extent than might have been imagined,' Fuller concluded. Connolly had adhered to the high standards he had proclaimed in *Enemies of Promise*: his essays were proof of his own claim that one of the benefits of being a regular reviewer was that one could go on educating oneself in public:

> It is style – language above all free from cliché and inaccuracy – that he has seen as the key to literary value. No doubt his largely unassuaged creativity has enabled him to apply this notion with remarkable resilience over the years. He avoided the stiff joints of the academic: he never acquired the hardened arteries of the hack.

Such words must have come as balm to their recipient – who, that very month, had indulged in a familiar bout of literary self-denigration in the *Sunday Times*, claiming that he found it very hard to write well myself; cheerfulness is no substitute for accuracy, nor warmth for concision. I can't pare my words down to the bone like Orwell or Hemingway, nor avoid overdone adjectives like real, fantastic, marvellous, boring, readable, compulsive, which blunt the critic's fire-power. I use too many dots... and dashes – and marks of exclamation – and I shall never improve!

In his memoirs, Alan Ross recalled how, in these later years, Connolly 'seemed moderately content to potter conjugally about the shops in Lewes and Eastbourne'. Every now and then they met for lunch at the White Hart in Lewes, 'all *froideurs* over women and misunderstandings about *Horizon* finally resolved'. Ross found Connolly still as avid for gossip as ever: 'there was nothing that could not be discussed, and such was his sensibility that confidences exchanged with him were as if with a woman.' 'Jealous to a degree, he could snap like a crocodile': he could be 'rude, cruel and vindictive', but his high spirits were as contagious as his gloom, 'he was never pompous, self-important and affected', and 'when his eyes lit up or he laughed he had irresistible charm, gaiety mixed with boyish mischievousness.' Ross was touched by Connolly's continuing and helpful interest in the *London Magazine* – the heir to *Horizon* in so many ways – and by his benign pretence to be interested in Ross's cricketing reports in the *Observer* (' "Tom Graveney must have hooked well yesterday," he would say, having mugged it up, and delighted at the incongruity of his own words').

*

'My own rude health is at last deserting me,' Connolly told Gerald Brenan in the spring of 1974,

> and I am now a case of mild angina (coronary insufficiency) which I thought was bronchitis – and incipient cataract in one eye – please give me some advice about this – but don't disclose it to anybody as I couldn't bear Janetta's loaded sympathy or Bill's horror of other people's illness. It is a bore when one has to read for one's living. It's crazy turning seventy, one feels more and more frivolous and impatient with Christianity, politics, love affairs, recriminations and pompous 'evaluations' of Lawrence, Leavis, Huxley and now the Powyses...

Far from being 'rude', Connolly's health had never been of the best – during his *Horizon* years he had suffered from chest pains and recurrent boils and rotting teeth and what Lys described, alarmingly, as an 'abscess' on the chest – and now, though by no means an old man, he began, quite suddenly, to deteriorate on all fronts: so much so that, as he lay dying, none of his friends seem to know whether it was his liver, or his heart, or a combination of the two that was responsible. As he put it to Barbara, after telling her that he was taking pills for his heart, 'My second-hand value is clearly deteriorating, mileage very heavy.' Some years before a dentist in Wimpole Street had alerted him to broken teeth and chronic abscesses in his upper jaw, and advised him to have them out since they were, in effect, poisoning his system; and as he approached, and then passed, his seventieth birthday, the dentist's gloomy prognostications must have seemed all too exact. At the *Sunday Times*, Jack Lambert noticed how loosely his clothes now hung about him, and Raymond Mortimer worried that he looked so ill.

In the early summer, he went to stay with Janetta in southern Spain – the Colour Magazine had commissioned him to write a piece entitled 'Cooking for Love', with photographs of his hostess hard at work in the kitchen – and on his return he booked into Moorfields Eye Hospital to have his cataracts examined by Patrick Trevor-Roper, the brother of the historian and, with Raymond Mortimer and Desmond Shawe-Taylor, one of the part-owners of Long Crichel, in Wiltshire. Although Connolly had cataracts in both eyes, Trevor-Roper decided to operate only on the left eye; and because of his bad heart, the operation was done under a local anaesthetic. According to Ali Forbes, Connolly had always dreaded blindness, but he proved the most stoical of patients, chatting away as Trevor-Roper went about his business.

While he was in Moorfields, Connolly wrote 'Poetry – My First and Last Love', but – in Alan Ross's opinion – the spark went out of him after his operation, never to return. Equipped with a new pair of glasses, he then went, with Shelagh, to stay with Barbara in her *mas* in the South of France. Barbara was now living with Bernard Frank, a temperamental French writer who had earlier been involved with Françoise Sagan: on an earlier visit, Connolly had narrowly escaped decapitation when an infuriated Frank hurled a jug of cream at Barbara, sending it skimming within inches of their visitor's head. Connolly had alerted Barbara to his angina, which gave him shooting pains in his chest and left him gasping and puffing for air, and the year before, when he and Shelagh were staying at the Mas du Colombier, he had found it hard to climb out of the pool and had complained of pains in his chest; and now, a year later, his heart was playing up again. He decided to give Barbara and Shelagh lunch to celebrate his seventy-first birthday – Bernard Frank declined the invitation – but when the time came for them to set out for the restaurant, Barbara found him sitting on the edge of his bed, dressed for the occasion, with his hat on his head, but in no condition to go. A heart specialist was summoned from St Tropez, and the next day Barbara drove him in for an immediate operation. Although the prognosis was discouraging – the surgeon who had conducted the operation, echoing Connolly's own motoring analogy, told Barbara that he was like an old car, every part of which was worn out and needed to be replaced – Connolly soon seemed back on form, complaining about the food in the hospital in Cannes to which he had been transferred. He asked Barbara if she could smuggle some *oeufs en gelée* into the ward, and still hoped to take her and Shelagh to lunch in a smart restaurant once he'd been discharged. As soon as he was fit to travel he was flown back to London by the *Sunday Times* for further tests. Ali Forbes and the Glenconners both recommended the best doctors they knew, and Sir Harry d'Avigdor-Goldsmid offered to pay the fees of the Harley Street Clinic, where he was to be admitted for tests. In the meantime, he continued to write his reviews and to see old friends – though Kenneth Clark told him that 'You looked so ill at the Society of Literature party that I was really worried.' The time came for him to be admitted to the Harley Street Clinic, and he left home for what proved to be the last time. 'Back in Eastbourne,' Ali Forbes later remembered,

> he laboriously dressed and shaved for a last family lunch, of which he could not bring himself to touch a bite; managed only the very minimum of tentative jokes; pondered whether to show me his case-notes from the French hospital he had just left, and by deciding against it confirmed in me the worst fears which had already been aroused by his appearance and deportment.

The Connollys spent the night before his admission at the Wilbraham Hotel. Anne Dunn – who had heard of his heart attack while in New York, and had hurried back to London – rang him there; his voice was weak and 'blurred with tears' for, as he told her, 'I keep crying from weakness.' Janetta saw him there, and was shocked by his 'shrunken and diminished appearance'; and, later, she and Anne Dunn grumbled together about the way in which Sonia Orwell, though not a bedside-visitor herself, seemed to be taking an almost proprietory interest in Connolly's illness, as if she were the exclusive channel of information and communication.*

Connolly was given a large room on the first floor at the Harley Street Clinic: building work was going on outside so it was very noisy, with workmen's drills and hammers sounding through the walls and great sheets of polythene flapping in the wind. He was seen by a top heart specialist, but

* Sonia Orwell may have been proprietorial, and bossy, and tiresome when drunk, but she had proved – from Deirdre's point of view – the best of friends: generous to a fault, kind, a first-class cook, and a favourite aunt to both Cressida and Matthew.

although she was told that he should be well again within six weeks or so, Deirdre knew, instinctively, that he was going to die. The pills he was given brought him out in a rash; he hated the apparatus of tubes and catheters and, though normally so considerate, he swore at the nurses. Two days after his admission, Anne Dunn went to see him. He was asleep when she arrived, 'his head fragile and bald, his mouth large on his face, hands puffy, covered in scabs, relaxed on the sheet'. When he woke, she noticed that his eyes were bloodshot, and that one seemed to droop at the corner; he kissed her, said how pleased he was with the flowers on the dressing-table, rummaged in a drawer and handed her a miniature bottle of Black and White whisky and then, half-dozing and half-awake, talked about mutual friends.

Shelagh told Barbara that although the food in the Clinic was good, Connolly would eat nothing; he suffered from breathlessness, particularly at night; the specialist had told him that he should remain there for at least another month, having vitamins injections and diuretics. When Barbara herself came to visit him, 'the first thing that struck me was the dust and the array of dead flowers cluttering the room': he was studying a medical encyclopaedia, and when the doctors appeared he asked them, querulously, why he didn't seem to be getting any better, and whether he was suffering from a heart or a liver complaint. He also arranged for Barbara to meet Cressida, and 'as she seemed prepared to brave my evil eye, we met for lunch in Knightsbridge.'

As Connolly had realised, no one seemed quite sure why he was so ill, or why – far from improving – he appeared to be getting steadily weaker. He was moved, briefly, to King's College, Denmark Hill, for a liver biopsy, and then taken back to the Harley Street Clinic, where – in Ali Forbes's words – 'he was cleared for the Final Departure. The consultants looked at their watches rather than their diaries and shrugged their shoulders.' By now he was fading fast: his voice had faded to a whisper, he could eat nothing but was kept going by intravenous drips and vitamin injections; he shed the fat of years and the thin man he had once been re-emerged, to be 'succeeded in turn by a sort of Calcutta street bundle hardly bigger than his son Matthew', curled up in the hospital bed in a 'foetal crouch'. Back in England from France, Anne Dunn rang Sonia Orwell for news: '"Cyril is dying," she announced, almost triumphantly.' Anne went to see him: he was 'yellow and withered as a mummy', with a patch over one eye 'at which he occasionally twitches a finger'; his great worry – reiterated in a telegram to Barbara in France – was that a demi-kilo of 'mangoteens' should be ordered for the Duke of Devonshire from Fauchon in the Place de la Madeleine.

Twenty-five years earlier, Connolly had prescribed, for a girl who had expressed a fear of dying, a 'cure for the fear of death, to be taken *logically*'.

In it he had tried to explain why death was not something of which she should be afraid, quoting Lucretius to the effect that 'Death therefore does not exist, neither does it concern us a scrap', and concluding

> while my reason inclines me to extinction and a few childish fears to hell, remorse and judgement, my temperament has constructed its own version: that when we die we become what we have loved, and that, were I to be vaporised tomorrow, the bulk of me would soon be staring out at the world through those topaz panes at which I now dream my life away looking in.

The calm, rational common sense and courage with which he had comforted his frightened friend were displayed on his own deathbed. 'He is dying without fuss or emotion, like an ancient Roman, philosophically, stoically,' Anthony Hobson noted in his diary: 'Cyril is dying like a poet, in the sense that Erasmus used the word of himself, that is, a humanist whose life is based on the study of classical ethics and ancient literature.' Hobson noticed that although his face and arms were wasted, his mind was as clear as ever. He was asleep when he got up to go, and Hobson left beside the bed a copy of the Hours Press edition of Auden's 'Spain', something Connolly had always wanted; propped up on the bedside table was *Fleurs de la Cuisine Française*, ordered from a Paris bookseller, and the last book Connolly ever bought.

'I'm so tired. I can't see anyone. I just want to sleep. Keep everyone away,' Connolly told Anthony Hobson, but a steady stream of visitors came and went, while others spoke to him on the telephone. Deirdre had to juggle family life and responsibilities with visits to the hospital, sometimes staying the weekend with Alan and Jennifer Ross in Pelham Crescent: 'Deirdre is apparently being marvellous, getting up at six to cook Cressida's lunch, getting Matthew off to school, then taking the train to London,' Anne Dunn noted, adding that Joan Leigh Fermor played an important diplomatic role in making sure that Deirdre didn't coincide at the bedside with Shelagh, who was there for most of the time, slipping away when visitors arrived; and that worries about money and Deirdre's future – there was now an overdraft of £27,000 at Coutts's Bank, which held the deeds of No. 48 – in some odd way assuaged the misery of his dying. Diana came and Connolly was pleased, feeling that another chapter of his life had been rounded off; John Betjeman called, and reported that 'Cyril is dying very fast'. 'I do not recommend dying,' Connolly told Stephen Spender, to whom he told things about his life that his visitor had never heard before, some funny, some so painful that he buried his face in his hands and cried. 'I still think of you as my only genuine mentor, who made even those beastly war years a joy on many, many occasions,' Philip Toynbee wrote: 'Somehow I manage to remember the fun – and I give you tremendous credit for keeping up the morale of at least one war-evading civilian. The voice of pleasure, sanity, wit and the imagination at a time when all were treated as almost treasonable.' But the voice, like its master, was fading fast: Peter Quennell could barely make out his words over the phone, noting that he said goodbye 'with what I felt to be a tragic emphasis,' while Alan Ross remembered how

> Shortly before he died I spoke to him in hospital. To my question about how he felt he replied, 'Liver's lousy.' Instead of his putting the receiver down I heard it drop from his hand and lie on the bed, the sounds of the room like the sea in a shell continuing to reverberate. They were the last words I heard him say.

Deirdre read aloud from Hugh Lloyd-Jones's recent collection of tributes to Maurice Bowra, Connolly's *Sunday Times* valediction among them – he was so taken with Noël Annan's contribution that he insisted on his being sent a congratulatory telegram – while Noël Blakiston, at his old friend's request, read from Ezra Pound:

> I am thy soul, Nykoptis. I have watched
> These five millennia, and thy dead eyes
> Move not, nor ever answer my desire.

'Cyril is dying beyond my means,' Sir Harry d'Avigdor-Goldsmid is supposed to have said, evincing a wit that Connolly would surely have relished under happier circumstances; but whatever the reasons, shortly before he died Connolly was moved from the Harley Street Clinic to St Vincent's Hospital in Ladbroke Grove. 'I'm nothing but a zombie now, but luckily I rather like lying here thinking about the past,' he told Ali Forbes: but when Stephen Spender came to see him, very near the end, he turned his face to the wall and whispered 'Who is it? Is it Stephen? Go away – I no longer belong to this world.' He was moved on a Friday; by Saturday he was being given morphine to relieve the pain; the Sunday was, according to Deirdre, 'the worst day I've ever known', with Connolly thrashing and moaning about the bed; on Monday he was himself again, 'and it was all right between us for ever.' The nuns who ran St Vincent's had told Deirdre that they were unable to look after terminal cases; but before he could be moved on again he had died, at 11.30 on the morning of November the 26th. Deirdre rang the Hobsons to tell them that 'Our darling has left us', and the next day

Anthony and Tanya Hobson went round to collect his possessions from the hospital, and the death certificate: the cause of death was given as cardiac failure, and the secondary causes as arterio-sclerosis and hypertension.

He was buried on the 2nd of December in Berwick Church, in the shadow of the Downs – where, some fourteen years earlier, Cressida had been christened. Will Carter, the Cambridge typographer, designed the headstone: his name and dates were subscribed with a quotation from the *Aeneid*, 'Intus aquae dulces vivoque sedilia saxo' – 'Within are fresh waters and seats from the living stone.' The Hobsons met Deirdre, Peter Levi and Cressida for lunch at the Cavendish Hotel in Eastbourne – the food was filthy, the wine very good – before driving over to Berwick; Stephen Spender travelled down on the train from Victoria with Diana, Noël Blakiston, Sonia Orwell and Jack Lambert, and at Lewes they were met by a cortège of Daimlers and driven to the church. It was a wet and windy day, and the church was crammed with mourners, shown to their places by Ali Forbes; at one point the porch door was flung open with dramatic effect, and Duncan Grant – whose lurid murals are, perhaps, the best known feature of Berwick Church – staggered in, clad in an astrakhan hat, a duffle coat and bright red trousers. The vicar made a short speech about Connolly's life and work, and Anthony Hobson read from 1 Corinthians 15, 'The last enemy that shall be destroyed is death;' and afterwards the mourners stood by the grave in the cold and wet before moving on to St John's Road, where drinks were handed round, Matthew sat on people's knees, and 'the party acquired the normality of any champagne party.' That evening, the Quennells invited Lady Diana Cooper and Michael Holroyd to dinner: poised in mid-carve over the joint, Peter Quennell suddenly remarked 'This is Cyril's first night under ground.'

Years before, Connolly had suggested that his memorial service should be held at Sotheby's: there would be a 'sung bibliography', a 'wants list' would be chanted, and – Deirdre suggested – he would be buried clutching a bottle of Worcester sauce 'in case the chef's British'. On another occasion, he imagined himself peering down on the gathering below, and how

> as the choir from the Abbey or Solesmes thunders out the Dies Irae (Palestrina's? or just plain chant?); as the orchestra gets down to Stravinsky's Symphony of Psalms, and the weeping multitude file out to the final irony of Debussy's Gigue, I can imagine but one thought. Who's going to pay?

Connolly's debts were no laughing matter – the Alexander Cozens, the Lucian Freud, many of his books and much of his silver and porcelain had already been sold, and a fund was being planned – but in the meantime a memorial service, organised by John Betjeman, was held on 20 December at St Mary-le-Strand. Michael Berkeley, the son of Sir Lennox, composed a motet for unaccompanied choir, and speeches and readings were given by Stephen Spender, John Betjeman and Peter Levi. 'Cyril used to say memorials most important for social climbers,' Bill Davis scrawled on the back of his order sheet; and then – presumably for the edification of his neighbour – 'Next to Deirdre important man Harrod's fruit department'. It seemed a good note on which to end.

REFERENCES

Where it is obvious from the text who is writing to whom, I have given the date only of letters (if known). I have listed in the Preface the libraries and collections consulted, and to save space I have referred to them here as briefly as possible ('Tulsa', for example). *DT* refers to the *Daily Telegraph*, *E of P* to *Enemies of Promise*, *H* to *Horizon*, *NS* to the *New Statesman*, *J and M* to *Journal and Memoir*, *TCP* to *The Condemned Playground*, *RF* to *A Romantic Friendship*, *TRP* to *The Rock Pool*, *TUG* to *The Unquiet Grave*, and *ST* to the *Sunday Times*.

vi What is there to say . . .': quoted in John Russell, *Reading Russell*, p. 99.

PREFACE

x 'No two biographies . . .': 'Sainte-Beuve' in *Previous Convictions*, p. 176.

CHAPTER 1: 'ANCESTRAL VOICES'

1 'Look, there's the Abbey . . .': unpublished MS of 'Happy Deathbeds', n.d., Tulsa.

2 'the refusal to face . . .': *E of P*, p. 183.

3 'my journalism is literature': interview with Simon Blow, *Guardian*, 8 Sept. 1974.

3 'who criticises everything': draft *TUG*, Austin.

3 'I hate colonels . . .': *Life and Letters*, Oct. 1929.

4 'My mother, with . . .': unpublished MS, private collection.

4 'reciting the "Dead . . ." ': *E of P*, p. 170.

4 'My father's forebears . . .': *ST*, 6 Aug. 1972.

4 'who, in their turn,': Major Connolly, unpublished family records, n.d., Tulsa.

4 'simple, bluff old sea dogs . . .': *ibid.*

5 'frugal, blue-eyed . . .': *E of P*, p. 157.

5 'from such a devastating . . .': n.d., Tulsa.

f.n. ' "This just links up perfectly" . . .': unpublished MS of 'Finest Hour' by Noël Blakiston, n.d., private collection.

5 'sunk under . . .': Percy King to CC, 14 June 1945, Tulsa.

5 'a worldly old man . . .': Percy King to CC, 13 May 1944, Tulsa.

6 'a great reputation . . .': *E of P*, p. 158.

6 'he was known as . . .': Mollie Connolly to CC, 26 March 1947, Tulsa.

6 'for the capture of an Indian': unpublished memoir by Admiral Connolly, n.d., Tulsa.

6 'a handsome old man . . .': Major Connolly, *op. cit.*

6 'The fifty thousand pounds . . .': draft of *E of P*, Austin.

7 'all the aunts except the mater . . .': Mollie Connolly, *op. cit.*

7 'something of a crank . . .': Major Connolly, *op. cit.*

7 'he was never normal . . .': Mollie Connolly to CC, n.d., Tulsa.

7 'hoarding, collecting passion . . .': CC to Mollie Connolly, n.d., Tulsa.

7 'a somewhat dismal pedant . . .': *The Times*, 27 November 1974.

7 'a mildly eccentric...': Quennell, *The Marble Foot*, p. 222.
8 'philatelic chat...': the *Stamp Collector*, Jan. 1903.
9 'I was the only child...': *ST*, 13 Feb. 1972.
9 'Major Connolly is very vulgar...': n.d., Tulsa.
9 'belching and coughing...': n.d., Tulsa.
9 'He would read...': CC to Clark, n.d., Tulsa.
9 'I always felt...': CC, n.d., Tulsa.
9 'Matt will never be happy...': CC to Lys Lubbock, March 1951, Lilly.
9 'It is noteworthy...': Major Connolly, *op. cit.*
10 'an old Welshman...': Major Connolly, *op. cit.*
f.n. 'trees felled...': *Journal and Memoir*, p. 255.
10 'someone one might see': PQ in conversation with the author.
10 'It is the loss': 10 Jan. 1955, BL.
11 'Love is the consequence...': unpublished MS, Tulsa.
11 'I sometimes think...': 17 Jan. 1957, Tulsa.
11 'your reading to me...': 20 March 1938, Tulsa.
11 'To my mind...': 29 March 1952, Tulsa.
11 'and the nightingales...': 21 May 1964, Tulsa.
11 'I have had many years...': n.d., Tulsa.
11 'My charge of you...': n.d., Tulsa.
11 'She and I...': 24 Dec. 1924, *RF*.
11 'I found two days...': CC to Longden, n.d., Tulsa.
12 'I have dreamt about you...': n.d., Tulsa.
12 'most "Palinuroid" traits': *The Marble Foot*, p. 222.

CHAPTER 2: 'INTIMATIONS OF EDEN'

13 'who discovered...': *E of P*, first edition, Chapter 18.
14 'my memories became': *E of P*, p. 159.
14 'something approaching': *ibid.*
14 'already my life...': *ibid.*
14 'To me it seemed...': draft of *E of P*, Austin.
15 'awoke in me...': *E of P*, p. 160.
15 'You must remember...': n.d., private collection.
15 'from that evening...': *E of P*, p. 162.
15 'I have always felt...': draft of *E of P*, Austin.
16 'From that moment...': *E of P*, p. 162.
16 'character began to deteriorate': *ibid.*
16 'like a vicious little...': *ibid*, p. 163.
16 'To this period I trace...': *ibid.*
17 'seemed always tired': MS of 'Happy Deathbeds', Tulsa.
17 'I had embarked...': *E of P*, p. 164.
17 'the smell of wet cardboard...': *ibid.*
17 'the licence permitted...': draft of *E of P*, Austin.
18 'seemed to be initiated...': *E of P*, p. 165.
18 'possessed an...': draft *E of P*, Austin.
18 'Young Billy...': MS, Tulsa.
18 'and sometimes there were mild...': draft of *E of P*, Austin.
18 'a typical schoolboy': *E of P*, p. 165.
18 'facetious little': *ibid.*
18 'Oh welcome!': unpublished MS, Tulsa.
19 'Scansion unexcellable': unpublished MS, Tulsa.
19 'Ahead of me stretches...': *E of P*, p. 166.
19 'I don't suppose...': 29 March 1952, Tulsa.
20 'We shall miss him...': 18 July 1914, Tulsa.
20 'I came to know...': *E of P*, p. 167.
f.n. 'Do you know how...': Tulsa.
20 'Here were horrible...': *E of P*, p. 167.
20 'Another bitter lesson...': draft of *E of P*, Austin.
20 'Grannie, lodgings...' *E of P*, p. 167.
20 'because another boy...': 20 Oct. 1912, Tulsa.
21 'lonely, romantic and affected...': *E of P*, p. 172.
21 'At night my fear...': *E of P*, p. 176.

22 'always snub...': draft of *E of P*, Austin.

CHAPTER 3: 'ST CYPRIAN'S'

25 'vast, gabled...': *My Life and Soft Times*, p. 36.
25 'the flat playing-field...': 'Such, Such Were the Joys', Collected Essays, Journalism and Letters, Vol. IV, p. 398.
25 '"Look what you've..."': *ibid*, p. 382.
25 'round-shouldered...': *ibid*, p. 381.
25 'cold, businesslike...': *E of P*, p. 174.
25 'tall, reserved, shy...': 'St Cyprian's Days', *Blackwood's Magazine*, May 1971, p. 394.
25 'a courtesy title...': *The House of Elrig*, p. 69.
25 'a strictly matriarchal...': *ibid.*
25 'a couple of silly...': *op. cit.*, p. 420.
26 'the most formidable...': *op. cit.*, p. 36.
26 'a stocky, square-built...': *op. cit.*, p. 380.
26 'regarded Flip...': *The Wandering Years*, p. 32.
26 'rosy cheeks': *ibid*, p. 30.
26 'ample figure': *op. cit.*, p. 394.
26 'the appearance of Flip...': *op. cit.*, p. 70.
26 'to be "in favour"...': *ibid.*
26 'no primitive farmers...': *op. cit.*, p. 394.
26 'Whenever one had...': *op. cit.*, p. 401.
27 'withering her chosen...': *op. cit.*, p. 86.
27 'When angry Flip...': *E of P*, p. 177.
27 'she was basically...': *op. cit.*, p. 87.
27 'women are notoriously...': Christie, *op. cit.*, p. 396.
28 'impatiently, with hair-pulling...': *op. cit.*, p. 395.
28 'I detected...': *op. cit.*, p. 389.
28 'little office boy...': Orwell, *op. cit.*, p. 389.
28 'an expensive and snobbish school': *ibid*, p. 384.
28 'We have an awful lot...': n.d., Tulsa.
28 'a wretched drivelling...': *op. cit.*, p. 384.
29 'the children of rich...': *ibid.*
29 'jump into an icy...': *op. cit.*, p. 30.
29 'we were always hungry...': *op. cit.*, p. 392.
29 'liquefied orange-coloured...': *op. cit.*, p. 37.
29 'sweaty stockings...': *op. cit.*, p. 398.
30 'the oasis of bed...': unpublished MS, Tulsa.
30 'big oak-lined...': Maxwell, *op. cit.*, p. 72.
31 'grey-uniformed veterans': *St Cyprian's Chronicle*, July 1914.
31 'through simple...': Longhurst, *op. cit.*, p. 39.
31 'a gas balloon...': *op. cit.*, p. 36.
31 'rubbed with a purring...': *op. cit.*, p. 71.
31 'haunting the radiators...': *E of P*, p. 175.
32 'I am *very* pleased...': Dec. 1914, Tulsa.
32 'I like St Cyprian's...': n.d., Tulsa.
32 'his grizzled cheek-tufts...': *E of P*, p. 179.
32 'I came down...': *St Cyprian's Chronicle*, July 1915.
32 'boys who read the best...': *ibid.*
32 'there was a fearful row...': Orwell to CC, 14 Dec. 1938, *Collected Essays, Journalism and Letters, Vol. I*, p. 400.
33 'Do you remember...': *ibid.*
33 'Of course you were...': *ibid.*
33 'certainly the strangest...': *op. cit.*, p. 31.
f.n. 'held out his hand...': Roy Fuller, *Spanner and Pen*, p. 171.
33 'I got a bit...': *op. cit.*, p. 31.
33 'What made me tremble...': *ibid.*
34 'a peppery, gruff...': draft *E of P*, Austin.
34 'the barking Wuf-wuf...': CC juvenilia, Tulsa.
34 'the rest were makeshifts...': draft *E of P*, Austin.
34 'one of those invaluable...': *op. cit.*, p. 393.
34 'the one master...': *op. cit.*, p. 78.
34 'about whom even...': *op. cit.*, p. 39.

34 'Visitors are requested...': CC juvenilia, Tulsa.
36 'revealed an artist...': *St Cyprian's Chronicle*, July 1917.
36 'mob-cap and curls...': *op. cit.*, p. 31.
36 'The whole school was mad...': CC to Mollie Connolly, n.d., Tulsa.
37 'perform his part and songs...': CC juvenilia, Tulsa.
37 'I got the chap who...': n.d., Tulsa.
37 'My dear Blair!...': n.d., Tulsa.
37 'The whole thing...': n.d., Tulsa.
38 'summoned by the Municipal...': *St Cyprian's Chronicle*, Jan. 1917.
38 'simply spiffing': CC to Mollie Connolly, 21 May 1916, Tulsa.
38 'I have been turned...': 29 Oct. 1916, Tulsa.
38 'He often visited us...': *St Cyprian's Chronicle*, Jan. 1917.
39 'I have inspected...': *ibid.*
39 'a *very* poor school': L.C. Vaughan Wilkes to Mollie Connolly, 26 Feb. 1917, Tulsa.
39 'was typical of England': *E of P*, p. 175.
40 'a stage rebel...': *ibid*, p. 178, and for CC on Blair and Beaton.
40 'He is extraordinarily...': 26 Nov. 1926. Quoted in Vickers, *Cecil Beaton*, p. 17.
40 'faced with a sea...': Beaton, *The Wandering Years*, p. 31.
41 'the eighty-odd Wulfricians...': *E of P*, p. 180.
41 'a ravishing Japanesey...': draft of *E of P*, Austin.
41 'kept him far too busy': *ibid.*
41 'the one reality': CC to Roger Mynors, n.d., Tulsa.
41 'one of the best friends...': St Cyprian's notebook, Tulsa.
41 'small and brown and wiry...': CC to Mynors, *op. cit.*
41 'moved in a fast-moving set...': *E of P*, p. 186
41 'Wilson the silent...': St Cyprian's notebook, Tulsa.
42 '"Now we are blood brothers,"...': draft of *E of P*, Austin.
42 'after a night of pillow-fighting...': *E of P*, p. 187
42 'We slept together...': CC to Mynors, *op. cit.*
42 'but a consideration...': draft *E of P*, Austin.
42 'tried to kiss me...': CC to Mynors, *op. cit.*
42 'they were in fact...': draft of *E of P*, Austin.
43 'was more faun-like...': CC to Mynors, *op. cit.*
43 for the 'four types', see *E of P*, p. 184–6.
43 for the 'Pair System', see *E of P*, p. 18.
44 'I had a moment...': *E of P*, p. 189.
44 'good in all branches...': St Cyprian's report, July 1917.
45 'a little inclined...': n.d., Tulsa.
45 'little clique...': *E of P*, p. 191.
45 'about as civilised': *ibid*, p. 189.
45 'a kind of "Souls"...': *ibid*, p. 191.
45 'as you will not write...': CC to Mollie Connolly, n.d., Tulsa.
45 'Stalk and sneak...': St Cyprian's notebook, Tulsa.
46 'My lack of character...': *E of P*, p. 190.
46 'The makers of St Cyprian's...': 12 Dec. 1938, Tulsa.
47 'I am deeply impressed...': n.d., Tulsa.
47 'I wonder how you can write...': 8 July 1938, *Collected Essays, Journalism and Letters, Vol. I*, p. 380.
47 'so shocked...': *My Life and Soft Times*, p. 39.
47 'capable and motherly...': 5 June 1967, Tulsa.
48 'never dared to re-read...': *The Evening Colonnade*, p. 372.
48 'history, if it can be bothered...': *ST*, 29 Sept. 1968.
48 'nobody spoke to me': *The Evening Colonnade*, p. 372.

CHAPTER 4: 'AUT COLLEGER AUT NIHIL'

49 'Mais qu'est que c'est...': CC, 'Memories of André Gide', *Adam*, 1970.
f.n. *A Life of Contrasts*, p. 202.

50 'Eton was our Eden...': CC to Blakiston, May 1927, *RF*, p. 304.
51 'Those days belonged...': *Pack My Bag*, p. 85.
51 'an absurd but lovable place': *The Seven Ages*, p. 26.
51 'it encouraged...': *Along the Road to Frome*, p. 40.
51 'Eton publishes a list...': quoted in Fox, *White Mischief*, p. 132.
51 'recall no sense...': *Infants of the Spring*, p. 72.
51 'the supposed difference...': *ibid*, p. 73.
52 'grudged the 70 scholars...': draft of *E of P*, Austin.
52 'You will find all Oppidans...': CC to William le Fanu, 9 Oct. 1922, Tulsa.
52 'College is the only possible...': le Fanu to CC, 22 Oct. 1923, Tulsa.
52 'a charm derived...': *The Whispering Gallery*, p. 95.
53 'the echoes of ancient tongues...': CC to le Fanu, n.d., Tulsa.
53 'quite lost and friendless': *E of P*, p. 195.
54 'The Master in College who...': draft of *E of P*, Austin.
54 'brooding, a sinister figure...': CC to Dannreuther, n.d., Tulsa.
55 'complete nonentity': unpublished MS, Tulsa.
55 'fagmasters were usually...': *E of P*, p. 195.
55 'A tousled wire terrier...': *E of P*, pp 195–6.
56 'who was quick to divine...': *E of P*, p. 196.
56 'To this day...': *E of P*, p. 199.
56 'poor advertisement...': *Infants of the Spring*, p. 125.
56 'I was staggered...': 29 Oct. 1938, Tulsa.
56 'the old College customs...': 8 Dec. 1938, Tulsa.
57 'total anarchy': Hollis, *Along the Road to Frome*, p. 38.
57 'decided that the traditional...': *ibid*, p. 40.
57 'a riot commenced...': quoted in Lancaster, ed., *Brian Howard*, p. 21.
57 'our elders had decided...': *The Road to Wigan Pier*, p. 122.
57 'certain Vile Old Men...': *E of P*, p. 210.
58 'bad influence': *E of P*, p. 203.
58 'cynical and irreverent': unpublished MS, Tulsa.
58 'a big, neat, handsome boy...': *E of P*, p. 200.
58 'Untidy, lazy yet energetic...': *ibid.*
58 'Such an end...': *ibid*, p. 202.
59 'dirty, inky, miserable...': *ibid*, p. 203.
59 'His work like his hair...': Eton school report, n.d., Tulsa.
59 'I have had sometimes...': 19 Dec. 1918, Tulsa.
59 'The boy certainly has a vein...': *ibid.*
60 'suggested the torture...': Proceedings of the Chamber Debating Society, 4 Oct. 1919, College Reading Room, Eton.
60 'All gentlemen in College...': Proceedings of the College Debating Society, 1 Oct. 1921, College Reading Room, Eton.
60 'inner culture': *E of P*, p. 231.
61 'Socrates roamed...': *ibid*, p. 234.
61 'an ogre for the purple patch': *ibid*, p. 232.
61 'his sensibility...': *The Bonus of Laughter*, p. 42.
61 'there was no doubt...': draft of *E of P*, Austin.
61 'the forbidden tree': *ibid.*
61 'romantic passions...': *Infants of the Spring*, p. 79.
61 'lay my personality...': *E of P*, p. 206.
61 'the toughest member...': draft of *E of P*, Austin.

CHAPTER 5: 'THE DREAM BROTHER'

62 'brown hair, not very dark...': MS of uncompleted story, Tulsa.
62 'the one person...': CC to Dannreuther, n.d., Tulsa.
62 'I first noticed you...': CC to Blakiston, n.d., Tulsa.
62 'wistfulness of...': *E of P*, p. 206.

62 'so generous with bananas and cream': *ST*, 16 March 1958.
63 'The Thames Valley climate...': *E of P*, p. 208.
64 'a charming, feline boy': *ibid*.
64 'the kindness and cruelty of a cat...': Anon. to CC, 15 Aug. 1925.
64 'His wit and range...': Rylands to Anthony Hobson, 3 Oct. 1984, private collection.
64 'knew by heart...': *E of P*, p. 239.
64 'foppish, melancholy and ironical dandy': *E of P*, p. 208.
64 'I have dwelt in spirit...': unpublished MS, Tulsa.
64 'heartless, soulful Noël': notebook, Tulsa.
64 'one of the few rooms...': CC to William le Fanu, n.d., Tulsa.
f.n. 'their paths only crossed...': CC to William le Fanu, n.d., Tulsa.
65 'very definite ideas...': *Miscellaneous Verdicts*, p. 299.
65 'He's one of the few people...': n.d., Tulsa.
65 'I said I thought...': CC to Beddard, n.d., Tulsa.
65 'I feel very honoured...': quoted in letter from CC to Beddard, *op. cit.*
66 'I am afraid I am gone on Eastwood...': quoted in letter from CC to Beddard, *op. cit.*
67 'dirty scug': *E of P*, p. 218.
67 'like an old hostess...': *E of P*, p. 220.
67 'Now years three...': MS, Tulsa.
68 'Here, Private Connolly...': *E of P*, p. 222.
f.n. 'our self-appointed jester...': quoted in Crick, *George Orwell*, p. 56.
68 'To this day...': *E of P*, p. 208.
f.n. 'Came out in the form...': 29 Nov. 1938, Tulsa.
69 'intolerable selfishness...': unpublished MS, Tulsa.
69 'at school his oscillating...': *ibid.*
69 'I don't know what...': Raymond Coughlin to R. Delves Broughton, n.d., Tulsa.
69 'His conversation...': le Fanu, unpublished journal, 25 June 1922, Tulsa.
69 'Even people one would never...': *ibid*, 29 June 1922, Tulsa.
70 'a charm in your outward...': 9 Sept. 1922, Tulsa.
70 'Intelligence was a deformity...': *E of P*, p. 230.
70 'Becoming ashamed of working...': draft of *E of P*, Austin.
70 'He is in danger...': Crace to Major Connolly, 20 April 1920, Tulsa.
70 'constantly the saving feature...': 28 July 1920, Tulsa.
71 'in leaving classics...': 18 Dec. 1920, Tulsa.
71 'they were teachers whose rebukes...': *E of P*, p. 238.
71 'sanest of schoolmasters': *ibid*, p. 237.
71 'a pre-Ruskinian culture...': *ibid.*
71 'In the aestheticism...': *ibid*, p. 238.
72 'not a place...': CC to Blakiston, 22 Dec. 1924. *RF*, p. 39.
72 'I am very fond indeed...': CC to Longden, n.d., Tulsa.
72 'We are so shut in...': CC to Dannreuther, n.d., Tulsa.
72 'the military horrors of Aldershot...': CC to Mynors, n.d., Tulsa.
72 'Damp is in the house...': n.d., Tulsa.
72 'foolishly afraid...': n.d., Tulsa.
73 'flirt and if possible fall in love...': n.d., Tulsa.
74 'produced no sudden ecstasy...': CC to le Fanu, n.d. Tulsa.
74 'as full of whores...': n.d., Tulsa.
74 'a truly Michael Fane experience...': CC to Dannreuther, *op. cit.*
74 'be telling you the nearest...': CC to le Fanu, *op. cit.*
75 'clerical reactionary': *E of P*, p. 229 .

CHAPTER 6: 'POP AND THE PERMANENT ADOLESCENT'

76 'most of the staff': *E of P*, p. 231.
76 'much too favourable...': 11 May 1961. *Lyttelton-Hart-Davis Letters*, Vol. II, p. 55.

76 'easy-going extroverts...': *E of P*, p. 245.
77 'idled into fame...': *ibid*, p. 243.
77 'gut a book...': *ibid*, p. 244.
77 'As a little boy...': draft of *E of P*, Austin.
77 'the most successful types...': *E of P*, p. 244.
77 'they were dandies...': *E of P*, p. 245.
77 'a votary...': *ibid.*
78 'remarkable for his vitality...': *NS*, 21 Dec. 1935.
78 'droll, idle, timorous little beetle': *E of P.*
79 'a bad institution...': *The Seven Ages*, p. 26.
79 'one of those angel-faced...': *E of P*, p. 250.
79 'a handsome red-haired Etonian': *Another Part of the Wood*, p. 84.
79 'an immense zest...': *ibid*, p. 96.
80 'man of angelic disposition': *Harold Nicolson*, Vol. I, p. 341.
80 'good-looking, enthusiastic...': *Part of My Life*, p. 82.
80 'good natured and cheerful...': miscellaneous notes, Tulsa.
80 'and after they had left...': *E of P*, p. 252.
80 'I cannot tell you...': *Antony*, p. 82.
80 'Is that the tug...': quotes in Powell, *Infants of the Spring*, p. 120.
80 'an Extreme Blond...': *E of P*, p. 202.
81 'I know only...': *ibid*, p. 256.
81 'Get into Pop...': CC to William le Fanu, n.d., Tulsa.
82 'for a month...': *E of P*, p. 260.
82 'Connolly was in Pop...': Powell, *op. cit.*, p. 119.
82 'I knew him, of course...': *ibid.*
82 'He occupied...': *The Whispering Gallery*, p. 97.
83 'an ugly and unimportant house...': *E of P*, p. 261.
83 'I felt about them...': draft *E of P*, Austin.
84 'the house was crammed...': William le Fan unpublished journal, 22 July 1922, Tulsa.
84 'signatures on my programme...': *E of P*, p. 261.
84 'like a Labour Party...': draft *E of P*, Austin.
85 'the most handsome boy...': quoted in Lancaster, *op. cit.*, p. 120.
85 'His big brown eyes...': *Memoirs of an Aesthete*, p. 79.
85 'a distinguished, impertinent face...': *E of P*, p. 265.
85 'like a lady...': *ibid.*
86 'subtle cramp of metre': quoted in Lancaster, *op. cit.*, p. 35
86 'I hear that Gow...': *ibid*, p. 96.
86 'neither of whom seemed...': Powell, *op. cit.*, p. 115.
86 'to a set of boys...': *E of P*, p. 266.
86 'most of us had not yet...': quoted in Lancaster, *op. cit.*, p. 56.
86 'literature meant...': *E of P*, p. 181.
87 'the full Tennysonian afterglow': *ibid.*
87 'the authentic romantic thrill...': *E of P*, p. 241.
87 'no modern poet...': 18 May 1926, *RF*, p. 131.
87 'Mediterranean clarity...': *E of P*, p. 232.
89 'always conscious...': Maud to CC, n.d., Tulsa.
89 'frightfully pushing...': miscellaneous notes, Tulsa.
89 'a cake of soap...': CC to Charles Milligan, n.d., Tulsa.
89 'wordly superior...': Dannreuther to CC, 9 Sept. 1922, Tulsa.
89 'all musical...': n.d., Tulsa.
89 'very sensual...': n.d., Tulsa.
89 'My God if Crace...': O'Dwyer to CC, n.d., Tulsa.
89 'I always hanker...': CC to O'Dwyer, n.d., Tulsa.
90 'I was supposed to be...': draft *E of P*, Austin.
90 'a private civilisation...': *E of P*, p. 270.
90 'but I just don't see...': draft *E of P*, Austin.
90 'kissed each other...': CC to O'Dwyer, n.d., Tulsa.
90 'So it has come...': miscellaneous verses, Tulsa.
91 'I am terrified...': n.d., Tulsa.

91 'Crace and the Head Usher...': n.d., Tulsa.
92 'corrupt the fags...': CC to O'Dwyer, n.d., Tulsa.
92 'I do not wish...': Headlam to CC, 27 June 1923, Tulsa.
92 'Tuppy told me...': n.d., Tulsa.
92 'bringing out friendship...': 20 Dec. 1922, Tulsa.
92 'There is not a thing...': *Antony*, p. 122.
92 'Reading about Eton...': unpublished notebook, Tulsa.
93 'I labour under...': n.d., Tulsa.
93 'nothing without one's friends...': 21 April 1927, *RF*, p. 295.
93 'the experiences undergone...': *E of P*, p. 271.
93 'Once again romanticism...': *ibid*, p. 272.
94 'For my own part...': *ibid.*
94 'Somewhere in the facts...': *ibid*, p. 278.
95 'Cultured middle-class life...': Collected Essays, Journalism and Letters, Vol. I, p. 566.

CHAPTER 7: 'BLOKEY BALLIOL'

96 'only lasting homesickness...': unpublished MS, Tulsa.
96 'I hanker...': n.d., Tulsa.
97 'My ambition...': unpublished journal, Tulsa.
97 'cold, tired and depressed': *ibid.*
97 'Christ I do miss you...': n.d., Tulsa.
97 'I would like to write a symphony...': n.d., Tulsa.
97 'a tempting book... very limp': unpublished journal, Sept.–Oct. 1922, Tulsa.
98 'My trouble is...': CC to le Fanu, n.d., Tulsa.
99 'Balliol stood out...': Powell, *Infants of the Spring*, p. 147.
99 'Balliol is the home...': 9 Sept. 1922, Tulsa.
99 'antagonistic to Balliol...': unpublished notebook, Tulsa.
99 'Denis I would never...': CC to O'Dwyer, n.d., Tulsa.
99 'Chesterto-Wembley...': CC to Milligan, n.d., Tulsa.
99 'unlimited drink...': CC to O'Dwyer, n.d. Tulsa.
99 'a little too hard...': *Memories*, p. 158.
100 'biscuits and oranges...': n.d., Tulsa.
100 'If it were a monastery...': n.d., Tulsa.
100 'without doubt the most gifted...': *Another Part of the Wood*, p. 97.
100 'I don't think you had...': n.d., Tulsa.
100 'complete with a brass band...': *With an Eye to the Future*, p. 97.
101 'Connolly was no less further removed...': Powell, *op. cit.*, p. 162.
102 'Anything connected with Oxford ...': CC to Balfour, n.d., Tulsa.
102 'and to make up for it...': Bowra, *op. cit.*, p. 157.
102 'slim and slight...': *ibid.*
102 'obviously an extraordinary person...': Clark, *op. cit.*, p. 85.
103 'he had read...': *ibid*, p. 97.
103 'His was a protean character': *The Marble Foot*, p. 118.
103 'It's been *extremely* nice...': 29 April 1923, Tulsa.
103 'lending colour...': *The Sign of the Fish*, p. 192.
104 'the squat tower of the castle...': misc. MS, Tulsa.
104 'too fastidious...': *A Little Learning*, p. 203.
104 'I am glad to find...': CC to O'Dwyer, n.d., Tulsa.
104 'kindly-looking man...': Clark, *op. cit.*, p. 85.
104 'mild, monkish...': Powell, *op. cit.*, p. 150.
104 'we should get the best men...': quoted in Hollis, *Oxford in the Twenties*, p. 12.
104 'lascivious blue lips...': *Glimpses of the Great*, p. 172.
105 'who attracted him by their looks...': *A Sort of Life*, p. 135.
105 'cultivated but not highbrow...': Bowra, *op. cit.* p. 119.
105 'down-to-earth approach...': Powell, *op. cit.*, p. 161.

105 'content to live in a society...': *The Marble Foot*, p. 123.
106 'As to women, I came...': n.d., Eton.
106 'strange, roistering character...': *The Seven Ages*, p. 51.
106 'kind and generous...': Bowra, *op. cit.*, p. 158.
106 'From Sligger comes...': unpublished verses, Tulsa.
107 'Whatever you hear about the war...': quoted in Lloyd-Jones ed., *Maurice Bowra*, p. 44.
107 'I was not nearly so sure...': *Memories*, p. 124.
107 'Noticeably small,...': *Infants of the Spring*, p. 179.
107 'When you were with him...': Lloyd-Jones, *op. cit.*, p. 61.
107 'passionately opposed...': *ibid*, p. 16.
107 'Endowed with...': *ibid*, p. 17.
107 'priggish fears...': *Another Part of the Wood*, p. 100.
107 'Here was a don...': *Infants of the Spring*, p. 179.
108 'stimulate the brilliant response...': *With an Eye to the Future*, p. 70.
108 'to meet him...': Lloyd-Jones, *op. cit.*, p. 49.
108 'great reserves...': Lancaster, *op. cit.*, p. 71.
108 'a slight sense of danger...': *Infants of the Spring*, p. 179.
108 'even those who were at heart...': *Oxford in the Twenties*, p. 21.
108 'The Bowra innovation...': *Infants of the Spring*, p. 180.
108 'gave tutorials...': Hollis, *Oxford in the Twenties*, p. 22.
109 'always talked as if...': Powell, *op. cit.*, p. 180.
109 'It has the most marvellous...': CC to le Fanu, n.d., Tulsa.
109 'comparing himself with Swann...': *Memories*, p. 158.

CHAPTER 8. 'MINEHEAD AND AFTER'

110 'call a masterpiece jolly...': unpublished notebook, Tulsa.
110 'revoltingly tawdry...': n.d., Tulsa.
110 'nice, odd, child-like boy...': CC to Mynors, n.d., Tulsa.
110 'perhaps the most admired...': *Personal Impressions*, p. 92.
111 'he was at heart a puritan...': n.d., Tulsa.
111 'become a complete prostitute...': CC to Mynors, n.d., Tulsa.
111 'Gloucester Road...': extracts quoted here are taken from an unpublished diary, 17 March to 4 April 1923, Tulsa.
112 'Spain of all countries...': unpublished MS, Tulsa.
112 'I am Catholique and Irlandais...': 23 July 1923, Tulsa.
113 'I look very sleuth-like...': 23 July 1923, Tulsa.
114 'never known the squalor...': CC to Longden, n.d., Tulsa.
114 'Work was the order of the day...': *Memories*, p. 120.
114 'pulses and stale bread': *Another Part of the Wood*, p. 98.
114 'as regards books...': 20 June 1923, Huntington.
115 'cold and haughty-looking...': CC to Longden, n.d., Tulsa.
115 'And then I start...': unpublished verses, Tulsa.
116 'Well, my dear infant...': CC to Longden, n.d., Tulsa.
116 'tristesse d'automne...': CC to le Fanu, n.d., Tulsa.
116 'an invincible mania...': n.d., Tulsa.
116 'I am much poorer...': 22 Dec. 1923, Tulsa.
117 'Christ! a horrible Sardinian face' *et seq.*: CC to Longden, n.d., Tulsa.
117 'happier than I have been...': n.d., Tulsa.
118 'As you know, I only tolerate Oxford...': n.d., Tulsa.
118 'I always want to sleep with you...': n.d., Tulsa.
118 'of course the purely mystical...': n.d., Tulsa.
118 'I agree about Noël...': Powell to Anthony Hobson, 2 Aug. 1983, private collection.
118 'The brown curtains...': n.d., Huntington.
119 'the next day Cyril...': James Lees-Milne, unpublished diary, 13 Dec. 1974.

119 'ugly, garrulous, rasping...': unpublished diary, Tulsa.
119 'I walked in the palms...': n.d., Tulsa.
120 'worst kind of pompous...': CC to Longden, n.d., Tulsa.
120 'the greatest thing in the world...': n.d., *RF*, p. 11.
120 'I'll tell Sir Arthur...': CC to Longden, n.d., Tulsa.
121 'vulgarity reigns...': CC to Longden, n.d., Tulsa.
121 'I hate Oxford...': *ibid.*
121 'this is the earthly...': n.d., *RF*, p. 12.
122 'less spinstered...': CC to Longden, n.d., Tulsa.
122 'he came and spoke...': CC to Balfour, 14 Sept. 1924, Huntington.
122 'a most Ionian city...': CC to Mynors, n.d., Tulsa.
122 'lovely Eritreans...': CC to Longden, n.d. Tulsa.
122 'so like my conception...': CC to Mynors, n.d., Tulsa.
123 'muffled autochthonous... homecoming': CC to Mynors, n.d., Tulsa.
123 'I think you are entirely right...': CC to Blakiston, n.d., *RF*, p. 15.
123 'a certain lack of robustness...': quotes are from Pater's *Imaginary Portraits*.
123 'fighting a losing battle...': CC to Blakiston, 18 Oct. 1924, *RF*, p. 20.
123 'so now I do 1688...': *ibid.*
123 'florid and bustling...': *ibid.*
124 'N. was fairly quiet...': unpublished MS, Tulsa.
124 'I agree with you...': CC to Blakiston, 31 Oct. 1924, *RF*, p. 23.
124 'everywhere malice reigns...': CC to Blakiston, 24 Nov. 1924, *RF*, p. 26.
124 'tasting innumerable kinds of cider...': CC to Longden, n.d., Tulsa.
124 'It was very ghostly...': n.d. *RF*, p. 30.
125 'It was horrible...': n.d., Tulsa.
125 'The chief snag in our relations...': n.d., *RF*, p. 31.
126 'Poverty and stupidity...': CC to Longden, n.d., Tulsa.
126 'My father has repeated...': CC to Blakiston, n.d., *RF*, p. 37.
127 'the Narcissus of the Balliol baths': unpublished MS, Tulsa.
127 'he really is a very great man...': n.d., Tulsa.
127 'nauseating...': CC to Balfour, 5 Jan. 1925, Huntington.
127 'incredibly peaceful...': CC to Balfour, 12 Jan. 1925, Huntington.
127 'surging sea': Synnott to Balfour, 7 Jan. 1925, Huntington.
128 'Dear Patrick...': 5 Jan. 1925, Huntington.
128 'If I slept with Noël...': *ibid.*
128 'Our friendship seems...': 8 Jan. 1925, Eton.
128 'I don't think I have ever been happier...': n.d., Tulsa.
129 'enjoyed them a lot...': Bowra to CC, n.d., Tulsa.
129 'in a fit of spleen...': n.d., Tulsa.
129 'I shouldn't worry...': Bowra to Balfour, 28 July 1925, Huntington.
129 'How many geese...': unpublished verses, Tulsa.
130 'with an adorable...': CC to Longden, n.d., Tulsa.
130 'which whenever I wear...': CC to Synnott, n.d., Tulsa.
130 'malignant leer...': CC to Blakiston, n.d., *RF*, p. 69.
130 'Oxford is just bloody...': CC to Blakiston, 27 April 1925, *RF*, p. 73.
130 'incredibly lovely...': unpublished MS, Tulsa.
131 'What worries me...': n.d., Tulsa.
131 'There was no need...': *A Little Learning*, p. 206.
131 'extremely lavish...': *The Marble Foot*, p. 114.
131 'highly successful...': unpublished MS, private collection.
132 'When days...': quoted in CC to Blakiston, n.d., *RF*, p. 83.
132 'What sort of a fellow...': quoted in Hollis, *The Seven Ages*, p. 51.
132 'I had thought...': *Memoirs of an Aesthete*, p. 133.
132 'long ago...': n.d., Tulsa.
132 'like a death struggle...': CC to Blakiston, n.d., Tulsa.

132 'Bobbie who was very hot...': *ibid.*
133 'the surprising name...': *A Cornishman at Oxford*, p. 232.
133 'How horrible...': n.d., Tulsa.
133 'about that absurd...': 3 Aug. 1925, Tulsa.
133 'I am glad Sligger...': 12 Aug. 1925, Tulsa.
133 'Oxford remains...': n.d., Tulsa.

CHAPTER 9. 'IN LIMBO'.

134 'You *must* bestir yourself...': n.d., Tulsa.
134 'Don't let yourself...': 10 Sept. 1925, Tulsa.
134 'Remember, Cyril...': n.d., Tulsa.
135 'Well, the great fight...': 7 Sept. 1925, Tulsa.
135 'Mr Cyril Connolly...': 8 Oct. 1925, Tulsa.
135 'a mild dose...': CC to Blakiston, 13 July 1925, *RF*, p. 98.
136 'Dependence does not suit Noël...': CC to Bowra, n.d., Tulsa.
136 'the dearth of good talk...': n.d., Tulsa.
136 'bury a token...': 5 Aug. 1925, Tulsa.
136 'which he did...': CC to Bowra, n.d., Tulsa.
137 'I got mixed up...': CC to le Fanu, 25 Aug. 1925, Tulsa.
137 'How beautifully brown...': le Fanu to CC, 15 Aug. 1925, Tulsa.
137 'He treated Noël...': 9 Dec. 1925, Huntington.
137 'I feel I have watched...': 2 Jan. 1927, Tulsa.
137 'Your going away...': 31 Oct. 1925, Tulsa.
137 'have nothing but spiteful...': 'John' to CC, n.d., Tulsa.
138 'extremely good value...': n.d., Tulsa.
138 'our relationship...': n.d., private collection.
138 'De Musset indeed!...': n.d., Eton.
138 'There is nothing to read...': 18 May 1926, Eton.
138 'I never thought...': n.d., private collection.
138 'and so far...': 10 Nov. 1925, Eton.
138 'Don't mind me': 29 Aug. 1926, Eton.
138 'the most precarious...': CC to Blakiston, n.d., *RF*, p. 103.
139 'weighed down with scholarships...': Bowra to Balfour, 22 Aug. 1926, Huntington.
139 'awfully sad and anxious': 5 Sept. 1925, Tulsa.
139 'pay some of your Oxford bills...': 27 April 1926, Eton.
139 'enormous bills...': 3 Nov. 1925, Tulsa.
139 'status of bank clerks...': n.d., Tulsa.
139 'I am more than disappointed...': 16 Nov. 1925, Tulsa.
140 'yellow little man...': CC to Blakiston, n.d., *RF*, p. 110.
140 'exquisite moment of nostalgia...': 4 March 1966, Tulsa.
140 'memories of you...': 10 July 1974, Tulsa.
140 'a fashionable suburb...': CC to Blakiston, 30 Nov. 1925, *RF*, p. 107. f.n. 'You would never...': n.d., private collection.
140 'black people are...': CC to Blakiston, n.d., *RF*, p. 111.
140 'I have given up...': n.d., Tulsa.
140 'I have never felt...': n.d., *RF* p. 111.
141 'Je suis porté...': misc MS, Tulsa.
141 'real greenness...': unpublished MS, Tulsa.
141 'Simon awoke...': untitled MS, Tulsa.
141 'I live in...': CC to Jack Blakiston, n.d., private collection.
141 'slip into a church...': 1 Jan. 1926, Tulsa.
141 'base ingratitude': 8 Feb. 1926, Huntington.
141 'I try to find romance...': n.d., *RF*, p. 113.
142 'I to return etc...': unpublished verses, Tulsa.
142 'Sorry if I have lost caste...': 22 May 1926, Tulsa.
143 'if I have learned...': unpublished notebook, Tulsa.

143 'the most awful old satyr . . .': CC to Blakiston, 16 May 1926, *RF*, p. 126.
143 'short and fat . . .': *The Familiar Faces*, p. 18.
143 'an unpleasant man . . .': 17 May 1926, Tulsa.
143 '*Cardinal* . . .': unpublished MS, Tulsa.
144 'Since friendship haunts . . .': CC to Blakiston, n.d., *RF*, p. 133.
144 'Has Bobbie or Sligger . . .': n.d., Tulsa.
144 'just the thing . . .': 1 Aug. 1926, Tulsa.
144 'provided you promise . . .': 1 Aug. 1926, Tulsa.
145 'intelligent and nice . . .': CC to Synnott, n.d., Tulsa.

CHAPTER 10: 'UNCLE BALDHEAD AND THE AFFABLE HAWK'

147 'The pleasure of giving . . .': Handbook of the 'Down with Cyril Society', Tulsa.
147 'he is the complete craftsman . . .': 14 Aug. 1926, *RF*, p. 162.
147 'strained off . . .': John Russell, Introduction to *A Portrait of Logan Pearsall Smith*, p. 17.
147 'a largish man . . .': *Recollections of Logan Pearsall Smith*, p. 2.
147 'a tall man . . .': Introduction to *A Portrait* . . ., p. 31.
147 'His tall frame . . .': *Another Part of the Wood*, p. 145.
148 'He is a very well-brushed . . .': 18 May 1919. *Diary*, Vol. I. p. 275.
148 'I don't want respect . . .': quoted in *A Portrait* . . ., p. 2.
148 'the most delicious and enduring . . .': quoted in *A Portrait* . . ., p. 5.
148 'cat and mouse . . .': A.L. Rowse, *A Cornishman at Oxford*, p. 133.
148 'When Uncle Logan . . .': *Julia*, p. 48.
148 'At the height . . .': *Another Part of the Wood*, p. 147.
149 'long, dark, sullen . . .': *Recollections*, p. 13.
149 'enjoyed the company . . .': *Another Part of the Wood*, p. 146.
149 'the steam from the banana . . .': *Julia*, p. 99.
149 'almost disappointed . . .': *Forty Years with Berenson*, p. 64.
149 'contrived to saturate . . .': *A Portrait* . . ., p. 29.
149 'a small Tudor farmhouse . . .': CC to Blakiston, 26 July 1926, *RF*, p. 153.
150 'in a position for which . . .': *Recollections* . . ., p. 47.
150 'He disclaimed . . .': *A Portrait* . . ., p. 5.
150 'the act of copulation . . .': Handbook of the 'Anti-Cyril Society', Tulsa.
150 'How do you pronounce . . .': *A Portrait* . . ., p. 14.
150 'was not really workable . . .': *ibid*, p. 27.
150 'to whom I stand . . .': Pearsall Smith to CC, 7 Dec. 1926, Tulsa.
151 'the worst thing so far . . .': n.d., Lilly.
151 'courteous, sympathetic . . .': 3 Aug. 1926, *RF*, p. 156.
151 'very adequate . . .': CC to Blakiston, 14 Aug. 1926, *RF*, p. 162.
151 'blithe old Chinaman . . .': CC to Synnott, 24 Aug. 1926, Tulsa.
151 'God knows how much . . .': 21 Nov. 1926, Tulsa.
152 'in the interest of the Republic . . .': n.d., Tulsa.
152 'always dreamed . . .': *Another Part of the Wood*, p. 146.
152 'That you should be at work . . .': 21 Nov. 1926, Tulsa.
152 'much struck with my promise . . .': CC to Blakiston, 3 Aug. 1926, *RF*, p. 156.
152 'I write quite a lot . . .': 13 March 1927, Huntington.
153 'She must be grown-up . . .': unpublished story, private collection.
153 'Love is a painful . . .': n.d., *RF*, p. 172.
153 'the greatest living writer . . .': CC to Blakiston, 3 Aug. 1926, *RF*, p. 156.
154 'The loss of Eden . . .': n.d., Lilly.
154 'I am chiefly occupied . . .': n.d., Tulsa.

155 'purely to teach myself... *et seq.*': unpublished notebook, Tulsa.
156 'a very good man indeed...': 14 Aug. 1926, *RF*, p. 161.
157 'Henry has fallen...': quoted in Cecil, *Clever Hearts*, p. 128.
157 'incapable of...': quoted in Holroyd, *Lytton Strachey*, Vol. II, p. 114.
157 'he possesses any faults...': 18 Feb. 1919. *Diary* Vol. I. p. 237.
158 'Desmond simply...': *Personal Record*, p. 184.
158 'used his voice...': *Memories*, p. 82.
158 'a pair of china birds...': *ibid.*
158 'a plump, warmhearted...': *Personal Record*, p. 185.
159 'Desmond's voice rises up...': CC to Blakiston, 18 Nov. 1926, *RF*, p. 189.
159 'Molly and I...': *ibid.*
159 'I regard you...': n.d., Lilly.
159 'Mind you...': quoted in CC to Blakiston, 18 Nov. 1926, *RF*, p. 188.
159 'Desmond and I...': *ibid.*
159 'moved heaven and earth...': CC to Blakiston, 25 Dec. 1926, *RF*, p. 200.
159 'I hear you have begun...': n.d., Tulsa.
159 'unguarded and thoughtless...': 18 Jan. 1927, Lilly.
160 'little round man...': 'Alpdodger' sketch, Tulsa.
160 'I am not very much in favour...': CC to Blakiston, 3 Aug. 1926, *RF*, p. 157.
160 'whose face...': CC to le Fanu, 25 Aug. 1925, Tulsa.
161 'Go to the Astoria...': unpublished guidebook, Tulsa.
161 'There was something sexually...': 'The Sisters Good', MS, Tulsa.
162 'since leaving Eton...': CC to Blakiston, 29 Dec. 1926, *RF*, p. 202.
162 'all curiously saturated...': unpublished MS, Tulsa.
162 'I miss you with grief...': unpublished notebook, Eton.
162 'to swerve away...': CC to Blakiston, n.d., Tulsa.
162 'use the letters...': n.d., Tulsa.
162 'confident and natural...': 13 Nov. 1926, *RF*, p. 184.
162 'I worship the past...': CC to Blakiston, 18 Nov. 1926, *RF*, p. 187.
163 'appalled to find...': CC to Blakiston, 16 Nov. 1926, *RF*, p. 184.
163 'must be alive...': n.d., *RF*, p. 191.
163 'relying entirely...': n.d., Lilly.
163 'Truth is revealed...': 25 Dec. 1926, *RF*, p. 198.
163 'a young girl's...': CC to Jack Blakiston, n.d., private collection.
163 'Alps, arguments...': CC to Balfour, 13 March 1927, Huntington.
163 'Don't you think...': 27 Jan. 1927, *RF*, p. 232.
164 'Handbook of...': unpublished MS, Tulsa.
164 'I am delighted...': 17 Nov. 1926, Tulsa.
164 'could not fathom...': CC to Blakiston, 5 Nov. 1926, *RF*, p. 181.
164 'Edith is tedious...': CC to Blakiston, n.d., *RF*, p. 191.
164 'one of the prettiest...': 3 Feb. 1927, Tulsa.
164 'This Debussy weather...': CC to Blakiston, 26 Jan. 1927, *RF*, p. 229.
164 'an old failing of mine...': CC to Molly MacCarthy, n.d., Lilly.
164 'much nicer than his novels...': CC to Balfour, *op. cit.*
164 'pre-war vodka...': CC to Jack Blakiston, private collection.
f.n. 'identified a fondness...': CC to Jack Blakiston, n.d., private collection.
165 'talks too much': 10 Feb. 1927, *RF*, p. 249.
165 'green Poussin woods...': CC to Blakiston, 11 Feb. 1927, *RF*, p. 251.
165 'we (you, me, Jack)...': CC to Blakiston, 13 Feb. 1927, *RF*, p. 255.
165 'I have been anti-French...': CC to Blakiston, 7 March 1927, *RF*, p. 280.
165 'forgotten, outworn...': unpublished notebook, Tulsa.
165 'about my only equal': n.d., Lilly.
165 'Bobbie will make...': CC to Balfour, 27 March 1927, Huntington.
165 'I feel now more than ever...': n.d., Tulsa.
166 'nursing a secret...': CC to Blakiston, 20 Jan. 1927, *RF*, p. 218.

166 'the nicest person...': CC to Blakiston, n.d., *RF*, p. 287.
166 'Dear me...': *In Another Part of the Wood*, p. 147.
166 'I haven't much taken...': CC to Blakiston, n.d., *RF*, p. 287.
167 'capable of fine...': CC to Blakiston, 21 March 1927, *RF*, p. 290.
167 'we will want...': 4 April 1927, *RF*, p. 292.
167 'The Sicilian expedition...': 9 Feb. 1963, Eton.
167 'I am in for a bad...': 21 April 1927, *RF*, p. 294.
167 'I am sorry...': 24 April 1927, Tulsa.
167 'with a Conrad crew...': CC to Blakiston, 27 April 1927, *RF*, p. 298.
168 'a very conservative young man' *et seq*...: 'The English Malady', unpublished MS, Austin.
169 'the most beautiful girl...': *A Boy at the Hogarth Press*, p. 61.
169 'trembling on the brink...': Diary, 10 Oct. 1927, Tulsa.
169 'the MacCarthys' quiet...': *Personal Record*, p. 185.
169 'the house I have long...': unpublished diary, 17 Aug. 1927, Tulsa.
169 'Early autumn...': *J and M*, p. 150.
169 'the only person...': CC to Blakiston, 5 May 1927, *RF*, p. 302.
169 'Have everything cut and dried...': *ibid.*
169 'malicious, boring and boastful...': Synnott to Balfour, 27 May 1927, Huntington.
170 'Five minutes with Quennell...': 31 May 1927, Huntington.
170 'I have rather come round...': CC to Balfour, 31 July 1927, Huntington.
170 'Jesus Christ...': n.d., Huntington.
170 'apart from complaining...': n.d., Huntington.
170 'a foul chalet': CC to Blakiston, n.d., *RF*, p. 310.
170 'a drear lot' *et seq.*: unpublished diary, July 1927, Tulsa.
171 'Since he suffered...': *Personal Record*, p. 185.
171 'has welcomed disillusion...': unpublished diary, 18 July 1927, Tulsa.
171 'He went through life...': *ibid*, 6 Nov. 1927.
171 'is really the misfortunes...': 1 Aug, 1927, Tulsa.
171 'when I start to write...': n.d., *RF*, p. 312.
172 'a comic old contraption...': unpublished diary, 14 July 1927, Tulsa.
172 'It is both difficult...': *ibid.*
172 'unless I marry someone...': *ibid.*

CHAPTER 11. 'YEOMAN'S ROW AND THE SEA LORD'S DAUGHTER'

173 'Oh, the superb...': Diary, 27 July 1927: reprinted in 'England not my England', *TCP*, pp. 196–210.
173 'That'll be the end...': unpublished diary, 3 Sept. 1927, Tulsa.
173 'We will grumble...': 31 May 1927, Huntington.
174 'we must decide on...': n.d., Huntington.
174 'We'll have a rule...': 2 July 1927, Huntington.
174 'quaint staircase...': unpublished diary, 27 July 1927, Tulsa.
174 'banished to work...': note by Molly MacCarthy, n.d., Tulsa.
175 'Solitude confirms...': CC to Molly MacCarthy, n.d., Tulsa.
175 'Nearly all my happiness...': CC to Molly MacCarthy, n.d., Lilly.
175 'Perfect summer's day...': Diary, 3 Aug. 1927: reprinted in 'England not my England'.
175 'the terrible flaw...': *NS*, 25 June 1927.
176 'a good many of...': 16 Sept. 1927, Lilly.
176 'The great difficulty...': *NS*, 17 Nov. 1928.
177 'to read all these...': *NS*, 8 Oct. 1927.
177 'dark spots...': *NS*, 7 Jan. 1928.
177 'The love of life...': *NS*, 17 March 1928.
177 'There is a growing...': *NS*, 3 March 1928.
177 'By an ever-deepening...': *NS*, 31 March 1928.

178 'Twice a year...': *NS*, 21 July 1928.
178 'that rare gift...': *NS*, 2 Feb. 1929.
178 'to enter a world...': *NS*, 18 Aug. 1928.
178 'reads like a painstaking...': *NS*, 3 Nov. 1928.
178 'such was the treatment...': *Memoirs of an Aesthete*, p. 203.
f.n. 'Well, my dear...': Waugh to Mitford, 14 Aug. 1946. *Letters of N.M. and E.W.*, p. 50.
178 'long, tedious...': *NS*, 25 Aug. 1928.
179 'romantic in outlook...': *NS*, 18 Feb. 1928.
179 'He is one of the few...': *NS*, 19 Jan. 1929.
179 'perfect laughter...': *NS*, 24 Dec. 1927.
179 'Once more our English...': *NS*, 7 July 1928.
180 'We at once...': *NS*, 26 Nov. 1927.
180 'collection of sincere...': *NS*, 23 Feb. 1929.
180 'the most remarkable...': n.d., Tulsa.
180 'I liked best...': 30 Nov. 1927, Tulsa.
181 'delighted': 11 Aug. 1928, Tulsa.
181 'tremendously enthusiastic...': n.d., Tulsa.
181 'odd that...': Diary, 27 Nov. 1927, *Wandering Years*, p. 145.
181 'neglecting you...': 17 Nov. 1927, Tulsa.
f.n. I am shocked...': n.d., Cambridge University Library.
182 'my introduction...': note by CC, private collection.
182 'In days of old...': from *Mirror of Fashion*: verses by 'Presto', adorned with scissor-cuts by Ada Steiner. The Medici Society, 1927.
183 'to find material...': note by CC, private collection.
183 'based on the qualities...': unpublished diary, 14 Aug. 1927, Tulsa.
183 'with a sense of...': *ibid*, 28 July 1927.
184 'I hope he will...': Pearsall Smith to CC, 10 Sept. 1927, Tulsa.
184 'this fag end London': Diary, 3 Sept. 1927: reprinted in 'England not my England'.
184 'dead form...': *ibid*, 1 Nov. 1927.
184 'Damn life...': *ibid*, 17 Nov. 1927.
184 'I am just...': *ibid*, 20 Sept. 1927.
185 'I get happier...': *ibid*, 10 Oct. 1927.
185 'cold, unsympathetic...': unpublished diary, 3 Sept. 1927, Tulsa.
185 'fair-haired, Grecian...': *ibid*, 10 Oct. 1927.
185 'Brown and gold...': *J and M*, p. 149.
186 'I have never known...': CC to Rachel MacCarthy, n.d., Tulsa.
186 'I had wept...': CC to Rachel MacCarthy, n.d., Tulsa.
187 'Philip's death...': unpublished diary, 15 Sept. 1927, Tulsa.
187 'The only person...': quoted in Cecil, *Clever Hearts*, p. 230.
187 'Cyril Connolly has been told...': 24 Nov. 1927. *Memories*, p. 135.
188 'I'm not a scheming...': 29 Oct. 1929, Tulsa.
188 'You can depend...': n.d. Tulsa.
188 'Molly seems...': *J and M*, p. 148.
189 'that nice feeling...': Molly MacCarthy to CC, n.d., Tulsa.
189 'Of course I do not...': n.d., Lilly.
189 'I fear it is...': 11 Jan. 1943, Tulsa.
189 'I can't thank you enough...': n.d., Tulsa.
189 'That horrible Connolly...': quoted in Cecil, *Clever Hearts*, p. 293.
189 'divinely English...': unpublished diary, 10 Oct. 1927, Tulsa.
189 'meanwhile I can...': *J and M*, p. 146.
189 'I am writing...': 5 July 1928, Huntington.
189 'with one of those...': CC to MacCarthy, n.d., Tulsa.
190 'one blue summer twilight...': *Encounter*, Jan. 1955.
191 'passion, equality...': unpublished diary, 15 Oct. 1927, Tulsa.

CHAPTER 12. 'A YOUNG BEETHOVEN, WITH SPOTS'

192 'snobbish thrill...': *J and M*, p. 130.

193 'general sense...': Diary, March 1928: reprinted in 'England not my England'.
193 'There is some very good...': 10 May 1928, *RF*, p. 318.
193 'real sense of release...': *J and M*, p. 137.
193 'Had a Moroccan...': *ibid.*
193 'instead I met Cecil...': CC to Balfour, 14 April 1928, Huntington.
193 'rather boring...': CC to Balfour, 14 April 1928, Huntington.
194 'All activity...': *J and M*, p. 144.
195 'rather a big man...': *J and M*, p. 144.
195 'imperiously rebuffed': James Lees-Milne, *Harold Nicolson*, Vol. I, p. 335.
195 'got on well...': *J and M*, p. 143.
195 'He is very clever...': quoted in Glendinning, *Vita*, p. 195.
195 'Cyril came yesterday...': 10 May 1928. *Vita and Harold* p. 195.
196 'most unpleasant book...': unpublished diary, 30 July 1927, Tulsa.
196 'real sense of balmy...': *J and M*, p. 145.
196 'We needs must love...': Gladwyn, *Memoirs*, p. 35.
196 'a bowl of porridge...': n.d., Tulsa.
197 'Dear Governor...': n.d., Tulsa.
197 'frankness and sincerity...': *J and M*, p. 211.
198 'Harold and Vita...': *ibid*, p. 159.
198 'begging not...': quoted in Glendinning, *Vita*, p. 195.
198 'Friendship, which survives...': n.d., Huntington.
198 'that crook Philby': n.d., Tulsa.
198 'both had been debagged...': MS of 'The English Malady', Austin.
199 'Back in England...': *J and M*, p. 146.
199 'One really cannot love London...': Diary, Nov. 1928.
200 'run my fingers...': p. 175.
200 'It is ghoulish...': n.d., Tulsa.
200 'the main feature...': *J and M*, p. 167.
201 'except for Philip Ritchie...': unpublished TS by CC, Tulsa.
201 'younger self...': *ibid.*
201 'Cyril and Tray...': 26 July 1928. Quoted in Lees-Milne, *Harold Nicolson*, Vol. I. p. 341.
201 'talk and company...': *London Magazine*, Aug–Sept. 1973.
201 'my fears...': Urquhart to CC, 20 Aug. 1928, Tulsa.
f.n. 'Thank you too for your harsh words...': Auden to CC, n.d., Tulsa.
'exposed like...': *Part of My Life*, p. 82.
202 'nothing memorable...': CC to Balfour, n.d., Huntington.
202 'what drugs or women...': unpublished diary, 17 Sept. 1927, Tulsa.
203 'General dissatisfaction...': *J and M*, pp. 173–4.
203 'I was speaking to Clifford Sharp...': *ibid*, p. 191.
f.n. 'A massive man...': *Midnight Oil*, p. 190.
203 'a music hall style...': *Personal Record*, p. 186.
204 'appealed to all the rake...': *J and M* p. 195.
204 'Too bad...': unpublished MS, Tulsa.

CHAPTER 13: 'JEANNIE'

206 'A tall dark girl...': *J and M*, p. 213.
206 'hideous green house *et seq*'.... : see unpublished memoir by Jean Bakewell, Tulsa.
207 'short, dark hair...': *J and M*, p. 202.
208 'not a lesbian...': Mara Andrew to Jean Bakewell, 1 June 1928, Tulsa.
208 'tall with narrow hips...': unpublished 'Alpdodger' MS, Tulsa.
209 'used perforated...': *J and M*, f.n. to p. 214.
209 'I have as much right...': 11 July 1929, Tulsa.
209 'Quand je pense...': Mara Andrews to Jean Bakewell, 2 Sept. 1929, Tulsa.
210 'At that we fell...': *J and M*, p. 214.
210 'If my parents...': Anthony Hobson, Diary, 4 July 1965.
210 'only expatriates...': *J and M*, p. 201.
f.n. 'That's a rum-shaped...': *ibid*, p. 186.

210 'Well, Cyril Connolly...': *Julia*, p. 111.
210 'felt that at last...': *J and M*, p. 201.
211 'wide forehead...': unpublished 'Alpdodger' MS, Tulsa.
211 'I am afraid...': *J and M*, p. 203.
211 'the allusion...': 25 March 1929, private collection.
212 'an analogy...': 15 March 1929. *Reflections on James Joyce*, Staley, ed. p. 8.
212 'a Tragic Sense of Life...': *Life and Letters*, Oct. 1929.
212 'the steady divorce...': misc. MS, Tulsa.
213 'adored...': MacCarthy to CC, 20 Feb. 1929, Tulsa.
213 'wail...': unpublished notebook, Tulsa.
213 'pre-Homeric...': Brenan to CC, 22 May 1929, Tulsa.
213 'Bless you...': n.d., Eton.
213 'I'm afraid...': n.d., Eton.
213 'in a sense...': *J and M*, p. 196.
214 'Peter has the drawback...': 11 July 1929, Tulsa.
214 'Can you – v. important...': n.d., Eton.
214 'Inside Cyril...': Quennell, unpublished diary, 19 April 1929, private collection.
214 'dumpy, hirsute...': *ibid*, 21 April 1929.
215 'the just torture': 'Alpdodger' MS, Tulsa.
215 'your references to me...': 17 Nov. 1929, Tulsa.
215 'rather grubby': Nicolson, quoted in Lees-Milne, *Harold Nicolson*, Vol. I, p. 370.
215 'Cyril is not perhaps...': 18 May 1929, *Vita and Harold*, p. 214.
216 'an awful nuisance...': CC to Enid Bagnold, n.d., Tulsa.
216 'paralysis of the will...': n.d., Tulsa.
216 'why buggers...': *J and M*, p. 208.
216 'I don't think Leigh...': 4 July 1929, Tulsa.
217 'in Harold's apartments...': *Second Son*, p. 37.
217 'almost sick...': Lees-Milne, *op. cit.*, p. 371.
217 'Depressed at being...': Diary, July 1929: reprinted in 'England not my England'.
218 'I fear the whip...': quoted in Sebba, *Enid Bagnold*, p. 166.
f.n. 'when he went down...': *Adam*, Cyril Connolly Commemorative Number, 1975.
218 'I hear good and bad...': n.d., Tulsa.
218 'moment of love...': Diary, 16 July 1929: reprinted in 'England not my England'.
219 'respectability and...': n.d., *RF*, p. 325.
219 'I have been hopelessly...': n.d. Tulsa.
219 'I thought the *Statesman*...': n.d., Lilly.
f.n. 'I soon came up...': *ST*, 21 April 1963.
220 'a sharp and candid...': *Midnight Oil*. p. 192.
220 'The martyred...': *ibid*.
220 'I think it would...': n.d., Lilly.
221 'Basle, Berne...': 'Alpdodger' MS, Tulsa.
222 'The reviewing of novels...': *NS*, 31 Aug. 1929.
222 'august and readable...': *J and M*, p. 183.
223 'I hate the little...': 6 Aug. 1929, Huntington.
223 'I must say...': n.d., Tulsa.
223 'WW got tight...': n.d., Tulsa.
223 'I am governed...': n.d., *RF*, p. 334.
224 'I like and need...': n.d., Tulsa.
224 'You will find me...': 6 June 1929, Tulsa.
224 'vague sense...': CC to Balfour, 6 Aug. 1929, Huntington.
224 'So Racy...': CC to MacCarthy, n.d., Lilly.
225 'I think I shall...': 6 Aug. 1929, Huntington.
225 'quite impossible...': Harmer to CC, n.d., Tulsa.
225 'almost entirely...': n.d., *RF*, p. 326.
226 'I don't think...': 29 Oct. 1929, Tulsa.
226 'lucrative work...': 1 Nov. 1929, Tulsa.
226 'I am sure...': 19 Sept. 1929, Tulsa.

226 'If you married...': 11 June 1929, Tulsa.
227 'cocktail parties...': CC to Balfour, 29 Aug. 1929, Huntington.
227 'toothless...': 17 June 1929, Tulsa.
227 'I can't be engaged...': CC to Balfour, 29 Aug. 1929, Huntington.
227 'retailing it...': 17 Sept. 1929, Huntington.
227 'All the pirate gang...': 29 Oct. 1929, Tulsa.
228 'perfectly awful...': CC to Balfour, 17 Sept. 1929, Huntington.
228 'I have a hatred...': n.d. Tulsa.
228 'spend my last months...': CC to MacCarthy, n.d., Lilly.
228 'obsessed with autumn': *J and M*, p. 236.
229 'I have a round bedroom...': 29 Oct. 1929, Tulsa.
229 'In mentioning me...': CC to Blakiston, n.d., Eton.
229 'stage a gladiatorial...': CC to Blakiston, n.d., *RF*, p. 329.
229 'thick brown fur...': *ibid.*
230 'if I am to marry...': CC to MacCarthy, 29 Oct. 1929, Tulsa.
230 'immense bowings...': CC to Jean Bakewell, n.d., Tulsa.
230 'The Eats are Swell...': n.d., *RF*, p. 334.
230 'perfectly bloody': 3 March 1930, Huntington.
231 'this is a bloody...': 2 April 1930, *RF* p. 336.
231 'amusing and cultivated *et seq*'...: CC to Balfour, 3 March 1930, Huntington.
231 'You couldn't have picked...': n.d., Tulsa.
231 'one was always being burst...': 8 April 1930, private collection.
232 'fabulous trousseau...': CC to Balfour, 3 March 1930, Huntington.
232 'I came to America...': 2 April 1930, *RF*, p. 337.

CHAPTER 14: 'LIVING FOR PLEASURE'

233 '1930 makes...': 30 Nov. 1973, Eton. f.n. ''ere's the man...': *J and M*, p. 259.
234 'All along the coast...': *TRP*, p. 50.
234 'an ideal life...': Pearsall Smith to CC, 3 Feb. 1931, Tulsa.
234 'rehabilitation of pleasure...': 'The Anonymous Voyage', unpublished MS, Tulsa.
234 '"Living for Beauty"...': *TUG*, p. 83.
235 'And "living for beauty"...': *ibid.*, p. 85.
235 'a life of definite...': 'Alpdodger' MS, Tulsa.
235 'the real disadvantage...': *J and M*, p. 239.
235 'have not been passed...': *Life and Letters*, Dec. 1931.
235 '£30,000...': 'Alpdodger', *op. cit.*
236 'The most important thing...': n.d., Tulsa.
236 'I don't think you...': 14 Dec. 1930, Tulsa.
236 'the social pinnacle...': *ST*, 2 April 1972.
236 'It would be fun...': 14 Dec. 1930, Tulsa.
236 'The Huxleys, with whom...': *ST*, 19 June 1966.
237 'We arrived...': *ST*, 2 April 1972.
237 'a bit elderly...': Jean Connolly to Jack Blakiston, 25 Jan. 1931, private collection.
237 'Edith has had...': 19 Dec. 1930. *Forty Years with Berenson*, p. 164. f.n. 'only surrender...': *ST*, 19 June 1966.
237 'I feel you somewhat...': 14 Dec. 1930, Tulsa.
237 'you were a great success...': 4 Jan. 1931, Tulsa.
237 'the books snapped back...': *ST*, 2 April 1972.
238 'overwhelming adoration...': *ibid.*
238 'unspoilt...': *Aldous Huxley*, Vol. I, p. 230.
238 '"Aldous!"...': *ST*, 13 July 1969.
238 'Cyril may have...': *op. cit.*, p. 262.
238 'slow, erotic charm...': PEN Club, 'Memories of Cyril Connolly', 13 June 1984.
239 'Neither she nor Aldous...': *Aldous Huxley*, Vol. I, p. 262.

f.n. 'the winter . . .': *ST*, 2 April 1972.
'I rather think . . .': 21 April 1972, Tulsa.
239 'The Huxleys . . .': *J and M*, p. 241.
239 'had nobody . . .': 25 Jan. 1931, private collection.
239 'whatever he attempted . . .': unpublished MS of 'Humane Killer', Tulsa.
239 'developed an inferiority . . .': *Picture Post*, 6 Nov. 1948.
240 'happiest and calmest . . .': *The Marble Foot*, p. 220.
240 'young and dirty . . .': 6 June 1933, *RF*, p. 339.
240 'gentle and fearless . . .': *TUG*, pp. 83–5.
241 'I did not realise . . .': 19 Nov. 1931, Tulsa.
241 'it will get . . .': n.d., Tulsa.
241 'We are both sick . . .': n.d., private collection.
242 'nearest approach . . .': *NS*, 5 Dec. 1931.
243 'no one is better . . .': *Architectural Review*, March 1930.
243 'our valued friend . . .': *J and M*, p. 242.
244 'young man on the make . . .': 'Alpdodger' MS, Tulsa.
f.n. 'These could do . . .': *Yesterday Came Suddenly*, p. 128.
'Joe Ackerley . . .': *The Gymnasium of the Mind*, p. 76.
245 'the brilliant give-and-take . . .': misc. MS, Tulsa.
246 'Giana and I . . .': 19 May 1930, private collection.
246 'Children dissipate . . .': *E of P* p. 126.
246 'fairly easy . . .': n.d., Austin.
247 'a tenth-rate Turkish . . .': *NS*, 18 March 1933.
248 'looked deliciously . . .': 'Brummell at Calais', *Art and Literature*, Spring 1967.
248 'a little rabbit . . .': Jean Connolly to Mrs Warner, n.d., Tulsa.
249 'inconceivably ugly . . .': CC to Blakiston, 6 June 1933, *RF*, p. 339.
249 'Mind you pay . . .': 17 June 1933, Tulsa.
249 'the moment I got back . . .': CC to Princess Bibesco, Eton.
249 'Cyril picked me up . . .': *The Bonus of Laughter*, p. 85.
f.n. 'Goodbye . . .': n.d., Tulsa.
250 'I was considerably surprised . . .': 7 Sept. 1933, private collection.
250 'I am afraid . . .': 8 Sept. 1933, Tulsa.
251 'the play should . . .': CC to Sykes, n.d., Tulsa.
251 'Julia and I . . .': Gathorne-Hardy to CC, 8 July 1933, Tulsa.
251 'I can't tell . . .': Strachey to Jean Connolly, 11 July 1933, Tulsa.
251 'Think if I died . . .': 14 Feb. 1933, *Letters*, Vol. 5, p. 157.
251 'I would have given . . .': Anthony Hobson diary, 12 March 1966.
251 'She gets in my way . . .': *J and M*, p. 155.
251 'the flavour of contemporary . . .': unpublished notebook, Tulsa.
252 'gave a cocktail . . .': Woolf to Quentin Bell, *Letters*, Vol. 5, p. 277.
252 'Byronesque gangster': in conversation with author.
252 'succession of cooks . . .': *Faces in My Time*, p. 27.
252 'amiable, tipsy . . .': *J and M*, p. 254.
252 'quite derelict . . .': *ibid.*
253 'We spent a night . . .': *Letters*, Vol 5, p. 299.
253 'baboon Connolly . . .': Diary, Vol. IV, p. 210.
f.n. 'second-rate . . .': Diary, Vol. IV, p. 188.
253 'absolutely outgrown . . .': *J and M*, p. 256.
253 'I have a reputation . . .': unpublished MS of 'Humane Killer', Tulsa.
254 'the Thirties . . .': misc. MS, Tulsa.
254 'Navy-blue . . .': *J and M*, p. 246.
254 'edit a monthly . . .': *ibid*, p. 244.
254 'one should have . . .': *ibid*, p. 248.
254 'He asked . . .': *ibid*, p. 271.
255 'perfectly normal . . .': *op. cit.*, p. 28.
f.n. 'very easily amused . . .': in conversation with author.
255 'Tell Cyril . . .': 17 Jan. 1931, Tulsa.

255 'You will find me sadly changed...': 6 Oct. 1932, Tulsa.
255 'There can be nothing...': *NS*, 2 Feb. 1935.
256 'My little Mollie...': Major Connolly to Jean Connolly, 23 Sept. 1934, Tulsa.
256 'I suppose because...': CC to Mollie Connolly, 9 Dec. 1935, Tulsa.
257 'most of the time...': CC to Mollie Connolly, 9 Dec. 1935, Tulsa.
257 'I thought you...': 3 June 1936, Tulsa.
257 'Cyril was no pauper...': *My Friend Henry Miller*, p. 29.
258 'These stories are really...': notebook, Austin.
259 'an artificial self-pity...': unpublished MS of 'Humane Killer', Tulsa.
261 'I doubt if...': 17 May 1935, Faber & Faber.
262 'we do not expect...': Introductory letter to *TRP*.
262 'a tall bulky man...': *Memoirs of a Booklegger*, p. 265.
262 'a lovely talker...': *ibid.*
f.n. 'the crocs got her...': Robin McDouall to Auberon Waugh, 22 Feb. 1976, private collection.
266 'better art,...': *ST*, 23 Aug. 1935.
266 'As Mr Cyril...': 23 July 1936. Collected Essays, Journalism and Letters, Vol. I, p. 254.
267 'I don't think...': 26 Aug. 1936. *ibid*, p. 259.
267 'I swallowed...': 3 June 1936, Tulsa.
f.n. 'Maurice Cranston...': *On My Way to the Club*, p. 178.
'very weak in verbs...': Baron, *Miss Ethel Sands and her Circle*, p. 272.

CHAPTER 15: 'MR MOSSBROSS GOES TO SPAIN'

268 'lazy, irresolute...': *E of P*, p. 106.
268 'Unfortunately...': draft of *E of P*, Austin.
269 'whole-time job...': *E of P*, p. 106.
269 'will talk about...': draft of *E of P*, Austin.
270 'to review...': *NS*, 16 Feb. 1935.
270 'extremely amusing...': *NS*, 2 March 1935.
270 'I can think of...': *NS*, 13 April 1935.
270 'I was asked...': *NS*, 3 Aug. 1935.
270 'three colossal...': *NS*, 23 Nov. 1935.
271 'snobbish and preposterous...': *NS*, 30 Nov. 1935.
271 'Mr Garnett is...': *NS*, 7 Dec. 1935.
f.n. 'I put out my hand...': quoted in Julian Symons, 'Meeting Wyndham Lewis', *London Magazine*, Oct. 1957.
272 'no new novels...': *NS*, 15 Feb. 1936.
272 'And now for...': *NS*, 30 March 1935.
273 'Phyllis Bentley...': *NS*, 13 June 1936.
273 'the most brilliant...': quoted in Hyams, *The New Statesman*, p. 165.
274 'as literary editor...': unpublished TS on Mortimer, Tulsa.
274 'The bareness...': *NS*, 8 Feb. 1936.
274 'I should like...': *NS*, 1 June 1936.
274 'I think Grigson...': n.d., private collection.
275 'Sometimes, at...': *NS*, 6 July 1935.
275 'At this moment...': *DT*, 4 Feb. 1936.
276 'the advantages...': *DT*, 10 Dec. 1935.
276 'fine writer...': *DT*, 30 June 1936.
276 'Galsworthy...': *DT*, 7 Dec. 1935.
277 'mystical but also...': *ST*, 3 May 1936.
277 'literature of...': *ST*, 5 April 1936.
277 'Politics, women...': *Green Hills of Africa*, p. 28.
277 'Whom the gods...': *NS*, 8 June 1935.
f.n. 'an advertising man...': *J and M*, p. 273.
277 'indigence...': MS, Tulsa.
278 'I could write...': MS of 'Humane Killer', Tulsa.
279 'mixture of ignorance...': *NS*, 30 Nov. 1935.
279 'The mill where I...': *TUG*, p. 72.
280 'the best weekend...': quoted in Wheen, *Tom Driberg*, p. 89.

280 'not boiled...': quoted in Julian Symons, *A.J.A. Symons*, p. 155.
280 'the seven joys...': draft of *TUG*, Austin.
280 'which my psychological...': CC to Orwell, n.d., UCL.
280 'Peeling off...': *TUG*, p. 62.
281 'real drugs...': misc, MS, Tulsa.
282 'extraordinary mixture...': *NS*, 21 Nov. 1936.
282 'shared no common...': Draft *E of P*, Austin.
282 'an arrangement...': *NS*, 21 Nov. 1936.
282 'bourgeois trembling...': *ST*, 13 April 1969.
282 'rugged, lion-like...': *NS*, 19 Dec. 1936.
282 'The population ate...': *The Spanish Civil War*, p. 502.
284 'I remember...': *ST*, *op. cit.*
284 'It seems certain...': *NS*, 26 Dec. 1936.
284 'in time to take part...': *ibid.*
284 'alert, full of curiosity...': *NS*, 16 Jan. 1937.
285 'it wasn't so much...': 20 Feb. 1937. *Letters to Christopher*, p. 130.
286 'often awkwardly...': *NS*, 4 May 1935.
286 'immensely tall...': *Lions and Shadows*, p. 173.
286 'arresting prominence...': *Behind the Battle*, p. 16.
286 'lived his ordinary...': *ibid*, p. 12.
286 'mottled complexion...': Pritchett to Gerald Brenan, n.d., Austin.
286 'with expensive tastes...': *Behind the Battle*, p. 90.
f.n. 'sexing and dining...': see Worsley in *Adam*, 1974–5.
287 'a detail which...': CC, 'Some Memories', in *W.H. Auden: A Tribute*, p. 69.
287 'eliminating the beast...': *NS*, 20 Feb. 1937.
288 'But if your lordship...': *Behind the Battle*, p. 95.
288 'much more social...': CC to Peggy Bainbridge, n.d. quoted in *J and M*, p. 282.
288 'There have been considerable...': *NS*, 20 Feb. 1937.
288 'with a hopeless...': *E of P*, p. 133–4.
288 'Looking back...': draft *E of P*, Austin.
289 'reason and scepticism...': *ST*, 21 Jan. 1973.
f.n. 'I remember reading...': *Robbery Under Law*, p. 22.
289 'I was just...': 8 June 1937, *Collected Essays, Journalism and Letters*, p. 300.
289 'admirable novel...': *NS*, 6 July 1935.
f.n. 'without Connolly's help...': *Collected Essays...*, p. 186 f.n.
290 'savage and bitter...': *DT*, 21 April 1936.
f.n. 'a harrowing and stark...': *NS*, 24 April 1936.
290 'I felt...': n.d., UCL.
290 'his greeting...': *Encounter*, Jan. 1962.
291 'editorial policy': Orwell to Rayner Heppenstall, 31 July 1937: *Collected Essays...*, p. 311.
f.n. 'probably under-estimated...': *Editor*, p. 230.
291 'I suppose...': 13 Oct. 1937, UCL.
291 'The defeat...': *ST*, 13 April 1969.
292 'He will support...': draft *E of P*, Austin.
293 'Literature is...': *NS*, 5 June 1937.
293 'which I don't think...': *NS*, 12 June 1937.
293 'Being political...': *E of P*, p. 110.
293 'good medium Auden...': *NS*, 5 June 1937.

CHAPTER 16: 'ENEMIES OF PROMISE'

294 'an untidy...': *Part of My Life*, p. 203.
294 'your role...': n.d., Tulsa.
294 'as someone determined...': n.d., Tulsa.
295 'My long dark...': misc. MS, Tulsa.
295 'a nice girl...': 10 July 1939, Tulsa.
295 'I couldn't be...': 11 July 1939, Tulsa.
295 'Well, this is...': quoted in Fisher, *Cyril Connolly*, p. 148.
f.n. 'one of those...': quoted in *White Mischief*, p. 129.

296 'around thirty . . .': 'Beulah', unpublished TS, Tulsa.
296 'I walked up . . .': quoted in *J and M*, p. 283.
297 'smell of the sun-warmed . . .': draft of *TUG*, Austin.
298 'Horror upon horror . . .': 10 July 1939, Tulsa.
298 'never had enough fucking . . .': *ibid.*
f.n. 'impudent . . .': see also *Christopher and His Kind*, p. 202 *et seq.*
'I must confess . . .': *ST*, 1 Nov. 1953.
298 'I remember a coldness . . .': *Christopher and His Kind*, p. 203.
299 'His big face . . .': *ibid*, p. 202.
300 'I don't think . . .': 28 Oct. 1937, Tulsa.
300 'a brilliant pasquinade . . .': *A Little Learning*, p. 205.
f.n. 'sandwiched in . . .': see Lancaster ed., *Brian Howard*, pp. 198–200.
301 'We are entering . . .': 'Into Philistia', unpublished MS, Tulsa.
301 'the ineffable . . .': *NS*, 29 Jan. 1938.
301 'I never realised . . .': 23 Jan. 1938, Tulsa.
302 'Salzburg was great . . .': quoted in Glendinning, *Elizabeth Bowen*, p. 121.
302 'Articles of . . .': *Night and Day*, 9 Sept. 1937.
f.n. 'ragged Audrey . . .': Bowra to CC, 11 Aug. 1939, Tulsa.
'*au fond* . . .': John Sutro to Auberon Waugh, 21 Jan. 1975, private collection.
303 'very patient . . .': 13 Aug. 1937, Reading.
303 'I've had a very bad . . .': n.d., Reading.
303 'If I can genuinely . . .': 15 Dec. 1937, Reading.
304 'dig at publishers': 10 Aug. 1938, Reading.
304 'So much depends on style . . .': *E of P*, p. 19.
305 'no more sombre . . .': *ibid*, p. 127.
305 'The pages . . .': draft *E of P*, Austin.
305 'so resembles . . .': *E of P*, p. 100.
306 'must obtain . . .': *ibid*, p. 103.
306 'fatal word . . .': *ibid*, p. 121.
306 'Sloth in writers . . .': *ibid*, p. 123.
307 'clasping tares . . .': *ibid*, p. 125.
307 'a return of emphasis . . .': *ibid*, p. 145.
307 'in "This England . . ."': *ibid*, p. 148.
307 'Solvency . . .': *ibid.*
307 'it is the duty . . .': *ibid*, p. 150.
307 'an analysis . . .': *ibid*, p. 155.
308 'This is the time . . .': *ibid*, p. 15.
308 'whom ill-famed . . .': *ibid*, p. 279.
308 'This curious . . .': *TLS*, 12 Nov. 1938.
308 'essential to . . .': *NS*, 12 Nov. 1938.
f.n. 'This reversion . . .': *Europe without Baedeker*, p. 15.
309 'The only man . . .': *Tablet*, 3 Dec. 1938.
310 'Mr Connolly's list . . .': *Scrutiny*, June 1939.
f.n. 'currency values . . .': in 'The Progress of Poetry', 1948; reprinted in *The Common Pursuit*, p. 297.
f.n. 'you scratch . . .': 14 March 1938, *Collected Essays . . .*, Vol. I, p. 343.
311 'to congratulate you . . .': n.d., Tulsa.
311 'since I know . . .': 30 Oct. 1938, Tulsa.
311 'We are still . . .': 6 Nov. 1938, Tulsa.
312 'I feel we ought . . .': 9 Dec. 1938, Reading.
312 'Now I understand . . .': n.d., Reading.
f.n. 'Milton, Pope . . .': n.d., private collection.
312 'Where Eton words . . .': n.d., Reading.
312 'I hope they make . . .': 17 May 1939, Reading.
312 'Having passed . . .': 'Flights into Egypt', unpublished MS, Austin.
315 'You are quite right . . .': n.d., private collection.
315 'ovarian injections . . .': Jean Connolly to CC, n.d., Tulsa.
316 'Δ situation . . .': 7 Nov. 1938, unpublished diary, Tulsa.
316 'signed . . .': marginal note, Tulsa.
316 'marks the end . . .': 21 Nov. 1938, unpublished diary, Tulsa.

316 'Noel was very sweet': unpublished diary, 22 Nov. 1938, Tulsa.
316 '£30 of dressmakers' . . .': 27 Nov. 1938, unpublished diary, Tulsa.
316 'homo dreams . . .': 4 Dec. 1938, unpublished diary, Tulsa.
316 'for good health . . .': unpublished MS, Tulsa.
317 'I love you more . . .': CC to Jean Connolly, n.d., Tulsa.
317 'a terrible shit . . .': n.d., Tulsa.
317 'sad, gray . . .': unpublished MS, Tulsa.
317 'dust and ashes': 13 Feb. 1939, Reading.
317 'skiing mad' . . .': CC to Jean Connolly, n.d., Tulsa.
317 'entertaining on . . .': n.d., Tulsa.
318 'if you write to Momma . . .': n.d., Tulsa.
318 'awful dream . . .': 1 April 1939, Tulsa.
318 'the two ugliest . . .': Janetta Parladé in conversation with the author.
318 'I hope you have fun . . .': n.d., Tulsa.
318 'who seem utterly . . .': *TUG*, p. 74.
319 'is really very sweet . . .': n.d., Tulsa.
319 'happiness is thrown away . . .': *TUG*, p. 74.
319 'in black cloak . . .': draft of *TUG*, Austin.
319 'for the rest . . .': CC to Jean Connolly, n.d., Tulsa.
319 'Madame n'est pas rentrée . . .': *The Wanton Chase*, p. 11.
320 'Darling is running . . .': CC to Jean Connolly, n.d., Tulsa.
320 'gradually split up . . .': 11 April 1939, Tulsa.
320 'I thought you were . . .': n.d., Tulsa.
320 'calamitous': *The Wanton Chase*, p. 11.
320 'tiresome and cross . . .': 15 July 1939, Tulsa.
321 'champion trouble-makers . . .': CC to Jean Connolly, n.d., Tulsa.
321 'really dotty . . .': 4 July 1939, Tulsa.
321 'fat is rolling back . . .': CC to Jean Connolly, 8 July 1939, Tulsa.
322 'I do feel . . .': 10 July 1939, Tulsa.
323 'I wish you would not . . .': n.d., Tulsa.
323 'mine and Jean's . . .': CC to Mollie Connolly, n.d., Tulsa.
323 'Ulster is . . .': n.d., Tulsa.
f.n. 'very dotty . . .': CC to Mollie Connolly, n.d., Tulsa.
324 'says I am . . .': CC to Jean Connolly, 19 Aug. 1939, Tulsa.
324 'Cyril developed . . .': Freya Elwes to Jean Connolly, n.d., Tulsa.
324 'when I have a difficult . . .': n.d., Tulsa.
324 'how can I love . . .': CC to Jean Connolly, 19 Aug. 1939, Tulsa.
324 'pierced by memories . . .': 25 Aug. 1939, Tulsa.
324 'When I think . . .': CC to Jean Connolly, 28 Aug. 1939, Tulsa.
324 'I will dance with you . . .': 24 Aug. 1939, Tulsa.
325 'I'm not ready . . .': n.d., Tulsa.
325 'pretty and rather nice . . .': Jean Connolly to CC, n.d., Tulsa.
325 'You say Jean . . .': n.d., Tulsa.
f.n. 'shabby humped': Dylan Thomas to John Davenport, 8 Jan. 1941. *Collected Letters*, p. 471.
'odious youth': Mitford to Mark Ogilvie-Grant, 23 Jan. 1930. *Love from Nancy*, p. 35.
'a large man . . .': *With Love*, p. 3.
'never to see . . .': CC to Jean Connolly, n.d., Tulsa.
326 'I'm sorry you've had . . .': 5 July 1939, Tulsa.
326 'Without your help . . .': n.d., Tulsa.
326 'very sweet . . .': diary entry, 31 Aug. 1939, Tulsa.
326 'Dieppe was full . . .': n.d., Tulsa.
326 'to keep the pot . . .': Diana to author.
327 'makes you comfortable . . .': n.d., Tulsa.
327 'Chamberlain and . . .': *ST*, 12 Sept. 1965.
327 'they were full of pop . . .': Mitford to Violet Hammersley, 15 Sept. 1939, *Love from Nancy*, p. 83.
328 'Mrs Connolly seems . . .': CC to Jean Connolly, 7 Sept. 1939, Tulsa.
328 'horrible old colonels . . .': *ibid.*
328 'dirty white coat . . .': Quennell to CC, n.d., Tulsa.
328 'the same air . . .': *More Memoirs of an Aesthete*, p. 86.

328 'You must come...': 19 October 1939, Victoria.
328 'The life I want...': n.d., Tulsa.
329 'Cyril told me...': 25 Oct. 1939, *Letters to Christopher*, p. 199.
329 'My poppet...': Jean Connolly to CC, n.d., Tulsa.
329 'pedantic, irrational...': Jean Connolly to CC, 10 April 1940, Tulsa.
f.n. 'phallus with...': quoted in Lees-Milne, *Prophesying Peace*, p. 41.
'I had to lunch...': 10 Aug. 1945. *ibid*, p. 220.
330 'Darling darling heart...': n.d., Tulsa.
330 'Cyril Connolly's...': unpublished MS, Tulsa.
330 'It is beginning...': 14 June 1940, Tulsa.
331 'O woman...': unpublished MS, Tulsa.

CHAPTER 17: 'NEW HORIZONS'

332 'Bouvard-Pecuchet...': *The Golden Horizon*, p. xiii.
332 'All I want...': n.d., Tulsa.
332 'No one was more...': Spender, journal, 5 May 1956, Tulsa.
333 'that hog...': see *Dear Nancy*, p. 107 f.n.
333 'coral-coloured...': *ibid*, p. 35 f.n.
333 'tall, gangling...': *The Wandering Years*, p. 222.
333 'I hear the new...': quoted in Glendinning, *Edith Sitwell*, p. 172.
333 'the last of...': *Down There on a Visit*, p. 160.
f.n. 'very pale...': *Palimpsest*, p. 179.
334 'his despair...': *op. cit.*
334 'I started...': n.d., Eton.
335 'Grigson and I...': quoted in *When I Was*, p. 91.
335 'spent hours...': *The Whispering Gallery*, p. 162.
336 'an inspired...': *ST*, 8 April 1951.
336 'Stephen would...': *I Am My Brother*, p. 43.
336 'deadly feud...': Woolf to Angelica Bell, 16 Oct. 1939, *Letters*, Vol. VI, p. 364.
336 'ivory tower...': *I Am My Brother*, p. 42.
336 'friendly rivalry...': quoted in Tolley, *John Lehmann*, p. 18.
f.n. 'The war has so far...': annotated *Horizon* galley of May 1940 'Comment', Austin.
337 'as the war...': *I Am My Brother*, p. 43.
338 'looked at me...': *Journals*, p. 51 f.n.
338 'suggests flatness...': *ibid.*
338 'I am sure...': 27 Oct. 1939, Tulsa.
338 'we bow...': Spender, *Journals*, p. 51.
338 'We must all...': 19 Oct. 1939, *Letters*, Vol. I, p. 243.
338 'How nice...': 1 Nov. 1939, Tulsa.
338 'I note that...': 7 March 1940. *Letters*, Vol. VI, p. 384.
339 'I know you...': n.d., Merton College, Oxford.
339 'very good poem...': n.d., Victoria.
339 'editorial policy...': *NS* advertisement, 18 Nov. 1939.
340 'very ornamental': SS in conversation with the author.
f.n. *A Room in Chelsea Square*, p. 99.
341 'remuneration will be...': n.d., private collection.
f.n. 'Cyril, over the port...': *I Am My Brother*, p. 173.
342 'Cyril fascinated...': *Journals*, p. 434.
342 'It isn't...': *ibid*, p. 435.
343 'David Herbert...': 12 Nov. 1942, Tulsa.
343 'less free...': *NS*, 7 Oct. 1939.
344 'Communist energy...': *ibid.*
345 'a blow': n.d., private collection.
345 'With an almost...': *NS*, 16 Dec. 1939.
346 'would enter...': *ST*, 11 March 1956.
346 'pressed that...': 30 Sept. 1939, *Letters to Christopher*, p. 191.
348 'the most important...': *H*, Feb. 1940.
348 'the soldier has the right...': *H*, July 1940.
f.n. 'at that time...': *A Chapter of Accidents*, p. 152.

349 'no longer possible . . .': *H*, Oct. 1941
349 'born editor . . .': *The Thirties and After*, p. 89.
349 'because he's like': quoted in *ibid*, p. 88.
349 'As an editor . . .': *World Within World*, p. 295.
350 'Editing a magazine . . .': *The Golden Horizon*, p. xii.
350 'Are you certain . . .': *World Within World*, p. 294.
350 'Please tell me . . .': Watson to CC, n.d., Tulsa.
351 'laughed till . . .': 17 Sept. 1942, *Journals of Denton Welch*, p. 9.
351 'It seems to me . . .': n.d. Tulsa.
351 'Hold on . . .': *Memoirs of the Forties*, p. 57.
352 'a row of small . . .': *ibid.*, p. 60.
352 'face was round . . .': *ibid*, p. 61.
352 'at sight . . .': *ibid*, p. 75.
353 'as soon as I say . . .': unpublished MS, Tulsa.
353 'they will not kill . . .': draft of *TUG*, Austin.
354 'I hear from Stephen . . .': n.d., Tulsa.
355 'Whereas Cyril . . .': Spender to Lehmann, 2 Nov. 1940, Austin.
355 'Could you get me . . .': Spender to Lehmann, 4 Dec. 1940, Austin.
355 'There is a little . . .': 11 Nov. 1940. *Dear Nancy*, p. 105.
355 'Cyril, Hog Watson . . .': 26 Dec. 1940, *ibid*, p. 107.
355 'sitting in Connolly's . . .': 8 April 1941, *Collected Essays . . .*, Vol. II, p. 392.
356 'carrying a case . . .': *The Wanton Chase*, p. 21.
356 'We don't know . . .': 7 Nov. 1939, Victoria.
356 'Cyril came here . . .': Georgiana Blakiston to Kinross, 17 Aug. 1942, Huntington.
356 'We don't like . . .': *Observer*, 1 Dec. 1974.
f.n. 'When the tin . . .': quoted in *Confessions of an Optimist*, p. 88.
357 'That it is . . .': 27 Sept. 1944, Tulsa.
357 'I spent . . .': *ST*, 21 March 1971.
357 'the new symbolic . . .': *I Am My Brother*, p. 23.
358 'he ought to . . .': Nicolson, *Diaries and Letters*, Vol. II, p. 388.
358 'fox without a tail': 'Comment', *H*, Jan. 1946.
358 'neo-Georgian paper . . .': *ibid.*
358 'slackness and flippancy . . .': 17 Dec. 1940, Berg Collection.
359 'you will have to show . . .': n.d., Berg Collection.
359 'I find *Horizon* . . .': n.d., *Durrell-Miller Letters*, p. 136.
359 'it makes me homesick . . .': 8 Jan. 1940. *Diaries*, p. 77.
359 'seductive, cigar-like . . .': 1 Feb. 1941, Tulsa.
359 'the miracle of . . .': 18 May 1940, Tulsa.
359 'felt as if . . .': quoted in John Pikoulis, *Alun Lewis*, p. 126.
359 'had always regarded . . .': *H*, Dec. 1940.
360 'is really . . .': *NS*, 3 Aug. 1939.
361 'sulky and down-trodden . . .': Roger Senhouse, unpublished diary, n.d., Eton.
f.n. 'How did you know?': *ibid.*
362 'I had only . . .': 17 Dec. 1940, Caversham.
362 'particularly wounding . . .': *The Thirties and After*, p. 89.
f.n. 'not only because . . .': BBC internal memo, 14 Feb. 1947, Caversham.
'one of the best . . .': Barnes to CC, 25 Sept. 1947, Caversham.
363 'How boring . . .': *Part of My Life*, p. 248.
f.n. 'One must . . .': *ibid*, p. 249.

CHAPTER 18: 'TE PALINURE PETENS'

364 'an absurd quarrel . . .': *The Wanton Chase*, p. 21.
f.n. 'I am not a friend . . .': 19 March 1945, Yale.
'lived up in . . .': 15 Dec. 1948, Yale.
365 'Cyril took me . . .': quoted in Iain Hamilton, *Koestler*, p. 76.
365 'for an educated . . .': quoted in *Koestler*, p. 77.
365 'That really is . . .': n.d., Tulsa.

365 'ill-advised...': 25 Dec. 1943, Tulsa.
365 'accomplice by omission': quoted in *Koestler*, p. 77.
f.n. 'after-dinner stories...': n.d., Tulsa.
366 'Cyril's household...': *The Wanton Chase*, p. 21.
366 'furnished in much...': unpublished diary, 10 Oct. 1942, Eton.
366 'Skeltie...': Quennell to CC, n.d., Tulsa.
367 'Have had several...': Diary, 13 Jan. 1943, private collection.
367 'actually had...': *ibid*, 18 March 1943.
367 'Don't you understand...': CC to Lys Lubbock, 18 May 1943, Lilly.
367 'Fancy, no mention...': Major Connolly to CC, 18 Feb. 1943, Tulsa.
f.n. 'hard-edged and unmellowed...': *W.H. Auden: A Tribute*, p. 71.
368 'all the musky flakes...': *NS*, 3 April 1943.
368 'as he grew...': *The Wanton Chase*, p. 22.
368 'playfully self-disparaging...': *Voices*, p. 166.
369 'PQ as a goat...': draft *TUG*, Austin.
370 'Did I tell you...': 24 Aug. 1942, Georgetown.
370 'Cyril is now Lit. Ed...': Beaton to Kinross, 12 Dec. 1942, Huntington.
371 'the best writer...': n.d., Tulsa.
371 'I am afraid...': 23 April 1942, Tulsa.
371 'ability and character...': 17 June 1942, Tulsa.
371 'You'll have to bear...': 1 July 1942, Tulsa.
372 '*in vino*...': 2 Dec. 1941, Tulsa.
372 'You'll think I've got...': n.d., Tulsa.
372 'I think you write...': n.d., Tulsa.
372 'I should add...': 21 Aug. 1943, Tulsa.
372 'I have chosen YOU...': n.d., Tulsa.
372 'I don't know...': 24 Sept. 1942, Tulsa.
372 'Mr Quennell...': Astor to CC, n.d., Tulsa.
373 'it still needs you...': 24 Sept. 1942, Tulsa.
373 'You have just flown...': 22 Feb. 1943, Tulsa.
f.n.: 'gamblers, lords and heroes': Waugh to Mitford, 10 Oct. 1949, *Letters of N.M. and E.W.*, p. 149.
'the only club...': Waugh to CC, 19 Oct. 1942, Tulsa.
373 'You seem to forget...': 20 Aug. 1943, Tulsa.
374 'expects to be...': Waugh to Laura Waugh, 19 Sept. 1943, *Letters*, p. 170.
374 'You must...': n.d., Tulsa.
374 'where the Indo-Russo...': 'Spring Assignment', unpublished MS, Tulsa.
375 'either he sang...': *The Bonus of Laughter*, p. 61.
375 'regularly filled...': *ibid*, p. 134.
375 'he soon began...': *The Wanton Chase*, p. 60.
375 'at the end...': *Julia*, p. 192.
375 'when he began...': quoted in Glendinning, *Elizabeth Bowen*, p. 136.
f.n. 'the pack of lions...': Eddie Sackville-West to James Lees-Milne, 3 Sept. 1943, *Ancestral Voices*, p. 235.
375 'In myself...': draft of TUG, Austin.
375 'Intense emotion...': *ibid.*
376 'little castrated': *H*, May 1943.
376 'one of the last...': *H*, May 1941.
378 'I have a list...': 5 Jan. 1944, Bristol.
378 'The galleries...': 1 Sept. 1944, Tulsa.
379 'incomparably...': *H*, Nov. 1944.
379 'The State now sits...': *H*, Dec. 1944
379 'Poor Cyril...': 10 Jan. 1945, *Dear Nancy*, p. 133.
379 'whatever I write...': draft *TUG*, Austin.
379 'nice and intelligent...': n.d., Tulsa.
380 'animal person...': *Down There on a Visit*, p. 159.

380 'Jean is much...': 13 Aug. 1940, *Diaries*, p. 118.
380 'I think about you...': n.d., Tulsa.
380 'I am so tired...': note by CC on back of letter of apology from Brian Howard, 9 June 1942, Tulsa.
381 'Everything connected...': draft *TUG*, Austin.
381 '*Visite angoissante*...': 14 Sept. 1943, draft *TUG*, Austin.
381 'A face seen...': *TUG*, p. 43.
382 '*Oh toi que*...': *TUG*, p. 59.
382 'Faint with excitement...': 8 Oct. 1943, draft *TUG*, Austin.
382 'Perhaps the most painful...': draft *TUG*, Austin.
382 'The world...': draft *TUG*, Austin.
383 'fine new typeface...': 26 March 1943, Austin.
383 'one of the most...': Hamilton to E.C. Aswell, 29 March 1945, Princeton.
383 'You write like...': 17 April 1944, Tulsa.
384 'As I waddle...': *TUG*, p. 22.
384 'Approaching forty...': *ibid*, p. 6.
384 'sense of total...': *ibid*, p. 64.
384 'When I consider...': *ibid*, p. 5.
384 'Happiness is...': *ibid*, p. 28.
384 'apathy...': *ibid*, p. 42.
384 'remorse about...': *ibid*, p. 22.
385 'Imprisoned in...': *ibid*, p. 44.
385 'consumed by...': p. 23.
385 'The more books...': p. 1.
385 'He said...': 24 Dec. 1944, *Prophesying Peace*, p. 147.
385 'which he carries...': 6 Dec. 1944, Austin.
385 'extremely touched...': 29 Nov. 1944, *Love from Nancy*, p. 130.
385 'but it makes...': 16 Dec. 1945, Tulsa.
385 'There is a very...': 5 Nov. 1946, *Letters*, p. 555.
385 'rapture and despair': 15 Dec. 1944, Tulsa.
386 'It has given...': 22 Dec. 1944, Tulsa.
386 'whether the best...': n.d., Tulsa.
386 'the whole of...': n.d., Tulsa.
386 'Your picture...': 5 Nov. 1944, Tulsa.
386 'a young man...': 11 July 1945, Tulsa.
f.n. 'sat in W.S. Gilbert's...': to CC, 5 Dec. 1944, Tulsa.
386 'I never wrote you...': 15 March 1948, Tulsa.
387 'the last flicker...': Read to Henry Treece, 29 Nov. 1941, quoted in King, *The Last Modern*, p. 209.
387 'his moralisings...': 29 Jan. 1945, *ibid*, p. 220.
387 'The middle ranks...': 28 Feb. 1946. *Durrell-Miller Letters*, p. 197.
387 'writers hundreds...': *NS*, 30 Dec. 1944.
387 'Even without...': 14 Jan. 1945. *Collected Essays*..., Vol. III, p. 318.
388 'in the literary...': *Classics and Commercials*, p. 280.
388 'What he writes...': 7 Jan 1945. *Letters*, p. 196.
388 'the literary ladies...': *Tablet*, 10 Nov. 1945.
f.n.: 'Poor Smarting...': 22 Nov. 1945, *Letters of N.M. and E.W.*, p. 23.
389 'what can only...': *H*, June 1946.
f.n. 'I think you...': 31 Jan. 1946, Yale.
390 'gentle, civilian...': *Tablet*, 27 July 1946.
390 'I thought...': 4 June 1946, BL.

CHAPTER 19: 'PAGING MR SMARTIBOOTS'.

391 'angelic': CC to Lys Lubbock, n.d., Lilly.
391 'getting to know...': n.d., Eton.
391 'undeservedly vicions...': Mitford to Waugh, 28 Jan. 1950, *Letters of N.M. and E.W.*, p. 176.
391 'disgustingly ugly...': quoted in Ziegler, *Diana Cooper*, p. 241.
391 'We've had C. Conelly...': 18 Jan. 1945, *Mr Wu and Mrs Stitch*, p. 81.
392 'is not a world...': *H*, May 1945.
392 'very much the official...': CC to Lys Lubbock, n.d., Lilly.
392 'grey sick wilderness...': unpublished journal, n.d., Tulsa.

392 'He said he...': 27 Jan. 1945, *Prophesying Peace*, p. 158.
392 'a frozen look...': *I Am My Brother*, p. 205.
392 'distinguished herself...': quoted in Glendinning, *Elizabeth Bowen*, p. 173.
393 'You say somewhere...': 28 Dec. 1945, Tulsa.
393 'not quite...': see *Classics and Commercials*, p. 283.
394 'I wish I had...': n.d., Yale.
f.n. 'Critics are...': *ST*, 10 June 1951.
'hideously bad...': Wilson to Mamaine Koestler, 19 June 1951, *Letters on Literature and Politics*, p. 440.
394 'top brass...': *I Am My Brother*, p. 288.
394 'a certain nostalgia...': 11 Sept. 1945, *Letters on Literature...*, p. 427.
395 'very dilapidated...': n.d., Lilly.
f.n. 'he ordered...': Vidal, *Palimpsest*, p. 179.
395 'bleached, tropical...': *H*, Sept. 1945.
395 'The French...': 29 Sept. 1945, BL.
396 'one can't be...': CC to Lys Lubbock, n.d., Lilly.
396 'vast thick cloud...': *H*, Sept. 1945.
f.n. 'There is...': *Europe without Baedeker*, p. 5.
396 'Connolly has moved...': 1 Aug. 1945, Huntington.
397 'superb grub': Waugh to Mitford, 7 April 1948, *Letters of N.M. and E.W.*, p. 97.
397 'stunned by...': *Everything to Lose*, p. 19.
397 'Oh my lord...': *ibid*, p. 28.
397 'Cyril is now...': 29 June 1947, *Diaries*, p. 681.
398 'Cyril obsessed...': 21 Oct. 1947, *ibid*, p. 690.
398 'I know that...': quoted in Glendinning, *Elizabeth Bowen*, p. 158.
399 'I've just had...': 17 Jan. 1946, *Love from Nancy*, p. 153.
399 'leisure and privacy...': *H*, Sept. 1946.
f.n. 'It must be...': *E of P*, p. 130.
400 'prep school voyage...': *H*, Oct. 1947.
400 'the charm of...': unpublished diary, 28 Nov. 1946, Tulsa.
400 'charming though...': *ibid.*
400 'greatest material...': 7 Aug. 1946, Princeton.
400 'Cyril's triumphant...': n.d., Eton.
400 'luxury of poverty...': unpublished diary, n.d., Tulsa.
401 'I could never...': n.d., Yale.
401 'it's time...': *H*, Oct. 1947.
401 '(1) to withdraw...': n.d., Lilly.
402 'I felt...': n.d., Yale.
402 'what he really...': 2 Sept. 1947, *Durrell-Miller Letters*, p. 203.
402 'seems to have...': *NS*, 7 April 1945.
402 'I loved him...': Bedford, *Aldous Huxley*, Vol. II, p. 77.
402 'one likes him...': 11 Aug. 1950, *Letters*, p. 627.
f.n. '*Aldous*: Who said that?...': Bedford, *Aldous Huxley*, Vol II, p. 113.
402 'I have thought...': n.d., Yale.
403 'Jean who comes...': unpublished diary, n.d., Tulsa.
403 'I have an American...': n.d., Yale.
403 'his evidence...': n.d., Lilly.
404 'I don't look...': 19 Oct. 1945, Tulsa.
404 'Think you are making...': n.d., Tulsa.
404 'Three months here...': 11 Nov. 1945, Tulsa.
404 'When you were in love...': 20 Nov. 1945, Tulsa.
404 'a kind of praying...': 7 April 1947, Tulsa.
405 'wonderful company': *High Diver*, p. 56.
405 'perhaps a way...': Anthony Hobson, diary, 24 Aug. 1965.
406 'his first wife...': unpublished MS, Tulsa.
406 'the brown plump...': unpublished MS, Tulsa.
406 'inescapable lunatic': Gathorne-Hardy to CC, 12 March 1946, Tulsa.
407 'eat the gilded...': 30 April 1941, Tulsa.

407 'the semi-colon . . .': 13 Aug. 1942, *Portrait of Logan Pearsall Smith*, p. 150.
407 'But in the serene . . .': 25 Oct. 1944, Tulsa.
407 'English better . . .': *H*, Nov. 1945.
407 'his ferocious . . .': Gathorne-Hardy, *op. cit.*
407 'How *dreadful* . . .': n.d., Tulsa.
407 'Civilisation will not . . .': *NS*, 9 March 1946.
408 'still lying . . .': CC to Mollie Connolly, 1 April 1947, Tulsa.
408 'with that lameness . . .': Mollie Connolly to CC, n.d., Tulsa.
408 'I'm just a little bit . . .': 'Crooked Neighbours', Tulsa.
408 'Dear brave . . .': 1 March 1947, Tulsa.
409 'He was so . . .': n.d., Tulsa.
409 'like being left . . .': 1 April 1947, Tulsa.
410 'This cold spell . . .': 'Happy Deathbeds', Tulsa.
410 'the final stronghold . . .': *H*, June 1947.
410 'I hear Legionnaire . . .': 30 April 1947, BL.
410 'so that Connolly . . .': 4 May 1947, BL.
410 'the largest, saddest . . .': *H*, April 1947.
411 'Cher Maître . . .': 1 Jan. 1947, King's, Cambridge.
411 'something like 16 . . .': Dylan Thomas to David Higham, 3 May 1948. *Collected Letters*, p. 575.
411 'disgraceful way . . .': n.d., Tulsa.
411 'I saw the inside . . .': 10 Oct. 1949, *Letters*, p. 311.
411 'I want it published . . .': 16 Sept. 1947, *Letters*, p. 260.
412 'failure of imagination . . .': MS of 1969 talk on *The Loved One*, Austin.
412 'Some days . . .': 28 Nov. 1947, *Diaries*, p. 691.
412 'an immensely agreeable . . .': 1 March 1948, Tulsa.
412 'Est, est, est!' . . .': n.d., BL.
412 'I anticipated . . .': 2 Jan. 1948, Tulsa.
412 'Evelyn (unaware . . .': CC to Oliver Simon, n.d., Cambridge University Library.
412 'May I say . . .': n.d., BL.
f.n. 'Osbert Lancaster . . .': 8 Sept. 1948, private collection.
413 'pen pal . . .': n.d., BL.
413 'I was moved . . .': 2 Jan. 1948, *Letters*, p. 265.
413 'you have to have . . .': n.d., BL.
413 'Did I tell you . . .': 16 March 1948, *Letters*, p. 273.
413 'Poor Cyril . . .': n.d., *Letters*, p. 270.
413 'Awful about . . .': Mitford to Waugh, 11 Feb. 1948, BL.
414 'What has happened . . .': Bowra to Waugh, 2 March 1948, BL.
414 'I was told . . .': *The Fifties*, p. 107.
414 'I have to go . . .': 2 Feb. 1948, BL.
414 'hell . . .': 1 March 1948, Tulsa.
415 'all that is nicest . . .': 21 April 1948, Princeton.
417 'a person with whom . . .': 11 Jan. 1949, Tulsa.
418 'who had just said . . .': diary, 7 June 1948, Tulsa.
418 'either a wild attempt . . .': quotes in this paragraph are from 'The Id's Journal', unpublished MS, Tulsa.
419 'Joan is . . .': n.d., Lilly.
419 'climbing the Dune . . .': *Art and Literature*, Autumn 1966.
420 'the feminine equivalent . . .': 6 Jan. 1949, Princeton.
420 'I can just imagine . . .': Hamilton to Canfield, 7 Jan. 1949, Princeton.
420 'Quite fantastic . . .': Hamilton to Canfield, 17 May 1949, Princeton.
420 'his reasons . . .': 9 June 1949, Princeton.
421 'I'm not a socialist . . .': 11 Jan. 1949, Tulsa.
421 'Cyril is a lumpish . . .': 6 June 1948, *Midway on the Waves*, p. 59.
421 'like Rubens's . . .': 13 Nov. 1947, *ibid*, p. 143.
f.n. 'the most brilliant . . .': 13 Jan. 1949. *ibid*, p. 206.
421 'reading, writing . . .': misc. MS, Tulsa.
421 'with the collapse . . .': *H*, April 1948.
421 'hugging a thimble . . .': *Partisan Review*, May 1949.
423 'I always regard . . .': n.d., Tulsa.
423 'bilious . . .': Sonia Brownell to CC, 10 Aug. 1948, Tulsa.

424 'I must say I love . . .': 29 Nov. 1949, private collection.
424 'forms part . . .': Mitford to Waugh, 25 Jan. 1948, BL.
424 'so devoted . . .': nd., Tulsa.
424 'for part of me . . .': n.d., Lilly.
424 'Lys is very pretty . . .': 28 Feb. 1946, *Everything to Lose*, p. 50.
425 'Cyril kept . . .': 16 April 1948, *ibid*, p. 75.
425 'Have you heard about . . .': 21 Feb. 1946, *Love from Nancy*, p. 162.
425 'with his long . . .': 12 Sept. 1948, *Everything to Lose*, p. 78.
425 '"Oh that must have been . . ."': *ibid.*
425 'sat upright . . .': *Adam International Review*, 1974–5.
425 'We have been naughty . . .': *Recollections*, p. 107.
f.n. 'Round the ring . . .': *Our Age*, p. 214.
425 'Good (about Cyril . . .': 9 June 1949, BL.
426 'Oh please God . . .': CC to Lys Lubbock, n.d., Lilly.
426 'I am sure . . .': n.d., Lilly.
426 'I wish you wouldn't . . .': n.d., Lilly.
426 'Get up, Cyril . . .': CC to Lys Lubbock, n.d., Lilly.
f.n.: 'He was quietly singing . . .': Pritchett to Gerald Brenan, 28 Jan. 1950, Austin.
427 'I am afraid . . .': CC to Lys Lubbock, 4 June 1949, Lilly.
428 'What would you do . . .': Anthony Hobson, diary, 10 Aug. 1969.
f.n. 'It *is* hard . . .': quoted in Nancy Mitford to Waugh, 13 April 1946, BL.
428 'I see Cyril's boom . . .': 2 Jan. 1948, *Diaries*, p. 694.
428 '"Cyril must have a rest" . . .': *The Ample Proposition*, p. 120.
429 'someone else's interest . . .': *Coastwise Lights*, p. 173.
429 'sterile, embittered . . .': *H*, Nov. 1949.
429 'desperate struggle': *H*, Dec. 1949–Jan. 1950.
429 'We closed . . .': *Ideas and Places*, p. ix.
430 'I enjoyed my funeral . . .': n.d., BL.
430 'I must tell you . . .': 4 Dec. 1949, Tulsa.

CHAPTER 20: 'OAK COFFIN'.

431 'adventurous young . . .': *The Wanton Chase*, p. 71.
431 'balding, stocky . . .': *Tears Before Bedtime*, p. 26.
431 'the pivotal heroine . . .': *Fourteen Letters* (no page numbers).
431 'She might have had . . .': *The Wanton Chase*, p. 20.
431 'As feline . . .': *High Diver*, p. 149.
432 'extraordinarily quick . . .': *The Wanton Chase*, p. 36.
f.n.: 'like some exquisite . . .': *Anything Goes*, p. 3.
433 'She is the warmest . . .': n.d., private collection.
433 'dim little creatures . . .': n.d., Lilly.
434 'the structure of . . .': n.d., private collection.
434 'Boots has gone off . . .': 30 April 1950, BL.
434 'what should rise . . .': n.d., private collection.
435 'base for fucking . . .': n.d., Lilly.
435 'I can't muster up . . .': n.d., BL.
436 'I suddenly saw . . .': 19 June 1950, BL.
436 'I expect I am . . .': n.d., Lilly.
436 'because he tells Robin . . .': Pritchett to Gerald Brenan, 21 Jan. 1951, Austin.
436 'Would you like to hear . . .': Mitford to Waugh, 25 Sept. 1950, BL.
437 'a huge sawdust . . .': *Tears Before Bedtime*, p. 91.
437 'Darling Wopsy . . .': n.d., private collection.
f.n. 'Memorandum for . . .': private collection.
437 'Cyril very nearly died . . .': n.d., private collection.
437 'sat and read . . .': Mitford to Waugh, 30 Sept. 1950, *Love from Nancy*, p. 265.
438 'Sorry to hear . . .': 25 Aug. 1950, private collection.
438 'the salutary mistake . . .': n.d., Lilly.
f.n. 'awful thoughts . . .': n.d., Lilly.

439 'hence my general...': 24 Nov. 1950, Bristol.
439 'after the first course...': n.d., *Letters*, p. 342.
440 'As to cottages...': n.d., Lilly.
440 'Bloody dark...': see *Tears before Bedtime*, p. 96 *et seq.*
f.n. 'beautiful witch...': Catherine Lambert to author.
442 'The Mayfair clubman...': n.d., Lilly.
442 'plodding up Bond Street...': *Tears Before Bedtime*, p. 97.
442 'We are doing...': n.d., Lilly.
442 'spent his all...': Ann Fleming to Hugo Charteris, 16 July 1952, *Letters*, p. 118.
f.n. 'Goodness...': 8 April 1951, *Letters of N.M. and E.W.*, p. 221.
443 'lamentable...': *ST*, 3 Sept. 1950.
443 'I admired him...': quoted in Russell *et al*, *The Pearl of Days*, p. 323.
443 'tendency to...': *ST*, 2 March 1952.
f.n. 'Look, General...': Pearson, *Life of Ian Fleming*, p. 97.
444 'outstripped...': 9 Dec. 1947, Tulsa.
444 'permanent contribution...': 2 Oct. 1951, Tulsa.
444 'How terrible...': n.d., Bodleian.
444 'warm, friendly...': *Memories*, p. 10.
445 'I always feel...': 10 April 1951, BL.
445 'it appears...': Pritchett to Brenan, 20 Jan, 1951, Austin.
445 'new "internal daydream"...': *The Ample Proposition*, p. 120.
445 'my Baudelaire...': n.d., Lilly.
445 'Anglo-American...': n.d., Bristol.
445 'I am pretty canny...': 12 Oct. 1951, Princeton.
446 'there remains...': 10 April 1952, Bodleian.
446 'I give Connolly...': Cass Canfield to Mike Bessie, 13 March 1953, Princeton.
446 'I had an awful time...': 20 Aug. 1951, BL.
446 'Cyril has many...': 21 Aug. 1951, *Letters*, p. 353.
446 'he approached me...': 29 Oct. 1951. *Letters*, p. 358.
447 'There are two...': unpublished *Time* TS, Austin.
447 'They looked...': *The Blessing*, p. 224.
447 'I don't want...': 28 March 1951, BL.
448 'flabby to the core...': Mitford to Waugh, 2 April 1951, BL.
448 'Bootikins won't speak...': 29 May 1952, BL.
448 'It seems...': 3 June 1952, BL.
448 'he gets his own back...': Mitford to Waugh, 8 March 1954, BL.
448 'Miss Mitford's...': *ST*, 7 March 1954.
448 'I feel as if...': n.d., Lilly.
f.n. 'a truly awful man...': CC to Lys Lubbock, 13 Aug. 1952, Lilly.
449 'She is a very saintly...': n.d., Tulsa.
449 'Do go...': n.d., Tulsa.
449 'Did I or did I not...': n.d., Lilly.
450 'I know all about you...': quoted in Boyle, *The Climate of Treason*, p. 367.
450 'What would you do...': quoted in Knightley, *Philby*, p. 172.
450 'innocent of...': n.d., Lilly.
451 'the clever, helpless...': for quotes from *The Missing Diplomats*, see *ST* 21 and 28 Sept. 1952.
451 'the Alcazar...': *ibid.*
451 'I didn't mean...': n.d., Tulsa.
452 'Politics beginning the nursery...': *The Missing Diplomats*.
452 'great offence...': *ST*, 2 Dec. 1956.
452 'I met with...': *ST*, 18 Feb. 1968.
453 'He is the first underwater...': Connolly to Knapp-Fisher, 1 March 1952, Bodleian.
453 'chase American...': CC to Lys Lubbock, n.d., Lilly.
453 'a kind of cosy cat...': Pritchett to Brenan, 21 Jan. 1951, Austin.
453 'Everybody complains...': Mitford to Waugh, 29 May 1952, BL.
454 'a draughty old Sunbeam...': reprinted in *Tynan Right and Left*, p. 268.
454 'You have no idea...': n.d., Lilly.
454 'longed to remain...': CC to Lys Lubbock, n.d., Lilly.
454 'honeymoon with myself...': unpublished diary, 24 July 1952, Tulsa.

454 'why he always wore...': Waugh to Mitford, 5 May 1954, *Letters*, p. 424.
454 'He has become...': 12 Jan 1951, *Everything to Lose*, p. 136.
454 'hopping mad...': Ann Fleming to Waugh, 20 Sept. 1952, BL.
455 '"Keep the Home..."': 21 Sept. 1952, *Letters*, p. 384.
455 'golden and perfect...': *ST*, 7 Sept. 1952.
455 'Evelyn refused...': *Evelyn Waugh*, p. 408.
455 'I deeply wish...': 9 Dec. 1953, *Letters*, p. 414.
455 'Of all the people...': n.d., BL.
f.n. 'always mesmerised...': *Journals, 1987–9*, p. 195.
456 'like Yeats...': *NS*, 13 March 1954.
456 'as caddish...': 13 March 1954, Tulsa.
f.n. 'How typical...': n.d., BL.
'his pale...': *Weep No More*, p. 9.
456 'All right, I had...': CC diary, n.d., private collection.
457 'For six months...': n.d., private collection.
457 'Like many artists...': *ST*, 6 Nov. 1952.
457 'Few existences...': *ST*, 18 Jan. 1953.
457 'death by boredom...': n.d., Lilly.
458 'an unspeakably flat...': Pritchett to Brenan, n.d., Austin.
458 'We all shuddered...': 17 Jan. 1953, *Journals*, p. 110.
458 'We've had the...': *As I Walked Down New Grub Street*, p. 67.
459 'they would be like...': 16 April 1952, Austin.
459 'Cyril greeted...': *Remembering My Good Friends*, p. 167.
460 'I love you...': 11 May 1953, Tulsa.
460 'Cyril's writing...': Mary McCarthy to Mike Bessie, 4 Oct. 1953, Princeton.
460 'His collected...': *Observer*, 17 May 1953.
460 'I thought...': n.d., private collection.
460 'I always enjoyed...': 9 Dec. 1953, *Letters*, p. 414.
461 'He coveted...': 15 June 1953, Austin.
461 'a good-looking...': Davis to CC, 6 Jan. 1962, Tulsa.
461 'big, balding...': *The Interior Castle*, p. 410.
461 'sweetly smiling wife': Brenan to Ralph Partridge, 16 Feb. 1953, *Best of Friends*, p. 168.
461 'delightful neighbours...': n.d., Austin.
462 'Thurber-simple...': Brenan to Pritchett, 27 Dec. 1956, Austin.
462 'His slow, droning...': 23 July 1953. *Best of Friends*, p. 177.
462 'Every conversation,...': Brenan to Ralph Partridge, 8 May 1954, *Best of Friends*, p. 199.
462 'house writer...': Kathleen Tynan, *The Life of Kenneth Tynan*, p. 130.
462 'a wonderful huge...': *The Dangerous Summer*, p. 16.
462 'loved good food...': *ibid*, p. 36.
462 'great slabs...': Brenan to Pritchett, 27 Dec. 1965, Austin.
462 'baggy, besandalled...': *Tynan Right and Left*, p. 265.
463 'all we need...': n.d., private collection.
463 'gazing at fat women...': quoted in *Weep No More*. p. 2.
463 'extraordinary capacity...': *Remembering My Good Friends*, p. 275.
463 'Why is there...': *ibid*.
463 'He chases...': quoted in *Weep No More*, p. 2.
464 'Fifty in September...': 28 March 1953, misc. MS, Tulsa.
464 'the main course...': journal, 13 Sept. 1953, private collection.
464 'Cyril was radiant...': *The Strenuous Years*, p. 273.
465 'the taint of homosexuality...': 7 Jan. 1954, *The Fifties*, p 105.
465 'like many wits...': *ibid* p. 106.
465 'vast unheated...': 6 Jan. 1954, *Tears Before Bedtime*, p. 182.
f.n. 'a large Victorian...': n.d., BL.
465 '"She's going..."': Partridge, *Everything to Lose*, p. 191.
466 'A lot of talk...': journal, n.d., private collection.
466 'I am terribly...': n.d., private collection.

466 'I spend...': journal, n.d., private collection.
466 'stricken with nymphomania...': journal, 28 June 1954, private collection.
467 'I am glad...': n.d., private collection.
467 'like swimming...': *Tears Before Bedtime*, p. 198.
467 'You will find me...': n.d., Lilly.
467 'We are tortured...': n.d., Lilly.
468 'I have never...': 22 Feb. 1955, private collection.

CHAPTER 21: 'E ARRIVATO WEIDENFELD'

469 'I like lunching...': n.d., private collection.
f.n. 'whenever I heard...': *Weep No More*, p. 6.
470 'at that moment...': unpublished TS, private collection.
470 'a paradise...': CC to Skelton, n.d., private collection.
470 'I cannot stand...': 27 June 1955, private collection.
471 'it is obvious...': 16 April 1955, private collection.
471 'Poor widowed...': 2 Aug. 1955, BL.
471 'Connolly's cuckolding...': Waugh to Diana Cooper, 20 Dec. 1955, *Mr Wu and Mrs Stitch*, p. 215.
471 'There is certainly...': n.d., Tulsa.
471 'You are the only...': 18 July 1955, Tulsa.
471 'I think it is...': 2 Nov. 1955, Tulsa.
472 'the only book...': CC to Waugh, n.d., BL.
472 'I really do love...': n.d., private collection.
472 'My life is really...': 4 July 1955, private collection.
472 'angry despatch-rider's...': Skelton, diary, 21 July 1955, private collection.
473 'I love Cyril...': n.d., private collection
473 'I really am...': n.d., private collection.
473 'it is a great pleasure...': CC to Skelton, 6 Aug. 1955, private collection.
473 'an absolutely staggering...': CC to Skelton, n.d., private collection.
f.n. 'Cyril read out...': diary, 19 Oct. 1955, private collection.
473 'monotonous diet...': diary, n.d., private collection.
473 'give us a fresh start...': n.d., private collection.
474 'I hope it is not...': n.d., BL.
f.n. 'I have Boots...': 30 July 1954, *Letters of N.M. and E.W.*, p. 341.
474 'I was not...': *ST*, 3 July 1955.
474 'I think he had better...': 12 July 1955, BL.
474 'I see his blue...': Waugh to Bowra, 14 July 1955, *Letters*. p. 444.
474 'with his alert...': *Weep No More*, p. 12.
474 'Mary Campbell...': *ibid*, p. 14.
474 'found his back...': ibid, p. 15.
475 'I cannot imagine...': *ibid*, p. 25.
475 'The Campbells...': *ibid*, p. 26.
475 'you will have to...': 18 Dec. 1955, private collection.
475 'It is not very...': n.d., private collection.
475 'a terrible, terrible...': 21 Dec. 1955, private collection.
476 'Gone to the Prado...': 29 Dec. 1955, Partridge, *Everything to Lose*, p. 240.
f.n. 'you have met...': CC to Skelton, n.d., private collection.
476 'red roses...': *Weep No More*, p. 27.
476 'He clamours...': 20 Jan. 1956, Partridge, *Everything to Lose*, p. 243.
476 'Hate is really...': n.d., private collection.
476 'First catch...': journal, n.d., private collection.
476 'I am more in love...': diary, 1 Feb, 1956, private collection.
477 'How I love them BOTH...': diary, 6 March 1956, private collection.
477 'really made the divorce...': CC to Brenan, n.d., Austin.
477 'This never-ending...': n.d., BL.
478 'You will realise...': 28 Oct. 1955, Tulsa.
478 'all he wanted...': Spender, *Journals*, p. 180.
478 'Terrible news...': 26 Aug. 1956, private collection.

478 'he gave a sigh...': *Journals*, p. 181.
479 'a dismal affair...': *Remembering My Good Friends*, p. 279.
479 'This must be the ugliest...': 4 Sept. 1956, private collection.
479 'Algeciras was...': n.d. Austin.
479 'I was on top...': 12 Sept. 1956, private collection.
f.n. 'a really odious...': n.d., Tulsa.
480 'Gush! Gush!...': *Weep No More*, p. 49.
480 'I chant...': *ibid*, p. 48.
480 'The last three...': n.d., Austin.
481 'He is not...': 21 Oct. 1956, BL.
481 'It is something...': 9 Aug. 1956, *The Fifties*, p. 373.
481 'Cyril Connolly/Behaves...': 'Scurrilous Clerihews' from 'A Christmas Stocking: Fun for Young and Old', 1953, reprinted in *Wilson's Night Thoughts*.
481 'always full...': *The Fifties*, p. 349.
482 'the bit about Jamie': n.d., Lilly.
482 'Sir Mortimer...': n.d., BL.
483 'hammy...': BBC Third Programme, 21 Jan. 1964, National Sound Archive.
483 'Of what is *Shade*...': *NS*, 31 March 1956.
483 'Perhaps I get...': n.d., Bristol.
483 'awful mackintoshes...': *The Restless Years*, pp. 44–5.
484 'Every few years...': *ST*, 29 Nov. 1953.
484 'Keats-struck...': *ST*, 17 Jan. 1954.
f.n. 'he had the...' *TLS*, 6 Dec. 1974.
485 'go back to...': *ST*, 15 March 1953.
f.n. 'he had the...': *TLS*, 6 Dec. 1974.
485 'initial horror...': *ST*, 7 Nov. 1954.
485 'Mr Blackmur...': *ST*, 16 Jan. 1955.
485 'This means that...': *ST*, 18 May 1969.
485 'What I dislike...': *ST*, 10 April 1960.
486 'unself-conscious, unsubsidised...': *ST*, 4 Feb. 1962.
486 'Yeats appears...': *ST*, 13 June 1965.
486 'What originally...': *More of My Life*, p. 124.
486 'one of the bad...': *ST*, 13 Jan. 1974.
487 'I do not believe...': 'Beyond Believing,' *Encounter*, April 1961.
487 'Malaise...': n.d., Tulsa.
487 'It was you...': n.d., Tulsa.
487 'no difference...': n.d., Tulsa.
487 'What you want...': Elizabeth Jane Howard to author.
487 'You are a mirage...': n.d., Tulsa.
488 'Cyril Connolly is hammering...': Fleming to Waugh, 20 Oct. 1956, BL.
488 'I really do love you': n.d., Tulsa.
f.n. 'dazzling and worshipful glances': *The Old Man and Me*, p. 58.
488 'When will you realise...': 28 June 1957, private collection.
488 'I should have thought...': n.d., Tulsa.
489 'At the relevant time...': n.d., Tulsa.
489 'frosty hostility': *High Diver*, p. 152.
489 'The much-heralded...': 17 Feb. 1957, *Everything to Lose*, p. 274.
489 'but when we moved...': 19 Feb. 1957, *ibid*, p. 274.
490 'But what an extraordinary...': 26 Feb. 1957, *ibid*, p. 275.
490 'brilliantly amusing...': 13 Jan. 1958, *ibid*, p. 296.
490 'he motioned me...': 20 Feb. 1959. *ibid*, p. 322.
f.n. 'some great sea bird's...': *The Adonis Garden*, p. 9.
'pretty, tender...': *ibid*, p. 217.
490 'I hate having...': n.d., Bodleian.
490 'The only solution...': diary entry, n.d., private collection.
491 'governed by...': *Remembering My Good Friends*, p. 278.

CHAPTER 22: 'BUSHEY LODGE'

495 'Even if you...': 15 March 1959, Tulsa.
495 'Do give...': n.d., Tulsa.
495 'Cyril (the final blow)...': 24 June 1959, private collection.
495 'After staying...': n.d., private collection.
495 'You should have come...': Deirdre Levi to author.

496 'I lived . . .': *ST*, 1 Aug. 1971.
496 'a delightful house . . .': *Cyril Connolly as a Book Collector*, p. 8.
496 'I don't know . . .': 1 March 1967, private collection.
496 'a spell about . . .': n.d., private collection.
497 'All in my mind's . . .': 25 July 1962, *Letters*, Vol. II, p. 234.
497 'so sadly empty . . .': n.d., private collection.
497 'so precociously . . .': CC to Skelton, 22 May 1963, private collection.
498 'She looks so much . . .': CC to Skelton, n.d., private collection.
498 'she was having tea . . .': CC to Skelton, 29 March 1962, private collection.
498 'squalling baby . . .': n.d., private collection.
f.n. '*Connolly* . . .': Anthony Hobson, diary, 24 Oct. 1964.
498 'desperate, lonely . . .': 18 Jan. 1961, private collection.
499 'Every afternoon . . .': n.d., private collection.
499 'I sit through . . .': CC to Skelton, n.d., private collection.
499 'more than ever . . .': CC to Skelton, 27 Oct. 1961, private collection.
499 'They bang around . . .': CC to Skelton, 8 Nov. 1961, private collection.
499 'I feel like . . .': 9 Jan. 1963, private collection.
500 'At the moment . . .': n.d., quoted in *Weep No More*, p. 87.
f.n. 'institutionalised selfishness': in conversation with author.
501 'Greatly distressed . . .': 6 April 1960, Penguin Books.
501 'luckily there . . .': 21 June 1961, BL.
502 'Hope he doesn't . . .': 12 Jan. 1961. Bristol.
502 'taken literally . . .': 21 May 1960, Tulsa.
502 'provided the expenses . . .': 15 June 1960, Tulsa.
f.n. 'True it is . . .': *Journey to Java*, p. 282.
'It is warm . . .': n.d., Bodleian.
'I find it . . .': 12 Oct. 1960. *Letters*, p. 272.
503 'Connolly was radiating . . .': Ann Fleming to Waugh, 29 May 1961, BL.
503 'the thinnest . . .': *ST*, 25 Sept. 1960.
503 'unquestionably . . .': 29 Oct. 1961.
503 'I am not surprised . . .': quoted in Ann Fleming, *Letters*, p. 295.
503 'A mischievous . . .': 23 Oct. 1961, *Letters*, p. 578.
504 'Gossip tells me . . .': quoted in Waugh, *Letters*, p. 578.
504 'I try to think . . .': 29 Oct. 1961, BL.
504 'I did not get . . .': 25 Oct. 1961, BL.
504 'Don't let . . .': 29 Oct. 1961, *Letters*, p. 578.
f.n. 'to see him. . . .': *Tablet*, 5 May 1951.
505 'I have told . . .': 20 Nov. 1961. *Letters*, p. 578.
505 'I do not think . . .': 30 Oct. 1961, BL.
505 'with a nose . . .': *ST*, 24 Dec. 1961, reprinted in *Previous Convictions*.
506 'It seems to me . . .': *The Sixties*, p. 260.
506 'Since I have . . .': n.d., Tulsa.
507 'that wretched Cyril Connolly . . .': *Yesterday Came Suddenly*, p. 257.
508 'Put on one side . . .': 10 May 1960, Tulsa.
508 'It was a spontaneous . . .': n.d., Tulsa.
509 'I happen to be . . .': *ST*, 1 Sept. 1963.
509 'Tapering off! . . .': *ST*, 24 Dec. 1967.
509 'It is sad . . .': 7 Dec. 1971, Tulsa.
509 'wild goose chase . . .': *ST*, 3 Feb. 1974.
509 'could only be . . .': 'Sotheby's as an Education', in *Sotheby's Review*, 1971.
510 'Connolly loved . . .': *Infants of the Spring*, p. 128.
510 'I should have . . .': in conversation with author.
510 'His own personality . . .': *Infants of the Spring*, p. 129.
510 'I am expecting . . .': 26 April 1962, *Hanging On*, p. 106.
510 'The arrival . . .': 27 April 1962, *ibid.*
510 'guards were lowered . . .': 12 Aug. 1962, *ibid* p. 117.

510 'People forget . . .': 1 May 1973, Brotherton Library.
f.n. 'I don't think . . .': Patrick Leigh Fermor to author.
512 'often thought of him . . .': reprinted in *A Man of Letters*, p. 154.
512 'he delights . . .': 20 May 1966, *Other People*, p. 221.
512 'conspiratorial purr . . .': *Coastwise Lights*, p. 194.
513 'he was more odious . . .': 13 July 1962, Huntington.
513 'About to be 59 . . .': misc. MS, Tulsa.
513 'The French . . .': *Les Pavillons*, p. 4.
514 'Cyril's book . . .': 3 Dec. 1962, BL.
514 'muttering with Maecenas . . .': *ST*, 19 Aug. 1962.
515 'Isn't "the Kitchen . . ."': 7 Dec. 1962 and 12 Dec. 1962, Austin.
515 'Imagine my delight . . .': 31 May 1963, Tulsa.
515 'a queer mixture . . .': *The Sixties*, p. 259.
515 'You did so much . . .': 23 Aug. 1964, Tulsa.
515 'I wish I could say . . .': n.d., *Letters of Ann Fleming*, p. 357.
516 'or rather he . . .': 2 April 1963, Bristol.
517 'Isn't this typical? . . .': n.d., Bristol.
517 'Secretly I am convinced . . .': *Previous Convictions*, p. xiii.
518 'It is very much a book . . .': 4 Jan. 1964, Tulsa.
518 'Though it is ghastly . . .': 21 Dec. 1963, Tulsa.
518 'come to terms . . .': *Sunday Telegraph*, 6 Dec. 1963.
518 'what is trivial . . .': *ST*, 15 Dec. 1963.
f.n. 'academic critics . . .': *Our Age*, p. 214.
518 'anything but . . .': *NS*, 6 Dec. 1963.
519 'I suppose what . . .': 21 Dec. 1963, Tulsa.
f.n. 'He thought talking . . .': Amis, *Memoirs*, p. 182.
'Let me now . . .': *ST*, 18 Sept. 1960.
519 'the result is . . .': *Listener*, 19 Dec. 1963.
519 'no on writing . . .': *Spectator*, 13 Dec. 1963.
520 'A different Connolly . . .': *Evening Standard*, 14 Jan. 1964.
520 'the benignity . . .': Fleming to Waugh, 6 Dec. 1963, *Letters*, p. 332.
520 'The trouble with Deirdre . . .': quoted in Ann Fleming to Waugh, 24 Jan. 1964, BL.
520 'I wake with the death wish . . .': n.d., BL.
520 'One is like . . .': n.d., Wadham.
520 'dix ans après . . .': 3 June 1963, Tulsa.
521 'usual jam . . .': *The Sixties*, p. 258.
521 'The self-consciously . . .': 6 June 1962. *Hanging On*, p. 111.
521 'a prose that was . . .': *Coastwise Lights*, p. 196.
522 'is one of those . . .': *London Magazine*, Dec. 1963.
f.n. 'Has it ever struck . . .': *Coming up for Air*, p. 23.
'The expression was . . .': *London Magazine*, Feb. 1964.
523 'Cyril Connolly has gone . . .': Fleming to Waugh, 4 Feb. 1964, *Letters*, p. 334.
523 'After the first evening . . .': CC to Skelton, 24 Jan. 1961, private collection.
523 'heavenly tropical grass smell . . .': CC to Skelton, 10 Feb. 1964, private collection.
523 'reconciliation, perhaps, . . .': *ST*, 19 April 1964.
f.n. 'The pair of them . . .': Introduction to Keith Vaughan, *Journals*, p. ix.
524 'like a train . . .': Raymond Hoffenberg to author.
524 'It seems like . . .': 25 March 1964, Tulsa.
524 'She had been saving . . .': CC to Skelton, 2 Jan. 1965, private collection.
524 'I always feel . . .': n.d., private collection.
525 'You were the first sympathetic . . .': 20 Aug. 1964, Tulsa.
525 'I must tell you . . .': Anthony Hobson, diary, 24 Aug. 1964.
525 'From now on . . .': *ibid*, 29 Aug. 1964.

526 'only the raising . . .': *ibid*, 28 Oct. 1964.
526 'I suffer . . .': *ibid*, 29 Oct. 1964.
526 '"Alan Ross . . ."': *ibid*, 17 Dec. 1964.
526 '*jusqu'à* your . . .': *ibid*, 14 Feb. 1965.
526 'Shall we risk . . .': 17 Sept. 1948, Eton.
f.n. 'both of them . . .': *Collected Stories of Noël Blakiston*, p. 74.
527 'I want to create . . .': 12 Jan. 1963, Eton.
527 'My life in some letters . . .': 21 Jan. 1963, Eton.
527 'but I lack . . .': n.d., Wadham.
527 'At night . . .': n.d., private collection.
527 'Next victim Freddie! . . .': CC to Blakiston, 12 Jan. 1963, Eton.
527 'his is going to write . . .': 5 Nov. 1962, BL.
f.n. 'farrago of old cat': flyleaf of Anthony Hobson's copy of *The Adonis Garden*.
527 'I don't like . . .': CC to Plomer, 2 Aug. 1964, Durham.
528 'I am touched . . .': 11 Aug. 1964, Tulsa.
528 'I would hate it . . .': 13 July 1964, Bristol.
f.n. 'It is infuriating . . .': Anthony Hobson, diary, 24 Oct. 1964.
529 'Dear Chum . . .': 29 Sept. 1972, Tulsa.
529 'Jean's mausoleum': 26 Oct. 1972, Tulsa.
529 'Cyril is doing . . .': 5 Aug. 1965, André Deutsch files, Tulsa.
529 'fills me . . .': 28 Nov. 1965, Tulsa.
529 'I can't tell you . . .': 2 Dec. 1965, Tulsa.
529 'I tried . . .': Anthony Hobson, diary, 7 June 1965.
530 'Mr Connolly's choice . . .': *Observer*, 5 Dec. 1965.
530 'all Mr Connolly's . . .': *Spectator*, 17 Dec. 1965.
530 'what Mr Connolly has written . . .': *TLS*, 23 Dec. 1965.
530 'preaching his own . . .': *DT*, 23 Dec. 1965.
530 'affectionate . . .': *NS*, 3 Dec. 1965.
530 'light, bright . . .': *Encounter*, March 1966.
531 'with a twisted . . .': Anthony Hobson, diary, 26 Aug. 1965.
531 'a little old bird . . .': *ibid*, 24 Aug. 1965.
531 'We intend . . .': 30 Oct. 1964, private collection.
532 'No other . . .': *Encounter*, Feb. 1964.
f.n. 'alas, Professor Praz's . . .': *ST*, 13 Sept. 1964.
'Suppose you had written . . .': 23 Sept. 1964.
534 'I felt . . .': Anthony Hobson, diary, 19 Jan. 1966.
535 'Cyril made fearfully . . .': 26 Aug. 1967, *Letters*, p. 386.
535 'I now regard . . .': n.d., Wadham.
535 'serenely happy . . .': CC at Mermaid Theatre celebration of Pound, 1973.
535 'When we met . . .': *ST*, 17 Sept. 1967.
536 'If only I had . . .': n.d., Yale.
536 'mild blue eyes . . .': 'Pound in Venice', MS, Austin.
536 'I couldn't remember . . .': 25 Nov. 1969, Yale.
536 'their droppings . . .': 'An Aesthete in Africa', *ST*, 31 Dec. 1967, 7 Jan. 1968.
537 'Most exhausting . . .': n.d., Bodleian.
537 'All my life . . .': *ST*, 17 Sept. 1967.
f.n. 'There once . . .': n.d., private collection.

CHAPTER 23: 'EASTBOURNE REVISITED'

539 'The more I think . . .': 17 Nov. 1967, *Letters*, Vol. II, p. 340.
539 'All the visions . . .': Anthony Hobson, diary, 10 Jan. 1968.
539 'If one wants . . .': *London Magazine*, Aug–Sept. 1973.
540 'first editions . . .': *Cyril Connolly as a Book Collector*, p. 9.
540 'It is a great . . .': n.d., private collection.
540 'the relief . . .': CC to Skelton, 25 March 1968, private collection.

540 'he welcomed . . .': *Customs and Characters*, p. 104.
541 'I should like to know . . .': CC to Jack Lambert, n.d., Bodleian.
541 'Who was responsible . . .': CC to Jack Lambert, n.d., Bodleian.
f.n. 'should give . . .': *Encounter*, May 1975.
542 'those celebrated cadenzas . . .': *ibid.*
542 'I suppose . . .': Russell *et al*, *The Pearl of Days*, p. 324.
543 'Not generally . . .': *ibid.*
543 '"But why . . ."': diary, 11 May 1968, Tulsa.
543 'My birthday . . .': CC to Skelton, n.d., private collection.
543 'I felt like . . .': n.d., Wadham.
544 'all the Elmstead . . .': n.d., private collection.
f.n. 'I am *so sick* . . .': Deirdre Levi to the author.
544 'lampooned . . .': CC to Francis Wishart, n.d., Tulsa.
545 'As you rang off . . .': 8 Oct. 1968, Bristol.
545 'Why, oh why . . .': n.d., Bristol.
545 'I am overdrawn . . .': 6 March 1969, Bristol.
545 'The best one . . .': misc. MS, n.d., Tulsa.
f.n. 'You don't realise . . .': Anthony Hobson, diary, 23 July 1967.
545 'It is a mark . . .': misc. MS, n.d., Tulsa.
546 'a touch of the tarboosh': Anthony Hobson, diary, 15 Oct. 1969.
546 'In this I feel . . .': Anthony Hobson, diary, 10 Aug. 1969.
546 'very maternal': CC to Skelton, 30 April 1970, private collection.
f.n.: 'I am sending you . . .': 17 April 1970, Yale.
'I am sure Matthew . . .': CC to Olga Rudge, 3 July 1970, Yale.
547 'I am in a way . . .': 17 May 1970, Tulsa.
547 'I seem to be sunk . . .': n.d., Wadham.
547 'the baby is always . . .': CC to Skelton, 17 June 1970, private collection.
547 'ray of sunshine . . .': CC to Skelton, 24 April 1971, private collection.
547 'I love his . . .': CC to Skelton, 17 June 1970, private collection.
547 'He has very . . .': CC to Skelton, 24 April 1971, private collection.
548 'I don't know . . .': CC to Skelton, n.d., private collection.
548 'a femme fatale . . .': CC to Olga Rudge, 16 Nov. 1970, Yale.
548 'crushed and miserable': Anthony Hobson, diary, 9 Aug. 1969.
548 'being dragged . . .': *ST*, 25 July 1965.
548 'affectionate in a . . .': CC to Skelton, 18 Dec. 1971, private collection.
548 'always smoking . . .': journal, n.d., private collection.
548 'Yackety . . .': misc. verses, Tulsa.
549 'I can't bear . . .': CC to Skelton, 24 April 1971, private collection.
549 'People say she is dull . . .': quoted in Anthony Powell, *Journals* 1987–89, p. 217.
550 'even at the best . . .': journal, n.d., private collection.
550 'Well, Timothy . . .': Tim Jones to author.
551 'I recognised . . .': *The Hill of Kronos*, p. 114.
551 'a great friend . . .': 16 Sept. 1969, Yale.
f.n. 'who is breathing . . .': misc. MS, Tulsa.
552 'affection and admiration . . .': *ST*, 17 Oct. 1965.
552 'that longed-for . . .': *White Mischief*, p. 133.
553 'unpaid invoices . . .': *ibid*, p. 141.
554 'there is also . . .': n.d., Austin.
554 'acolyte': 'Memories of Cyril Connolly', PEN Club, 13 June 1984.
554 'Some find . . .': n.d., Austin.
556 'wicked godmother . . .': *ST*, 6 June 1971.
556 'Of course we all . . .': 6 June 1971, Tulsa.
556 'the candour . . .': 12 July 1971, Tulsa.
556 'horrible remarks . . .': 7 June 1971, Tulsa.
556 'saved me from despair . . .': reprinted in Lloyd-Jones, *Maurice Bowra*, pp. 44–7.
557 'My life would only . . .': n.d., Tulsa.

557 'harder to be...': *ST*, 1 Dec. 1974.
557 'Good news...': *Encounter*, Feb. 1956.
557 'Only the tears...': *London Magazine*, Jan. 1963.
f.n. 'Please alter...': 9 Jan. 1963, private collection.
558 'We're back...': *ST*, 25 March 1973.
558 'Emotionally, Cyril...': *Customs and Characters*, p. 104.
559 'bad conscience...': misc. MS, n.d., Tulsa.
559 'The truth is...': 13 June 1972, *Love from Nancy*, p. 517.
559 'I was much...': 7 July 1972. *ibid*, p. 518.
559 'I cannot remember...': *Coastwise Lights*, p. 126.
560 'You must think...': n.d., private collection.
560 'the nearest wild elephants...': 'Destination Atlantis' was never published in the *Sunday Times*, but it was included in *The Evening Colonnade*, pp. 117–138.
561 'we are linked...': Graves to CC, 14 Sept. 1972, Tulsa.
561 'to be Alice B. Toklas...': quoted in Carpenter, *W.H. Auden*, p. 316.
561 'totally uninterested...': misc. MS, n.d., Tulsa.
561 '"Why, Cyril..."': *W.H. Auden: A Tribute*, p. 73.
f.n. 'It's like being asked...': Peter Levi to author.
'my sacred book': quoted in Andrew Motion, *Philip Larkin*, p. 202.
562 'the old...': *W.H. Auden: A Tribute*, p. 68.
562 'though I find...': CC to Brenan, 15 March 1963, Austin.
562 'In his deeper layers...': *Personal Record*, pp. 186–9.
562 'Cyril is funny...': 2 May 1973, Brotherton Library.
562 'It seems to me...': 18 April 1974, Tulsa.
562 'Your strong changing...': 1 May 1974, Tulsa.
562 'GB confuses...': quoted in Gathorne-Hardy, *The Interior Castle*, p. 551.
562 'horrible preparations...': CC to Olga Rudge, 28 Aug. 1973, Yale.
564 'Top Secret...': n.d., private collection.
564 'Cyril looked calm...': *The Parting Years*, p. 418.
565 'Cyril looked like...': 2 Sept. 1973, Bodleian.
565 'the claret was...': Powell to Lambert, 15 Sept. 1973, Bodleian.
565 'Cyril's seventieth...': Betjeman to Lambert, 19 Sept. 1973, Bodleian.
565 'What fun...': Hamilton to Lambert, 11 Sept. 1973, Bodleian.
565 'how blissfully...': n.d., Bodleian.
565 'looking like...': *J and M*, p. 294.
565 'Is not my work...': *Evening Colonnade*, p. 13.
565 'the small fry...': *Evening Colonnade*, p. 519.
566 'the more subjective...': reprinted in *Miscellaneous Verdicts*, pp. 297–9.
566 'how much I have...': 23 Aug. 1973, Tulsa.
567 'one of the very few...': *ST*, 10 Oct. 1963.
567 'obstinately Mediterranean...': *ST*, 9 Sept. 1973.
567 'desultoriness...': *Sunday Telegraph*, 7 Sept. 1973.
567 'It's destroyed...': *Guardian*, 8 Sept. 1973.
568 'Strange to be reviewing...': 20 May 1973, Brotherton Library.
568 'like a commando course...': *Art and Literature*, March 1964.
568 'too soft on...': *London Magazine*, Aug.–Sept. 1973.
569 'very hard to write...': *ST*, 12 Aug. 1973.
569 'seemed moderately content...': *Coastwise Lights*, p. 193.
569 'My own rude health...': 19 Feb. 1974, private collection.
570 'My second-hand...': n.d., private collection.
571 'You looked...': 2 Oct. 1974, Tulsa.
571 'Back in Eastbourne...': *TLS*, 6 Feb. 1976.
571 'blurred with tears...': 'Cyril', unpublished memoir.
572 'the first thing...': *Weep No More*, p. 150.

572 'succeeded in turn...': Forbes, *op. cit.*
572 'cure for the fear...': written for Jennifer Fry, published in *London Magazine*, Feb.–March 1975.
573 'Cyril is dying...': Anthony Hobson, diary, 8 Nov. 1974.
573 'Cyril is dying very fast': Betjeman to Penelope Betjeman, 6 Nov. 1974, *Letters*. Vol. II, p. 450.
573 'I do not recommend...': Spender, 'Cyril Connolly', *TLS*, 6 Dec. 1974.
573 'I still think...': 6 Nov. 1974, Tulsa.
574 'with what I felt...': *Encounter*, May 1975.
574 'shortly before...': *Coastwise Lights*, p. 196.
574 'the worst day...': Deirdre Levi to author.
574 'Our darling...': Anthony Hobson, diary, 26 Nov. 1974.
575 'the party acquired...': Spender, *Journals*, p. 281.
575 'This is Cyril's...': quoted in Drabble, *Angus Wilson*, p. 468.
575 'sung bibliography...': Anthony Hobson, diaries, 4 March 1965.
575 'as the choir...': *ST*, 4 Feb. 1973.
576 'Cyril used to say...': 20 Dec. 1974, Tulsa.

BIBLIOGRAPHY

Acton, Harold *Memoirs of an Aesthete* London: Methuen, 1948
—— *More Memoirs of an Aesthete* London: Methuen, 1970
Allen, Walter *As I Walked Down New Grub Street* London: Heinemann, 1981
Amis, Kingsley *Memoirs* London: Hutchinson, 1991
Annan, Noël *Our Age* London: Weidenfeld & Nicolson, 1990
Ayer, A.J. *Part of My Life* London: Collins, 1977
—— *More of My Life* London: Collins, 1984
Baron, Wendy *Miss Ethel Sands and Her Circle* London: Peter Owen, 1977
Beaton, Cecil *The Wandering Years. Diaries: 1922–1939* London: Weidenfeld & Nicolson, 1961
—— *The Strenuous Years. Diaries: 1948–1955* London: Weidenfeld & Nicolson, 1973
—— *The Restless Years. Diaries: 1955–1963* London: Weidenfeld & Nicolson, 1976
—— *The Parting Years. Diaries: 1963–1974* London: Weidenfeld & Nicolson, 1978
Bedford, Sybille *Aldous Huxley: A Biography. Volume I: 1894–1939* London: Chatto & Windus and Collins, 1973
—— *Volume II: 1939–63* London: Chatto & Windus and Collins, 1974.
Berenson, Bernard *Sunset and Twilight: Diaries, 1947–58*, ed. Nicky Mariano London: Hamish Hamilton, 1964
—— *Selected Letters* ed. A.K. McComb London: Hutchinson, 1965
Berlin, Isaiah *Personal Impressions* London: Hogarth Press, 1980
Betjeman, John *Letters Volume I: 1926–1951* ed. Candida Lycett-Green London: Methuen, 1994
—— *Letters Volume II: 1951–1984* ed. Candida Lycett-Green London: Methuen, 1995
Blakiston, Noël *Collected Stories* London: Constable, 1977
Brenan, Gerald *Personal Record: 1920–1972* London: Jonathan Cape, 1974
—— *Best of Friends: The Brenan-Partridge Letters* ed. Xan Fielding London: Chatto & Windus, 1986
Bowra, Maurice *Memories, 1898–1939* London: Weidenfeld & Nicolson, 1966
Boyle, Andrew *The Climate of Treason* London: Hutchinson, 1979
Callard, D.A. *The Case of Anna Kavan* London: Peter Owen, 1992
Capote, Truman *Answered Prayers* London: Hamish Hamilton, 1986
Carpenter, Humphrey *W.H. Auden: A Biography* London: Allen & Unwin, 1981
Cecil, Hugh and Mirabel *Clever Hearts: Desmond and Molly MacCarthy* London: Gollancz, 1990
Clark, Kenneth *Another Part of the Wood* London: Murray, 1974
—— *The Other Half* London: Murray, 1977
Cockett, Richard *David Astor and the Observer* London: Deutsch, 1991
Connolly, Cyril *The Rock Pool* Paris: The Obelisk Press, 1936. Rev. ed. London: Hamish Hamilton, 1947
—— *Enemies of Promise* London: Routledge & Kegan Paul, 1938. Rev. ed. 1948
—— *The Unquiet Grave* London: Horizon, 1944. Rev. eds. London: Hamish Hamilton 1945 and 1951
—— *The Condemned Playground* London: Routledge & Kegan Paul, 1945
—— *The Missing Diplomats* London: Queen Anne Press, 1952
—— *Ideas and Places* London: Weidenfeld & Nicolson, 1953

——*The Golden Horizon* ed. London: Weidenfeld & Nicolson, 1953
——*Les Pavillons: French Pavilions of the Eighteenth Century*; with photographs by Jerome Zerbe London: Hamish Hamilton, 1962
——*Previous Convictions* London: Hamish Hamilton, 1963
——*Hundred Key Books of the Modern Movement* London: André Deutsch/Hamish Hamilton, 1965
——*The Evening Colonnade* London: David Bruce & Watson, 1973
——*A Romantic Friendship: The Letters of Cyril Connolly to Noël Blakiston* ed. Noël Blakiston London: Constable, 1975
——*Journal and Memoir*, ed. David Pryce-Jones London: Collins, 1983
——*Shade Those Laurels*, completed by Peter Levi London: Bellew, 1990
Cockett, Richard *David Astor and the Observer* London: André Deutsch, 1991
Cowles, Virginia *The Rothschilds* London: Weidenfeld & Nicolson, 1973
Crick, Bernard *George Orwell: A Life* London: Secker & Warburg, 1980
E.E. Cummings *Selected Letters* ed. F.W. Dupee and George Sade London: André Deutsch, 1972
Drabble, Margaret *Angus Wilson: A Biography* Secker & Warburg, 1995
Dundy, Elaine *The Old Man and Me* London: Gollancz, 1964
Durrell, Lawrence *The Durrell-Miller Letters* ed. Ian S. MacNiven London: Faber, 1988
Ferris, Paul *Dylan Thomas* London: Hodder & Stoughton, 1977
Fielding, Daphne *The Adonis Garden* London: Eyre & Spottiswoode, 1961
Fisher, Clive *Cyril Connolly: A Romantic Life* London: Macmillan, 1995
Fitzgibbon, Theodora *With Love* London: Century, 1982
Fleming, Ann *Letters* ed. Mark Amory London: Harvill Press, 1985
Ford, Hugh *Published in Paris* London: Garnstone Press, 1975
Fox, James *White Mischief* London: Jonathan Cape, 1982
Fyvel, T.R. *George Orwell: A Personal Memoir* London: Weidenfeld & Nicolson, 1982
Garnett, David *The Familiar Faces* London: Chatto & Windus, 1962
Gascoyne, David *Journal: 1936–37* London: Enitharmon Press, 1980
Gathorne-Hardy, Jonathan *The Interior Castle: A Life of Gerald Brenan* London: Sinclair-Stevenson, 1992
Gathorne-Hardy, Robert *Recollections of Logan Pearsall Smith: The Story of a Friendship* London: Constable, 1949
Gilbert, Stuart *Reflections on James Joyce* ed. Thomas F. Staley and Randolph Lewis Austin: University of Texas Press, 1993
Gladwyn, Lord *Memoirs* London: Weidenfeld & Nicolson, 1972
Glendinning, Victoria *Elizabeth Bowen: Portrait of a Writer* London: Weidenfeld & Nicolson, 1977
——*Edith Sitwell: A Unicorn Among Lions* London: Weidenfeld & Nicolson, 1981
——*Vita: The Life of Vita Sackville-West* London: Weidenfeld & Nicolson, 1983
Green, Henry *Pack My Bag* London: The Hogarth Press, 1940
Green, Martin *Children of the Sun* London: Constable, 1977
Greene, Graham *A Sort of Life* London: Bodley Head, 1971
Grigson, Geoffrey *Recollections* London: Chatto & Windus, 1984
Grindea, Miron ed. *Adam International Review*: Cyril Connolly Commemorative issue. London, 1974–5
Hamilton, Denis *Editor-in-Chief* London: Hamish Hamilton, 1989
Hamilton, Iain *Koestler* London: Secker & Warburg, 1982
Hamilton, Ian *The Little Magazines: A Study of Six Editors* London: Weidenfeld & Nicolson, 1976
Hastings, Selina *Nancy Mitford* London: Hamish Hamilton, 1985
——*Evelyn Waugh: A Biography* London: Sinclair-Stevenson, 1995

Hawkins, Desmond *When I Was: A Memoir of the Years between the Wars* London: Macmillan, 1989
Hawtree, Christopher ed. *Night and Day* London: Chatto & Windus, 1985
Hemingway, Ernest *Green Hills of Africa* London: Jonathan Cape, 1935
—— *The Dangerous Summer* London: Hamish Hamilton, 1985
Herbert, David *Second Son* London: Peter Owen, 1972
Hewison, Robert *Under Siege: Literary Life in London 1939–45* London: Weidenfeld & Nicolson, 1977
Hillier, Bevis *Young Betjeman* London: John Murray, 1988
Hinks, Roger *The Gymnasium of the Mind: Journals* ed. John Goldsmith Wilton: Michael Russell, 1984
Hobson, Anthony *Cyril Connolly as a Book Collector* Edinburgh: The Tragara Press, 1983
Hollis, Christopher *Along the Road to Frome* London: Harrap, 1958
—— *The Seven Ages* London: Heinemann, 1974
—— *Oxford in the Twenties: Recollections of Five Friends* London: Heinemann, 1976
Holroyd, Michael *Augustus John. Volume II: The Years of Experience* London: Heinemann, 1976
Huxley, Aldous *Letters*, ed. Grover Smith London: Chatto & Windus, 1969
Hyams, Edward *The New Statesman: The History of the First Fifty Years, 1916–63* London: Hutchinson, 1963
Hynes, Samuel *The Auden Generation* London: Bodley Head, 1976
Isherwood, Christopher *Down There on a Visit* London: Methuen, 1961
—— *Christopher and his Kind* London: Eyre Methuen, 1977
—— *Diaries. Vol. I: 1939–60* ed. Katherine Bucknell London: Methuen, 1996
Jones, Nigel *Through a Glass Darkly* London: Abacus, 1992
Kahane, Jack *Memoirs of a Booklegger* London: Michael Joseph, 1939
Kennedy, Ludovic *On My Way to the Club* London: Collins, 1989
King, Francis *Yesterday Came Suddenly* London: Constable, 1993
King, James *The Last Modern: A Life of Herbert Read* London: Weidenfeld & Nicolson, 1990
Knightley, Phillip *Philby: KGB Masterspy* London: André Deutsch, 1988
Koestler, Arthur and Cynthia *Stranger on the Square* ed. Harold Harris London: Hutchinson, 1984
Lancaster, Marie-Jacqueline ed. *Brian Howard: Portrait of a Failure* London: Blond, 1968
Lancaster, Osbert *With an Eye to the Future* London: John Murray, 1967
Leavis, F.R. *The Common Pursuit* London: Chatto & Windus, 1952
Lees-Milne, James *Ancestral Voices* London: Chatto & Windus, 1975
—— *Prophesying Peace* London: Chatto & Windus, 1977
—— *Caves of Ice* London: Chatto & Windus, 1983
—— *Midway on the Waves* London: Faber, 1985
—— *Harold Nicolson, A Biography, Vol. I: 1886–1929* London: Chatto & Windus, 1980.
Lehmann, John *The Whispering Gallery* London: Longmans, 1955
—— *I Am My Brother* London: Longmans, 1960
—— *The Ample Proposition* London: Eyre & Spottiswoode, 1966
Levi, Peter *The Hill of Kronos* London: Collins, 1980
Lewis, R.W.B. *Edith Wharton: A Biography* London: Constable, 1975
Lewis, Wyndham *Letters* ed. W.K. Rose London: Methuen, 1963
—— *Men Without Art* London: Cassell, 1934
Lloyd-Jones, Hugh ed. *Maurice Bowra: A Celebration* London: Duckworth, 1974
Longhurst, Henry *My Life and Soft Times* London: Cassell, 1971
Luke, Michael *David Tennant and the Gargoyle Years* London: Weidenfeld & Nicolson, 1991
Lycett, Andrew *Ian Fleming* London: Weidenfeld & Nicolson, 1995
Lynn, Kenneth *Hemingway* New York: Simon & Schuster, 1977

Lyttelton, George *The Lyttelton-Hart-Davis Letters. Volume I: 1955–56* London: John Murray, 1978
—— *The Lyttelton-Hart-Davis Letters, Volume II: 1957* London: John Murray, 1979
—— *The Lyttelton-Hart-Davis Letters Volume VI: 1961–62* London: John Murray, 1984
Lytton, Earl of *Antony: A Record of Youth* London: Peter Davies, 1935
MacCarthy, Desmond *Memories* London: MacGibbon & Kee, 1953
McCabe, Cameron *The Face on the Cutting-Room Floor* London: Gollancz, 1937
Maclaren-Ross, Julian *Memoirs of the Forties* London: Alan Ross, 1965
Mariano, Nicky *Forty Years With Berenson* London: Hamish Hamilton, 1966
Martin, Kingsley *Editor* London: Hutchinson, 1968
Maxwell, Gavin *The House of Elrig* London: Longmans, 1965
Mitford, Nancy *The Blessing* London: Hamish Hamilton, 1952
—— *Love from Nancy: The Letters of Nancy Mitford* ed. Charlotte Mosley London: Hodder & Stoughton, 1993
—— *The Letters of Nancy Mitford and Evelyn Waugh* ed. Charlotte Mosley London: Hodder & Stoughton, 1996
Muggeridge, Malcolm *Like It Was: The Diaries of Malcolm Muggeridge* ed. John Bright-Holmes London: Collins, 1981
Meyers, Jeffrey *Edmund Wilson: A Biography* London: Constable, 1995
Nelson, Michael *A Room in Chelsea Square* London: Jonathan Cape, 1958
Nicolson, Harold *Journey to Java* London: Constable, 1957
—— *Diaries and Letters 1930–39* ed. Nigel Nicolson London: Collins, 1966
—— *Diaries and Letters 1939–45* ed. Nigel Nicolson London: Collins, 1967
—— *Vita and Harold: The Letters of Vita Sackville-West and Harold Nicolson* ed. Nigel Nicolson London: Weidenfeld & Nicolson, 1992
Orwell, George *The Collected Essays, Journalism and Letters*, ed Sonia Orwell and Ian Angus
—— *Volume I: An Age Like This. 1920–1940* London: Secker & Warburg, 1968
—— *Volume II: My Country Right or Left. 1940–1943* London: Secker & Warbug, 1968
—— *Volume III: As I Please. 1943–1945* London: Secker & Warburg, 1968
—— *Volume IV: In Front of Your Nose. 1945–50* London: Secker & Warburg, 1969
Partridge, Frances *Memories* London: Gollancz, 1981
—— *Julia: A Portrait of Julia Strachey* London: Gollancz, 1983
—— *Everything to Lose: Diaries 1945–60* London: Gollancz, 1985
—— *Hanging On: Diaries 1961–63* London: Collins, 1990
—— *Other People's Diaries 1963–66* London: HarperCollins, 1993
—— *Good Company: Diaries 1967–70* London: HarperCollins, 1994
Pater, Walter *Imaginary Portraits* London: Macmillan, 1887
Pearsall Smith, Logan *A Portrait: Drawn from his Letters and Diaries* ed. John Russell London: Dropmore Press, 1951
—— *An Anthology* ed. Edward Burnham London: Constable, 1989
Pearson, John *The Life of Ian Fleming* London: Jonathan Cape, 1966
Perles, Alfred *My Friend Henry Miller* London: Neville Spearman, 1955
Penrose, Roland *Scrapbook 1900–1981* London: Thames & Hudson, 1981
Powell, Anthony *To Keep the Ball Rolling. Volume I: Infants of the Spring* London: Heinemann, 1976
—— *Volume II: Messengers of Day* London: Heinemann, 1978
—— *Volume III: Faces in My Time* London: Heinemann, 1980
—— *Miscellaneous Verdicts: Writings on Writers 1946–1989* London: Heinemann, 1990
Pritchett, V.S. *Midnight Oil* London: Chatto & Windus, 1971
Prokosch, Frederic *Voices: A Memoir* London: Faber, 1983
Pryce-Jones, Alan *The Bonus of Laughter* London: Hamish Hamilton, 1987
Quennell, Peter *The Sign of the Fish* London: Collins, 1960
—— *The Marble Foot* London: Collins, 1970

——*The Wanton Chase* London: Collins, 1980
——*Customs and Characters: Contemporary Portraits* London: Weidenfeld & Nicolson, 1982
Rees, Jenny *Looking for Mr Nobody: The Secret Life of Goronwy Rees* London: Weidenfeld & Nicolson, 1994
Ross, Alan *Coastwise Lights* London: Harvill Press, 1988
Rowse, A.L. *A Cornishman at Oxford* London: Jonathan Cape, 1965
——*A Cornishman Abroad* London: Jonathan Cape, 1976
——*Glimpses of the Great* University Press of America, 1985
Russell, Leonard *et al. The Pearl of Days: An Intimate History of the Sunday Times, 1822–1972* London: Hamish Hamilton, 1972
Sebba, Anna *Enid Bagnold* London: Weidenfeld & Nicolson, 1986
Shelden, Michael *Friends of Promise: Cyril Connolly and the World of Horizon* London: Hamish Hamilton, 1989
——*Orwell: The Authorised Biography* London: Heinemann, 1991
Skelton, Barbara *Born Losers* London: Alan Ross, 1965
——*A Love Match* London: Alan Ross, 1969
——*Tears Before Bedtime* London: Hamish Hamilton, 1987
——*Weep No More* London: Hamish Hamilton, 1989
Smith, Adrian *The New Statesman: Portrait of a Political Weekly* London: Frank Cass, 1996
Sonnenberg, Ben *Lost Property* London: Faber, 1991
Spender, Stephen *World Within World* Hamish Hamilton, 1951
——*The Thirties and After: Poetry, Politics, People (1933–75)* London: Fontana/Macmillan, 1978
——*Letters to Christopher: Stephen Spender's Letters to Christopher Isherwood, 1929–39* ed. Lee Bartlett Santa Barbara: Black Sparrow Press, 1980
——*Journals 1939–1983* ed. John Goldsmith London: Faber, 1985
——ed. *W.H. Auden: A Tribute* London: Weidenfeld & Nicolson, 1975
Stannard, Martin *Evelyn Waugh: The Early Years, 1903–1939* London: Dent, 1986
——*Evelyn Waugh: No Abiding City, 1939–1966* London: Dent, 1992
Stansky, Peter and Abrahams, William *The Unknown Orwell* London: Constable, 1972
Strachey, Barbara *Remarkable Relations* London: Gollancz, 1980
Sykes, Christopher *Evelyn Waugh: A Biography* London: Collins, 1975
Symons, Julian *A.J.A. Symons: His Life and Speculations* London: Eyre & Spottiswoode, 1950
Topolski Feliks *Fourteen Letters* London: Faber, 1988
Thomas, Dylan *Collected Letters* ed. Paul Ferris London: Dent, 1985
Tolley, A.T. *John Lehmann: A Tribute* Ottawa: Carleton University Press, 1987
Tynan, Kathleen *The Life of Kenneth Tynan* London: Weidenfeld & Nicolson, 1987
Tynan, Kenneth *Tynan, Right and Left* London: Longmans, 1967
Vaughan, Keith *Journals* ed. Alan Ross London: John Murray, 1989
Vickers, Hugo *Cecil Beaton: The Authorised Biography* London: Weidenfeld & Nicolson, 1985
Waugh, Evelyn *Robbery Under Law* London: Chapman & Hall, 1939
——*Unconditional Surrender* London: Chapman & Hall, 1961
——*A Little Learning* London: Chapman & Hall, 1964
——*Diaries* ed. Michael Davie London: Weidenfeld & Nicolson, 1975
——*Letters* ed. Mark Amory London: Weidenfeld & Nicolson, 1980
——and Cooper, Lady Diana *Mr Wu and Mrs Stitch: The Letters of Evelyn Waugh and Diana Cooper* ed. Artemis Cooper London: Hodder & Stoughton, 1991
Weidenfeld, George *Remembering My Good Friends* London: HarperCollins, 1994
Weld, Jacqueline Bograd *Peggy: The Wayward Guggenheim* London: Bodley Head, 1986
Welch, Denton *Journals* ed. Michael de-la-Noy London: Allison & Busby, 1984
Wheen, Francis *Tom Driberg: His Life and Indiscretions* London: Chatto & Windus, 1990
Wilson, Edmund *Europe without Baedeker* London: Secker & Warburg, 1948

——*Classics and Commercials* New York: Farrar, Straus, Giroux, 1950
——*The Fifties* ed. Leon Edel New York: Farrar, Straus, Giroux, 1986
——*The Sixties* ed. Lewis M. Dabney New York: Farrar, Straus, Giroux, 1993
——*Letters on Literature and Politics: 1912–1972* ed. Elena Wilson New York: Farrar, Straus, Giroux, 1973
Wishart, Michael *High Diver* London: Blond & Briggs, 1977
Woolf, Virginia *The Sickle Side of the Moon. The Letters of Virginia Woolf: Volume V, 1932–1935* ed. Nigel Nicolson London: Hogarth Press, 1979
——*Diary. Volume IV: 1931–1935* ed. Anne Olivier Bell London: Hogarth Press, 1979
——*A Moment's Liberty* London: Hogarth Press, 1990
Worsley, T.C. *Behind the Battle* London: Robert Hale, 1939
Wyatt, Woodrow *Confessions of an Optimist* London: Collins, 1985
Wyndham, Joan *Anything Once* London: Sinclair-Stevenson, 1992
Ziegler, Philip *Diana Cooper* London: Hamish Hamilton, 1981

I am extremely grateful to the following authors or their estates for permission to quote from published and unpublished works:

Lord Annan; W.H. Auden (Copyright by the Estate of W.H. Auden); Cecil Beaton (the Literary Estate of the late Sir Cecil Beaton); Sybille Bedford; Sir Isaiah Berlin; Sir John Betjeman (Candida Lycett-Green); Elizabeth Bowen (Curtis Brown Ltd, London, Literary Executors of the Estate of Elizabeth Bowen); Sir Maurice Bowra (All Soul's College, Oxford); Gerald Brenan (Margaret Hanbury); Randolph Churchill (Winston S. Churchill); Lord Clark (John Murray Ltd and Margaret Hanbury); Lawrence Durrell (Curtis Brown Ltd); T.S. Eliot (Valerie Eliot); Theodora Fitzgibbon (David Higham Ltd); Ann Fleming (Hon. Fionn Morgan); Jonathan Gathorne-Hardy (Sinclair-Stevenson Ltd); Robert Gathorne-Hardy (Constable Ltd); Hamish Hamilton (Penguin Books Ltd); Christopher Hollis (Heinemann Ltd); Christopher Isherwood (Curtis Brown Ltd); Francis King (A.M. Heath Ltd); Arthur Koestler (Peters, Fraser & Dunlop Ltd); Osbert Lancaster (John Murray Ltd); James Lees-Milne (David Higham Ltd); the Estate of John Lehmann; Henry Longhurst (Macmillan Inc); Julian Maclaren-Ross (London Magazine Editions); Gavin Maxwell (© The Estate of Gavin Maxwell 1965: Gavin Maxwell Enterprises Ltd); Nancy Mitford (Peters, Fraser & Dunlop Ltd); Harold Nicolson (Nigel Nicolson); George Orwell (© Mark Hamilton as literary executor of the Estate of the late Sonia Brownell Orwell, and Martin Secker & Warburg Ltd); Frances Partridge (Rogers, Coleridge & White Ltd); Anthony Powell (David Higham Ltd: unpublished letter © Anthony Powell 1977); V.S. Pritchett (Peters, Fraser & Dunlop Ltd); Sir Peter Quennell (Lady Quennell); Alan Ross; Osbert Sitwell (David Higham Ltd: unpublished letters © Frank Magro 1997); Sir Stephen Spender (Lady Spender, Faber & Faber Ltd for *Journals 1939–1983*, Peters, Fraser & Dunlop Ltd for *World Within World* and *The Thirties and After*); the Estate of Kenneth Tynan; Christopher Sykes (Peters, Fraser & Dunlop Ltd); Evelyn Waugh (Peters, Fraser & Dunlop Ltd); Edmund Wilson (Farrar Straus & Giroux Inc); Woodrow Wyatt (HarperCollins Ltd); Joan Wyndham (Peters, Fraser & Dunlop Ltd). Every effort has been made to contact copyright owners, and the author and publishers apologise for any inadvertent omissions. Unless otherwise stated, the photographs were provided by Deirdre Levi.

INDEX

Works by Cyril Connolly (including occasional and minor writings) appear under title, works by others under author's name